advertising media
strategy and tactics

advertising media

strategy and tactics

Donald W. Jugenheimer
Fairleigh Dickinson University

•

Arnold M. Barban
University of Alabama, Tuscaloosa

•

Peter B. Turk
University of Akron

WCB Brown & Benchmark

Book Team

Editor *Stan Stoga*
Production Editor *Connie Balius-Haakinson*
Designer *Eric Engelby*
Art Editor *Mary E. Swift*
Photo Editor *Lori Gockel*
Permissions Editor *Vicki Krug*
Art Processor *Andréa Lopez-Meyer*

WCB Brown & Benchmark

A Division of Wm. C. Brown Communications, Inc.

Vice President and General Manager *Thomas E. Doran*
Executive Managing Editor *Ed Bartell*
Executive Editor *Edgar J. Laube*
Director of Marketing *Kathy Law Laube*
National Sales Manager *Eric Ziegler*
Marketing Manager *Carla Aspelmeier*
Advertising Manager *Jodi Rymer*
Managing Editor, Production *Colleen A. Yonda*
Manager of Visuals and Design *Faye M. Schilling*

Design Manager *Jac Tilton*
Art Manager *Janice Roerig*
Photo Manager *Shirley Charley*
Production Editorial Manager *Ann Fuerste*
Publishing Services Manager *Karen J. Slaght*
Permissions/Records Manager *Connie Allendorf*

Wm. C. Brown Communications, Inc.

Chairman Emeritus *Wm. C. Brown*
Chairman and Chief Executive Officer *Mark C. Falb*
President and Chief Operating Officer *G. Franklin Lewis*
Corporate Vice President, Operations *Beverly Kolz*
Corporate Vice President, President of WCB Manufacturing *Roger Meyer*

Copyeditor *Mary Monner*

Line art by Illustrious, Inc.: Figures 1.2, 1.3, 1.4, 2.2, 2.3, 2.4, 2.5, 2.6,
2.7, 2.8, 2.9, 2.11, 3.1, 5.9, 9.1, 9.2, 10.1, 10.2, 10.3, 10.4, 11.1, 12.1,
12.2, 13.2, 15.1, 15.4, 15.6, 15.9, 16.1, 16.2, 16.8, 16.12, 17.1, 17.6a and
b, 17.11a–g, 17.12a–c. Text art on pages 53, 71, 91, 111, 169, 185, 207,
223, 239, 263, 271, 285, 323, 345, 357, 369, 391, and 440. Line art by
Diphrent Strokes, Inc.: Figures 5.5 and 16.4.

CONTENTS

Chapter 5

The Role of Syndicated Research 90

Chapter 6

The Role of Uncontrollable Factors 110

PART III ANALYTICAL CONCEPTS 127

Chapter 7

Quantitative Factors in Media Decisions 129

Chapter 8

Qualitative Factors in Media Decisions 145

List of Media Spotlights

*M*edia costs represent the major portion of advertising investments, yet media often take a secondary position in advertising education, behind copywriting and other more "creative" aspects of the business. But every student and practitioner of advertising must understand the media function, not only because of the costs involved but because the media are the sole channel by which the advertising message is transmitted to the right (or wrong) audience.

Advertising Media: Strategy and Tactics provides a thorough yet basic grounding in advertising media as practiced in modern advertising work. The number of advertising educational programs has been rapidly increasing during the past few years, as have student enrollments in advertising classes, yet few good textual materials deal with advertising media. This book presents this essential information in a logical, organized, and understandable format that follows the same phases as the actual practice of advertising media planning and buying.

Although this book is primarily intended for undergraduate and graduate students majoring in advertising at colleges and universities, the information is also of great use to entry-level advertising and media employees. The book follows the logical sequence of steps in the advertising media business, with a focus on a central model of advertising media planning. Using this model, the reader can comprehend the total advertising media process while also understanding how each step and each individual topic fits into the overall picture.

The book begins with an overview of media decision making and a discussion of the organization of the media function and its role within general marketing. Then some basics of advertising research are explored, along with an examination of external factors that affect advertising media planning. Next, analytical concepts are introduced, with separate treatment of quantitative and qualitative factors in media decisions. Strategic media decisions are discussed next, including how to set objectives, define markets, establish a media mix, and determine continuity in scheduling. Tactical decisions about each of the major types of media are explored in some detail. Finally, advertising trends and projections for the future are discussed. A complete glossary of advertising media terminology appears at the end of the book.

Pedagogy

Each chapter opens with a chapter outline and a list of learning objectives. At the end of each chapter is an overview summary, along with review questions to aid understanding and application of the chapter materials. For those who wish to delve more deeply and thoroughly into individual topics, additional readings are also suggested. Throughout the book are "Media Spotlights" of information—real advertising applications and explanations of the materials covered in the chapters. These highlighted sidebars provide indications of how the material and information can be applied, and they can aid in understanding why the facts are important and why the processes are essential.

The learning process should begin with a reading and *thorough understanding* of the first chapter, not just because it offers background information for the rest of the book but because it provides a comprehensive learning model. One problem in teaching is deciding where to start, because it is easy to understand individual items of knowledge but difficult to place these topics in a larger framework of understanding. The comprehensive model of how the advertising function operates helps overcome this obstacle, by providing an overview of the entire advertising media planning and buying process, with all its functions and interrelationships. This model is detailed in chapter 1, with portions of it then repeated throughout the book in appropriate places, aiding in the understanding of where each topic fits into advertising media operations.

This book has been written by three experienced professors who have taught advertising media for a total of more years than we care to remember! In the development of this book, we have consciously attempted to include vital information, presented in a logical and understandable format, that fits most advertising media course organizations while providing essential knowledge that every student needs to know. We have used approaches known to work through years of experience. We have contributed external examples and explanations that help the reader understand how the information can be applied to real-life, real-world advertising situations.

We hope that students will enjoy this book, while simultaneously learning the basics of advertising media strategy and tactics.

Acknowledgments

We would like to thank the following reviewers for their comments and helpful suggestions:

Alan D. Fletcher, Louisiana State University

Karen W. King, University of Georgia

Mark M. Secrist, University of Idaho

Daniel NG, Iowa State University

PART I

INTRODUCTION

An Introductory Look at Media Decision Making

Outline

Learning Objectives

In the study of this chapter, you will have the opportunity to:

- Explore how the media function is viewed by advertising practitioners.
- Assess the importance of media operations.
- Note the division of U.S. advertising dollars among media, and observe which media are used for local and national advertising.
- Understand the relationship of the media function to other advertising and marketing efforts.
- Observe how media decision making can be approached in a systematic way.

*A*ssume that you work as a media specialist for the advertising agency responsible for preparing a new advertising campaign for Kellogg's Nutri·Grain breakfast cereals. You are asked to do the following:

I. Prepare a media plan for Nutri·Grain for the next fiscal year:
   A. Suggest research that should be undertaken and assess existing research.
   B. Coordinate marketing strategy with the media effort.
   C. Establish workable and measurable media objectives.
   D. Develop media strategies for advertising the brand, including:
      1. The target audience to whom the advertisements and commercials will be directed.
      2. The various media to use.
      3. The timing schedule of the plan.
      4. The various contingencies and alternative decisions that must be considered.
      5. The various influences that you cannot control but that may influence the results of the campaign.
   E. Implement your strategies by:
      1. Negotiating for the purchase of specific media vehicles and units.
      2. Maintaining a budget so that costs do not exceed the amount appropriated.
      3. Scheduling media buys to fit the plan.
      4. Paying all bills on time to take full advantage of available discounts.
II. Establish a system of measurement so that you can determine whether the media objectives were attained, and use this information as feedback for the planning of future Nutri·Grain campaigns.

The goal of this book is to provide you with a reasonable level of competence so that you would feel qualified to develop a workable media program for Nutri·Grain cereals. You may say, "Who cares? I'm not really interested in being a media specialist; I want to work in the creative area of advertising, as a copywriter." This book, however, will not necessarily make you a media *expert* or encourage you to seek a career in media; rather, it will provide you with an understanding of and appreciation for the media function. The more you know and understand each of the advertising functions, the better you will be able to perform your own specialty and the better prepared you will be for future management positions, for which a knowledge of the whole advertising process is essential.

Media Decision Making Today

Advertising media decision making, as a significant part of the advertising process, has only come into its own within the last fifteen years or so. For a long time, the media function in advertising received less than its share of attention, and media people typically were paid notably less than others. The "creative" function, as copywriting and artwork are termed, as well as the account management function, received most of the emphasis. Even today, not all advertising functions are viewed as equal, but changes in the advertising business have increased the perceived importance of media decision making. As noted by Carol Hall:

While no one is suggesting the elimination of the account staff, media options have become far more complex, making it hard for the nonmedia person to stay abreast of the changes. "The account team is no longer in a position to carry the ball themselves," declares Joel Kushins [media director at Bozell, Jacobs, Kenyon & Eckhardt, Inc.]. Gone, he says, are the days where you "troop out the media people once a year for the annual meeting, and that's it."

Another explanation for the emergence of the media department has to do, of course, with the agency itself. Plainly put, it is looking to media people to assume more of the burden of selling. While it is still largely the creative effort that wins or loses an account, both advertiser and agency realize that, with the glut of clutter out there, the media plan can make or break the success of that creative. It's now up to agency people to not only sell a creative concept but, increasingly, a media plan, too.[1]

The emergence of the media function has driven home the realization that the media department not only controls and spends most of the monies that flow through advertising, but also commands most of the campaign expenditures. Commonly, about 80 to 90 percent of all money spent on advertising is devoted to the media placements or to the media function, and the remaining amount is left for all the other advertising functions: research, copywriting, art, layout, evaluation, planning, budgeting, and the like. With the realization that most of the advertising budget is, in one way or another, expended on media, the media function has risen higher in the hierarchy of the advertising process. (See figure 1.1.)

Added to the growing importance of media operations is the recognition that, in times of economic difficulties, saving money has become most important. Rising inflationary spirals, even when at modest levels, pressure advertisers, their agencies, and the advertising media to avoid overspending resources, especially financial resources, and to become more frugal. Budget stretching has suddenly become an important goal, and deriving every possible benefit from a set amount of money has evolved into an important advertising objective.

Part of the problem, however, has been that little savings is possible in most areas of advertising.

On August 29, you can help Hal Riney spend $100,000,000.

Of course, that's just a rough figure. But, nevertheless, one that represents a huge opportunity.

An opportunity called the Saturn Corporation.

Soon, Hal Riney & Partners will introduce the world to a very different kind of car company. And we want to use a very different kind of automotive advertising to do it.

What we're looking for from you are some unique media proposals with which to showcase that work.

On August 29th, at 2:00 p.m., we're inviting media sales representatives to join us at the Palace of Fine Arts in San Francisco for a briefing on the Saturn launch. We'll share with you some of our initial media and marketing thoughts, in hopes that you'll soon get back to us with some interesting thoughts of your own.

Invitations are already on their way to many media sales representatives. Attendance is limited, and you must have a pass and proper identification to be admitted. If your ad director or San Francisco sales representative has not yet been contacted, please call us by August 11th at (415) 955-4227.

We encourage you not to miss this event. It is, most definitely, the start of something big.

HAL RINEY & PARTNERS
INCORPORATED

FIGURE 1.1 An Advertising Agency Advertisement in a Trade Magazine. Note that the agency, Hal Riney & Partners of San Francisco, calls special attention to the importance of media in its plans to develop advertising for the Saturn Corporation.
Courtesy of Hal Riney & Partners, Inc.

Creative work is essential, and scrimping on copywriting and artwork is self-defeating. Research also typically is necessary, although advertisers could perhaps save by relying on already-available facts rather than by performing their own primary research surveys and experiments. While the media function, too, makes an important contribution to the total success of an advertising campaign, it is the one area where many people have reasoned that advertising can become more efficient. Attempting to reach more people in larger audiences with less waste provides real opportunities in advertising to economize without sacrificing communication effectiveness. In fact, efficient media operations not only can save money but also focus on the best prospects and thereby make the advertising *more* effective and productive.

TABLE 1.1

Amount of Advertising Monies Spent in the Various Media

Medium	1989 Millions of Dollars	1989 Percent of Total	1990 Millions of Dollars	1990 Percent of Total	Percent Change
Newspapers					
National	$3,704	3.0%	$3,867	3.0%	4.4 %
Local	28,664	23.1	28,414	22.1	(0.9)
Total	**$32,368**	**26.1%**	**$32,281**	**25.1%**	**(0.3) %**
Magazines					
Weeklies	$2,813	2.2%	$2,864	2.2%	1.8%
Women's	1,710	1.4	1,713	1.3	0.2
Monthlies	2,193	1.8	2,226	1.8	1.5
Total	**$6,716**	**5.4%**	**$6,803**	**5.3%**	**1.3%**
Farm Publications	$212	0.2%	$215	0.2%	2.0%
Television					
Network	$9,110	7.4%	$9,383	7.3%	3.0%
Cable (national)	1,197	1.0	1,393	1.1	16.4
Syndication	1,288	1.0	1,589	1.2	23.4
Spot (national)	7,354	5.9	7,788	6.1	5.9
Spot (local)	7,612	6.1	7,856	6.1	3.2
Cable (non-network)	330	0.3	396	0.3	20.0
Total	**$26,891**	**21.7%**	**$28,405**	**22.1%**	**5.6%**
Radio					
Network	$476	0.4%	$482	0.4%	1.3%
Spot (national)	1,547	1.3	1,635	1.3	5.7
Spot (local)	6,300	5.1	6,609	5.1	4.9
Total	**$8,323**	**6.8%**	**$8,726**	**6.8%**	**4.8%**
Yellow Pages					
National	$1,011	0.8%	$1,132	0.9%	12.0%
Local	7,319	5.9	7,794	6.0	6.5
Total	**$8,330**	**6.7%**	**$8,926**	**6.9%**	**7.2%**
Direct Mail	$21,945	17.7%	$23,370	18.2%	6.5%
Business Papers	$2,763	2.2%	$2,875	2.2%	4.0%

TABLE 1.1 CONTINUED

Medium	1989 Millions of Dollars	1989 Percent of Total	1990 Millions of Dollars	1990 Percent of Total	Percent Change
Outdoor					
National	$653	0.5%	$640	0.5%	(2.0)%
Local	458	0.4	444	0.3	(3.0)
Total	**$1,111**	**0.9%**	**$1,084**	**0.8%**	**(2.4)%**
Miscellaneous					
National	$10,998	8.9%	$11,608	9.0%	5.5%
Local	4,273	3.4	4,347	3.4	1.7
Total	**$15,271**	**12.3 %**	**$15,955**	**12.4%**	**4.4%**
National Total	$68,990	55.7%	$72,780	56.6%	5.5%
Local Total	54,940	44.3	55,860	43.4	1.7
Grand Total	**$123,930**	**100.0%**	**$128,640**	**100.0%**	**3.8%**

Source: From *Advertising Age,* May 6, 1991, page 16. Copyright ©1991 Crain Communications Inc., Detroit, MI. Reprinted by permission.

Because of this potential return on investment in advertising media analysis, marketing-media managers can contribute even more to the overall success of advertising. Efficient media operations also save time for media audiences because people who are not bona fide prospective customers for a product or service are now less likely to see advertising for items that do not interest them. More people are being reached for each dollar of advertising investment. Greater selectivity on the part of the media themselves has replaced the once-popular consideration of audience size as the only critical factor. Fewer messages need to be directed to people who are not interested or who are not prospective customers.

How Advertising Monies Are Allocated to the Various Media

Although each brand and service advertised establishes its own unique mixture of media allocation, seeing how advertisers on the whole allocate their advertising investment to the various forms of advertising media is useful. Table 1.1 provides information for such expenditures during a two-year period.

Almost $129 *billion* was spent in all advertising media in 1990, a 3.8 percent increase over the amount spent in 1989. Newspapers received the

MEDIA SPOTLIGHT
1.1

A Day in the Life of Lesley Meyer Luca

FIGURE 1 Lesley Meyer Luca

Lesley Meyer Luca (figure 1) is media supervisor in the Chicago office of DDB Needham Worldwide. She is an advertising graduate of the University of Texas at Austin.

8:45 A.M.—Arrive at office; pick up coffee.

9:00 A.M.—Review list of active projects on national brands and test products including:

• *Packaged dinner*
  - get approval on print plan
  - negotiate print positions
  - review cable recommendation
  - status on radio creative?
  - possible incremental funds
• *Packaged cake mix*
  - purchase cycle?
  - new competition?
  - inclusion of print in media plan?
• *Packaged side dish—test*
  - review final media options
  - get telexed to client by 12:30
  - conference call 1:45
• *Packaged dessert—test*
  - write objectives
  - write strategies
  - discuss cannibalism of current brands
• *Microwave dinner*
  - issue network television buying requirements

9:10 A.M.—Check in with media planners and assistant planners—review today's schedule and assignments.

9:15 A.M.—Review with assistant planner quantitative media information needed for new side-dish product media plans:
• reach/frequencies
• GRPs/impressions by subtarget
• budget summaries

9:25 A.M.—Account executive calls with client approval on packaged dinner print plan.

9:30 A.M.—Meet with media and account groups for final review of media plan recommendation and options for new side-dish product.

10:20 A.M.—Meet with planner to discuss direction on network television buying specifications for microwave dinner, including demographics, psychographics, personality of advertising, ideal environment, ideal program types, etc.

10:30 A.M.—Meet with sales representative from *Parents* magazine:

- feasibility of including *Parents* on the print plan recommendatin for new side dish
- positioning of national ads for packaged dinner
  - food section
  - opposite full page of black-and-white editorial on pasta or quick-dinner recipes

10:55 A.M.—Make sure media plan recommendation and options have been faxed to client.

11:00 A.M.—Return A.M. phone calls; set up two meetings and a lunch with magazine sales representatives.

11:30 A.M.—Call client—discuss media recommendation for possible incremental funds on packaged dinner. What is objective?

- additional weeks for continuity versus
- incremental weight within current dayparts for frequency versus
- new medium or dayparts for reach

11:50 A.M.—Review cake-mix print plan with account group; discuss the possible role of print from both a media point of view (efficiencies) and a creative point of view (communication).

12:20 P.M.—Grab a sandwich for lunch; write media objectives for new packaged dessert; think about media strategies.

1:45 P.M.—Conference call with client; present test-plan options and make recommendation; agree on revisions to be discussed at meeting in two days.

2:35 P.M.—Meet account group on dessert test to discuss possible cannibalism of current products; determine if new product will add sufficient sales volume to overall division to merit national introduction.

3:15 P.M.—Call various magazines to begin negotiating print positions.

4:00 P.M.—Call client's media department to discuss positions; agree to send out final negotiated print position statements by end of the week.

4:15 P.M.—Join rest of agency for Chicago Cubs Day in reception areas—hot dogs, pretzels, beer, and peanuts.

4:45 P.M.—Review with planner information on purchase cycle, sales patterns, and competition of packaged cake mix; determine impact of information on media plan.

5:15 P.M.—Review cable television recommendation with buyers; make revisions before client presentation:

—more cherry-picked networks for targeted reach

5:35 P.M.—Find out radio creative will not be ready until after first air date; call buyer to determine if purchased radio weight can be moved or exchanged with another brand.

5:50 P.M.—Go through "in" box—read mail, catch up on memos, letters, correspondence, and trade magazines.

6:45 P.M.—Revise list of active projects for tomorrow.

6:50 P.M.—Leave office.

Photo and text courtesy of Lesley Meyer Luca.

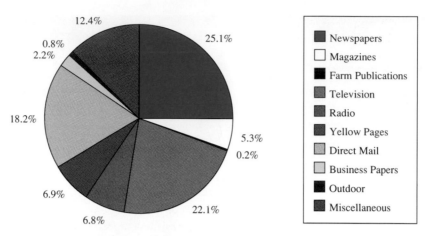

FIGURE 1.2 Allocation of Advertising Monies, by Media Type, 1990

Source: From *Advertisisng Age,* May 14, 1990, page 12. Copyright © 1990 Crain Communications Inc., Detroit, MI. Reprinted by permission.

TABLE 1.2		
Percentages of Advertising Monies Spent by National and Local Advertisers in the Various Media		
Media Type	Percent by	
	National Advertisers	Local Advertisers
Newspapers	12.0%	88.0%
Television	70.9	29.1
Radio	24.3	75.7
Yellow Pages	12.7	87.3
Outdoor	59.0	41.0

largest share of the total—25.1 percent in 1990 ($32.281 billion), followed by television with 22.1 percent ($28.405 billion). Direct mail was the third largest recipient of advertiser monies—18.2 percent. Figure 1.2 charts the share of total for each of the ten media types shown in table 1.1, including the miscellaneous media category (which includes such media as transit advertising). Overall, national advertisers spent somewhat more than local advertisers—56.6 percent of the $128.64 billion

versus 43.4 percent, respectively—in 1990. The split among national and local advertisers, however, varied among different media types in 1990, as shown in table 1.2. Thus, newspapers, radio, and the Yellow Pages were used predominantly by local advertisers, while national advertisers focused on television and outdoor advertising.

How the Media Function Relates to Marketing and Advertising

The media function is part of the overall advertising effort, but then advertising is but part of the overall marketing effort. Advertising's contributions to marketing must be thoroughly understood before we examine the media contribution to advertising (see also chapter 3).

Within marketing, there are four basic variables, which marketing educator E. Jerome McCarthy identified as the four P's: product, place, price, and promotion.[2] Collectively, these four variables constitute the marketing mix, which Philip Kotler defines as "the set of controllable marketing variables that the firm blends to produce the response it wants in the target market."[3]

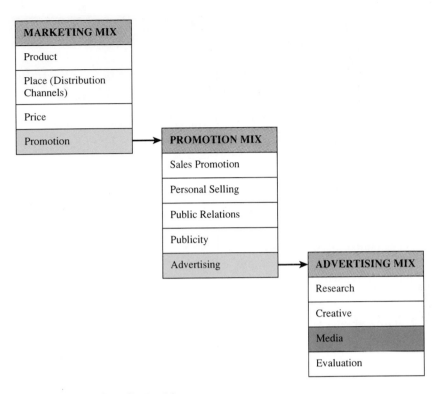

FIGURE 1.3 The Relationship of Media Decisions to Marketing, Promotion, and Advertising

The *product* can be an actual good to be marketed, or it can be a service or an idea. In the study of marketing and advertising, it is convenient to think of a product as a brand that is being sold and advertised, but the principles that apply to goods apply equally well to ideas and services. The *place* portion of the marketing mix involves distributing the product, service, or idea to the proper target. *Price* is the agreed-upon value of the item to be sold. And *promotion* is communicating with the customer about the product for sale, helping the sale to take place. Other incidental variables may arise within the marketing mix, such as packaging (which may be considered part of the product variable, or of promotion, or a combination of both), product planning (which is usually involved with the product itself), brand policy, service, and other similar considerations. Most marketing functions, however, involve one of the four basic variables.

The promotion variable of marketing is where advertising becomes important, although promotion also may involve a variety of other functions, such as sales promotion (coupons, premium offers, cents-off deals, contests, and the like), personal selling (sales clerks in stores or sales representatives calling on businesses), public relations, and publicity. The advertising function can itself be broken into a kind of advertising mix that includes research, creative and evaluative efforts, and, of course, media. Figure 1.3 shows how these three mixes—the marketing mix, the promotion mix, and the advertising mix—are related to one another.

Finally, one aspect of media decision making relates to how a particular set of media types is combined to reach a target market. Such a **media mix** is discussed initially in this chapter and examined in more detail in chapter 12.

Media Terminology

Although this book deals primarily with providing an understanding of the principles and concepts involved in advertising media decisions, a secondary goal is to acquaint you with many of the terms used in the media field. (Many of these terms are also defined in the "Glossary" at the end of the book.)

The word *media* is plural; the singular form is *medium. Media* comes from the Latin for "middle," and that is exactly what an advertising medium is: something in the middle that acts as a go-between or intermediary, which serves to join together a writer or performer with an audience, or a marketer with potential customers. Modern American usage allows for the plural form to be *mediums,* but *media* is the word most often used in advertising.

The term *media type* refers to the broad, general categories of communication channels available for placing advertising messages; thus, media types include newspapers, magazines, television, radio, direct mail, directories, supermarket shopping carts, and the like. Because of the inherent complexity of the media systems in most parts of the world, precise terminology can be confusing. For example, most media types typically can be classified into a number of subcategories: Newspapers can be classified as *daily* or *weekly* (as well as *tabloid* or *broadsheet*); magazines can be subdivided into *consumer, business,* or *agricultural;* radio can be categorized as *AM* or *FM.* Generally, in discussions of aspects of media decisions, the term *media type* refers to the broadest categorization. Thus, a particular media mix might consist of newspapers, radio, and magazines. The strategy for this mix of media types would need to identify the media subcategories recommended.

A **media vehicle** means a specific, single carrier within a media type. Thus, *USA Today* is a vehicle for newspapers, while radio station KXYZ-FM and "60 Minutes" on CBS network television are vehicles for their respective media. Again, defining media vehicles can be confusing because not all media types lend themselves to the same vehicular classification scheme. For example, some would argue that there are no *vehicles* within direct mail.

TABLE 1.3		
Relationships between Media Type, Media Vehicle, and Advertising Unit		
Media Type	Media Vehicle	Advertising Unit
Newspaper	*New York Times*	Four columns × 12 inches
Magazine	*Vogue*	Full page, four colors
Television	CBS Evening News	Thirty-second commercial
Radio	WBBM-AM	Sixty-second commercial
Outdoor	Patrick Outdoor/ Birmingham	Bleed poster

The same could be argued for outdoor advertising, although the outdoor company within a particular city could be considered the vehicle.

The designation following the selection of a media vehicle is the advertising **unit** purchased—that is, the size of a print advertisement or the length of a broadcast commercial. The relationships between a media type, a media vehicle, and an advertising unit are shown with examples in table 1.3.

Three additional terms of general importance are **objectives, strategy,** and **tactics.** Objectives are the tasks to be accomplished through the development and execution of the media effort. Media objectives, or goals, must be as specific as possible so that, as the plan evolves, measurement of whether the objectives are attained is possible. (The terms *objectives* and *goals* are used interchangeably in this book, although some writers distinguish them as the long- versus short-range tasks, respectively, to be accomplished.) Media objectives must be set within the context of the broader advertising plan and, most importantly, to complement the full marketing efforts of the firm or organization.

Media strategies are the broad courses of action recommended to accomplish the stated objectives.

TABLE 1.4		
Media Plan for New High-Fiber Cereal		
Media Objective	Media Strategies	Media Tactics
• Reach 60 percent of the target market with an average of three messages during the introductory month of the plan.	• Target to current users of high-fiber bran cereals who are in the 50–65 age category. • Use a 90/10 mix of primetime network television and general editorial magazines.	• Two thirty-second commercials per month on "60 Minutes," "Murder She Wrote," and "The Cosby Show." • Full-page, four-color ads in *Modern Maturity, American Health, Life,* and *Changing Times.*

Strategies include the definition of the target audience on which media efforts will be concentrated, the mixture of media types directed to the target, the variation of media effort over the life of the plan, and the planning for various contingencies and alternatives.

Media tactics are the specific, detailed activities used to implement media strategies. Table 1.4 shows proposed objectives, strategies, and tactics in the media plan for the introduction of a new wheat-bran, high-fiber cereal.

An Overview of the Media Decision-Making Process

A framework for systematically studying the advertising media decision-making process is provided in figure 1.4.[4] Marketing scholars who have studied the matter of decision processes (usually relative to the field of consumer behavior) have commented that a decision process can be described in terms of (1) a list of variables that make up its content and (2) a list of functional relationships through which these variables affect each other.[5] Accordingly, figure 1.4 contains two major sets of constructs: decision variables and functional relationships.

Decision Variables

The primary decision variables that operate in media decisions—background inputs, objectives, strategies, tactics, constraints and uncontrollable influences, and measurement—are shown in figure 1.4. These are the factors that a media decision maker (generally referred to as a **media planner** in this book) considers and utilizes directly in developing a media plan or program for a particular brand, service, or idea.

Background Inputs

The media planning process usually begins with a careful consideration of the situation within which the brand, service, or idea to be advertised exists. (The term *brand* is used in this discussion to refer to all three—brand, service, and idea.) Media planners ask, "What do we know, and need to know, about our brand from research, experience, and marketing strategy?" They might begin by studying available research information, including what is known from experience with this or similar brands.

Research Inputs

Media planners often have a broad array of existing research from which they can learn much about the product situation. In cases where little information exists, such as for a totally new product category, original research data, known as primary research, may need to be gathered. Whether examining existing research or primary research, planners likely will look at four broad categories of research inputs: consumer research, product research, market analysis, and the competitive situation.

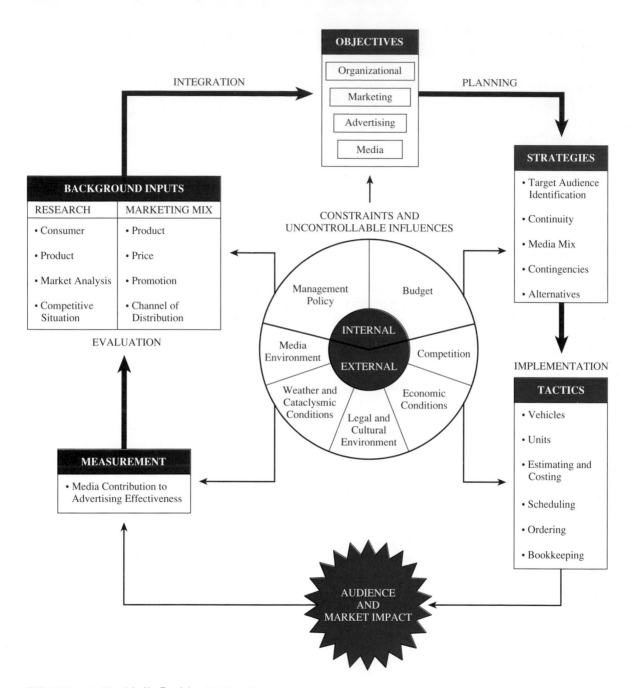

FIGURE 1.4 The Media Decision-Making Process

Consumer research provides information about a particular buying situation and can answer such questions as:

- Who are the primary users of the product category?
- What are their demographic, product usage, and/or psychographic characteristics?
- What are people's views, attitudes, knowledge, and motivations toward the product category and/or brand?
- What media types and vehicles reach category users, and to what degree?

For example, if you were developing plans for a new wheat-bran, high-fiber breakfast cereal, consumer research might tell you that (1) 50 percent of present users of bran cereal are between fifty and sixty-five years of age; (2) bran cereal users have favorable attitudes about the health value of bran fiber, yet know relatively little about proper levels and frequency of use; and (3) current bran cereal users watch television at less-than-average levels, but that, nevertheless, certain television programs reach relatively large numbers of bran cereal users.

Product research is a special type of consumer research. It attempts to find out how people feel about specific attributes of a product or brand. Often, this type of research is done *before* a particular brand is produced, in order to know what consumers want from the product. For example, if you were developing a new brand of 35-millimeter camera, knowing where the shutter release should be located (in terms of consumer preferences), whether auto-focus is a desired feature, whether other lenses can be added, and the like might be useful. For a packaged good, you might want to assess how consumers feel about the package in which the product comes: Can the package be reused? Does it easily fit retail shelves, and can it be easily stored at home? Is the package biodegradable?

Market analysis is research that determines the manner in which specific products and brands are used on a geographical basis. Currently, many marketers are paying particular attention to this issue, and companies are using regional marketing, where different strategies (including, in some instances, media strategy) are developed for specific geographic regions. As a media planner, you would want to know whether your brand is consumed relatively equally across the regions of the United States. If it is, then network television and/or national magazines may be efficient media types; if it is not, spot broadcasts, regional magazines, or newspapers may better pinpoint target audiences. In addition to looking at patterns across broad regions, media planners may also consider other geographical divisions: sizes of individual cities and counties, metropolitan versus suburban versus rural areas, and so on.

An analysis of the *competitive situation* is yet another type of research input. Some of the kinds of questions about the competitive situation that media planners might want answered include:

- What kinds of marketing mixes are being used by competitors?
- What share of the market does each brand have?
- How much money have competitors spent on advertising media in recent years?
- What media mixes are competitors using?
- What media vehicles have competitors purchased? How many? How often?

Although media planners may choose not to duplicate competitors' marketing and advertising efforts, this informational input usually is helpful. Research is discussed more fully in chapters 4 and 5.

Marketing Mix

The concept of marketing mix was introduced earlier in the chapter. The variables involved need not be repeated here. Instead, several examples of how marketing strategy can serve as valuable background input in the media decision-making process are presented. Media planners usually do not develop the marketing mix; rather, this typically is done by marketers and given to planners as background material. Yet, media planners must understand all aspects of marketing strategy to draw the linkages between marketing and media planning.

The *product* to be advertised can have significant media implications. For example, if many complex product features must be explained to prospects, then print media, which can present lengthy explanations, may be needed. Television might then be used as a follow-up, featuring only one or two attributes in a particular commercial. If a particular brand requires constant repetition of its availability, radio might be an effective medium to achieve high levels of frequency. Similarly, a national advertiser of a frequently purchased product might encourage its dealers also to advertise the brand in local media by offering incentives, such as cooperative advertising monies.

The *price* element in the marketing mix also can interrelate with media decisions, as well as other marketing-mix variables, in several ways. If the price suggested for a brand is at the high end of the price continuum, this factor may "position" the brand with a certain image. The media vehicles selected for this brand should have an image consistent with the brand. For example, Christian Dior cosmetics may find *Vogue* magazine's editorial environment more compatible with its pricing and brand strategy than, say, *True Story* magazine. The amount of price markup a marketer provides its dealers can affect the relative amount of money that marketer may be willing to devote to the media budget.

Promotion decisions have a direct impact on the media budget. Marketers must decide, for example, the relative amount of money to spend for advertising versus that spent for sales promotion and personal selling. When sales promotion is a part of the marketing mix, there may be a concurrent need to use certain media to advertise and/or distribute the promotion. Thus, coupons may be advertised in newspapers or magazines, and the number of coupons to be distributed affects the media placements.

The *place* variable—or *channel of distribution*—affects media decisions in some of the following ways:

- "Long" channels of distribution (many different channel members between the manufacturer and the final consumer) may require that additional media efforts be directed to channel members.

- How extensively a product is distributed at the retail level often relates to the brand image, which, in turn, affects media placements. Brands that have limited or exclusive retail outlets may need media vehicles with matching prestige; for example, Christian Dior cosmetics generally are available only through certain department and specialty stores.

- Brands sold largely in self-service outlets, where little if any personal selling is involved, may require media that permit detailed explanation of product benefits.

- The degree of a brand's placement in a geographic area affects media planning. Without adequate placement, there is little point in advertising in the area.

See chapter 3 for additional discussion of marketing mix.

Objectives

In figure 1.4, objectives are presented hierarchically, ranging from broad organizational goals down to specific media goals. The point is that media goals derive from the advertising goals, which, in turn, relate to broader marketing and organizational objectives. Although media planners may be responsible only for setting media objectives, they also must take the higher-level advertising, marketing, and organizational goals into account.

Strategies

The specific strategies derived for a media plan will, of course, vary according to such things as the type of product, stage in the product life cycle, and product turnover. As such, any number of strategies may be needed in a particular brand situation. Thus, the strategies shown in figure 1.4 do not necessarily exhaust all possibilities but represent the key strategies that typically must be considered.

In developing a media program, media planners at the minimum must: (1) carefully identify the target audience to whom the media efforts will be directed, (2) decide which media types are to be included and the allocation of budget among types (known as media mix, media weighting, or media allocation), and (3) develop a strategy that determines when media dollars should be spent over the life of the plan (usually called scheduling or continuity strategy). In addition, many planners develop various contingency strategies that take possible marketplace changes into account. Contingency strategies usually result in the preparation of alternative strategies that are based upon a certain number of possible outcomes. (For example, if you predict that economic conditions will be positive throughout the plan, what should you do if the economy suddenly turns downward?)

Tactics

Tactics involve the implementation stage of the media process; broad, strategic elements must be given specificity. Once a target audience has been defined and media types selected to reach the desired audience, the task becomes one of selecting specific media vehicles and deciding which advertising units to purchase. The continuity strategy must be executed by developing a media schedule that shows exactly when each unit will appear in each vehicle.

A number of other activities support these tactical decisions, typically called media buying. Along the way, media delivery must be estimated, costs must be determined for the various units to be purchased, orders must be placed with specific media companies, the spending budget must be monitored on a systematic basis, and a host of bookkeeping functions (sending production materials, paying media invoices, checking what was actually run, and so on) must be performed.

Constraints and Uncontrollable Influences

Although constraints and uncontrollable influences are not technically decision variables per se, they must nevertheless be considered *throughout* the decision process. These are the factors over which the media decision maker has no direct control, yet must nevertheless take into account as decisions are formulated. These factors are shown in figure 1.4 as a sphere with two major parts—internal and external constraints—each consisting of different elements, with arrows indicating the relationship between constraints and several key decision variables.

Internal constraints derive from within the organization itself: (1) the budget for a media plan typically is provided by company management as a given (although, of course, a media planner can recommend changes), and (2) various company policies may impinge on media selections (for example, there may be a management policy regarding the placement of advertising in vehicles that feature unacceptable editorial or entertainment content, such as television programs that contain excessive violence or deal with inappropriate topics).

External constraints involve a host of factors that occur in the environment, yet may have direct impact upon a particular plan. For example, if economic conditions change during the course of a media plan, contingency planning might be influenced; the manner in which competitors operate in the marketplace during the time of a plan could affect outcomes, and media objectives may then have to be modified; changing weather conditions could alter scheduling; and so on. Constraints are discussed further in chapter 6.

Measurement

Once background inputs and uncontrollable influences are considered, objectives and strategies established, and the plan tactically implemented, there is an audience/market impact. Such impact could be based on several criteria: How many units of the brand were sold? Did the advertising communicate what was intended? What percentage of the target market received messages, and how frequently were the messages received?

Ideally, the measurement part of the media decision-making process determines the degree to which the media effort contributed to overall advertising effectiveness. This, however, would require isolating media effects from all other influencing variables. (For example, if you see an advertisement for a brand, decide you like the brand, and eventually go to the store and purchase it, what role did the placement of the advertisement itself, so that you saw it, influence your final purchase decision?) Generally, this type of measurement is not possible, given current understanding of how advertising works. Therefore, the measurement stage normally involves determining whether the media effort has been able to achieve the stated media objectives and whether media placements have provided adequate exposure opportunities.

Functional Relationships between Decision Variables

If advertising decision making, including the media component, were totally scientific and if just how advertising influences consumer choice were understood, *decision rules* that show precisely how different media decision variables are "linked" to each other could be established. As has already been indicated, however, this information is currently not known. Nevertheless, the bold arrows in figure 1.4 show that there should be certain functional relationships (or decision rules, or "linkages") between the decision variables.

The functional relationships between decision variables are *integration, planning, implementation,* and *evaluation. Integration* means that, before media goals are set, media planners must carefully and systematically assess research inputs and marketing strategy. Although there currently are no precise decision rules for doing this, there nevertheless must be a thought process that attempts to link what is known from the background with what should be accomplished through the plan. For example, if research shows that a brand is unknown to many in the targeted audience, the advertising objective may logically call for certain levels of awareness, which, in turn, may be translated into a media goal of high reach.

By the same token, the linking of objectives and strategies involves a process of *planning,* whereby planners attempt to determine the functional relationships between a specific goal (say, to achieve a high degree of reach) and a certain strategy (say, use primetime television because data show a high percentage of the target delivered by this media type). Although this is still a subjective process, data sources are available that can assist planners.

Strategies are linked to tactics by the functional relationship labeled *implementation.* Tactical media specialists attempt to understand every aspect of a strategy to provide a workable execution. For example, by having a precise target audience definition and knowledge of which media types are recommended—coupled with an understanding of what the plan seeks to achieve—media buyers generally can use existing data sources to determine which media vehicles are most efficient.

Finally, following media measurement, there must be an attempt to relate what has been learned to the beginning of the next cycle of media decision making; this process is called *evaluation.* In evaluating the results of a particular media effort, planners consider changes and adjustments that they might make if they could start over. And, in fact, since many brands continue with media effort period after period, planners have the opportunity to apply what they have learned. Evaluation thus serves as a feedback loop into the next campaign period, making the whole process dynamic.

How the Media Decision-Making Process Relates to This Book's Organization

Much of this book is organized around the systematic description of the media decision-making process presented in figure 1.4. Each remaining chapter in the book relates to the overview flowchart of figure 1.4 as follows:

- Chapter **2** ("How the Media Function Is Organized") does not directly correspond to figure 1.4 but provides background information for understanding the advertising media business.

- Chapter **3** ("The Role of Marketing") corresponds to BACKGROUND INPUTS, Marketing Mix, of figure 1.4.

- Chapters **4** ("The Role of Research") and **5** ("The Role of Syndicated Research") correspond to BACKGROUND INPUTS, Research, of figure 1.4.

- Chapter **6** ("The Role of Uncontrollable Factors") corresponds to CONSTRAINTS AND UNCONTROLLABLE INFLUENCES of figure 1.4.
- Chapters **7** ("Quantitative Factors in Media Decisions") and **8** ("Qualitative Factors in Media Decisions") do not directly correspond to figure 1.4 but provide information for understanding strategic decisions.
- Chapter **9** ("Setting Objectives") corresponds to OBJECTIVES, especially Media, of figure 1.4.
- Chapter **10** ("Identifying Target Audiences") corresponds to STRATEGIES, Target Audience Identification, of figure 1.4.
- Chapter **11** ("Determining Scheduling Strategies") corresponds to STRATEGIES, Continuity, of figure 1.4.
- Chapter **12** ("Evaluating Media Mix Opportunities") corresponds to STRATEGIES, Media Mix, of figure 1.4.
- Chapter **13** ("Considering Other Strategic Factors") corresponds to STRATEGIES, Contingencies and Alternatives, of figure 1.4.
- Chapter **14** ("General Tactical Decisions") corresponds to TACTICS of figure 1.4.
- Chapters **15** ("Print Media: Newspapers and Magazines"), **16** ("Broadcast Media: Television and Radio"), **17** ("Direct Mail and Out-of-Home Media"), and **18** ("Other Media") correspond to TACTICS (by specific media type) of figure 1.4.
- Chapter **19** ("Trends and Projections") does not directly correspond to figure 1.4 but provides a perspective of media in the future.

Summary

The advertising media function has received increased attention in recent years as a result of several changing conditions, including the greater complexity of media options, the influence of general economic circumstances, and a recognition that media effort is one area of the advertising process where efficiencies often can be achieved.

In terms of overall advertising media expenditures, newspapers have the largest share, followed by television and direct mail. Whereas national advertisers predominate in television and outdoor advertising, local advertisers spend larger shares in newspapers, radio, and the Yellow Pages.

In making media decisions, media planners must always be mindful of the relationships that exist between the media effort and overall advertising and marketing strategies. The starting point of the process is the marketing mix, which consists of the blending of the product, place, price, and promotion variables. Media planners also look to research as an additional input. Research and marketing mix, then, serve as the background for the media decision-making process: for determining the objectives to be accomplished, the strategies that must be formulated, how the strategies will be tactically implemented, and finally, how results will be measured so that evaluations can influence the next cycle of the media process. Media planners also must take into account other factors over which they have no control but that may significantly influence decisions.

Questions for Discussion

1. What future conditions or circumstances might serve to increase further the importance of the media function?

2. Why do you feel that some media types are used mainly by national advertisers while others are predominantly used by local advertisers?

3. Using a recent issue of your local newspaper, count the total number of advertisements in the paper (exclude the classified or "want ads" section), and compute what percent of the total are for national advertisers and what percent are for local advertisers. Do a similar analysis for television by keeping track of the commercials shown for, say, 1 1/2 hours of viewing.

4. What factors do you feel contribute to the fact that more money is spent for newspaper advertising than for any other media type?

5. Assume that you are doing a media plan for Diet Coke. Discuss how various marketing-mix variables might affect your plan. Start by making assumptions about what you think the marketing strategy is for this brand.

6. Do the same thing asked in question 5, but this time assume the media plan is for the U.S. Army (recruitment of new enlistees into the voluntary defense forces).

7. Using the list of "Constraints and Uncontrollable Influences" shown in figure 1.4, speculate on how these might affect media planning for Diet Coke, as well as U.S. Army recruitment advertising.

8. If you were asked to develop a media program for Kellogg's Nutri·Grain breakfast cereal, list the set of questions you would like answered from research.

Endnotes

1. Carol Hall, "And Now, the Media Department Presents . . . ," *Marketing & Media Decisions,* January 1987, 31.

2. E. Jerome McCarthy, *Basic Marketing: A Managerial Approach* (Homewood, Ill.: Irwin, 1960).

3. Philip Kotler, *Principles of Marketing,* 3d ed. (Englewood Cliffs, N.J.: Prentice-Hall, 1986), 43.

4. The flowchart of the media decision-making process was originally developed by one of the authors of this book for a course in advertising media planning and has been modified a number of times over the past twenty years. It was initially published in Arnold M. Barban, Donald W. Jugenheimer, and Lee F. Young, *Advertising Media Sourcebook and Workbook* (Columbus, Ohio: Grid, 1975), and has also appeared in the second (Barban, Jugenheimer, Young, and Peter B. Turk; Grid, 1981) and third (Barban, Jugenheimer, and Turk; Lincolnwood, Ill.: NTC Business Books, 1989) editions of this source. Earlier versions also were in Jugenheimer and Turk, *Advertising Media* (Columbus, Ohio: Grid, 1980), and Arnold M. Barban, Steven M. Cristol, and Frank J. Kopec, *Essentials of Media Planning: A Marketing Viewpoint,* 2d ed. (Lincolnwood, Ill.: NTC Business Books, 1987).

5. See, for example, Francesco M. Nicosia, *Consumer Decision Processes* (Englewood Cliffs, N.J.: Prentice-Hall, 1966), 12.

Suggested Readings

• Aaker, David A., and John G. Myers. *Advertising Management.* 3d ed. Englewood Cliffs, N.J.: Prentice-Hall, 1987. Chapter 2.

• Barban, Arnold M., Steven M. Cristol, and Frank J. Kopec. *Essentials of Media Planning: A Marketing Viewpoint.* 2d ed. Lincolnwood, Ill.: NTC Business Books, 1987. Chapter 1.

• Barban, Arnold M., Donald W. Jugenheimer, and Peter B. Turk. *Advertising Media Sourcebook.* 3d ed. Lincolnwood, Ill.: NTC Business Books, 1989. Pages 1–7.

• Boone, Louis E., and David L. Kurtz. *Contemporary Marketing.* 7th ed. Hinsdale, Ill.: Dryden Press, 1992. Chapters 9–20.

• McGann, Anthony F., and J. Thomas Russell. *Advertising Media.* 2d ed. Homewood, Ill.: Irwin, 1988. Chapter 1.

• Sissors, Jack Z., and Lincoln Bumba. *Advertising Media Planning.* 3d ed. Lincolnwood, Ill.: NTC Business Books, 1989. Chapter 1.

• Surmanek, James. *Media Planning: A Practical Guide.* Lincolnwood, Ill.: Crain Books, 1985. Part II.

How the Media Function Is Organized

Outline

Learning Objectives

In the study of this chapter, you will have the opportunity to:

• Analyze the organizational structure of advertisers and the role of the advertising manager.

• Examine how national and local advertisers handle the media function.

• Explore the reasons for and against using a house agency.

• Observe the functions advertising agencies perform, the manner in which they are compensated, and how they organize their media department.

• Note how media advertising departments are organized and how they function.

*I*f you asked a friend, "What kind of work do you do?" and she answered, "I work in *advertising media,*" what would this mean? Well, it could mean a lot of things! This chapter seeks to clarify such ambiguity by providing some insights into how the media function is organized—what organizations are involved in making decisions about advertising media and what media tasks are performed by people within these organizations.

Although the subject matter of this chapter does not directly relate to the overview flowchart presented in chapter 1 (figure 1.4), it provides background information for understanding the media business, which can be of value to you in two important ways: (1) knowing who does media tasks provides assistance in understanding the decision process itself, and (2) you can assess whether working in the media end of the advertising business meets your personal career objectives.

The chapter is structured according to the major organizations that perform the media function. (In this chapter, an organization is often referred to as a "company," even though that word typically is used in a fairly restrictive sense. For example, one usually would refer to, say, Procter & Gamble as a *company,* but would label the American Red Cross an *institution* or *organization.* Using the word *company* for both examples merely simplifies the reference.) Chapter content revolves around the following three groups:

1. *Advertisers.* These are the companies that pay for the advertising produced under their name. Advertisers can be national (for example, Kraft General Foods advertising its JELL-O brand dessert) or local (for example, a bank, a department store, or a dry-cleaning establishment in your community). Likewise, advertisers can be profit-making entities, or they can be nonprofit organizations, such as the local library, the American Cancer Society, or the U.S. Internal Revenue Service.

2. *Advertising Agencies.* These are independent business firms that perform all, or a limited number, of advertising activities. They are hired by an advertiser to accomplish specific advertising tasks. For example, a particular advertiser might use an advertising agency to plan and execute a complete advertising campaign. Or an advertiser might use an agency only for the buying of advertising media vehicles.

3. *Advertising Media.* These are the firms that create and distribute the specific vehicle in which advertising is carried. Many media vehicles provide informational and/or entertainment content along with advertising, although some carry only advertising. The *Denver Post* newspaper, *Cosmopolitan* magazine, and the CBS television program "60 Minutes" are examples of the former; a direct-mail brochure, an outdoor poster in Los Angeles, and a transit advertisement on the outside of buses in Houston exemplify the latter.

Although other organizations can assist in the performance of the media function—for example, independent research firms that monitor media

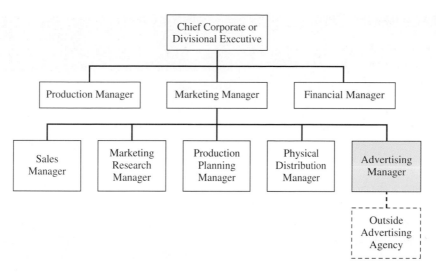

FIGURE 2.1 Organization Chart of a National
Advertiser with Advertising As a Marketing Function

spending by advertisers in various media types—
discussion in this chapter is limited to the three categories just mentioned.

Advertisers

The ways in which companies organize the advertising function are quite diverse and may depend on
the type of product in question. Thus, a company
marketing a consumer durable product (for example, an automobile) may organize differently
from a company selling a nondurable, packaged
good (for example, a laundry detergent). Regardless of how the advertising function is organized,
however, companies that place importance on the
advertising function, including the media component, usually designate an individual as the advertising manager or director. We look now at that
position.

Advertising Manager

Figure 2.1 shows a simplified organization chart for
a national advertiser, with the advertising manager
reporting to the chief marketing executive. The
three major functions of a business organization—

production, finance, and marketing—are on the first
level below the chief executive officer; five major
functions of marketing are shown reporting to the
top marketing officer. When advertising managers
also manage the company's sales promotion activity, their title is advertising and sales promotion
manager.

Local retail stores that have an advertising manager typically position the function under a director
of sales promotion. Under such an arrangement, the
advertising manager—along with managers of special events, public relations, and displays—reports
to the sales promotion manager. The advertising
manager coordinates all aspects of the store's advertising: planning overall strategy, creating and
producing the advertisements, placing the advertisements in local media, and assessing effectiveness.

The advertising manager typically coordinates
the company's advertising with an outside advertising agency (or with a house agency, as described
later in the chapter). However, local advertisers do
not use outside agencies to the same extent as national advertisers.

Although the specific duties of an advertising
manager vary widely according to the size of the

MEDIA SPOTLIGHT

2.1

How the Top One Hundred National Advertisers Spent Their Media Dollars in 1990

The top one hundred national advertisers spent almost $20 billion in 1990 in ten different types of media. These one hundred advertisers accounted for 28 percent of the media dollars spent by all advertisers, including local companies. Table 1 shows how these one hundred leading national advertisers invested their monies by media type.

TABLE 1

How One Hundred Leading National Advertisers Invested Monies, by Media Type

Media Type	Dollars Spent (in millions)	Percent of Total
Magazines	$2,882.1	14.5%
Sunday magazines	247.3	1.2
Newspapers	2,009.5	10.1
Outdoor	267.0	1.3
Network television	7,846.8	39.5
Spot television	3,938.7	19.8
Syndicated television	1,258.5	6.3
Cable television networks	633.9	3.2
Network radio	417.4	2.1
Spot radio	391.5	2.0
Total	**$19,892.7**	**100.0%**

As shown in the table, network television was the primary medium used, accounting for almost $8 billion, or 39.5 percent of the total. Spot television expenditures—advertising bought by national advertisers in local television markets—were almost $4 billion (19.8 percent of the total). All forms of television—network, spot, syndicated, and cable—were 68.8 percent of the total for the top one hundred national advertisers.

Source: Table from *Advertising Age*, September 25, 1991, page 67. Copyright © 1991 Crain Communications Inc., Detroit, MI.

company, the nature of its product or products, and the importance of its advertising, the following are some common responsibilities:

• *Planning the Overall Advertising Effort.* This is the advertising manager's most pervasive duty. Planning must involve the coordination of advertising with marketing and other company activities. If a company, for example, decides to use a contest or sweepstakes as a promotional event, and advertises it, the advertising manager works with the legal department to see that there is compliance with all laws governing such use.

• *Supervising the Execution of Advertising Plans.* Much day-to-day work revolves around the actual execution of advertising—for example, the placement of company advertisements in specific media and the creation of the advertising itself. The advertising manager works with department personnel or with individuals in an advertising agency to accomplish this.

• *Selecting and Evaluating the Work of an Advertising Agency.* When an advertising agency is being used, the advertising manager develops criteria by which agencies are chosen and assessed. The selection process typically involves top management of the company—in particular, the chief marketing executive.

• *Informing and Advising Top Management of Advertising Issues.* The advertising manager must be aware of the ways in which advertising impinges on the company as a whole and keep the appropriate executives informed of these implications. For example, if consumer groups have objections to certain types of advertising— say, advertising on television programs that have questionable content—the advertising manager must assess the possible effect on sales of company brands and keep marketing people appraised of the situation.

• *Coordinating Advertising Functions with Other Marketing Activities.* The advertising manager must be especially aware of the specific ways in which advertising interrelates with marketing tasks. Thus, the creation of advertising

messages, and the placement of these messages in media vehicles, must be coordinated with, for example, the company's selling and sales promotion strategies.

• *Coordinating Advertising Functions with Other Communication Activities.* By the same token, the advertising manager is responsible for coordinating advertising with the company's general communication strategy. For example, the public relations program may involve creating and placing advertising that communicates general company policy and philosophy.

• *Developing the Advertising Appropriation and Monitoring the Budget.* Although the advertising manager often does not have sole responsibility for deciding how much is to be spent for advertising, he or she works with top company officials in arriving at a decision. Once an amount is appropriated, the manager is responsible for monitoring the advertising budget   for example, by determining how much should be spent among alternative media, which vehicles in each medium should be bought, what size of print advertisements and what length of television commercials should be purchased, and when the messages should be scheduled. The manager also works with the accounting department to see that media bills are paid on time.

Brand-Management Approach

Companies that market several brands, especially those in the packaged-goods category, often use what is known as a **product-** or **brand-management approach.** Under this system, each of the company's brands is headed by a brand manager who is responsible for the overall marketing efforts for that particular brand.

One of the major advantages of brand management is that each product receives special attention. If one individual is responsible for several brands, particular brands may not receive the marketing effort needed to make them successful. Further, brand managers usually can react quickly to

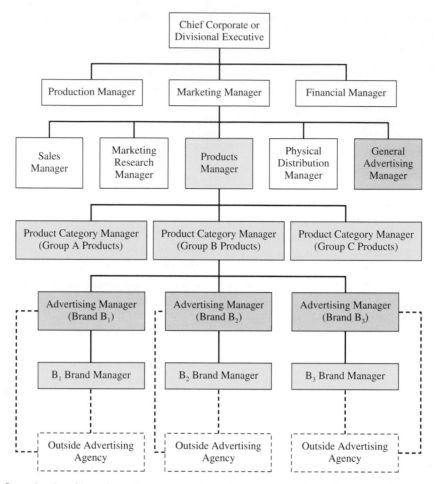

FIGURE 2.2 Organization Chart for a Company with Category and Brand Managers. (**Note**: The product category managers for Group A and Group C products have the same type of organization as that shown for Group B products.)

changing market conditions that may affect their brand. In addition, since brand managers work directly with their advertising agencies, advertiser-agency problems can be readily solved.

The use of brand managers, however, has some limitations. First, brand managers often do not have extensive control over the line functions needed to carry out the advertising plan. Second, because brand managers are often placed at a low organizational level, the position tends to be staffed with young, relatively inexperienced personnel. Third, because the job often is considered a stepping-stone to higher-level jobs, rapid personnel turnover is common. Despite these disadvantages, many com-

panies continue using the brand-management system because of the benefits it offers.

Figure 2.2 shows a type of brand-management organization currently used by many packaged-goods companies. On the level immediately below the major marketing functions are product category managers, who are responsible for a set of products in the company's marketing lineup. Procter & Gamble, for example, has a category manager for bar soap products (for example, Ivory, Camay, Safeguard) and another for its laundry detergent products (for example, Dash, Tide, Oxydol, Dreft). Each brand within a product category is, in turn, assigned to a specific brand manager. The advertising function is handled in two ways. First, a general advertising manager reports to the top marketing executive. The responsibilities here primarily are at the policy level, with the aim of coordinating all of the company's advertising. Second, an advertising manager is assigned to each brand to set overall ad strategy and approve all advertising and promotions for that brand, in addition to supervising the brand manager.

Advertising Media Function

So far, we have discussed advertising activity in general, without regard to the specific ways in which *media* decisions relate to a company's organization. Any advertising decision maker must, of course, be concerned with the media effort in planning and executing an advertising program. Thus, advertising managers—regardless of where they are positioned in the company hierarchy—deal in one way or another with media planning and placement.

In recent years, however, many advertisers have adjusted the organization of the advertising function to take the media effort into account more specifically. This usually is accomplished by establishing a small group of media experts—often called a media services department—who report to the advertising manager. In a company using the brand-management approach, shown in figure 2.2, the media services department usually is placed under the general advertising manager, rather than being a part of each brand's advertising manager setup. In this way, the media services department can provide media assistance for the advertising programs of all brands and can ensure media coordination across the advertised brands. As one company media expert (Robert Viscardi of Best Foods) put it:

I think more clients will see the need to have experts on the staff with media experience. Then there's one person in the company who knows where all the pieces fit.[1]

A media services department usually focuses on the two major media tasks: *planning* and *buying*. An understanding of what planning must take place for the successful advertising of a brand and (when

a company markets several brands) an ability to coordinate the planning for all of them is necessary. Where a multi-brand advertiser uses outside advertising agencies, the need to coordinate the different agency recommendations is critical. By the same token, media buying also requires special attention. Given the complexity of most media schedules, as well as the magnitude of costs involved, a company often finds it useful to have its own buying experts. Buyers assess the media placements for all brands and coordinate "buys" suggested by agency media people. Taking into account the complex discount structures of most media placements is reason alone for having buying experts on hand.[2]

House Agencies

Some companies choose not to use an outside, independent advertising agency, but rather to establish their own **house agency** (also called **in-house agency**).[3] Under this arrangement, the advertiser sets up a separate organization to perform all or some of the advertising effort. A house agency may have a limited focus, consisting only of the media-buying function, or it may perform all of the advertising task for certain products, with other brands handled by outside agencies. For example, a company may use advertising agencies for its regular brands but its house agency for brands being developed and placed in test markets. Then, once the test market brand is established, it is assigned to an outside agency. Let us now look at some of the reasons why a company may or may not want to use a house agency.

Reasons for Using a House Agency

Some of the reasons for using a house agency, either totally or partially, include:

Cost Savings. House agencies typically receive commissions from advertising media and therefore may be able to perform the advertising function at less cost than if the advertiser used an outside advertising agency. For cost savings, however, media commissions must be larger than the costs of in-house personnel and other operating expenses.

Confidentiality. Some companies prefer to keep certain marketing and advertising information confidential. They feel more secure working with an in-house group, rather than sharing information with an outside agency. This also may allow in-house personnel to have more complete data for developing advertising plans.

Communication. A house agency may have more direct contact with key company executives. In contrast, the lines of communication between an advertiser and its outside agency can become complicated, thus creating problems in the development and execution of plans.

Coordination and Control. Some executives feel that the in-house approach functions better in terms of coordinating the advertising effort with the marketing situation and controlling advertising expenditures.

Company and Product Familiarity. House agency personnel, as employees of the advertiser, may have more knowledge of the company's brands and its philosophy of doing business.

Reasons Against Using a House Agency

A company may choose not to establish a house advertising agency for the following reasons:

Objectivity. Outside, independent advertising agencies can bring objectivity to their view of a company's advertising problems. These agencies typically represent many different advertisers, with varied marketing situations, which provides them with a broad perspective of the marketplace. In-house people may be too close to the problem, resulting in a narrow view.

Quality and Number of Personnel. For a house agency to be cost effective, the quality and number of personnel may be limited. Much depends here on who can do a better job in advertising the company's brands.

Specialized Personnel. House agencies may not have as extensive a group of skilled specialists as an independent agency. Outside talent may need to be hired to provide many of the specialized services needed for the development and production of the advertising.

Working Relationship. Often, a company may find it easier to deal with an outside advertising agency whose personnel do not have to be managed in the same way as its own in-house employees. If the work of an independent agency becomes unsatisfactory, the agency can be replaced, whereas a similar situation with a house agency could not be handled so easily.

Most advertisers primarily use independent agencies to advertise their products. As Victor Buell commented, in comparing the results of his studies of advertisers in the 1970s and 1980s:

Some companies tried managing advertising in-house, but most gave it up. There were exceptions, such as those who retained the media-buying function. And some continue to provide special creative services for such things as new product concept testing or market testing. But the heralded revolution never came off. It does appear, however, that the companies that have in-house capabilities like the flexibility this gives them, even though they continue to rely primarily on their advertising agencies for their principal product campaigns.[4]

Advertising Agencies

Advertising agencies can be either **full service** or **limited service.** Victor Bloede defines a full-service agency as "an advertising agency that is capable of providing all the services necessary to handle the total advertising function."[5] A limited-service agency concentrates on one of the major advertising tasks—for example, the creative function (these are often called creative boutiques) or the media function (a **media-buying services agency**). The discussion that follows concentrates mostly on the full-service agency.

Advertising agencies are located throughout the United States, although they are concentrated in relatively few large cities. Table 2.1 shows the top twenty-five cities, in terms of the local office billings, in which agencies are located. The top twenty advertising agencies in the United States are listed in table 2.2. These are primarily headquartered in New York. The largest agency in 1990 was Young & Rubicam, with a gross income of $450.6 million.

TABLE 2.1

Top Twenty-Five U.S. Cities, by Local Agency Billings, 1990

Rank	City	Local Office Billings (in millions of dollars)	Number of Local Offices
1	New York	$24,728.4	174
2	Chicago	6,867.1	72
3	Los Angeles	4,321.9	55
4	Detroit	3,609.4	27
5	San Francisco	1,922.6	30
6	Dallas/Fort Worth	1,302.7	17
7	Minneapolis	1,091.3	21
8	Boston	922.8	17
9	Atlanta	861.1	20
10	Philadelphia	830.1	26
11	St. Louis	716.1	13
12	Cleveland	669.6	13
13	Stamford, Conn.	515.9	11
14	Houston	435.7	11
15	Pittsburgh	314.8	8
16	Baltimore	305.4	8
17	Milwaukee	296.3	13
18	Seattle	292.7	8
19	Washington, D.C.	257.3	4
20	Richmond, Va.	230.9	4
21	Kansas City, Mo.	217.1	8
22	Rochester, N.Y.	212.9	6
23	Miami	180.6	10
24	Winston-Salem, N.C.*	152.2	3
25	Dayton, Ohio	135.7	4

*Includes Asheville, Winston-Salem, and Highpoint, N.C.
Source: From *Advertising Age,* March 25, 1991, page S–36.
Copyright © 1991 Crain Communications Inc., Detroit, MI.
Reprinted by permission.

TABLE 2.2

Top Twenty U.S. Advertising Agencies in Terms of U.S. Gross Income, 1990 (in millions of dollars)

Rank	Agency	Headquarters	U.S. Gross Income
1	Young & Rubicam	New York	$450.6
2	Saatchi & Saatchi	New York	388.3
3	BBDO Worldwide	New York	370.4
4	Ogilvy & Mather Worldwide	New York	321.7
5	Backer Spielvogel Bates	New York	311.2
6	Leo Burnett Company	Chicago	299.3
7	DDB Needham Worldwide	New York	297.8
8	Foote, Cone & Belding	Chicago	292.4
9	J. Walter Thompson	New York	285.2
10	D'Arcy Masius Benton & Bowles	New York	276.7
11	Grey Advertising	New York	256.3
12	Lintas: Worldwide	New York	253.0
13	McCann-Erickson Worldwide	New York	210.1
14	Bozell, Inc.	New York	155.5
15	Ketchum Communications	Pittsburgh	121.3
16	Ross Roy Group	Bloomfield Hills, Mich.	106.0
17	Wells, Rich, Greene	New York	105.0
18	N W Ayer	New York	99.4
19	Della Femina, McNamee	New York	94.3
20	Chiat/Day/Mojo	Venice, Calif.	88.7

Source: From *Advertising Age,* March 25, 1991, page S–6.
Copyright © 1991 Crain Communications Inc., Detroit, MI.
Reprinted by permission.

A significant trend in recent years has been the merging of agencies into large mega-groups. For example, the WPP Group includes such previously independent agencies as Ogilvy & Mather; Scali, McCabe, Sloves; and J. Walter Thompson. Another mega-group, Saatchi & Saatchi Communications, includes Backer Spielvogel Bates; Campbell-Mithun-Esty; and Rumrill-Hoyt. Although this trend may have peaked, the implications of such mergers are likely to continue for some time. One of the main problems created by mergers is that different agencies within a group may each handle advertiser brands that are in direct competition with one another. Chapter 19 provides further discussion of the merger trend.

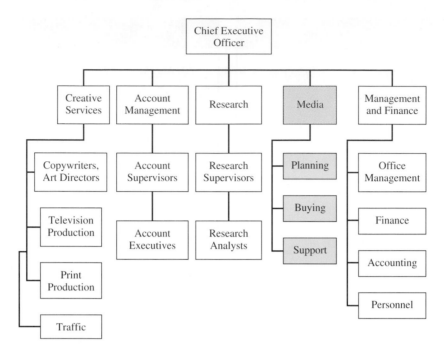

FIGURE 2.3 Typical Full-Service Advertising Agency Organization Chart by Functions

Agency Functions

A full-service advertising agency usually is organized according to the major functions it undertakes in working for a variety of advertiser clients. Figure 2.3 shows a typical agency organization chart by functions. Thus, the major functions performed are: creative services (message development and execution), account management, research, and media planning, buying, and support. In addition, an agency typically has an internal management and finance function.

Creative Services

A major function provided by a full-service advertising agency is the creation and execution of the advertising messages to be communicated to an intended audience. Copywriters and art directors develop a creative idea and then transform the idea into appropriate words and pictures. The next step is to produce the message as print advertisements and/or broadcast commercials. Traffic personnel maintain the flow of the work within the agency.

Account Management

The account management function is handled by account supervisors and account executives, who serve as the agency's liaison officers. They coordinate all of the agency's activities in developing a full advertising plan for a client and maintain close contact with the advertiser. They must know as much as possible about their clients' businesses. In large agencies, account executives may handle only one brand; then they, in turn, report to an account supervisor, who coordinates several brands and account executives.

Research

A large advertising agency usually has a research director responsible for advising agency personnel about research needs for particular situations. Agencies that do extensive research for their clients employ a number of research supervisors and research analysts.

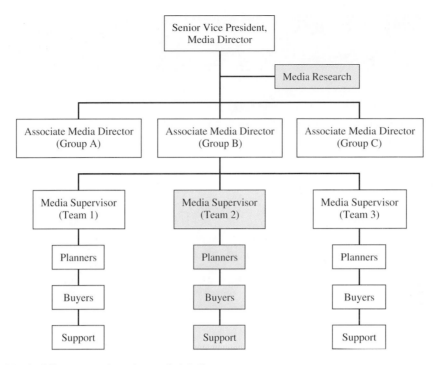

FIGURE 2.4 Vertical Structure of an Agency's Media Department. (**Note**: Groups A and C have the same organization as that shown for Group B.)

Media

The media department in a full-service agency generally is responsible for two major functions: (1) *planning* the media strategy and (2) executing that strategy by *buying* specific media vehicles. Other people within the department often *support* these major tasks. For example, experts are available to estimate media costs and the delivery of audiences from particular media buys. Sometimes, a small group of media research specialists are located within this group rather than in the research department.

Management and Finance

The management and finance function in a full-service agency is no different than that required of most business organizations: Clerical needs must be provided; expenses and revenues must be managed; bills must be paid; consideration must be given to such matters as cash flow and investment of agency profits; personnel must be hired and fired; employ-

ment benefit programs must be established and maintained; and so on.

Media Department Organization

Having glimpsed agency organization in general, we now turn our attention to the organization of the media department itself. We first look at some general material about agency media departments and then discuss how three specific agencies handle their organizational structure.

General

The two general approaches to organizing the media function within a full-service advertising agency are: *vertical* and *horizontal*. The vertical structure, or group system, builds on a series of self-contained media units, each unit handling a particular client's account from planning through execution. Figure 2.4 shows the vertical approach. In the figure, media

MEDIA SPOTLIGHT

2.2

Advertising and Marketing Salaries among Advertisers and Advertising Agencies, 1991

The average salary information provided here for a number of positions in marketing and advertising companies and agencies was obtained from a study conducted by *Adweek*, a trade publication. *Adweek*, as well as sister publications, *Adweek's Marketing Week* and *Mediaweek*, asked for the amount of their respondents' salaries in spring 1991, as well as what they had been earning one year earlier. Tables 1 and 2—for advertisers and advertising agencies, respectively—show the average salaries for a selected number of positions. The figures given are *base* salaries; 59 percent of *Adweek*'s sample received additional compensation (for example, bonuses).

TABLE 1

Average Salaries for Advertisers

Position/Title	1991 Salary	Percent Increase Over Previous Year
Marketing/Brand Management		
Vice President	$82,200	4.6%
Supervisor, "Director of"	58,500	4.5
Marketing Manager, Brand Manager	50,900	4.1
Assistant Marketing/Brand Manager	39,200	5.9
Advertising Management		
Vice President	85,900	6.8
Supervisor, "Director of"	53,600	7.4
Advertising Manager	44,600	2.5
Planner/Buyer	30,800*	−0.3
Media Buying/Planning		
Media Buyer, Media Planner	45,800	34.7
Advertising Research/Marketing Research		
Supervisor, "Director of"	61,100	−4.4

*Small sample size.

As can be seen in table 1, in 1991, a media buyer or planner, typically within a separate media services department, earned, on average, somewhat more than an assistant marketing or brand manager—$45,800 versus $39,200. A planner/buyer within the main advertising department earned noticeably less—$30,800—but the figure here was based on a small number of replies.

Table 2 shows that 1991 salaries for agency media people generally were lower than for those in the creative and account management departments. Averages for all positions in each respective department (and increases over the previous year) were: creative department—$62,700 (14.8 percent); account management department—$53,200 (6.4 percent); media department—$39,200 (9.8 percent).

TABLE 2

Average Salaries for Advertising Agencies

Position/Title	1991 Salary	Percent Increase Over Previous Year
Creative Department		
Executive or Senior Vice President	$152,700	11.4%
Vice President	78,900*	4.5
Creative Supervisor/Director	63,000	16.7
Manager	37,600*	−1.8
Copywriter	41,700	14.6
Art Director	39,200	4.3
Account Management Department		
Executive or Senior Vice President	110,400	6.6
Vice President	71,700	6.9
Supervisor, "Director of"	53,700	4.7
Account Manager	41,100	2.2
Account Representative	32,600	1.9
Media Department		
Executive or Senior Vice President	110,400	1.4
Vice President	60,400	−0.7
Media Supervisor/Director	41,500	3.5
Media Manager	33,100*	−2.7
Media Buyer/Planner	25,200	0.0

*Small sample size.

Source: *Adweek*, 3 June 1991, 27–32.

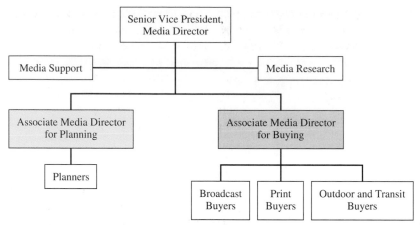

FIGURE 2.5 Horizontal Structure of an Agency's
Media Department

research is shown as a unit within the overall media department, which permits research specialists to advise all groups on research matters. Immediately below the media director are a number of associate media directors, who are responsible for coordinating several media teams. Each media team likely is headed by a media supervisor, with planners, buyers, and support people reporting to him or her. A media team usually is assigned one brand (or relatively few brands), and the team does the media planning and buying for that brand. The support function assists the planners and buyers by providing such information as media cost estimates and the likely audience delivery of specific media vehicles. The self-contained team, therefore, is a key element in the group system, with planning, buying, and support activities organized vertically.

The horizontal structure, or specialist approach, places the two major media tasks—planning and buying—on parallel, or horizontal, levels (see figure 2.5). Support activity is shown as a staff or service function for all planners and buyers, as is media research. Typically, an associate media director coordinates all of the planners in the media department, with each planner assigned one or more of the agency's accounts. Another associate media director specializes in the buying function; in turn, buyers typically are specialists in a particular media type (for example, broadcast, print, or out-of-home). When a planner completes the media plan for an

account, and it is approved by the associate media director and the client, the task of purchasing specific media vehicles is assigned to the buying group.

The vertical and horizontal approaches to media department organization can be thought of as abstractions. That is, no particular agency is likely to follow either structure exactly as shown here, but rather, organizes in a way that works best for its particular needs.

Specific Agencies

In this section, we look at the organization of the media task for three specific full-service advertising agencies by: (1) examining the agency's media department organization chart and (2) discussing brief job responsibilities for the major positions in the department.

Young & Rubicam/New York Office

As shown in table 2.2, *Advertising Age's* 1991 "Advertising Agency Income" issue reported that Young & Rubicam was the number one U.S. agency in terms of U.S. gross income. The agency had 1990 billings in the United States of over $2.1 billion. Clients handled by the New York office included: Adidas USA, Colgate-Palmolive Company, Eastman Kodak, General Foods Corporation, Holiday Inns, Time Inc., U. S. Postal Service, and Metropolitan Life Insurance Company.

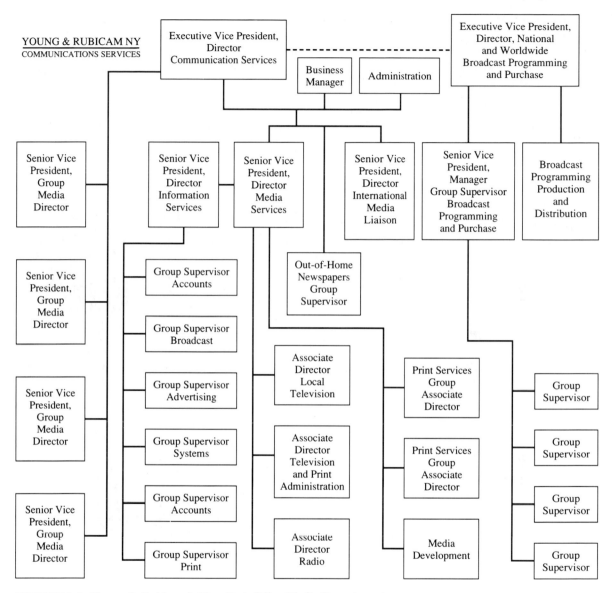

FIGURE 2.6 Young & Rubicam's New York Office Media Department
(Communications Services) Organization Chart
Source: Young & Rubicam, New York, NY.

Figure 2.6 shows the overall organization of Young & Rubicam's media department, which it calls Communications Services. The broad array and size of the companies and brands represented results in an organizational structure that is of necessity quite extensive, with a number of management levels to coordinate the work of many individuals.

Each of the four major *planning* groups—shown at the far left side of the chart—is headed by a senior vice president, who has the title group media director. A group, in turn, typically has about three planning group supervisors, who each is assigned a number of client accounts. Reporting to each group supervisor are between seven and nine planning supervisors, who, in turn, coordinate the work of a host of media planners, some of whom carry the title senior planner.

Buying activity is handled by separate groups, generally with responsibility broken down according to media type: broadcast, print, and out-of-home. A number of media research, as well as resource and development, personnel assist in the activity of the overall department.

The major responsibilities and duties of some of the key people in the media department are:[6]

• *Planning Group Supervisor:* The senior line media representative with overall responsibility for media output quality and service on assigned accounts. Reports to the group media director and supervises assigned planning supervisors. Has ongoing contact with other Communications Services groups and also deals with account management personnel on long-range planning and strategy; also has contact with all levels of the client companies. Has two areas of responsibility: (1) top-level leadership and supervision and (2) long-range marketing and media strategy planning.

• *Planning Supervisor:* Directs the day-to-day media activity on assigned accounts, assists the planning group supervisor in developing media strategy, and oversees translation of client marketing and advertising objectives into media strategies. Also responsible for developing the skill and knowledge base of assigned senior planners and planners. Responsible for
(1) planning, analyzing, and evaluating, and
(2) leading, coordinating, and managing.

• *Senior Planner:* Develops media plans in accordance with the strategy of the media work plan on assigned accounts, and then implements and monitors the approved media plan. Responsible for developing the skill and knowledge base of any planner assigned to him or her. Has three areas of responsibility:
(1) implementing strategy and direction,
(2) providing media expertise, and
(3) implementing, coordinating, and monitoring.

• *Planner:* Assists with the development of media plans in accordance with the strategy of

the media work plan on assigned accounts and then implements and monitors the approved media plan. Has the same responsibilities as the senior planner, except that "assisting" with the process is part of the training aspect for this position.

• *Group Supervisor, Network Television:* Manages the day-to-day purchasing of all national television commercial time, including network, cable, and syndication. Has key involvement in the development of network television supervisors, associate buyers, and network specialists. Responsible for
(1) supervising broadcast buying and
(2) providing commercial broadcast purchasing expertise.

• *Supervisor, Network Television:* Negotiates and implements network television buys and helps develop the skill and knowledge base of network specialists.

• *Group Supervisor/Associate Director, Local Broadcast and Network Radio:* Negotiates and executes spot television and spot radio buys within specified markets and also purchases network radio. Responsible for developing the skill and knowledge base of assistant supervisors and purchase service assistants.

• *Supervisor, Print Services Group:* Serves as an information resource for the planning groups and clients in matters concerning the magazine industry. Responsible for participating in/ overseeing as appropriate client or brand specific pricing, positioning, and added-value negotiations. Plays a key role in helping to develop pricing strategies and added-value programs. Has responsibility for specific accounts and for developing the skill and knowledge base of assigned print service assistants.

• *Director, Information Services:* Responsible for ensuring effective management of information services to optimize the quantity and quality of research produced. Responsible for fostering innovative media research approaches that answer planner, buyer, and related departments' needs.

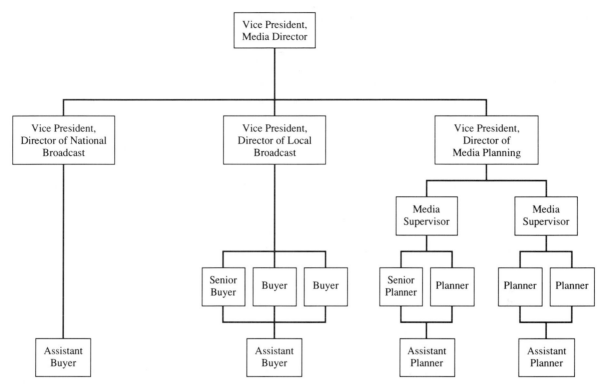

FIGURE 2.7 The Bloom Agency's New York Office
Media Department Organization Chart
Source: The Bloom Agency, New York, NY.

The Bloom Agency, Inc./New York Office

The Bloom Agency operates out of offices in New York and Dallas. Ranked sixty-eighth in the *Advertising Age* survey, it had gross income in 1990 of $20.0 million and $174.1 million in billings. Among its accounts were Scott Paper Company, Hiram Walker, Ross Laboratories, and Block Drug Company.

The organization of the New York office of the Bloom Agency is shown in figure 2.7. Three sub-departments report to the vice president and media director—national broadcast buying, local broadcast buying, and media planning. Print media and out-of-home (outdoor and transit) buying is handled by the media-planning unit. All media functions are supported by a full array of outside media-research services.

The major responsibilities within the department are:[7]

• *National Broadcast Buying:* The vice president, director of national broadcast is responsible for the analysis and purchase of network television, national cable television, syndicated television, and network and syndicated radio for all Bloom clients. The department seeks efficient, highly visible programming opportunities that will enhance clients' advertising messages.

• *Local Broadcast Buying:* Headed by the vice president and director of local broadcast, the unit's group of media buyers, also known as market specialists, purchase spot television, spot radio, and local cable television for the agency's clients. These local-market buyers are fully involved with each brand's unique marketing, creative, and promotional needs; they develop buys and coordinate merchandising/promotional opportunities to achieve highly effective local market efforts.

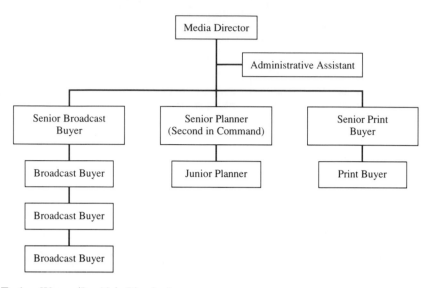

FIGURE 2.8 Tucker Wayne/Luckie's Birmingham
Office Media Department Organization Chart
Courtesy of Tucker Wayne/Luckie & Company—Linda Rountree.

• *Media Planning:* The media planning
subdepartment is led by the vice president and
director of media planning and is staffed by a
group of media planning supervisors, senior
planners, planners, and assistant planners. These
individuals oversee the placement of all
advertisements and commercials. They develop
the media mix, deciding how much to spend,
where, when, how often, and in which medium.
They map out the broad strategy (for example,
use print media) and the finer details (for
example, specific magazine titles). The planning
group also prepares the buying specifications used
by the broadcast negotiators and is responsible
for the negotiation and placement of all print and
out-of-home media as well as for maintaining
brands' budgets and billing. It maintains a close
partnership with people in the account
management, creative, and research departments
of the Bloom Agency, as well as with client
marketing groups to achieve the brands'
marketing objectives.

Tucker Wayne/Luckie & Company— Birmingham Office

With a ranking of eighty-eighth in *Advertising
Age's* survey of agencies, Tucker Wayne/Luckie &
Company had gross income in 1990 of $15.5 mil-
lion and billings of $116.2 million, and employed
180 people in two offices, Atlanta and Birmingham.
It represented such clients as BellSouth Services,
McKee Baking Company, Liberty National Life
Insurance, and Blue Cross/Blue Shield.

Figure 2.8 shows the organization of the media
department in Tucker Wayne/Luckie's Birmingham office. Three major units are under the
media director: broadcast buying, print buying, and
media planning. The major responsibilities * of the
positions shown in figure 2.8 are:[8]

• *Media Director:* Responsible for overall
media product of the agency. Keeps abreast of
new trends, current standards, and new methods
in all aspects of media planning, buying, and
research. Maintains strong relationships with

*Courtesy of Tucker Wayne/Luckie & Company—Linda Rountree.

media and rep firms. Has constant communication with account services regarding all media activity on their accounts. Involved in client meetings, new-business research and presentations, and planning and buying for network broadcast, syndication, and cable television. Supervises media research projects and source library.

• *Senior Planner:* Plans media independently or assists media director as assigned. Services agency accounts on a continuing basis through regular contact with account services, by troubleshooting, and by providing client-requested information on a regular or as-needed basis. Assists media director with network television buying. Assists with research and special projects, with new-business preparations and presentations, and in maintaining media resource and research library. Serves as department head in absence of media director.

• *Junior Planner:* Assists senior planner and media director with research projects and new-business preparation, and in maintaining media resources and research library. Tracks media budgets by client and media types. Prepares all flowcharts by computer program.

• *Broadcast Buyer:* Under supervision of media director and senior broadcast buyer, implements services appropriate to specific client's needs as directed by account services and department management. Maintains effective professional relationships with media sources and representatives. Continues to broaden base of knowledge regarding media analysis, selection, and the buying process.

• *Print Buyer:* Under supervision of media director and senior print buyer, implements services appropriate to specific client's needs as directed by account services and department management. Maintains effective professional relationships with media sources and representatives. Continues to broaden base of knowledge regarding media analysis, selection, and the buying process.

Media Buying Services

A media buying service is a limited-service agency that concentrates on the media function. If the media department, or part of it, was taken out of a full-service agency and set up as an independent company, it would be a media buying service. Although most media buying services concentrate, as their name implies, on the *buying* aspects of media, some offer a full complement of media services.

Many advertising organizations find a media buying service useful. For example, some advertisers prefer to have different outside specialists develop and execute their advertising. Thus, they use a creative boutique for message strategy and execution and a media buying service for media planning and buying. An advertiser that has its own house agency sometimes prefers to develop all of the advertising strategies for its brand or brands, but due to the inherent complexity of media buying, uses a buying service to execute the media plan. A full-service advertising agency also might hire a media buying service to do part of its execution under certain circumstances. For example, if a full-service agency's media buyers are overloaded at certain times of the year, using a buying service may be more economical than hiring new personnel for a limited period. Or an agency may find that a buying service can be more efficient than its own staff in placing certain kinds of media—for example, television.[9]

Agency Compensation

Advertising agencies generally are compensated in three ways: media commissions, agency charges, and fees.

Media Commissions

The **media commission system** has been around since the origin of advertising agencies in the 1860s. Originally, advertising agents started as space brokers: They bought advertising space from a publication at one price and sold the space to advertisers at a higher price, making their profit from the price difference. This evolved into the situation whereby media offer an agency a commission—usually 15 percent—on the stated price of space the agency buys for an advertiser. Thus, if a magazine lists a particular advertising unit for $1,000, the charge to an agency is 15 percent less, or $850. The agency, in turn, bills the advertiser for $1,000, leaving it a gross profit of $150. The agency provides the advertiser with certain services, such as creating the messages and handling media placements; from its $150 gross profit, it pays its personnel, rent, utilities, and other expenses, and (hopefully) has some money left over as a net profit.

Agency Charges

Certain costs that an agency incurs in handling an advertiser's account typically are not included as part of its basic service, for which media commissions apply. For example, the *production* of advertisements and commercials usually is charged to the advertiser in a special way. In making a television commercial, the agency has expenses for such items as hiring the actors in the commercial, making props, hiring studios, filming or taping, and the like. Print advertisements involve buying artwork, composing type, and producing finished printing plates. Such charges usually are handled on a "cost plus" basis. Traditionally, agencies have handled these expenses by marking them up 17.65 percent. Thus, if it costs $10,000 to produce a television commercial, the agency adds $1,765 to the $10,000 in charges and bills the advertiser $11,765. The unique figure—17.65 percent—amounts to 15 percent of the amount billed ($1,765 gross profit divided by the billed amount, $11,765, is 15 percent). Thus, the 15-percent media commission system has carried over to the area of other charges.

Agencies also charge for other services they might supply to an advertiser client. For example, the expense of doing a research project, where outside companies are hired by the agency to do the research study, typically is charged to the advertiser. In addition, some media—for example, direct mail—are not by their unique nature commissionable; thus, an agency that develops such advertising for a client adds a charge to its out-of-pocket expenses to make a profit.

Fees

The fee system of compensation came about because some individuals believed that the media commission system was a holdover from earlier days and was no longer applicable to modern advertising. The principle here is that an advertising agency should be compensated for its expertise in the same manner as any other profession, such as lawyers or accountants.

There are a number of approaches to fee compensation, but they basically work in the same way. The advertiser and its agency decide what kind of work is to be done and arrive at a reasonable fee for such work. For example, the advertiser and agency might agree to a cost-plus method: The agency keeps careful records of the costs incurred in serving a client—including hourly costs of agency personnel who work on the account—and periodically bills the advertiser for these costs, plus some agreed-upon profit margin. Or the agency and client might establish a fixed-fee arrangement, whereby a particular fee is paid for prescribed work. Regardless of the particular fee arrangement used, the normal commissions the agency receives from media are credited against the fee.

The Compensation Situation Today

The straight 15-percent media commission system was the dominant type of agency compensation for over one hundred years. Since the mid-1980s, however, this method no longer predominates. Some companies believed that the advertising agencies were making too much profit from the 15 percent they received from media commissions, and they renegotiated the figure downward. For example, industry observers estimate that most automobile advertisers presently allow their agencies only a 12-percent commission. In this situation, the agency still receives a 15-percent commission from most media but can only bill the advertiser for 12 percent.[10] This trend is not limited to automobiles and extends to a number of other product companies.

Other advertisers have switched from a commission to a fee arrangement, and still others have developed unique variations on the fee system. For example, Carnation Company's agency-compensation program is based on how advertising scores in research tests.[11] Other advertisers have announced plans to develop compensation plans related to sales results.[12] While the 15-percent commission probably will continue to be used in many instances, many advertisers in the near future will experiment with new and unique options.[13] We discuss this further in chapter 19.

Advertising Media

The companies that produce the media vehicles in which advertising is carried are the third major organization involved with the media function. These are companies involved in distributing newspapers, magazines, television and radio programs, outdoor advertising, and the like. Many of these companies focus on a single vehicle, such as a weekly newspaper in a rural community. Others are multibillion-dollar corporations that own and operate several different types of media, with alternative vehicles within a media type.

Table 2.3 shows the top twenty media companies, along with their percent of revenues by media type, in the United States. Some of these companies concentrate on one media type, whereas others are more diversified in their media involvement. For example, CBS Inc. earns all of its media revenues from broadcast, through its ownership of the CBS Television Network as well as television stations in major markets in the United States. Likewise, TCI, the seventh-ranked media company, operates only in the cable field and owns cable television systems throughout the country. On the other hand, the Hearst Corporation has ownership in four of the five categories shown in table 2.3. Although the majority of Hearst's media revenues are from newspapers (33.4 percent) and magazines (47.9 percent), it also has income from its television and radio stations and other media activities.

Media Advertising Department

A media vehicle, such as the *New York Times* newspaper or *House & Garden* magazine, has a number of major functions it must perform in is-

suing its publication. For example, there is the "editorial" side of the business, with reporters, editors, and the like responsible for the news/informational/entertainment content of the publication. On the other hand, the vehicle also must be responsible for generating income (and profit) for the company, the "business" side of the activity. A print medium, for example, may secure income from the sale of the publication—its distribution or "circulation" function—and from the revenues it receives from advertisers who buy space.

Our concern is with the medium's advertising activity and advertising department. The advertising department of any media vehicle is primarily concerned with the *sale* of advertising space or time. Usually, however, there are individuals in the department who are not directly involved in selling but who assist salespeople. For example, research people may collect and analyze information about their vehicle's audience or market characteristics. Promotion people design materials that a salesperson can use in calling on prospective advertisers. Creative talent may be employed by the medium to help develop the advertising of its clients. We now examine advertising department organization for several of the major types of media.

Newspapers

The main advertising sales activities of a newspaper usually are represented in three subdepartments: retail (or display) advertising, classified advertising, and general or national advertising, as shown in figure 2.9. Research and promotion serves to assist the sales activity.

The retail advertising unit sells advertising space to local retailers and service organizations, such as banks, dry cleaners, theaters, and the like. Retail advertising accounts for over half the advertising revenues of a typical newspaper. Retail salespeople help their customers plan and execute their newspaper advertising program. When necessary, newspaper service personnel may assist a customer with the writing and artwork used in an advertisement. The retail advertising unit often has a person who is responsible for coordinating cooperative advertising funds, which are monies and services available to local retailers from national advertisers.

TABLE 2.3

Top Twenty U.S. Media Companies, 1990

Company	Media Revenues (in millions of dollars)	Percent of Revenues by Media Type
1. Capital Cities/ABC	$5,175.4	10.1% / 7.1% / 74.2% / 8.6%
2. Time Warner	4,964.8	39.2% / 60.8%
3. Gannett Company	3,441.6	80.6% / 11.5% / 7.9%
4. CBS Inc.	3,261.2	100.0%
5. General Electric Company	3,236.0	99.0% / 1.0%
6. Advance Publications	3,039.6	59.1% / 27.8% / 13.1%
7. TCI	2,942.0	100%
8. Times Mirror Company	2,855.2	72.3% / 11.0% / 13.0% / 3.7%
9. News Corporation	2,234.4	7.8% / 31.7% / 37.3% / 23.2%
10. Hearst Corporation	2,137.6	33.4% / 47.9% / 13.5% / 5.2
11. Knight-Ridder	2,106.1	94.6% / 5.4
12. New York Times Company	1,776.8	76.5% / 19.1% / 3.9%
13. Cox Enterprises	1,710.9	43.5% / 24.5% / 32.0%
14. Tribune Company	1,703.0	70.3% / 29.7%
15. Thompson Corporation	1,404.0	46.6% / 53.4%
16. Washington Post Company	1,356.1	51.0% / 25.1% / 13.2% / 10.7%
17. Viacom International	1,337.5	12.3% / 87.7%
18. E. W. Scripps Company	1,220.0	64.4% / 19.3% / 16.3%
19. Turner Broadcasting System	1,069.1	100.0%
20. Dow Jones & Company	983.7	100.0%

Key: Newspapers ▢ Magazines ▢ TV and Radio ▢ Cable ▢ Other ▢

Source: From *Advertising Age*, August 12, 1991, page 21. Copyright © 1991 Crain Communications Inc., Detroit, MI.

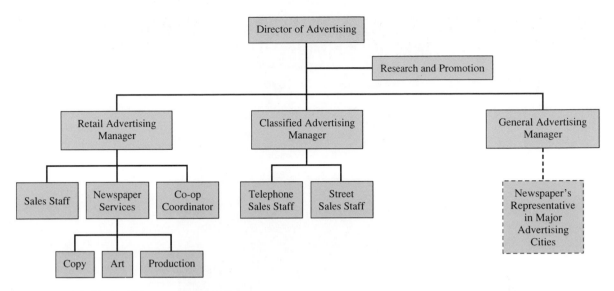

FIGURE 2.9 Typical Newspaper Advertising Department Organization Chart

The **classified advertising** unit sells, prepares, and services individuals and businesses that use the newspaper's classified section. Much of the classified advertising in a newspaper, typically straight lines of copy, is by individuals who want to sell something to others in the community—say, a piece of furniture, items in a garage sale, or an appliance. Selling of classified ads often is handled over the telephone. Businesses also use the classified section to advertise such things as automobiles, help wanted, or real estate. These advertisements often use illustrations and look much like regular retail advertisements, but they are in the classified section (called **classified display**). Business accounts can be handled by telephone but also are called upon in person by street salespeople. An average newspaper gets about 38 percent of its advertising sales from classified advertising.

The general advertising unit is usually a small department and deals solely with national advertising, which accounts for 11 percent of a newspaper's advertising revenue. However, personnel in general advertising do not themselves typically sell the advertising; rather, national advertising is sold by outside newspaper representatives who have offices in the major advertising markets of the United States. (Such newspaper reps are discussed later in this chapter.) What people in the general advertising unit do, therefore, is "service" the national advertisements sold by reps. For example, they see to it that an advertiser's special requests—say, where the advertisement is placed within the newspaper—are met whenever possible. They also help a national advertiser **merchandise** its advertisements in the local community by calling on local dealers to be sure they have adequate stock and are using the national advertiser's point-of-purchase displays that tie in with the newspaper advertising.

Broadcast Stations

Local radio and television stations operate much like local newspapers, except that there is no counterpart to the classified unit. The advertising department typically is headed by a sales manager, who generally has two people reporting to him or her—one for local or retail sales and one for national sales. The national sales manager works with the station's time rep, who sells advertising to national advertisers and their agencies for inclusion on the station. (This type of advertising is known as national spot.) The local sales manager has a staff of salespeople who sell and service the needs of local advertisers.

FIGURE 2.10a Samples of Sales-Support Material
Developed by WBMG-TV, the CBS Affiliate Station in
Birmingham, Alabama
Courtesy of WBMG-TV.

They also provide help with the planning and execution of their clients' broadcast advertising—for example, in the writing and production of a commercial. Also included as broadcast station advertising is the use of cable programs sold by a staff hired by the local cable system.

Broadcast stations provide their customers and prospective clients with merchandising assistance, and also have research and promotion materials that help their sales staff. Figures 2.10*a* and *b* show a packet of information used by the sales staff of WBMG-TV, the CBS affiliate station in Birmingham, Alabama.

Broadcast Networks

In radio, more than twenty companies link together various radio stations throughout the country to comprise a specific **network,** such as the Mutual Broadcasting System. Television networks can be assembled "over-the-air" (such as ABC, CBS, NBC, and Fox) or by cable systems (such as ESPN, USA Network, Arts & Entertainment, and The Discovery Channel).

By definition, network advertising is used by national advertisers who distribute their products throughout the United States. Network sales are handled by account executives who work with advertisers and their agency broadcast negotiators in arriving at a schedule of broadcast commercials. The salespeople are supported by their network's research and promotion unit. Network buying is a fairly complex process. Prices of commercials are negotiated, as are a host of other factors, such as the guarantee of audience delivery, placement of commercials within a program, replacement procedures for canceled programs, and the like.

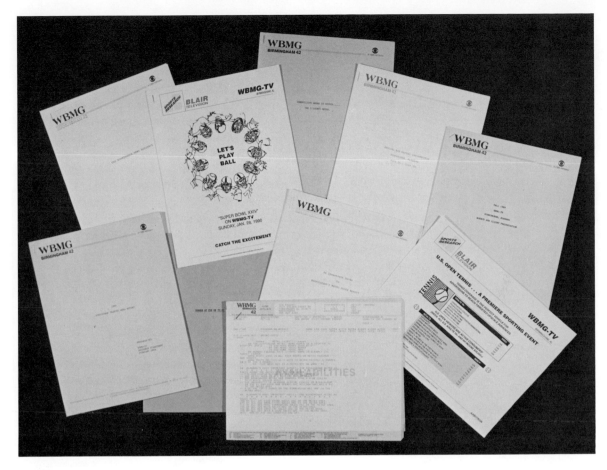

FIGURE 2.10b

Magazines

Magazines, like broadcast networks, are primarily used by national advertisers; accordingly, they operate in a similar manner. Magazine salespeople work with advertisers and their agencies in selling magazine space, and they are supported by research, promotion, and merchandising groups.

In some instances, a particular magazine may use outside magazine representatives to do all or part of its selling. For example, a magazine might have its own sales staff to cover certain markets (say, New York and Chicago) but use magazine representatives in other major advertising cities. (Such magazine reps are discussed later in the chapter.) Figure 2.11 shows the advertising department of

Chicago magazine, which concentrates its circulation in the Chicago market. Account executives are primarily responsible for advertising sales within Chicago and national accounts in the Midwest, whereas independent rep firms focus on national advertisers in major markets outside of Chicago.

Out-of-Home (Outdoor and Transit)

Outdoor advertising is handled by companies (called plant operators) that operate in one or more local markets. Local salespeople sell outdoor posters and painted bulletins to retailers and service companies in the region. Space to national advertisers usually is sold by an industrywide sales organization. Transit

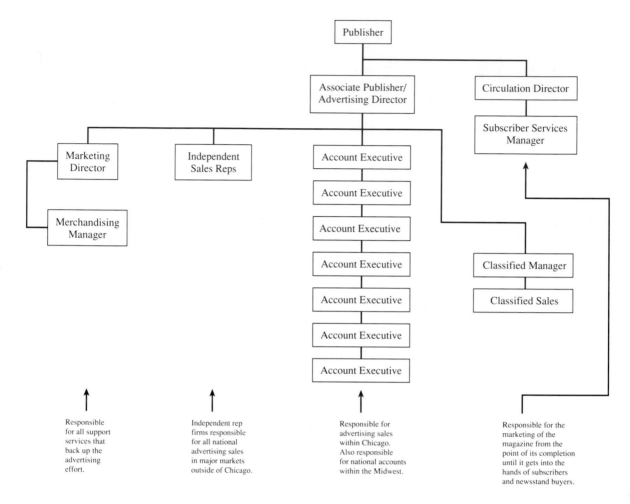

FIGURE 2.11 Organization of *Chicago* Magazine's Business Function
Courtesy of *Chicago* magazine.

advertising—advertisements on the sides and interiors of buses, on taxicabs, and inside transit stations—is handled similarly, except that specialized outside companies represent different transit systems in selling advertising space.

Media Representatives

Media representatives (**reps**) work in the print and broadcast media to sell advertising for a particular media vehicle that does not want to have sales offices in the major advertising cities. For newspa-

pers, and television and radio stations, a rep firm (usually a *company* with a sales force and support personnel) typically operates along the following lines:

- Maintains a sales staff in major advertising markets to call on national advertisers and particularly their advertising agencies.
- Handles only one newspaper or station in a specific market and has exclusive rights to sell the newspaper or station to national advertisers (but handles, overall, many different papers or stations throughout the United States).

- Has a threefold sales job: sell the value of the medium (for example, television), sell the value of the market (for example, Birmingham, Alabama), and sell the value of the particular station it represents (for example, WBMG).

- Operates as an independent business, not owned by the paper or station it represents. It derives its income primarily from commissions paid by the medium. The usual commission ranges between 10 and 15 percent of the price of the space or time sold. Thus, if a newspaper prices a page of its advertising at $5,000 for a national advertiser and hires a rep firm on a 15-percent commission basis, the newspaper earns $4,250 (85 percent of $5,000) for the space and pays the rep $750 (15 percent of $5,000).

The economic justification for a local medium using a media rep is that a sales staff representing a number of newspapers or radio and television stations can do a better job at less cost than the medium could by itself. The rep may be able to secure an added amount of national advertising that a local vehicle could not.

Offshoots of the outside, independent media representatives are the company-owned subsidiaries that handle national advertising sales for a chain of newspapers or broadcast stations. With the trend toward the concentration of media properties, this approach has proven efficient for many companies. These subsidiaries operate much like reps, except that they are owned by the media they represent. For example, Gannett National Newspaper Sales—with offices in New York, Atlanta, Detroit, Los Angeles, San Francisco, and Chicago—handles national advertising sales for the approximately eighty-nine newspapers owned by the Gannett Company. In the broadcast area, NBC Spot Sales deals exclusively with the seven television stations owned by the NBC Television Network (which is owned by General Electric).

Summary

The three major organizations that perform the advertising media function are the advertisers, the advertising agencies, and the advertising media in which advertising is placed. Among advertisers, the advertising manager is the key executive who supervises and coordinates media activity with other advertising functions. Some national advertisers use a brand-management approach, which involves advertising at two levels: at the company level, where broad policies are established and overall coordination is achieved; and at the individual brand level, where specific decisions are made, executed, and coordinated with an outside agency or in-house personnel. Some advertisers have established a media services unit within their advertising department to provide specific expertise in making media decisions. In addition, some companies have their own house agency to perform all or some of the advertising functions. There are both advantages and disadvantages to this approach.

Advertising agencies offer an advertiser either a full array of advertising services or concentrate on a specific, limited task, such as media buying. Full-service advertising agencies provide assistance in creative services, account management, research, and media planning and buying. The media department generally is organized either vertically or horizontally, with specialists in the areas of media planning, buying, and support activities. Specific agencies structure their media department according to the needs of their overall organization and the unique needs of their accounts. Some advertising organizations use media buying services, which are limited-service agencies that concentrate on the media function. Advertising agencies are compensated through the receipt of media commissions, agency charges for noncommissionable services, and/or through fees for the amount of work they do for an advertiser.

The advertising departments of media are strongly sales-oriented, although they are also involved in creative services, research, promotion, and merchandising. Local media—for example, newspapers, and radio and television stations—have their own staffs for selling and servicing local accounts, but they often use independent national representatives to sell to national advertisers and their agencies. These independent media reps have exclusive rights to the local medium and handle only one newspaper or station in a given market. They are compensated by a commission received from the medium for space and time bought by national advertisers and agencies. Some media companies, such as newspaper or broadcast chains, have their own subsidiaries to sell national advertising.

Questions for Discussion

1. Why would the advertising manager of a company using a full-service advertising agency need to be knowledgeable about the media function?

2. If a company was presently marketing ten different brands and had a single advertising manager, would you recommend the company reorganize under a brand-management approach? What factors would you look at in arriving at a recommendation?

3. Visit a large local retailer or service establishment (or one in a nearby city) that has an advertising department. Ascertain how the department is organized and what functions are performed. What importance does the establishment place on media decisions?

4. Why are the largest advertising agencies concentrated in relatively few large cities?

5. Why might an advertising agency organize its media department vertically, as opposed to horizontally?

6. If an advertising agency bought $120 million of media time and space for advertisers in a given year and was on a straight 15-percent commission plan with its clients, how much gross income would the agency receive? Is this amount likely to be the only income the agency receives?

7. Why would an advertiser use a media-buying service?

8. Visit a local medium, such as a newspaper, radio or television station, or outdoor company. How is the advertising department organized? How many people are in the department? What are the major responsibilities of the people in the department?

9. If you were the national representative for your hometown newspaper or radio or television station, what information would you want from the medium to help you sell space or time to national advertisers?

Endnotes

1. Jim Brosseau, "How Much Must Marketers Know about Media?" *Adweek's Marketing Week,* 17 April 1989, 22.

2. For further discussion of media responsibility among advertisers, see Victor P. Buell, *Organizing for Marketing/Advertising Success* (New York: Association of National Advertisers, 1982). See also Judann Dagnoli, "Media Synergies," *Advertising Age,* 6 November 1989, 4.

3. Some of the material in this section is excerpted from S. Watson Dunn, Arnold M. Barban, Dean M. Krugman, and Leonard N. Reid, *Advertising: Its Role in Modern Marketing,* 7th ed. (Hinsdale, Ill.: Dryden Press, 1990), 160–61.

4. Buell, *Organizing for Marketing/Advertising Success,* 75.

5. Victor G. Bloede, *The Full-Service Advertising Agency* (New York: American Association of Advertising Agencies, 1983), 3.

6. From materials supplied to the authors by Bruce Wager, senior vice president and group media director. The authors thank Young & Rubicam for providing this information.

7. These responsibilities were supplied by Bonnie Barest, vice president and media director. The authors thank the Bloom Agency, Inc., for its help.

8. The description of major responsibilities was supplied by Linda Rountree, media director of the Birmingham office. The authors appreciate the cooperation of Tucker Wayne/Luckie, with special thanks to Frank Lee, vice chairman and president/Birmingham, and Linda Rountree.

9. For additional discussion, see Fred Pfaff, "Media for Hire," *Marketing & Media Decisions,* October 1987, 34–40; and Gary Levin, "More Agencies Rely on Media Shops," *Advertising Age,* 6 August 1990, 6.

10. Raymond Serafin, "How Much Is Saturn Really Worth?" *Advertising Age,* 6 June 1988, 6.

11. Marcy Magiera, "Admen Question Carnation Plan," *Advertising Age,* 13 March 1989, 4.

12. Raymond Serafin and Gary Levin, "Saturn Plans Agency Pay Tied to Sales," *Advertising Age,* 9 May 1988, 1, 101.

13. For an interesting discussion of the 15-percent commission system, see "15% System: Fair or Faulty?" *Advertising Age,* 1 May 1989, 20, 76.

Suggested Readings

- Aaker, David A., and John G. Myers. *Advertising Management.* 3d ed. Englewood Cliffs, N.J.: Prentice-Hall, 1987. Chapter 1.
- Bloede, Victor G. *The Full-Service Advertising Agency.* New York: American Association of Advertising Agencies, 1983.
- Buell, Victor P. *Organizing for Marketing/ Advertising Success.* New York: Association of National Advertisers, 1982.
- Dunn, S. Watson, Arnold M. Barban, Dean M. Krugman, and Leonard N. Reid. *Advertising: Its Role in Modern Marketing.* 7th ed. Hinsdale, Ill.: Dryden Press, 1990. Chapter 6.
- Gamble, Frederic R. *What Advertising Agencies Are—What They Do and How They Do It.* New York: American Association of Advertising Agencies, 1976.
- Kotler, Philip. *Principles of Marketing.* 3d ed. Englewood Cliffs, N.J.: Prentice-Hall, 1986. Chapter 21.
- McGann, Anthony F., and J. Thomas Russell. *Advertising Media.* 2d ed. Homewood, Ill.: Irwin, 1988. Pages 128–34.
- Shimp, Terence A. *Promotion Management and Marketing Communications.* 2d ed. Hinsdale, Ill.: Dryden Press, 1990. Chapter 13.

PART II

BACKGROUND OF MEDIA DECISIONS

Chapter 3

The Role of Marketing

Outline

Learning Objectives

In the study of this chapter, you will have the opportunity to:

- Learn about the economic considerations that form the background for advertising efforts.
- Study the elements that comprise the marketing mix.
- Understand the marketing concept.
- Learn about the universal marketing functions.
- Understand that positioning is an essential contributor to media planning.
- Assess how the advertising process fits into the marketing process.
- Comprehend the management considerations that contribute to advertising media plans.

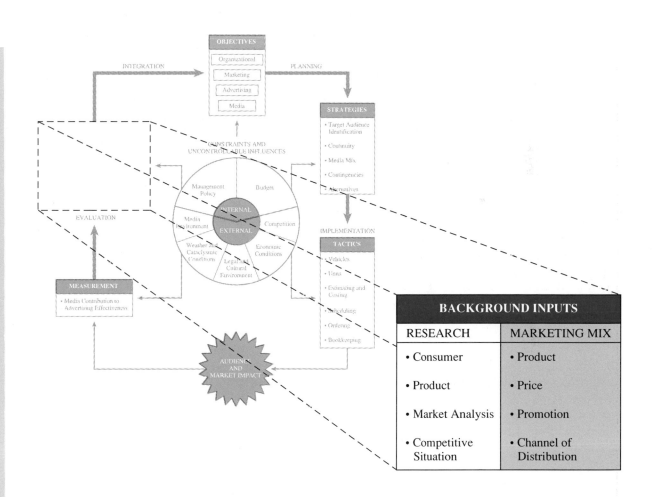

OBJECTIVES

Organizational

Marketing

Advertising

Media

INTEGRATION

PLANNING

CONSTRAINTS AND
UNCONTROLLABLE INFLUENCES

STRATEGIES

• Target Audience
  Identification
• Continuity
• Media Mix
• Contingencies
• Alternatives

Management
Policy

Budget

INTERNAL

EXTERNAL

Media
Environment

Competition

Weather and
Cataclysmic
Conditions

Economic
Conditions

Legal and
Cultural
Environment

EVALUATION

IMPLEMENTATION

TACTICS

• Vehicles
• Units
• Estimating and
  Costing
• Scheduling
• Ordering
• Bookkeeping

MEASUREMENT

• Media Contribution to
  Advertising Effectiveness

AUDIENCE
AND
MARKET IMPACT

BACKGROUND INPUTS	
RESEARCH	**MARKETING MIX**
• Consumer	• Product
• Product	• Price
• Market Analysis	• Promotion
• Competitive Situation	• Channel of Distribution

*A*n understanding of how advertising media operate requires comprehension of the general principles of advertising. Similarly, an understanding of how advertising functions requires a background in marketing, as well as the basics in economics and communications. In fact, advertising is often referred to as "marketing communications."

Before we consider marketing directly, we examine a few basic principles of economics. An understanding of economics is important to all business functions because the total economy affects how business as a whole operates and prospers and because a firm's internal economics must also be considered. We also discuss a number of advertising considerations that are based on the marketing role, along with management considerations to enact the marketing and advertising plans.

Economic Considerations

Advertising is an essential part of a competitive economic system because it provides critical information upon which consumers can base their purchase decisions. In this way, advertising has an impact on a country's macroeconomic system—that is, on the national economy.

Advertising serves several macroeconomic functions:

1. It stimulates the economy by letting consumers know what products and services are for sale, what new items are being introduced, how much things cost, and where products can be purchased.

2. It fosters competition among companies and brands by providing information about competing items.

3. It subsidizes the mass media by paying for most of the costs of newspapers and magazines and for almost all the costs of broadcast stations and networks.

4. It reaches large numbers of people at a relatively low cost.

5. And, as mentioned earlier, it provides information, which is necessary for a competitive economic system to operate simply and easily.

Of course, not everyone feels that advertising is always a positive influence. Promotion of brand image and brand loyalty through advertising may permit some marketers to charge higher prices. Advertising may also help established firms stay entrenched in their positions, serving as entry barriers for new competitors.

Yet, average advertisers are concerned more about their individual companies than the economy as a whole. In this respect, advertising plays an essential role in microeconomics, the economics of the firm. The cost of advertising must be calculated and included in the costs charged for the services and products being advertised, although advertising can actually lower such costs. For example, the effectiveness of advertising may bring larger sales volume, allowing each unit to be produced at a lower cost, through what is known as the economies of scale. In addition, advertising may bring increased sales and more productive use of the marketing investment, which can result in higher profits for the firm.

Thus, advertising has both a macroeconomic and a microeconomic effect. The entire advertising business has an impact on the macroeconomic system, and an individual organization's advertising has a direct effect on the organization's microeconomic well-being.

Marketing Considerations

Marketing (how it operates and what it accomplishes), the marketing mix, the marketing concept, the basic functions of marketing, and positioning are all essential to the study of advertising media. The sections that follow analyze these concepts in detail.

Marketing Defined

What exactly is marketing? At one time, marketing was the study of the market itself, the physical place where the buyer and seller would actually meet to conduct business. Business practices have changed, however, and there is no generally accepted marketplace for many kinds of goods and services. Now we can purchase via telephone or by using a personal computer to scan available merchandise, check prices, place an order, and charge and arrange for delivery. So marketing is constantly changing. Both parties—buyer and seller—want to satisfy their needs or wants.

Today's marketing concentrates on the *exchange* of goods and services for something of value. In addition, we are less concerned with the market as a physical place; instead, we tend to think of marketing as a way to overcome market separations, which are things or concepts that separate the buyer and seller, rather than bring them together. Separations between buyer and seller may be geographic, temporal, perceptual, or valuational differences.

Buyers and sellers are often geographically separated. To resolve the geographical differences, a store may deliver its wares, or a decorating service may come directly to the home with fabric and paint samples, or an auto mechanic may come to an office parking lot to service a vehicle. Persons on the East Coast can buy from businesses in California about as easily as persons in suburban areas can buy from stores in central-city business districts.

Buyers and sellers also may be separated by time constraints—for example, many people have to work and cannot go shopping during normal store hours. To compensate, a shopping mall may stay open until 10:00 P.M., a garden center may open early on Saturday, or a mail-order firm may have operators available twenty-four hours every day. This gives buyers a flexible shopping schedule, rather than one that must match the convenience of the store's schedule.

Perceptions may also separate buyers and sellers. A college student may think that paying $50 for a rock concert is a good deal while parents may feel that it is a waste of money. A traveler from a rural area may be astounded to be charged $10 an hour for parking in a big city. A particular style in women's clothing may be perceived as fashionable by one person, odd or undesirable by someone else. We have different tastes and preferences, and our perceptions are influenced by our background, environment, friends, and experiences.

This also relates to values, another market separation. An exhausted office worker may value a vacation more than a raise. A suburban dweller may value comfort and peace over the convenience of nearby shopping. A teenager may value music while studying or reading, while an older person may value quiet for these pastimes. An individual can place differing values on the identical situation or thing, depending on the circumstances: Seeing one movie may be worth the several-dollar charge, while another movie may not be attractive even if it is free; when one has discretionary income, money may be spent on items that are eliminated from the budget when money is less plentiful.

Advertising can help to overcome these market separations. It can eliminate geographic separations by telling shoppers what items are available where and how to order them. It can cancel time separations by letting the customer shop when it is convenient. It can overcome perceptual separations by explaining the hidden features of an item or by targeting the message to an audience that appreciates and holds similar perceptions. And it can reduce value separations by listing all that is being offered and by making the commodity appear to be worth the price.

MEDIA SPOTLIGHT

3.1

The New Marketing Litany: Four P's Passé; C-Words Take Over

by Bob Lauterborn

Bob Lauterborn is James L. Knight Professor of Advertising at the University of North Carolina. He formerly was director of marketing communications and corporate advertising for International Paper Company.

It's time to retire McCarthy's famous Four P's, the Rosetta Stone of marketing education for twenty years.

"The trouble with our newly minted MBAs," a package-goods marketing executive said recently, "is that they're wonderfully well prepared for a world which no longer exists."

When Jerry McCarthy and Phil Kotler proposed their alliterative litany—Product, Price, Place and Promotion—the marketing world *was* very different. Roaring out of World War II with a cranked-up production system ready to feed a lust for better living, American business linked management science to the art of mass marketing and rocketed to the moon.

In the days of "Father Knows Best," it all seemed so simple. The advertiser developed a product, priced it to make a profit, placed it on the retail shelf, and promoted it to a pliant, even eager consumer.

Mass media simultaneously taught consumptive culture and provided advertisers with efficient access to an audience which would behave, Dr. Dichter assured us, perfectly predictably, given the proper stimulation.

That was then. This is now.

Desperately, some marketers still try to make the formula work. They strew twelve thousand new products across the shelves in a single year. Eighty percent are stillborn.

Retailers declare their independence. Consumers don't listen, can't be found, *talk back* for God's sake. What's going on here?

It's time for a new formula: Lauterborn's Four C's.

Marketing Mix

As explained in chapter 1, marketing is usually considered to have four components, known as the four P's, which collectively constitute the **marketing mix.** They are (1) the *product* or service being promoted, (2) the *place* of distribution of the product or service, (3) the *price* of the product or service, and (4) *promotion.*

The products or services are critical elements, of course, because they are the focus of the advertising effort. The goal may be to provide information, build an image, generate dealer store traffic, produce inquiries, or attract actual sales, but all of these occur for the product, service, or idea being marketed.

Distributing the items to a convenient or proper place is another essential part of marketing. Goods must be shipped from the manufacturers to stores, which must stock items in convenient and logical locations. Direct marketers need an adequate supply of items to send to purchasers. Customers should be able to purchase the items with minimum difficulty and in a convenient place. Distribution channels are very competitive, with marketers continually trying to gain some advantage over competitors. Advertising directs buyers to the place where they can purchase a product or service. As distributive channels are compressed and fewer entities separate the manufacturer from the consumer, advertising's role becomes increasingly important.

Forget product. Study *consumer wants and needs*. You can't sell whatever you can make any more. You can only sell what someone specifically wants to buy. The feeding frenzy is over; the fish are out of school. Now you need to lure 'em one by one, with something each particularly wants.

Forget price. Understand the consumer's *cost to satisfy* that want or need. Price is almost irrelevant; dollars are only one part of cost. What you're selling against if you're selling hamburgers is not just another burger for a few cents more or less. It's the cost of time to drive to your place, the cost of conscience to eat meat at all, versus perhaps the cost of guilt for not treating the kids. Value is no longer the biggest burger for the cheapest price; it's a complex equation with as many different correct solutions as there are subsets of customers.

Forget place. Think *convenience to buy*. People don't have to go anyplace any more, in this era of catalogs, credit cards, and phones in every room. On the other hand, when they do decide to go somewhere, it's no longer only to Kroger's. What's a poor marketer to do? Think beyond those nice, neat distribution channels you've set up over the years. Know how each subsegment of the market prefers to buy, and be ubiquitous.

Forget promotion. The word is *communication*. All good advertising creates a dialogue. Promotion is us—out, manipulative, 1960s. Communication is from the buyer—in, cooperative, 1990s.

That contrast is, in fact, the fundamental difference between the Four P's, which served so well for so long, and the Four C's, which may be the formula for success as we leave the second millennium.

Product, price, place and promotion are passé. Consumer wants and needs, cost to satisfy, convenience to buy, and communication are the catechism for our times.

Source: Bob Lauterborn, "The New Marketing Litany: Four P's Passé; C-Words Take Over," *Advertising Age,* 1 October 1990, 26.

Prices for consumer products are set by the seller, such as the retailer, and not by the manufacturer. As a result, manufacturers' advertisements usually omit price information, while retailers' advertisements often state the price. Advertising can stress low prices, as in Kmart advertisements, or it can focus on the quality implied by a high price, as in advertisements for L'Oreal cosmetics.

Advertising relates most directly to promotion, but it is not the only kind of promotion. Sales promotion supports advertising, personal selling, and other promotions, often through short-term incentives. In the past few years, investment in sales promotion in the United States has grown larger than that in advertising, and sales promotion is still growing faster than advertising. Much advertising is intended not to complete a sale but to direct customers to the point of sale, where personal selling takes over. In fact, advertising works best before and after the actual transaction, but other forms of promotion can also be effective and can work with advertising to make it more effective.

Marketing Concept

As the previous discussion has shown, advertising is only one of the many variables that operate to produce a sale. And sales volume alone is not the way to profits. The **marketing concept** is the idea that the consumer is essential at both ends of the

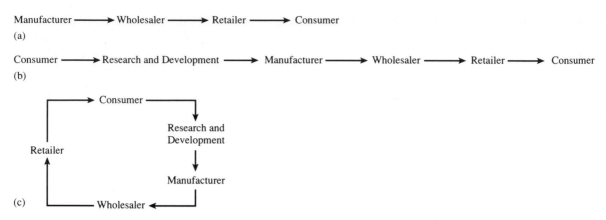

FIGURE 3.1 The Marketing Concept. (a) The Traditional Marketing Channels. (b) The Marketing Channel Utilizing the Marketing Concept. (c) The Cyclical Marketing Channel, Showing the Role of the Consumer in the Marketing Concept.

marketing channel: at the beginning of the process when the service or product is being developed, and at the end of the process in making the final purchase. (See figure 3.1.) In essence, the marketing concept consists of determining the needs and wants of the target groups and then trying to meet those needs with products and services. The emphasis is on the customer rather than the seller: Selling places the focus on the seller, but marketing concentrates on the needs of the buyer.[1]

The marketing concept also emphasizes marketing instead of production. When the emphasis is on selling, a company manufactures a product and then tries to persuade customers to buy it, so the company is trying to make consumer demand conform to its production supplies. With the marketing concept, the company finds out what consumers want and then tries to manufacture an item that will meet that need at a profitable rate. In other words, the company conforms its business to consumers' needs and wants.[2]

To illustrate the marketing concept, consider two companies. One company decides that it can make a candy bar profitably by using cheap ingredients, but then has difficulty selling the item, even after heavy advertising. Another company tests the taste preferences of groups of consumers, then develops a candy bar that satisfies these tastes, and finds a ready market for its product. This latter firm is utilizing the marketing concept.[3]

Under this approach, all marketing plans, policies, and strategies are designed around the consumer. Moreover, the activities of the business are focused on satisfying consumers' needs. Marketing and communications, and in particular, advertising, are difficult tasks that are made considerably easier with the use of the marketing concept. Even though low in price, poor products are difficult to sell or can only be sold once. Few products or services can survive without repeat purchases, which result from providing an item that meets needs.[4]

Although the marketing concept appears to be hidden in the writing of the famous economist Adam Smith, General Electric Company was likely the first company to apply this philosophy in the 1950s.[5] Since that time, many companies have become marketing-oriented and have utilized the marketing concept.

The marketing concept involves:

- Focus on consumer needs
- Integration of all activities of the organization, including production, to satisfy identified consumer needs

- Achievement of profits by satisfying consumer needs
- Attainment of profitable sales volume rather than simple maximization of sales

The marketing concept also requires knowing in what business you actually operate. A window manufacturer believed that its business was wooden windows, so it refused to consider expanding to include aluminum windows. An inventory of the company's expertise showed that its real talent was in woodworking, so the company branched out into making wooden cabinets, stairways, and banisters. When one famous chain of hamburger restaurants ran into a period of static sales, it re-examined its business. It had always believed that it was selling food, but it found that it was actually offering convenience to its customers.

Marketing Functions

At least seven basic marketing functions seem to occur in every marketing situation: (1) analysis, (2) communications, (3) differentiation, (4) positioning, (5) segmentation, (6) valuation, and (7) exchange. Advertising can contribute to the success of every one of these functions.

Analysis

Analysis of the market involves gathering information from many sources, including potential customers. The information gained from such analysis can make the advertising effort, which provides information to these same customers, more efficient and effective. Market analysis is essential in the marketing process to help determine the baseline measure for increases by both the target firm and the competition. Analysis is also an essential part of the background inputs necessary for advertising media planning.

Communications

Advertising is likely the most visible and the best-known form of marketing communications. As mentioned earlier, however, other forms of communications may be more important than advertising for accomplishing certain marketing tasks. These other forms include the so-called promotional mix, those functions that comprise the field of promotion, which are publicity, public relations, sales promotion, personal selling, packaging, and advertising.

Differentiation

Advertising is often utilized to differentiate a marketer's products and services from those of competitors. Media can help to differentiate items by using different media approaches and by reaching various targets. One common advertising technique, called the unique selling proposition (USP), concentrates on identifying some promotable factor that helps to differentiate a product or service from that of competitors. This differential may be some real product advantage, such as a faster-acting medicine or a less expensive shampoo. But it can also be a perceived difference, such as quality or taste. It may even be some attribute that can also be ascribed to competing items but that the competitors, for whatever reason, have not promoted. For example, a bread company might advertise that it adds twelve nutritional supplements to its bread, while most other bakers also add these nutrients but do not promote them. Or a beverage company might promote the idea that its product is pasteurized. Although competitors' goods may also be pasteurized, if they also begin promoting that attribute, they appear to be "me, too" products who are imitating the category leader.

Positioning

Positioning involves where the marketed item fits in consumers' memories and how consumers view the item versus alternative items. The positioning statement is a good basis for advertising strategies, and the position may even become the actual slogan or "tagline" for the advertising message. Positioning is a very important marketing and media function that is discussed in greater detail later in the chapter.

MEDIA SPOTLIGHT

3.2

Scanners and the Framing Effect

by John Deighton, Caroline Henderson, and Scott Neslin

Scott Neslin and Caroline Henderson are on the faculty at Dartmouth College. John Deighton is on the faculty at the University of Chicago.

Advertisers have long sought an answer to the question of how advertising affects sales. Only very recently, scanner panel data have become available that record both household purchases and household exposure to television advertising. Our research suggests that, for mature brands, advertising primarily works by reinforcing and enhancing the loyalty of current users of the brand, rather than by attracting new users.

The traditional view of advertising effectiveness is based on the "hierarchy of effects" model of consumer behavior. In this model, consumers become aware of a brand, then form beliefs about product attributes, which in turn translate into purchase behavior. Advertising is seen as enhancing awareness and beliefs and, therefore, could attract a nonuser of the brand.

A new view of advertising effectiveness, called advertising "framing," is based on the idea that advertising could also work in conjunction with actual brand usage. Many television ads portray the brand-usage experience—consumers are shown admiring the softness of their laundry or trying to get extra-thick ketchup out of the bottle. The commercial by itself does not convince consumers that the product will deliver on these claims, but instead tells the consumer what to look for in the product-usage experience. This framing effect creates an enhanced-usage occasion and results in higher brand loyalty.

Until now, the framing effect has undergone only limited empirical investigation, due to a lack of appropriate data. Now, scanner panel data that compile a computer file of all purchases made by the panelist at scanner-equipped stores are available. The advertising data are provided by a device attached to the panelist's household television set. The device records when the television is turned on, and to which channel. Of course we cannot be

Segmentation

Segmentation divides prospective consumers into various categories so that they can be communicated to more easily and more directly. Advertising uses different media to reach these different targets.

Markets can be segmented according to geographic criteria, such as state, county, city, or regional divisions. For example, there is a market for egg creams in New York City but not in most of the rest of the country. Antifreeze is sold in early fall in the northern tier of states but not until winter in the South—if ever.

Demographic criteria involve population characteristics and may help sell briefcases to professionals and disposable diapers to new mothers. Demographics can also help to differentiate the types of movies people attend, the cars they buy, and even whether they own a video recorder or a cellular telephone.

Psychographic criteria are personality and character traits, and to some extent, may overlap with some demographics. Thus, BMWs are promoted to upwardly striving young people, while advertisements for Buicks are directed at those who value comfort over flashy outward appearances. Psychographics also influence the brand of beer consumed, sure that the panelist actually watched the television at the exact time a particular commercial was aired, but we do know that the television was on and tuned to the appropriate channel.

We analyzed scanner panel data to determine the impact that advertising has on the likelihood that a particular household will purchase the brand. We did this among those who did and did not recently purchase the brand. We found that advertising tends to be most effective at enhancing the likelihood of repeat purchasing among those who recently purchased the brand. This is consistent with the framing concept.

There are several important implications of this finding. First, it supports the strategy of advertising to current users, for it is among current users that the advertising will be most effective.

Second, the framing effect supports the strategy of using sales promotion and advertising together to build and nurture the brand franchise. Sales promotion is known to attract light users of the brand—that is, it attracts brand switchers. The framing effect of advertising could then enhance the usage experience for these consumers, making it more likely they will purchase the brand again.

In sum, promotion attracts new customers, and advertising helps retain them.

Third, the findings support the notion that advertising is more likely to pay out for large share brands. Large share brands, by definition, have relatively more current users, and advertising works best among current users.

We emphasize that the view of advertising working as a framing mechanism among current users is an emerging one and needs to be tested in several additional product categories. Research to date has investigated mature brands in mature categories. We also need to study which types of creative ad executions are most conducive to this effect.

In summary, newly available scanner panel data, coupled with advertising exposure measures, have allowed us to investigate in detail the question of how advertising affects sales. The conclusion from this research is that advertising primarily works by framing the brand-usage experience, thereby retaining and enhancing the brand loyalty of current users.

Source: John Deighton, Caroline Henderson, and Scott Neslin, "Scanners and the Framing Effect," *Marketing & Media Decisions*, October 1989, 112.

the willingness to try new products, and the likelihood of telling others about one's experiences with a particular brand.

Lifestyle criteria are oriented around the way one lives, which may lead to promotions of Michelob for weekends and evenings. Lifestyles also impact on vacation destinations, clothing purchases, and decisions regarding whether to add additions to homes and landscaping to yards.

Usage criteria involve dividing the audience into the amount of product or service consumed. If only a small number of people drink Scotch whisky regularly and they account for most of its consumption, why advertise it to anyone else?

Situational criteria involve the current problem or setting in which a person is placed. If you ate onions at lunch, and then remembered an important afternoon meeting with a client, you would want to do something about your breath. That could result in the purchase of mouthwash or perhaps breath mints.

Benefit criteria concentrate on the actual benefits a person might receive from the advertised item—and those benefits may differ from one individual to another. Thus, benefit segmentation may help sell mortgage insurance to new home owners or high-quality luggage to a business traveler.

MEDIA SPOTLIGHT

3.3

Mass Retail and Its Micro Markets

by Michael F. Smith

Michael Smith is on the faculty of Temple University.

As today's headlines suggest, retailing is one of the most exciting, frustrating, challenging, exasperating, and fascinating segments of the American economy. It is also one of the most brutal, and as competition intensifies, retailers will take a harder look at the effectiveness of their promotional expenditures.

Several factors have important implications for how retailers will communicate with the consumer. They are: time compression, aging of the population, geomarketing, and market fragmentation.

For families where both spouses work, time is a valuable commodity. Marketers who can provide convenience in terms of how people acquire and consume products will reap huge rewards. Similarly, creative avenues must be found to reach consumers with messages that are short and sweet.

The aging of the population means a more savvy consumer who is adept at shopping and has definite opinions on the value of brand names and the relationship between price and quality. In light of the increasing personal cost (that is, fighting traffic, finding a parking space, etc.) of patronizing traditional fixed-location retailers, consumers are more willing to purchase products by description rather than by inspection—either by telephone or through the mail.

As the attractiveness of direct marketing for the consumer increases, retailers will have to reorient their media strategies. In this instance, the mass media is not just a vehicle for stimulating interest and desire; it is a viable alternative (versus face-to-face) for stimulating and closing the sale.

Geomarketing is a phenomenon that describes the increasing diversity in tastes and preferences.

Overall, then, segmentation makes advertising more efficient by narrowing the general population down to specific segment targets.

Valuation

Valuation relates to the price a seller places on a product or service and to the price a buyer is willing to pay. Both parties must feel that they are receiving at least that much value, and the ideal is for both parties to believe that they got more than they gave up. Advertising expresses the seller's value and contributes to the buyer's value. It also can lend additional value to a product or service, sometimes in nonphysical terms. For example, while valuation is most often expressed in monetary units, it can also

be experienced in terms of pleasure, taste, appearance, and other ways. Lite Beer promotes its value on the basis of what is missing: "It's less filling."

Exchange

Exchange is the actual trading of money for a product or service. While advertising may not contribute much to the actual sales transaction, it still contributes to the function of exchange. Advertising's effect may be most evident in a nonphysical exchange, such as when a mail-order catalog customer telephones an order and pays by credit card. In such a case, advertising provided all the selling information from the seller to the buyer.

The exchange is the end result of marketing, although *not* necessarily the end of the marketing

Traditionally, demographers concentrated on differences between larger regions, such as East, West, North, and South. Now manufacturers are developing marketing strategies to tap the idiosyncrasies exhibited by consumers across more narrowly defined geographic settings. Similarly, retailers are attempting to develop offerings to appeal to consumers in different parts of the country as well as in different neighborhoods in the same suburb.

Geographic marketing must be accompanied by geographic targeting. Newspapers, for instance, allow retailers to target specific areas within the newspaper's "territory." As geographic markets become scrambled, retailers are going to demand that audiences be delivered in even smaller geographic parcels. Some would say that there are too many stores attempting to appeal to too few people. Many specialty retailers try to differentiate themselves on the basis of a unique offer to a narrowly defined group of consumers. Consumers are becoming more demanding about what they require from retailers. The interaction between these two forces has led to market fragmentation.

Markets will continue to decrease in size as competitors fine-tune market segments along the lines of value, lifestyle, demographics, geographics, and benefits. The focus will be on developing a unique niche that matches the comparable strengths of the retailer and the requirements of the target market. Promotional strategies will place greater emphasis on developing the appropriate image to match the consumers' lifestyle and less on price promotions. To accomplish this, retailers will communicate through media that can deliver a specific audience. As retailers become more cost conscious, the media must deliver not only the message, but also the consumer.

Source: Michael F. Smith, "Mass Retail and Its Micro Markets," *Marketing & Media Decisions,* April 1990, 88.

effort. Final steps include evaluation of the success of the marketing effort. Since this evaluation can be viewed as a type of *analysis,* it can also be considered the first function of the next round of marketing. Thus, marketing is an ongoing, cyclical process.

Positioning

As mentioned earlier, where the product or service fits into the minds of prospective customers is called positioning. Positioning also overlaps into how the product or service fits in the marketplace in relation to competitors.

Entire books have been written about positioning, so only a small part of the concept can be summarized here. Positioning encompasses how sellers want to be envisioned by their principal customers, and their position must be incorporated into their main selling theme. To achieve a favorable position, sellers take two actions that may, at first glance, seem to be opposites of one another: They generalize and they specialize.

When sellers advertise, they concentrate on one central idea that is generalized as *the* identity of the product, service, or idea that they want to promote. This one essential element becomes the theme of the advertising and the identifier for the product or even the entire company: "Coca-Cola is the real thing!"

At the same time, sellers specialize. They narrow down the consumer group to which they want to sell and to which they want to target their advertising.

MEDIA SPOTLIGHT

3.4

Going for the Long Bomb

by Bob Rueff

Bob Rueff is chief executive officer and director of account services at Clarity Coverdale Rueff Advertising in Minneapolis.

Marketers are too often guilty of aiming at the market—or worse, lingering behind the market—rather than leading it. Perhaps it feels safe and predictable, but it's a form of short-term thinking.

It's like a football team that relies on an offense of short flair-out passes. The pass has a good chance of being completed, but the gain is likely to be small. Granted it's more difficult, but when a quarterback hits his deep receiver in full stride behind the defense, things really happen. It's the team that accomplishes this with some consistency that breaks the game open.

The American automobile industry is a classic example of falling behind the market. It was obvious for several years before Detroit's troubles that its emphasis on large cars and holding to status quo quality and engineering was like throwing short passes at best, while the teams they competed against had much more aggressive game plans.

Detroit lost to the much better coached and drilled Japanese, who won with precision, efficiency, and the recognition that American consumers would accept small cars (even though Detroit's research still showed Americans wanted "big" cars). And they lost to the innovative tactics of the European car manufacturers, who consistently "threw long," leading the market often out of principle.

Any consideration of what I call "lead marketing" should involve the question: Is it better for the consumer, whether or not the consumer is currently aware of the benefits?

European car builders have done this in spades. Front-wheel drive, antiskid brakes (ASB), radial tires, and aero design, to name a few, were first introduced across the Atlantic.

To be sure, American car manufacturers did their market research. But customer prospects were asked what they wanted and liked, and that's what Detroit gave them—a clear example of aiming at the market, not leading it.

Even if asked, could consumers comprehend the benefits of independent four-wheel suspension, fuel injection, and rack-and-pinion steering before they had experienced them in their cars? Many innovative features on today's automobiles were first developed in the United States, including those just

They selectively differentiate their product or service, which relates to the unique selling proposition (USP) discussed earlier. Then they use this narrow focus to position their product or service in the minds of their special market segmentation.

A seller's position is then summarized in a positioning statement, which simply refines and encapsulates the position. The positioning statement should be a clear, concise summary of the product or service's position goal, in simple language. The statement should be spelled out, even if it seems ob-

vious. The position should differentiate the seller from competitors and should establish a leadership role. Very important, of course, is that the product or service lives up to the promise made by the position.

Advertising Considerations

Once the marketing role is firmly established, the advertising process may begin.

listed. None of them were first marketed by Detroit in any meaningful way. Mostly, they were resisted.

Has Detroit learned from its experience? Granted, there has been a frantic scramble to adopt the tactics of the competition. There is finally a commitment to smaller cars. Emphasis on trendy styling is giving way to more functional, aerodynamic design. Front-wheel drive has become the dominant setup. Handling characteristics have gradually improved, at least on some models. There remains, however, a disturbing reliance on what is termed psychoengineering—appearance priority over function priority (anathema to German car manufacturers).

Recent studies indicate that the American consuming public is becoming Europeanized. This translates to a demand for higher quality and overall value in cars intended for longer life and wider usability. Cars from Europe are benefiting from this trend, as might be expected. So when Ford introduced the Mercur XR4Ti, a respectable European-made performance automobile, only five western states were scheduled to get it with a firmer "European-style" suspension. Why? Because surveys showed that all but these five states prefer a softer suspension.

Back into the same old trap.

Is Ford leading the market here? No. Can a soft-sprung Mercur hope to gain the acceptance of enthusiasts? No. And, applying the question: "Is it the way it ought to be done because it's better?" The answer is still no.

Detroit has a way to go. It's still plagued with anachronistic perceptions as to what the public will buy. It needs to be concerned with doing things because they are better from a pure product standpoint.

Detroit is an easy target. We all know the sad story, and hindsight makes wise critics of us all. The hard part is practicing lead marketing here and now. To do it right, you need to "read" trends and anticipate demand. Lead marketing can be chancy. It plows new ground. What if the market veers? Doesn't follow your lead? Consumers don't respond? The question to ask yourself to increase your odds of success is: "Is it the way it ought to be done because it's better for the consumer?" If you can answer "yes" to this question and other indicators are in place, do it.

Source: Bob Rueff, "Going for the Long Bomb," *Marketing & Media Decisions,* February 1990, 80.

The Advertising Process

As discussed in chapter 1, advertising objectives are set first. Strategy planning and implementation, which may need to be supported by other kinds of activities, follow.

Advertising objectives must match up with the organization's general marketing objectives of, for example, intending to promote or to sell a new product. Objectives are most valuable if expressed in quantifiable measures, rather than in quality terms only.

Strategies are plans. They are the means to meet the objectives, the ways in which objectives can be accomplished. "Using advertising media" is not an objective; rather, it is a strategy for achieving an objective. Advertising media themselves are means to achieve objectives through the use of advertising.

At this stage, no actual advertising work has yet been done. That involves tactics. Tactics are the implementation of the plan and include preparing advertising messages, selecting advertising vehicles, ordering media time and space, and running the advertisements.

Market research is important but may be performed by some other firm hired specifically for this purpose. Logistical or support activities are not central to the advertising strategies and tactics, yet are necessary for the success of the plan. Typesetting, photography, coupon redemption, broadcast production, and account billing are all examples of logistical support. These are all essential to the success of the marketing and advertising efforts, but they are not the central focus of the campaign.

Targets

Our discussions of the marketing functions, positioning, and advertising have mentioned targets. But more than one kind of target is involved.

A **target market** is a general term that may refer to a physical location where prospects live or work, to a group of prospective customers, or to a kind of individual or group that may be in the market for the good or service being promoted. Thus, a target market might be the northeastern United States. Another target market could be housewives with small children at home. Still another target market could be users of a competing product.

The terms *target group* and *target audience* are more specific than target market; both deal with groups of people. Target group refers to the kind of persons who may constitute good prospects for the selling effort. The target audience is the actual media audience reached with the advertising. The target group and the target audience are rarely the same group. Advertisers may know what group they would like to reach with their message, but there may be no advertising medium that reaches that particular group. For example, the target group for dog food may be all dog owners, but no advertising vehicle reaches *all* dog owners or *only* dog owners.

To avoid confusion, it may be helpful to think of markets as physical locations, so target markets might be cities or regions where the products or services are to be sold. Target groups and target audiences are kinds of people, not locations.

All of these different targets can be thought of as a prospect group that includes persons who are primary targets and those who represent only the slightest sales potential. From these people, the target audience group is identified for the campaign messages. So **target prospect** may be an easier way to think of target groups and target audiences.

Targets for advertising media strategies are discussed in detail in chapter 10.

Management Considerations

In addition to the economic situation, marketing plans, and the advertising process, corporate management must also be involved in overseeing the functioning of the advertising effort. Management may be involved in decision making, coordination and budgeting, and perhaps in test marketing as well.

Decision Making

Management's primary concerns are the prospect groups—where they are located, when they should be reached with advertising, how much financial and other resources should be devoted to advertising, and how those resources should be allocated.

These are essential decisions, most often involving top management. The media planner, and even the advertising manager, may not be empowered to make these decisions. In most cases, top management is consulted, even if it does not make the actual decisions. Middle management has a different role, that of coordination and execution.

Coordination

The primary task of any manager is coordination. Coordination is difficult because so many variables are involved—and most of those variables are people. In fact, managers spend an estimated two-thirds of their time with personnel and related matters. The situation with people is even more critical in advertising because people (and the ideas that they come up with) are the basic raw material with which advertising operates and from which advertisements are born.

Advertising managers want good creative work, but the creativity must be focused on achieving the objectives of the campaign. One large advertising agency promotes itself as having a combination of creative flair and business acumen. But these tasks involve different attributes and require different kinds of people. A firm that is too homogeneous is not progressive and far-reaching, but a firm that has too many different kinds of people working for it is difficult to manage and coordinate. Good managers attract different kinds of persons and combine their varied talents to serve a central purpose.

Managers find it easier to coordinate similar activities. Thus, a financial manager can coordinate a cashier's office, accounting office, and payroll office without too much difficulty. Advertising managers, however, must coordinate creative activities (copywriting, art, layout), media activities (planning, estimating, buying, checking), client service activities (liaison, service, reports, personal calls), research activities (planning, contracting, conducting, analyzing, reporting), along with accounting, payroll, production, traffic, and many other activities.

While advertising coordination is a demanding task, the dynamic, deadline-oriented nature of advertising means that managers can see results—and experience positive or negative feedback—in a relatively brief time. In addition, managers work with talented and interesting people in a fast-moving yet rewarding enterprise.

Coordination is also an essential skill for media planners and buyers who must establish and carry out a media plan.

Budgeting

One task that all managers deal with is the budget, and the advertising budget can be complicated. A basic knowledge of accounting and of how the financial system works at the particular firm one manages is helpful.

In some cases, the advertising budget may be determined by some higher level within the firm, or by the advertiser client, so that the amount of the budget is not an issue. Budget determination is beyond the scope of this discussion. Suffice it to say that determining an advertising budget is a complicated and time-consuming task.

For most advertising management, the budget issue is how to allocate the monies—that is, how to divide the advertising budget into different uses. These allocations can be made on the basis of territory, product lines, target groups, or many other divisions. Again, budget allocations are beyond the scope of our advertising media discussion, but media planners need to know how the budget impacts their work.

The media plan must stay within the budget constraints. In making a media plan, media planners are allocating the advertising budget because each media "buy" spends part of the budget on some activity, for some product or service line, or on some particular media vehicle. In addition, the large majority of the advertising budget is expended for the media function; only a small part goes for creative, research, and other advertising activities.

Test Marketing

Decision making, coordination, and budgeting are universal management responsibilities. An additional responsibility in advertising media management is **test marketing.**

A test market involves a trial run of the advertising and marketing campaign, usually on a small scale, to test its efficacy and effectiveness. A test-market situation also can involve testing the use of various media against one another, which is expensive.

A test market permits media planners to try out the media plan on a small scale, for less money, so that the entire budget is not at risk and so that various factors can be manipulated and varied until they appear to maximize their efficiency and effectiveness and perhaps even achieve a degree of synergy.

Summary

Economic, marketing, and advertising considerations all must be taken into account in preparing an advertising media plan. No single element can be structured without consideration of the others.

Economics underlies all business, including advertising. Advertising has both a macroeconomic and a microeconomic effect. The entire advertising business has an impact on the macroeconomic system, and an individual organization's advertising has a direct effect on the organization's microeconomic well-being.

Because advertising also can be considered "marketing communications," it is especially important that a strong marketing element is present in the media-planning process. Marketing can be better understood through comprehension of the marketing mix, which is usually broken into four elements: product, place, price, and promotion. The marketing concept, which is the idea that the consumer is essential at both ends of the marketing channel, can bring close coordination, greater profits, easier selling, and a better-defined mission to the firm. Detailed analysis of the various marketing functions—analysis, communications, differentiation, positioning, segmentation, valuation, and exchange—rounds out the marketing effort and allows preparation of a more complete and comprehensive plan. Much advertising effort also focuses on the positioning strategy, which carries over into media-planning considerations.

Advertising decisions are, of course, paramount when formulating media plans. The advertising objectives must complement the marketing objectives while also influencing the specific research, creative, media, and evaluation plans. Individual target markets, groups, and audiences are then defined, based on all of these foregoing objectives.

Management considerations also must be factored into any media-planning activity. Top management's primary concern is decision making with regard to prospect groups—where they are located, when they should be reached with advertising, how much financial and other resources should be devoted to advertising, and how those resources should be allocated. The overall task of middle management is coordination, an essential element in advertising where so many different elements are contributing in varied ways to the success of the eventual campaign plan. Management also establishes the advertising budget appropriation, which is a strict limit on how much advertising can be done, especially in terms of how much media time and space are affordable. Test marketing of a media plan also requires management involvement.

Questions for Discussion

1. How does modern marketing's emphasis on the concept of exchange provide opportunities for advertising?

2. In what ways can each of the four P's of the marketing mix be utilized in advertising media planning?

3. In what ways do product and service differentiations have implications for market segmentation through media selection?

4. Does advertising media selectivity gain from the increasing specificity in segmentation, or vice versa?

5. Is advertising media strategy taken into account in the process of positioning? If so, how?

6. Is it likely that there is a target audience that matches exactly with a target group? Why or why not? Give specific examples.

7. To what extent is management actually involved in the process of planning advertising media selections?

Endnotes

1. Philip Kotler, *Marketing Essentials* (Englewood Cliffs, N.J.: Prentice-Hall, 1984), 15–16.

2. William J. Stanton, *Fundamentals of Marketing,* 7th ed. (New York: McGraw-Hill, 1984), 12–13.

3. Michael L. Rothschild, *Marketing Communications: From Fundamentals to Strategies* (Lexington, Mass.: D.C. Heath, 1987), 4.

4. Rothschild, *Marketing Communications,* 5–6.

5. Thomas C. Kinnear and Kenneth L. Bernhardt, *Principles of Marketing* (Glenview, Ill.: Scott, Foresman, 1983), 14–16.

Suggested Readings

- Kaatz, Ron. *Advertising & Marketing Checklists.* Lincolnwood, Ill.: NTC Business Books/National Textbook Company, 1989.
- Kinnear, Thomas C., and Kenneth L. Bernhardt. *Principles of Marketing.* Glenview, Ill.: Scott, Foresman, 1983.
- Kotler, Philip. *Marketing Essentials.* Englewood Cliffs, N.J.: Prentice-Hall, 1984.
- Rothschild, Michael L. *Marketing Communications: From Fundamentals to Strategies.* Lexington, Mass.: D. C. Heath, 1987.
- Stanton, William J. *Fundamentals of Marketing.* 7th ed. New York: McGraw-Hill, 1984.

Chapter 4

The Role of Research

Outline

Learning Objectives

In the study of this chapter, you will have the opportunity to:

- Explore the difference between primary and secondary research.
- Learn why and when primary research is used in advertising media planning.
- Discover the considerations that support research decisions.
- Examine the different types of market analysis used in advertising.
- Discuss modern media research technologies.

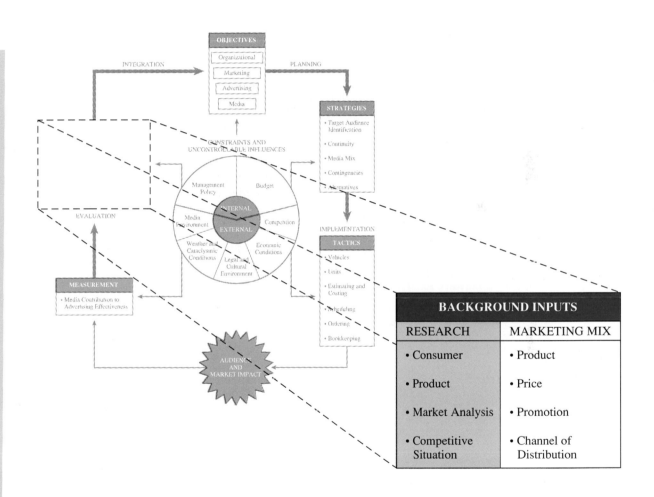

P**rimary research** is research that has not been conducted before, such as information gathering for some specific purpose. **Secondary research,** on the other hand, involves using information already collected. For example, gathering all the names, addresses, and telephone numbers to be published in a telephone book is primary research since it involves collecting information, not available elsewhere, for some specific purpose. Looking up someone's name and telephone number is secondary research since it involves using information that someone else has prepared.

Advertising media work requires extensive use of secondary research, as we will see in chapter 5. Original research must also sometimes be conducted, however, so an understanding of primary research methods is important. Primary research is required when suitable current data are not available from a secondary source, when special confidentiality may be required, when a product or service is new or has changed so drastically that available research may not pertain, and when special details, special audiences, or special characteristics must be included in the study.

Numerous research considerations are involved in the decision of whether or not to employ primary research in advertising media work. This chapter concentrates on some of these research considerations but does not explain how to conduct primary research, which is beyond the scope of this book. Many excellent textbooks on research methods, including social science and behavioral science research, are available, and some of these books focus specifically on advertising research.

Research Considerations

Whether to use any research at all, and then whether that research should be primary or secondary research, is a function of at least four major considerations:

1. How much will it cost? Is the potential return worth the investment? Are adequate funds available?

2. How long will it take? Is there enough turnaround time? Will the findings still be current by the time we receive them? What is the risk of not waiting?

3. How valuable is the information? Do we really need this information, or will it only be of marginal assistance? Is its value worth the expense? Are there alternatives to using primary research?

4. How reliable is the information? Does it actually answer the research questions? Does it accurately reflect the actual facts? Can these results be projected onto the population at large?

These and related factors are addressed in greater detail in the sections that follow.

Cost Versus Value

Gathering information through primary research requires time and money. Obtaining information through secondary research may require less time, but the information source still often must be paid. The question is, how much time and money are available?

A media planner who must decide whether or not to place an order for a $4,000 magazine advertisement can easily see that it is not worthwhile to spend $5,000 on research to support that decision. More troublesome is the question of whether or not it is worthwhile to spend $500 of research money on that decision. Such an expense would increase the cost of the magazine advertisement to $4,500 (original cost of $4,000 plus $500 for research), which actually changes the scope of the decision: A media expenditure that made economic and marketing sense for $4,000 might very well not be worth $4,500.

Even more troublesome are research decisions without an immediate or measurable decision payoff. An advertising agency that handles advertising for a breakfast-cereal maker may want to order research on cereal consumers, but does it also want to pay for research on alternatives to cereal, such as toast, pancakes, and eggs? How would the media manager ever know if such information was really worth what it cost to gather and analyze? Even if the manager could make that evaluation after the research information was in hand, the decision must be made in advance, before the research information is available for evaluation—in fact, before the research is even begun.

Another constraining factor is that research takes time. Many advertising media decisions must be made within very short time constraints. Even if the proposed primary research on, say, a particular broadcast time could be completed in two weeks, the broadcast time that was being researched may, after two weeks, no longer be available; some other advertiser may have bought it, so the research turns out to be worthless. A more serious situation exists when the developer of a new item tests it fully in the marketplace, but a competitor sees the test, duplicates the item, and introduces it on a large scale while the original is still in the test stage. This actually happens, and not just occasionally. The result is that the originator is second to the large marketplace and thus appears to be a "copycat" product because the real imitator is first in the minds of customers.

The cost of primary research is rarely minor. And not just the cost of the research is at stake: If a competitor wins the race to the market because the developer was delayed by the research process, the entire project and the entire investment may be lost. A large-scale research study may take months to complete, and during this interim, a competitor may forge ahead with a similar idea and capture a huge advantage in lead time, introductory time, credit for innovation, and initial sales.

The questions that must be asked are:

1. How much is the potential information worth?

2. How does that compare to the price of the research?

3. How much time will the research require? Will a competitive advantage still be available then?

4. What risks are involved in commissioning the research?

5. What risks are involved if the research is *not* conducted?

6. How else might this or comparable information be obtained?

7. Is this information really needed?

Relying on Results

While the results of primary research should be used, relying too heavily on research results can be a mistake. No matter how good primary research is, it is not perfect. There always will be errors.

Perhaps the wrong subjects were studied, or maybe respondents' answers were not truthful. Sometimes, the entire study is completely valid internally, but the subjects were not representative of the entire population. One common problem is that the questions being asked are biased. The project manager may want the venture to succeed so much that personal perceptions and perspectives are allowed to creep into the question development. Occasionally, the order in which the questions are asked affects the responses. Even the choice of words can have an impact: Emotionally charged words and terms can induce personal rather than rational responses from individuals.

Obviously, all sorts of problems can crop up in a research study. While researchers must try to be aware of these problems, advertising managers also have a responsibility to be wary, to anticipate errors and forestall them. Advertising media planners, too, must realize that the reliance placed on the information at hand must be limited.

Marketers who rely entirely on research results, without judging whether the information is correct, may make poor decisions. Their personal assessment of the research should be balanced with the variety of other factors on which their decisions must be based. The evidence to support a certain approach may be overwhelming, while the marketer's experience and instinct indicate that the research results are misleading, if not absolutely wrong. Every observation, in every situation, can be viewed as a research study: Information is gathered from a wide variety of sources, and all of this information is weighed against the results of formal research studies.

In addition, managers who always rely on research may be unable to make a decision when supporting research is not available. Such managers are lost when faced with ordinary everyday decisions that do not warrant conducting primary research.

Finally, there is never enough research. The research may deal with specific situations in rather general settings, but these may not apply to the particular situation and setting currently in need of research. Finite resources of time, money, and personnel all limit the scope of any study. Compromises creep into the research plan. Various kinds of pressures force the research plan to be reduced. Whatever the situation, no matter how good the research, individual human judgment is still needed. Even the best research is subject to interpretation, as the Nielsen advertisement in figure 4.1 suggests.

Ignoring Research Results

Obviously, it would seem ridiculous to conduct primary research and then ignore the results—but it happens. Sometimes, a marketer has already decided what course of action to pursue, but to support this decision, orders a small, hurried study. If the results support the marketer's original decision, the marketer is reinforced but also feels good about already making the correct decision without research assistance. In this situation, perhaps no real harm has been done—except for the wasted time, money, and effort that have gone into the research.

Along these same lines, the marketer who has already made the decision prior to ordering research may request the wrong kind of research. The research objective may actually be to support the course of action already selected, rather than to determine whether the course of action is optimal. A study that sets out to prove that the chosen approach is right can certainly do exactly that, but nothing has been learned. Research that attempts to determine *whether* a decision is right, or preferably, *what* the optimal decision should be, is far superior.

If research results run counter to the marketer's original decision, the researcher may be asked whether the results are accurate and reliable. The truthful answer must be that only a "quick and dirty" study was requested, and as a result, it is neither large enough nor complete enough to be entirely reliable. In that case, the marketer may ignore the research results and go back to the original decision. Again, resources have been wasted and nothing of value has been gained from the research.

Sometimes, research is ignored because the marketer feels more knowledgeable and competent than any research. Persons with self-made careers, who have learned their business through the traditional "school of hard knocks," may believe that they know the right decision inherently, and do not need supporting research. As mentioned earlier, it

FIGURE 4.1 An Advertisement Promoting Nielsen's
Marketing Research Services
Source: Nielsen Media Research.

is possible to rely too much on research, and a competent manager may have the experience and knowledge to overrule what the research indicates. But such decisions must be made carefully—in a way that is fully justifiable—and never simply to support an ego.

Research also may be ignored when a decision is made in haste or ignorance. Perhaps there was insufficient time to gather appropriate information, or maybe a careless or lazy person went ahead without consulting the available information. Maybe those involved did not know that the information was attainable or did not check all the resources thoroughly. This may not be a conscious or vindictive decision; it may simply occur in the press of the advertising business, where time truly is money.

Quality of Information

Any decision is only as good as the research information supporting it. Evaluation of research results requires consideration of the research's accuracy, relevance, and reliability. Information gathered in a hurried or sloppy manner may not be worth much and certainly should not be used as the basis for major decisions. Important decisions may require stronger research support, and the corollary is that lesser decisions may make use of research that is less stringent in its approach. Still, the research should be accurate and reliable: A question of lesser importance does not excuse shoddy research work.

There is always the danger of relying on research that simply is not correct. Managers must learn to judge the reliability and truthfulness of research results. Constant questioning and challenging is preferable to major errors because of blindly following the research directions. The data should be checked against other sources. Managers should then make their own calculations to determine whether the research results are correct, should draw their own conclusions from the raw research data, rather than rely only on someone else's interpretation. Managers should judge for themselves whether the values, proportions, and recommendations actually make sense.

Another problem is giving the research findings a degree of accuracy that they simply do not have. A researcher may find that, of some certain group of consumers, 45.8 percent are male and 14.4 percent are college-educated. A casual analyst might combine these figures and conclude that 6.5952 percent are college-educated males ($0.458 \times 0.144 = .065952$). But the initial figures were accurate only to the nearest one-tenth of 1 percent, so it is faulty reasoning to combine these data and assume an accuracy to the nearest one ten thousandth of 1 percent. In fact, it may not even be accurate to combine the data: Males may be more likely or less likely to be college-educated than is the overall population.

In summary, decisions are only as good as the information that goes into them. Managers should check the procedures, questions, samples, answers, statistical calculations, results, and conclusions, and use only information in which they have confidence. As the Quest advertisement in figure 4.2 says, you need the facts behind the figures.

Market Analysis

Primary research can be applied to advertising to analyze various problems and decisions that arise in the media business. These topics most often deal with distribution, usage, markets, targets, and competition. These areas are not always mutually exclusive—there may be some overlap from one to another. For example, distribution analysis may also involve competitive distribution, so distribution analysis and competitive analysis might overlap in this case.

Distribution Analysis

All aspects of the marketing channel, including the types of intermediaries within the distribution channel—whether they be wholesalers, jobbers, retailers, or salespersons—and even direct-marketing channels, are involved in distribution analysis. The markup or payment required by the various entities in the distribution channels, whether any special

FIGURE 4.2 An Advertisement Promoting an On-Line Computerized Advertising Data-Base Service
Courtesy of Leading National Advertisers.

handling may be needed (for example, for perishable items), the degree and kind of service desired, and the relationship to the ultimate customer are all distribution analysis considerations.

Primary research into distribution can be very simple in advertising: One of the best, yet most direct, approaches is for the analyst simply to visit stores or other outlets where the merchandise may be for sale to examine shelf space and shelf position, final price, competitive items, in-store promotions, and stock supplies. Just because they are simple and relatively inexpensive does not mean that store inspections should be minimized. Some of the largest advertisers make constant use of store visits: When a member of the advertising department at Procter & Gamble travels for business purposes, a short list of stores often is inserted into the travel documents, and the P&G marketer is expected to visit those stores while in the destination city. These store visits are really a form of research, used for exactly the purposes just discussed: to check on point-of-purchase displays, to determine whether the shelf position is appropriate, to find out if special promotions are attracting customers, and to make certain that the store has an adequate stock of merchandise.

Usage Analysis

Who uses a service or product? What kinds of people are they? Where do they live? What other goods and services do they buy? Media planners and buyers need these answers, along with the answer to an even more important question: What media do these people see and hear?

Through primary research, marketers may be able to determine who these people are and where they are located, but they may not be able to match them exactly with a media group. So different levels of analysis are necessary to find a suitable match between a target group and available media audiences.

Marketers start with usage: Who uses the product or service? Most often, they collect this information in demographic terms: age, income, gender, educational attainment, employment status, marital status, children's ages, and similar data.

Sometimes, they also collect psychographic information or other personality or social traits. For more detail, refer to the chapter 3 discussion of segmentation in marketing.

Market Analysis

Once marketers have determined who uses the product or service, the next step is to find out where these people live and where they work. Getting access to persons in their homes is not as easy as just finding out where they live. In addition, while locating a person's place of residence is relatively easy, that person may not spend as much time at home as at work or elsewhere.

A large service corporation in the New York City metropolitan area knew what kinds of people were its best potential customers, and it knew where they lived. But most customers wanted to be able to obtain the service after work, while on the commute home, and the corporation used primary research to determine that most of its clientele worked within 12 miles of at least one of its outlet locations. The corporation's advertising problem then became one of determining how to reach people at work with advertising.

Markets are geographic in nature, so by definition, they are physically separated from one another. Thus, market analysis requires travel and expense. Relying on information from too few markets provides too narrow a view.

In most cases, advertisers are interested in the kinds of people who live in the various markets, but other types of information can also be useful. A detergent manufacturer may want to know the water quality in each locale, to determine how well the washing agent will work. A gasoline refiner may wish information on the number of automobiles, while a cereal maker may be interested only in the children's market segment.

One modern approach to marketing involves the use of geodemographic analysis. Different kinds of people live in different parts of the country, and advertising directed at certain geographic territories can sometimes be used to reach certain kinds of people. Conversely, a large-scale advertising campaign may not be equally effective with all the different categories of people, so different campaigns

MEDIA SPOTLIGHT

4.1

Focus on Focus Groups

by Gerald J. Eilers

Gerald Eilers is director of marketing services at Isadore & Paulson, Inc., in New York City.

As a general rule, media planners are seldom (if ever) invited to attend consumer focus groups. And that's a shame, because an important person on the team is not being given an opportunity to be creative to the fullest extent in determining the marketing of a brand.

Yes, I know that some account people "tell" media people what they learned from the groups or occasionally let a media planner or buyer read the report. But that's not the same as seeing and hearing consumers talk about the category and the product.

Fifteen years ago, I had a real lesson in the importance of involving all members of a product group, including media people, in the research function. I was at an agency that had a fashion account. Because of a change in management, we felt we had to demonstrate our commitment to innovatively service the business. So we filled the room with our account and creative people and invited the associate media director to attend the groups.

At this time, sales of the client's basic product lines (very structured, full-coverage, underwire bras for the older, full-busted woman) were declining. Meanwhile, a line of contemporary, fashionable, designer bras was the rage. While the client felt his basic customer didn't buy this merchandise, his company had introduced similar goods in A, B, and C cups to expand the franchise. In spite of the fact that we advertised this new merchandise in the younger fashion books rather than the older Seven Sisters books we used for the basic line, we had difficulty getting distribution on these products, and sales lagged behind projections. The trade did not feel that the prospects for this type of merchandise were our customers.

Given this lack of success, we scheduled several focus groups with our present buyers (that is, mature, fuller-busted women). Imagine our surprise when we learned that these women wanted this sexier, more fashionable merchandise in C, D, and DD cups!

A quick change of strategy was in order. We made the new merchandise in C, D, and DD cups, and our media maven talked us into doing a mini-catalog featuring the basic and new merchandise using the same model. And then he got brilliant—he proposed a dealer listing (which helped us to get the distribution we needed) and charged the whole media cost back to co-op. The ad budget only got hit with the production costs.

Since that time, I've made it a practice to invite media people to focus groups when appropriate or at least let them view edited tapes of the groups. While it hasn't always produced brilliant media plans or buys, I know that my clients got more than traditional thinking.

Some of the more interesting examples include buying DIY cable shows for a faucet filter system . . . or buying sports talk shows on cable systems for a beverage being sold in stadiums when we were locked out of the actual team telecasts . . . or using off-campus college newspapers and "with it" local newspapers such as *LA Weekly* to promote a mixed drink targeted to sociable young adults.

At the very least, the agency got a better-informed planner/buyer. And that meant people who could defend the plan or buy to the client because they shared common knowledge and business insights from a hands-on exposure to the target.

Source: Gerald J. Eilers, "Focus on Focus Groups," *Marketing & Media Decisions*, July 1990, 51.

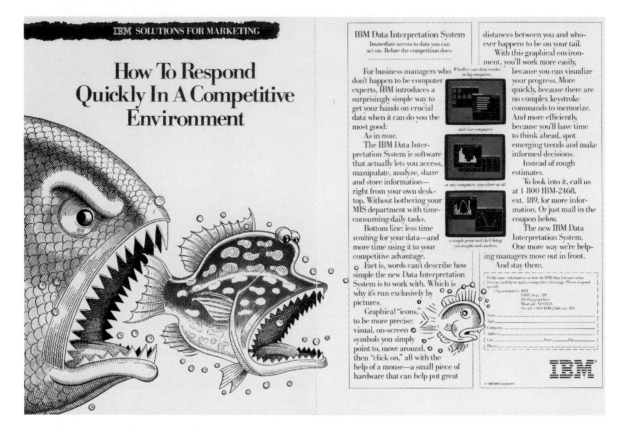

FIGURE 4.3 An Advertisement for Computer Data Services Specifically Developed for Advertising Applications
Source: International Business Machines, Inc., Montvale, NJ.

may be developed to match the characteristics of the populace in particular areas. One soft-drink marketer has reportedly used dozens of individualized advertising themes and campaigns, matching each to specific markets where it will be most effective.

Maximization of the efficacy of this approach requires conducting sales audits. These can be done privately, or market research specialists can be hired. Tracking sales by city, county, metropolitan area, or other geographic category is essential in allocating media resources geographically, including the use of a brand or category development index, which is discussed in chapter 11. The IBM advertisement in figure 4.3 offers a direct solution to these problems.

Target Analysis

Knowing the market, then, means knowing the physical or geographic location of the prospects—the *target market*. Knowing the demographic characteristics of these same people identifies the *target group* to which they belong, usually divided by demographic segments or according to other segmentation characteristics. Knowing what print media they see and which broadcast media they hear determines the *target audience* that can be reached through a certain advertising medium or some combination of media. Knowing the kinds of people and their location is not as critical to advertising media success as is knowing the mass media of which these prospects are audience members.

As discussed in chapter 3, those people who can be reached through mass-media advertising—the target audience—are not exactly the same people as those in the target group. However, because advertising media strategy concentrates on media audiences, marketers can focus on that concept rather than worrying about a separate target group. Therefore, marketers' major concerns are the target market (geographic locations where they want to sell) and the target audience (the persons they wish to reach through advertising). As noted in chapter 3, all of these terms—target market, target group, and target audience—can be grouped under the heading of **prospect targets.**

In trying to market videotape rentals, marketers may know the target markets (locations) and target groups (kinds of people). But no advertising medium reaches videotape renters, all videotape renters, and only videotape renters. Any advertising medium that communicates with large numbers of videotape renters also reaches some persons who do *not* rent videotapes, which results in waste circulation. And yet, reaching all potential videotape renters, even with a combination of media and vehicles, is impossible. Not only can marketers not reach all members of the target audience, but the very fact that these people view videotapes may interfere with their viewing of broadcast television, which might be an otherwise natural medium to use in promoting videos.

Information about the target audience is best for advertising media planning because it is through the mass media that these audiences can most efficiently and effectively be reached. In some ways, the media develop entertainment and information content that attract an audience so that they, the media, can then turn around and sell that audience to advertisers. Advertising media planners are very interested in those audiences and their composition.

Target analysis, then, utilizes consumer data. It groups consumers according to their profiles, describing them by their demographic and geographic characteristics. If these traits can be matched with their usage of certain products, their attitudes toward certain brands, or their reactions to advertising, the media planner can use the con-sumer profile descriptions to aim messages at specific prospect groups. When media reading and viewing patterns are included, marketers obtain a complete matchup of consumers with their product and brand usage, their media usage, and their consumer profiles, permitting much more accurate media targeting and much less waste.

Analysis of Competition

Any marketer wants to know what the competition is doing and planning. This aspect of primary research can range from very quick and simple to very time consuming and complicated. A restaurant owner can easily count the number of customers who enter a nearby competitor's restaurant to determine whether the other's business is improving. Multiplying the approximate number of customers by the approximate average bill provides a very rough idea of the daily gross proceeds of that competing business. It may not be totally accurate—but it is closer to the truth than a random guess, it is fast and easy, and it is primary research!

Advertising media planners often want information regarding competitors' advertising. Simply by looking at the competitors' advertising, they can determine how much use is made of print advertising, what kinds of publications the advertisements tend to appear in, how much color and bleed advertising is used, the usual sizes of the advertisements, patterns of scheduling advertisement placements, common advertising themes, and so on. Similar information can be gained for local broadcast advertising, but with greater difficulty because of broadcasting's transient nature. Almost any skilled person can collect and analyze this kind of information. Then these data can be used for planning prospect impact strategies and for media scheduling.

More formal primary research, conducted by professional research firms, can examine details of competitors' advertising expenditures, their media and vehicle choices, broadcast commercial message lengths, and the like. Because gathering this information is so detailed and thus expensive, because so many competitors may be involved, and because many different advertisers would like to have this kind of information, the research is often conducted by a firm that syndicates the data to individual firms that subscribe to the researcher's service. These data thus become **syndicated research,** which is discussed in chapter 5.

The professional research organizations are conducting primary research, even though the users of the information are at other firms and thus are utilizing secondary research. We now examine some of the research techniques utilized in advertising media by these primary researchers.

Media Research Technologies

More research gadgetry is utilized in the copy and creative-strategy research portion of advertising than in advertising media research, which in some ways, is rather simple by comparison. Advertising media research uses a combination of mechanical and paper research instruments, although computer programs and electronic information-gathering equipment are becoming more common. Most of the research involves surveys, collecting information from persons who respond to questions, record their purchasing and media-consumption habits, or express their opinions regarding specific topics. As primary research techniques become more sophisticated and utilize advanced technologies, the one-time divisions between the various media are beginning to diminish, and a single research approach may be applied to several different kinds of media, providing more compatible and comparable research data.

People Meters

The earliest mechanical audience measurements were done with the **audimeter,** developed by the A. C. Nielsen Company, which recorded broadcast tune-ins by tracking stations and times when a receiving set was in use. The resulting data were combined with those gathered by other methods, helping to overcome the shortcomings of each.

In recent years, the so-called **people meter** added a new dimension, allowing each audience member within a household to "punch in" as a member of the audience at specific times during the broadcast day. At the same time, however, broadcast audience levels began to decline, especially for network television. Naturally, the question arose as to whether fewer persons were actually watching television or whether the apparent decline was at least partially the result of the change in measurement techniques. A concomitant concern was whether the old audimeter figures had been correct; perhaps the audience actually had been smaller than previously estimated and was only now being accurately measured by the people meter.

People meters have the advantage of collecting information without excessive human interference, resulting in more accurate data unclouded by interpretation, bias, or lying. Of course, viewers must cooperate by entering their codes when requested, and the resulting data still must be analyzed and interpreted. A disadvantage is that people meter respondents grow tired of reporting their attendance, so their viewing can be undercounted. And audimeters may indicate television viewing when nobody was actually watching the television set. With both the audimeter and people meter, there also can be problems with the selection of individuals or households so that the panel as a group does not exactly represent the population as a whole.

To counter these concerns, Nielsen Media Research is developing a passive people meter, which uses a camera and artificial intelligence to record who is watching television when, without any viewer inputs required. One outcome may be the ability to measure all television viewing, including out-of-home viewing in hotels, taverns, restaurants, college dormitories, and second homes.[1]

Scanners

The electronic price scanners now familiar in grocery and similar stores have helped simplify and speed up the checkout process while increasing accuracy. At the same time, scanners record what items are selling, which automatically helps to keep track of inventory.

Scanners can be helpful in primary research if certain customers answer a few questions and record demographic data along with purchase information. Members of a consumer panel may answer complicated questionnaires and then, when shopping, show a small card with scanner markings so that their identifier code can be recorded along with the list of items being purchased. A match of demographics, purchase patterns, and media habits can provide useful insights into consumers' behavior as well as the best ways to reach them with advertising messages.

Advertisers use these data to find out what kinds of persons are buying what product, in what volume, in which parts of the country, and at what price. This information can even be compared with the characteristics of competitors' customers and matched with panel members' reported media consumption habits and patterns.

As with any mechanical measuring instrument, the data collected by scanners are pure and not influenced by human intervention in the research process. Yet, the scanners were designed primarily for retail inventory control, not advertising media research, and matching an individual's purchases with his or her demographic characteristics is difficult, while a matchup with the person's media habits is almost impossible. Other complications are that those respondents who agree to serve as members of a panel may not be entirely representative of the population as a whole, and scanner data from one locale may not be representative of a larger area or other regions.

Information Networks

Combinations of media, consumption, and demographic information are of obvious value to advertising media planners. Major advertisers or their agencies may subscribe to information networks—large data compilations that provide cross-comparisons of these categories. The two major information networks are the Simmons Market Research Bureau (known commonly just as "Simmons" or as SMRB) and Mediamark Research, Inc. (MRI). Both firms collect their information from surveys of large groups of consumers, gathering detailed information on product and service usage, amounts of consumption, media-usage patterns, and demographic and psychographic characteristics.

From this information, media planners can determine the best media match for reaching a certain kind of customer—in essence, match a target group with a target audience. Instead of simply knowing consumers in demographic terms, this kind of information permits knowing consumers in terms of their media consumption patterns. This allows communication of the advertising message to the intended target group with more efficiency and less waste.

The immense volume of data that research firms must collect, analyze, and compare lends itself to computer storage and recall of the data. The computerized information sources can then be accessed by on-line computers so that huge quantities of information are available to both large and small businesses. These information networks are available by subscription to advertisers and their agencies, and the syndication of the research work spreads the costs among a larger number of concerns.

Information gathering for research firms can be problematic. Because the interview process may require several hours of time, many potential respondents may decline to be interviewed, throwing off the representativeness of the sample. In addition, respondents may not provide truthful answers, either because they have forgotten the actual facts or because they are trying to impress the interviewer. Although information networks provide invaluable data for media planning, the potential for inaccuracies means that relying too heavily on these research aids can mislead the media decision maker.

Chapter 5 discusses syndicated and other kinds of secondary research, and samples of these advertising data sources are shown there.

Interviews

Much consumer information is gained by interviewing respondents, asking questions regarding pertinent subjects. With regard to advertising, such interviews can be conducted coincidentally with the

MEDIA SPOTLIGHT

4.2

The Print-Plus Payoff

by Wally Wood

The evidence is piling up from the Netherlands, Italy, Canada, Great Britain and, most recently, West Germany: Campaigns that employ both television and print media advertisements are more effective than either television or print alone. True, the media environments in these countries are different from ours, as well as from each other, and critics may question methodologies. But all the studies point the same way.

One of the most comprehensive studies, "Media Mix and Advertising Effectiveness," comes from Axel Springer Verlag (ASV), the Hamburg-based publisher. Rolf Speetzen, ASV's international research officer, recently came to the United States to share the results.

Axel Springer previously had surveyed 246 German brands to establish advertising effectiveness (*Marketing & Media Decisions,* February 1987, 130). For the current study, they looked at 43 of these brands—those that spent one million deutsche marks or more during the survey period (January 1986–May 1987) and spent at least 20 percent of the budget in either television or radio. The print/television mix ranged from 75/25 to 24/76.

Their findings: The brands reached 22.9 percent of all consumers exclusively through print, 29.4 percent exclusively through television, and 39.7 percent through a combination of both. Neither print nor television was able to reach 8.3 percent of consumers (although some might have been reached through radio).

Reach is one thing; what about impact? Axel Springer tested three advertising effectiveness criteria: unaided brand awareness, aided brand awareness, and potential buyers. The unaided brand awareness scores were, in virtually all cases, much higher among consumers who had been exposed to a mix of television and print (see table 1.) As the report concludes, "The highest effectiveness levels are scored among people who were exposed to a mix of media." In addition, "among people who can be reached mainly or solely through television, only a very high dosage of contacts shows an adequate effectiveness level."

Bill Landgraf, director of media planning at Kraft General Foods, says the findings are "another indication that a media mix makes more and more sense. The nay-sayers might argue that German television is a different situation: Media patterns aren't like ours, commercial television has certain restrictions, etc. But so what? I think the concept is right—a media mix, or synergy, or a multiplier are all telling me the same thing."

A Canadian study, "The Multiplier Effect," a joint research venture of McLean-Hunter, *Reader's Digest,* Telemedia Publishing, and MacLaren: Lintas, looked at four different campaigns. It concludes that "adding magazines to a schedule contributes more than adding more television."

For example, if "television without print" is indexed at 100, the main message for a Kraft Miracle Whip Light campaign of "television with print" is 118 for the "light and healthy" main message, and 126 for the "taste" main message.

Another British study, "Multiplying the Media Effect 2," commissioned by the Press Research

Council, looked at twelve cases, ranging from Peugeot to Sarsons Pickling Vinegar. The report concludes, "Print can lead people to perceive the television commercial in new ways and can also convey new information that is not in the television commercial. The result of adding print to a television campaign is a richer, more complete communication."

This study looked at both newspaper and color-supplement advertising, as well as magazine ads. "Although there are undoubtedly differences in the ways different kinds of publications communicate, the distinctions are small compared with the major differences between print and television."

Marian G. Confer, vice president and research director of the Magazine Publishers of America, says they are testing three female-oriented brands in the field to see how the media mix affects advertising effectiveness. They hope to have the results by the end of March.

Confer says that the studies are so interesting, "we're trying to get together a meeting in London this spring to share what we've been doing. Since there is so much interest in global marketing, there may be one global methodology—the best of the best—to do this research."

TABLE 1

Mixed Media and Unaided Brand Awareness
(Index: Score for No Exposures = 100 [=25.7%])

| | Print | | Television only | | Mix Print and Television | |
	Awareness Percentage of All Consumers	Index	Awareness Percentage of All Consumers	Index	Awareness Percentage of All Consumers	Index
1–12 Exposures	4.5%	144	15.4%	91	23.7%	139
13–24 Exposures	30.8	181	21.2	125	31.5	185
25+ Exposures	32.6	192	32.4	191	40.7	239
All Contacts	27.5%	162	19.9%	117	30.9%	182

Source: Axel Springer Verlag
Source: Wally Wood, "The Print-Plus Payoff," *Marketing & Media Decisions,* March 1990, 90.

advertising exposure or following the exposure. Coincidental interviews are most often done by telephone, which permits reaching large areas and lots of people, although calls may not be welcomed early in the morning or later at night.

Follow-up interviews can also be by telephone but are often conducted in person. Such interviews can be door-to-door, but that involves a lot of travel and results in loss of information because so few persons may be at home at any given moment. For these reasons, follow-up interviews are usually done in convenient locations, such as shopping areas. This technique is called the "mall intercept" approach.

As mentioned earlier, any interviewing is subject to error: Respondents may forget what they actually did, or they may try to please the interviewer by giving answers intended to bring approval. Follow-up interviewing about advertising exposure is especially subject to error: Respondents really cannot be expected to have memorized what they saw on television the night before or in what publication they first read a certain advertisement. Without prompting, respondents recall very little. With prompting, however, respondents may provide answers that were suggested, rather than the actual facts.

Tracking

Tracking studies record who buys certain brands, how they make use of these items, the frequency of the purchase cycle, media habits, and prospect profiles. Most often, a panel of consumers are recruited to maintain tracking records of their purchases, applications, and satisfaction with various brands. The members of tracking panels may be paid directly for their cooperation, or they may be offered premiums or gifts in return for their time and effort.

A panel is used so that the research can track the same individuals' purchase decisions over a substantial period. If a different panel were recruited for each survey, purchase-pattern changes might reflect different persons with different tastes and habits, rather than changes within the individuals themselves. Because tracking panels do not change for each survey, changes in purchase patterns can be traced back to a specific individual, who

can be interviewed in depth for more detailed information. In addition, alterations in a panel's purchase patterns are obviously the result of some change, whether conscious or unconscious, on the part of panel members. These changes may then be correlated with a brand's advertising campaign.

Diaries

Diaries are records kept by members of a consumer panel to keep track of their media usage, their purchase decisions, or similar information. The most common advertising media use of diaries is to record household members' television viewing and radio listening. The diary information can then be matched with the data gathered by mechanical devices, with the diaries providing detail on which persons were present during each period of media use.

Diaries are also used to record the purchases consumers make at, say, a grocery store. Recording information while standing in a supermarket line is somewhat more difficult than while at home seated in front of the television set, however. Sometimes, the shopping patterns can be compared with the media habits to determine the influence of the advertising messages received by audience members, although these kinds of conclusions must be drawn carefully and the results viewed with a healthy dose of skepticism.

The advantage of using diaries is primarily that data can be collected on individual consumers, rather than on entire households or families. The major disadvantage is that respondents may forget to complete the diary at the time of reading, viewing, or shopping, and then may try to reconstruct the information afterward. This results in guesswork and the errors of faulty memories. Using diary information in conjunction with data gathered by other means can help to offset this disadvantage.

Opinion and Attitude Research

Various methods have been devised to gather public opinion on such topics as products, services, media, and vehicles. One problem is that opinions and attitudes are both "feelings" about something.

MEDIA SPOTLIGHT

4.3

Get Involved

by Joe Mandese

For nearly three decades, researchers have debated the impact that viewers' involvement with television programing has on ad effectiveness. Over this period, two major, contradictory theories have evolved: the negative and positive effects hypotheses. The first theory says that the more involved viewers are with programing surrounding an ad, the weaker the ad response will be. The latter theory claims just the opposite. However, a review of the varying methodologies used by past researchers, in addition to a new study, now appears to lend support in favor of the positive hypothesis.

At the Advertising Research Foundation's recent Media Research Workshop, Boston College professor David Lloyd revealed the findings of the new study with Yankelovich Clancy Shulman that clearly makes a case for a correlation between program involvement and positive ad response. As a result, they advocate that, instead of planning television on the basis of CPMs [costs-per-thousand], media planners should now plan the medium based on "cost per thousand people involved, or impacted," which they claim significantly improves both costs and effectiveness of the medium.

Source: Joe Mandese, "Broadcast Beat: Get Involved," *Marketing & Media Decisions,* August 1989, 134.

Because attitudes are internalized, however, they are assumed to be more "truthful." Opinions are shared with others and thus may be influenced by circumstance, by the desire to impress the interviewer, by problems with recall, by lack of factual information, and by poor interview techniques and leading questions.

Some of these problems can be countered by using mechanical or paper-and-pencil measuring devices. The **Q-Sort** utilizes printed opinion statements that the subject sorts into categories of agreement, partial agreement, neutrality, and disagreement. Respondents can apply these statements to various situations, persons, brands, or institutions, providing a breadth of opinion information. The **semantic differential** allows respondents to indicate where on a continuum with bipolarized adjective extremes their actual opinion is positioned. As with the Q-Sort, the semantic differential eliminates some of the problems common with direct interviewing, but care still must be taken in the administration and analysis of the test results.

Summary

Primary research is a study conducted for the first time for some specific purpose. It is expensive and time consuming, which must be weighed against the value of the information to be gained and the purpose to which it may be applied. It is possible to rely too heavily on research results, just as it is possible to ignore the results of primary research. Advertising media managers can reduce these hazards through experience and by comparing the data with other sources and their personal knowledge. The resulting advertising media decisions are only as good as the research that goes into them.

Primary research can be applied to many kinds of marketing situations, including distribution, product and service usage, markets, target groups and audiences, and competitors and their advertising. In addition to more traditional methods of advertising media research methods, such as interviews and diaries, modern media research technologies that may involve computer programs and electronic information-gathering equipment are being introduced. These include the so-called people meters, shopping scanners, and information networks.

Questions for Discussion

1. Can research really cost more than it is worth? Is there not value in all information?

2. Why would anyone order and pay for research and then not use it in the resulting decision-making process?

3. Is it really a problem to take research answers to as many decimal places as possible? Is not the resulting accuracy desirable?

4. What are the problems inherent in people meters? What could be done to improve people meters?

5. What innovations have scanners brought to research methods? To research results?

6. If diaries have disadvantages, why are they so widely used in advertising research?

7. What is the difference between attitudes and opinions? Do opinions reflect attitudes? Can attitudes actually be tested and recorded?

Endnote

1. Wayne Walley, "Nielsen Passive Meter Test Near," *Advertising Age,* 10 September 1990, 64.

Suggested Readings

- Fletcher, Alan D., and Thomas A. Bowers. *Fundamentals of Advertising Research.* 4th ed. Belmont, Calif.: Wadsworth, 1991.

- Fletcher, Alan D., and Donald W. Jugenheimer. *Problems and Practices in Advertising Research.* Columbus, Ohio: Grid, 1982. Pages 3–18.

- Lawrence, Ron. "Mediology: Personalizing the Process." *Marketing & Media Decisions,* August 1989, 123.

- Leigh, James H., and Claude R. Martin, Jr., eds. *Current Issues & Research in Advertising.* Ann Arbor, Mich.: Division of Research, Graduate School of Business Administration, University of Michigan, annual series.

- Walley, Wayne. "Nets Force Nielsen Showdown." *Advertising Age,* 24 September 1990, 3 and 60.

- Walley, Wayne. "Nielsen Passive Meter Test Near." *Advertising Age,* 10 September 1990, 64.

Chapter 5

The Role of Syndicated Research

Outline

Learning Objectives

In the study of this chapter, you will have the opportunity to:

- Learn about the use of secondary research in advertising media.
- Explore the kinds of syndicated media research available.
- Assess examples of actual syndicated research data.
- Understand the applications of secondary research to media planning and buying situations.
- Learn how to manipulate secondary data to meet specific situational needs.

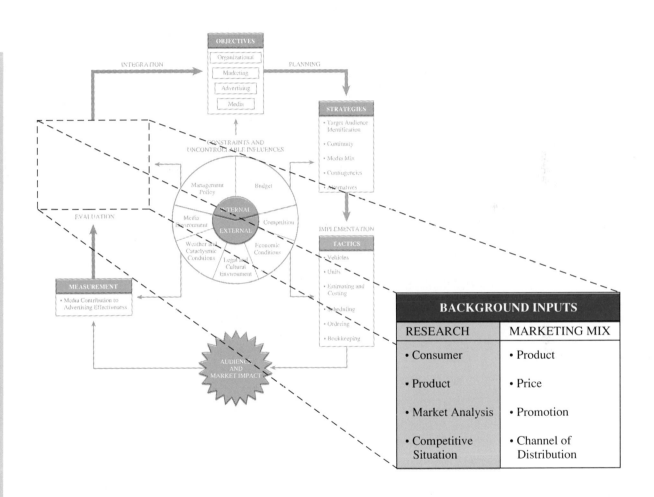

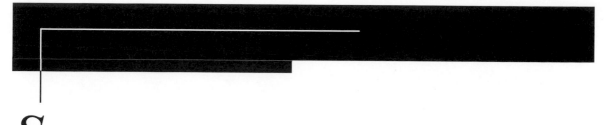

*S*econdary research is information that has already been gathered by some other entity and for some other purpose than the specific application at hand. Secondary data are used along with the results of primary research or original research, which is discussed in detail in chapter 4. Media planners generally seek out secondary research *before* resorting to primary research. If the necessary information is already available somewhere else for a reasonable price, it is not cost effective to duplicate that effort and conduct an entirely new study.

Because most secondary research used in advertising media work comes from syndicated information sources, this chapter focuses on the role of syndicated research. First, however, we discuss how all secondary research may be used in advertising and examine some internal sources of this kind of information.

Role of Secondary Research

Secondary research has some innate advantages over primary research. First, the use of secondary data is usually less expensive than paying for original research. Subscribing to a syndicated research service helps to spread research costs among several subscribers, creating savings for each one. Second, existing secondary research can be used much faster than an entirely new study that must be authorized, designed, tested, conducted, tabulated, analyzed, and applied. Third, and perhaps most important, secondary research information may actually be more accurate than that provided

by primary research. Secondary research is done without a specific purpose in mind, which tends to eliminate the possible bias or prior conclusions that can exist in a primary research situation. In addition, because secondary research may be shared by several firms or institutions, a more complete, larger-scale, and more detailed research study is affordable.

The key to successful secondary research is knowing what kinds of information are available, where that information can be found, and how to apply that information to the particular situation or problem at hand. The remainder of this chapter focuses on what information is available in advertising media work. In this section, however, we address the problem of applying the available information.

One common problem is that the secondary data are not in categories that match other findings or that can be directly applied to a particular situation. Perhaps an advertiser knows its customers according to the following age groupings: 18–24, 25–39, 40–49, 50–64, and 64+. With regard to buying spot-television advertising time, however, the broadcast ratings service may provide information in the following age categories: 18–24, 18–39, 40–49, 50–64, and 64+.

The obvious problem is that the ratings service does not specifically address the 25–39 age group. The total audience size for the 18–24 group, however, can be subtracted from the total audience size for the 18–39 group, leaving the figures for the 25–39 age group. The point is that, while the secondary data may not exactly fit the problem at hand, they can be manipulated and "massaged" to apply to a particular situation or problem.

Perhaps a researcher finds that 49 percent of a target group is male and 18 percent is college educated. A fairly reasonable conclusion may then be that 8 to 9 percent of the group consists of college-educated males ($0.49 \times 0.18 = 0.088$). While not exact, this figure is probably close enough for the purposes of estimating and calculating.

Perhaps an automobile manufacturer wants to target college-educated adult males, 35–49 years of age, working in professional and managerial positions and earning annual household incomes of $50,000 and higher. After consulting various sources, the manufacturer may calculate that only 4.8 percent of the U.S. population fits into all those categories, which is only about 120,000 persons. Of those 120,000 men, if even as many as 2 percent of them could be persuaded to purchase this make of automobile this year (a rather ambitious goal, incidentally), sales would amount to only 2,400 automobiles.

This kind of calculation by the automobile manufacturer can check several factors:

1. Is the target group an appropriate size? In this case, its narrow focus probably makes it too small.

2. Is it an appropriate target group for an advertising budget of $10 million? There are two problems here. First, that budget amounts to an advertising expenditure of $83+ for each target group member, so the target group of 120,000 may be too small to warrant such a large budget, or contrarily, the budget may be too large for such a small target. Second, the advertising expenditure would amount to $4,167 for each car sold, which is probably too high an amount.

3. Are the sales goal and advertising budget logical and reasonable? Is there a match between the sales objective, the advertising budget, and the target group? How much reach and frequency would be possible from applying this advertising budget against this target group?

Thus, the secondary information available can be applied to a variety of questions and concerns, even though the data may not specifically address the situation at hand.

Internal Sources of Secondary Information

Before dashing down the street to the public library in search of secondary research, or even down the hall to the media library, media planners should explore information on hand that might be suitable for answering questions and solving problems in advertising media. For example, the company undoubtedly has sales results from previous years, probably broken down by quarter or month, by product line, and perhaps by sales regions and type of selling outlet. Previous advertising budgets and media plans probably also are available for scrutiny. Past advertising budgets could be compared with respective years' sales to determine if there is a positive correlation. Also feasible is matching past years' media plans with sales successes, although causal relationships cannot be assumed without caution. Perhaps past public opinion surveys are available to relate the firm's public image to advertising efforts.

Within the organization, the obvious locations of such information are the advertising department, the marketing department, and the individual sales or brand managers. Less obvious, perhaps, are the public affairs, customer relations, investor services, and institutional research departments. Even the accounting department may have useful information in its records, accounts, and ledgers.

Although not technically part of the firm, trade associations in the industry might be considered internal sources of information. Such industry sources may provide information regarding direct competitors, industry trends, category advertising expenditures, and public concerns and image.

MEDIA SPOTLIGHT

5.1

Networks and Sponsors Vie in $4 Billion Game of Chance

by Bill Carter

The war being waged over the hearts and eyes of America escalated significantly last week. The television networks invited a British company to become the new official scorekeeper. And they set up a new method of counting viewers and charging advertisers for them.

The main result of these developments: confusion edging toward chaos. "It was the most incredible week I have ever experienced," one network executive said.

The event that boggled his mind was not the news that the networks had invited the AGB television research company of Britain to introduce a new rating system to challenge the venerable A. C. Nielsen Company. To many network executives, that was merely the most visible sign that the networks' offensive against Nielsen is for real.

What left this executive perplexed were the maneuvers that the networks made to alter the established system of paying for primetime advertising. The moves came on the eve of the orgy of spending that precedes every fall television season.

Within the next few weeks, advertisers will spend more than $4 billion to buy commercial time on primetime network programs—even though they now have no idea exactly what they are buying.

But then, the networks have no idea exactly what they are selling.

With more than $4 billion on the table, it might be logical to think that somebody would have a better grasp of what is going on than a tourist playing three-card monte or shell games in Times Square. But the network television business is increasingly taking the shape of a floating game with all but indecipherable rules.

Even before the AGB counterattack against Nielsen was announced, ABC declared that it had decided to line up behind NBC in bringing a new element to the measurement of television audiences. (After some delay, CBS also said it would go along with the NBC system.)

The networks plan to use what they call a linear regression model. This technique would plot the trend in overall television viewing levels over the last eight years to determine the accuracy of next season's "HUT," "PUT," and "WUT" levels.

This is not a joke. In the arcane business of audience measurement, **"HUTs," "PUTs"** and **"WUTs"** refer to "homes," "people," and "women using television."

The networks decided to resort to a linear regression model for the same reason they decided to bring back AGB, a rating company they snubbed two years ago: They now feel that Nielsen

External Sources of Secondary Information

Most secondary research information is found in external sources, outside the firm and outside its particular industry. Some of this information is general in scope, dealing with marketing and advertising matters, while other types may be applied directly to the media operation.

The external information used in advertising media planning is most often syndicated research. Because many advertisers and agencies require similar types of information, and because individual studies for each firm would be prohibitively is the enemy and has grossly undercounted all three of those "UT" levels, starting in January.

Nielsen, which has been reporting a drop in overall television viewing, has strenuously defended its system.

The truth is probably somewhere between. Even the networks' own research executives concede that viewing is down; they just do not believe it is down by nearly as much as Nielsen has reported. Nielsen executives admit that their figures for the first three months of the year are odd, and they cannot entirely reconcile them with statistics available from individual television markets.

The larger question may be: What difference does it make? Network television may be a diminished three-headed monster, but it is still the only monster in the national forest. Fox Television is a growing young beast, but it is no monster yet. Cable television is a herd of smaller creatures, living well but on the fringes.

If the networks decide that they are going to change the scorekeeper, the rules, and the prices of the advertising game, the sponsors are not in the best position to fight. In the television lottery, they *have* to play to win.

Some advertising executives are mad and would like to be able not to take it anymore.

For instance, Betsy Frank, senior vice president for Saatchi & Saatchi Advertising, warned that the networks' maneuvers may backfire.

"More people are asking seriously about alternatives," she said, referring to Fox Television and the cable channels.

But even if the *pas de deux* between the networks and advertisers turns out to be just more posturing, the confrontation between the networks and Nielsen is now too nasty to be dismissed. The appearance on the scene of a credible challenger to Nielsen, one that the networks appear to be sanctioning, has to be taken by Nielsen as a serious threat.

Either Nielsen will make adjustments in its methodology to make the networks happy, or its three best customers may put it out of business.

The networks concede it may take years for a new, credible ratings system to be established. But they have seen the light: Having a monopoly ratings service determining profit levels is not an ideal way to run an ever more difficult business.

There are not enough viewers to go around for the three networks (let alone for Fox). Every scrap of viewing is precious and will apparently be fought for with the desperation of the unjustly deprived.

And after the fight, they will probably demand a recount.

expensive, research companies conduct this research in the marketplace at large and then syndicate the research results. **Syndication** means that the research is sold to subscribers, who pay for the right to use the research findings and apply them to their own marketing and advertising problems. In this way, research expenses are spread across many customers, who share both the costs and the outcomes of the studies. Figure 5.1 shows an advertisement for Leading National Advertisers (LNA) and Arbitron, two of the best-known syndicated research firms.

In many cases, large advertisers and agencies with large accounts are asked to pay more of the

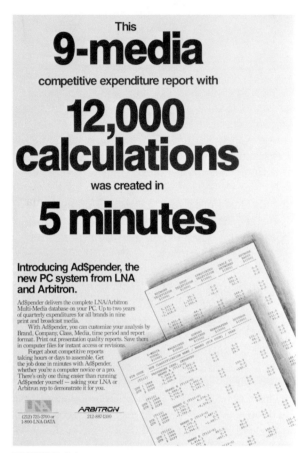

FIGURE 5.1 An Advertisement Promoting a Computerized Advertising Media Data-Base Service Offered Jointly by LNA and Arbitron
Source: Copyright 1991. The Arbitron Company. Reprinted by permission.

While all the advertisers in a category may have identical information, their approaches to their media and other campaign decisions are often different because interpretation and application of the data are essential parts of the process: Each entity must examine, evaluate, interpret, and decide which data are important, which are not, and how they affect the plans and tactics that result. Five marketers of chocolate candy may take five different marketing approaches, even though they are selling similar goods and have similar goals, because each firm has utilized its research and other information in different ways.

As we examine some of the actual sources of advertising media information, keep in mind that syndicated research information changes, in two ways. First, syndicated research is usually conducted continuously on a regular schedule: New sets of findings may be issued every month or every six months or every year. The respondents, purchase habits, competition, advertising plans, and execution all change, so the research must be conducted in an iterative manner.

Second, the syndication firms themselves change. New research firms come into the business; existing firms merge or change or go out of business. For that reason, providing completely current information about these firms and the research they supply is difficult. In the sections that follow, we examine some of the best known of the syndicated research sources, but keep in mind that their topics, research methods, report formats, and even their existence are subject to change. As the advertisement in figure 5.2 shows, LNA and Arbitron have joined together to offer a new level of advertising research.

Marketing and Advertising Data

Although general marketing and advertising information may not be applicable to specific media questions, it is still essential in directing media efforts in the most profitable direction, coordinating the media plan with advertising and marketing objectives, and working with the advertising research,

syndication costs, with smaller firms making reduced contributions. This method assumes that the information is of more value in large-scale situations, where more is at risk and where advertising investments are greater; those who have less to gain pay less of the cost.

The affordability of syndicated research involves trade-offs, however. For example, syndicated research cannot be tailored to each party's situation. In addition, all subscribers, including competitors, have access to exactly the same information.

Another important point is that having information provided by syndicated research is not as important as what is done with the information.

HOW TO BREAK THE SPEED LIMIT

Now With 5 Years of Data for 10 Media!

In five minutes flat, you can produce customized advertising expenditure reports with AdSpender 2.0.

Load AdSpender 2.0 on your PC and you'll have the complete LNA/Arbitron Multi-Media database at your fingertips. With AdSpender 2.0, you can obtain up to five years of advertising expenditures for all brands in ten media.

New features in AdSpender 2.0 enable you to track spending on a monthly basis. Break out network and spot TV by dayparts. Sort, rank and trend all data.

With AdSpender 2.0, you can customize your analysis. Select just the information you need by Brand, Company, Class, Media and time period. In the report format of your choice.

Whether you're a computer novice or genius, AdSpender 2.0 can make your job a lot easier. It's fast, easy-to-use, flexible and up-to-date. With AdSpender 2.0, there's no limit to what you can do.

LNA

ARBITRON

212-789-1400   1-800-LNA-DATA   212-887-1300

FIGURE 5.2 An Advertisement Promoting the Speed of Using a Computerized Advertising Data-Base Service
Source: Copyright 1991. The Arbitron Company and Leading National Advertisers. Reprinted by permission.

creative, and account-service operations. While the categories of information sources often overlap, the external sources of marketing and advertising information most often provide information about sales, product and brand usage (the competition), and consumers.

Sales and Brand Share

There is more to sales information than simply the volume of sales. Sales volume can be expressed in dollar volume, units sold, or in other units, such as 100–pound equivalents of breakfast cereal. These figures can also be broken down by product line, model, color, size, options, and price category. Sales volume also can be divided according to market, region, type of retail outlet, and city size. Customer demographics, previous purchase history (brand loyalty), most important feature, and information source (where did the consumer first learn about the product?) are other possible ways of organizing sales data.

Trade associations or other industry organizations often provide these data, or the information may be published in one of the tens of thousands of **trade papers** or the even greater number of newsletters and "insider" publications. The primary syndicated source from which sales information can be purchased is the **A. C. Nielsen Company,** whose Nielsen Marketing Research Services cover sales in grocery stores and drugstores, with the information provided by scanners that record items sold and their prices. The trade name for this service is Scantrack.

Product and Brand Usage

Advertising media planners require strategic information regarding matches of target markets, target groups, and media coverage. At first glance, these strategic secondary research data appear cumbersome and puzzling because of their complexity, detail, and terminology. A clear understanding of these data requires practice in applying the numbers to real situations.[1]

Strategic information helps in the media-planning process, but the decisions still must be made by media planners. In marketing chewing gum, for example, strategic information sources may indicate the kinds of people who use gum, how much and how often they use it, what brands they use, their demographic characteristics, and their media usage patterns. If a manufacturer is going to introduce a new brand of chewing gum, would it be best to advertise it to people who already chew a lot of gum and try to induce them to change brands, or to advertise it to people who do not chew gum and try to induce them to start chewing gum, or to advertise it to people who chew only a little gum (and thus may be less brand loyal than heavy users) and try to induce them to switch to the new gum and chew more, or to advertise it to people who usually chew candy or tobacco instead of gum and try to induce them to switch to gum? Information about these groups can be found in strategic media sources, but media planners must decide how to apply this information.

The strategic information used in media planning is less specific than tactical information. Strategic sources indicate which media types are used by what persons, but except for network television programs and magazine names, there is little indication of specific media vehicles. Those decisions are more commonly made by media buyers during the tactical implementation of the media plan.

The most commonly used strategic information source in advertising media is the *Study of Markets and Media* by the Simmons Market Research Bureau (SMRB). The Simmons study is available in printed form, which consists of about fifty volumes of data annually, on computer diskettes, and from on-line computer information networks. Mediamark Research, Inc. (MRI), offers a similar source of strategic advertising media information, as does the Mendelsohn Media Research Company (MMR).

Consumer Analysis

Another category of marketing and advertising information needed by media planners revolves around the groups into which consumers can be categorized. Standard classifications of consumer groups have been established by the American Association of Advertising Agencies, and for compatibility and ease of cross-reference, most of the standard sources use identical categories that allow demographic characteristics to be seen according to geographic divisions.

Some of this kind of information is available from government sources, such as the U.S. Census and its annual update—the *Statistical Abstract of the United States.* Data aimed at marketing applications are found in the *Survey of Buying Power,* published annually by *Sales & Marketing Management* magazine; its "Buying Power Index" is especially helpful in allocating resources to markets according to population income and retail sales ratios (figure 5.3). This information can also be found in certain volumes of *Standard Rate & Data*

Service (SRDS), which reports advertising rates for many media. Some *SRDS* reports are organized geographically and have good summaries of market information at the beginning of each state's section; these volumes include the reports for daily newspapers, spot television, and spot radio.

Competitive Media Data

Any good marketer wants to know what the competition is doing, and industrial espionage is not required to gather this information. In fact, an amazing array of this information can be located in standard commercial reference sources. Of course, this information is somewhat dated because the sources are involved in tracking what competitors have already done with past advertising investments, and there may have been delays in reporting the information. In addition, the past does not guarantee the future, and a competitor may not continue past patterns into future advertising.

Still, media data about competitors obviously are useful, and any advertising practitioner, in media or in other aspects of the business, should be familiar with them.

General Information

Specialized commercial sources of competitive media data deal with advertisers' budgets, media used, agencies employed, and personnel. Trade publications, such as *Advertising Age,* publish annual compilations of major advertisers and their strategies. The same trade papers feature advertisers' creative approaches, test markets, new product introductions, and media plans in almost every issue.

Syndicated sources of competitive advertising media information monitor advertisements to track individual companies' advertising placements—accessible by brand name, product category, or parent company. Competitive sources for individual advertising media are discussed in the next section. The competitive advertising expenditures in several media are combined in Leading National Advertisers' (LNA) *Multi-Media Report* (figure 5.4). Although this source does not provide the detail

Wisconsin

POPULATION—12/31/89

RETAIL SALES BY STORE GROUP—1989

S&MM ESTIMATES

METRO AREA County City	Total Population (Thousands)	% Of U.S.	Median Age Of Pop.	% of Population by Age Group				Households (Thousands)	Total Retail Sales ($000)	Food ($000)	Eating & Drinking Places ($000)	General Mdse. ($000)	Furniture/ Furnish/ Appliance ($000)	Auto-motive ($000)	Drug ($000)
				18-24 Years	25-34 Years	35-49 Years	50 & Over								
APPLETON–OSHKOSH–NEENAH ...	315.4	.1262	31.6	11.7	17.2	19.9	24.2	117.9	2,329,010	382,816	214,263	354,666	140,031	538,177	53,373
Calumet	35.9	.0143	30.5	10.0	16.5	19.9	22.8	12.4	153,057	62,007	16,751	6,988	8,145	35,254	2,268
Outagamie	139.2	.0557	30.8	11.1	17.2	19.9	22.9	51.0	1,115,454	164,478	101,283	204,278	55,261	267,900	19,094
• Appleton	65.6	.0263	31.9	11.7	17.9	19.6	24.8	25.8	487,803	111,744	47,131	51,753	36,644	89,535	11,439
Winnebago	140.3	.0562	32.6	12.8	17.1	20.0	25.9	54.5	1,060,499	156,331	96,229	143,400	76,625	235,023	32,011
• Neenah	24.0	.0096	32.5	10.2	17.0	20.9	24.8	9.4	187,604	31,491	14,658	13,327	6,569	69,786	10,766
• Oshkosh	53.1	.0213	32.2	17.4	16.7	16.8	28.5	21.5	548,869	86,513	58,325	93,825	21,066	99,094	11,902
SUBURBAN TOTAL	172.7	.0690	31.1	10.2	16.8	20.9	22.6	61.2	1,104,734	153,068	94,149	195,761	75,752	279,762	19,266

EFFECTIVE BUYING INCOME—1989

EFFECTIVE BUYING INCOME—1989

METRO AREA County City	Total EBI ($000)	Median Hsld. EBI	% of Hslds. by EBI Group: (A) $10,000-$19,999 (B) $20,000-$34,999 (C) $35,000-$49,999 (D) $50,000 & Over				Buying Power Index
			A	B	C	D	
APPLETON–OSHKOSH–NEENAH ...	4,023,194	27,573	20.7	32.1	20.2	13.7	.1269
Calumet	446,885	29,757	19.0	32.3	22.5	15.4	.0123
Outagamie	1,795,409	28,628	18.9	33.1	21.1	14.4	.0579
• Appleton	910,869	28,202	19.7	32.1	20.7	14.4	.0276
Winnebago	1,780,900	25,962	22.8	31.1	18.9	12.6	.0567
• Neenah	330,551	28,373	19.1	33.0	20.7	14.9	.0102
• Oshkosh	636,594	21,832	27.6	29.1	14.6	10.3	.0235
SUBURBAN TOTAL	2,145,180	28,979	19.0	32.8	22.0	14.4	.0656

METRO AREA County City	Total EBI ($000)	Median Hsld. EBI	% of Hslds. by EBI Group: (A) $10,000-$19,999 (B) $20,000-$34,999 (C) $35,000-$49,999 (D) $50,000 & Over				Buying Power Index
			A	B	C	D	
MILWAUKEE–RACINE CONSOLIDATED							
AREA	23,157,104	30,490	18.3	26.9	21.3	20.4	.6837
RACINE	2,290,587	29,258	18.2	29.5	22.3	16.0	.0710
Racine	2,290,587	29,258	18.2	29.5	22.3	16.0	.0710
• Racine	1,044,747	25,804	21.1	29.3	20.1	12.1	.0345
SUBURBAN TOTAL	1,245,840	32,484	15.1	29.8	24.6	20.0	.0365
SHEBOYGAN	1,404,175	29,355	19.6	29.9	22.0	16.1	.0411
Sheboygan	1,404,175	29,355	19.6	29.9	22.0	16.1	.0411

FIGURE 5.3 An Example of *Sales & Marketing Management's Survey of Buying Power*
Source: Reprinted by Permission of Sales & Marketing. Copyright: Survey of Buying Power, August 13, 1990.

found in the individual media competitive sources, it does publish a good summary of estimated advertising expenditures by brand in each major media type.

Specific Media Expenditures and Activity

Available competitive data for print media include the names of the publications in which advertising appeared; the size, dates, and frequency of those insertions; estimated approximate costs of the advertising; and whether color or bleed advertising was employed. In the broadcast media, similar information details the programs on which network advertising appeared and markets in which spot advertising appeared, along with dates, commercial length, and estimated costs. Compilation of broadcast advertising records is somewhat difficult because, unlike the print media, there are no actual copies or issues that can be read; the research firms must watch or listen to all the local stations, maintaining records of what items are promoted, how long each commercial lasts, and when each commercial is broadcast.

LNA/ARBITRON MULTI-MEDIA SERVICE

CLASSIFICATION TOTALS
January - March 1991

MAJOR	CLASS CODE	YEAR-TO-DATE MAJOR CLASS DOLLARS (000)							
		10-MEDIA TOTAL	MAGAZINES	SUNDAY MAGAZINES	NEWSPAPERS	OUTDOOR	NETWORK TELEVISION	SPOT TELEVISION	SYNDICATED TELEVISION
READY-TO-WEAR	A110	84.803.8	58.509.6	3.285.6	963.2	1.029.7	12.518.2	3.789.3	1.165.0
UNDERCLTHNG, SLEEPWEAR & LOUNGING APP	A120	13.577.4	2.884.0	368.3	13.8	62.9	6.614.8	1.238.0	1.964.9
FOOTWEAR	A130	78.303.5	20.936.2	752.3	783.9	406.6	32.022.1	9.421.5	7.344.5
ACCESSORIES, NOTIONS & MISC APPAREL	A140	4.888.0	2.981.1	736.3	- -		783.9	190.5	36.5
HATS	A150	180.0	140.6	- -		4.5			
HOSIERY	A160	12.877.0	4.262.9	115.0	- -	10.7	5.206.2	125.7	1.375.9
APPAREL FABRICS & FINISHES	A170	6.933.2	1.624.7	140.5	- -	11.1	3.846.5	216.1	
LUGGAGE & ACCESSORIES INCL BRIEFCASES	A180	506.4	489.9	- -		6.3		10.2	
ENGINEERING & PROFESSIONAL SERVICES	B110	194.402.7	8.399.4	976.1	140.465.9	1.433.8	1.764.7	26.118.3	4.058.0
CREDIT CARDS & TRAVELERS CHECKS	B120	73.408.1	8.436.2	213.9	1.060.6	0.5	22.450.6	27.934.8	1.203.7
SCHOOLS & CAMPS	B130	26.794.0	5.882.1	1.542.8	7.838.0	356.9	- -	8.250.8	202.9
COMMUNICATIONS & PUBLIC UTILITIES	B140	214.221.1	12.542.4	1.380.1	24.684.5	1.925.2	81.195.1	57.437.2	8.474.0
FINANCIAL	B150	194.600.7	22.393.6	1.259.6	95.037.0	6.135.0	17.535.3	40.622.1	363.0
GOVERNMENT ADVERTISING	B160	39.310.9	4.022.3	1.022.4	5.088.0	1.326.9	4.700.8	16.317.6	317.4
MISC CORPORATE ADVERT (NOT ELSE CLASS)	B170	36.931.0	11.354.1	299.7	1.365.2	65.2	13.420.5	6.851.4	829.4
ORGANIZATION ADVERT (NOT ELSE CLASS)	B180	24.371.0	5.883.3	558.0	9.577.0	1.049.8	1.455.6	2.813.8	49.0
MILITARY EQUIPMENT	B190	1.319.6	1.072.6	- -	114.3	1.5		21.8	
LIFE & MEDICAL INSURANCE	B210	70.620.3	14.028.3	944.5	8.522.4	556.5	24.394.3	15.058.2	2.113.0
PROPERTY CASUALTY & INSURANCE NEC	B220	53.335.1	11.034.2	326.5	3.284.7	534.1	22.178.5	6.677.6	491.0
REAL ESTATE, R.E. BROKERS & DEVELOPERS	B230	51.600.6	4.891.3	1.525.4	29.672.7	3.543.1	7.756.9	2.184.2	- -
COMPUTERS & DATA PROCESSING EQUIPMENT	B310	50.313.6	26.646.7	1.547.0	9.383.6	394.8	9.049.5	659.1	443.3
OFFICE MACHINES & EQUIPMENT	B320	30.060.1	11.067.0	- -	2.424.1	236.6	8.118.0	2.168.8	
STATIONERY & OFFICE SUPPLIES	B330	25.308.5	6.858.7	898.2	1.993.9	313.5	12.681.6	498.4	1.661.7
COMPUTER SOFTWARE	B340	8.125.0	5.693.4	- -	2.173.6			171.1	
BOOKS & MUSIC	B410	15.691.2	4.023.1	885.6	6.931.8	9.0	145.9	1.836.5	34.4
MAGAZINE, NEWSPPR, NEWSLTR & MISC MEDIA	B420	6.307.3	1.467.2	478.3	1.127.6	217.4		2.530.4	
RADIO STATIONS	B430	25.628.1	146.9	140.2	3.833.6	5.839.6		15.667.8	
TELEVISION & CABLE TELEVISION STATIONS	B440	113.231.7	41.465.8	1.151.5	35.362.9	2.862.0	5.487.2	11.682.6	2.082.8
MANUFACTURERS MATERIALS & SUPPLIES	B510	15.354.8	3.947.3	93.6	167.2	190.2	7.829.9	1.399.5	
INDUS MACH, INSTR, ELEC COMPON, FIX&ACC	B520	9.184.1	6.746.3	161.1	1.084.3	132.1	792.1	64.7	
FREIGHT	B610	34.996.5	3.591.5	7.8	1.064.0	- -	21.306.9	7.816.3	
INDUSTRIAL & AGRICULTURAL DEV (AREA)	B620	3.322.7	2.733.3	33.7	335.3	2.7		37.9	
BUSINESS PROPOSITIONS	B710	5.821.7	4.834.2	53.0	408.0	2.1	- -	404.6	
EMPLOYMENT RECRUITMENT	B720	3.025.7	1.411.5	1.5	- -	17.9	1.327.1	100.0	
COSMETICS & BEAUTY AIDS	D110	147.645.4	68.491.1	2.175.5	570.1	18.5	47.592.8	12.878.1	10.148.5
PERSONAL HYGIENE & HEALTH	D120	243.944.1	32.116.1	1.744.9	1.825.1	101.7	137.322.9	26.075.6	30.638.4
BATH TOILETRIES & MISC TOILET GOODS	D130	8.574.8	4.641.2	- -	64.6	- -	2.340.9	540.2	280.3
HAIR PRODUCTS	D140	112.727.4	28.084.7	336.7	30.1	336.5	50.839.0	14.425.5	12.339.7
PERSONAL CARE APPLIANCES	D150	1.222.2	986.8	- -				86.2	
MEDICINES & PROPRIETARY REMEDIES	D210	414.634.9	28.068.2	6.082.8	5.446.6	118.8	237.633.9	49.107.3	44.642.2
MEDICAL EQUIPMENT, APPLIANCES & SUPPLIES	D220	11.944.2	2.272.7	- -	135.4		5.523.4	1.323.1	1.442.9
PHYSICAL CULTURE	D240	70.477.5	4.644.2	1.501.0	16.357.8	2.427.6	6.330.3	35.019.9	457.7
COOKING PRODUCTS & SEASONINGS	F110	171.451.4	24.422.7	1.059.8	521.6	57.6	78.714.7	36.973.8	20.870.7
PREPARED & CONVENIENCE FOODS	F120	360.522.6	29.544.3	3.113.8	3.661.8	349.2	165.200.6	99.829.9	34.426.6
DAIRY PRODUCTS & SUBSTITUTES	F130	83.648.9	14.437.9	639.8	671.7	383.4	25.809.3	26.761.4	9.167.6
FRUITS, VEGETBLS, GRAINS & BEANS (ALL)	F140	69.439.6	14.402.4	319.5	169.5	154.2	25.633.0	18.611.2	1.905.9
MEATS, POULTRY & FISH	F150	52.432.0	7.992.0	183.3	2.185.6	116.1	13.956.6	18.471.2	3.006.8
BAKERY GOODS (FRESH, FROZ, REFRIG, ETC)	F160	87.838.3	4.864.3	54.0	63.9	128.6	37.773.1	22.471.8	16.988.5
FOOD BEVERAGES	F170	132.009.9	13.713.0	1.414.0	691.4	261.2	52.712.9	38.471.1	8.760.7
COMBINATION COPY FOOD & FOOD PROD & GP	F190	12.475.3	1.374.2	67.1	379.9	162.5	6.333.0	1.257.3	1.888.0
CONFECTIONERY & SNACKS	F210	173.296.1	7.427.5	113.5	77.8	319.3	62.459.6	37.976.0	40.998.4

FIGURE 5.4 An Example of Leading National Advertisers' (LNA) *Multi-Media Report* on Competitive Advertising Expenditures
Source: Leading National Advertisers/Arbitron. Reprinted by permission.

Other media, such as transit, outdoor, and direct mail, do not have regular syndicated sources, but much can be gleaned by simple observation or by utilizing primary research. This information, however, is not as reliable as that obtained by more sophisticated research methods, and the results are not projectable.

Competitive information is more complete for print media because actual copies of the publications can be surveyed, as noted earlier. The Publishers Information Bureau (PIB) of the Magazine Publishers Association and Leading National Advertisers (LNA) together publish a report on consumer magazine advertising expenditures that is known by the two sets of initials: *LNA/PIB*. Arranged by product or service category and then by brand names, this report shows, for each consumer publication, when advertisements were run, their size, whether color was used, and a cost estimate. A simplified source of competitive business publication advertising is compiled by the *Rome Reports*.

Newspaper advertising expenditures traditionally have been reported by a firm called Media Records, but the service has been taken over by the *LNA Newspaper Report*. Out of habit and tradition, however, this source is often referred to as *LNA/ Media Records*.

For television, advertising expenditure information is available from Broadcast Advertisers Reports, Inc., whose network television report is known by its initials, **BAR.** It provides the names of advertisers and products, the times when commercials were run and on which network they appeared, and an estimate of the cost of that advertising. In all such reports, advertising costs are estimated because the actual price paid is privileged information held by the advertiser and the media vehicle. Because of discounts, combinations, and special offers, outsiders can only estimate the costs of an advertising campaign.

A primary source for advertising expenditure information for spot television is again available from Broadcast Advertisers Reports, which calls its spot service *BARCUME. BARCUME* provides information similar to that for network, along with the various spot-broadcast markets that have been used. Two other services, Media Watch and Monitor-Plus, also monitor competitive spot-television expenditures.

Broadcast Advertisers Reports is also active in network radio with its *BAR Network Radio Service.* For spot radio, *Radio Expenditures Report (RER)* provides names of products or services, individual markets, and competitive expenditure estimates.

Outdoor advertising is reported by Leading National Advertisers, in its *LNA Outdoor Advertising Expenditure Report*. In comparison to other media, the outdoor information is rather simple in format, showing the markets, advertising schedule, and an expenditure estimate for each brand. For other media, such as transit and direct mail, there is little tracking of competitive advertising.

Media Audience Data

Media audience data provide audience information for specific vehicles within a media type. This kind of information is highly specialized, which means that more experience and skill is required to use it properly. It is also more expensive because the costs of conducting and disseminating the research cannot be spread across as many functions and organizations. Finally, smaller samples may provide data that are less reliable than those from larger-scale studies.

Media audience data are especially helpful to media buyers, who tend to need tactical media information to implement media plans. Although general types of media may have been determined in the media plan and perhaps the general time periods established, individual media vehicles, such as specific radio and television stations and newspapers, must now be selected. If specific markets or even program types have been called for, media buyers must negotiate for the most appropriate times, locations, competitive advertising protection, and prices.

In general, for broadcast media, media buyers refer to the established radio and television ratings services, which provide information on audience shares, projected audience numbers, and demographic categories of listening and viewing, in addition to the program ratings themselves. The best-known ratings services are offered by the **A. C. Nielsen Company** and Arbitron, Inc. The Nielsen ratings are more widely recognized for network television ratings, but Arbitron may be used more for local television and radio.

The print media have no media audience source comparable to the ratings services, although the Scarborough service refers to itself as a ratings service (discussed in more detail later in the chapter). As for local newspaper coverage, there is little problem in most markets because few cities have

A-16

| Nielsen | NATIONAL TV AUDIENCE ESTIMATES | | | | | | | | | | | | | | | | EVE. SUN. SEP. 24, 1989 |

TIME	7:00	7:15	7:30	7:45	8:00	8:15	8:30	8:45	9:00	9:15	9:30	9:45	10:00	10:15	10:30	10:45	11:00	11:15
HUT	53.3	55.2	56.8	58.2	60.1	61.9	63.3	64.6	66.7	67.7	67.4	66.6	63.8	62.5	60.5	57.7	51.1	44.3

ABC TV — ◄—LIFE GOES ON—► —► FREE SPIRIT HOMEROOM ◄—— ◄—— ABC SUNDAY NIGHT MOVIE ——► THE PREPPIE MURDER (PAE)

ABC TV																		
AVERAGE AUDIENCE	9,210				9,580		8,010		14,000									
(Hhlds (000) & %)	10.0	9.3 *		10.8 *	10.4		8.7		15.2	13.7 *		15.8 *		15.7 *		15.5 *		
SHARE AUDIENCE %	18	17 *		19 *	17		14		24	20 *		24 *		25 *		26 *		
AVG. AUD. BY 1/4 HR %	8.7	9.8	10.6	11.1	10.2	10.6	8.5	8.9	13.6	13.8	15.7	15.8	15.9	15.6	15.6	15.5		

CBS TV — ◄— 60 MINUTES —► ◄—MURDER, SHE WROTE—► ◄— ISLAND SON SPEC (PAE) — ◄— WOLF SPEC ►

CBS TV																		
AVERAGE AUDIENCE	17,040				19,060				14,640				11,700					
(Hhlds (000) & %)	18.5	16.9 *		20.0 *	20.7	20.2 *		21.2 *	15.9	15.5 *		16.2 *	12.7	13.1 *		12.3 *		
SHARE AUDIENCE %	33	31 *		35 *	33	33 *		33 *	24	23 *		24 *	21	21 *		21 *		
AVG. AUD. BY 1/4 HR %	15.7	18.0	20.1	20.0	20.0	20.5	21.4	21.0	15.4	15.7	16.5	16.0	13.2	12.9	12.5	12.1		

NBC TV — (1) | ALF TAKES NETWORK (7:25-8:00) (PAE) | SISTER KATE | MY TWO DADS | ◄—— SNL 15TH ANN. SPC ——►

NBC TV																		
AVERAGE AUDIENCE		5,990			8,200		10,870		18,700									
(Hhlds (000) & %)		6.5		6.4 *	8.9		11.8		20.8	19.3 *		21.1 *		22.1 *		21.1 *		17.7 *
SHARE AUDIENCE %		11		11 *	15		18		33	29 *		31 *		35 *		36 *		37 *
AVG. AUD. BY 1/4 HR %	13.6	6.9	6.1	6.7	8.6	9.3	10.9	12.8	18.5	20.0	20.6	21.6	22.4	21.8	21.4	20.9	19.8	15.6

INDEPENDENTS (INCL. SUPERSTATIONS)																		
AVERAGE AUDIENCE	11.5		12.6		14.2		14.8		15.7		11.4		9.6		7.7		6.0	
SHARE AUDIENCE %	21		22		23		23		23		17		15		13		13	

SUPERSTATIONS																		
AVERAGE AUDIENCE	2.3		2.3		1.9		2.2		2.5		2.8		2.4		1.9		1.7	
SHARE AUDIENCE %	4		4		3		3		4		4		4		3		3	

PBS																		
AVERAGE AUDIENCE	1.5		1.6		2.4		3.0		1.7		1.8		1.2		1.2		1.0	
SHARE AUDIENCE %	3		3		4		5		3		3		2		2		2	

CABLE ORIG.																		
AVERAGE AUDIENCE	6.8		8.6		7.2		6.5		5.6		5.4		4.9		4.4		3.8	
SHARE AUDIENCE %	12		15		12		10		8		8		8		8		8	

PAY SERVICES																		
AVERAGE AUDIENCE	2.7		2.5		3.7		4.1		4.1		3.5		3.5		3.1		2.5	
SHARE AUDIENCE %	5		4		6		6		6		5		5		5		5	

U.S. TV HOUSEHOLDS: 92,100,000

For explanation of symbols, see page B.

(1) NFL GAME 2, VARIOUS TEAMS AND TIMES, (PAE), NBC, (MULTI SEGMENT)

FIGURE 5.5 An example of the Nielsen Television Index Network Ratings
Courtesy of Nielsen Media Research.

competitive daily newspapers: If there is only a single newspaper in a market, media buyers have little choice. For consumer magazines, the Simmons Market Research Bureau's *Study of Markets and Media* provides an indication of media audience by publication title. Print media vehicles distribute their own research to advertisers and their agencies, and media buyers may rely on these primary sources to supplement the syndicated research data. Outdoor media purchase decisions are usually based on market coverage, rather than ratings.

We now look more closely at some of the specific media audience information available.

Network Television

For network television, the best-known source of audience data is the **Nielsen Television Index (NTI),** provided by the A. C. Nielsen Company (figure 5.5). The NTI *Pocketpiece* provides weekly network ratings in a manageable format. Nielsen also makes available daily network audience information, which it gathers from mechanical meters.

Long-term network audience data are provided by Simmons Market Research Bureau in the product and media volumes of its *Study of Markets and Media*. This information covers network viewing habits of audiences for an entire year. A similar source is available from Mediamark Research, Inc. (MRI).

Spot Television

Spot-television audience data for more than two hundred markets are provided by the Arbitron Ratings Company. Viewing for categories of audience members is given in terms of ratings, share of market, and projections of actual audience size for every commercial station within each market (figure 5.6). The local ratings surveys, commonly known as **sweeps,** are conducted four times annually in large markets, with only two or three surveys per year in the smaller markets. Similar information comes in a **Nielsen Station Index (NSI)** report.

Network Radio

Audience data for network radio are somewhat less specific than that for television because network radio is no longer as important a medium as is television. Rather than reporting on specific programs, these data cover only general patterns of network radio listening.

Specific network radio audience data are available from RADAR, which gives share of audience and ratings along with general estimates of costs. Summary information also is reported by Simmons Market Research Bureau in the media and product volumes of its *Study of Markets and Media*.

Spot Radio

Arbitron, Inc., provides information on audiences in local radio markets. The format is similar to that for spot television: ratings, shares, and market-by-market audience composition projections, by station. Because there are more radio markets than

television markets, and many times more radio stations than television stations, the spot-radio data do not cover every station in all markets.

The *Birch Radio Qualitative Report* provides information on spot-radio audiences for stations in more than sixty markets. Unique among this type of source, however, is that Birch also provides information on product usage in those markets, to allow an easier match between targets and media outlets.

Magazines

Modern media audience information started with magazines, so it is somewhat ironic that today magazines are able to obtain less syndicated information about their audiences than are other media. The media and product volumes from Simmons Market Research Bureau's *Study of Markets and Media,* along with data from Mediamark Research, Inc. (MRI), supply detailed information that matches brand usage with media habits, for magazines as for most other advertising media (figure 5.7). This media and purchase habit matchup is extremely useful to media planners and buyers. For upscale audiences, Mendelsohn Media Research, Inc., publishes similar data in its *Survey of Adults and Markets of Affluence (SAMA)*.

Newspapers

A standard source for newspaper audience information is the *Scarborough Newspaper Audience Ratings Study*. It concentrates on the largest U.S. markets, so there is little information on the many smaller cities. Even though this company refers to itself as a newspaper "ratings" service, the data differ substantially from the usual formats of the broadcast ratings data. Information about the coverage of certain audience segments by the publications in various markets, as well as a breakdown of vehicle audiences, are provided, but brand and product data are not included.

Time Period Estimates

DAY AND TIME STATION PROGRAM	ADI TV HH RATINGS BY WEEKS				ADI TV HH		ADI TV HH SHARE/HUT TRENDS				METRO TV HH		ADI RATINGS																						
													PERSONS										WOMEN							MEN					
	1 OCT 31	2 NOV 07	3 NOV 14	4 NOV 21	RTG	SHR	JUL 90	MAY 90	FEB 90	NOV 89	RTG	SHR	2+	18+	12-24	12-34	18-34	18-49	21-49	25-54	35+	35-64	50+	18+	12-24	18-34	21-49	25-49	25-54	W	18+	18-34	18-49	21-49	25-49	25-54
	1	2	3	4	5	6	59	60	61	62	8	9	11	12	13	14	15	16	17	18	19	20	21	22	23	24	25	26	27	28	29	30	31	32	33	34	35

Relative Std-Err Thresholds (1σ): 25% — 11 12 12 12 / 3 / 5 / 3 2 11 5 7 3 3 3 2 3 4 / 3 21 11 6 6 7 6 9 / 4 12 6 6 7 6
50% — 3 3 3 3 / – / 1 / – – 3 1 1 – – – – – 1 / – 6 3 1 1 1 1 2 / 1 3 1 1 1 1

FIGURE 5.6 An Example of Arbitron Spot Television Ratings

Source: Copyright 1991. The Arbitron Company. Reprinted by permission.

Notes:
* SAMPLE BELOW MINIMUM FOR WEEKLY REPORTING
** SHARE/HUT TRENDS NOT AVAILABLE
– DID NOT ACHIEVE A REPORTABLE WEEKLY RATING
‡ TECHNICAL DIFFICULTY
♦ COMBINED PARENT/SATELLITE
▲ SEE TABLE ON PAGE v

CHATTANOOGA   91   SUNDAY   NOVEMBER 1990 TIME PERIOD AVERAGES

Time Period Estimates

STATION BREAK AVERAGES

DAY AND TIME / STATION PROGRAM	ADI RTG TN 12-17	CH 2-11	CH 6-11	TSA: TV HH	PERS 18+	PERS 12-34	WOM 18+	WOM 18-34	WOM 18-49	WOM 25-49	WOM 25-54	WKG WOM	MEN 18+	MEN 18-34	MEN 18-49	MEN 25-49	MEN 25-54	TNS 12-17	CH 2-11	CH 6-11	TIME ADI TV HH RTG	MET TV HH RTG	TSA TV HH	WOM 18+	MEN 18+
(col ref)	36	37	38	39	42	41	45	46	47	48	49	50	51	52	53	54	55	56	57	58	5	8	39	45	51
RELATIVE STD-ERR 25%	20	18	22	14	20	22	16	18	17	16	15	15	16	19	17	16	16	19	35	27	3	5	14	16	16
THRESHOLDS (1σ) 50%	6	5	6	3	5	5	4	4	4	4	4	4	4	5	4	4	4	5	9	7	-	1	3	4	4
SUNDAY																									
MDNGHT-12:15A																									
WRCB WHEEL OF FOR			1	7	8	4	5	2	2	1	2		3	2	2	1	1		1	1	3	2	9	7	4
WTVC LIFESTYLES			2	4	3	2	2	1	2	2	2	1	1	1	1	1	1								
BIG ORNGE SU				6	6		5		3	3	3	3	1		1	1	1								
--4 WK AVG--			4	5	5	1	3	3	3	3	3	2	1		1	1	1				2	2	7	7	2
WDEF ENTRTN TN 60			1	1	1	1	1	1	1										1	1					
NWCTR12 SU L				2	5		2						3												
--4 WK AVG--			1	1	2	1	1	1	1	1	1	1	1		1	1	1				1	1	4	4	3
WFLI SOUL TRAIN																									
WTCI PTV																									
HUT/PVT/TOT		1	1	12	15	6	9	4	6	5	6	3	5	2	4	3	3		1	1	10	8	20	18	9
12:15A-12:30A																									
WRCB WHEEL OF FOR			1	5	6	2	4	2	2	1	2		2	1	1	1	1		1	1	2	2	6	4	3
WTVC LIFESTYLES			2	2	3	2	2	1	2	2	2	1	1	1	1	1	1								
BIG ORNGE SU				3	3		3		1	1	1	2													
--4 WK AVG--			3	3	3	1	2	1	1	1	1	1	1		1	1	1				1	1	4	3	1
WDEF ENTRTN TN 60			1	1	2	1	1	1	1	1	1	1	1		1	1	1					1	1	1	1
WFLI SOUL TRAIN																									
WTCI PTV																									
HUT/PVT/TOT		1	1	9	11	4	7	4	4	3	4	2	4	1	3	3	3		1	1	6	5	11	8	5
12:30A-12:45A																									
WRCB MAGNUM PI-S				6	9	5	6						3												
QUANTUM MRKT				2	1	1	1	1	1				1												
KENT MRKTING				5	4		4																		
--4 WK AVG--			1	4	4	2	3	1	1		1	2	1	1	1	1	1		1	1	1	1	4	4	1
WTVC BIG ORNGE SU				3	2	2	2						3												
RNWY RCH FMS				4	7	4	4						3												
LIFESTYLES				2	2		2					2													
--4 WK AVG--				3	3	1	2	1	2	2	2	1	1		1						1	1	3	2	1
WDEF CBS SUN NEWS				1																					
ENTRTN TN 60				1	3		1	1	1	1	1		2		2	2	2								
--4 WK AVG--				1	1		1	1	1	1	1		1		1	1	1						1	1	1
WFLI SOUL TRAIN																									
WTCI PTV																									
HUT/PVT/TOT			1	8	8	3	6	2	4	4	5	2	3	1	3	2	2		1	1	5	4	8	7	3
12:45A-1:00A																									
WRCB MAGNUM PI-S				3	5	5	2						3												
QUANTUM MRKT				2	2	1	1	1	1				1												
KENT MRKTING																									
--4 WK AVG--			1	2	2	2	1		1	1	1	1	1	1	1	1	1		1	1	1	1	3	2	1
WTVC BIG ORNGE SU				3	2	2	2						3												
RNWY RCH FMS				2	3	1	1																		
LIFESTYLES				2	2		2					2	1		1										
--4 WK AVG--				2	2	1	1	1	1	1	1	1	1		1						1	1	2	2	1
WDEF PRO ED INST				1																					
ENTRTN TN 60				1	4		2		1	1	1	1	2		2	2	2								
--4 WK AVG--				1	2		1		1	1	1	1	1		1	1	1						1	1	1
WFLI SOUL TRAIN																									
WTCI PTV																									
HUT/PVT/TOT			1	5	6	3	3	2	3	3	3	2	3	1	3	2	2		1	1	4	3	6	5	3
1:00A-1:15A																									
WRCB MAGNUM PI-S		2	3	3	5	5	2	2	2	2	2		3	3	3	3	3		2	2	1	1	2	1	2
WTVC BIG ORNGE SU				2	3	1	2						3												
ABC WKND NWS																									
LIFESTYLES				2	2		2					2													
--4 WK AVG--				1	2		1					1	1		1						1		2	1	1
WDEF PRO ED INST																									
CBS SUN NEWS																									
ENTRTN TN 60				2	7		4						3		1	1	1								
--4 WK AVG--					2		1		1	1	1	1	1		1	1	1						1	1	1
WFLI STHRN SPRTSM																									
WTCI PTV																									
HUT/PVT/TOT			1	4	9	5	4	2	3	3	3	2	5	3	5	4	4		2	2	3	3	5	3	4
1:15A-1:30A																									
WRCB MAGNUM PI-S		2	3	3	5	5	2	2	2	2	2		3	3	3	3	3		2	2	1	2	3	2	3
WTVC BIG ORNGE SU				2	2		2					2													
LIFESTYLES				1	1		1					1													
--3 WK AVG--																							1	1	
WDEF CASH ASKING																									
GOOD LIFE																									
CBS SUN NEWS				2	7		4						3												
STAIN A RATR																									
--4 WK AVG--					2		1		1	1	1	1	1		1	1	1						1		1
WFLI STHRN SPRTSM																									
WTCI PTV																									
HUT/PVT/TOT			1	4	8	5	4	2	3	3	3	2	4	3	4	4	4		2	2	3	2	4	4	4
1:30A-1:45A																									
WTVC ABC WKND NWS				1	1		1					1											1	1	
WDEF CASH ASKING																									
GOOD LIFE																									
PRO ED INST				2	7		4						3												
STAIN A RATR																									
--4 WK AVG--					2		1		1	1	1	1	1		1	1	1							1	1
WFLI QUANTUM																									
WTCI PTV																									
HUT/PVT/TOT			1	1	3		2		1	1	1	2	1		1	1	1				2	2	1	2	1
(col ref)	36	37	38	39	42	41	45	46	47	48	49	50	51	52	53	54	55	56	57	58	5	8	39	45	51

Daily

FIGURE 5.6 Continued

	TOTAL U.S. '000	ADULTS A '000	B % DOWN	C % ACROSS	D INDX	MALES A '000	B % DOWN	C % ACROSS	D INDX	FEMALES A '000	B % DOWN	C % ACROSS	D INDX	FEMALE HOMEMAKERS A '000	B % DOWN	C % ACROSS	D INDX
TOTAL	178193	178193	100.0	100.0	100	85056	100.0	47.7	100	93136	100.0	52.3	100	85531	100.0	48.0	100
SPORTS ILLUSTRATED	20432	20432	11.5	100.0	100	16345	19.2	80.0	168	4087	4.4	20.0	38	3541	4.1	17.3	36
STAR	10958	10958	6.1	100.0	100	3083	3.6	28.1	59	7875	8.5	71.9	137	6944	8.1	63.4	132
SUNDAY MAGAZINE NETWORK	40439	40439	22.7	100.0	100	19887	23.4	49.2	103	20553	22.1	50.8	97	19007	22.2	47.0	98
SUNSET	3438	3438	1.9	100.0	100	1040	1.2	30.3	63	2397	2.6	69.7	133	2358	2.8	68.6	143
TV GUIDE	40204	40204	22.6	100.0	100	17393	20.4	43.3	91	22811	24.5	56.7	109	20641	24.1	51.3	107
TENNIS	1334	1334	0.7	100.0	100	795	0.9	59.6	125	539	0.6	40.4	77	460	0.5	34.5	72
TIME	24570	24570	13.8	100.0	100	13660	16.1	55.6	116	10910	11.7	44.4	85	9903	11.6	40.3	84
TRAVEL & LEISURE	2162	2162	1.2	100.0	100	1048	1.2	48.5	102	1114	1.2	51.5	99	1047	1.2	48.4	101
TRUE STORY	3712	3712	2.1	100.0	100	354	0.4	9.5	20	3359	3.6	90.5	173	2937	3.4	79.1	165
USA TODAY	6326	6326	3.6	100.0	100	4231	5.0	66.9	140	2095	2.2	33.1	63	1981	2.3	31.3	65
USA WEEKEND	29461	29461	16.5	100.0	100	14187	16.7	48.2	101	15274	16.4	51.8	99	14127	16.5	48.0	100
U.S. NEWS & WORLD REPORT	12099	12099	6.8	100.0	100	7477	8.8	61.8	129	4621	5.0	38.2	73	4301	5.0	35.5	74
US	4625	4625	2.6	100.0	100	1587	1.9	34.3	72	3039	3.3	65.7	126	2709	3.2	58.6	122
VANITY FAIR	1487	1487	0.8	100.0	100	*262	0.3	17.6	37	1224	1.3	82.3	157	1028	1.2	69.1	144
VOGUE	5441	5441	3.1	100.0	100	537	0.6	9.9	21	4905	5.3	90.1	172	3943	4.6	72.5	151

FIGURE 5.7 An Example of Simmons Market Research Bureau's *Study of Markets and Media*
Source: Simmons Study of Media & Markets. Reprinted by permission.

Media Cost Data

A media buyer must negotiate prices for the advertisement insertions desired. This bargaining process takes place directly with the individual media vehicle or its representative firm, but the starting point is to determine the general range of prices. For most media, the advertising rates are indicated in *Standard Rate & Data Service (SRDS),* which also contains some general audience information in some cases (figure 5.8). The rates in *SRDS* are provided by the media vehicles and are generally the highest applicable advertising rates; negotiation may bring savings through discounts, combinations, or special arrangements. *SRDS* covers most media advertising rates, except that network broadcast rates must usually be obtained directly from networks' sales representatives, and outdoor advertising rates are found in *The Buyer's Guide to Outdoor Advertising.* Transit advertising rates are usually available from the respective transit systems, and some regions or states with extensive transit networks may have a central office that supplies advertising rate information.

Media buyers use estimating guides to judge how much media and vehicle coverage can be expected from a certain "buy," what is a reasonable price for a certain media purchase, and how many markets or vehicles can be included as the budget is being committed to actual media purchases. This type of estimating information is found in media buying guides, such as *Adweek*'s *Marketer's Guide to Media* (figure 5.9.). Here there is a summary of general advertising rates, to provide a quick estimate of the coverage and costs of many media and some vehicles. These estimating guides are used by advertising media planners to gauge the general cost of the media plan or to fit the plan to the available budget. Estimating guides are also used by media buyers in the tactical stage of the advertising media process.

A good way to understand how all these kinds of media information sources can be used is to look over the actual examples in an advertising media workbook.[2] Such workbooks also contain explanations of how to understand the source data, examples of how to apply the information to real media problems, outlines of how the information is collected, and references on how to contact the services themselves.

122 Radio, TV & Video

TWICE—cont

3	—Mfrs' reps.
4	—Others Allied to the Field
TL	—Total.

TL. Total. A. Management. B. Buying. C. Merchandising.
D. Sales. E. Other titled & non-titled pers.

	TL	A	B	C	D	E
1—	37,757	31,863	1,395	614	2,142	1,743
1-1—	18,672	16,397	331	126	680	1,138
1-2—	6,533	5,878	144	48	364	99
1-3—	418	358	36	5	11	8
1-4—	291	237	26	2	22	4
1-6—	727	621	20	5	55	26
1-7—	227	196	16	4	6	5
1-8—	3,756	2,785	372	214	226	168
1-9—	2,800	1,788	250	133	524	105
1-10—	588	443	72	28	27	18
1-11—	2,127	1,725	101	38	144	119
2—	2,050	—	—	—	—	—
3—	1,542	—	—	—	—	—
4—	1,216	—	—	—	—	—
TL—	42,565	31,863	1,395	614	2,142	1,743

TWICE•TODAY

The Show Daily of CES

Location ID: 7 BLST 122   Mid 052188-000
Published twice a year/daily during the show by Cahners
Publishing Corp., 245 W. 17th St., 11th Fl, New York,
NY 10011. Phone 212-337-6994. FAX: 212-337-7066.

PUBLISHER'S EDITORIAL PROFILE
TWICE TODAY is edited for people attending the Consumer Electronics Show. The publication covers news
from the exhibit floor, new products introductions and
trends. Rec'd 5/23/91.

1. PERSONNEL
Pub—Marcia Grand.
Adv Mgr—Sherri Regnault.

2. REPRESENTATIVES and/or BRANCH OFFICES
Los Angeles, CA 90064—Nick West, 12233 West Olympic
Blvd., Suite 236. Phone 213-826-5818. FAX: 213-207-
1067.

3. COMMISSION AND CASH DISCOUNT
15% to agencies if bill paid within 30 days; net 30 days.

ADVERTISING RATES
Effective January 01, 1991. (Issue)
Rates received October 01, 1990.

5. BLACK/WHITE RATES
Tabloid:

	1 ti	3 ti		1 ti	3 ti
1 page	2895.	2450.	1/4 page	1400.	1300.
1/2 page	2000.	1850.	1/8 page	850.	810.
1/3 page	1650.	1500.			

Junior:

	1 ti	3 ti		1 ti	3 ti
1 page	2500.	2000.	1/2 page	1800.	1575.
2/3 page	2150.	1875.	1/3 page	1300.	1100.

Show Special:
Buy 3 tabloid pages for 7500.00 earn 1 page.
Buy 3 junior pages for 6000.00, earn 1 page.
3 time advertisers earn 4 pages for the cost of 3.

6. COLOR RATES

2 Color, per spread	800.
Matched color, per spread	1000.
Per page	525.
4 color, per spread	1600.
Per page	900.
2-color per page	450.

7. COVERS
2nd cover, extra ___ 20%   4th cover, extra ___ 40%
3rd cover, extra ___ 15%

8. BLEED
Extra ___ 10%

10. SPECIAL POSITION
Extra ___ 10%

15. GENERAL REQUIREMENTS
Also see SRDS Print Media Production Data.
Printing Process: Offset Full Run
Trim Size: 11 x 14-1/2.
Binding Method: Saddle Stitched.

TABLOID AD PAGE DIMENSIONS
Sprd 2-3/8 x 13-1/2   1/2 h 4-3/4 x 13-1/2
1 pg 9-3/4 x 13-1/2   1/4 h 2-1/4 x 13-1/2

JR AD PAGE DIMENSIONS

Sprd	15 x	10	1/3 sq	7 x	7
2/3 h	4-3/4 x	10	1/4 h	9-3/4 x	3
1/2 h	9-3/4 x	6-5/8	1/8 h	2-1/4 x	4-1/2
1/3 v	4-3/4 x	5-5/8			

16. ISSUE AND CLOSING DATES
Published twice a year.

Issue:	Closing (*)	Issue:	Closing (*)
Jan	12/1 12/15	Jun	5/1 5/15

(*) Material

18. CIRCULATION
SWORN June 1991 Convention
Non-Paid Controlled Circulation (daily average) ___ 25,000
Publisher states: Effective with June 1992 issue,
guaranteed non-paid circulation average of 25,000.

A Cahners Publishing Co. Publication

475 Park Avenue South, New York, NY 10016. Phone
212-779-1100. FAX: 212-779-2706.
See listing under classification No. 95.

Via Satellite

▽ BPA

Location ID: 7 BLST 122   Mid 039782-000
Published monthly by Phillips Publishing, Inc., 7811
Montrose Rd., Potomac, MD 20854. Phone 301-340-
2100. FAX: 301-340-0542.

PUBLISHER'S EDITORIAL PROFILE
VIA SATELLITE covers video, voice and data. Via Satellite showcases hands-on feature articles, company
profiles and market analysis on trends, opportunities and
challenges throughout the industry. VSAT marketplace
coverage includes video news releases, TV and radio
broadcasting, corporate networks, launch services, data
transmission, teleports, mobile satellite, transmission
services, international issues and more. Rec'd 1/17/89.

1. PERSONNEL
Pub—David J. Durham.
Editor—Scott Chase.
Sales Mgr—Angela M. Cook.

3. COMMISSION AND CASH DISCOUNT
15% of gross charges including space, color, premiums
and inserts if paid within 30 days of invoice date. Net 30
days.

4. GENERAL RATE POLICY
Cancellations not accepted after closing date.

ADVERTISING RATES
Effective January 01, 1991. (Card 3)
Rates received October 22, 1990.

5. BLACK/WHITE RATES

	1 ti	3 ti	6 ti	12 ti	15 ti
1 page	2995.	2505.	2095.	1795.	1595.
2/3 page	2275.	1890.	1585.	1450.	1275.
1/2 pg isl	1995.	1675.	1385.	1280.	1195.
1/2 page	1925.	1615.	1365.	1190.	1020.
1/3 page	1460.	1140.	1035.	925.	790.
1/4 page	1150.	975.	820.	680.	595.

5a. COMBINATION RATES
Combination rates with other Phillips Publishing, Inc. publications are available to Via Satellite magazine advertisers.

6. COLOR RATES

	1 ti	3 ti	6 ti	12 ti	15 ti
2 Color:					
1 page	3220.	2730.	2320.	2020.	1820.
2/3 page	2500.	2115.	1810.	1675.	1500.
1/2 pg isl	2220.	1900.	1610.	1505.	1420.
1/2 page	2150.	1840.	1590.	1415.	1245.
1/3 page	1685.	1365.	1260.	1150.	1015.
1/4 page	1375.	1200.	1045.	905.	820.

	1 ti	3 ti	6 ti	12 ti	15 ti
4 Color:					
1 page	3620.	3130.	2720.	2420.	2220.
2/3 page	2500.	2515.	2210.	2075.	1900.
1/2 pg isl	2220.	2010.	1905.	1820.	
1/2 page	2150.	2240.	1990.	1815.	1645.
1/3 page	2085.	1765.	1660.	1550.	1415.
1/4 page	1775.	1600.	1445.	1305.	1220.

	Extra
Standard printers color, per page	225.
2-page spread, per color	325.
Special/matched color, per color	325.
Metallic color, per page	500.
4-color, per page	625.
4 color spread	950.

7. COVERS
4-Color:

	3 ti	6 ti	12 ti
2nd cover	3600.	3130.	2785.
3rd cover	3285.	2855.	2540.
4th cover	3600.	3130.	2785.

8. INSERTS

	3 ti	6 ti	12 ti	15 ti
2-pages (1 sheet front and back)	4260.	3562.	3052.	2712.
4 pages	7515.	6285.	5385.	4785.

Rates for more than 4 pages available.
Binding charge (non-commissionable) per insertion . 350.
Business-reply card inserts (must be accompanied by full
page ad in book) cost is 50% of earned page rate.

9. BLEED
No charge.

10. SPECIAL POSITION
Extra ___ 10%

11. CLASSIFIED/MAIL ORDER
See Business Publication Rates & Data Classified
section.

15. GENERAL REQUIREMENTS
Also see SRDS Print Media Production Data.
Trim Size: 8-3/8 x 10-7/8; No./Cols. 2.
Binding Method: Saddle Stitched.
Colors Available: Black and white only; Black and
one color; 4-color process; Matched; GAA/SWOP;
5th cylinder.

AD PAGE DIMENSIONS

Sprd	14-1/2 x 9-3/4	1/2 h	7-1/4 x 4-3/4
1 pg	7-1/4 x 9-3/4	1/3 v	2-1/4 x 9-3/4
2/3 v	4-3/4 x 9-3/4	1/3 sq	4-3/4 x 4-3/4
1/2 isl	4-3/4 x 7-1/4	1/4 v	3-1/2 x 4-3/4
1/2 v	3-1/2 x 9-3/4		

16. ISSUE AND CLOSING DATES
Published monthly.

Issue:	Closing (+) (*)	Issue:	Closing (+) (*)
Jan/91	11/20 11/26	Jul	5/15 5/17
Feb	12/21 12/26	Aug	6/14 6/18
Mar	1/18 1/21	Sep	7/15 7/18
Apr	2/14 2/19	Oct	8/15 8/19
May	3/14 3/18	Nov	9/13 9/18
Jun	4/15 4/18	Dec	10/15 10/18

(+) Space
(*) Material

18. CIRCULATION
Established 1985.
Summary data—for detail see Publisher's Statement.
B.P.A. 6-30-91 (6 mos. aver. qualified)

	Total.	Non-Pd	Paid
	14,676	12,914	1,762

Average Non-Qualified (not incl. above):
Total 5,238

NETWORK TV
ANNUAL NETWORK TV AVERAGE COST DATA

	Average Rating		Cost/:30(000)		:30 CPM/HH***	
	Low	High	Low	High	Low	High
Daytime						
Early Morning (7:00–9:00 A.M.)	1.3	4.4	$2.2	$19.0	$1.69	$4.32
Weekday (10:00 A.M.–4:30 P.M.)	2.2	8.1	4.6	30.0	2.30	4.02
Weekend—Children	1.3	6.7	3.0	23.4	2.51	3.79
Sports						
Low						
(Multi-Sports Series and Low-Draw Sports)	3.0	8.0	15.0	55.0	5.43	7.46
Middle						
Football—Regular Season	5.0	18.0	25.0	225.0	5.43	13.57
Basketball—Regular Season	3.0	6.0	18.0	42.0	6.52	7.60
High						
(Bowl Games and Championship Events)	—20.0*—		—270.0*—		—14.65*—	
Prime Time	6.9	26.4	45.4	307.6	7.15	12.65
News	1.5	11.5	5.5	65.0	4.00	6.14
Late Night**	1.0	3.5	1.8	40.0	1.95	12.41
Syndication						
Prime Access	2.5	12.5	9.2	86.3	4.00	7.50
Fringe	1.5	4.5	2.7	20.4	1.96	4.92

*Average of top events, for example, Rose Bowl, World Series, etc.
**Does not include overnight news programs.
***CPMs reflect average daytime schedule.

FIGURE 5.9 An Example of Information from an Advertising Media Buying Guide
Source: "Reprinted with Permission of Adweek's *Marketer's Guide to Media*."

Summary

Secondary research is widely used in advertising media work because it is usually less expensive, faster, and more accurate than primary research. Whenever possible, media planners should first consult internal sources for information that might be suitable for answering questions and solving problems in advertising media. Most useful data, however, are found in external sources and are syndicated research.

Syndication means that research is sold to subscribers, who pay for the right to use the research findings and apply them to their own marketing and advertising problems. For general marketing and advertising information, sources most often supply research information on sales, product and brand usage (the competition), and consumers. More specific information on competitive media, media audience, and media cost is provided by strategic information sources and tactical information sources. For the novice, learning to use the syndicated media information sources can be a problem, but advertising media workbooks can be of great help.

Questions for Discussion

1. How could secondary research ever be preferable to primary research?

2. What are the problems inherent with using internal sources of information?

3. Is research worthwhile if it does not provide precise information?

4. Why do marketers and advertisers use syndicated research that is also available to competitors?

5. How can syndicated research be customized for use by an individual advertiser?

6. What are some of the problems associated with competitive research data?

7. Why do we need to know the research methods used by syndicated research firms? Is it not enough to have the results?

8. What are the benefits of using consistent categories of consumer groups?

9. What are the differences between strategic information and tactical information in advertising media research data?

10. Why are the most useful research data likely to be supplied by external sources, rather than by internal sources?

Endnotes

1. For additional insight into these sources and how to use them, consult Arnold M. Barban, Donald W. Jugenheimer, and Peter B. Turk, *Advertising Media Sourcebook,* 3d ed. (Lincolnwood, Ill.: NTC Business Books/National Textbook Company, 1989).

2. An example of an advertising media workbook is: Barban, Jugenheimer, and Turk, *Advertising Media Sourcebook.*

Suggested Readings

- *Adweek's Marketer's Guide to Media.* New York: A/S/M Communications, quarterly issues.
- Barban, Arnold M., Donald W. Jugenheimer, and Peter B. Turk. *Advertising Media Sourcebook.* 3d ed. Lincolnwood, Ill.: NTC Business Books/National Textbook Company, 1989.
- Kaatz, Ron. *Advertising & Marketing Checklists.* Lincolnwood, Ill.: NTC Business Books/National Textbook Company, 1989.

Chapter 6

The Role of Uncontrollable Factors

Outline

Learning Objectives

In the study of this chapter, you will have the opportunity to:

- Assess how advertising is affected by a variety of natural environmental factors that are outside the realm of anticipated occurrences.

- Understand the complications that the media environment itself may introduce to an advertising media plan.

- See what can be done to reduce media clutter.

- Learn how competitors can affect an advertiser's media plan.

- Explore the economic, cultural, and legal and political factors that may force large-scale changes in even carefully planned media programs.

- Examine the role of management in creating problems for media planners.

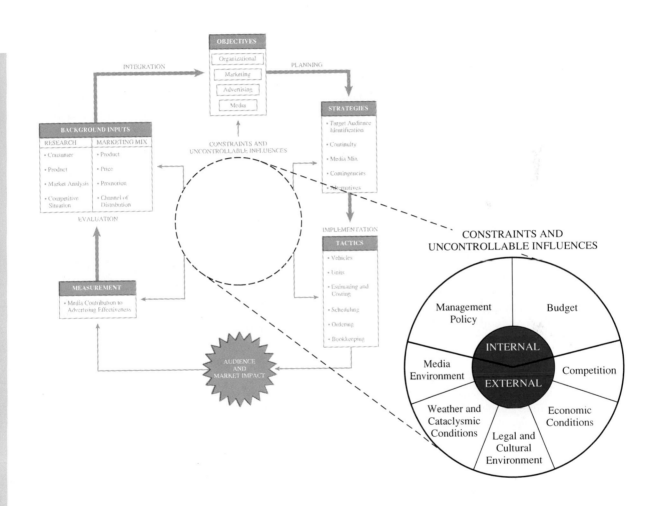

*A*fter all the careful budgeting, planning, and buying of media time and space, the advertising media plan still may not run as intended. All sorts of things can go wrong. Some of these problems are only inconveniences, but others can throw the plans out of alignment and force large-scale changes in even the most carefully planned media programs.

Some of these problems may involve outside forces, such as the weather, unforeseen disasters, and legal, political, and cultural shifts. Some may be the result of internal organizational functions, including management decisions, the media environment, and the possibility of simply making mistakes. Still others may involve external forces, such as competitive shifts and economic changes, that may sometimes be influenced by internal measures and policies. The diagram of the media-planning process at the beginning of this chapter clarifies how these internal and external factors influence media planning.

Natural Environment

The most obvious uncontrollable variables in the media decision-making process are natural occurrences, such as weather and unforeseen disasters. Weather can produce both favorable and unfavorable advertising conditions. For example, weather certainly must be taken into consideration in the promotion of a retail store's winter holiday sale: A blizzard may prevent customers from going to the store, forcing the sales event to be postponed or canceled. Weather can also create opportunities for advertising, which may result in previously planned media efforts being redirected. For example, a period of hot weather may make it easier to promote and sell air conditioners and cold drinks. Cold weather might create obvious sales opportunities for automobile antifreeze and snow tires, overcoats, weather stripping, fireplace logs, furnaces and their fuel, snowblowers, ski equipment, and Caribbean vacations, just to name a few. Heavy rains may bring sales of sump pumps and drainage tiles, while light rain can help retailers by making such items as umbrellas, raincoats, lawn seed, and windshield wipers easier to advertise and market.

Even weather in remote areas can affect an advertising media plan. Several years ago, a summer drought in the Midwest reduced the size of the corn crop; as a result, Quaker Oats had to cut back the advertising efforts for its Instant Grits product because there was not enough corn to make the grits and because the corn shortage raised the price level such that demand for grits was reduced.

Disasters

Unforeseen disasters also can affect advertising media usage. If a Caribbean hurricane struck St. Croix, damaging hotels and tourist resort facilities, the island's tourism advertising schedule would have to be changed. An explosion at a chemical plant in India might result in the plant's U.S. owner deciding to reduce corporate image advertising until the bad news was not so fresh in people's minds.

The uncontrollable environment of the airline industry certainly affects airlines' advertising operations. Airlines often include a cancellation clause in their advertising contracts that permits advertising to be withdrawn on short notice in the case of a major airplane crash. Most airlines cut back on their advertising after an air disaster, even if some other airline is involved. The bad publicity hurts all airlines and makes some customers wary of air transportation for a period of time following the accident. Airline advertising during this time period could simply heighten those people's concerns.

Other advertisers may experience similar uncontrollable influences. External events may cause preemption of broadcast schedules. For example, a major news event may be of such public interest and concern that programming is canceled. Nobody is really at fault here, but the advertising schedules change dramatically, and media planners and buyers may be forced to make adjustments on very short notice.

Media Environment

While the weather or an unforeseen disaster is beyond anyone's control, marketers may be able sometimes to influence the media environment. Some media content is uncontrollable, however, so advertising media planners must deal with it as they would with other uncontrollable variables. (The media and message environments are also discussed elsewhere, for other contexts and situations.)

Program Content

Program content can sometimes influence the advertising media plan as, for example, when a television program focuses on or includes some topic that audience members find offensive. The offended viewers often complain to the advertiser whose commercial announcements appear on that program. To avoid this kind of difficulty, many network advertisers try to prescreen the programs on which they have commercials scheduled; some advertisers even hire screening services that preview all the programs and then alert their advertiser customers to possible problems. In one case, a cosmetics marketer canceled its planned commercial insertion for red lipstick on a dramatic program that featured a particularly gory murder, with red blood gushing from the female victim's mouth immediately before the commercial break.

Some advertisers formulate a planned policy to avoid advertising on programming that includes extreme violence, suggestive materials, or controversial topics, for fear of upsetting audience members who might blame the advertisers for the situation. In the past, certain advertisers have made it known to programmers and networks that they will not authorize any commercial time if the programming discusses or shows certain topics. Such a warning can be effective, but it raises questions about advertising influence over media content.

Media content can also be influenced by advertisers by more direct but perhaps less intrusive ways. A peanut-butter manufacturer requested a change in program dialogue, from a child asking his mother for a bologna sandwich to the child requesting a peanut-butter sandwich. As a result, the child asked only for "a sandwich," which avoided mentioning a competing product category while not interfering with the program content.

Media Clutter

A media problem actually created by advertising is media **clutter.** Broadcasting is especially vulnerable to clutter because the commercial announcements may be lined up one after another, sometimes resulting in more than a dozen commercials in a row. The result can be that an individual advertiser's message, surrounded by so many competing messages, gets lost in the shuffle. The standard commercial length has been shortened from a full minute to thirty seconds, with some announcements lasting only fifteen, ten, or even five seconds—the result being that more commercials are packed into a single commercial break. Ironically, advertisers themselves are responsible for exacerbating this situation: To combat the problem of competing advertisements, they often respond by scheduling even more commercials.

This situation does not arise only because direct competitors advertise more and more often. When many advertisers increase their levels of advertising, the resulting clutter affects all advertisers, whether directly competitive in the same industry or not. In a sense, all advertisers are competing with one another because they all want to utilize the same media time and space.

Fighting clutter with still more clutter, however, is perhaps not the best way to solve this dilemma; other options are available. Research shows that longer television commercials attract more attention and score higher on audience recall than short commercials, so a longer commercial may stand out from the competition, although it is a very expensive solution. Switching to another medium, away from clutter, can help if the right audience combinations are available with a different media mix. Avoiding head-on competition may be an oversimplified solution, however, because matching advertising to the target audience remains a critical factor. If desirable advertising time or space allotments are available, staying in the same medium but running the advertising at a different time can also help, again if the proper audience can be reached. Clutter in broadcast media is most prevalent during **station breaks** on the hour and half-hour, so scheduling program announcements within the body of a program can help, although, again, it is often more expensive. Such a tactic may also require avoiding local spot advertising, which may force the choice toward expensive network time and may eliminate the use of local independent broadcast stations. If avoiding the competition results in greatly increased costs, the strategy may be self-defeating.

Media are more willing to cooperate with large, regular advertisers. A large advertiser with lots of advertising monies to spend may be able to influence broadcasters to schedule a commercial at a favorable time. Scheduling regular advertising to run in a certain mass-media vehicle may also win favors from the media.

New Media

One solution to media clutter may be the use of new media. Original advertising approaches are constantly being developed and tested for advertisers who are willing to try unconventional avenues.

Cable television is a relatively new medium that advertisers might want to try if there is too much advertising on regular broadcast television stations or networks. Cable networks now reach a sizeable portion of the television audience, and cable audience measurements and statistics are also now included on a few of the ratings services' surveys.

Media planners and buyers who want to use cable television, however, at this point are handicapped by partial audience information, or information that may be biased because it is provided by the cable service, or even no information at all for their media decision making.

Another new advertising media development involves telemarketing—calling potential customers on the telephone or letting customers call the marketer through the use of inward-WATS "800" numbers. If advertising in general is too cluttered and not audience specific, then telemarketing can work in specific cases.

If advertising seems too expensive for the brief message time available, nonadvertising promotions, such as sweepstakes, sponsorship of sporting events, giving away token specialty items, and special marketing programs directed at affluent target groups may be substituted. In fact, advertising expense is one reason why sales promotion has been growing faster than advertising in the United States in recent years. The money budgeted by marketers for nonadvertising promotions in the United States is now estimated to be larger than the total monies expended for advertising.

Some advertisers have begun subsidizing videotape versions of motion pictures in return for inserting commercial messages at the beginning and end of the tape. This novel approach may reach a substantial audience, but how can information on audience demographics, purchasing habits, or even numbers be gathered? New media may present novel opportunities, but they must also be considered uncontrollable factors in advertising media selection.

Ten years ago, hardly anybody was using personal computers. Then newer and less expensive machines were introduced, sales picked up, and now suddenly, the market is highly competitive, and some strata are even saturated. This has provided opportunities for computer networks. Prodigy—a service of IBM and Sears, Roebuck & Company—permits direct marketing via telephone hookups with the personal computer. While the shopper is perusing the available merchandise categories, there are on-screen cross-references to advertising messages, which can be accessed with a few simple keystrokes on the computer keyboard. This new advertising medium was not even contemplated only a decade ago.

Other types of new media developments are discussed in greater detail in chapter 19.

Negative Publicity

Another factor that may affect the media environment involves when an advertiser receives bad publicity. If a local newspaper published a particularly critical article about a company, the advertising personnel for that company could react by avoiding all advertising until the ill effects of the bad publicity disappeared. "Why advertise and maintain public awareness of our situation," they might ask. Or they could try to retaliate by pulling all of the company's advertising from that newspaper, thereby withholding advertising monies from the vehicle that carried the unfavorable report. The newspaper, however, may not suffer as much from the resulting loss of revenue as the advertiser does from the resulting loss of sales. In most instances, the local newspaper or radio station has many advertisers who use that media vehicle, so the loss of a single advertiser may not be critical. A local company or retail store, on the other hand, probably has only a few available broadcast stations and very likely only one daily newspaper to carry its advertising messages, so cutting the advertising in one of those few vehicles may well have a devastating effect on the retailer.

The advertising personnel for the negatively publicized company could also take out a special advertisement in that very newspaper to explain the company's point of view. What better way to reach the right audience—those who saw the "bad news"—than to present the other side of the story in the same medium? And what better way to control the perspective of the story being told than to write the message for paid advertising use?

Negative publicity about one business can also affect the competitors of that business. If there is news that one car dealer has misled customers, the general public may simply feel that all car dealerships are crooked, so other dealers in that town are hurt by the misdeed and the story.

Media planners must be vigilant over a wide area and for the entire industry because any kind of factor could affect the media environment and the media plan.

Competition

The competition is one of the most important factors taken into account in establishing marketing and advertising plans of all kinds, including media plans. But because the competition may take actions that result in a need for adjustments in the media plan, the competition must be considered an uncontrollable variable, and media planners must devise strategies for dealing with it.

For example, what would you do if a competitor introduced a product similar to yours for less money? The most obvious solution might be to compete on a price basis, but there are alternatives. For example, you could also advertise that even though your product costs more, it is worth more. L'Oreal cosmetics has done this for years, with wonderful sales success ("It costs more, but I'm worth it"). Who would deny that they themselves are worth a little extra attention and expense, especially when it comes to personal appearance and attractiveness?

Another approach might be to increase the amount of media time and space used to increase your competitiveness. Overwhelmingly the cheaper competition may provide a leadership position for your product or service, and most people expect the leader to be worth a little more of an investment.

What would you do if a competitor brought out a product that was superior to yours? Your first reaction might be to go back to research and development and try to develop an item just as good or (preferably) even better. In that way, you might beat the competition at its own game. But you could also change your advertising, focusing on your product's unique features. Or you might select a certain target

MEDIA SPOTLIGHT

6.1

Outdoor Ads Coming Down

by Alison Fahey

Outdoor board companies will relocate more than two thousand tobacco- or alcohol-related ads by mid-September, in compliance with newly adopted industry guidelines.

The action results from the Outdoor Advertising Association of America's new policy, announced in June, to encourage members to voluntarily ban tobacco- or alcohol-related ads on boards located within 500 feet of primary and secondary schools, established places of worship, and hospitals.

The group also has asked members to place decals on those boards to signal that they're "off limits" to tobacco- or alcohol-related ads.

The 5-by-5-inch decal features a symbol of a child and will be posted on the pole or board structure but won't obscure the ad. They're primarily for industry use but will be visible to passersby.

The relocation process has taken several months because companies first had to identify off-limit boards, notify the advertisers, and then fill the void with other advertisers.

Some companies have also been waiting for long-term contracts with tobacco marketers to expire rather than pulling those ads.

Three of the leading outdoor advertising companies—Gannett Outdoor, Patrick Media Group, and Lamar Advertising—said they will move some two thousand plus tobacco- or alcohol-related ads and put decals on some 9,200 structures.

Together, the three companies represent nearly 20 percent of the nation's five hundred thousand boards.

"Every board that has tobacco or liquor ads within the 500-foot rule will be moved by September 1," said John Hope, senior vice president-public affairs at Gannett Outdoor.

Gannett, which has thirty thousand boards in fourteen major markets, said it has identified "close to three thousand [boards] that will require the decal." More than a thousand of those feature tobacco or liquor ads that have been or will be moved, he said.

Gannett will also move some eight hundred tobacco or alcohol ads on bus shelters in New York.

Politics and advertising can indeed make strange bedfellows. For example, although a company may have the legal right to market in new territories, it may not be politically wise to do so since it may upset the population or bring down the wrath of powerful competitors.

Advertising that announces some questionable new product ingredient may alert government regulators, who then might take some political action to restrict the use or promotion of that ingredient. This has happened in recent years to marketers of breakfast cereals, who introduced new products with ingredients that were considered by some to be con-

trolled by the medical and pharmaceutical industries.

Cigarette manufacturers and liquor marketers are now more careful in their media plans to avoid directing advertising at young people, although many critics feel that more drastic steps still are needed. Even though they would like young people to start using their products early in life, liquor and cigarette marketers know that advertising campaigns aimed at these target audiences would bring about a backlash from large sectors of the public as well as from government.

Patrick, which operates forty-one thousand boards, said by mid-September it plans to have relocated more than a thousand tobacco- or alcohol-related ads. More than four thousand of its boards will feature the decal.

Lamar said about two thousand of its boards will soon feature the decal, but Tommy Teepell, vice president-marketing, said the company has pinpointed only fifty to one hundred tobacco- or alcohol-related ads that need to be moved.

Lamar, with twenty-five thousand boards in more than thirty markets, operates largely in more rural areas.

Whiteco Outdoor and Penn Advertising also said they're abiding by the industry policy, but Whiteco won't use the decals. Whiteco's boards are primarily on highways, and it will instead identify boards within the 500-feet range by computer.

The industry has been bracing for financial losses due to the new restrictions. But outdoor companies said they haven't been hurt yet financially by the relocation, and they're quickly replacing vacancies.

Mr. Hope said Gannett hasn't lost any tobacco or liquor business as a result of the relocation process.

"Those locations the tobacco people are willingly giving up are excellent advertising locations," said Lamar's Mr. Teepell. "The tobacco [marketers] are giving other advertisers the front row."

Patrick, which has added playgrounds to the list of off-limits areas, said it's been fielding phone calls from marketers that are looking to snap up the vacancies.

"We're getting calls from toy and cereal [marketers] and those types of companies that advertise on Saturday morning cartoon shows that are interested in those locations," said Mary Ellen Coleman, director of public relations.

Some outdoor companies believe the new policy will give the industry a needed image boost.

"The whole landscape of outdoor advertising will change," said one outdoor executive, who asked not to be named. "Once a tobacco or liquor ad comes down today, they will never go up on those [particular] boards again. I don't see that changing . . . ever."

Source: From Alison Fahey, "Outdoor Ads Coming Down" in *Advertising Age*, August 27, 1990, pages 3 and 35. Copyright © 1990 Crain Communications Inc., Detroit, MI. Reprinted by permission.

The media plan for a fast-food chain that packages food in plastic foam containers may advocate that the heat-retention qualities of that packaging not be promoted since such promotion might also alert environmentalists who oppose use of those items. After using plastic foam containers for more than a decade, McDonald's switched back to paper products, even though the foam packages had a better shape, protected the product better and kept it warm, and were easier to work with in the fast pace of their chain stores. The negative outcry from environmentally concerned segments of the population created a perilous situation that McDonald's simply wanted to avoid, even if it meant higher costs and a less desirable alternative package.

Regulatory restrictions can affect the advertising media selection as well. For example, in their advertising, cruise lines must provide registry information for their ships so that customers know about the protective elements of the various governments' registration requirements. Including that required information for several ships with several different countries of registry may preclude the use of radio because of the limited message time; such information, however, might be superimposed on the screen of a television commercial of identical length.

MEDIA SPOTLIGHT

6.2

A Specialized Advertising Situation with Economic Concerns

Research findings suggest that short-term population growth has less of an influence than the economy on total Hispanic market purchasing power. Hispanics as a group have lower incomes and could be affected in tight economic times. However, some large-ticket advertisers are not concerned. Automobile advertisers who target Hispanics are encouraged by the growth potential in the Hispanic market. What occurs in the general market appears to be magnified in the Hispanic market.

Source: Christy Fisher, "Hispanic Car Buys Down As Ads Surge," *Advertising Age,* 24 September 1990, 42.

Similarly, required loan information might take up too much time in an automobile dealer's broadcast commercial. As a result, the media plan may call for the broadcast commercial not to include any mention of loans. In print media, however, the required clarifications can be footnoted, where they will not detract as much from the major theme of the advertised message. Prescribed-dosage, side-effect, and contraindication directions may similarly limit a pharmaceutical advertisement to print media only, where there is enough space to include all the "small print."

Culture

Television commercials for birth-control products are common in Scandinavian countries, but they would probably create an uproar of protest if they were shown in the United States. German advertisements use nudity more casually than do American advertisements. Britons find humor in depicting personal situations that many Americans would find objectionable.

Cultures vary. Americans like shiny white teeth and fresh breath. But another culture admires stained teeth because the stains were caused by chewing betel nuts, and only wealthy persons have enough discretionary income to spend some of it on a luxury item like betel nuts. Promoting toothpaste on American television is worthwhile, while it probably would be wasteful in the other culture. Similarly, print advertising may not be worthwhile in areas where the literacy rate is very low—including parts of the United States where more than one-third of adults are functionally illiterate.

Cultures vary even within a single country. U.S. midwesterners may buy "sweet rolls" for breakfast, which would mystify New Yorkers, who are accustomed to eating a "Danish," which is the same thing with a different name. Ask for a breakfast roll in New York City, and you will likely be served a dry, hard dinner roll, which is what comes to mind there when the word *roll* is used. Similarly, New Yorkers who ask for a "soda" to drink would not get what they want in St. Louis, where that would be called a "soft drink" or a "soda pop." Midwesterners think of a "soda" as an ice-cream dessert with carbonated water—that is, an ice-cream soda.

Advertising media plans must take cultural differences into consideration. As cultures differ, the advertising message must likewise differ, which affects the scope and units of the advertising media plans. Special advertising campaigns may be needed if a particular group is to be targeted. These campaigns might require particular media placements, along with separate plans for targeting, message strategies, and even positioning.

Management

Changes occur regularly in business simply because of shifts in management directions and goals, alterations in budget allocations, price increases or other adjustments, and related changes. Top management makes adjustments that have far-reaching repercussions throughout the firm and even into the industry at large. Even though these changes are controlled by top managers, the changes are in response to conditions not entirely under managerial control. What is more, lower-level mangers in the organization may have these changes imposed on them without full consultation, so the net effect is an uncontrollable change with which the middle manager must deal.

Budget Appropriations

Budget changes affect those working with the budget and those whose work is funded by that budget. For example, if monies that were allocated for television advertising are shifted by management into print advertising, the advertising plan obviously is affected. It also means that the media reservations for space and time must be changed. Any budgetary change is very likely to cause concomitant changes throughout the plan, not just in advertising, but in the entire marketing effort.

If a competitor takes some unanticipated action during the course of another advertiser's campaign period, the advertising may need to be redirected or its budget reallocated. One advertiser may increase advertising to be competitive, while another may retrench to save money. A given situation does not necessarily result in a given solution: Every strategy and tactic is subject to human interpretation and intervention.

Corporate Objectives

In these days of buy-outs and mergers, a company may be taken over by another firm, which will change the objectives, operations, and work, including advertising. This often results in hiring a different advertising agency as well. In fact, the most common reason for changing advertising agencies is because of a change in marketing and advertising personnel on the part of the client advertiser.

Sometimes, a firm alters its own objectives. This may be necessary to meet changes in the marketplace or among competitors. Other reasons might

be to keep pace with the business category or the economy, as well as to provide for product or service upgrades. Changes in objectives may be necessary for macroeconomic reasons, such as to shift corporate investments of time, material, and money to more productive categories. Whenever corporate objectives change, the advertising effort must be altered as well.

Pricing Policy

Changing the pricing policy for a brand also affects the advertising plan. Management may decide to change pricing strategies so as to meet competitive threats, to take advantage of increased sales that arise from the increased demand curve reaction to price reductions, to bolster sales in a lagging category, or to extend the product life cycle for an item. Such price machinations can also be ways to test the marketplace for shifts in consumer interest and to experiment with various pricing strata.

Inflation can also cause prices to be increased or can create a shortage of raw materials. In these circumstances, the advertiser may need to cut back on advertising a certain category or line of goods, or make an increased advertising investment to offset the price increase and supplement selling efforts.

Errors and Mistakes

While it is generally recognized that everybody makes mistakes, the problem is that other persons are often affected. This is true in advertising as much as in any other kind of business. For example, suppose that an advertising schedule has been ordered and that (as is usually the case) a certain television placement is due at the broadcast station seventy-two hours in advance of the scheduled commercial time. For some reason, the delivery of the tape or film is delayed. If the advertiser or agency is responsible, that operation must suffer whatever financial penalty results, but a substitute advertising schedule may also be required. If the delay was because of a transportation failure, the responsibility and liability are less certain, but changes in the advertising schedule may still be necessary.

MEDIA SPOTLIGHT

Fifteen-Second Spots: Help or Hindrance?

by Kim Foltz

As the use of fifteen-second commercials becomes more prevalent—they now represent about 40 percent of all television ads—many advertisers and agency executives have questioned the effectiveness of using so many short spots. Some have also worried that the use of fifteen-second commercials could spiral out of control, creating a hopelessly glutted television advertising environment.

A new report by the Association of National Advertisers has some revealing insights into the future of short commercials. The report, "15-Second Television Commercials: Improved Marketing Productivity or Advertising's Vietnam?" was compiled by the association's advertising research committee over seven months and relies on information gathered from leading advertising research, media, and creative executives.

The report by the New York-based industry group was a response to numerous questions about the effectiveness of the commercials.

First and foremost, the report said, fifteen-second commercials are "here to stay." Since they were introduced on network television in 1983, the number of such spots has steadily increased, and the report predicted that, by the end of the decade, they would account for more than half of all commercials.

This fall, for example, Kmart will begin a television campaign that consists of dozens of short spots that quickly pitch a product on sale. Another big advertiser, RJR Nabisco, has increasingly used fifteen-second commercials for products like Ritz crackers and Oreo cookies.

But the report warned that advertisers who continued to rely too much on fifteen-second commercials—whose messages almost seem as though they are over before they begin—run the risk of damaging the brand equity that has been established for their products through longer commercials.

Recently, some agency executives have speculated that the clutter caused by the proliferation of fifteen-second spots would eventually cause a movement toward longer ones. During the last year, a few advertisers, like American Telephone and Telegraph and Porsche Cars North America, have broadcast spots that were at least two minutes long.

Creative executives prefer longer commercials because the format allows more time for spectacular effects or riveting emotional appeals. As some creative directors have lamented, fifteen-second spots do not win awards.

Sometimes, broadcast media overestimate a program's anticipated audience level. If the audience delivery is less than was predicted, a broadcast network may be forced to schedule make-goods so as to meet promises of audience level delivery or cost-per-thousand guarantees.

As another example, suppose that there is a mechanical problem in carrying the advertisement in the media: Maybe the sound engineer neglects to turn up the audio portion of a television commercial, so the soundtrack cannot be heard; perhaps a newspaper forgets to insert the new prices in a grocery advertisement; maybe the typesetter makes a typographical error that is not caught by the proofreader—in fact, with today's computerized composition, there may be no proofreader. In situations like these, the advertiser is entitled to a **"make-good"** that allows the advertisement to be run again

But the short spots remain attractive to advertisers because they cost about half as much as a thirty-second commercial, which averages about $120,000 on prime-time television. Research has also shown that the shorter commercials are 60 to 80 percent as effective as thirty-second spots, in terms of recall or the ability to persuade consumers.

But the report warned that the fifteen-second spots may be far less of a bargain in the future. Some networks are already charging premiums for the commercials when broadcast during the most popular television programs, and the report forecasts that prices in general will continue to rise.

The report concluded that fifteen-second commercials were most effective when used with thirty-second ones for the same product. And not surprisingly, the report underscored the well-established belief that fifteen-second spots were best when used to hammer home the names of well-known brands.

The researchers also said that original fifteen-second spots were more effective in reaching consumers than short commercials that were simply "cut-down" versions of thirty-second ads. In making a fifteen-second spot that is "lifted" from a longer version, the report said, the message that reinforces the sales pitch is inevitably cut or dropped, and the commercial will therefore "not be effective."

The report recommended that advertisers not use fifteen-second spots to introduce products because the spots offer too little time to fully explain a product's benefits.

One way of making fifteen-second commercials more effective, the report said, was to use them as "bookends"—splitting in two a commercial for one product and separating the parts by spots for other products. In one for Excedrin, for example, the first fifteen-second spot shows a woman talking about her headache and then taking two Excedrin tablets. When she reappears in the final segment after a couple of unrelated commercials, the woman happily announces that the pain has passed.

As fifteen-second commercials become more commonplace, the report concluded, thirty-second ones will become far more valuable by the sheer nature of their uniqueness.

Although the report did not speculate on the fate of already scarce sixty-second spots, these anachronistic ads clearly seem destined to pop up only occasionally during special events, like the annual Super Bowl telecast, when advertisers traditionally show their most spectacular commercials.

free of charge—that is, with no additional charge beyond the original contracted price.

Yet, sometimes, these kinds of errors can be even more costly. For example, a customer may demand the advertised product at the advertised price, even though the printed price was obviously an error. There may be legal repercussions that entitle the buyer to make a reasonable purchase at the advertised price, even when the stated price was a mistake. Such errors in advertising can be very expensive. If there is a magazine advertising insertion scheduled at a cost of $40,000 and the advertising media department fails to get the materials to the publisher on time, the advertiser or agency may still be billed for the agreed-on cost. One error like that will make any media planner or buyer more attentive to deadlines in future work.

Above and beyond any penalties or additional costs incurred, the advertising plan may need to be examined for any adjustments necessitated by the mistake.

Summary

Many uncontrollable factors may alter the advertising plan and operation. The natural environment, in the form of weather or unforeseen disasters, can affect advertising, even in far-off places and in rather obscure ways. So can the media environment, in program content, media clutter, new media developments, and negative publicity. The competition, the economy, the culture, and legal and political factors can also interfere with the advertising media plan, resulting in changes even after the media plan appears to be firmly established and completed. Management changes in budget appropriations, corporate objectives, and pricing policies can also affect the media plan, as can simple but expensive human mistakes.

All of these factors can alter the advertising media objectives, plans, and executions, and the changes can be expensive in both monetary and personal terms. The changes may also force concomitant changes in corresponding operations. To whatever extent possible, media planners and buyers should try to anticipate these uncontrollable factors and plan for them.

Questions for Discussion

1. Should advertisers make any attempt to bring so-called uncontrollable factors under control? How might they do so?

2. Why should we be concerned with things that are beyond our control?

3. How can a company's budget appropriation be considered an uncontrollable variable?

4. Is it ironic that advertising itself creates the problem of media clutter? How can an advertiser counter the problem of clutter?

5. Developers seem to be turning every object and process into new advertising media. Are there any problems with this trend? How does it affect advertising?

6. If government regulates advertising, why would the advertising industry also want to resort to self-regulation?

7. What are the best ways to counter errors and mistakes in advertising?

Suggested Readings

- Barban, Arnold M., Steven M. Cristol, and Frank J. Kopec. *Essentials of Media Planning: A Marketing Viewpoint.* 2d ed. Lincolnwood, Ill.: NTC Business Books/National Textbook Company, 1987.

- Bozell, L. Brent III, and Brent H. Baker. *And That's the Way It Isn't: A Reference Guide to Media Bias.* Alexandria, Va.: Media Research Center, 1990.

- Grass, Robert C. "Satiation Effects of Advertising." Paper presented at fourteenth annual conference of the Advertising Research Foundation.

- Kaatz, Ron. *Cable: An Advertiser's Guide to the New Electronic Media.* Chicago: Crain Books, 1982.

- Schneider, Robert A., and Donald E. Siebert. "Viewer Attitudes toward Commercial Clutter on Television and Media Buying Implications." Paper presented at eighteenth annual conference of the Advertising Research Foundation.

ANALYTICAL CONCEPTS

Quantitative Factors in Media Decisions

Outline

Learning Objectives

In the study of this chapter, you will have the opportunity to:

- Examine the characteristics of quantitative media decision factors.
- Understand the basis for the importance of quantitative factors in media decisions.
- Know the limits or the weaknesses of quantitative factors in media decision making.
- Become acquainted with quantitative decision tools.
- Observe how media cost balances audience size/profile.

*S*election criteria for advertising media are plentiful, but only those criteria that are subject to precise measurement are considered objective. These audience dimensions, recognized across the advertising industry as standard measures of media performance, are known as the quantitative aspects of media analysis. Their limitations and applications in media decision making are the subject of this chapter.

Recognizing Quantitative Factors

While no standard officially determines what is or is not quantitative, quantitative measurements have features that separate them from other media selection factors:

- **Direct Measurement.** They can always be expressed as an absolute value (for example, thousands of people, dollars) or as a percentage.
- **Simplicity.** Though often developed from a complex series of calculations (numbers), a quantitative value can usually be reduced to or summarized as a single number value (for example, "reach," "frequency").
- **Wide Recognition.** Quantitative values have industry-wide acceptance that is standardized and uniformly understood by advertising professionals (for example, "share").

These three features—direct measurement, simplicity, and wide recognition—make quantitative measures the foundation of media evaluation.

Practical Importance of Quantitative Factors

Quantitative factors dominate the media selection process because they make a complex procedure easier to comprehend. They have a practicality, a bottom-line personality, characteristics of which include:

- *Media Roots.* Many of these values originated as descriptions of media audiences. They have a long history of use in communications as well as in business.
- *Convenience.* Many of the decision makers in advertising planning do not care for the volume of research necessary for media selection. Quantitative measures, for better or worse, are easily conformed into a rule of thumb, a guideline, or even a principle.
- *Reduction.* A "report card" mentality often forces complex relationships into a summary or single value. People who are more comfortable with all interactions reduced to a bottom-line grade feel that quantitative values are perfectly suited for this purpose.

Limitations of Quantitative Factors

Quantitative measures, then, have a number of comfortable features, but they are far from infallible. In fact, overreliance on these quantitative criteria can result in questionable media strategies and tactics. The following are some of the shortcomings that media planners have to avoid:

Media Exposure or Advertising Exposure?

The quantitative measure of a media audience is not the same as an audience exposed to advertising. If five million people read a consumer magazine, it does not mean that five million people will see each marketer's advertisement. Audience members do not necessarily read every ad in a magazine or see every commercial in each television program they watch.

Quantitative measures are based on the media vehicle's audience. While a high percentage of audience members are assumed to see or hear the message, determining the actual proportion that have is not at this point practically possible. (See the discussion of the A. C. Nielsen Company's people meter for television in chapter 16.)

Much of media audience research is retrieved from the memories of audience members. Yet, memories are faulty and somewhat unreliable for even the most recent things people have done. If people have difficulty remembering the shows watched, or stations heard, how can they accurately recall the commercials or the ads seen? Frankly, for most people, advertising has a lower priority than the entertainment and information obtained from the media. Thus, research is not likely to be able to consistently measure advertising message audiences. No matter how precise the media audience numbers are, there are no precise measures of those exposed to the advertising message. Media exposure and advertising exposure are two different things.

Media Audiences Not Tightly Defined

The nature of media research and its cost greatly limit how well media audiences are described. Consumer magazine reader research is fairly thorough, but radio, television, newspaper, and outdoor audience reports are limited primarily to age and gender. These data rarely provide the specificity that many marketers need for their much more narrowly defined target audiences. Media planners, searching for these specific prospects, often have to rely on personal judgments in selecting the right media vehicles.

Questionable Research Accuracy

Though audience research technology continues to advance, many media researchers express concerns about the reliability and validity of the research results. Even the measuring technologies—people meters (television), diaries (radio), personal interviews (magazines), and traffic counts (out-of-home media)—have been questioned. Sometimes, sample sizes are suspect. In other cases, researchers challenge the use of statistical probabilities that are part of audience projections. While these criticisms do not deter media professionals from using quantitative data, media planners often feel the need to support decisions with nonquantitative measures, such as those discussed in chapter 8.

Major Quantitative Variables in Media Decision Making

Some of the most common quantitative measures used are factors related to: size and composition of media audiences, how these audiences can be combined for a schedule effect, and audience/cost relationships. We begin with audience size.

Audience Size

Marketers naturally want advertising messages exposed to the largest group of customers and prospects allowed by the budget. This is as fundamental a principle in media planning as it is in many other contexts: Bigger is better. Not surprisingly, then, the

MEDIA SPOTLIGHT

7.1

Working with Reach Estimators

Bill Roberts was an assistant media planner at the Hendrix Advertising Agency, and he was about to attend his first client meeting, where he would be a primary advisor for the media strategy questions discussed. In preparation, Bill stopped by the office of his supervisor, Carol Kenda. He explained that he was sure that spot television would be discussed, and he was worried about calculating audience reach estimates for various schedule alternatives. Carol explained that no one calculates reach "on the spot" because it would tie up the meeting too long. She then told Bill about the media department's reach estimation tables. The file Carol placed in front of Bill looked like the information in table 1.

Carol emphasized that, although the information was based on Arbitron and Nielsen data from hundreds of schedules, the averages shown were rough estimates. She explained that these were optimum levels based on schedules that used many different programs (known as dispersion). She told Bill never to promise reach based on the table estimates because the actual schedule's reach could be significantly lower than the table figures. The value of the table, she advised, was in its ability to provide fast estimates once the affordable gross rating points (GRP) was known.

Carol instructed Bill to first calculate the GRP from the dollars per daypart and then to find the appropriate GRP row and trace across the table until the vertical daypart column was located. She explained that the figure at the intersection of the two points was the highest reach of adults possible from the monthly GRP in that part of the broadcast schedule.

TABLE 1

Media Department Reach Estimation

| Gross Rating Points Four Weeks Total | Adult Viewer Reach | | |
	Early Evening	Prime	Late Evening
100	41%	57%	36%
150	53	68	43
200	64	74	52
250	66	78	56
300	68	81	59
400	72	86	65

Bill said that the table was easy to use for a single daypart, but he was confused on how to estimate reach when different parts of the day were involved. Carol told him that, first, he should never add reach levels together because that was absolutely invalid. Instead, he should use a simple statistical approach to combine different reach levels. To demonstrate, Carol set up a short problem with the steps to the solution:

1. The schedule alternative calls for 150 (four-week) GRP in prime evening and 100 GRP in early evening.
2. Use the table to find each respective reach level (prime 150 = 68 percent, and early evening 100 = 41 percent).
3. Subtract the highest reach level percentage from 100 (100 − 68 = 32).
4. Multiply the next lowest reach level (41 percent = 0.41) by the remainder from step 3 (32). (0.41 × 32 = 13).

5. Add the product from step 4 (13) to the first and highest reach level (68) to obtain the combined estimated reach (68 + 13 = 81).

Carol again stressed that these were estimates and were never to be offered to clients as an accurate outcome. She said that once everyone in Bill's meeting understood the limitations, the table and the combination formula would enable the planning to examine all sorts of alternatives.

Questions to Consider

1. What are the table estimates for monthly levels of 300 GRP in early evening and 150 in prime?
2. What is the combined estimate of both daypart reach levels?
3. Why was Carol Kenda so careful about explaining the limitations to Bill Roberts?

TABLE 7.9

Reach and Frequency Comparisons for Alternative Schedules—Alpha Brand, October 199___

| | Schedule | |
	A	B
Message Units	10	14
Gross Impressions	50,000	70,000
Unduplicated Audience	15,000	14,000
Gross Rating Points	50	70
Reach	15	14
Average Frequency	3.3	5.0

$$F = \frac{50}{15} \qquad F = \frac{70}{14}$$

or

$$F = \frac{50,000}{15,000} \qquad F = \frac{70,000}{14,000}$$

complete and valid as the frequency distribution, is easier to calculate and more commonly reported. Two formulas for calculating average frequency are:

$$\text{Average frequency} = \frac{\text{Gross rating points used}}{\text{Reach}}$$

and

$$\text{Average frequency} = \frac{\text{Gross impressions}}{\text{Unduplicated impressions}}$$

Table 7.9 demonstrates these methods based on a simulated schedule selection procedure. If the audience research is available, media planners would rather make frequency selections on a complete distribution and not trust judgment to the questionable accuracy of *averages*.

Frequency is achieved in the same ways described earlier for reach or accumulation—within the same vehicle and across vehicles.

Within-Vehicle Frequency

The first aspect of within-vehicle frequency involves determining the medium's natural pattern—whether the rate of distribution set by the medium is hourly, daily, weekly, or monthly. Obviously, media vehicles operating on a daily schedule (newspapers, radio formats, daytime television) offer more of a frequency than the NCAA Basketball Championship Game, a monthly magazine, or a Yellow Pages directory. Media plans that call for a high level of repetition first have to consider the vehicle's natural frequency.

Within-vehicle frequency also involves the permanence (or conversely, the perishability) of the medium. Some media vehicles, such as radio and television, "disappear" with the sweep of the clock's second hand. Others have forms of longer life—such as the hobby magazine that receives repeated use, or the Yellow Pages yearlong reference, or the outdoor bulletin on an annual contract. Multiple-exposure opportunities are clearly a bonus to certain businesses.

Another consideration of within-vehicle frequency is the pattern of consumer use that reflects on the content of the vehicle itself. The examples are endless—the television shows that we will not miss if possible, the newspaper sections or columns we try to read daily, or the late-evening radio music show that for us is an integral part of the day's end. Not all television shows, newspaper segments, or radio programs are this way. But if media planners choose vehicles with a high degree of favored participation, the chance for frequency of exposure is expanded.

Note that frequency and reach have opposite objectives: Reach involves looking for different people; frequency involves looking for the same people.

Across-Vehicle Frequency

Combining different media vehicles to achieve a frequency objective is more difficult than using the within-vehicle approach for two reasons:

1. The research available is only marginally successful in accurately tracking all mass-media activities for each individual target

member. With most media research today focused on a single medium, all-media tracking studies are unlikely to become a reality. Instead, across-vehicle exposure can be estimated with mathematical probability models such as those covered in chapter 13.

2. Using different vehicles is more likely to attract reach than achieve frequency.

The difficulties in achieving message repetition through different media seems to beg a question— why bother? Would it not be easier to simply use the same vehicles? The answer may be yes, but there are other circumstances to consider.

The Natural Frequency of the Vehicle

Some media (monthly magazines, weekly or monthly television programs) do not have concentrated repetition and therefore lack enough opportunities for duplicated exposure. To increase frequency in these situations, media planners need more vehicles.

Vehicle Availability

Vehicles popular with advertisers may not always be available for all the space or time desired. The marketer might want to use Fox Television's "The Simpsons," but what if some of the desired program episodes are already sold out? Replacement programming is often needed to satisfy frequency goals in television.

Goal Conflicts

Frequency is seldom the sole objective of the media plan. Media planning usually has accumulation (reach) goals that also need attention. In fact, the effective reach strategy discussed earlier is actually a form of compromise between reach and frequency because it tends to avoid situations where these independent goals conflict.

Cost of the Media

Whether the advertiser is General Motors or a local shoe-repair service, the most expensive part of the advertising process is media cost. Marketers use a higher proportion of promotional budgets for media time or space than any other facet of advertising. Media cost does not reflect the quality of the idea or the production values. It does not respect good talent or creative ideas. Marketers have to pay the price for a good ad or a lousy one. And because most of the mass media have increased prices at rates higher than inflation, many advertisers are becoming preoccupied with the price paid for media.

Media costs are the central focus of the quantitative factors in media selection and planning. Cost interacts with audience size, composition, audience reach, and message frequency. Ultimately, all media-planning decisions are in some way influenced by media cost.

Detailed explanations of costs for each medium are found in chapters 14 through 18.

Media Audience Efficiency

Selection of media and, specifically, media vehicles should be based on the ability of the medium to expose the largest possible audience of prospects at the lowest possible price. While selecting media types and vehicles with the highest proportion of target prospects is clearly one part of this task, the other aspect is equally significant: The selection must be cost efficient. This means that the audience size (and composition) must justify the price paid for the space or time. Media planning uses two different but closely related procedures to determine audience efficiency: cost-per-thousand and cost-per-rating-point.

Cost-Per-Thousand Procedure

In essence, the cost-per-thousand procedure involves finding the cost to deliver (expose) one member of the target audience, however that audience is described (for example, households, readers, viewers, demographic audiences, or some description that is sales related, such as "heavy user" or "brand loyal"). In practice, the size of media audiences has made the cost of delivering one audience member an awkward (it could be a fraction of a penny) calculation, so the industry computes the relationship on a per-thousand-member

TABLE 7.10

Major Media Cost-Per-Thousand Percentage Changes 1989–1991

Medium	1989 to 1990	1990 to 1991
Television:		
Prime-Network	+10.9%	+7.7%
Day-Network	+8.4	+6.8
Spot Market	+5.6	+5.4
Syndication	+7.7	+5.7
Daily Newspaper	+6.5	+5.8
Consumer Magazines	+5.6	+5.7
Outdoor	+4.0	+3.0
Spot Radio	+4.5	+4.7

Source: "Media Costs," *Marketing & Media Decisions,* August 1990, 23.

Note: All 1990 and 1991 figures are based on agency estimates.

basis. The **cost-per-thousand** (or **CPM,** where "M" is the Roman numeral for 1,000) formula involves multiplying the unit cost of the media vehicle by one thousand and dividing that answer by the estimated size of the target audience:

$$CPM = \frac{\text{Cost of message unit} \times 1,000}{\text{Size of the audience}}$$

Chapters 15 and 16 provide a complete explanation of this tactical analysis for print and broadcast media vehicles. The trends of cost-per-thousand are shown in table 7.10.

Cost-Per-Rating-Point Procedure

Another method of efficiency analysis uses the rating (or percentage) instead of the raw audience number. This is a popular method for comparing broadcast alternatives because a rating is the fundamental measure of broadcast popularity. This process can also be used to compare newspaper or magazine coverage or penetration figures as long as the audience value is listed in percentage form. The

technique is known by several names: **CPP (cost-per-point)**, **CPR (cost-per-rating)**, and **CPRP (cost-per-rating-point).** Each uses the following formula:

$$\text{Cost-per-rating-point} = \frac{\text{Unit cost}\left(\begin{array}{l}\text{for example, cost of one}\\\text{thirty-second commercial}\end{array}\right)}{\text{Audience rating}}$$

Again, chapter 16 provides a full discussion of cost-per-rating-point.

Guidelines for Efficiency Analysis

While the CPM and CPRP have been key factors in the selection of media and media vehicles, over-reliance on these efficiency calculations for choosing the best vehicle can be a problem. The following are some important points to remember:

- Efficiency only relates price with size; it does not reflect quality or the impact of the media opportunity.
- Highly specialized products (durable goods and special services) often involve very narrow target audiences. Marketers of such products or services are usually encouraged to ignore efficiency to assure target reach.
- Efficiency analysis is best applied to within-media analysis (television compared to television) and not across-media analysis (outdoor to newspaper).
- To compare different communication patterns is to equate their impact. If media are not the same in impact, they should not be compared on CPM.
- Because cost is a critical element in efficiency, underpriced media alternatives can look better than they actually are. Media that are heavily discounting their message units may have an important reason for doing this that could affect the advertiser's eventual success. The old axiom "You get what you pay for" also applies to advertising media.

Summary

Much of the decision making in selecting media types and vehicles is based on a series of standardized, measurable, and numerical factors known as the quantitative dimensions of the media. These factors include: audience size, accumulation rates of media vehicles, exposure frequency, cost (prices), and cost-efficiency analysis. Though they do not reflect every aspect of media performance and may even disguise potential weaknesses, these are the criteria that media professionals and marketers rely upon for selection.

Audience size reflects the measured popularity of each media vehicle and is a fundamental principle in the selection process. Media planners deal with size estimates as either raw audience counts (number of viewers, readers) or as percentages of the target population. Media selections based on size must be carefully considered to ensure that the general audience measured reflects the marketer's more specific target audience. Failure to differentiate can prove to be a costly error since unwanted ("waste") members of a media vehicle's audience are invariably reflected in the vehicle's price.

Audience size is also a dynamic process in that media habits (audiences) change over time. Marketers base their media planning on a media vehicle's ability to "collect" or accumulate different target individuals as the advertising schedule continues. Accumulation also is concerned with the number of times each target audience member is exposed to the advertising message. Accumulation (or reach) and repetition (or frequency) are part of the media selection process so that a desired proportion of the target audience will see or hear the marketer's message a sufficient number of times to be influenced in a positive way.

Inevitably in the media selection process, audience size and/or composition of a medium is compared to the price for space or time. The interaction of these major quantitative factors has resulted in an analysis procedure known as media audience efficiency. Two procedures for determining audience efficiency predominate: cost-per-thousand (CPM) and cost-per-rating-point (CPRP). Both are designed to identify media opportunities that provide an audience at the most efficient cost. As is true with the other quantitative features of media selection, audience efficiency analysis is not a panacea for choosing media vehicles but must be combined with other criteria to present a more balanced picture of opportunity.

Questions for Discussion

1. The quantitative factors used in media selection are, in part, justified as "practiced" evaluators. Explain.

2. Quantitative research is primarily based on media exposure and not advertising exposure. What does this mean? Is the industry capable of measuring advertising exposure?

3. If magazine A had a RPC factor of 4.3 and magazine B had a RPC of 2.8, would A be the most logical choice if type of audience and cost were equal?

4. Both gross impressions and the gross rating point (GRP) are known as "duplicated" measures of audience. What does this mean? Is this duplication something to be avoided in media selection?

5. Explain this relationship: The narrower a company's target-audience definition, the greater the likelihood that mass-media options will be judged on audience "waste."

6. Using a daily newspaper as your illustration, explain what within-vehicle and across-vehicle audience accumulation mean? Which has the larger capacity for reach and why?

7. A television program has an average household rating of 15. An advertiser bought a commercial position in each of four consecutive episodes of the program. Research analysis of the program estimated its four-week household reach as 35 percent. The average rating (15) indicates that the audience summary should

have been higher than 35. If the program gets 15 percent each week for four consecutive weeks, where did the other portion of the share's audience go?

8. In table 7.6, the accumulation potential of *Newsweek* magazine is demonstrated. If your company considered buying four issues of the magazine instead of one, how many new (different) adult readers would be added? What percent increase is that above the single-issue audience?

9. A weekly radio schedule generates 75 GRP for the target audience. The estimated reach is 25. What is the average frequency of exposure? What does average, in this situation, mean?

Suggested Readings

- Barban, Arnold M., Steven M. Cristol, and Frank J. Kopec. *Essentials of Media Planning: A Marketing Viewpoint.* 2d ed. Lincolnwood, Ill.: NTC Business Books, 1987.

- Sissors, Jack Z., and Lincoln Bumba. *Advertising Media Planning.* 3d ed. Lincolnwood, Ill.: NTC Business Books, 1989. Chapters 3, 5, 14.

- Surmanek, James. *Media Planning: A Practical Guide.* Lincolnwood, Ill.: Crain Books, 1985.

Qualitative Factors in Media Decisions

Learning Objectives

In the study of this chapter, you will have the opportunity to:

- Identify and classify qualitative influences on media decisions.
- Understand the importance of qualitative factors in media decisions.
- Recognize qualitative factors that can increase or decrease message effectiveness.
- Assess how media qualities can improve media evaluation.

*T*he following signal phrase will undoubtedly be repeated by a growing list of consumer marketers in the 1990s and beyond: "We want something more—something extra beyond the audience numbers in a media buy." That "something" comes in a multitude of forms, many of which involve intangible values of media that are clearly different from the media advertising staples of audience reach, frequency, and cost-per-thousand (CPM). No specific label classifies these aspects of media performance, but because they embrace subjective decisions, decisions not anchored in numbers, they are called qualitative decision factors.

In this time when competitors look for anything that will increase sales share levels, media advertising deals are including complex activities far from the traditional mainstream. This chapter explores the more elusive values that surround media dealing and how advertising media planners are coping with the evaluation process.

Recognizing Qualitative Factors

Prior to any discussion of the meaning of qualitative factors or how they are identified, you should know that media planners have not fully accepted qualitative factors of media-message performance as standard criteria for the selection of media types or vehicles. They have found it awkward to employ qualitative dimensions in their decision making because of the limited measurement of the effects of qualitative factors and also because of their professional unwillingness to use subjective arguments.

Even so, the use of qualitative evaluation grows each year. Increasing numbers of planning groups work with schemes that can accommodate quality above and beyond audience dimension and cost. To appreciate that these factors go beyond the strict boundaries of media audiences, you need to understand the characteristics or conditions that relegate some values of exposure potential to the side called qualitative. Here, briefly, are some of these conditions. They are explained in greater detail as the chapter continues.

Message Environment

Quality in media evaluation often involves the creative side of the message, or the mood or atmosphere during the exposure opportunity. Do some circumstances improve the chance to "connect" with a target audience? Do some lessen the connection? The variety of positive and negative media environments ensures that message placements with identical audience levels will not communicate equally. Message environment also implies that creative message elements (copy, pictures, and so on) interact with the media content to the benefit or liability of the advertiser. That is, the right environment can increase creative effectiveness; the wrong one can decrease it.

Nonadvertising Activity

A qualitative aspect of a media proposal could offer nonadvertising activity in the form of public relations, merchandising, or sales-promotion services as part of the medium's package. If a medium, in addition to its audience level and CPM, is prepared to offer a promotional contest as a bonus, media planners should consider the value of the contest.

Measurement Difficulties

As discussed in chapter 7, research is the foundation of quantitative factors, but many of the dimensions called qualities must be estimated.

Suppose you wondered if an advertisement would attract more readers' attention in the front of a magazine or in the back. No reader or circulation analysis would give you even a clue. You would need special testing to compare awareness levels from front and back. Even then, the research company would, no doubt, warn you that the test might be "confounded" (results confused) by other influences that have nothing to do with *where* the ad is positioned. As you read about other qualitative factors in this chapter, think about how research could be designed to measure each factor's contribution to advertising effectiveness.

Subjectivity

Without uniform and absolute measurement, the significance or importance of a quality of a medium becomes a matter of personal judgment. Ask five media directors how many additional commercials should be planned if the commercial length is fifteen seconds, and you are liable to get five different estimates. Qualitative factors do not deal in black or white, but in shades between. Media professionals, usually in the absence of research, use personal judgment or intuition. While not a bad situation, it often forces arguments of one opinion against another.

No Uniform Acceptance

As noted earlier, there is some inconsistency among advertisers and their agencies on if and how a qualitative factor should be used in media planning. These same professionals would not apply the same scrutiny to the quantitative dimensions covered in chapter 7. In part, this reflects on the lack of evaluation standards and possibly also on ignorance of how a qualitative factor may influence the communication success or failure of a brand.

Why Qualitative Factors Should Be Used More in Media Decisions

Why should subjective, inconsistent, underresearched, and nonstandardized factors have any

place in media decisions? Clearly, media analysis is a less complicated procedure without them. Just the same, qualitative factors lend valuable aspects to media selection. Qualitative factors:

1. Address the changing media environment. *Environment,* here means the occasion of advertising reception. The technology of home information and entertainment shows no signs of arrested development (for example, FAX transmission, VCR usage, computer linking, and digital processing). Competition for consumers' leisure time and interests has intensified. The pace of daily lives has seriously changed the way consumers search for products and services. Past traditional approaches used to expose mass audiences are in question. Advertisers need more sensitive measures to assure that target audiences will receive the product message in the time and place of optimum effectiveness. Qualitative factors can better address the need for effective exposure opportunities.

2. Adjust gross impression levels. Some of the qualitative factors to be discussed operate on the downside of exposure. That is, they address the negative aspects of media that would limit or reduce effectiveness. By showing a negative influence, these factors force media planning to anticipate shortfalls and compensate for them in advertising schedules. When schedules are adjusted upward to offset certain weaknesses before the starting date, the advertiser has a better chance to achieve the campaign's objectives.

3. Develop media and creative bonding. Once media planners move beyond audience numbers to communication effects, they better appreciate the creative writer/ visualist's job. This is the opportunity for specialists from divergent operations to share ideas and strategies. In this way, qualitative thinking can develop a synergy that rewards both the media and creative departments.

MEDIA SPOTLIGHT

8.1

'Meddling' in Creative More Welcome*

by Gary Levin

There's a creative revolution taking root in ad agencies today. The thing is, it isn't necessarily coming from creatives.

More and more creative directors are turning to media departments to make their best ideas work harder.

Important in some cases, media people are even initiating ideas for new campaigns.

"There's an increasing amount of fraternization and discussion with creatives," says Richard Kostyra, executive vice president-U.S. director of media services at J. Walter Thompson Company. "The idea is to exploit to the maximum program-type positioning or magazine placement. It's becoming a more competitive market and it's harder to stand out."

Media planning is no longer an after-the-fact complement to a new campaign.

Media executives say they're working more closely than ever with creatives to allow media selection to help shape the creative process, often before a single ad is written. They say account planning and the increasing push for breakthrough advertising are the major forces behind the new harmony.

Single-sponsor magazine issues and "bookend" split-30s wrapped around other television spots are merely the start of the trend toward media-creative collaboration.

Among the more noteworthy campaigns based on tight media-creative partnerships is the one for Carillon Importers' Absolut vodka.

Carillon and TBWA, its New York agency, meet with a slew of magazines once each year to set big-selling Absolut's annual media schedule, which consists of up to one hundred magazines.

After that process is completed, the agency's creative department is charged with creating several media-specific ads to run, for example, in business publications or theater playbills or *Playboy.* An "Absolut Bravo" ad in playbills has roses adorning the clear bottle, while business magazines trumpet a *Mad*-magazine style "Absolut Merger" foldout.

Sometimes, however, creatives will develop an ad for a magazine not even on the schedule, as was the case with *Playboy's* "Absolut Centerfold" ad, which portrayed its playmate bottle ("11-inch bust, 11-inch waist, and 11-inch hips") (see figure 1).

The process doesn't require a major reorientation of TBWA's media department, but it has had an impact on the agency.

"What Carillon has done for us is give us a more open mind and put more demand on all departments to be creative in their ideas than might be the case otherwise," says Richard Costello, TBWA's president and chief operating officer.

**Marketers need to take more risks to cut through the advertising clutter, says Michel Roux, president and chief executive officer of Carillon.

Roux, who helped turn Absolut into the nation's no. 1 imported vodka and the tenth-best-selling liquor brand, attributes much of Absolut's success to a willingness to take chances.

"Building a brand requires passion and courage," Roux told an International Events Group's sponsorship conference, "If you believe in a brand, make the investment and stay the course."

Last year, in a period of flat vodka industry sales, Absolut's sales were up 30 percent, Roux says.

Reaching that point has involved a number of risks. In the late 1970s, Carillon turned its back

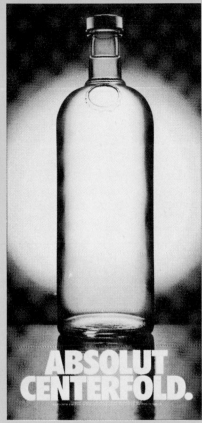

FIGURE 1 For its ad to run in *Playboy,* Carillon Importers ran an "Absolut Centerfold," complete with its ambitions: "To always be cool, with or without ice." *Advertising Age,* "Absolut Centerfold."

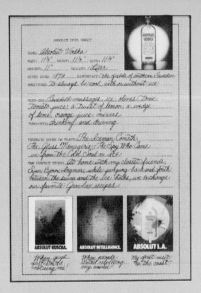

on $65,000 in market research that said that Americans would never buy a Swedish vodka with a misspelled name sold in a clear, difficult-to-pour bottle.

"We nearly always accept the advice of our consultants but never blindly," Roux says.

Later, Carillon committed to using the works of cutting-edge designers and artists, such as the late Andy Warhol, as part of its advertising before knowing what they would produce.

The result, though not always what might have been expected, reinforced Absolut's image of being for consumers on the cutting edge of taste and fashion. The new images were spotlighted in art opening events.

Finally, Carillon was willing to forego price discounting and the quick sales it might generate in the interest of developing brands.

Roux says the key to successful marketing is starting with a good product, developing positioning, then making sure all subsequent events and programs reflect that positioning.

"The impressions you make in ads, publicity, sponsorships, point of purchase, the way the brand is handled at retail—all of these impressions have to integrate to produce a powerful, focused brand image," he says.

*From Gary Levin, "Meddling in Creative More Welcome" in *Advertising Age,* April 9, 1990. Copyright © 1990 Crain Communications Inc., Detroit, MI. Reprinted by permission.
**Remaining text: From "Absolut Built on the Edge" in *Advertising Age,* April 9, 1990. Copyright © 1990 Crain Communications Inc., Detroit, MI. Reprinted by permission.

not every product advertised in *Good House-keeping* seeks to obtain the "Seal of Approval," an extra degree of credibility still flows from *Good Housekeeping* to its advertisers, as if to say that an advertisement has more believability if found in the pages of *Good Housekeeping* magazine.

Good Housekeeping is an exceptional case of an earned reputation, but it is not alone. In nearly every editorial content area, certain magazines have some measure of this special authority. In some cases, such as *Good Housekeeping, Reader's Digest,* or *National Geographic,* respect comes from credibility. Other magazines, such as *GQ, Cosmopolitan,* and *Sassy,* have acquired the authority to direct which ideas in fashion, entertaining, or personal relationships are "correct."

Authority or prestige is not reserved for only magazines. Some newspapers enjoy it (for example, the *New York Times,* the *Wall Street Journal*), as do some television programs (CBS's "60 Minutes," NBC's "Bill Cosby Show," and ABC's "Nightline with Ted Koppel"). In nearly all media, some vehicles stand out. They are not always the most popular in terms of readers/viewers, but they carry a perceived belief and loyalty that, to some media planners, compensate for what might be lacking in audience size.

While many advertisers acknowledge the importance of authority or prestige, marketers of innovative products or those with some special news aggressively seek vehicles whose audience reputations can accelerate awareness, acceptance, and adoption.

Compatibility between Vehicle and Product

A parallel value similar to authority concerns a natural compatibility or affinity between the editorial content or the programming and the marketer's product or service. If media vehicles are so closely related to the product that the advertisement or commercial may be perceived as an extension of the vehicle's content, then the advertising exposure audience may be nearly the same size as the media exposure audience.

TABLE 8.1

Advertising Enjoyment Level by Magazine Reader Demographics

"Does Advertising Increase Your Magazine Reading Enjoyment?"

Audience Category	Percentage Agreeing
Adult Males:	
Ages 18–34	47%
Household Income $25,000+	40
Professionals/Managers	39
College Graduates	37
Adult Females:	
Ages 25–54	35
Household Income $25,000+	36
Sales/White-Collar	41
College Graduates	30

Source: Magazine Publishers of America.

What would a fashion magazine be without fashion advertising? What would a sports/recreation issue be without advertisements on equipment or apparel? What would a televised golf tournament be without commercial promotions of golf balls and clubs? Though most consumers view advertising as an intrusion, these particular audiences welcome the messages because they add to the desired experience—appreciation of a hobby, interest, or sport. Table 8.1 provides reader reactions to magazine advertising.

While the degree of compatibility does not add more target readers, viewers, or listeners, it may reduce the difference between vehicle and advertising audiences. This extra dimension concerns how the advertising is treated by the audience and how often it is used. Consumers have reported that magazines directed to their interests have pages of advertising that they sometimes read and reread for reference and enjoyment. This repeated, purposeful exposure is the intriguing dimension. First, the magazine has continued "life," but even more valuable, the advertising receives repeated attention.

Compatibility is also found in broadcast vehicles. The programming choices now available through syndication and cable outlets assure that numerous special-interest programs are available, from programs on hunting/fishing and home projects to sports and fitness. If broadcast vehicles such as these cannot guarantee repeated exposure, they still can claim higher attention values for related commercials.

Most advertisers must rely on judgment and intuition in deciding how much additional impact a compatible arrangement could provide, although magazine readership studies attempt to provide some clues.

Position/Placement to Enhance Attention

Purist baseball fans shook their heads in disbelief. They were going to watch the Chicago Cubs play *night* baseball at beloved Wrigley Field. Chicago's decision to use lights like every other major league ballpark was not without major controversy. By the time the lighting was installed and the inaugural game scheduled, media hype (baseball style) had turned this game into a nationally televised event. At B.B.D.O., the advertising agency for General Electric, the creative team asked the media-planning group for a special position for General Electric lighting—they wanted the first commercial position after the lighting ceremony. The creative people had developed a commercial that reenacted the historical event when General Electric engineers and technicians played the very first baseball game under lights (a then brand-new General Electric lighting concept). The perfect "window" for releasing this commercial was following the Wrigley Field lighting ceremony. It probably took some negotiation (and perhaps special cost consideration), but the special positioning quality for this particular commercial was too good to pass up.

The underlying reasoning for placement is that not all advertising positions in a media vehicle are equal. Quantitative audience measures do not indicate if some will read one section of the newspaper more than another, or if radio positions adjacent to the news have higher attention, or if the first commercial break in a television movie is more audience tolerable than the last or next to last. Even without consistently documented research, however, media analysts often negotiate for what are believed to be preferred positions.

Advertiser interest in position strategy is usually based on either a desire to improve the attention opportunity or a recognition that certain positions preselect desired target groups. The latter reason is especially important when different audiences use the same vehicle (for example, readers of a newspaper do not all seek the same news features). In this case, the special placement is primarily intended to fulfill target-audience objectives.

How helpful are the advertising media in placing the advertiser's message in an advantageous position? It depends on three considerations. First, the media vehicle must have the available position desired. A magazine has only one back cover, and it may already be filled. Second, the medium's cost for accepting every special-position request must be calculated. Some requests may demand extra time and labor. If a daily newspaper allowed every advertiser complete control over where each ad was placed, the makeup of each edition would go well past deadline. Third, the medium's willingness to accommodate advertisers is a question. If a pattern of accommodation is established, the medium had better be prepared to offer these goodwill gestures to most, if not all, advertisers. Once this "extra" attention is started, it is hard to stop. Because there are substantial differences in how the media react to these considerations, it is best to discuss some of the media individually.

National Television (Network/ Cable Network)

The placement strategy involves the commercial positions *within* the program. Positions have two

MEDIA SPOTLIGHT

8.2

The Quality Question

"Advertisers should be looking at the relationship that a magazine has with its readers. From there you can make a determination about how responsive the readers will be to the advertising," says Richard Thompson, publisher of *U.S. News & World Report.*

Lou Schultz, executive vice president and director of media services for Lintas:USA, urged media researchers at the Advertising Research Foundation's July workshop to take up the cause of the expansion of qualitative data options. Other agencies are investigating new ways of applying existing measures to the planning process.

Are such efforts for real?

For some, they are. In a recent survey, Helen Johnston, vice president and associate media director at Grey Advertising, finds that among forty-three magazine planners at nine agencies, nearly all planners frequently use qualitative data. Among those nearly universally used are advertising to editorial ratios, editorial content, and degree of competitive advertising. Almost equally used are circulation analyses, which include growth, subscription renewals, and reduced-price subscriptions. Data about where the publication is read, how much time is spent with it, and what percentage are primary readers are also considered relevant, but are used only slightly more than half the time.

"There is clearly a strong belief that readers approach different magazines differently," concludes Johnston. That belief centers on the notions that "magazines are read with varying degrees of intensity and involvement and that the greater the reader's involvement, the better the ad will fare," concludes Johnston.

Certainly, agencies are encouraging planners to use qualitative measures in decision making. For example, at J. Walter Thompson in Chicago, media supervisor Sharon McDonald says she tries to strike a balance between quantitative and qualitative factors for nearly every magazine buy. No client places equal importance on all the criteria within these factors, so each account gets a separate evaluation.

The analysis can become "pretty complicated for some clients," tells McDonald. She says that for Kraft, qualitative and quantitative data are weighted according to what the client and agency agree to be the most important information for the particular campaign. Then a grade is given on how well each magazine scores on both quantitative and qualitative factors.

---

elements. First, there are a specified number of program interruptions called **breaks** within each program. Then, within each break is a group of commercials called a **pod.** Network operations schedule when the commercial breaks occur, and they determine both the length of the pod and the position of each commercial within the pod. (See table 8.2.) Technically speaking, advertisers have no say on where the breaks occur, how long the breaks are, or how many commercials are allowed in a pod.

Networks are reluctant to allow clients to dictate the position of a commercial. Perhaps, they fear that all clients would want to be first or last in the pod position and would desire the later pods because of heightened audience interest. Local or spot-market television stations generally follow network procedures where applicable.

Bernard Guggenheim, senior vice president and director of media information services at Lintas:USA, relates how reliant Lintas is on qualitative measures. In one case, an automotive trade magazine was excluded from the schedule strictly because of quality issues. Lintas, which handles advertising for Chevrolet, examined what percentage of editorial was devoted to foreign-made vehicles. "The editorial mind-set wasn't on the kind of vehicles we're selling," he notes. "While the numbers from a cost-efficiency basis were terrific, from a qualitative standpoint, the magazine didn't make it on the schedule," he emphasizes.

At J. Walter Thompson in Chicago, Debbie Solomon, vice president and associate media research director says, "We are big advocates of qualitative measures." A checklist of factors to consider includes editorial environment, reader response judged by letter-to-editor and reader panels, competitive advertising, graphics, positioning, and merchandiseability to the trade.

She cautions, however, that Thompson judges these factors for each brand. "Sometimes, cost efficiency is the most important," she says. "Other times, it could be the reader's loyalty, the subject matter, or advertising clutter."

She notes that the numbers need to be interpreted individually for each type of advertiser. For instance, buyers generally consider that a high score on readership at home is good. However, it would be good to read a health ad in the doctor's office. The most commonly used measures are ABC data to examine circulation vitality. The planning groups also look at ad-to-edit ratios and "sometimes rely on syndicated qualitative measures," Solomon says. "If the numbers were more predictable and we had more confidence in them, then we would rely on them more," she explains. "We would like as much information as possible, but we need to know how to interpret it," she cautions.

Most agency planners would like to see a lot more valid information. With that goal in mind, the magazine council of the Advertising Research Foundation (ARF) has recently drafted a paper on how editorial environment contributes to the effect of advertising. "Of all the different issues, this subject had the highest interest," says Guggenheim, who sits on this research committee. Unfortunately, the ARF report doesn't offer any new answers. "We focus on identifying the problem, and then set forth how it can be researched. But every approach we have come up with has certain kinds of problems tied to it," Guggenheim says. "There's no Holy Grail here."

Source: Abridged Article by Rebecca Fannin, *Marketing & Media Decisions*, September 1989, 53–58.

Newspapers

With newspaper advertising, special positions are more the rule than the exception. Because of highly segmented editorial composition, newspapers understand that advertisers need to be located in certain sections (sports, business-financial, food, editorial). This is usually arranged without charging the advertiser a premium or extra cost. If, however, the advertiser demands a position *within* a section ("main news—opposite editorial" or "sports—second page"), only a premium charge for the extra production effort will guarantee it. Similarly, demands for back pages of the section are usually secured only by larger, long-term contracts.

Business/Consumer Magazines

The nature of magazines provides so many options in positioning that position consideration must be

TABLE 8.2		
Voluntary Time Guidelines, Network Television Stations (Selected Dayparts/Lengths)		
	Prime Evening	Daytime
Nonprogram Minutes Per Hour	11	16
Number of Interruptions Per Pod:		
2-Hour Programs	7	16
1-Hour Programs	5	8
30-Minute Programs	3	4
Number of Commercials Per Pod:		
1-Hour Programs	5	5
30-Minute Programs	5	5

Source: *Adweek's Marketer's Guide to Media* (1990).

part of nearly every contract. Chapter 15 provides a discussion of the many possible options.

Qualitative Factors That May Detract from Advertising Message Effectiveness

The previous section sampled some of the qualities that can increase exposure value. Many advertisers pursue these advantages routinely, with no particular imagination. Others explore every possible enhancement for maximum exploitation of the creative opportunity. While certain circumstances or conditions can improve the communication effect, some environments increase the difficulty in connecting with the targeted audience member. In other words, some conditions test audience tolerance, produce brand confusion, or otherwise destroy the mood for communication. The discussion here highlights the more serious concerns but is not meant to suggest that most messages are doomed or to imply that the circumstances are without remedy. There are remedies to reduce the effect: Foremost among them is an advertising message that is fresh, informative, and entertaining. For the media planner's part, knowledge is strength. Awareness of the potential danger leads to strategies and tactics designed either to avoid or offset poor communication conditions.

Overcrowded Media (Clutter)

Some anonymous "expert" once claimed that the average metropolitan adult is exposed to over seven hundred advertising messages each day. The reliability of such a generalization is questionable, but whether the average is one hundred or one thousand, there is no denying that American adults are exposed to far too many advertising messages, and in too many different ways—in the home, on the road, in schoolrooms, offices, stores, and even public restrooms. Eventually, the whole advertising industry will suffer from this advertising **clutter.** Clutter affects exposure opportunities, awareness levels, brand attitudes, and is also primarily responsible for the low esteem with which the American public regards advertising. Until the competing interests can be reconciled, however, media planners must recognize the most seriously cluttered areas and develop strategies to limit the worst effects. A few examples follow.

Television

Usually identified as the leading perpetrator of clutter, television has an awkward position. Because it is the primary outlet for entertainment and information, most audiences consider its advertising a serious intrusion. Yet, television is also a powerful means to communicate attributes and images, an advertiser's dream. Economic forces pressure networks and stations to keep prices competitive, but they compensate by allowing more commercials. The effect is a wider and deeper commercial stream (river?), as shown in table 8.3.

In the past five years, greater use of the fifteen-second commercial has accelerated these cluttered

TABLE 8.3

*Depth of Message Stream—
Commercial Announcements Per Week
for Network Television*

	1975	1980	1985	1988	1989*
Units Per Day (Avg.)	245	582	732	893	957
Units Per Week (Avg.)	3,500	4,075	5,125	6,250	6,700+
Index	100	116	146	179	191

*Projected.
Source: From TV Bureau of Advertising. Reprinted by permission.

TABLE 8.4

*Growth of Shorter-Length
Commercials in Network Television*

Commercial Length	Breakdown by Percentage				
	1975	1980	1985	1988	1989
:60	6.0%	2.0%	2.0%	1.5%	1.5%
:30	93.0	96.0	84.0	60.7	57.5
:15	—	—	10.0	35.3	37.9
Others	1.0	2.0	4.0	2.5	3.1

Source: From TV Bureau of Advertising. Reprinted by permission.
Note: Data are based on a four-month sample.
Key: :60 = sixty-second commercials; :30 = thirty-second commercials; :15 = fifteen-second commercials.

effects, as demonstrated in table 8.4. This is because of audience perception. Even when the length of a commercial pod stays the same, an increase in the number of commercials (that is, using more fifteen-second commercials) is perceived by the audience as a *longer* interruption (see table 8.5). The experimental results in table 8.5 were obtained from identical pod lengths of ninety seconds. The only change was in the number of commercials. The index level was three thirty-second commercials. The audience tested was adults, ages 18–34. Viewer feelings about the length of the interruption were directly related to negative attitudes: As the break got longer, the audience was less and less interested in viewing.

What can be done? Clutter in television is very unlikely to go away. Media planners, therefore, develop defensive positions. Those who expect that client commercials may run in breaks of longer than ninety seconds might give serious thought to reducing the gross-rating-point (GRP) value of the position, if the position cannot be avoided altogether. The reason for this is simple: Longer interruptions are an invitation to change channels, to become distracted, or to leave the viewing area. When viewer attention to evening programs is already low (see table 8.6), attention levels to commercial pods are probably significantly worse.

TABLE 8.5

*Perceived Pod Length with Increasing
Numbers of Commercials*

Ninety-Second Pod	Index
Three Commercials	100
Four Commercials	220
Five Commercials	220
Six Commercials	280
Eight Commercials	380

Source: "Reprinted from the *Journal of Advertising Research* © Copyright 1984, by the Advertising Research Foundation."

One so-called solution has been to increase the volume (number) of television commercials for a given client. This may improve the isolated situation, but the combined effect of these "solutions" is to pour fat on the fire.

TABLE 8.6	
Primetime Viewer Attention Levels	
Mode Description	Percentage of Viewers Agreeing
Attentive to Program	40%
Partly Attentive	24
Not Attentive	36

Source: Agency Compilations.

Local Radio

Local radio is one of the most competitive in advertising media today. The more than 10,200 U.S. commercial radio stations struggle constantly to maintain respectable audience shares. Few things are overlooked in a station's desire to attract listeners. Some music-oriented stations (regardless of format) began promising listeners more and more plays without commercial interruptions ("five in a row" or "ten in a row"). Such policies are good for the audience, but bad for advertisers. Why? Successful (profit) stations need to run commercial time for about a third of each hour. With each music unit running fifteen minutes or longer, the math is obvious: The commercial breaks must be long ones. Consider your own reactions to this situation: If you were a listener and had easy access to a dial, a push button, or a remote device, would you change stations? Restricted interruption policies attract listeners, but they discharge them just as quickly. Media buyers are aware of such listener migration and try to balance a station's high ratings with close scrutiny of its commercial policies.

Magazines

Although not one of the major culprits with regard to general clutter conditions, magazines (especially monthlies) do have seasonal issues where the ratio of advertising pages to editorial pages is four to one,

or higher. Even so, because magazine readers have a measure of control over what advertising they look at, they are more tolerant of clutter. In addition, where the compatibility of editorial and advertising content is high, advertising pages are treated as a reader bonus. A particular clutter problem that some magazines share involves competing advertising, which is the subject of the next section.

Problems with Share-of-Voice (SOV)

Share-of-voice (SOV) means one brand or company's proportion of the total competing messages used in a medium or media vehicle. By "competing" are meant the messages used by all those firms directly competing in the same product/service category. For example, if Ajax Cereal's evening television for May amounted to thirty gross rating points and the combined GRP for all competing cereal brands was three hundred, Ajax's share-of-voice would be 10 percent.

Numerous studies have shown a high positive correlation between SOV levels and brand-awareness levels, brand attitudes, and indications of interaction. This is particularly true for new brand market entries and with low-involvement convenience goods. The reverse is also documented.

Since convenience-product target prospects tend to follow the same media patterns, marketers for competing brands invest in the same media vehicles. A good media vehicle for one competitor tends to be equally valuable to others. But is it? What happens if audience members are exposed to all sorts of competing claims? Can they recall who said what? In table 8.7, the effect of target-audience saturation is evident in recall (awareness) scores. More brand messages for toothpaste and pain relievers did not improve recall. In fact, this agency study suggested that the more brand message seen, the harder it was to separate them. Table 8.7 shows that the lightest-exposure group had *better* recall than the heaviest.

Such research suggests a twofold SOV strategy. First, because the absolute weight of advertising pressure (GRP) can be neutralized by competitors'

TABLE 8.7

Comparison of Television Exposure Groups on Brand Recall

Viewing Group	Total GRP Exposure	Percentage of Brands Recalled
Very Heavy Exposure	1,020	34.0
Very Light Exposure	100	37.0

activities if the messages occur in the same vehicles, media planners should avoid "crowded" media vehicles. Second, companies with smaller advertising investments should also consider scheduling advertising to avoid routine seasonal increases in competitors' advertising. This may be particularly advantageous if the product or service is one of the so-called low-involvement items to target consumers. Those brands are of only limited interest to buyers.

While SOV strategy is usually considered a defensive plan (avoiding confusion), it could also be an offense. Powerful brand leaders may concentrate their schedules to dominate lesser brands. "Confusion" (the inability of consumers to differentiate brands) invariably rewards the better-known brand.

Negative Context (The Wrong Editorial/Program Environment)

In the spring of 1989, consumers, tired of television networks' ineffective response to their complaints about television program content, took a more direct protest route: They threatened advertisers and agencies with store reactions to "trash-TV." While audience dissatisfaction with program content has been documented for many years, this time such major marketers as Sears Roebuck, Chrysler, Mennen Company, and Ralston Purina removed

advertising support from the most offensive programming.[2] Furor over program themes is cyclical, but it underscores the fundamental difficulty of selecting advertising placements that do not reflect badly on the advertising message or the advertiser.

It is ironic that popular program themes or editorial positions can run directly counter to the mood needed for the advertising message. Research by advertising agencies has demonstrated that even recognition and recall scores can be affected by program themes using crime, violence, political controversy, and sexual matters. The psychological theory behind this is complex, but it is enough to say that, today, media planners and buyers must exercise care not to choose positions that may produce audience antagonism or create tensions or anxieties that reduce advertising effectiveness. Graphic violence displayed in magazines, newspapers, and television does not mix well with appeals for sentiment, appreciation, and love.

Media-Offered "Extras" As Qualitative Values

Up to this point, our discussion has concentrated on factors that affect advertising exposure—factors that may increase or decrease effectiveness. Qualitative media measures, however, are not confined to exposure. In many instances, media planners must evaluate advertising opportunities on additional criteria or activities offered as a bonus.

These "extras," as inducements for media space or time sales, have been available for years and are unlimited in variety. They are incentives proposed by the media to gain advertisers in the same way that marketers offer extras to consumers (premiums, contests, and so on). Their common denominator is that they involve promotional activities and materials in addition to the space or time purchased. The examples that follow give some idea of the inventory of these extras. They also emphasize the difficulty in judging how much, if any, assistance they provide. Either way, the decision of the media expert is far removed from audience profile and CPM. Though the following examples are fictitious, each accurately portrays realistic situations:

1. Advertising Assistance. In perhaps the oldest extra of all, a newspaper approaches a prospective retailer and offers to design, write, and produce all the advertising for the client at no cost beyond the space. The newspaper may also offer to contact and arrange for cooperative advertising with the retailer's marketers.

2. Extra Advertising. A radio station offers a soft-drink company a summer-long contract. If the media planner or buyer accepts the station's proposal, the station will create a special contest—a listener promotion that will award the client's soft drinks as the prizes. The contest will include many on-air "mentions" and a van painted in the client's colors to roam the area for prospective winners. The additional announcements and use of the van are at no additional cost to the advertiser beyond the donated product. In another scenario, a magazine approaches food marketers with an offer to have their products featured in the recipes in a special, detachable, cooking supplement for no additional charge.

3. Additional Media. A radio station purchases a schedule of outdoor billboards for its own promotion but also shares the display space with advertisers. Half of each board location is large enough to present a product picture, and the radio station does not charge extra for the outdoor production or the space. Another radio station has a long-term arrangement with a supermarket chain for end-aisle (point-of-purchase) displays in each of the chain's stores. When an advertiser purchases a time contract with this radio station, the advertiser's product is promoted and displayed in the supermarket chain as well.

4. Distribution Assistance. Local media, such as newspaper and radio, frequently have continuing business relationships with the retail community. As "middlemen" between marketer and retailers, these media are in a position to assist in trade promotion for the manufacturer. Special meetings, newsletters or flyers, and sporting events arranged by the local media have considerable influence in gaining and maintaining distribution for media clients. A specific program of merchandising extras for *Southern Living* magazine is detailed in chapter 15.

More direct assistance has been documented in black and Hispanic media, where local media representatives make store-level sales calls to successfully negotiate shelf space and positions for marketers.

Integrating Qualitative and Quantitative Values in Media Selection

In a literal sense, a qualitative dimension of media performance does not lend itself to measurement. If it did, then, by nature, it would be quantitative. But virtually everything discussed in this chapter is capable of affecting or influencing awareness, attitude, or behavior. Effects are measurable. If the media planner is determined to assign a value (number) to qualitative features, it can be done and is. Nor is it a complicated process, as is demonstrated shortly. The challenge is to assign the measures or values *accurately*.

Some magazines or television programs may be said to improve the advertising exposure opportunity. But by how much? 10 percent? 20 percent? The point is simply this: If a media planner demands performance scales for qualitative factors, there must be a reasonably objective and scientific basis for the number assigned. Without research, assigning value is a pointless guessing game.

MEDIA SPOTLIGHT

8.3

MRI Measures Reader Interest

Many of the questions relating to magazine authority and compatibility are too product-specific to be generally surveyed by syndicated audience services. That has not stopped one research firm—Mediamark Research, Inc. (MRI)—from giving magazine buyers some insight into qualitative value. In its semiannual interviews of over twenty thousand adults, MRI employs a series of questions clearly intended to offer some insight into the form and substance of readership. Examples include:

1. Reader Habits (by title)
   - *Where do you usually read the magazine*? Home, office, work, waiting rooms, and friends'/relatives'/neighbors' residences are the usual categories.
   - *When do you usually read it*? Weekday? Weekend? Morning, afternoon, evening? While doing something else?
   - *How often*? (number of days for a given issue) In most cases, a higher number of days indicates the magazine's status and degree of value to the reader.
   - *Percent of all pages (per issue) opened*? The higher the percentage, the better

the chances of ad exposure. Issue pages also reflects the reader's interest in the publication.

2. Reader Appreciation
   - *How much do you enjoy each issue*? Media habits are not confined to only the most enjoyable. People may read several or more but usually have particular favorites.

3. Advertising Interest
   - *Do you enjoy the advertising in this magazine*? It is a general response, but it tries to capture the relative significance of advertising to the reader's pleasure.

Questions to Consider

1. Which, if any, of these questions would help to establish authority or prestige? Explain.

2. Which, if any, of these questions would help to establish the potential for compatibility with certain products? Explain.

3. If you *did* want to use the response patterns to these questions in your planning decisions, how would you do it? Can you fit this information with readership size or profile?

Careful research under controlled and field conditions provides some measure of a qualitative factor. The problem with this is the time and cost involved in such testing. Unlike research that measures the number of readers or viewers to a vehicle, this research should be product-specific. And the research must be repeated under similar conditions to establish a valid pattern. The answers found for one brand or one company are not necessarily the right answers for others. Each company's media situation may be unique. Therefore, a major reason why media qualities stay unmeasured is because of scarce resources.

<table>
<tr><td colspan="4">TABLE 8.8</td></tr>
</table>

Brand Awareness Scores of Five Magazines

Magazine	Readers	Awareness Factor	Adjusted Readers
A	1,000,000	1.1	1,100,000
B	2,000,000	1.0	2,000,000
C	3,000,000	0.9	2,700,000
D	1,000,000	1.0	1,000,000
E	2,000,000	1.0	2,000,000

If the hurdle of research is overcome, the mechanical process of conforming the qualitative to the quantitative is relatively easy. Two illustrations follow.

Suppose a food company learns from its own research that magazine *A* consistently produces brand awareness scores that are 10 percent above competing magazines. Further, magazine *C,* though having a large reader base, performs below average by 10 percent. To ease the adjustment, media analysts might use readership and factor in the reader awareness score. As shown in table 8.8, the average magazines in awareness show a factor of 1.0. This is the same as an index average of 100. Above-average magazines would use a factor of 1.0+, and those below would use a factor below 1.0. Here, magazine *A* has an awareness factor of 1.10, and *C* has an awareness factor of 0.90. Readers and factors are then multiplied to show the adjusted figures. What the planning did was to adjust audience size (relatively) by the qualitative (awareness) score. The number has no absolute value, but it serves as a comparative measure of potential.

For another example, assume a sport-shoe company uses television in its promotion. Company interviews with buyers and prospects indicate that they enjoy seeing the shoe commercials on college basketball telecasts. The research "value-added score" for these commercials is 15 percent greater than primetime or other sports events. The qualitative factor improves the target cost-per-rating-point because the "value-added score" raises the rating by 15:

Event	Cost/ :30	Target Rating	"V-A" Score	CPRP	"V-A" CPRP
NCAA	$35,000	4.5	1.15	$7,778	$6,763

With the adjustment factor procedure, any opportunity for placement can be raised and/or lowered by one or more qualitative aspects. The weighting process is easily employed in computer analysis.

Can qualitative factors be used without research to establish some level of performance? The answer depends on the company's attitude toward decision making. Some media analysts have the freedom to make qualitative judgments intuitively (without numbers). Others must pursue a bottom-line approach where all decisions are derived or validated with *measured* performance. In the latter case, a planner must assign some sort of number to every qualitative factor; otherwise, the qualitative factors cannot be used.

Summary

The qualitative dimensions in media evaluation embrace a wide variety of elements that can either increase or decrease the effectiveness of an advertising plan. Some deal with the environment of the media vehicle's content, others concern the influence of the media on the advertising message, and still others involve a mixture of media and nonadvertising activities. Most qualitative factors are difficult, if not impossible, to measure in the way that quantitative factors are. Further, advertising professionals do not all completely agree on whether some qualities should even be considered in media selections.

Despite the lack of uniform acceptance and the measurement difficulties, qualitative factors deserve an important place in media decisions. These factors are sensitive to the changing environment of communication technology and its impact on the public. Their close look at audience reaction to advertising allows advertisers a better understanding of consumer expectations. Above all, qualitative factors move beyond the threshold of exposure opportunity to mirror those aspects of media that can help or hurt advertising effectiveness.

Qualitative features of media show that certain media vehicles with authority or prestige actually improve communication of the advertising message. Qualitative factors also indicate that compatibility between a media vehicle's content and the product can enhance awareness of and appreciation for the creativity of the advertising message. Similarly, qualitative factors demonstrate the importance of position or placement (front versus back, or pod position). Qualitative factors may also detract from the effectiveness of an advertising message. Through qualitative analysis, media planners deal with such problems as severe media clutter from too many competing messages, crowding by direct competitors (SOV), and incompatible content environments.

Beyond advertising exposure effects, qualitative factors also concern the collateral extras or bonus activities offered by the media to marketers. These incentives include: direct assistance in creating and producing advertising messages, offering participation in additional media or audience contests and promotions, and even direct assistance to manufacturers in retail distribution.

Though qualitative factors resist research measurement, there are still ways to incorporate a value scale, particularly if the marketer is willing to engage in careful field testing of the effects of these qualitative factors. Though costly and time consuming, this research can establish strict value priorities, which enable qualitative standards to be applied to audience size, composition, and cost.

Questions for Discussion

1. What makes an audience value qualitative? If some so-called qualitative values can be measured, then why are they still considered nonquantitative?

2. Explain and illustrate the difference between "controllable" and "uncontrollable" qualitative media factors.

3. Identify a media selection factor that would enhance an advertising message's effectiveness. Identify one that might detract from effectiveness. Use personal observations to illustrate each situation.

4. If a media vehicle believed that its reputation carried a positive image for its advertisers (for example, credibility), how could the media vehicle "prove" this extra value to prospective advertisers? What sort of evidence might be accepted?

PART IV

STRATEGIC DECISIONS

Chapter 9

Setting Objectives

Learning Objectives

In the study of this chapter, you will have the opportunity to:

- Appreciate the importance of planning in achieving success.
- Compare and contrast objectives, strategies, and tactics.
- Understand basic rules for developing a functional objective.
- See how various types of objectives are applied to marketing, advertising, and advertising media.
- Assess the importance of media objectives in giving the advertising plan a strategic focus.

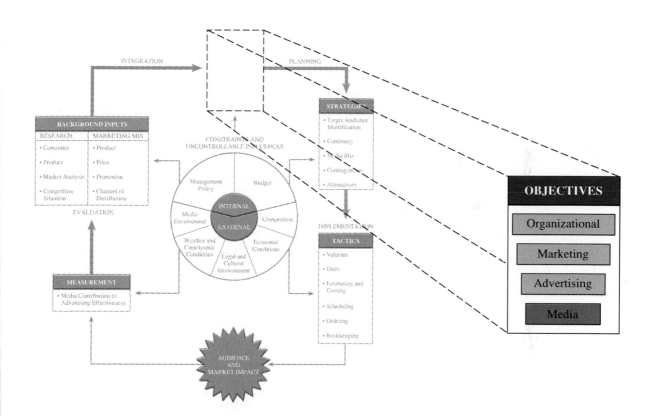

The media-planning group was receiving its first briefing on the advertising plan recommendations for the coming fiscal year for a famous condiment (food) corporation. On this particular day, the brand involved was barbecue sauce, and the leader of the media planning group—the executive vice president of media/marketing services—led the briefing. He told the media group of the complexity of the marketing direction and how it would affect media planning. His face indicated that this was not an occasion for celebration.

The planning group leader then passed around the following summary outline reviewing the situation and setting out the marketing guidelines for the next campaign:

• *Brand Profile*: Brand is entering third year in distribution. It has two flavors (regular and spicy), each in two bottle sizes.

• *Competition*: One other contending national brand is from the same company. Primary competition in above-average CDI areas (CDI is a way to compare market size and sales performance) came from local and regional brands that tend to have high loyalty from heavy- and medium-usage segments.

• *Distribution*: Four shelf facings per store was the ideal goal, but few chains or buying groups carried this way. In heavier sauce-usage areas, distribution was difficult to secure and maintain. In low-usage areas, three shelf facings was possible, but a shorter outdoor cooking season restricted store interest.

• *Sales Performance*: Growth Year I (second year in the marketplace) sales were acceptable, but serious improvement was necessary for payout (marginal revenue has offset introductory year spending). Sales were fair in the South and

Pacific West, but brand was a follower in key barbecue markets. Spicy flavor was not well accepted in the North and East.

The next sheet highlighted the brand's marketing objectives:

• Increase case volume by 10 percent over preceding year. Goal to be achieved by share increases in low BDI markets (trial) and usage increases in higher BDI areas. (BDI is a way to compare market size and sales performance.)

• Develop a national promotional program specifically tuned to four separate use zones based on the length of the outdoor barbecue season.

• Concentrate promotional activity against highest CDI markets in each use zone.

• Direct advertising to a dual audience of females and males (ages 18–55) with females the key target (70 percent) and males secondary (30 percent).

• Adjust combination of advertising and sales promotion activities to parallel distribution and market-by-market sales goals.

The planning group leader recapped the changes as (1) a new dual audience, (2) a changing media mix according to market profiles, (3) at least four different continuity sequences (it later worked out to *eleven* schedule variations), and (4) media selections that allowed maximum flexibility (meaning changes).

The planning group members sat in stunned silence. It seemed as if they had to develop objectives for five or six separate campaigns for the same brand. It took the media-planning group four months to complete its initial recommendations.

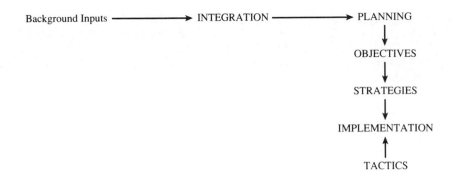

FIGURE 9.1 Interrelationships of Objectives, Strategies, and Tactics

And that was only the beginning. The objectives were revised by the condiment corporation twice, and the strategy and tactics were changed too many times to count. Much later, the media-planning group learned that the condiment corporation missed its sales increase by only one percentage point. The group believed that its plan goals had certainly been a major contributor to the corporation's success.

This factual vignette is not unique or even unusual. Yet, it illustrates how complicated objective planning can be and the careful preparation needed for plan objectives. For advertising campaigns, nothing is more important than developing a set of clear objectives. It is the essence of successful strategy. Overall planning was introduced in chapter 1. Now it is time to look at the engine that drives the plan.

The Plan Anatomy: Objectives, Strategies, and Tactics

This chapter focuses on objectives, one of the three elements in an advertising plan, or more specifically, a media advertising plan. Figure 9.1 borrows from the "Media Decision-Making Process" in figure 1.4 to show how objectives, strategies, and tactics comprise a plan anatomy.

Objectives

As chapter 1 indicated, **objectives** are a series of statements that set out what exactly the media plan intends to accomplish. Media objectives identify the directions or path of the campaign decisions. They are goals or a set of specifications that carefully represent how each activity can assist the company's marketing plans. When the planner identifies these goals or specifications, the media objectives are formed. The form and function of objectives are discussed in more detail later in this chapter.

Strategies

Strategies follow objectives because they explain how objectives will be achieved. Media strategies are the alternative ways that can get the job done.

Invariably, in media, there is more than one way to meet objectives, and the strategy section of each advertising plan recommends the best approach. Further, multiple strategies develop because there are a number of objectives. Media planners must try to select the best strategies by analyzing a number of objectives and alternative approaches at the same time. "Best" strategies are usually approaches that match as many objectives as possible within the budget limits. Illustrations of advertising campaign strategies as a response to an objective appear later in this chapter.

Tactics

Tactics are a series of specific recommendations for implementing or fulfilling a recommended strategy. If magazine advertising was the recommended strategy, the tactics would be the recommended list of titles and the number of ad insertions for each. If the strategy was to concentrate advertising pressure prior to Father's Day, the tactics would recommend the gross-rating-point levels week by week. Any of the detailed steps, including vehicle selection, cost estimation, and scheduling, are tactical recommendations in a media plan.

Chapters 7 and 8 evaluated quantitative and qualitative aspects of vehicle performance. These features are essential in the tactical section of a media plan. Tactical decisions are discussed in more detail in chapter 14.

The Form and Function of Plan Objectives

The creation of objectives for an advertising campaign demands careful research, analysis, some luck, and for many, the nerve to make a reasonable forecast. Planning objectives reflect the past (recent history), current conditions, and reasonable projections for the future. Objectives have three key roles in the planning process:

1. Strategic Decision Making. This is probably the most critical role for objectives. Objectives create a tighter focus on the strategies essential to company success. They provide the basis for the sifting of alternatives. They are the directional path of the planning process.

2. Personnel Coordination. Promotional campaigns are complex activities requiring teams of individuals from the company, its advertising agency, and other suppliers. In the advertising segment alone, research people, creative staff members, the account planning team, and the media department all work on the plan simultaneously. Plan objectives are instrumental in maintaining a single continuity for all individual efforts.

3. Campaign Assessment. Experience has taught many marketing organizations not to rely solely on sales for evaluating the success or failure of an advertising campaign. Objectives help to identify specific goals in a number of performance areas beyond sales (for example, awareness, attitude shift, exposure to messages). They set explicit levels of performance that simplify the evaluation process.

In summary, the role of objectives is found in the answers to the following two questions: (1) What are the most important things for this campaign to accomplish? (2) What levels of performance are needed for a successful effort?

Characteristics of Objectives

There is a right way and *many* wrong ways to develop solid planning objectives. There are no shortcuts or simplified guides. It involves a deep understanding of the company's situation and the marketplace, and competency requires extensive experience. Four important characteristics exemplify correct objective development: (1) significance, (2) specificity, (3) measurability, and (4) achievability.

Significance

One of the telltale signs of weakness in student media planning is a long list of objectives. Lengthy exposition of goals clearly indicates indecision with regard to what is important to the campaign. Implicit in planning is a reduction of thoughts and ideas to those with priority, the ones that are critical to the brand's success. There is no rule of thumb on the number. It depends on brand circumstances. Table 9.1 lists common objective categories. The test is to determine if each stated goal is really important or just something comfortable to include. A later section in the chapter discusses some popular media objectives, but even these are illustrations and not always mandatory.

Specificity

Vagueness has no place in objective development. If the objective is quantitative, then it should be expressed numerically. "An increase in awareness" is a poor objective because awareness should be expressed in a ratio (percentage) and the amount of increase should be specified. An objective that identifies "special activity in the top markets" needs to be reworded to specify what "top" means (top population? sales? potential?) and at least the minimum number of markets. The objective that deals with a time frame also should be specific. For example, the objective, "Achieve a distribution factor of 70," should also specify when—the end of the campaign? the third month? Not every objective category is based on numbers, but media planners still must be specific in describing what must be done.

Measurability

Measurability is a logical characteristic of an objective. An objective that is either incapable of measuring or unavailable for measuring cannot be used to assess success or failure. Measurability is a fairly common problem in both advertising and media objectives. A good example is response levels (awareness/attitude). If the company has not done recent research in these areas and is unwilling to begin a research program, there is little point in using communication responses as objectives. In media objectives, the effective reach level may be significant, but if the necessary audience research on message distribution is unavailable, the objective that focuses effective reach is useless.

Achievability

Achievability pertains to all objectives and particularly those with quantitative bases. It reflects reasonable forecasting of *possible* levels of improvement—levels that are neither ridiculously low nor foolishly high (beyond speculative reason). Low estimates may reflect indecisiveness or low personal security, while unrealistically high estimates may reflect ignorance and/or inexperience. Media planners are warned about setting reach and frequency levels or seeking geographic coverage levels that are beyond the scope of the budget. Similarly, they should not specify cost-per-thousand (CPM) goals that do not reflect audience delivery and media

---

TABLE 9.1

List of Common Subjects for Planning Objectives (But Not Necessarily Required)

Marketing Objectives	Media Objectives
Regions, States, or Markets to Be Covered	Level of Exposure (Reach)
Consumer Profiles of Prospects	Frequency (Repetition)
Sales (in Market Shares)	Target Audience Emphasis
Sales (in Units or Dollars)	Media Dominance or Mix
Distribution Levels Sought	Efficiency (Cost-Per-Thousand [CPM] Levels)
Market Priority Indicators (Brand Development Index [BDI], Category Development Index [CDI])	Media/Message Environments
Retailer Allowance Cooperation Levels	Geographic Emphasis
Seasonal Emphasis	Continuity Needs
Competitor Pricing Parity	Media/Merchandising Needs
Field-Testing Opportunities	Market Coverage Levels
Sales Increases from Increased Usage	
Sales Increases from New Users	

Advertising Objectives*

Creative Emphasis
SOV (Share-of-Voice) Levels
Benefit/Attribute Segmentations
Prospect Lifestyle Priorities
Product Image Priorities
Message Environment Needs
Communication Response Goals (Awareness/Attitude Change)

*Some subjects are not the exclusive domain of advertising or media. Company policy often dictates which topic belongs where.

costs. Achievable objectives reflect the reality of the marketplace; they show historical perspective and good judgment with regard to the future.

Identifying "Bogus" Objectives

Knowing the purpose and function of objectives helps in planning. The same is true of learning the right approach to objective construction, as discussed in the preceding section. Still, knowing the right way to do things is not enough training for evaluating good objective development. In the same way that banking employees are trained to spot counterfeit bills, one has to see the fraudulent to know the difference.

One media director has made it a point to collect examples of plan objectives that are "off," as he puts it. Staff training involves examining these polished statements to diagnose what is wrong with them. Many of these pseudo-objectives, on the surface, look very smart. Underneath the professional words, however, are serious deficiencies. Some of the media director's favorite bogus objectives follow, along with an analysis of their shortcomings. Try to determine each objective's deficiencies before reading the explanation. While these objectives are taken out of context, each should be able to stand alone for purposes of evaluation.

• *"Direct the brand's advertising impressions primarily to current category users with secondary emphasis to consumer segments considering market entry."* •

While this objective sounds professional, it has two serious faults. First, media planners deal with media audiences, which are never described as specifically as "category users." A better audience description for media purposes is needed. The second problem concerns vagueness. The objective refers to a dual audience (users and nonusers), and the first is to receive more effort ("primarily"). "Primarily" and "secondary" are nice phrasing, but what do they mean? Will there be a 60–40 split in focus? An 80–20 split? "Primarily" only says better; media planners need to know *how much better.*

• *"Use television to maximize creative intensity in market areas of highest developmental potential."* •

This objective is a collector's item. To begin with, it does not even qualify as a media objective. Recommending a medium is a strategy, not an objective. The medium should never be cited in media objectives. The objective also has some problem words, like "maximize" and "intensity." Such words are too vague and may lead to different interpretations of the objective. Media planners must find more precise ways of expressing the sort of creative effect desired. Finally, not even an experienced marketer could know what "highest" means in terms of sales development. These ratios or indices are specific. The objective writer should have expressed the lowest acceptable development number. For example: ". . . in markets with a development index of 115 or more." Companies that use development potentials know the indexing for every market.

• *"Select media that will facilitate a 30 percent increase in reach levels above last calendar quarter's reach level of 75.0."* •

While this objective is specific and states the reference point clearly, it is unrealistic. The objective probably cannot be accomplished. A 30 percent increase on a 75 reach means an increase of 22.5 points in exposure. Thus, this objective is calling for exposure levels of 97.5 percent or more. A 10 percent increase is probably reasonable, but setting goals much above that is naive.

• *"Schedule advertising to coincide with optimal consumer intention-to-buy attitude levels."* •

The "intention-to-buy" is a common consumer behavior dimension that parallels a purchase conviction. It, however, is not measurable as a *forecast.* No one can know when this will happen with the certainty that advertising can be scheduled. The company cannot predict intention. Scheduling could be based on past (historical) patterns, but even that is very risky.

• *"Select media that offer optimum effectiveness."* •

This type of "throw-in" objective infects too many plans—it is nothing but planning hype. No one knows the context of "effectiveness." And even if "effectiveness" was defined, what would an "optimum" be? Such objectives are deadwood and have no value.

Designing accurate and specific objectives is a skill not easily mastered without experience. Even experienced professionals can miss a point. The preceding examples certainly suggest more caution in the approach.

Marketing/Promotion Objectives: Illustrations

The media decision-making process profiled in figure 1.4 shows that most advertising campaign plans include three types of objectives: marketing objectives, advertising objectives, and media objectives. (The fourth type—organizational objectives—shown in figure 1.4 seldom reflects on media analysis and is not covered in the discussion here.) While we will discuss each of these three types of objectives individually, we first need to understand how they fit together.

Objective Coordination

Figure 9.2 illustrates the relationship between marketing, advertising, and media objectives. The order of presentation is important. Media objectives are at the bottom because they are guided by and based on relevant marketing and advertising goals. Advertising is guided by the larger marketing perspectives. The marketing objectives have priority and provide direction. Media activity is only one of the specialized duties that composes the advertising activity in promotion. Similarly, advertising is only one function in marketing, which encompasses all consumer-related opportunities.

Marketing Objectives

Chapter 3 explored the role of advertising in a marketing context. While advertising does not interact with every marketing element, all marketing ele-

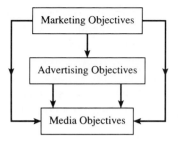

FIGURE 9.2 Relationship Between Marketing, Advertising, and Media Objectives

ments that have direct consumer relationship do influence advertising plans. A full compilation of planning objectives is shown in table 9.1. Those that bear most directly on media decisions are:

Promotional Mix Objectives. The marketing operation known as promotion includes sales operations, publicity, sales promotions, merchandising, public relations, and, of course, advertising. Virtually all marketing companies use a combination, or mix, of activities. A broad-based promotional objective identifies promotional intentions and indicates their respective proportions of investment. For example:

"The 1992–1993 Alpha Products communications program should be equally divided between consumer and trade promotion spending, with particular attention to seasonal advertising programs and in-store merchandising plans."

Sales (Share or Unit) Objectives. A marketing plan without sales goals is difficult to imagine. Sales objectives can be stated in shares (proportion of total category sales) or in units (boxes, cases, or dollars). The following sales objective reflects geographic intentions:

"For 1992–1993, Alpha seeks an overall 10 percent share of sales increase in its consumer products division. Sales performance will be realized in this manner: Maintain 1991–1992 share levels in the South and Southwest, 20 percent share increases in the Northeast and North Central, and a 5 percent share increase in the Far West."

Continuity Objectives. Marketing plans often include calendar arrangements. Few companies equalize marketing efforts throughout the year (that is, treat each quarter or month the same) even if consumer demand is relatively consistent. The major reason for variation is competition. Here is the Alpha version of a continuity objective:

"1992–1993 Alpha promotional spending should reflect historical demand patterns. In addition, 10 percent of the promotional budget should be targeted for two new sales events (Spring and Winter). Each of the 5–week periods stresses new model incentives."

Advertising Objectives

Because advertising is but a part of the marketing effort, its activity should work in concert with other marketing variables. What sets advertising objectives apart is that they are usually shorter range and involve tasks that can be accomplished through communication. Communication, in turn, concerns: (1) providing the advertising exposure opportunity, (2) delivering product image and information, and (3) producing positive communication influences (persuasion). Some illustrations follow.

Exposure Objectives—Target-Audience Profiles. Successful communication is very dependent on knowing who the target customers are and how they feel about those things associated with the company and its products. Marketers realize that no product or service suits everybody. Careful segmentation is necessary to identify those individuals best inclined to be receptive to the benefits offered. The following is an Alpha advertising objective based on the scenario that Alpha's products reflect serious environmental concerns:

"The 1992–1993 Alpha advertising should be directed to adults (25–55) living in better-income households ($40K+) who are balancing comfortable lifestyles with fears over our deteriorating environment. They are family-oriented and active in the neighborhood and the community. These people are opinion leaders.

They are also highly motivated to do what they can to improve environmental conditions. Importantly, they are strongly motivated to search for and reward companies that demonstrate similar concerns."

With this objective, the creative professionals have a much better "feel" for what to say and show, and media planners also have some guidelines for improving vehicle selections.

Creative Emphasis Objectives (Attributes/Benefits). Creative planners must decide what would be the most influential and interesting information to the target audience. What would capture attention and stick in the prospect's memory? The first step is choosing the ideas to highlight. Creative planning begins with emphasis selection. For many companies, no advertising objective has greater importance. The following objective reflects Alpha's creative direction:

"The creative approach used in 1992–1993 advertising must concentrate on two major concepts: (1) Alpha products are engineered for highest convenience satisfaction; and (2) No other company has performed more research and development to produce environmentally sound products (packaging through performance). Both concepts are to have equal treatment in any proposed concept, strategy, or theme."

Communication Effects Objectives. Most large, consumer-products companies monitor the impact of advertising through tracking studies on recall, recognition, comprehension, and attitude change. If done regularly, this communication effect scoring could be used to measure advertising accountability. Companies with a rigorous evaluation program learn the relationship between sales goals and specific awareness and/or attitude scores. Alpha might approach this subject with the following objective:

"Alpha advertising objectives on communication performance are threefold. 1992–1993 advertising should produce: (1) top-of-mind company awareness scores 25 percent above 1991–1992 levels; (2) key-line recall scores on

the "convenience" benefit should be 20 percent better than 1991–1992 by the end of the second quarter and finish at a minimum of 35 percent; (3) the environmental approach should account for a +15 attitude shift among users by campaign end."

Media Objectives

Media objectives, as explained at the beginning of this section, are based on relevant marketing and advertising objectives, and are dictated by marketing and advertising directions. As a highly specialized activity, media planning may not interact with every other objective, but its influence is widespread.

The section that follows fully explores a number of media-oriented goals. For now, it is enough to list the major questions asked by marketing and advertising objectives that can be addressed by media goals and strategies:

1. **Who**: Target-audience identification
2. **Where**: Sales geography (market selection and advertising weight priority)
3. **When**: Campaign timing of advertising activity
4. **Extent of coverage**: Level of desired reach of target audience
5. **How long**: Campaign length (continuity)
6. **How often:** Level of desired message repetition (frequency)

A Closer Look at Some Important Media Objectives

Training sessions for assistant media planners often offer the following advice:

- The media you recommend are never the objective. They are strategic and tactical solutions to the challenge posed by an objective.
- Because budgets are always a constraint on plans, certain objectives will work against each other. This is *not* inconsistent. Goals must be balanced so that, in fully achieving one, you do not cause an unnecessary sacrifice of another.
- Understanding the limitations of the dollar allocation and the limits of each medium's performance will guide you away from "overpromising" campaign effects.
- Do not treat objectives as enemies. Well-considered goals offer you a solid foundation for your own decision making. Objectives act as customized justifications for recommended actions.

This type of advice helps to offset the frustration that inexperienced media planners sometimes feel from trying to balance so many variables at the same time. What follows are descriptions of the more common media objectives.

Target-Audience Identification

As emphasized at the beginning of this chapter and in chapter 1, objectives are separate and different from strategies. Yet, "target audience" appears as a strategy in figure 1.4 and in chapter 10 but is listed here as an objective. Can it be both? The answer in this case is yes.

Directing advertising to the correct audience is a fundamentally important aspect of any campaign. The objective is to expose certain individuals to the advertising message. The strategy is to identify the ways to accomplish the exposure. How can media planners be sure that the media audiences actually contain the objective targets? Setting the identification of the target audience is the objective, and the research approach becomes the strategy. Media planners look for the common identity between the target consumer and the media audience member.

Many target-group descriptions used in the marketing objective sections use profile dimensions that never appear in media audience research. Several years ago, the AVIA Group International campaign (athletic shoes) had a marketing target of younger adults who either were, or wanted to be, fitness addicts who practiced weekly routines. Media

MEDIA SPOTLIGHT

9.1

Ducking the Objective Responsibility

My assignment involved the advertising campaign for one of the home-product divisions for ALCOA (the aluminum company). An early task was to meet with a marketing manager to cover plan "requirements." These, I assumed from my agency training, to be the ALCOA objectives.

The manager began by telling me what size ads and what kind of television programs they would use. I interrupted long enough to ask the manager if we shouldn't first talk about the marketing objectives.

"Objectives?" he asked. "We don't use objectives here." I thought we were having a semantic problem.

"Well, maybe you call them goals," I responded.

"Sure, ALCOA has goals—to increase sales," he replied. Then he informed me that he didn't really like to use goals or objectives because "they pin you down" and reduce "manager flexibility to do different things."

When I asked him how he could tell if things were going well for the brand, he told me ALCOA top management was the judge of that, and if they were unhappy, they let him know. When I reported this meeting to my boss, he explained that there were not many managers like my ALCOA client but enough of them to make the media-planning job a challenge.

Today, I doubt if there is a single product manager at ALCOA who is not an expert at identifying and expressing the marketing objectives for each brand. At the same time, professional managers must still feel a certain amount of anxiety about setting down the levels of achievement on which their performance will be evaluated.

research on audiences does not reflect mind-sets or exercise routines. Television rating reports do not indicate which viewers work out four or more times a week. Similarly, the Alpha target-audience profile presented earlier in the chapter described the target audience's social action activity and environmental motivations. For media objectives, only some of this can be transferred.

Chapter 10 covers the use of target-audience profiles in detail. Some descriptions (demographics and common-product usage levels) are available in media research. However, many are not. Technically, if an audience dimension sought is not measurable (either by syndicated or custom research), then it cannot be used as an objective criterion. What is the solution? Many media professionals prefer target translations in a two-stage process:

1. Use available common-denominator audience variables in the media objective.

2. Create a *media selection* objective that seeks media vehicles whose content reflects target-audience interests or activities.

Here is how the media plan for AVIA athletic shoes *might* have approached the situation:

1. "Direct advertising impressions to younger adults (specify age range), both men and women."

While very general and rather vague, this media objective can be improved with a media selection objective like the following that closely parallels the audience direction:

2. "Select media types and vehicles whose content features and/or supports individual fitness and athletic activity, including running/jogging, athletics, walking, bicycling, personal nutrition, weight

training, and tennis." The media planners for AVIA now have a target that can be measured through editorial and content descriptions. Each activity associated with a particular shoe model could be isolated.

For many broad-based products and services, a series of social and economic measures (demographics) is perfectly suitable as a media audience goal. When a tighter focus involves either unmeasured or unavoidable dimensions, the interpretation and translation skills must be incorporated to create a viable audience objective. Because consumer and media audience targets are so crucial today, chapter 10 explores this campaign dimension fully.

Sales Geography

Even for the top-share brands, leading retailers, or durable-goods manufacturers, sales patterns are seldom equal across areas or markets. For all sorts of reasons, these companies face market circumstances that preclude using identical levels of advertising intensity. Adjustments up and down are necessary. For each approaching campaign, most firms analyze the most recent sales results and try to forecast trends. One result of this analysis and forecasting is that the sales picture is translated into indexing that identifies each area's need for advertising activity. One of the more popular indexing systems—brand development and category development (BDI/CDI)—is demonstrated in chapter 11.

Once a marketing decision on sales area objectives has been made, the media plan often translates those intentions into geographic allocation goals. These objectives have the effect of distributing advertising dollars among market areas.

A national floor-care manufacturer must provide some increment of advertising support to every one of its sales districts, while also seeking to intensify the activity in a small group of markets. Its sales objective reads:

"The geographic allocation plan for 1992–1993 should deliver the minimum ('sustaining') level to all brand markets. Remaining budget should then be proportionally allocated to markets

having a BDI of 100 or greater and a CDI of 105 and above."

With this objective, markets that have demonstrated the strongest sales for the preceding year receive both a "sustaining" level and a special high-performance allocation. This direction indicates that marketing management for the brand believes that sales in high BDI/CDI markets can be increased from higher advertising levels. In chapter 11, we discuss how geographic emphasis is handled strategically.

Reach: The Exposure Level

In chapter 7, **reach** is defined as a percentage of different target-market members potentially exposed to the advertising message within a specified time frame. Generation of a reach objective requires that several elements be in place:

1. Media research must be available that can verify whether the target-market level was achieved. The narrower the target description, the less likelihood of accurate reach estimation.

2. Reach level should not be arbitrarily selected. It should reflect what previous levels have been. Media planners realize that the exposure level must coordinate with other media goals. For example, reach must operate within continuity and frequency guidelines. Stressing one restricts the others.

3. Reach levels are often based on statistical probability. As such, they are not empirically precise. Media planners who know those limitations use a range of performance over an absolute number.

Once these considerations are addressed, the expression of a reach objective is rather straightforward. In the following situation, the planner has a relatively broad target audience and two intensity levels (introductory and sustaining) with which to deal:

"Achieve a minimum reach level of 75 with adult women (ages 18–49) during the initial

introductory quarter of the 1992–1993 campaign. The following sustaining period will achieve a target reach of at least 60."

In practice, the reach objective is often stated in concert with a frequency objective. Further, it is becoming more common to literally combine the reach and frequency levels (see chapter 12).

Frequency: The Degree of Repetition

At one time, reach was, by far, the most important measure of advertising impact. The more people exposed, the better it was for the brand. Today, frequency has an equal or even superior position to reach. **Frequency** is the number of times a target audience member may be exposed to the brand message within a set time frame. Perhaps, in this era of crowded brand categories, cluttered media environments, and falling audience attention levels, marketers realize that repeated exposure is the only chance to leave some impression with a target prospect.

As is true with the reach objective, media planners must have the necessary media research available, use some benchmark for frequency goals, and realize that frequency is an estimate and not absolutely precise.

How many times is enough? This is a good question that has no set answer. Frequency needs for a brand embrace many different variables, including consumer involvement, competitive pressure, message appeal, purchase cycle, and size/length of the advertising unit.

Frequency objectives are best set from brand-specific testing of alternative levels. The expression of the objective is a comparatively simple process:

"Media selections for 1992–1993 should deliver a target-audience exposure frequency of four times in each purchase cycle of thirty-five days."

The objective, then, is to schedule the vehicles at sufficient weight so that each member of the target audience has at least four chances for exposure within each five-week period. That some audience members might see or hear more than four messages in the cycle is acceptable. However, anyone under four exposures has not been acceptably "reached," and thus the frequency objective is not satisfied.

Other Media Objectives

Briefly, the following are some other subjects that may be suitable for objectives:

• *Target-Audience Priorities.* When multiple-target audiences are involved, recommended proportions of the advertising impressions can be distributed among the target segments (for example, 60 percent to adult women, 40 percent to adult men).

• *Scheduling Objectives.* This type of objective sets the calendar for advertising. Key days, weeks, months, or quarters may be recommended for exclusive advertising activity.

• *Share-of-Voice (SOV) Goals.* The SOV is the percentage of all competing product messages controlled by one brand. While hard to control, some firms insist on minimal-share objectives.

• *Cost-Per-Thousand (CPM).* No longer as popular as it once was, this type of objective does not allow purchase of a media vehicle when its audience-to-cost relationship is above the CPM goal.

Summary

Planning, at any level in marketing or advertising, cannot be effectively done without strategies, tactics, and above all, clear and precise objectives. Objectives are formal expressions of the most important tasks for successful sales performance. Objectives are based on recent history, current conditions, and expectations for the near future. They have three key roles in the planning process: (1) as guides to strategic decision making, (2) as personnel coordinators for the activities of campaign design, and (3) as a basis for campaign performance evaluation. To perform these important functions, objectives need certain characteristics: They should identify the most important decision areas, and they must be expressed in specific terms that are both measurable and achievable.

Many advertising campaigns utilize three levels of objectives: marketing, advertising, and media. Each successive set of goals reflects the antecedent objectives. Marketing objectives are sales and profit-oriented and give a general direction to advertising objectives. Advertising objectives, in turn, set out the principal needs of the communication plan, which involves objectives for media selection and scheduling.

Marketing objectives cover a broad base of company intentions. However, some of these (sales objectives, promotional mix objectives, and continuity objectives) are especially important in the development of advertising plans.

The role of advertising in the total plan is expressed in advertising objectives. These goals generally set directions regarding: (1) who the messages should be directed to, (2) what information and images should be conveyed, and (3) what communication effects are needed.

Media objectives translate relevant marketing and advertising needs into specific goals for media selection and scheduling. These objectives can dictate the media audience to be focused upon, the level of exposure (reach) and the frequency of the advertising, the timing and length, and the geographic pattern. Objective setting gives decision making the direction needed to search for the best advertising opportunities.

Questions for Discussion

1. Using your own illustration, compare and contrast objectives, strategies, and tactics.

2. In Media Spotlight 9.1, what were the Alcoa manager's reasons for not using campaign objectives? Do you see any reasons for his position? If you were the advertising agency representative, would you have designed objectives anyway (without Alcoa's help)? Why or why not?

3. The Ajax marketing/advertising planning group has designed an objective for every possible performance outcome. What is the central problem in overidentifying goals in a plan? Why do you suppose Ajax managers have tried to convert all measured outcomes into objectives?

4. The objectives that follow reflect some questionable approaches to objective setting. Identify the problem, and then recommend a necessary step or two that would improve or correct the situation.
   a. "Direct advertising to target markets showing superior performance."
   b. "Concentrate effort against current brand users."
   c. "Increase brand sales share from its introductory level of 1.2 to better than 5 percent by the end of the fiscal year."
   d. "Use media that offer optimum compatibility with target users."
   e. "Establish brand Alpha as a franchise to be feared by competitors."

5. Which marketing objective topics would have *direct* influence on media decisions? Name three such areas and discuss the influence.

6. In an objective, should marketing management use unit sales goals or share goals when the

firm's brand is (a) a new category entry? (b) an existing brand in a stable category? (c) an existing brand in an expanding category?

7. Why is ongoing research necessary to set many advertising communication objectives for an established brand?

8. Media objectives often are based on these questions: Who? Where? How often? and How long? Explain the connection of each question to the media strategy required.

9. The New Land Product Company develops products that are environmentally responsive. Its target audience for consumer magazines indicates a homemaker audience, 25–55 years of age, who live in *A* and *B* density countries, and who demonstrate an active concern for environmental problems. Set up a two-stage objective process to assist in magazine selection.

Suggested Readings

- Barban, Arnold M., Steven M. Cristol, and Frank J. Kopec. *Essentials of Media Planning: A Marketing Viewpoint.* 2d ed. Lincolnwood, Ill.: NTC Business Books, 1987. Chapter 4.

- Sissors, Jack Z., and Lincoln Bumba. *Advertising Media Planning.* 3d ed. Lincolnwood, Ill.: NTC Business Books, 1989. Chapter 12.

Identifying Target Audiences

Outline

Learning Objectives

In the study of this chapter, you will have the opportunity to:

- Appreciate the importance of targeting for media.
- Understand the different target labels: groups, markets, audiences.
- Learn the basic sources of target audience identification.
- Examine the different current methods of audience profiling and their limitations.
- See how the various audience profiles are applied in media planning.
- Assess direct matching as a revolutionary media selection approach.

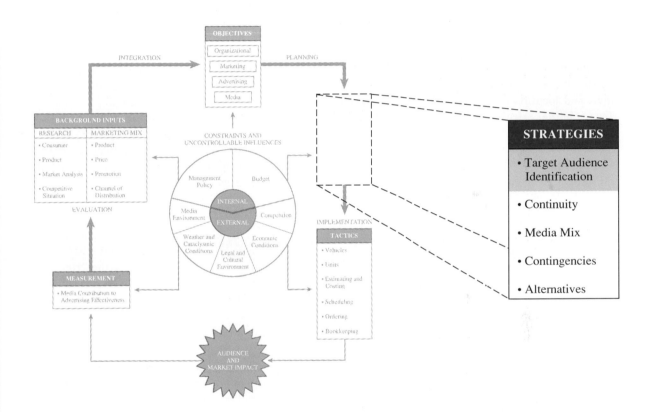

OBJECTIVES
- Organizational
- Marketing
- Advertising
- Media

INTEGRATION   PLANNING

BACKGROUND INPUTS

RESEARCH	MARKETING MIX
• Consumer	• Product
• Product	• Price
• Market Analysis	• Promotion
• Competitive Situation	• Channel of Distribution

EVALUATION

CONSTRAINTS AND
UNCONTROLLABLE INFLUENCES

Management Policy   Budget
Media Environment   Competition
INTERNAL
EXTERNAL
Weather and Cataclysmic Conditions   Economic Conditions
Legal and Cultural Environment

IMPLEMENTATION

MEASUREMENT
- • Media Contribution to Advertising Effectiveness

TACTICS
- • Vehicles
- • Units
- • Estimating and Costing
- • Scheduling
- • Ordering
- • Bookkeeping

AUDIENCE
AND
MARKET IMPACT

STRATEGIES
- • Target Audience Identification
- • Continuity
- • Media Mix
- • Contingencies
- • Alternatives

W hen planning objectives set the parameters of who to reach and when and where, they form the ideal opportunity for advertising exposure, called the target window. The media planners hope to locate an opening to expose the best prospects at a time and location that favor optimum persuasion. This chapter deals with part of that target window—the identification of key prospects in media audiences; that is, the separation of current and prospective consumers from other members of the media audience. Chapter 11 covers place and time, the other "dimensions" of the target window.

Why Targeting Is So Important

Currently, nothing challenges media professionals more than investigating media audiences for the profile characteristics desired. Here briefly listed are the major challenges. Factors that make this task most difficult are examined in the sections that follow.

1. Continued Source Expansion. In the past, people's television viewing was limited to only two or three channels. Today, cable and satellite technology offers what seems to be near limitless alternatives. Even in tight economic times, magazines flourish, radio stations multiply, and direct-response channels (mail and telemarketing) abound. Where once market segments were tightly confined by limited media, today they are widely spread. What was once a concentrated target has been replaced by many smaller and dispersed targets.

2. Mass Markets Are Anonymous. Time was when many retail businesspeople knew their customers by name. Now, with fewer salespeople in direct contact, regular customers are only recognized at the checkout registers. With the mass merchandiser, it has always been worse. Marketers are too far removed from the retail level to operate with any close surveillance of users and prospects. Instead, these firms operate with survey research profiles that offer only vague descriptions of who the customers are.

3. Adversity Costs Prohibitive. Six-figure rates for television and magazine unit costs increase the pressure of using the "right" media vehicles. Few advertisers can afford to blanket the airwaves and newsstands with messages.

4. Growth Niche Marketing. At one time, products used wide advertising nets for product introductions and brand development. Marketers today use narrow product positions directed at smaller (fractional) consumer groups. This small-segment strategy, known as niche marketing, demands more tightly focused advertising plans aimed at carefully defined target segments.

Target Labels: Groups, Markets, Audiences

The marketing terminology historically used to describe consumers has been imprecise. Even professionals occasionally interchange and confuse terms.

The three target classifications are groups, markets, and audiences, and these are described in detail in the sections that follow.

Prospect Groups

Some products and services have a general appeal to many consumers. To be in a **prospect group,** individuals only have to have some probability of purchasing. For example, even if you never personally consume soft drinks but will buy them for friends or guests, you are considered a member of the soft-drink prospect group as much as if you consumed a twelve-pack of the product every week. Similarly, airlines sell seats to all sorts of people for all sorts of reasons. A prospect could be any individual with some need, sooner or later, for air travel.

The difficulty with the prospect definition is that it does not separate the heavy users from the light, the brand loyal from the brand switchers. The cost of advertising demands that some prospects receive much more promotional attention than others. To achieve this, a tighter consumer portrait is needed.

Target Markets

The definition of prospects involves describing them geographically. Advertising and other promotional devices can then be directed to the areas where the best population concentrations for sales and profit opportunity are found. **Target markets** are the geographic boundaries (for example, regions, states, towns/cities, and metro segments) marketers use to locate customers and prospects.

Target markets are used in planning by all sizes of marketers. As we will see in chapter 11, even the largest companies set specific geographic priorities for campaigns.

Target Audiences

Target audiences are certain prospect groups, living in the selected target markets, who are identified for special advertising emphasis. Media planners and buyers must then select the media vehicles that will best expose these target audiences to the advertising message. For example, the advertising plan for an airline with a wide prospect group would select the kinds of travel to be emphasized. Marketing research would then provide a consumer description of those who do more of this type of travel and where they are located. The media planners would use target-audience descriptions to locate the priority individuals, and these are the profiles used to screen various media alternatives.

Target-Audience Sources

A number of research sources provide primary target-audience statistics. Some of these sources offer relatively general information, while others focus on the prospects of a single company or its brands. Some sources can be used at no cost, while others are very expensive. Chapters 4 and 5 discussed many source opportunities; here we review the highlights.

1. Government Sources. Most federal population sources are based on U.S. Census data collected every tenth year (last done in 1990). Projected updates are then provided in *The Statistical Abstract of the United States,* released yearly by the Department of Commerce. While a necessary foundation for population trends and the base for many selective profiles, these governmental data are too general for most marketing strategies.

2. Marketing (Sales) Sources. Independent market research firms provide much research on the marketplace and market audiences. Such companies as A. C. Nielsen monitor consumer retail activity. Other syndicated companies hire consumer panels that reflect changes in consumer behavior. Buyers and nonbuyers are carefully described. The combination of audience descriptions and buying patterns can be of immense help in selecting target audiences. Much of this information is shared among marketers to reduce research costs.

3. Media Audience Sources. As noted in chapter 5, virtually every medium's

audiences are monitored by independent research companies. Some, such as Arbitron, A. C. Nielsen, and Scarborough, provide basic social characteristics (for example, gender), while others, such as Simmons Market Research Bureau (SMRB) and Mediamark Research, Inc. (MRI), describe media audiences on purchase tendencies (brand users). Such services are expensive but are invaluable in media planning.

4. Customized Sources. Those marketers who can afford to underwrite special target-audience studies obtain the most precise information on target groups. These studies can involve one-shot survey forms or detailed, ongoing consumer panels. These sources are more fully discussed in the section on direct matching at the end of the chapter.

How Research Describes Marketing/Media Audiences

Advertisers have a number of different ways to describe audiences for media selection. The choice is dictated by company resources and, more importantly, by the needs of the product strategy. The challenge is straightforward: Which characteristics separate consumers into discrete segments that can be located in media audiences? More importantly, which characteristics best identify individuals who are sales prospects from those who are not? The following are some of the criteria used to evaluate which description method is best for a company:

1. Accuracy/Reliability. All descriptions are based on sample surveys of the population. The sample design and its size must be large enough to project the survey results to the full population. These sample estimates must also operate within acceptable levels of sample error. If the sample error is too large, the population projection loses much of its credibility and value.

2. Ability to Discriminate. Advertisers want audiences who are willing and able to make purchases. The best descriptions separate potential customers from noncustomers.

3. Segment Sizing. It is not practical to use an audience identification that so separates consumers that the marketer ends up with too many very small segments. Personality classifications are a good example. While some feel that personality types can separate consumer intentions, personality methods use so many categories that a mass communication strategy is impossibly complex. This means that each identified segment is so small that no mass medium could provide efficient coverage.

4. Contemporary Descriptions. Markets change, people change. "Female homemakers" was an adequate category in the past, but now homemakers must be separated by sex, and whether or not they are employed, and to what degree they are employed.

5. Application to Media Audiences. Consumer descriptions, regardless of detail, are of no benefit in media selection unless the same descriptions are found in audience analysis. Media planners need common denominators. To illustrate, a planner may have a brilliant set of personality characteristics that can neatly separate prospects from nonprospects. But this does not do any good if not a single magazine, newspaper, radio, or television program is measured in the same way. Media selection needs profile descriptions that can either be directly applied to media audiences (such as in demographics) or easily translated to media audience research.

Current Methods in Audience Profiling

This section highlights and illustrates some of the most popular methods of target identification. "Popular," in this case, refers to use and not

TABLE 10.1

Female Homemakers
Consumption Indices for Frozen Meals

Food Category	All	Unemployed	Working*
Frozen Pizza	100	90	115
Frozen Entrees	100	86	113
Frozen Dinners	100	95	108

*Working at least part-time.
Source: *Niche Marketing,* Mediamark Research, Inc., Spring 1987 Data, p. 7.

necessarily to the quality of performance. In fact, all the methods discussed have flaws, some more than others. No single method is perfect or ideal.

Demographics

Demographics is the oldest method used to describe target audiences and is also the most common because the information is easy to collect. Syndicated media research firms, such as MRI or SMRB, can report on sixty or more demographic characteristics. Still, the most usable social and economic profiles are usually: gender (sex), age, marital status, income, education achieved, and occupation.

Recently, changes in social trends have increased the value of certain more specialized categories, including working women and mothers, ages of children in household, home ownership, and individual employment income. Table 10.1 shows the influence of female employment on frozen meal purchases. Demographic research is also concerned with the size of characteristic groups in terms of trends and forecasts. These studies are particularly valuable when they identify expanding market segments, such as working women and the so-called mature market (adults over fifty).

Demographic research is used to describe purchasing segments (characteristics of those with buying/consumption patterns). It is also the most popular method for identifying media audiences. The depth of description depends on the media research source, although all media audiences are measured at least by age and gender.

Even though demographic research results in the easiest and most inexpensively learned characteristics, demographic data are often far from the ideal solution for targeting for the following reasons:

• *Too General.* Many of the segments used are too broad to identify a target audience without including many nonprospects. Peoples' buying habits do not always follow segment lines.

• *No Discrimination.* A demographic audience profile can have five to seven description categories. But which of these actually separates prospects from nonprospects? Using a characteristic that describes both product users and nonusers is pointless.

• *Not Reflective of Needs/Wants.* Social and economic status figures might reflect capability, but they are not based on marketing patterns, such as frequency of use, brands selected, and degree of loyalty.

• *Overprofiling.* When too many demographic elements are combined (that is, a prospect must have four or five of the valued characteristics), the audience becomes so small that the media planner is faced with searching for "the needle in the haystack." (See figure 10.1.)

While demographics have been used longer than any other profile measure, and are the easiest and least expensive to acquire, they are better utilized when "married" to other description methods, such as psychographics.

Psychographics

If two people were the same gender, age, and marital status, and if they both were home owners, were in the same occupation, and had similar educational backgrounds, would not their activities, priorities, and purchasing patterns be very similar? Not necessarily. Your college friends and acquaintances are mostly similar in basic demographics, but

MEDIA SPOTLIGHT

10.1

Who Are the Targets?

by Joe Mandese

Everyone seems to want a brand of their own. For mass marketers looking to put their finger on the next hot consumer trend, this is quite a dilemma. How can you efficiently develop new national brands for a population of individualists—a nation of rapidly moving targets brandishing increasingly smaller bull's-eyes?

"We're running out of ordinary people to have any kind of realistic target to shoot for," lamented social commentator/author Tom Wolfe, while addressing the recent annual conference of the American Association of Advertising Agencies. Wolfe pointed out that the advertising industry is confronted with the ultimate endangered marketing species: the American mass market.

"There used to be this wonderful category that was very predictable, no matter where you found them in the United States—the blue-collar worker," noted Wolfe. "He's disappeared. For one thing, he's wearing a Giorgio Armani elephant-collared shirt with cross sections of okra embroidered on the front panels. Remember the housewife? Not only is there no longer this great category known as the housewife, there are almost no housewives left. Fewer than 10 percent of households in the United States have, in residence, a woman who looks after children and the house."

Although there still are some pretty sizeable segments out there worth targeting, we asked consumer trends experts to give us a picture of what consumers will be like by the year 2000 and how their attitudes and lifestyles will affect branding opportunities.

These trends can be divided into five primary areas—demographics, psychographics, economics, geographics, and shifting lifestyle patterns—all of which are undergoing dramatic change.

Demographically, America is experiencing an enormous sea change, as the massive baby-boom generation enters midlife and approaches old age. The lead edge of the boomers will turn fifty in just eight years and will bring with them a whole new set of values and needs than those of previous mature markets. Indeed, by the year 2000, half of all Americans will be over the age of thirty-eight. The entire 18–34-year-old demo will shrink, along with the 25–34-year-old segment, which is where most ad dollars are currently directed. Growing the fastest will be the 45–54-year-old group, the 35–44s, and the over eighty-five population. Obviously, there is a whole lot of homework for an American marketing community raised on the youth culture to catch up on.

"Marketers that are relying on the young market have to recognize that franchise is declining in size, and they will have to target older consumers," notes J. Walter Thompson, senior vice president, and U.S. director of consumer research Peter Kim. "The problem is that for some of these brands, there may be little brand equity among older consumers, meaning they need to develop new products."

While the graying of the boomers certainly is an important demographic fact, it is not the only significant one taking place. The American household also is undergoing radical change as the percentage of working women increases. While the female head of the household still is the primary shopper in most homes, purchase decisions increasingly are being made by spouses and children, and this holds significant consequence for brands. Furthermore, divorce has created a society where there are more men and women living alone or heading households where children play an extremely active role in purchase decisions.

"Once upon a time, Dad worked and Mom stayed home and made the purchase decisions," notes Bozell senior vice president and director of strategic planning Larry Chiagouris. "Mom was very loyal to brands because part of her identity was based on the brands she bought. But today, the male head of the household is spending more time making purchase decisions, and kids—12–16 years old—are making more of the decisions," he notes.

Psychographically, American consumers are being affected by a multitude of changes. The aging phenomenon promises to create the most unique generation of old folks America has ever known as the boomers begin to mellow.

While older consumers tend to be particularly brand loyal, Campbell Mithun Esty's vice president of strategy development Tom Jonas points out that they may be harder to please than past generations. "Since the baby boomers are better educated than any generation before them, they're going to be much more discriminating consumers."

Meanwhile, several other psychographic trends appear to be emerging, including a new regard for socially conscious issues. "People are tired of being ripped off, whether it is someone polluting the environment, putting pesticides in their food, or investing in South Africa. People want to see companies become more accountable," observes Peter Flatow, president of the Brain-Reserve. He adds that he sees a "matriarchal swing" is currently reshaping consumer attitudes, meaning that traditionally "feminine" issues like the environment and ethics are seeping their way into the population at large.

Economically, consumer purchasing patterns also are in the midst of rampant change. The trend toward two-wage-earner households has contributed to the largest class of affluent Americans ever. Today, 57 percent of all households have two wage-earners, compared to 51 percent eight years ago. At the same time, however, a "bifurcation" of the marketplace is occurring, in which the lower-middle class—some forty-five million consumers earning between $15,000 and $30,000 annually—are getting economically squeezed. Although they had traditionally been one of the most brand-loyal segments, their economic pressures are leading to an erosion of brand loyalty.

Like the previously mentioned trends, geographic shifts in America promise to accelerate the proliferation of market segments. "There will be a continued shift to the Sunbelt, but this will be more communal living (for example, retirement communities)," forecasts Jim Reider, a senior staff professional of the consumer-products group of Arthur D. Little. "There will be more urbanization as working couples seek to live closer to the work place, but the escalating costs of housing will mean more apartment/condo/townhouse living. There will be a premium on living space."

"We've become a multitude of segments," noted Comart Associates senior vice president Calvin Hodock, in his introduction of the American Marketing Association's New Products Conference last spring. "Each segment is an individual entity endowed with its own uniqueness screaming for recognition of its needs. And, unfortunately or fortunately, the needs and wants of these segments are constantly shifting, creating inevitable new-product opportunities."

Source: Joe Mandese, "Who Are the Targets?" *Marketing and Media Decisions*, July 1989, 29–33.

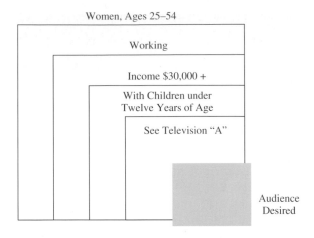

FIGURE 10.1 How Multiple Factors Affect Target Size

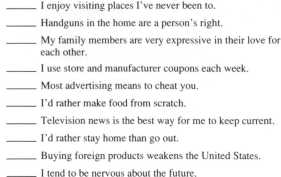

FIGURE 10.2 Sample Checklist for Psychographic Profiling

do they all like the same subjects, professors, music, clothes, and so on? Something besides demographics controls needs and wants.

Psychographics is a hybrid picture of consumers made from psychology, sociology, and some cultural spice. This research uses personal and group influences to describe market segments of similar beliefs, opinions, interests, and behaviors. Psychographics describes consumer segments bonded by common thoughts, feelings, and actions.

Psychographics may reflect personality traits (for example, serious, funny, aggressive), shopping principles (buy for best quality, lowest price, or well-known brand names), or how the consumer approaches new products or new brands (for example, likes to experiment, likes being the first, or waits until things have been well-tried and tested). The consumer's self-concept and shopping perspectives are obtained from samples of adults who fill out long questionnaires about all sorts of subjects. Figure 10.2 shows a selection of typical psychographic questions.

Researchers code questionnaire responses to form segments that hold a shared view (for example, economy shopper), an outlook (for example, traditional conservative), or a form of personality (for example, energetic/outgoing). These types of categories indicate: (1) reaction to different product positions: innovative, contemporary, or environmentally sensitive; (2) willingness to accept advertising and other sources of product information; (3) acceptance of risk or change.

The use of psychographics is primarily dictated by the product. New or introductory products might look at measures that indicate a person's willingness to try something new, to experiment, or to share initial reactions with others. A brand that is price-positioned may be looking for people who show conservative patterns, such as heavy coupon use, approval of store and generic brands, or rejection of frills and extras. Sample psychographic research on shopping tendencies is shown in figure 10.3. Because only a limited number of psychographic measures are found in media audience measurement, these characteristics are often used in conjunction with other target segmentations (for example, demographics, usage categories, and even geographic zip codes).

Although psychographic research can offer special insights to media planning, it has some serious shortcomings as a planning device. The following illustrate some of the limitations of psychographic research for media selection:

• *Risky Reliability.* The personal nature of psychographic characteristics puts the reliability of psychographic research results at risk. When an individual is asked whether he or she is one way or the other (for example, "Are you innovative?"), there is a great temptation to misrepresent feelings and positions to researchers (respondents tend to indicate how they would like to be, not how they are). To avoid this problem, survey questions must be more subtle, more indirect. But this forces researchers to use a number of situational evaluations that may or may not be pertinent to the segment category, which also may produce unreliable results.

• *Limited Availability.* Both SMRB and MRI provide some psychographics for their media audiences, but the accurate measurement difficulties, as just described, have limited the number of research companies featuring this sort of profiling. No regular psychographic measurement is done for some major media (for example, television, newspaper, radio, and direct mail).

• *Limited Translation to Media Audiences.* If the psychographic information comes from a nonmedia source, media planners probably cannot apply psychographics to a media evaluation process. Without a direct link to media habits, how could a planner know, for example, which television or radio programs have an audience of "experimental buyers" or people who are "socially outgoing"?

Lifestyles (Psycho/Demographics)

While lifestyle measurement is sometimes lumped in with discussions of psychographics, this method is sufficiently different to warrant a separate discussion. **Lifestyle profiles** are intended to reflect the consumer's priorities—that is, they measure commitment of time, money, and energy to activities, interests, and viewpoints. To gain perspective, lifestyle surveys cover all sorts of things we do and care about. Table 10.2 lists a number of lifestyle subjects, from which researchers can segment the population into some living patterns.

To make these categories functional for marketing and advertising, research firms design lifestyle categories that enable media planners to see the different segments. Perhaps the most famous

---

TABLE 10.2

Composite of Items That Reflect Lifestyles

Activities:	Sports, Other Recreation, Entertainment
Hobbies:	Collections, Leisure Pastimes
Interests:	Family Orientation, Sports, Music, Movies, Books, Art
Preferences:	Political, Social Causes, Media Sources
Attitudes/Positions:	Issues, Personalities
Career/Work:	Values, Satisfaction, Ambitions
Purchasing Habits:	Risk Taking, Search versus Impulse

---

lifestyle research is done by Stanford Research Institute International through its VALS-2 program. (The letters are an acronym for "values and lifestyles.") SRI reports three major social streams: (1) principle orientation, (2) status orientation, and (3) action orientation. Within these segments are eight subcategories, such as achievers, strivers, and strugglers. With such a category system, SRI believes it can assist marketers by predicting consumer purchasing behavior.

Problems of lifestyle measurement for media planning include:

• *Limited Availability.* Although SMRB has included some lifestyle data from SRI, this information is not generally available for media. This means that companies desiring lifestyle descriptions must contract for custom research, committing time and expense. For now, media planners have only limited access.

• *Limited Compatibility.* Lifestyle research has only limited application to media selection procedures. While advertisers might request some media data from lifestyle samples, this is not a major purpose for the research. Without direct

BUYING STYLE (FEMALE HOMEMAKERS)

	TOTAL U.S. '000	ECONOMY MINDED A '000	B % DOWN	C ACROSS %	D INDX	EXPERIMENTER A '000	B % DOWN	C ACROSS %	D INDX	IMPULSIVE A '000	B % DOWN	C ACROSS %	D INDX	PERSUASIBLE A '000	B % DOWN	C ACROSS %	D INDX
TOTAL FEMALE HOMEMAKERS	79807	35396	100.0	44.4	100	22950	100.0	28.8	100	18733	100.0	23.5	100	20116	100.0	25.2	100
BARRON'S	*236	**136	0.4	57.6	130	**81	0.4	34.3	119	**36	0.2	15.3	65	**17	0.1	7.2	29
BETTER HOMES & GARDENS	15586	7240	20.5	46.5	105	4345	18.9	27.9	97	3760	20.1	24.1	103	3966	19.7	25.4	101
BON APPETIT	2194	880	2.5	40.1	90	447	1.9	20.4	71	528	2.8	24.1	103	452	2.2	20.6	82
BUSINESS WEEK	1313	584	1.6	44.5	100	372	1.6	28.3	99	239	1.3	18.2	78	271	1.3	20.6	82
CAR AND DRIVER	314	*214	0.6	68.2	154	**152	0.7	48.4	168	**80	0.4	25.5	109	**33	0.2	10.5	42
CBS MAGAZINE NETWORK (GROSS)	2463	1196	3.4	48.6	109	910	4.0	36.9	128	602	3.2	24.4	104	569	2.8	23.1	92
CHANGING TIMES	1087	433	1.2	39.8	90	285	1.2	26.2	91	260	1.4	23.9	102	235	1.2	21.6	86
COLONIAL HOMES	1233	546	1.5	44.3	100	384	1.7	31.1	108	*226	1.2	18.3	78	355	1.8	28.8	114
CONDE NAST MAG. PKG. (GROSS)	12548	5484	15.5	43.7	99	3824	16.7	30.5	106	3125	16.7	24.9	106	3396	16.9	27.1	107
CONSUMERS DIGEST	1138	525	1.5	46.1	104	257	1.1	22.6	79	339	1.8	29.8	127	270	1.3	23.7	94
COSMOPOLITAN	6885	2809	7.9	40.8	92	2210	9.6	32.1	112	1677	9.0	24.4	104	1687	8.4	24.5	97
COUNTRY LIVING	1904	750	2.1	39.4	89	608	2.6	31.9	111	418	2.2	22.0	94	377	1.9	19.8	79
CUISINE	1341	623	1.8	46.5	105	363	1.6	27.1	94	313	1.7	23.3	99	326	1.6	24.3	96
CYCLE WORLD	*206	**105	0.3	51.0	115	**152	0.7	73.8	257	**109	0.6	52.9	225	**35	0.2	17.0	67
DECORATING & CRAFT IDEAS	2244	1043	2.9	46.5	105	661	2.9	29.5	102	560	3.0	25.0	106	494	2.5	22.0	87
DEC CRFT ID/SOUTH LIV (GROSS)	6102	2916	8.2	47.8	108	1761	7.7	28.9	100	1458	7.8	23.9	102	1491	7.4	24.4	97
DISCOVER	775	329	0.9	42.5	96	241	1.1	31.1	108	*198	1.1	25.5	109	*161	0.8	20.8	82
EBONY	3579	1616	4.6	45.2	102	1068	4.7	29.8	104	749	4.0	20.9	89	961	4.8	26.9	107
ESQUIRE	744	319	0.9	42.9	97	*212	0.9	28.5	99	*120	0.6	16.1	69	*157	0.8	21.1	84
ESSENCE	1812	805	2.3	44.4	100	613	2.7	33.8	118	461	2.5	25.4	108	490	2.4	27.0	107
FAMILY CIRCLE	15476	7411	20.9	47.9	108	4537	19.8	29.3	102	3683	19.7	23.8	101	3914	19.5	25.3	100
THE FAMILY HANDYMAN	1038	515	1.5	49.6	112	282	1.2	27.2	94	292	1.6	28.1	120	351	1.7	33.8	134
FAMILY WEEKLY	12311	5789	16.4	47.0	106	3584	15.6	29.1	101	3276	17.5	26.6	113	3460	17.2	28.1	112
FIELD & STREAM	1750	871	2.5	49.8	112	529	2.3	30.2	105	507	2.7	29.0	123	556	2.8	31.8	126
FOOD & WINE	572	*160	0.5	28.0	63	*108	0.5	18.9	66	*165	0.9	28.8	123	**95	0.5	16.6	66
FORBES	855	344	1.0	40.2	91	*242	1.1	28.3	98	*175	0.9	20.5	87	**112	0.6	13.1	52
FORTUNE	820	271	0.8	33.0	75	*305	1.3	37.2	129	*165	0.9	20.1	86	*164	0.8	20.0	79
GENTLEMEN'S QUARTERLY	698	287	0.8	41.1	93	*204	0.9	29.2	102	*204	1.1	29.2	125	**98	0.5	14.0	56
GLAMOUR	4561	1848	5.2	40.5	91	1373	6.0	30.1	105	1190	6.4	26.1	111	1260	6.3	27.6	110
GOLF DIGEST	590	*216	0.6	36.6	83	*166	0.7	28.1	98	**105	0.6	17.8	76	*171	0.9	29.0	115
GOLF DIGEST/TENNIS (GROSS)	1113	459	1.3	41.2	93	380	1.7	34.1	119	*181	1.0	16.3	69	307	1.5	27.6	109
GOLF MAGAZINE	385	*148	0.4	38.4	87	**121	0.5	31.4	109	**91	0.5	23.6	101	**123	0.6	31.9	127
GOLF DIGEST/SKI (GROSS)	843	291	0.8	34.5	78	*241	1.1	28.6	99	*176	0.9	20.9	89	*206	1.0	24.4	97
GOOD HOUSEKEEPING	15927	7175	20.3	45.0	102	4926	21.5	30.9	108	3861	20.6	24.2	103	4266	21.2	26.8	106
GRIT	1505	914	2.6	60.7	137	546	2.4	36.3	126	427	2.3	28.4	121	386	1.9	25.6	102

FIGURE 10.3 Simmons Market Research Bureau's Psychographic Measurement Data
Source: Simmons Market Research.

measures of media preferences, media planners have no direct means of locating the lifestyle category in media audiences.

• *Limited Validity.* The research community has complained about VALS applications, saying that many product-purchasing segments do not fit into VALS categories or that the VALS segments cannot predict product interest.[1] What seems good in theory may be less valuable in practice.

Usage and Usage Levels

A more sales-oriented segmentation method can classify audience members by their purchasing patterns of products and services. The **usage-level method** is fairly simple. Sample group members are asked whether they use the product category. The answer puts them in either a user or nonuser segment. If in a user segment, questioning then determines the intensity or level of use. Degrees of use

BUYING STYLE (FEMALE HOMEMAKERS)

	TOTAL U.S. '000	ECONOMY MINDED A '000	B % DOWN	C % ACROSS	D INDEX	EXPERIMENTER A '000	B % DOWN	C % ACROSS	D INDEX	IMPULSIVE A '000	B % DOWN	C % ACROSS	D INDEX	PERSUASIBLE A '000	B % DOWN	C % ACROSS	D INDEX
TOTAL FEMALE HOMEMAKERS	79807	35396	100.0	44.4	100	22950	100.0	28.8	100	18733	100.0	23.5	100	20116	100.0	25.2	100
HARPER'S BAZAAR	2218	847	2.4	38.2	86	672	2.9	30.3	105	484	2.6	21.8	93	514	2.6	23.2	92
HEALTH	1452	692	2.0	47.7	107	522	2.3	36.0	125	313	1.7	21.6	92	323	1.6	22.2	88
HEARST MAG. CORP. BUY (GROSS)	41949	18420	52.0	43.9	99	12927	56.3	30.8	107	10171	54.3	24.2	103	10743	53.4	25.6	102
HEARST MAN POWER (GROSS)	1883	936	2.6	49.7	112	590	2.6	31.3	109	444	2.4	23.6	100	432	2.1	22.9	91
HEARST WOMAN POWER (GROSS)	29909	13302	37.6	44.5	100	9255	40.3	30.9	108	7629	40.7	25.5	109	7873	39.1	26.3	104
HOUSE BEAUTIFUL	3784	1575	4.4	41.6	94	1148	5.0	30.3	105	786	4.2	20.8	88	916	4.6	24.2	96
INC.	*207	**68	0.2	32.9	74	**59	0.3	28.5	99	**32	0.2	15.5	66	**15	0.1	7.2	29
JET	2697	1174	3.3	43.5	98	867	3.8	32.1	112	539	2.9	20.0	85	780	3.9	28.9	115
LADIES' HOME JOURNAL	11122	5196	14.7	46.7	105	3340	14.6	30.0	104	2862	15.3	25.7	110	3020	15.0	27.2	108
LHJ FAMILY GRP COMBO (GROSS)	14614	6814	19.3	46.6	105	4551	19.8	31.1	108	3684	19.7	25.2	107	3895	19.4	26.7	106
LIFE	3988	1821	5.1	45.7	103	1179	5.1	29.6	103	1013	5.4	25.4	108	951	4.7	23.8	95
L.A. TIMES HOME MAGAZINE	1120	422	1.2	37.7	85	191	0.8	17.1	59	253	1.4	22.6	96	206	1.0	18.4	73
MADEMOISELLE	2597	1276	3.6	49.1	111	886	3.9	34.1	119	693	3.7	26.7	114	756	3.8	29.1	115
MC CALL'S	13358	6297	17.8	47.1	106	4240	18.5	31.7	110	3278	17.5	24.5	105	3589	17.8	26.9	107
MC CALL'S/WRK MOTHER (GROSS)	14302	6753	19.1	47.2	106	4513	19.7	31.6	110	3555	19.0	24.9	106	3775	18.8	26.4	105
MECHANIX ILLUSTRATED	699	361	1.0	51.6	116	*201	0.9	28.8	100	**125	0.7	17.9	76	*197	1.0	28.2	112
METROPOLITAN HOME	821	284	0.8	34.6	78	231	1.0	28.1	98	**229	1.2	27.9	119	*152	0.8	18.5	73
MONEY	1568	725	2.0	46.2	104	532	2.3	33.9	118	262	1.4	16.7	71	311	1.5	19.8	79
MOTHER EARTH NEWS	1235	552	1.6	44.7	101	420	1.8	34.0	118	346	1.8	28.0	119	*246	1.2	19.9	79
MS.	852	349	1.0	41.0	92	*183	0.8	21.5	75	*140	0.7	16.4	70	*152	0.8	17.8	71
NATIONAL ENQUIRER	10228	4708	13.3	46.0	104	3108	13.5	30.4	106	2826	15.1	27.6	118	2791	13.9	27.3	108
NATIONAL GEOGRAPHIC	9123	3893	11.0	42.7	96	2476	10.8	27.1	94	2082	11.1	22.8	97	2078	10.3	22.8	90
NATIONAL SUNDAY MAGAZINE PKG	46735	20633	58.3	44.1	100	13614	59.3	29.1	101	11306	60.4	24.2	103	12261	61.0	26.2	104
NATURAL HISTORY	549	*209	0.6	38.1	86	*128	0.6	23.3	81	**82	0.4	14.9	64	**103	0.5	18.8	74
NEWSWEEK	6275	2504	7.1	39.9	90	1618	7.1	25.8	90	1574	8.4	25.1	107	1348	6.7	21.5	85
NEW YORK INCLUDING CUE	574	163	0.5	28.4	64	*131	0.6	22.8	79	*156	0.8	27.2	116	*91	0.5	15.9	63
THE N.Y. TIMES DAILY EDITION	1179	391	1.1	33.2	75	331	1.4	28.1	98	243	1.3	20.6	88	*138	0.7	11.7	46
THE N.Y. TIMES MAGAZINE	1720	591	1.7	34.4	77	435	1.9	25.3	88	311	1.7	18.1	77	230	1.1	13.4	53
THE NEW YORKER	1148	407	1.1	35.5	80	282	1.2	24.6	85	241	1.3	21.0	89	309	1.5	26.9	107
OMNI	652	247	0.7	37.9	85	*198	0.9	30.4	106	*207	1.1	31.7	135	*134	0.7	20.6	82
ON CABLE	834	380	1.1	45.6	103	280	1.2	33.6	117	252	1.3	30.2	129	*199	1.0	23.9	95
1001 HOME IDEAS	2040	926	2.6	45.4	102	689	3.0	33.8	117	509	2.7	25.0	106	552	2.7	27.1	107
ORGANIC GARDENING	1657	885	2.5	53.4	120	473	2.1	28.5	99	343	1.8	20.7	88	497	2.5	30.0	119
OUI	*176	**129	0.4	73.3	165	**90	0.4	51.1	178	**73	0.4	41.5	177	**57	0.3	32.4	128
OUTDOOR LIFE	1054	606	1.7	57.5	130	327	1.4	31.0	108	*240	1.3	22.8	97	*252	1.3	23.9	95
PARADE MAGAZINE	22500	10064	28.4	44.7	101	6676	29.1	29.7	103	5494	29.3	24.4	104	5843	29.0	26.0	103

are then combined. The most common way to indicate each group usage level is by heavy use, medium use, and light use.

Level of use is a good discriminating variable when the volume of purchasing is controlled by a disproportionately small segment of the population. The skew (intensity) of usage signals that some segments are much more valuable as brand customers than others. For example, an airline is likely to target its advertising message to those individuals who make over twenty-five trips per year, instead of to those who make three or less. See table 10.3 for more of these categories where heavy users dominate.

For advertisers wanting a bottom-line audience identification method, classification by usage is effective. For media-planning purposes, usage segment can simplify vehicle selection *if* usage-level

MEDIA SPOTLIGHT
10.2

A Mature Perspective

by George P. Moschis

The increasing size and wealth of the older adult population has captured the attention of marketers and advertisers. However, practitioners know relatively little about this segment, and many decisions are based on intuition or common beliefs about older people. Unfortunately, many of these beliefs are simply not true, and they could result in costly, wrong decisions.

Examples of common myths about the senior market include:

- *Older people are all alike.* When one looks more closely at this segment, she or he discovers that the older consumer market is heterogeneous; it consists of people who look different, think different, and act different. And the longer the people live, the greater the differences between them.

- *Older people are unwilling to try new things.* Although older consumers may not be early adopters of new products and services, they do not necessarily resist new products. Studies show that, for example, they would quickly adopt high-tech products and services to the extent that

these products provide them with direct benefits.

- *Older adults are brand loyal and will not switch.* Not necessarily so. The less affluent tend to switch brands to get the most value for their money. The more affluent are more likely to remain loyal primarily for convenience, although they switch for variety.

- *Older people feel and act differently than younger people.* Research shows just the opposite, suggesting that perceived age is a more reliable indicator of a person's behavior and lifestyle than chronological age.

- *The older consumer market is static. The things we know about the market today will also hold true tomorrow.* This is a fallacy. As cohorts move through time, they become different because of social and cultural changes, age norms, and cumulative effects of previous experiences. What appeals to older people today might not appeal to the elderly of tomorrow.

Decision makers should take another look at the available evidence regarding the mature market and begin formulating strategies based upon facts, not misconceptions. Unfortunately, even facts are often difficult to interpret in such a way that they would prove of maximum benefit. Marketing

Matching Target Groups with Target Audiences

Matching is the process of comparing consumer target-group characteristics with the available media audience profiles. However, as already stressed, this matching process is far from perfect. Media planners and buyers cope with imperfect

matches in different ways. As the sections that follow show, some of these remedies are no more than translations from one data form to another, while others call for more intuitive and creative responses.

How does a media planner select media when the characteristics of the target consumer are not used in measuring media audiences? This situation is common with radio, newspapers, television, and managers and market researchers do not have adequate background in the fields of aging, social psychology, and other areas that help provide rich understanding into the behavior of older adults. It is no surprise, therefore, that much of the existing market research has placed emphasis on gathering descriptive information on older consumers and has contributed very little to our understanding of the reasons for their behavior. Social scientists, on the other hand, have been studying the aging person's behavior for several decades, but they have provided little information that could be easily interpretable and implemented into strategy.

Experts from various fields must begin to work closer together. Marketers must also be willing to dismiss certain assumptions and begin reevaluating the available methods for reaching markets in the specific context of marketing to older consumers.

For example, while existing segmentation criteria and methodologies enjoy a fairly high level of sophistication, segmentation of the older consumer is currently at a primitive stage of development and application. In most cases, the market is segmented by age, and only a few cases are found where other bases, such as cognitive age and lifestyles, have been suggested. There is a greater need in developing effective bases for segmentation than simply suggesting a number of possible ways. Given our limited understanding of this market, companies must be willing to use, compare, and validate various methods and to choose those most viable for their products.

We must also be willing to evaluate existing marketing practices in the context of new information about older persons. For example, because older consumers do not like to be "stereotyped" or singled out as a special segment, products should be positioned by feature (benefit or value-added) rather than target (for older people).

In sum, successful marketing to older adults requires dismissal of unfounded beliefs about older people, greater reliance on valid data, ability to understand and interpret the evidence prior to implementation, and a broad-minded perspective on existing marketing tools and use of strategies that have the highest likelihood of being effective with older consumers.

Source: George P. Moschis, "A Mature Perspective," *Marketing and Media Decisions*, May 1988, 168.

out-of-home media. There is no simple way or standard procedure to translate one profile to the other with high reliability. Some marketers surrender and conform their target research to simple demographic variables that can be monitored in the media. Others instruct their media people to use content judgments to estimate the attraction of certain audience types. Still others resort to periodic or even informal surveys of customers to learn of customers' media preferences (see the section on direct matching later in this chapter).

Using Multidimensional Target Profiles

A target group profile for a housewares or food manufacturer often appears as follows:

- Working women
- Ages 25–54
- Household income over $30,000
- Children under twelve years of age

TABLE 10.4

An Age-Segment Profile of Two Magazines

Magazine	Readers	Readers 25–54 yrs.
A	1,000,000	600,000
B	1,000,000	400,000

What this means is that the ideal media audience prospect has all of these variables. Target descriptions of this nature pose several problems. The first, already discussed, is that virtually none of the media can readily break out (separate) an audience with this special combination of characteristics. Cross tabulation of four or five variables (employment status, gender, age, income, and presence of children) is not attempted in syndicated reports for the practical reason that the statistical limitations of such a combination would render the audience estimate meaningless.

As figure 10.1 demonstrates, each additional variable makes the target smaller and smaller. In a general media survey done by SMRB or MRI, which may consist of twenty thousand or so interviews, fewer than a hundred women are likely to fit each of the manufacturer's target specifications. And that small group would be further split by individual media preferences. Who would believe a national estimate of *Good Housekeeping* readers in this custom profile if that estimate was based on ten or twelve women? A media professional would not even consider it.

Yet, multidimensional profiles are a reality. And to deal with such situations, media analysts employ a different approach for selecting media or vehicles. Instead of a composite profile (all variables used simultaneously), each variable's audience is used separately to show the strength of an individual profile factor. For example, suppose a media planner had a profile of three demographics (males, ages 25–44, professional or managerial work). If the intended medium is magazines, each of the desired audience segments could be pulled from syndicated research. Table 10.5 shows a sample arrangement.

To select the strongest magazine in the three audience categories, media planners could compare the summed totals. Obviously, the totals are not necessarily different readers. A magazine with the same reader in all three segments would be counting that reader three times. The totals, then, are only for comparison purposes. The logical assumption is that the magazine with the largest number is most likely to deliver the most males with the other two demographic features. An alternative to using the audience figure is to rank each vehicle (for example, first place, second place, and so on) on a dimension and sum the rankings. Either evaluation method is relatively effective when a multidimensional target is demanded by the plan.

Using Target Variable Priorities

In the previous section, three audience dimensions were treated with equal importance. What if the audience strategy dictates that each feature varies in its contribution to the target—for example, that occupation is more important than age? Similarly, in another situation, suppose a marketer has two very different audiences for a product or service. This is common for family-oriented products that must be promoted to parents and children.

When media planners must cope with either multiple characteristics or audiences, the vehicle selection process involves a weighted evaluation system. Weighting is a statistical method of assigning numerical priorities to each variable. The following are the steps in weighting the variables:

1. Identify the audience characteristics to be used. Each variable must be available from audience research.

2. Assign value or importance priorities to each characteristic. This task is usually done at a marketing management level and should be directed by the company's market research.

TABLE 10.5

Sample Profile of Readers of Four Magazines

| | Readers (in Thousands) | | |
Magazine	Male	25–44 yrs.	Prof/MGR
A	250.3	120.2	50.4
B	320.5	100.6	40.6
C	200.4	90.4	78.5
D	350.0	170.3	60.3

TABLE 10.6

Adult Women Readers of Three Newspapers

| | Women Readers (in Thousands) | | | | | | |
Newspaper	18–24	Weighted	25–34	Weighted	35–44	Weighted	Total
A	54.3		91.3		72.7		
B	23.9		66.2		52.2		
C	28.1		49.0		41.6		

3. Apply the number priorities as factors to each media vehicle's audiences.

4. Combine (sum) the adjusted audiences for comparisons between the media alternatives.

The following example bases newspaper selection on an age demographic. A cosmetic product has an adult women target audience in three age ranges: 18–24, 25–34, and 35–44. While each segment has strategic importance, the younger the woman, the better the prospect. From research, the marketer has determined that the 18–24 group has a target value of 0.50, that the 25–34 group has a target value of 0.30, and that the 35–44 group has a target value of 0.20. The media buyer begins by compiling a table (see table 10.6). The weights are then ap-plied by multiplying the target value factor by the reader audience in each segment. The "weighted" columns are then totaled, with table 10.7 showing the results.

The weighted figures in table 10.7, when compared with space costs (CPM analysis), give media analysts a much better comparison for the newspapers. These weighted numbers have no function or value other than to compare one newspaper's audience value with another. Weighting can be applied to any medium and can be adapted to any of the audience profile categories (for example, psychographics, usage levels, and so on). Weighting is also popular in geographic scheduling (discussed in chapter 11).

TABLE 10.7							∘ ∘

Weighted Reader Values of Three Newspapers

	Women Readers (in Thousands)						
Newspaper	*18–24*	*Weighted*	*25–34*	*Weighted*	*35–44*	*Weighted*	*Total*
A	54.3	27.2	91.3	27.4	72.7	14.5	69.1
B	23.9	12.0	66.2	19.9	52.2	10.4	42.3
C	28.1	14.1	49.0	14.7	41.6	8.3	37.1

Dealing with New or Changed Media Vehicles

A perplexing matching problem concerns media vehicles that are so new that audience research is unavailable. Some analysts would conclude that these media opportunities should be avoided until reliable media audience data are available. This is a safe approach, but shortsighted in certain situations. Some examples follow.

Television programming is a rather unstable commodity. It is constantly changing. Old programs are canceled and replaced by others. Others are continued from season to season but scheduled for different days or time periods, usually with different lead-in programs. Invariably, media professionals are faced with program alternatives that are not reflected in past research, if they have been measured at all!

Television is not the sole proprietor of change. Radio stations change personalities and formats, as do magazines and, to some extent, newspapers. All changes can affect the size and composition of the audiences.

The question is: Can media analysts accurately forecast either current or future audience composition without benefit of audience research? Unfortunately, there are no surefire techniques or solutions. The best judgments are made with professional experience, insight, and a well-organized research history of patterns and trends.

Because television planning usually requires more of this type of forecasting than the other consumer media, it is the best medium for illustration. Some of the major questions to be considered in forecasting a television program's audience size (popularity) and composition are:

* *Type of Content.* Programming content tends to preselect the sorts of individuals who are interested. Rating evaluations of past and current profiles of sports events, nighttime dramas or situation comedies can give planners a pattern of audience attraction.

* *Program Profile.* The style or approach of the specific program is also considered. "Murphy Brown" and "Alf" were both (topically) situation comedies, but the respective entertainment approaches attracted widely divergent audiences.

* *Time-Period Slotting.* Audience size and composition are strongly influenced by day of the week and time of day. Television researchers use past usage patterns by target characteristics to create adjustment factors to be applied to the "new" time conditions. For example, table 10.8 shows television use indicators between working and nonworking women. Note that a program's chances of reaching a working woman increase (with an early-morning exception) as the day progresses.

Direct Matching: Aggressive Methods of Learning about Media Audience Preferences

TABLE 10.8

Television Viewing Differences between Employed and Nonemployed Women

	Indexed to Total Women Viewers (100)	
Daypart	Employed	Nonemployed
6–9 A.M. (M–F)	73	133
9–4 P.M. (M–F)	50	158
4–7 P.M. (M–F)	74	131
8–11 P.M. (M–F)	92	106

Source: MRI Report, Spring 1989.

In this age of intensified segmentation, when target-consumer segments become narrower and narrower, media analysts and market researchers show increased dissatisfaction with target identification procedures. Use of demographics, psychographics, and other such "social statistics" often amounts to crude guesswork in consumer identification. Media planners face serious hurdles in selecting media vehicles from some generalized or indirect profile. The problems in matching have prompted some marketers to consider a more positive method of target definition. The system is called **direct matching.**

Media selection from direct matching involves a logical, uncomplicated, four-step procedure:

Step 1: A sample of people who will identify their use of the product category and brand preferences is selected. Such a survey might include the following segments: (1) those not using the category now but who intend to do so in the near future, (2) those using the company's brand on a somewhat exclusive basis (brand loyal), (3) those using competing brands on a loyal basis (other brand loyals), and (4) those who buy the category but have no particular loyalty (brand switchers).

Step 2: Sample members are questioned about their media habits: newspapers and magazines read, television shows watched, stations listened to, and so on. This audit of media preferences and priorities should be specific enough to clearly identify preferences.

Step 3: Those groups to be targeted for the advertising campaign are selected.

Step 4: The media preferences of the target audience are studied. Media planners determine which media alternatives offer the highest concentrations of brand loyals, switchers, and so on. This allows some forecast potential based on program types.

- *Competing Programming.* VCR use notwithstanding, people have to choose which program to view in a time segment. History shows that new programs usually have a hard time attracting audiences from well-entrenched competing programs.

- *Lead-ins (Preceding Program).* Though each program is capable of attracting its own audience, a strong audience base flows from one show to another. New shows following established programs are assured better tune-in. Conversely, a low-popularity program preceding a new show puts a heavy burden on the new show's audience attraction. Through careful analysis of past lead-in patterns, forecasters can accurately adjust audience potentials for new programs or for those that receive new slottings.

Forecasting audience acceptance is an intuitive process that demands thoughtful analysis of past trends and patterns, experienced evaluation, and some luck. It is a highly desired skill for media professionals.

In effect, this single source (users of products/ users of media) uses custom research as a substitute for syndicated media research. With direct matching, a selection of magazines, for example, would not be influenced as much by the number of readers as by the proportion (percent) of readers who are other-brand loyals or any other desired segment. Single-source analysis does not ignore audience size, but it does hold it to a lower influence on media selection.

What these specifications lead up to is a research program that commands serious corporate investment of time and money. To gain the rewards of customized research, a company has to be willing to dedicate its energy to a long-term project. And it has to use the findings as a central focus in its marketing and advertising plans. To date, such commitments are fairly rare, despite continued displeasure with the normal audience measurements.

Marketing interest in direct matching, however, has prompted some media research companies (for example, A. C. Nielsen, SMRB, MRI, and Arbitron) to provide advertisers with more single-source research. If these services develop and are accepted, direct matching of buying audiences with media audiences may become the norm, rather than the exception. Media planning might then become more of a reliable science than an art.

Summary

The continued increase in media cost and the potential of wasted advertising make the identification of campaign targets a vital step in media planning and buying. Target identification involves three levels. Prospect groups identify all individuals who have at least minimal sales potential. Target markets are the geographic areas where target audiences live. These areas may be described as regions, states, metropolitan markets, or counties. Target audiences are those within the prospect group that have been selected for advertising emphasis. Selection could be based on numerous factors, including current brand(s) being used, amount of use of the product category, or individuals about to purchase for the first time.

Whether target-audience research comes from government data, syndicated sources, or the firm's own research studies, the method of audience identification must pass certain standards. Audience research must be accurate and reliable, must discriminate reasonably between target and nontarget members, and must present up-to-date identification categories of reasonable size. Above all, for media planning, the characteristics should be compatible with available audience descriptions from the media.

Six major approaches used to describe target audiences are: demographics, psychographics, lifestyles, usage-level segments, geodemographics, and company-sponsored profile research. Each method has some capability of identification as well as specific limitations. The choice of methods should carefully parallel the market circumstances of the advertiser's product.

Media planning has to adapt target-audience profiles to the media selection procedure. Particular difficulties in this task arise when the consumer profile is substantially different from available media audience profiles. Special techniques are also required in handling multidimensional profiles and for campaigns that involve two or more separate audiences. Particular planning skill is needed when the available media vehicles are new or significantly changed so that available audience research is inappropriate or simply nonexistent.

Marketers in complicated circumstances and those using sensitive segmentation strategies may undertake a special audience identification procedure called direct matching. Direct matching uses customized survey samples to simultaneously measure purchasing segments and media preferences. While this method involves serious investments in time and expense, its potential for highly reliable media placements is unrivaled.

Questions for Discussion

1. For a fictional brand of your choice, set up the three possible descriptions: prospect group, target market, and target audience. Which of these will *least* affect the media plan? Why?

2. Why do most consumer-product advertisers use target-audience descriptions found in syndicated research? What is the definition of a syndicated source?

3. Each profiling method is somewhat limited in its use as a target-audience descriptor. Which of the limitations seems to affect media planners and buyers? Explain.

4. Psychographics and lifestyle profiles are often described as a single method, but in the chapter, they were pointedly separated. How was this justified?

5. Usage-level segmentation is particularly valuable when volume is skewed to certain identified groups. What does this mean? Give some personal examples where consumption appears to be skewed.

6. What social principle seems to explain why demographics and geographics can be combined? What is the source of the geographic control?

7. Develop a step-by-step evaluation scheme for a brand directed to adult males by age categories. All age segments should have some target value. Assume that your scheme would be used to evaluate which late-night television news show should be recommended for sponsorship.

8. A magazine has some editorial direction that could be valuable for your client. The problem is that the magazine is only nine months old and will not have SMRB or MRI measurement for at least twelve to eighteen months. Is there anything you can do to estimate a target audience? Explain.

9. In what ways can direct matching improve the media selection process?

Endnote

1. "New VALS-2 Takes Psychological Route," *Advertising Age,* 13 February 1989, 24.

Suggested Readings

• Barban, Arnold M., Steven M. Cristol, and Frank J. Kopec. *Essentials of Media Planning: A Marketing Viewpoint.* 2d ed. Lincolnwood, Ill.: NTC Business Books, 1987. Chapter 3.

• Sissors, Jack Z., and Lincoln Bumba. *Advertising Media Planning.* 3d ed. Lincolnwood, Ill.: NTC Business Books, 1989. Chapter 8.

Chapter 11

Determining Scheduling Strategies (Where, When, How Long?)

Outline

Learning Objectives

In the study of this chapter, you will have the opportunity to:

- Understand how scheduling (placement) is vital to successful media planning.
- Learn how to set up a sales-performance analysis that produces "fair-share" allocations to target markets.
- Appreciate how the selection of advertising time frames improves the selling opportunity.
- Recognize how pulse and flight strategies can balance reach, frequency, and continuity objectives.

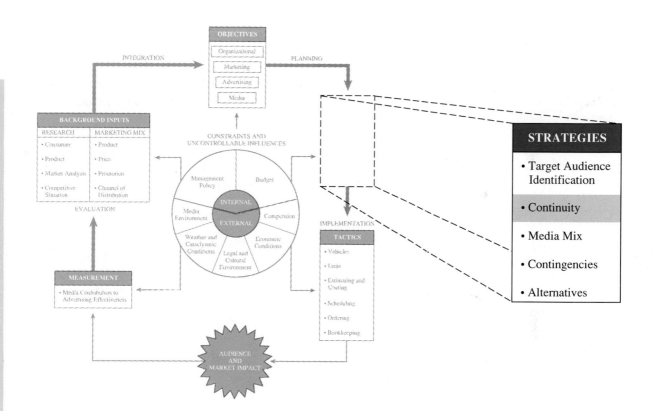

*A*s discussed in chapter 10, media planners' ideal goal is to provide an exposure opportunity to a target audience. While finding *the* target prospect is vitally important, so are the time and place of the connection. The "Media Decision-Making Process" in figure 1.4 indicates a strategy called continuity, which involves decisions regarding where, when, and for how long? This chapter deals with these scheduling dimensions of the "advertising window."

Scheduling and the "Advertising Window"

The goal for strategic answers to where, when, and for how long is based on finance (advertising investment). The funds available for an advertising campaign are absolute and limited. This forces media planners to prioritize. In chapter 10, this meant not advertising to everyone. The same principle applies in scheduling. Marketing regions are not alike; some have much more sales potential than others. Similarly, the sales calendar is not equal, month after month, week after week, and day after day; some time frames are much better than others. Scheduling priorities also involve the length of the schedule. For example, while advertising funds might be stretched to cover every week, the level of advertising would then probably become too thin. All of these dimensions call for strategies—strategies to find the "advertising window."

Media planners approach priorities through a process of allocation, not to be confused with budgeting. Budgeting, the initial determination of available advertising dollars, is not a media function and is performed by top company managers in consultation with marketing professionals. Media planners and buyers must live with the dollars set aside for advertising, especially the dollars designated for time and space. How these dollars are divided is the process of allocation. Priorities are set by allocating more dollars to one group, to one market, or to one time frame than another.

Scheduling Priorities and the Marketing Plan

Countless strategies may contribute to the scheduling process, but the three used most often are:

1. Sales Area Strategy. Marketing success invariably centers on location. Sales geography is a mix of distribution, consumer demand, and the study of competitors' activity, and can produce widely divergent sales performance. When advertising dollars are appropriated, decisions have to be made about which area gets how much. Two of the many ways to monitor and project sales territory performance in consumer marketing are demonstrated in this chapter.

2. Timing Strategies. Fiber-optic scanning at retail stores, in addition to its other contributions, has proven that consumer purchasing patterns are highly complex. The timing of when consumers decide and when they purchase is hardly simple. The "window" for advertising effectiveness can be either at the time of brand decision (home) or at the point of selection (store). Media planners work closely with marketing staffs to devise the exposure strategies

needed. Timing is very important because target-audience members do not carry the brand profile in their collective memories for long. This chapter discusses some of the factors that come into play in deciding the month, day, and even hours of scheduling.

3. Continuity Strategies. Budget limitations always force some sort of compromise between reach, frequency, and continuity because each of these media objectives is dollar driven. One cannot be increased without a corresponding investment decrease in another. Continuity is translated as the length of the advertising periods. Media planners must often balance the impact of the campaign (levels of advertising to produce awareness and positive brand attitudes) with how long the campaign can run. Two campaign-length strategies designed to protect impact without seriously shortening campaign length are examined in the chapter.

Geographic Considerations in Media Scheduling

Any company that has more than one store, distributor, or sales district has to deal with priorities because even if the brand's marketing situations are identical, sales will vary from area to area. This is true for all types of companies—local, regional, and national.

Local or Single-Market Firms

Service businesses and retailers know that location has an enormous influence on a store's sales results. Some stores have all the traffic they can handle. Others need constant promotion to keep consumers visiting. Even use of the same advertising and sales-promotion activities produces different results. How can the consumers from a tightly defined area (the same town) behave so differently? There are many possible answers to that question. The challenge for media planning is to match advertising investment with each store's sales potential.

Regional Firms

When the business territory involves multiple markets or states, the differences in potential and performance grow. Regional firms may have new sales areas, along with markets that are much more established. Markets may also have different target-audience descriptions, which contribute to differences, or they may encounter different levels of competition. Differences mean that carbon-copy advertising plans are not effective.

National Firms

At first glance, the term *national* may seem to suggest one complete market. But *national* does not mean that the brand must be universally distributed and sold or that each market or region produces its proportional level of sales. Even category leaders (number one in sales "nationally") find that they are the first choice in some markets and the fifth or sixth in others. National consumer product marketers know that consumers differ, competitors differ, and even advertising media differ from place to place. Therefore, even if it is mandatory that all areas or markets receive some of the advertising effort, all areas do not need to receive the same amount. We now look more closely at some factors that signal market differences.

Factors That Establish Market/Advertising Priorities

Media planners use several key factors to establish advertising priorities. Specific examples of conditions that influence priority follow.

Product Sales Performance

Table 11.1 is a brief excerpt of market-by-market sales shares for two of the more than thirty Kellogg cereal brands. The markets shown are from the

---

TABLE 11.1

Sales Share Indices* of Kellogg Cereal Brands (Adult) for Selected Eastern Region Markets

Dollar Shares of Cereal Sales

Brand	Baltimore/ Washington	Boston	New York	Philadelphia
Corn Flakes	110	86	144	89
Raisin Bran	93	114	115	113

Source: SAMI Market Resume 1987.
*National share of sales to local share of sales.

---

same region. The brands are both old and well established, and each comes from the adult cereal segment. Yet, in spite of all these similarities, table 11.1 shows substantial performance differences. Kellogg is a national advertiser and uses such national media as network television and magazines. While it may seem logical to assume that using the same network advertising schedule for Corn Flakes in both Boston and New York would be fair and equitable to both markets, this obviously is not the case. How Kellogg media planners might want to handle this is discussed shortly.

Competitive Conditions

An advertising agency developing an advertising/ promotional program on the West Coast (five markets) for Calgon's electric dishwasher detergent (Calgonite) found that the Pacific region showed a high demand for the category because of the percentage of households with dishwashers. A coupon for 75 cents off was scheduled for newspapers in each market. Word was then received from the area that a new competitor (Electra-Sol) had just embarked on an astonishing entry promotion. The competitor was offering a "two-for-one" sale on its 60–ounce size, which meant 7.5 pounds of detergent at a giveaway price. Calgon's ads and coupon promotion were canceled and the funds diverted to

other (less competitive) areas. In Calgon's view, spending extra advertising dollars in an area inhabited by a reckless competitor was pointless.

Companies do not sell products in a vacuum. Marketers must compensate for competitor strategies. In some cases (as in the Calgon example), compensation may mean a strategic withdrawal from action. In other situations, a firm may decide to attack with an even stronger advertising barrage.

Brand Cycle

Many of the branded goods consumers buy move through age cycles, just as people do: They experience "birth" (introductory stage); they develop (growth stage); they have a sustaining period (maturity stage); and finally, they fade away (decline stage). Each brand operates on a cycle within a target market area. More importantly, groups of markets can be in different brand cycles. In this case, the allocation strategy for markets is, in part, dictated by the brand's cycle stage. Some examples follow.

Introductory Markets

The initial release of a brand demands heavy promotional effort. The trade must be shown that a strong marketing program supports the brand.

Consumers must be educated about the brand's existence and its ability to satisfy their needs. Sales momentum must be developed from zero. All of this takes a substantial advertising investment at a time when sales revenues are very modest. The investment is based on potential.

Late-Maturity Markets

Sales may be stable with certain brand loyalties, but increased shares are unlikely. The brand has a proven record with the trade. Most consumers know of the brand and have either accepted or rejected it. Advertising can do little more than sustain awareness. Allocations to such market stages are modest in comparison to introductory or growth markets, where potential is yet to be realized. Further, additional advertising may not be paid off by additional sales. A primary responsibility of mature markets is to deliver profits to offset the losses expected in younger markets.

Uneven Distribution of Target Segments

As target-audience segmentation becomes narrower, it is increasingly likely that particularly ethnic or demographic segments will not be found in even proportions across target markets. The skew to particular markets automatically elevates the market's value. Two examples follow.

Mature Adults (50+ years old)

Mature adults could easily be the most dominant group in the 1990s. They currently make up more than 41 percent of adults, and with the maturing of the "baby boomers," their numbers are only going to increase. Table 11.2 shows how they are unevenly distributed across U.S. regions.

Hispanic Households

Hispanics, the nation's fastest-growing ethnic minority, are highly localized. The top ten U.S. population areas contain more than 57 percent of the nation's Hispanics. The top twenty Hispanic markets cover only 37.2 percent of the U.S. population but 72.8 percent of the Hispanic population.

TABLE 11.2

Index of Mature Adults to Total Adults by Census Region

	Age of Household Head		
Region	*50–64*	*65–69*	*70+*
New England	114	108	129
Middle Atlantic	96	108	112
East Central	103	99	89
West Central	91	99	105
South	110	103	102
Pacific	85	87	87

Source: Simmons *1989 Study of Media & Markets.* Reprinted by permission.

Systematic Approach to Geographic Allocation

Companies that want to address geographic differences within a marketing area can adopt any sort of analytical system that suits their priorities. The system used depends on the way target markets are evaluated and the form of the market information available to the firm. The two representative systems for target-market allocation discussed here (there are many) are based on either sales contribution or media performance. Either can suit a company, depending on the marketing situation.

Prior to discussions of the operation of these systems, however, some brief comment is needed on how geographic boundaries are determined. As with allocation, companies have a good deal of freedom in choosing which boundary systems best suit their needs. The following are some options beyond a firm's customized design:

1. Governmental (Census) Boundaries. Companies can use census regions or the metropolitan definitions called the **Standard Metropolitan Statistical Areas,** better known as **SMSA.**

2. Industry Boundaries. Two major industry associations (American National Advertisers and American Association of Advertising Agencies) provide guidelines for regional divisions and for descriptions of county sizes (A-, B-, C-, and D-size counties).

3. Media Research Boundaries. Many companies have found it very practical to use the media market borders set up by the A. C. Nielsen Company and Arbitron, Inc. (**Designated Market Area [DMA]** and **Area of Dominant Influence [ADI],** respectively) for television viewer research. The research firms measure each county's household viewing habits and determine which home-television stations dominate the viewing of the county (for example, 50 percent and above). The county is then credited to whichever home-television market it "belongs to." The value of these county allocation programs increased when radio, newspapers, and magazines also adopted the television system.

Using a Sales-Performance/ Potential System (BDI/CDI)

A common market-appraisal system used in consumer marketing is the Development Index. It has two components: (1) the individual market's contribution to brand sales (called the **Brand Development Index [BDI]**), and (2) the individual market's contribution to total sales in the category by *all* competitors (called the **Category Development Index [CDI]**). The BDI and CDI are easily figured from the following formulas:

BDI: $\dfrac{\text{Market } A\text{'s Share of Total Brand Sales}}{\text{Market } A\text{'s Share of U.S. Population}} \times 100$

CDI: $\dfrac{\text{Market } A\text{'s Share of Total Category Sales}}{\text{Market } A\text{'s Share of U.S. Population}} \times 100$

If Market A is Chicago with 3.5 percent of U.S. ADI population and has a share of brand X sales of 4.2 percent and a share of all category sales of 3.1 percent, the BDI/CDI would be calculated as follows:

$$\text{BDI} = \frac{4.2}{3.5}(100) = 120$$

$$\text{CDI} = \frac{3.1}{3.5}(100) = 89 \text{ (rounded)}$$

In this situation, Chicago is an important market to the brand (the higher the index, the better) but is not doing as well for all brands (the lower the index, the weaker). The use of population as the comparing number is important in reflecting efficiency or, as some call it, effectiveness. If size of the sales share were the only indicator, the largest cities or markets would always be at the top. With the use of population share, smaller markets can receive attention because they might have a greater proportion of sales in relation to their size.

The BDI reflects the sales *performance* of the market. It shows how the market has accepted the brand. But what about *potential*? Is the market capable of providing higher sales shares? The CDI pattern gives some indication, since a high index suggests that a number of brands are doing well.

If a marketer's sales analysis uses both the BDI/CDI indices, it makes sense to use them as one combined index instead of two separate ones. To do this, sales management must decide the relative importance of each index, which we learned in chapter 10, is called weighting.

A combined (weighted) BDI/CDI gives media planners a faster way to evaluate markets. The following are some simple illustrations that suggest different weighting possibilities:

• Young brands with limited sales history might weight the CDI more because potential is a better indicator of what the brand can do in the future. Sales may be slow to develop at first.

• Mature brands might tend to give more weight to the BDI because an established share pattern is more indicative of what the brand will do next year.

TABLE 11.3

Weighted BDI/CDI Process for Brand Alpha

Market	BDI	.20 Wtd.	CDI	.80 Wtd.	Wtd. BDI and CDI Value*	Fair Share (Percent)
Chicago	84	16.8	110	88.0	105	24.4%
Dallas	96	19.2	98	78.4	98	22.8
Denver	102	20.4	140	112.0	132	30.7
St. Louis	82	16.4	98	78.4	95	22.1

*Rounded figures.

Table 11.3 demonstrates how a weighted index is created. In this situation, Brand Alpha is only in its second year, and management has decided that the BDI should be only a small consideration. Thus, the BDI factor is set at 0.20 and the CDI at 0.80. The allocation process could then follow a **fair-share** basis, where each market receives some advertising dollars based on its index size. In table 11.3, the indices are added ($105 + 98 + 132 + 95 = 430$) and the sum divided into each market's index (for example, Chicago: $105/430 = 24.4$ percent) to find the market's percentage of the total. In this case, whatever dollars are available, Chicago will receive 24.4 percent (that is, a fair share).

An alternative BDI/CDI allocation idea is to group markets by index level and give each market in a particular level group (for example, "high" BDI group) the same advertising weight. If the top-priority group cutoff was a weighted index of 100 or above, then, from the example in table 11.3, Chicago and Denver would be eligible for a top allocation. In this method, both of these cities would receive the same additional advertising weight (for example, GRPs or more insertions), the next group of markets would receive less allocation, and so on, until the advertising dollars were used up.

Which allocation scheme is best? With the fair-share plan, every market has different advertising dollars. Some media planners consider that a mistake, and experience proves this out. Under the fair-share system, the lowest-ranked target markets can end up with trivial dollar amounts, perhaps so low that the advertising would be wasted. The market-group allocation has some problems, too, however. First, the design treats all markets within a given group the same, which reduces flexibility. Also, with this grouping system, which demands that the best markets are treated first, the dollars usually are exhausted before all markets are covered. Thus, the lowest-rated markets may go unfunded.

Using a Media-Performance Compensation System

Companies whose experience dictates the need for a threshold level of advertising (a minimum amount) across all markets often use a media-oriented allocation design to ensure that all target markets have an equal advertising pressure prior to any extra allocations. It can be considered an intermediate allocation step to compensate for any underdelivery of advertising impressions from first-stage planning.

For example, Beta Company is a hypothetical national firm selling liquid housekeeping cleansers. In addition to its national scope, the company also identifies its top thirty sales markets for special (extra) attention. Beta has traditionally relied on national or network television as the dominant advertising medium.

Through market research and sales analysis, Beta knows that its advertising plans must develop a certain level of reach and frequency. Its media plans are specifically designed to generate the mix of participation (rating points) necessary to achieve these minimum levels. Once the national level of advertising is planned, the priority allocations can be made to the most deserving markets.

However, before the allocation procedure (for example, based on a BDI/CDI system) is employed, media planners run a performance compensation analysis in each of Beta's top thirty markets. This system is designed to: (1) identify target markets where the national media plan will underdeliver (perform at less than the average) and (2) allocate the additional dollars to bring each market up to minimum Beta plan standards. Once these tasks are done, the BDI/CDI allocation system can be used to distribute the remaining dollars.

At this point, an explanation of how "underdelivery" happens is necessary. Vehicles, such as a national television program, are negotiated on a national delivery of an estimated rating. If a show has a household rating of 10.0, it means that approximately 10 percent of U.S. television homes view the program. It does *not* mean that 10 percent of *every* market will see the show. Historical research often shows wide variations in individual market show performance: Some markets are higher than 10.0; some markets are lower. Media planners are concerned with the markets where the program performs at levels below 10.0.

The same pattern of overdelivery and underdelivery is found in all national media (radio, cable networks, national newspapers, and magazines). The reasons are plentiful, but they all are anchored in public preference. And preferences in media choices are as varied as product choices. Media planners are not as concerned with why this happens as they are with fixing the problem.

In the Beta situation, for example, media analysts could use all available research to project market-by-market ratings for each of the television programs Beta has contracted for. If any of the

TABLE 11.4

Average Television Household Ratings Indices by Calendar Quarter

Time of Day	Yearly Average	1st	2d	3d	4th
Early News	100	109	95	91	104
Prime Evening	100	121	100	75	103

markets in Beta's top thirty showed a serious deficiency (perhaps more than 5 percent under), then additional dollars could be allocated to purchase more advertising units. This compensation system ensures that all markets have about the same advertising pressure before any other funds are allocated.

Timing Considerations in Media Scheduling

Proper timing of the advertising plan is the media equivalent of being "in the right place at the right time." Media planning deals with locating the most opportune time frames for placing the advertising message before the target audience. The principles of timing are logically clear; still, the strategic implications can be very sophisticated, especially when the match between shopping behavior and media behavior is not a good fit.

Media planners understand that target consumers are operating on two schedules, one for shopping and purchasing, and the other for media habits (preferences). Choices for media placement become difficult when media availability does not coincide with shopping patterns. Which is the right choice—popular target vehicles at the wrong time or weaker target vehicles at the best time? As one example, table 11.4 shows the serious seasonal fluctuations in television viewing across the year for two key dayparts (prime evening and early evening).

Note that prime evening is weak in the third quarter. If this is an above-average sales period for the brand, should television be used? Is it better to use television in the first quarter, even if sales are lower? These are typical media quandaries.

The use of units of time (time frames) in media planning is primarily dependent on two elements: (1) the timing flexibility of the medium considered and (2) the type of product involved in the campaign.

Timing flexibility concerns the precision of the communication channel in exposing the advertising message. For example, broadcast media have the highest control over exposure opportunity—isolating day-by-day, minute-by-minute opportunities. Magazines (especially monthlies) have one of the weakest flexibility patterns. Exposure to advertising is up to the reader, regardless of when the magazine arrives at the home or office.

The type of product also relates media timing to buying behavior. Retailers and service businesses (for example, fast-food restaurants) are most dependent on timing. Their sales are based on consumer traffic, and advertising is a major tool for traffic incentives. Some time-frame illustrations used by marketers and retailers follow.

1. Seasons/Calendar Quarters. Many products and services are weather related, from snow tires to lawn-and-garden supplies. Even items that are not weather dependent have seasons, such as public release of new models (durable goods, movies).

2. Weeks in the Month. Americans are more inclined to buy when the money is available, and payroll schedules may strongly influence demand for eating out, recreation, and other nonessential products and services. In smaller towns and cities, no retailers are unaware of when local workers are paid.

3. Days of the Week. Weekends are traditionally popular for families to shop for larger purchases. Display ads for movies also increase in size at this time. More

---

TABLE 11.5

Day-by-Day Viewing by Working Women

Day of Week	Viewing Time Index
Monday	104 (minutes)
Tuesday	103
Wednesday	97
Thursday	101
Friday	89
Saturday	90
Sunday	115

Source: From Nielsen Media Research. Reprinted by permission.

---

advertising is placed on those days of the week when most consumers are available and, as importantly, when they can participate with the media. (See table 11.5 for viewing patterns of working women.)

4. Hours of the Day. Chapter 15 examines marketing use of daily newspapers. One reason why afternoon editions are disappearing is that advertisers want to expose prospects in the morning, while the day's planning is still ahead. Daypart timing is also critical in broadcast advertising, where marketers try to design advertising schedules that support impulse buying wherever possible.

What underlies timing strategy in media planning is the product's **purchase cycle**: the nominal length of time between purchase and repurchase, between use and reuse. Some cycles deal with rapid consumption (beverage, gasoline), while others are long-range considerations (insurance, carpeting, appliances). Each time the cycle repeats, the marketer has an opportunity to maintain, gain, or lose a customer. We look at purchase cycles again in chapter 12.

MEDIA SPOTLIGHT

Keeping Time by the Consumers' Clock

by Ed Papazian

In the past, I have addressed the importance of timing in media selection and scheduling. Clearly, there are certain seasons of the year and certain times of day or days of the week when consumers are more receptive to product sales pitches. Heeding this, coffee marketers can be found advertising on early-morning television, a time when many Americans are about to or have just had their breakfast cup of java. In a similar vein, sleeping-aid marketers are more inclined to mid- or late-evening scheduling, and cold-remedy advertisers try to beef up their media weight when flu epidemics are rampant.

But is the concept taken far enough? While many timing aspects are taken into account by marketers, some of the more subtle nuances are often ignored. In most cases, timing is geared to direct consumer actions, such as shopping or product usage. When do people think about using or trying products? When are they more inclined to contemplate switching brands?

The "lead time" angle is recognized by astute marketers, but since it is difficult to quantify, action is rarely taken. We know of an exception, however. In this case, a day-by-day study, based on the previous twenty-four hours' activities, was conducted. Adult respondents were queried about their purchase, use, and, most important, their consideration of various products. The results for some categories were noteworthy (see table 1). Nutritional snack foods, for instance, were more likely to be bought on an average weekday

(11 percent) compared to Sunday (8 percent), while weekdays led handily in future buying consideration (9 percent to 5 percent). But Sunday was by far the best day for consumption of the product (26 percent versus 13 percent).

When the day-by-day consideration, purchase, and use patterns were plotted for the various products, definitive cycles were developed, indicating when consumers were most inclined to plan their next purchase, to actually make it, and to use the product, after which the cycle repeated itself. Intertwined within these cycles were brand-switching decisions—usually after a disappointing experience with the user's current product or exposure to a rival brand's ad.

When appropriate, time-of-day scheduling offers a way to enhance day-of-week strategies, especially when there are clear distinctions between shopping, preparation, and consumption times. In this manner, the advertiser has an opportunity to influence consumers when they are more interested in what the company has to say, while competing brands, which ignore the lead time or receptivity aspect, pound away more or less randomly—often at times when consumers have other things on their minds.

While broadcast offers time-of-day and day-of-week flexibilities, these are most effectively employed when homemakers or older persons are the prime consumer target (because such persons can be used throughout the day or week). When adults who are employed away from home are the primary target, a combination of print and broadcast media seems more appropriate. For example, television in the early mornings, prime time, or the late evenings might be coupled with daytime radio plus newspaper ads providing shopping (price/location) information for a more effective media mix.

TABLE 1

Involvement of Adult Population with Various Products "Yesterday"

	Average Weekday	Sunday
Nonsweetened Cold Cereal		
Bought	9%	5%
Used	13	16
Considered	6	5
Total*	**24**	**22**
Nutritional Snack Foods		
Bought	11%	8%
Used	13	26
Considered	9	5
Total*	**28**	**34**
Cake Mixes		
Bought	6%	3%
Used	4	10
Considered	3	6
Total*	**13**	**15**
Premium Brand Soup		
Bought	8%	1%
Used	8	19
Considered	5	—
Total*	**18**	**20**
Coffee		
Bought	13%	7%
Used	42	41
Considered	7	3
Total*	**51**	**46**
Tea		
Bought	5%	6%
Used	22	34
Considered	5	3
Total*	**28**	**38**
Diet Soft Drinks		
Bought	8%	5%
Used	25	21
Considered	6	2
Total*	**33**	**25**

*Totals may not add evenly due to multiple answers.

Source: Ed Papazian, "Mediology," *Marketing and Media Decisions*, July 1989, 103.

Campaign-Length Considerations in Media Scheduling

It is one thing if a business is an ice-cream stand in Montana or is selling ice-fishing supplies in Ohio, but most product/service businesses must sustain year-round sales performance. Campbell's sells soups in August, and Lipton sells iced-tea mixes in February. Some times are better than others, but most businesses do not close when sales are less than peak. The same is true of advertising. Very few firms would feel comfortable with six-to-nine-month pro-motion vacations.

Maintaining advertising programs for a long duration (continuous scheduling) is a concern because seasons are long and advertising dollars are short. Many firms must operate on schedule priorities. Simply put, advertisers cannot sustain needed advertising levels month after month. General Motors cannot. Budweiser cannot. Procter & Gamble cannot. The reason that even these powerful firms do not use a continuous advertising strategy is that length or continuity is not the campaign's only objective. As mentioned in chapter 9, media objectives are keyed to reach, frequency, and continuity. Each element is important, but strengthening one demands sacrifices from the others. Dollar limits force compromises or trade-offs. Media planners must find strategies that can maintain a longer advertising campaign without drastic reduction in reach or frequency. If reach is limited, fewer customer prospects are exposed. If frequency is limited, fewer advertising messages reach the audience. With regard to continuity, planners need to know the results of shortened schedules. What does limited duration do to campaign objectives?

Brand Threats from Weak Continuity

The previous section described purchase cycles as a logical guide to scheduling strategy. Failure to support enough purchase cycles eventually leads to a weakened brand franchise and lower sales. The following are some symptoms of inadequate scheduling:

1. Lower Brand Awareness and Attitudes. The phrase "out of sight, out of mind" applies to advertising in the same ways it applies to a myriad of other situations. A major goal of media planners, then, is to design a campaign that keeps the brand before the public—long enough to maintain levels of awareness and positive attitude. How long a schedule needs to be to support the communication response goals is a question answered only on a case-by-case basis.

2. Weakened Trade Relations. Retailers who deal with the public daily are not enthusiastic about brands that cannot maintain continuity in advertising. Their thinking is linear. Without brand advertising, consumers either forget a brand or never get to know it. Without consumer awareness, the brand stays on the shelf, and shelf movement is the life of a retailer.

3. Increased Competitor Interest. In the battle for consumer satisfaction and loyalty, advertising is a weapon to gain territory as well as to protect it. Brands with limited advertising schedules invite competitors to increase promotional intensity. The competition may well feel that customers can be attracted away when advertising defenses are low.

Schedule length is a dilemma for many companies. How long can consumers be out of contact with brand advertising? How long will the chain of distribution be satisfied with little or no advertising activity? How long can a brand restrict its schedules before competitors try to exploit a weakness? Finally, how much schedule length can be borrowed to support higher reach and frequency levels when advertising is used? Although there are no surefire remedies or easy answers to these questions, strategic scheduling methods may satisfy trade-off circumstances. One is known as "pulsing" or "wave" strategy. The other is called "flight" strategy.

TABLE 11.6

Pulse Scheduling for National Pain-Reliever Brand (1,200 Total GRP)

Calendar Month	Jan.	Feb.	Mar.	Apr.	May	June	July	Aug.	Sept.	Oct.	Nov.	Dec.
GRP/Month	200	200	150	50	50	50	50	50	50	50	150	150

TABLE 11.7

Flight Scheduling for National Pain-Reliever Brand (1,200 Total GRP)

Calendar Month	Jan.	Feb.	Mar.	Apr.	May	June	July	Aug.	Sept.	Oct.	Nov.	Dec.
GRP/Month	300	—	300	—	300	—	—	—	—	—	300	—

Pulse (Wave) Scheduling

Certain brands have year-round sales activity with some key sales concentrations during the year. Many of these have reasonably short purchase cycles. Dry cleaners have customers each week of the year, but heavier use of "dry clean only" fabrics during the winter months certainly creates usage peaks. Soft drinks are a staple beverage of people through young adulthood. They are consumed year-round, but there is no question that warmer weather increases usage. Companies that have products with these characteristics cannot promote and advertise only during key seasonal periods. At the same time, the higher demand periods should also have heavier levels of activity.

With the **pulse** technique, a minimally acceptable schedule of advertising is used during most of the sales year. These lower schedules allow media planners to "save" dollars for high-demand periods. For example, suppose a pain-reliever brand (aspirin, acetaminophen) has a yearly budget that can afford 1,200 gross rating points (GRP) in television. It needs a sustaining schedule of moderate activity, along with some much-higher levels for the cold/flu season. The pulse strategy (high-low) fits

this circumstance very well. As table 11.6 demonstrates, instead of 100 rating points every month ($12 \times 100 = 1,200$), this brand lowers the spring-summer scheduling to build much higher reach and frequency levels from November through February.

Flight Scheduling

While the pulse or wave strategy probably fits the vast majority of consumer brands, others demand a different approach. These brands may be operating under strong budget limitations, or they may face severe competitive pressure. They may also have steeper demand highs and lows. Any of these conditions (and often a combination) might lead these advertisers to a more dramatic strategy called **flight scheduling.**

Flight scheduling is characterized by dormant periods of no activity followed by relatively intense flights (bursts) of high-reach/high-frequency scheduling that switch the campaign year on and off. Flights are arranged to precede and continue through peak demand periods.

Table 11.7 shows a demonstration of flighting with the pain-reliever brand discussed previously,

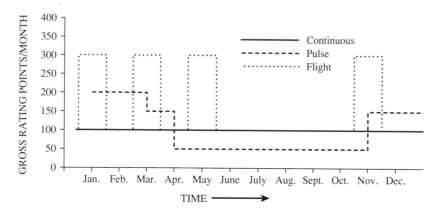

FIGURE 11.1 Scheduling Pattern Comparison for National Pain-Reliever Brand Using 1,200 Yearly Gross Rating Points (GRP)

which now must contend with one other condition—fierce competition during the cold and flu season. (See the share-of-voice discussion in chapter 8.) To combat strong advertising by competitors, the brand is willing to forego television advertising from June through November to finance much more serious GRP levels during the other months.

Flighting strategy gambles that awareness and attitude from high GRP levels will not seriously erode between advertising periods. If, indeed, the **carryover effect** is good, then the gamble may work. While not a recommended strategy for brands in the introductory and growth stages of development, flight scheduling is a lower risk for brands with established loyalty.

The three possible scheduling strategies for the fictional brand of pain reliever are shown in figure 11.1. Which strategy would work best would depend on the marketplace or on a careful testing program for schedule effectiveness.

Summary

This chapter continues to explore the "advertising window"—the ideal opportunity to place an advertising message before a target audience. While chapter 10 dealt with audience identification, this chapter examines the three dimensions of time and place that fill out this strategic optimum sought by all media planners: (1) where to place the advertising, (2) when to place it, and (3) how long to place it.

Geographic strategies involve setting area priorities for advertising investment. Any firm that has more than one sales outlet must decide on the amount of advertising that each geographic segment should receive. Decisions can be based on each area's past sales performance, the age cycle of the brand in the area, the degree of competitive activity, and the location of target segments. All of these factors assist in determining the correct advertising allocation.

Two representative systems for analyzing geographic market areas are based on sales contribution or media performance. Each one represents a carefully designed approach to both evaluate market potential and direct the appropriate dollars or advertising weight (for example, GRP).

In sales performance and potential, the best-known system is the Brand/Category Development Index (BDI/CDI). This approach uses the market's share of brand sales (BDI) or total category sales (CDI) in conjunction with the market's share of population to produce indices reflecting sales effectiveness. The two indices can be combined into one indicator to give media planners a faster way to evaluate markets and a means of allocating advertising dollars.

The media-performance compensation system is employed when the marketer's first priority is to ensure that all target markets receive an equal threshold level of advertising pressure. These strategies are designed to compensate first for media performance unevenness across target markets.

The timing element in the "advertising window" acknowledges that *when* an advertising message is exposed may seriously influence brand selection and purchase action. Time frames used by marketers include seasons/calendar quarters, weeks in the month, days of the week, and hours of a single day. Media planners deal with two separate behaviors in timing—shopping/consumption and media habits. Timing strategy recognizes the purchase-cycle time frame and the availability of target audiences to media vehicles.

The length of an advertising campaign is often a forced compromise between continuity (the number of consecutive purchase cycles used in the advertising plan) and the reach and frequency objectives. In many situations, campaign length must be compromised to provide adequate levels of advertising pressure (impact). Two trade-off strategic scheduling methods are: pulse (wave) scheduling and flight scheduling. Each of these approaches is designed to release dollars for reach and frequency without harming long-term brand awareness and attitude levels.

3. According to the text discussion, if two markets were similar in size and sales performance, but one was in an early brand cycle, that market might receive a higher advertising allocation. How does brand cycle influence the market's investment?

4. Why would a marketer with a history of using television advertising be more likely to define its market areas by television coverage (DMA or ADI) than by governmental SMSA?

5. If Chicago had 3.5 percent of population and 2.9 percent of Beta's total sales, and Kansas City had 0.8 percent of population and 2.2 percent of Beta's total sales, what would each market's BDI be? Why, if Chicago is larger and has more sales, does Kansas City have the larger index?

6. What does weighting the BDI/CDI mean? What factors should be contemplated in considering the relative importance of each index?

7. Imagine you are planning the advertising schedule for a store that sells compact discs and tape cassettes. Would you consider the need for seasonal adjustments? Weekly? Daily? Hourly? Set up a fictional situation that would support your views.

8. Explain how the pulse strategy works. Under what conditions would you believe that pulse would be superior to flight strategy?

Questions for Discussion

1. Media planners' central control on where, when, and how often is money. Explain how budget limits influence each of these "advertising window" areas.

2. The chapter suggests that all levels of company size can effectively use geographic priorities. Find and be prepared to discuss a local retailer, a regional (more than one town/city outlet) retailer, and a national marketer who could use market-area priorities.

Suggested Readings

• Barban, Arnold M., Steven M. Cristol, and Frank J. Kopec. *Essentials of Media Planning: A Marketing Viewpoint.* 2d ed. Lincolnwood, Ill.: NTC Business Books, 1987. Chapter 5.

• Sissors, Jack Z., and Lincoln Bumba. *Advertising Media Planning.* 3d ed. Lincolnwood, Ill.: NTC Business Books, 1989. Chapter 8.

Chapter 12

Evaluating Media-Mix Opportunities

Outline

Learning Objectives

In the study of this chapter, you will have the opportunity to:

- Appreciate how different advertising and marketing elements can be combined or integrated for desired effect.

- Understand the strengths and weaknesses of either concentrating or diversifying media or media vehicles.

- Learn why combining reach and frequency into a single measure (effective reach) improves strategic evaluation of media alternatives.

- Examine the development of cross-promotional opportunities and how such opportunities expand media planning.

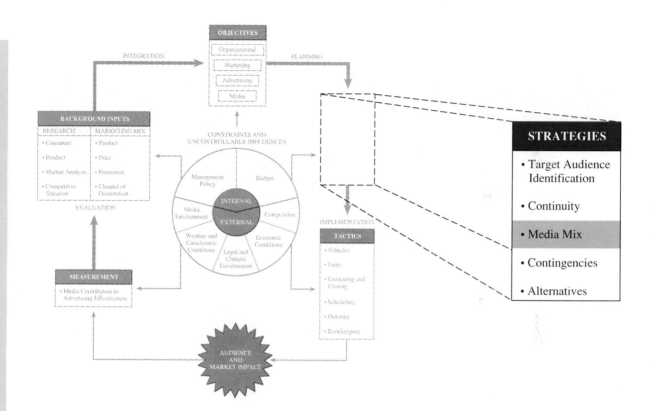

*T*he essential premise of mixing is to make something of a pure state (singular) better by combining it with something else. For example, iron is strong but made better if combined with other ingredients to form steel. Mixing also has potential value for advertising. A mix of numerous creative production, and financial skills is vital to the activity. In fact, virtually every area within advertising, including media strategy and planning, similarly demands multiple elements mixed for a desired result.

Of the many examples of **media mixing,** three have been selected for special discussion here. Mixing media or media vehicles is an alternative strategy that, under the right conditions, may improve the campaign's communication effect. Mixing two major quantitative factors (reach and frequency) solves an evaluative dilemma for planners and brings planning closer to solving the communication objective. Mixing promotional tools (for example, advertising, merchandising, sales promotion, and public relations) is the latest development in the mixing concept. It reflects the desire to integrate individual actions into a more cohesive operation. Examination of each of these "mixes" also encourages an appreciation for the complexity and sophistication of media planning in the 1990s.

Mixing Media/Media Vehicles: The Best Solution?

The previous discussion suggests that mixing is an ideal solution. In many cases and situations, this has been proven. On the other hand, in some circumstances, the issue is less sure. Our discussion of mixing strategies begins with a situation that is less than clear-cut. Should media plans concentrate on one "pure" communication channel, or is a combination of channels better? We examine the question at two levels: (1) concentrating all dollars in one medium versus more than one, and (2) concentrating all dollars in one vehicle (within a medium) versus more than one.

For example, suppose that LA Gear has developed a new athletic shoe that is designed to compete with NIKE and Reebok on performance and comfort. Perhaps the mass appeal and the creative demonstration potential of television advertising has made it the top media choice. Should LA Gear's planning group commit all dollars into television? Magazines, on the other hand, could reach some special-use groups with efficiency. Thus, magazine messages might be better able to educate consumers about the new shoe's technical features than television. Whether some television money should be directed to magazines is a mixing decision at the media-type level.

A typical media-vehicle mixing decision might involve a small, but developing women's clothing (sportswear) company choosing among magazine alternatives. *Vogue* has the image and the type of readers desired, but so does *Mademoiselle*. Should the sportswear company pick one of these and gain the maximum discounts, or use two magazines for a higher reach, but higher cost?

The Case for Concentration

Media planners choose media or vehicles that *best* fulfill a brand or company's marketing objectives. They concentrate advertising investment to provide optimum values. Concentrating the advertising effort makes good business sense for a number of reasons:

Impact Value

Impact value, in this context, refers to a special quality in the message placement that attracts notice and comment. It is an audience reaction that embraces interest, surprise, appreciation, and even drama. It is a quality that puts the advertising above the "typical," the "everyday," or the "expected." It is special.

Media's role in creating impact is to give the advertiser's message a special arena, a spotlight that showcases the brand. Football's Super Bowl telecast provides this stage, and such advertisers as Apple Computer (1984 commercial) and Budweiser ("Bud-Bowl Games") have made advertising history with it. A small hand-lotion company (Rose Milk) also made advertising history by successfully committing its entire budget to the telecasts of the Rose Bowl Parade. Spending nearly all of an annual budget in one day and on one telecast is a terrible risk. Fortunately, the risk was balanced by the impact it had on consumers and the retail trade. The Department of Tourism for the Commonwealth of Pennsylvania once spent most of the departmental budget on a twenty-eight page color insert in *one* issue of a national magazine. The agency reasoned that the impact potential in that single insertion would be more powerful than anything else the department could do. Hallmark has sponsored years of television specials that showcase the seasonal greeting cards. These are all examples of concentration for impact.

Positive Trade Reaction

Distributors, retailers, and other people in the middle may judge a brand's campaign on how well it is concentrated. They see this strategy as having the power to direct consumer traffic. Concentration is also seen as an easier way to tie in promotion and merchandising. While more diversified campaign strategies may deliver more advertising impressions, or cover more audiences, they do not gather the trade attention or excitement that a concentration plan does.

Negotiation Strength

The more a given marketer commits to a media company (newspaper, television network/station, or magazine), the more leverage the marketer has. It is a natural law of business—the bigger the contract, the better the deal potential.

Nearly all cost schedules for space and time have built-in discount systems. The more spent for time or space in total, the less paid per message unit (see the discussion of "common rate and discount policies" in chapter 14, as well as specific rate structures for the media in chapters 15–18).

Concentration of media dollars can also enable advertisers to negotiate with the media for special merchandising and promotional assistance (see the section on media-offered extras in chapter 8). If the advertising allocation is spread around, no media outlet has much incentive to make special arrangements.

Creative Opportunities

Many advertising campaigns are specifically designed for different messages to the same audience. Each creative unit, though different, builds upon the others already exposed. For example, many different commercials were interrupted by Eveready's drumming rabbit, and many different celebrities (all fields) have explained their need for the American Express Card. The list of multiple executions goes on and on (Excedrin headaches, Bud Lights, Bartles & James). The strategy is clear: Find the best medium or vehicle, and use it over and over with changing versions of the creative theme. Marketers cannot establish theme developments without concentration.

Lower Creative and Production Costs

All basic economic courses teach the economies of scale. It is less expensive to do all television commercials or magazine ads or newspaper layouts or thirty-sheet billboards than it is to do *one of each*. Often, the arrangements to set up one "shoot" for magazine photography are the same whether one advertisement is involved or five. Television studio and production facility arrangements are often done on a per-day basis. Concentrating advertising in one medium rather than over multimedia significantly reduces costs.

The Case for Media Mixing

While there are some powerful arguments for concentrating media activity, the case for mixing media is equally forceful. Spreading dollars among media opportunities is much more than following the old adage about not putting all of the eggs in a single basket. It is more than spreading the risk or "hedging" the bet. In media-planning situations, there are a number of specific advantages in *not* concentrating media activity:

Multi-Audience Segmentations

Many marketing strategies today are directed to narrowly defined consumer segments. Trying to be "all things to all people" does not produce the success it once did. Further, media habits borne of a variety of choice seem also to be more narrowly defined. The term *mass media* does not characterize advertising channels of communication as it has in the past.

There are literally hundreds of situations where the product user, the purchaser, and the decider are different people—different people who also have different media habits. Toy, video game, cereal, soft-drink, and fast-food marketers often use a combination of media and/or media vehicles for this reason. In such situations, concentration rarely can provide the desired coverage levels.

Expanded Reach and Frequency

Mixing media and media vehicles can improve the chance to fulfill basic objectives of reach and frequency. With a mix, the media plan can add customers and prospects not exposed by a single media outlet. Similarly, by mixing, media planners can more evenly distribute the number of exposure opportunities (frequency). Some illustrations of these capabilities follow.

TABLE 12.1

Reach Analysis (4 wk.) Working Women (One vs. Two Media)

Plan	Cost (Millions)	GRP	Reach (4 wk.)
A	$3.0	188	56%
B	$3.0	190	60

Source: Simmons Market Research Bureau. Reprinted by permission.

Reach Extension

Assume that one of the key target-audience segments for a branded hay-fever remedy is working women. Assume also that the media planner for this brand has an arbitrary yearly allocation level of $3 million and must compose schedule alternatives based on this amount. Schedule *A* is dollar-divided between a daytime television schedule and a prime-time evening one (8:00 P.M.–11:00 P.M. EST). Schedule *B* equally divides the allocation between two media: daytime television and consumer magazines. Table 12.1 shows the two schedules analyzed for working women reach potential. Schedule *B*, while identical in cost to *A*, can deliver 7 percent greater reach by combining television (day) with magazines. An equal-dollar comparison of one media vehicle versus two or more vehicle schedules often produces the same result. Diversity usually extends reach.

Frequency Expansion

Audience media patterns follow daily habits. Habits are formed by the availability of the individual and his or her preferences. A concentration strategy skews the frequency of exposure toward target-audience members who are the heaviest viewers, listeners, or readers. They receive a disproportionate share of messages. Conversely, those who

TABLE 12.2

Frequency Distribution Radio & TV vs. TV Only

Exposures	Target Reach	
	TV Only	TV & Radio
1 time	24%	18%
2 times	16	13
3–5 times	11	15
6–8 times	7	13
9+ times	12	9
Total Reach	**70%**	**68%**

view, listen, or read the least receive the fewest exposures or the smallest proportion. Increasing the amount of advertising does not improve the situation; in fact, a heavier concentration makes matters worse.

One remedy for frequency distortion is to mix media. With a combination of media, the highs and lows balance exposure opportunity. Table 12.2 shows a frequency distribution improvement from a radio to a television plan. Plan *A* is composed exclusively of nighttime television commercials rotated in eight programs. Plan *B* exchanges half of the nighttime television for a schedule in daytime radio. While Plan *B* loses some of the exposure (reach), it more than compensates by a superior distribution of the midrange frequency level. For example, nearly one-fourth (24 percent) of *A*'s audience would have only one exposure and 12 percent would have nine or more. In *B,* these peaks are smoothed (18 percent once, and only 9 percent nine or more times) with little sacrifice in overall reach.

Better Creative Treatments

Chapters 15–18 discuss the creative strengths and weaknesses of each medium. The bottom line of these discussions is that *no* medium is a creative superhero. None can do it all. Some are visually ex-

citing, some are dramatic, some have great potential for detail and information, and some have motion, but none have it all. Marketers are very reluctant to compromise the creative approach. Media mixing allows them to exploit the creative power of each medium.

Creative Synergy

Synergy is a term from the field of chemistry and describes an action-reaction from combining certain parts. The effect of the total is *greater* than the sum (parts added) of the parts. In media application, a synergism is believed to occur when the total communication effect (for example, awareness) is greater than the response measured from each part used in advertising. The combined reaction has more impact.

While this theory has not been heavily tested, there are two logical explanations: Contrast in message source may produce stronger memory storage. For example, reviewing the textbook and class lecture notes is often a better test preparation than relying on one or the other.

Using the text, notes, and discussion with classmates may be the best memory preparation. Something happens in the interaction of different sources that improves performance. The same could be true with consumers. Watching a commercial for a brand on television, seeing the brand on an outdoor billboard, and hearing the brand advertised on the radio might make a more lasting impression than if only a single source were used.

Message wear-out (overexposure to the advertising message) can produce a mental turnoff. Consumers sometimes encounter an ad so often that the instant they recognize it, they break their attention because they have heard it all before. Advertisers can measure this phenomenon where awareness scores go down in the face of a continuous advertising schedule. If continued repetition produces disassociation with the brand, a lower awareness is very possible. A campaign theme designed from different media sources reduces the potential of wear-out by simply approaching the target audience from different perceptual directions (media mix).

Mixing Versus Concentration

There are no formulas for making the mixing versus concentration decision. Each brand's situation is unique. Every medium has some sort of maximum effectiveness level—a relationship between its audience delivery and its cost. Marketers are ill-advised to use a second or a third medium (or vehicle) just for the sake of mixing.

Further, in media mixing, planners have to determine the weighting or relative allocations to each medium. Thus, it is not only a decision to mix, but also a decision on the best way to divide the dollars among the media. Concentration might be vital where competitive advertising levels are high. On the other hand, too much concentration could produce wear-out and might fail to cover the target market adequately. Media planners who know the brand situation and optimum media effectiveness levels can make a reasoned choice.

Combining Reach and Frequency Objectives

The principles of reach and frequency were introduced in chapter 7, and the following is a recap of the characteristics associated with each of these quantitative media dimensions:

- **Reach** is a measure of how many target-audience members might be exposed to a schedule within a predetermined time frame. This accumulation process counts each audience member with at least one exposure opportunity. Reach is *not* expanded by repeat exposures, only by new individuals with the first-exposure opportunity.

- **Frequency** is the estimate of the *number of times* a target-audience member might be exposed during a predetermined time frame of the advertising schedule. Repetition of the message is considered very important for two reasons: (1) consumers must have duplicate exposure to "learn" what the message says, and (2) purchase cycles are different for each household, and periodic reminders are needed before the brand decision is made.

- Advertising campaigns are designed to satisfy objectives for both reach and frequency. Adequate coverage of the target audience is necessary to bring the advertising message to as many prospects and customers as possible. Duplication of the exposure process is necessary so that consumers can remember the brand and its benefits.

- The goals of reach and frequency do not work in easy harmony. Research has proven that, under all budget conditions, the pursuit of a reach goal reduces frequency potential, and vice versa. With budget and schedule length held constant, attempts to extend or expand one dimension force a sacrifice of the other.

Blending the Objectives

During the 1970s, advertising professionals viewed reach and frequency as two separate plan functions. Objectives stated reach and frequency goals individually, even though the concepts of exposure and repetition are symbiotic (physically related). While both reach and frequency were valued, marketers preferred reach over frequency, although why reach had higher priority has never been adequately explained. Perhaps it was because coverage of the target is so fundamental (the more people covered by the message, the more chances for a sale). Reach might have also had priority because its standard was so simple (the more customer/prospects the better). On the other hand, frequency standards were more difficult (how many times is enough?). Regardless of the justification, marketers aimed first at satisfying reach and only then tried to maintain adequate frequency.

The emergence of frequency as a more dominant plan factor seems to have coincided with the rapid expansion of media choices and the increasing message clutter caused by advertising and media promotions. Media professionals were worried about target consumers who might come in contact with brand messages only once or twice during a brief campaign. Was that enough? Would people remember the message until the next purchase-cycle level was at hand? Would the popular thirty-second commercial have adequate time to communicate

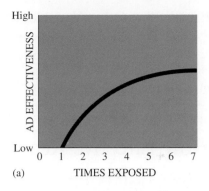

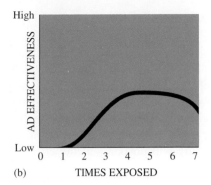

FIGURE 12.1 Two Theories of Frequency's Influence on Message Effectiveness. (a) Convex Theory. (b) *S*-Shaped Theory

images and information? Questions without answers produce doubt. Frequency became equal to or more important than reach. However, higher status for frequency only complicated the choice between the two and emphasized the need to combine the two goals.

The Theory of Effective Reach

Reach and frequency were combined to support the argument that, for an advertising campaign to be successful, the target audience must not only be exposed (that is, reached) but must also receive a minimum number of exposures within a certain time period. Media and other research specialists were saying that those exposed below the threshold level of frequency were not "reached" at all. In effect, this reshaped the curve of advertising influence.

Figure 12.1*a* depicts the traditional convex shape of the advertising influence curve. That is, each exposure, beginning with the *first,* contributes to audience awareness and understanding. Each additional exposure increases the effect. Figure 12.1*b* shows the effect of the **effective reach** theory: the first and second exposures have little influence, and awareness and comprehension begin to show only after the third exposure. The delayed effect gives this curve part of an *S* shape. The second bend reflects the idea that continued exposures eventu-

ally find an optimum level of effectiveness. Frequency beyond that point serves only to waste money—thus, the downward bend.

The Influence of Effective Reach on Planning

The media-planning concept of effective reach has some of the following immediate effects on media-planning strategy:

Lower Reach Levels

For a given budget, the objective audience exposure expectations are seriously reduced. The television campaign alternative in table 12.2 illustrates this. Each of the percentages listed in the television column is the proportion of target audience reached at the listed frequency range. The total reach, based on the convex curve, is 70 percent. But if the *S* curve is applied with assumptions that the effective reach for the advertiser is no less than three exposures and no more than eight, then only those exposed between three and eight times are counted. Thus, the reach drops from 70 percent to 18 percent (a reduction of nearly three-quarters of the original level)! While this example is fictitious, audience mass-media habits usually ensure that most schedules have a significant proportion of target audiences at both extremes (too few times or too many times).

Establishing a Basis of Effectiveness

Since the whole theory of effective reach is based on measures of advertising effectiveness, there must be a decision on how "effectiveness" is determined: By recognition of the package? By recall of key copy points? By a positive attitude change toward the company? Whichever measure is chosen should also be tested by audience research. If this is not monitored, the company will not know if the effective range is correct.

Establishing a Brand-Specific Range

There is no norm for a threshold level of frequency. Does a sales advertisement with unusual price discounts need as many exposures as one that features technical specifications for a new product? Does a brand in low advertising competition need the same range as one in a highly competitive category? It is shortsighted for media planners to adopt an arbitrary effectiveness range simply because it is convenient. Effective reach should be tested to learn brand-specifics.

Establishing an Effective Reach Time Frame

The traditional time period for reach and frequency is different for each medium. Television and out-of-home media work on four weeks. Radio and newspapers use one- and four-week periods. Magazine reach and frequency is based on an average issue life. But are any of these relevant? The foundation of frequency is keyed to the length of the product-to-purchase cycle. Arbitrary time frames only confuse the purpose: to create so many exposure opportunities within the time when the product is bought, used, and repurchased. As explained earlier, many cycles vary. Advertisers sincere about effective reach strategy need to establish frequency ranges within an accurate cycle for each product.

Establishing Other Variables of Influence

Chapter 8 discussed many aspects of media that could influence effectiveness (media environment, clutter, share-of-voice situations). These elements must be specifically involved in modifying the effective reach levels desired. Figure 12.2 identifies many of the variables.

How Effective Reach Is Used in Media Planning

The operational principle for effective reach is identical to that used in the more traditional measures of target-audience size, reach, frequency, and target cost-per-thousand (CPM): evaluation of media alternatives. The idea is to find the one combination of media (or of vehicles in the same medium) that best satisfies plan objectives. In the case of effective reach, this means determining which media schedule distributes the most exposure opportunities within the predetermined effective range. The following is an illustration of how this process might work for a metropolitan department store:

Bigham's is a large department-store chain with three locations in a midwestern city. In addition to weekly product advertising, the chain also schedules seasonal promotions designed to enhance image and service capabilities. Bigham's target audience is women, ages 18–54, living in households with a combined income above $30,000 per year. Bigham's media planner makes plan recommendations based upon CPM target audience, reach, and effective reach. The effective reach range for Bigham's is two to five exposure opportunities within each campaign month. The media planner is looking at two alternative plans that are nearly identical in cost. (See table 12.3.) The comparative impact summary based on table 12.3 is presented in table 12.4. Though both plans cost about the same and are very close in reader and average frequency, plan 2 is obviously superior in effective reach.

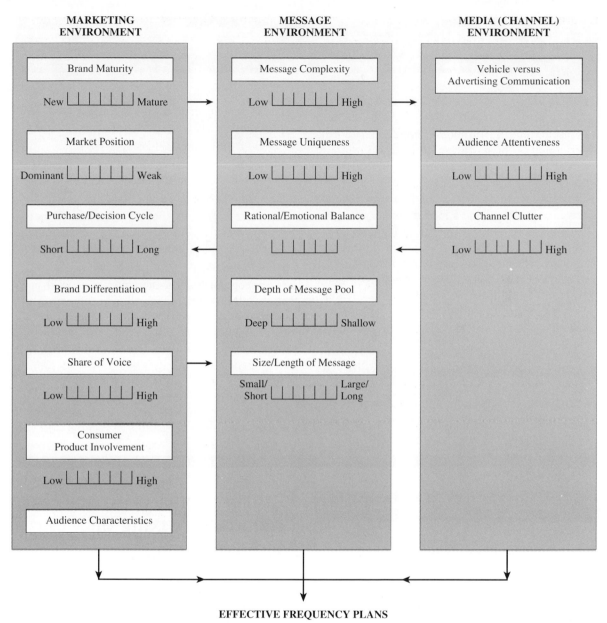

FIGURE 12.2 Descriptive Model Showing Variables
That Could Modify Effective Reach Ranges
Source: From Peter Turk, "Considerations in Setting Effective
Frequence Levels" in *Journal of Media Planning*, Spring 1987.
Copyright © 1987 *Journal of Media Planning*, Evanston, IL. Reprinted
by permission.

MEDIA SPOTLIGHT
12.1

Mixing Pizza with Kidvid

A fascinating illustration of revolutionary media packaging is the partnership between Pizza Hut and the Nickelodeon children's cable television network. It is a natural alliance: a cable programming source dedicated to children's information and entertainment and a food marketer with children and parents as a vital target segment. However, what was once a standard advertising association for media time has blossomed into a substantial multilayered advertising/promotional program. In addition to advertising on Nickelodeon programs, Pizza Hut contracted for the following:

- Charter advertiser in *Nickelodeon* magazine, with distribution of the first issue from Pizza Hut restaurants.
- Rights to develop premiums, contests, and other promotions based on Nickelodeon's programming and characters.

- Sponsorship (partial) of the Nickelodeon studios at the Universal Studio theme park and entertainment attraction in Orlando, Florida, which opened in the summer of 1990.
- Sponsorship of Nickelodeon's twenty-city shopping-mall tour to select contestants for the network's game shows.
- Exclusive rights to the aforementioned marketing activities, even though the arrangement does not exclude other fast-food advertisers from using network time.

The scope of this partnership has reward potential for Nickelodeon as well. The publicity the network receives from the food marketer's activities is unmeasurable. This is goodwill exposure needed by any cable operation seeking a specialized audience niche.

This sort of multimillion-dollar agreement has to be evaluated, but by what measures? Such is the nature of qualitative media decision making.

TABLE 12.3

Comparison of Two Plans for Effective Reach

Plan 1

Media: Television Only	30% in daytime 70% in prime nighttime Total Messages 41

Plan 2

Media: Television and Magazines	75% Television (30% daytime, 45% prime nighttime) 25% Magazines Total Messages 40

Future Impact of Reach/Frequency Mixing on Media Planning

The development of effective reach as a key media strategy could have a profound impact upon media planning in the 1990s. With channel clutter, diversified media audiences, and demand forcing higher media costs, media planning needs a more reliable and sensitive measure of advertising effectiveness. But, as noted earlier, effective reach demands a strong commitment to brand research. Without ongoing programs to measure effectiveness and the other necessary dimensions, the practical contributions of effective reach planning are minimal.

TABLE 12.4

Comparative Impact Summary

						Reach Distribution				
Plan	GRP	Reach	Freq.	1 Ti	2 Ti	3 Ti	4 Ti	5 Ti	6+ Ti	Effective Reach*
TV	387	86	4.5	20	22	14	7	14	9	57
TV & Mag.	370	84	4.4	13	21	20	16	10	4	67

*Eff. Reach Range: 2–5 Exposures.

Mixing Promotional Tools

Until recently, media planning dealt exclusively with the opportunities limited to advertising. Now, however, advertising is sometimes mixed with various combinations of other promotional tools. These multifunction offerings by the media may substantially influence campaign strategies. Here, briefly, is how they developed.

A New Age in Media Proposals

In this age of mergers, takeovers, and acquisitions, media corporations are active participants. Some media companies (for example, Gannett, CBS, Meredith, and Time-Warner) have become highly diversified operations with multicommunication outlets. With cross-media and other informational divisions, it was only a matter of time before the conglomerates began to package unique combinations of promotional tools for marketers.

Since the packages are, for the most part, custom-designed for individual marketers, a summary description or definition is difficult. However, most proposals feature advertising media, as well as merchandising, licensing, sales promotion, and public-relations events. Contracts offer special ser-

vices from the media's editorial/programming staff, production divisions, and promotion departments.

The degree of cooperation between the marketer and the communication company can be so integrated that it borders on a joint-venture concept—with each company taking specific steps to promote the other. Some current illustrations follow:

- The CBS Television Network signed agreements with major advertisers to participate in national sports events (college and professional football, golf, college basketball, and auto racing). What made these deals atypical was an extra participation for each sponsor in a twenty-eight-city tour of a shopping-mall exhibit and fair called "Sports Dream Season." Each corporate participant (for example, NIKE, AT&T, VISA, and others) was entitled to a booth or display for use as a selling outlet, or for public-relations or sales-promotion activities. The eight-month tour was expected to reach millions of Americans, many of whom might not have seen the sponsor's commercials during the sports telecasts.

- The Meredith Corporation (consumer magazines [*Better Homes & Gardens*], book divisions, broadcast stations) may have been the first media company to develop cross-promotional media proposals (1988). In 1989,

233

Meredith signed a deal with the Sherwin-Williams Paint Company that included pages of magazine advertisements, publication of a home decoration book featuring Sherwin-Williams products, a Meredith "how-to" videotape series featuring Sherwin-Williams products, and promotional tie-ins between Meredith's national real estate agencies and local Sherwin dealers. Each of these activities is designed for the mutual benefit of the sponsor and the media company.

- To attract Pepsi-Cola, (a brand with a traditionally low magazine advertising investment), Time-Warner's *Sports Illustrated,* designed a series of cosponsored activities and events. Along with magazine space, Pepsi will participate in a national contest promotion featuring fantasy sports-vacation prizes, a videotape series on fitness with Pepsi advertising, and a series of store promotions running concurrently with national sports events featuring Diet Pepsi and *Sports Illustrated* as partners.

The Attraction of Mixed-Promotion Packages

Much of the mixed-promotion activity is very fresh, which limits evaluation from experience. However, cross-promotional investment has some logical advantages over standard advertising alone, including:

- *Increased Reach and Frequency.* When used in conjunction with regular advertising, mixed-promotion packages undoubtedly reach more prospects and consumers. Licensed products, such as books, videotapes, and other merchandise, have frequency-of-impression potential that can last for months and even years.

- *Enhanced Communication Effects.* The impressive synergy possibilities from approaching the target audience from so many directions cannot fail to raise awareness, improve attitudes toward firms and products, and increase intention to buy.

- *Improved Sales Influence.* Many aspects are tied directly to sales opportunities (in-store Pepsi activities, Pizza Hut locations at Universal's theme park). Gaining trial from new prospects and brand switches is a built-in feature of many cross-promotions.

- *Goodwill.* In a time of consumer skepticism toward commercial motives, some of these packages can provide solid family-value images for the public. The public-relations images can seriously influence consumer choice in years to come. While hard to measure, anything that can bond the public's loyalty is a solid-gold opportunity.

Why Mixed-Promotion Proposals Are Planning Problems

Mixed-promotion opportunities are far from what media analysts consider "mainstream" options. As such, these offerings pose some interesting challenges for media planners. Some of the early transitional problems include:

- *Budget or Allocation Fit.* The custom nature of these proposals usually does not fit within the parameters set for space or time. How should a media planner react to a proposal that involves media activities well beyond the planner's dollar limits? For example, a magazine's offer might not only exhaust the *total* magazine allocation but absorb half the television dollars, too.

- *Campaign Time Frame.* Regular advertising arrangements seldom exceed one year (the advertiser's fiscal boundary). Mixed promotions demand especially long planning that often necessitates multiyear contracts. Further, the media see the efficiency of long-term arrangements and are anxious to push for exceptional length. How does a media planner recommend a plan that demands a two- or three-year participation?

• *Quantitative/Qualitative Evaluation.* Estimating the reach, frequency, and CPM evaluations for these special deals is especially difficult. How does a media planner estimate the exposure potential of books, videos, T-shirts, and the licensing of toy premiums? This is a set of judgments for which virtually no media planner has ever been trained.

The initial reaction of media departments at advertising agencies was to ignore or dismiss mixed-promotion proposals because they did not fit normal evaluation guides, were too long, and cost too much (*vis-à-vis* the media budget or allocation). These negative positions prompted media representatives to contact marketers directly (bypassing not only the media department but the agency and even client advertising staffs). Though threatened somewhat, the advertising staffs of agencies and marketers realized that, since the deals were going through, it made little sense to obstruct their development. Today, some advertising agencies are investigating the possibility of setting up teams of specialized personnel to actively solicit mixed-promotion proposals. If these unique campaigns prove to be successful, media operations in the 1990s could be much different.

Summary

The idea of combining or integrating different elements in the advertising/marketing process is a challenging opportunity for media planning in the 1990s. Along with challenges are risks that involve finding the balance point between a mix and the path of concentration. The chapter examines three decision points concerning a variety of combinable elements.

Whether media should be mixed in campaign strategy is one of the most debated questions in media analysis. Concentrating the budget in a single medium or on a single media vehicle has clear advantages in impact value, negotiation strength, creative opportunities, cost leverage, audience quality, and the promise of some dominance. Use of a primary vehicle assures more control and provides satisfactory trade acceptance. On the other hand, media mixing (combining media, or combining different vehicles in the same medium) is a valued asset when confronting highly segmented target audiences or where campaign objectives demand strong levels of reach and frequency. Media mixing can also assist communication of the product's theme by exploiting the creative power of each medium. More creative assistance comes through synergy of different media channels. When consumer targets are approached from several different directions, the chance for stronger communication response improves. The decision point on media mix versus media concentration lies with the product's situation and the needs of the campaign.

A different sort of challenge comes from quantitative evaluations involving reach and frequency. A relatively new theory recommends that these vital communication dimensions be combined into a single measure of media performance called effective reach. The premise of effective reach is that successful exposure (reach) must have minimum repetition (frequency) before the desired communication effects are realized. The establishment of a frequency minimum acts as a qualifier of exposure. Target individuals who do not receive a predetermined minimum number of exposure opportunities are, in effect, not reached at all. The impact of effective reach has brought about a re-evaluation of the function of media placement in advertising. Under this evaluation scheme, media plans are directly tied to advertising "effectiveness," instead of to the traditional role of simply providing audiences for the message. The "price" of effective reach is a system of market research that can identify the "effectiveness" factors, monitor campaign performance, and establish the product cycles in which effective reach must operate.

The most recent mixing decision point is also the most radical. It involves the packaging of advertising and nonadvertising promotional activities for sale to marketers. The opportunity for these combination arrangements is a result of the growth of communication companies with widely diverse media portfolios. Media companies are designing special campaigns for marketers that include merchandising, product licensing, sales promotion, and public relations. The combination of elements offers a marketer a chance to fully integrate marketing promotion in a single contract. Promotional mixes are too new to have a proven success factor, but it seems clear that advertisers fully intend to learn if these arrangements can improve sales and market shares.

Questions for Discussion

1. In deciding whether to concentrate or mix media, the advice is to follow the product's marketplace situation. How would you resolve the decision in these cases: (a) limited budget in a competitive product category; (b) local bank with target audience: mature adults and young executives; (c) new model of automobile with unique technical features. In each case, explain your reasoning.

2. What is the relationship between media rates and media mixing, reach and frequency, and media concentration?

3. How does message wear-out influence media concentration? Why is mixing preferred when seeking creative synergy?

4. If reach and frequency goals are both used in media planning, why can the attainment of one force a sacrifice of the other?

5. Explain this statement: In effective reach, frequency is used to *qualify* total reach estimates.

6. How should marketing/media planners decide what the effective reach range should be for a brand? What sources of information should be used in the decision?

7. Why does the text claim that use of the effective reach theory brings media planning much closer to realizing a product's communication needs?

8. If a company had a separate department for each marketing promotion area (common situation), why would acceptance of a mixed-promotion package create a technical reorganization of company operation?

9. Why are some of these mixed-activity promotions considered joint-venture partnerships between the marketer and the media company?

Suggested Readings

- Barban, Arnold M., Steven M. Cristol, and Frank J. Kopec. *Essentials of Media Planning: A Marketing Viewpoint.* 2d ed. Lincolnwood, Ill.: NTC Business Books, 1987. Chapter 5.

- Sissors, Jack Z., and Lincoln Bumba. *Advertising Media Planning.* 3d ed. Lincolnwood, Ill.: NTC Business Books, 1989. Chapter 10.

- Surmanek, James. *Media Planning: A Practical Guide.* Lincolnwood, Ill.: Crain Books, 1985.

Chapter 13

Considering Other Strategic Factors

Learning Objectives

In the study of this chapter, you will have the opportunity to:

- Understand how the budget-setting process affects the advertising media operation.

- Learn some of the methods by which advertising budgets are determined and allocated.

- Explore some of the basic advertising media allocation models.

- Be exposed to the standard advertising effectiveness model proposed by the Advertising Research Foundation.

- See how media effects can be tested.

- Learn about other media functions that occur in the postscheduling phase.

- Understand the importance of contingency plans in advertising media work.

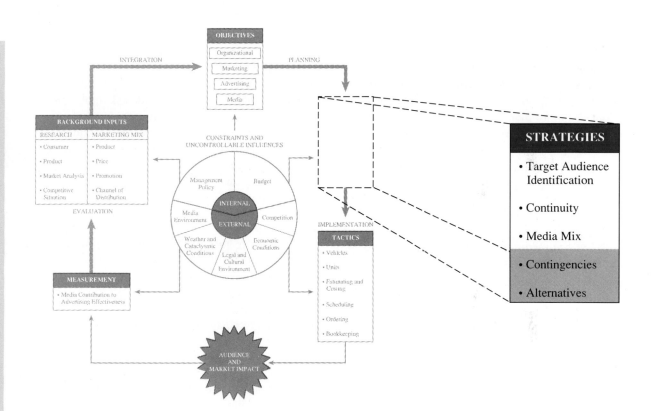

*A*dvertising media planning is more than working within a budget to select targets and media that reach those targets. Background information about the theoretical and practical ideas that underlie successful media campaigns is essential. So is determining whether the proposed plan will work. And after the plan has been completed, other aspects still must be examined before the plan can be put into place.

Experts and researchers who have explored advertising media strategies believe that the media allocation models discussed in this chapter are the most efficient and effective means of using media to accomplish advertising campaign objectives. Pretests of the media plan permit trial-and-error processes without risking the entire advertising budget or large-scale failure in the marketplace. Other steps introduce and implement the plan, as well as prepare for unforeseen contingencies. Before we discuss these topics, however, we need to acquire a basic understanding of advertising media budgeting.

Budgeting for Media

Most of the money spent on advertising goes for media. Of a large advertiser's budget, the bulk of the money—usually 85 percent—goes to the media used, and the remaining portion is for the advertising agency. In addition, a portion of the agency's share is spent for media planning and buying. Since most of the advertising dollar is designated for media, one might think that the media function should determine the advertising budget. With few exceptions, however, that is not the case.

In most situations, the budget is established before it is given to the media people. The advertising budget may be a function of the general marketing budget. More likely, the advertising budget is dependent on sales goals, share-of-market objectives, competitive spending for advertising, the number of units or outlets, inflation, and even economic projections.

One method of determining the advertising budget, called the objective-and-task approach (or simply the task method), may permit media planners to have input into the advertising budget determination decision. The objective-and-task approach begins with the sales goal and tracks backward to the amount of advertising needed to achieve that goal, then to the media necessary to carry and present that advertising, and finally to the amount needed for the total advertising effort. With this approach, the media function's requirements are factored into the sum that is eventually determined as the advertising budget. Thus, the media function has an impact on what the total sum of money available for advertising will be. Usually, however, advertising media planners are simply assigned an amount of money with which to work in creating the media plan.

Once the advertising budget has been determined, it is then allocated (divided) into various expenditure groupings, and some of the money is then available for media. Sometimes, the allocation is according to media types, and media planners receive a budget that has already been subdivided according to media type.

Within the media function is another allocation process: that of dividing the media monies into new categories. These categories may be according to media types, if that has not already been done, with specific amounts allotted for daily newspapers, weekly newspapers, consumer magazines, business publications, network television, spot television, spot radio, and so on. Once allocated by media type, the money must be allocated again; for example, the consumer magazine allocation must be reallocated into each specific magazine vehicle.

Media monies also can be allocated according to categories other than the types of media, such as:

Seasons or times of year

Geographic territories or markets

Primary, secondary, and tertiary target groups

Stages of product or service development

Primary media and supplemental media

Sales-oriented and image-oriented approaches

Information and persuasion

Demographic categories

Relationship to selling events and special offers

Retail outlets

Regular campaigns and special campaigns

There also could be combinations of these categories. Evidence of advertising's investment impact is seen in the announcement from AAAA (see figure 13.1).

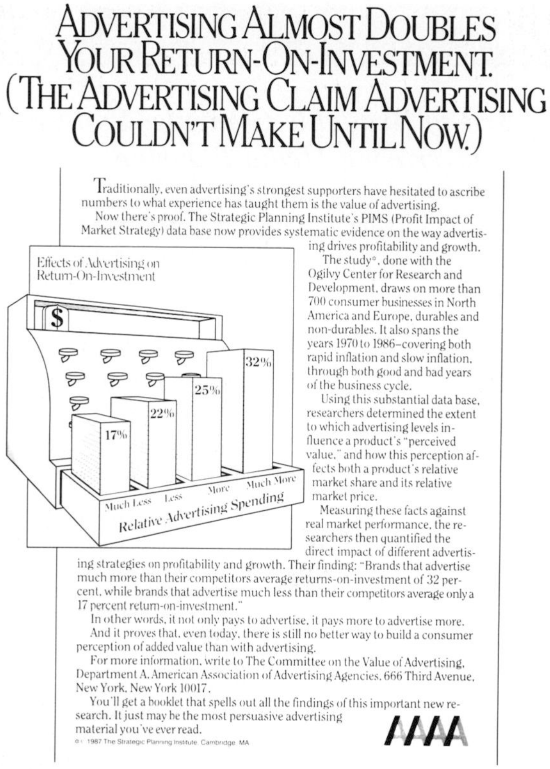

Media Models

Various theories of media planning have been developed into models that help explain the most efficient and effective ways to use media in accomplishing the advertising campaign objectives. Although the models themselves are not valuable without the ability to apply them to actual media-buying situations, understanding of the models can guide important advertising media decisions and support media choices. Of course, media planners must consciously decide whether a particular model fits the problem at hand. In addition, in some situations, assigning quantitative values to various aspects of a model may be difficult, so special care is required to avoid a situation where arbitrary values may be used to make concrete decisions.

We first examine models of how best to combine reach and frequency in media planning, and then models of media exposure and distribution. More general media-planning models also are discussed. Models of advertising media results are examined later in the chapter, in the "Response Functions" section.[1] Modern media models may be most useful if they can be utilized in computerized media planning, as shown in table 13.1.

FIGURE 13.1 **An Advertisement Promoting the Value of Advertising**
Courtesy of American Association of Advertising Agencies.

Reach and Frequency Models

If an advertisement is to be run only one time in a single medium, then reach is the only questionable factor because the insertion frequency is predetermined (that is, a frequency of one). In most advertising situations, however, multiple insertions are used in a combination of media and vehicles, so the proper balance of reach and frequency becomes critical. The problem is that vehicles' audiences overlap: Persons who read an advertisement in one magazine may also see the same advertisement in another magazine. Media planners are faced with the problem of trying to expand reach (through the

---

TABLE 13.1

A List of Available Computer Software for Advertising Media Planning

Primarily Buying and Research Software

Name of Software	*What It Does*	*Users*	*Price*
AdWare	Calculates buyer's estimates of media costs, and media-buy goals (GRPs); records station affidavits; draws up bills for clients.	Mostly midsize and small agencies.	$2,000–$20,000 a month, depending on number of terminals.
CHOICES	Generates cross-tabulations and magazine reach-and-frequencies based on Simmons data.	All-size shops, including largest like Young & Rubicam and Interpublic.	Depends on number of workstations; must be Simmons subscriber.
Conquest	Sophisticated geodemographic marketing tool that can pinpoint media target with precision; access to enormous data base, including census updates.	Larger agencies.	N.A.
Donovan	Prebuying, media research, accounting and billing tool, with access to four-year syndicated data bases.	Bulk of large shops and many midsize shops.	Percentage of agency's billing.
Jefferson-Pilot Data Services Media Line	Range of functions from media planning to buying to tracking and billing.	About 28 large and midsize shops.	$3,000 a month and up, based on percentage of agency's billing.
Marketron	On-line system generates spot-radio rankings, CPMs, reach and frequencies, and audience flow analyses.	J. Walter Thompson/ Chicago, some small shops; mostly station reps.	Hourly fee ranges from $85–$90 per hour.
Media Management Plus	Prebuy negotiating tool—allows buyers to rank stations in each market, calculate projected television and radio ratings.	More than 900 mostly midsize agencies.	$150–$7,000 a month, depending on usage, billings, and data requested.
MEMRI	Generates tabulations, reach and frequencies, and optimizations using syndicated data bases that include everything but SMRB.	Many of largest agencies.	$10,000 a year.
Tapscan	Calculates television and radio reach and frequency, offers access to syndicated data; combines reach and frequency reports for radio, newspaper, and television.	Mostly midsize agencies.	$200–$4,000 a month, depending on number of markets requested.

Primarily Planning Systems

Name of Software	What It Does	Users	Price
IMS Passport	Helps rank media options by cost and audience, create flowcharts; linked to most syndicated data bases.	35 of top 50 agencies, as well as many of the small and midsize shops.	Anywhere from $1,000–$15,000 a year, based on which software and number of workstations.
Lotus 1–2-3	Documents and calculates media-plan data; "Always" enhancement prints out presentation-quality spreadsheets.	All-size agencies.	$495 per diskette.
MANAS	Produces color, high-quality flowcharts; calculates cost and audience estimates using Nielsen data base.	More than 100 agencies worldwide, including many of the largest.	$1,500–$50,000 a year for three-year contract, depending on number of workstations.
Telmar MicroNetwork II	Analyzes media data, devises media plans, creates flowcharts.	More than 100 agencies, primarily small and midsize agencies.	$2,000–$75,000 a year, depending on number of software packages.

Competitive Systems

Name of Software	What It Does	Users	Price
Ad-Spender	New product that helps planners compute competitive spending reports based on *BAR/LNA* nine-media data.	Hill, Holliday, Connors, Cosmopulos is only user; expects to sell to 15–20 shops by year's end.	User must subscribe to *BAR/LNA* multimedia reports; pricing based on agency total billings.
Arbitron's BrandTraQ	Combines *BAR* television data with Arbitron ratings.	Advertisers only; no agencies subscribe due to high cost.	Based on ad categories, ad volume, and market share; nominal cost to agencies when piggybacked on client's contract.
LNA On-Line	Multiyear summaries of competitive expenditures by brand, parent company, and Publishers Information Bureau classification for nine media.	Magazines, print-heavy agencies, and 25–30 large agencies.	$10,000–$100,000 a year to access service, plus $100 per hour for usage on-line.

Source: "Hard Facts on Software," *Marketing & Media Decisions,* Special Report, October 1989, 68.

use of multiple vehicles) while controlling frequency. The frequency that results from vehicle overlap is not necessarily undesirable; more often, the question is how to count the overlap to know what level of exposure frequency is being achieved.

For the most part, models of reach and frequency combinations are derived from standard patterns of mathematical combinations. These models estimate the numbers of persons who are exposed to a media schedule. The persons exposed to an advertising campaign in more than one vehicle are called the **duplicated audience.** The number of persons who are reached at least once by a combination of vehicles, whether or not they are duplicated, is the **unduplicated audience.** Those persons who are reached at least once by multiple insertions within a single vehicle, whether or not they are duplicated, constitute the **accumulative audience** (or **cumulative audience**). They may be more important to media planners than the duplicated audience because the unduplicated and accumulative audience measures indicate how many different persons were exposed to an advertising campaign (that is, they represent the **reach** for the campaign), while the duplicated audience counts only those audience members communicated to at least twice and only then by some media combination.

Exposure Models and Distribution Models

Exposure and distribution models are used to plan the complete media schedule for an advertising campaign, which accounts for their being referred to as "comprehensive media-planning models." In these models, information about audience exposure to vehicles is used with exposure duplication figures (in exposure models) to derive optimal media vehicle selection and optimal advertisement insertion frequency, to maximize the message distribution (in distribution models) within the budget constraints.

Some such models utilize only a single variable as the input factor, while others use multiple variables. Still another category relies on the concept of aggregation. Both single-variable and multiple-variable models tend to be separated according to media, with different models for print and broadcast media, while aggregate models concentrate on print media only.

Single-Variable Models

Most of the print-media models focus on consumer magazines. Some of these models are quite accurate in their estimates of total reach achieved through some combination of magazines in a print advertising campaign, when compared with actual tabulated reach figures.[2] This checking is usually only valid for combinations of two magazines, however, because the syndicated research data concern only two-vehicle and two-issue combinations. Thus, when more or fewer than two insertions per magazine are selected for the actual campaign, accuracy of the models may diminish. Various studies have shown the more accurate models to be the full stochastic distribution models developed by Hofmans.[3]

Limited stochastic reach models are single-variable models. They provide only the final answer in summary form for all vehicles and all insertions in the media schedule, so they do not preserve each vehicle's individual data. These models deliver only an estimate of reach, not repeat exposure distribution.

Stochastic reach-distribution models combine a recognized and widely used formula for reach with the exposure distribution gained from probability statistics. The estimated reach is applied to a probability distribution to improve both the reach and frequency estimates.[4]

For broadcast media, deterministic models use a probability curve applied to actual research results to estimate overall reach and gross-rating-point (GRP) figures. Various sample schedules that represent those under consideration are compared to the statistical curve using standard multiple regression techniques to find the "best fit" among the plans tested. The actual gross rating points are easily calculated from known syndicated sources, so they are entered into the formula to arrive at an estimate of total reach.

Another technique, the combined deterministic stochastic distribution model, applies a similar approach to the research parameter to produce direction for achieving specific reach and frequency goals.[5] This technique, then, is almost the reverse of the one just discussed because the audience exposure figures are established as initial goals rather than as outcomes of a test plan.

Finally, limited-information stochastic distribution models use the audience data from a single broadcast advertisement insertion, which are available from syndicated research services. These models assume random duplication of vehicles, which tends to produce underestimates of the total achieved reach.[6]

Multiple-Variable Models

While single-variable models tend to average together all the media vehicles being considered for the campaign plan, multiple-variable models try to save information on the audiences of individual vehicles by preserving as many data dimensions as the number of vehicles. This can result in a huge number of cells containing individual vehicle data, so the number is often lowered by using approximation techniques. Even with this approximation approach, the multiple-variable models tend to be more accurate than single-variable models in estimating audience exposure and distribution.

Aggregate Models

Another way to counter the problem of the huge amounts of data that derive from multiple-variable models is to use aggregate models of exposure distribution. These models provide more accurate estimates of reach, which tends to decline with the addition of more vehicles in other kinds of models. Additional vehicles are aggregated into the results from existing combinations so that individual vehicle data are retained while simplifying the calculations.[7] As mentioned earlier, aggregate models have so far been applied only to print-media situations.

General Media-Planning Models

More comprehensive media models permit the application of specific media objectives, rather than only the reach and frequency estimates that result from the models discussed previously. Other portions of the media process also can be applied to these models to facilitate actual selection of media, vehicles, and units for the advertising plan. The data inputs are usually cost, availability, ratings, and similar data. The results are most often in the form of vehicles or media being considered, with recommended numbers of insertions, total cost figures, and projections of the impact on inquiries, sales, lead generation, or store traffic. Some of these models even provide optimal schedule timing. These general media-planning models include arithmetic programs, simulations, and the so-called heuristic models.

Arithmetic Program Models

Arithmetic program models were the earliest general media-planning models. They use linear programming techniques, which involve linear equations (the mathematical representation of a straight line) to which the data are fitted. If there are three variables in a linear equation and two of them are known, the third can then be calculated. So the known values of vehicle audience and duplication can lead, for example, to estimates of actual numbers of readers. The media can then be compared on the basis of, say, penetration of some particular target group.

There are constraints, such as budget limits, on arithmetic program models, just as there are in real-life situations. The most obvious limit is that linear solutions must be applied to all problems, but not all relationships among variables can be expressed as straight-line equations. Many variables, such as audience duplication figures and media cost figures, simply are not linear. As a result, audience exposure estimates can be relatively far from the mark. Although variations on the arithmetic program models have been proposed to deal with these sorts of problems, the variations tend to be piecemeal solutions that have not been successfully combined into an integrated approach.

Simulation Models

Because most use of simulation models has been by advertising agencies, which understandably retain the procedural information as proprietary, only a few general details are known. A computer uses various population data to calculate hour-by-hour exposures, providing some idea of each audience member's exposure to the advertising campaign, based on individual geographic, social, and economic characteristics.[8] The computer can quickly total the exposures for each possible media combination, although media planners must evaluate the resulting audience characteristics and select the ones that most closely represent the campaign goals.

Whether simulation models represent real audiences is questionable. Advertising agencies that have developed such models may be hesitant to check them against actual test results because of the high cost of such tests and because the tests might point out problems with the models themselves.

Heuristic Models

The most recent developments in media models are the heuristic models, which use computers to apply incremental searches to create a media schedule in stages. This permits introducing the decision that leads to greatest efficiency, audience size, exposure frequency, or effectiveness at each successive stage of the process.

At the beginning of the campaign, the initial media are evaluated and selected. The resulting duplication figures are entered into the computer to provide estimates of unduplicated audience size and exposure frequency. Even rate discounts can be added into the consideration. Then the next-stage media decision is made, attaining optimal levels of whatever characteristics are considered most important, and again, the resulting duplication figures are used to make new calculations. This process is iterative and continues until the goals have been achieved or the budget has been expended.[9]

Newer heuristic models include the MEDIAC model, which calculates the sales potential for each market segment or target group, along with the group's media habits. The audience exposures that would result from a given advertising media insertion are combined with data on memory retention and forgetting curves to obtain optimal patterns of media continuity.[10]

The Advertising Decision Model (ADMOD) is able to deal simultaneously with media decisions, copy decisions, and budget decisions. It also takes into account audience awareness, attitude change, and trial-purchase behavior characteristics of audience members.[11] With ADMOD, the best schedule can be chosen for each alternative copy approach. Because it connects behavioral information with media exposure data, ADMOD is viewed as an advance in modeling evolution, but it still has limits. The amount of information needed is very expensive and time consuming to gather, and each copy approach requires new media response estimates.

A newer heuristic model, VEDIAC, has been applied only to network television schedules.[12] Although similar to MEDIAC, this new model assigns factors based on product usage by various market segments, which provide some indication of sales potential by segment. VEDIAC can be applied at various levels of intensity as well, permitting media planners more experimentation with the plan under study, although some other media components are not included in the VEDIAC model.

Heuristic models, then, are more sophisticated and more complex than other general media-planning models, which means that they require more data, money, and finesse. They also tend to be more efficient than simulation models because they deal with marginal changes.

Response Functions

Of major concern to media planners is the actual response that can be traced to the media effort. This is highly complex because, first, most advertising response measures are linked to copy effects rather than media effects. Copy and media effects within a single advertising campaign effort are very difficult to separate. Second, attempting to trace effects

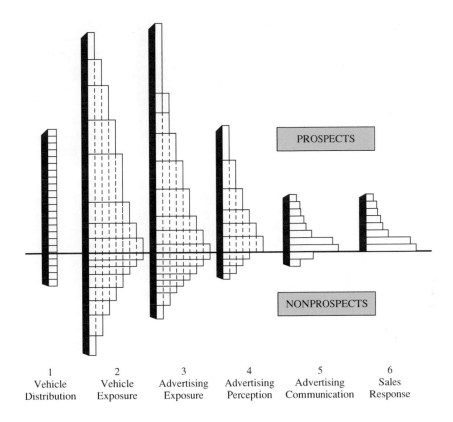

FIGURE 13.2 The Advertising Research Foundation
(ARF) Model for Evaluating Media
Source: "Reprinted from *Toward Better Media Comparisons*
© Copyright 1961 and 1983, by the Advertising Research Foundation."

back to advertising at all, and especially to specific entities within advertising, is risky because of the fallacy of assuming causal relationships.

How media work on an audience and how this impact can be tracked is explored next, using a standard model of advertising effectiveness. Then, various testing techniques employed in advertising media work are examined.

The ARF Model

For the past thirty years, the advertising industry has relied on a model for evaluating media effects that was developed by the Advertising Research Foundation (ARF). Although this model provides

some insights into how the media transmit the message and then how that results in communication, recall, and sales responses, it has recently come under question, so this topic is in a state of current development and change.

The ARF media evaluation model is divided into two major sections: prospects, shown in the upper part of figure 13.2, and nonprospects, below the center line. By definition, anyone who eventually makes a decision to purchase a product or service is a prospect.

The media evaluation process is then divided into six stages:

1. Distribution of the advertising media vehicle

MEDIA SPOTLIGHT

13.1

A Reconsideration of the ARF Model

by Stephen P. Phelps

Mr. Phelps is senior vice president and director of media services for Ross Advertising, Inc., in St. Louis.

If it isn't broken, why fix it? Strange as it may seem, this somewhat trite argument for status quo is at the heart of a two-year effort undertaken by the Advertising Research Foundation's (ARF) New Model Committee.

Over thirty years ago, when television was still in its infancy, a committee headed by Dr. Seymour Banks, then head of media research at Leo Burnett, and comprised of industry research leaders, was formed by the ARF to examine the means of measuring the effectiveness of advertising through use of the various media.

Three years later, in 1961, what emerged from these efforts was the ARF model for evaluating media. By employing a schematic of the advertising process to serve as the basis for isolating/identifying media-research needs, the committee was able to construct a simple but technically complete model that has stood the test of time.

But the question remains: Does the model, which has served us so well, still have relevance in today's marketing/media environment?

As chairman of the ARF's New Model Committee, formed to address this question, I can report that the committee wrestled long and hard during our initial meetings until we were able to hammer out a charter statement that accurately expressed our two interrelated objectives:

• First, "to examine the completeness of the 1961 model as a media evaluation tool in light of such factors as emergence of new media vehicle types, heightened interaction between the consumer, and the electronic media."

• And second, whether or not changes are deemed necessary in the basic model, "to explore the feasibility/appropriateness of incorporating the model into a larger schematic/s of the overall marketing process," based upon increased spending emphasis on promotion (consumer and trade) and the emergence of interactive marketing/media/advertising research tools (à la single source).

One year later, in mid-December 1988, the committee published, for internal ARF use only, its preliminary findings, which concluded: "The

2. Audience exposure to the vehicle

3. Audience exposure to a specific advertisement in the vehicle

4. Audience members' perception of the advertisement

5. Communication of the advertising message to the audience

6. Eventual decision regarding whether to purchase the advertised item

The model also displays the reach and frequency of the individual advertisement insertion. Reach is shown vertically: The distance above or below the center line indicates the comparative degree of reach achieved. Of course, reaching prospects (indicated by distance upward from the center line) is more desirable than reaching nonprospects (distance downward from the center line).

Frequency is indicated by the diagram's horizontal width for each stage of the process. Stage 1, model as originally designed is, in fact, not a singular model, but rather, a composite of two models. First, it is a model for evaluating media alternatives, and second, it is a model of the advertising process."

In this regard, it was the committee's recommendation that:

• As it has traditionally been used in the past, the first three stages of the model should form the basis for evaluating media options. By stopping short of phase four, it is believed that we should be better able to focus on the value of the media, while minimizing contamination from external factors (for example, the creative message).

• Once isolated, the media evaluation model should next be integrated into a broader model of the overall marketing communication process.

Finally, rather than publish these findings, it was the recommendation of the committee to convene a symposium of leading industry professionals to address the committee's original charter statement. The result, hopefully, will serve as a springboard for development of new models for the 1990s.

In this regard, on 27 June 1989, thirty industry leaders, including Dr. Banks, met at North-

western University in Chicago to air their thoughts on the subject. Even though a consensus was not reached at that time as to the specific shape a new model might take, it was generally agreed that the model as conceived in 1961 was in need of a "face-lift." Specific suggestions included: broadening the definition of the term *media,* better explaining placement of prospects and nonprospects relative to the horizontal axis, and considering a new title for stage 6 to replace "Sales Response."

As to next steps, in addition to preparation of a committee report on the symposium, it is planned that the papers presented will be published in the *Journal of Media Planning* by Professor Jack Sissors, the New Model Committee member who arranged for Northwestern to host the symposium.

Assuming all signs point in this direction, the last step would be the convening of an ARF workshop to explore the possibility of developing a more encompassing schematic of the marketing/advertising/media process, one that includes an updated media evaluation model as a key building block.

Source: Stephen Phelps, "A Reconsideration of the ARF Model," *Marketing & Media Decisions,* November 1989, 98.

"Vehicle Distribution," is narrow because the evaluation is of a single insertion. Some persons may see that insertion many times, resulting in a wider diagram for stage 2, "Vehicle Exposure."

Both reach and frequency decline (progressively narrower and shorter diagrams) as the process continues through the six stages. More persons are exposed to the entire vehicle than to any individual advertisement, and fewer still actually perceive the advertising message and understand it. Repeated

exposure to the advertisement by a single individual also declines: A magazine reader is more likely to reread some of the magazine than to reread any particular part of the magazine, such as a given advertisement. A logical conclusion is that exposure frequency, perception, and comprehension are more likely to be higher among prospects than among nonprospects, and the model shows that.

Much has been learned, however, during the years since this model was first introduced by the

ARF, and many critics and researchers have suggested various updating approaches. Even the ARF itself has a New Model Committee at work on the problem. Criticisms center on the model's overly simplistic nature, on whether the correct types of media impact are being measured, and on the difficulties of quantitatively applying real-world data to the model. The ARF model has been the best available, however, because it is relatively complete, sensible, and easy to comprehend.[13]

Testing

No matter what kind of model is employed to evaluate the effectiveness of a particular media effort, it is still necessary to gather data from advertising campaign outcomes. The data can then be evaluated to determine the efficacy and effectiveness of the media plan. The most common tests of advertising media involve split runs, coupons, and larger market tests.

Split Runs

The **split-run** technique directs different advertising approaches at separate, matched groups of audience members. For example, two different newspaper copy appeals might be tested by running both in a single issue of the newspaper, with half the circulation receiving one version and the other half the other version. Various response measures, such as telephone inquiries, coupon redemptions, research surveys, and merchandise turnover, can be employed to determine which version of the advertisement created more response. Split runs can be applied to copy tests as well as to media tests.

Sometimes, a certain medium or even a certain vehicle provides a better match with a particular advertising creative approach. In these cases, split runs can help to determine which media selections provide the most effective avenue for delivering the message or copy. Although split runs can be more easily used with print media, they also can be applied to broadcast situations.

Coupons

Coupons are widely used by advertisers to induce trial of an advertised item or to reward regular customers, usually with price-off offers or combination offers. Yet, coupons are also a valuable response measure for advertising media.

Several vehicles under consideration can be tested by inserting the same advertisement in each, along with a coded coupon. This coded **key** permits tracing coupon responses back to the individual vehicle in which they appeared, even though the keying may not be apparent to the audience.

While coupon distribution is an obvious attribute of print media, it is also feasible with broadcast advertising. Listeners can be asked to bring in a particular item, rather than a specific coupon ("Two dollars off your admission price with any item containing the words 'Coke' or 'Coca-Cola' "), or to make their own coupon ("Just write your name and phone number and the word 'Ford' on a three-by-five-inch piece of paper, and drop it in the entry box"). While these may be less orthodox methods of using coupons, the principles are the same.

Market Tests

The best test of media effectiveness is an actual experience in the marketplace. In most instances, trial and error at a full-scale level is far too expensive and risky: If the media plan turns out not to be solid, the campaign fails; it is difficult to know whether an alternate campaign would have worked better; and by the time the results are in, there is no opportunity to revise and start over. For these reasons, smaller-scale tests are conducted in only a few markets. New computer software, such as that depicted in figure 13.3, can aid modern media research tests.

Test marketing usually involves several markets, so interference or other problems in one market permit discarding of those results. Potential problems include: (1) interference from a competitor, who might run an advertising "blitz" to throw off the test; (2) a drastic change in the local economy,

FIGURE 13.3 An Advertisement Promoting
Computer Software for Advertising Media Planning
Courtesy of Dave Carlisle/Tapscan, Inc.

maybe because of a weather disaster or the closing of a major employer; (3) data collection problems, perhaps due to the inability to recruit qualified research aides; and (4) difficulties with local media, such as a lack of availabilities on local television or a strike at the local newspaper.

Test markets are usually paired with a set of **control** markets. The control areas receive the standard advertising media plan, perhaps following the pattern that has been used in the past, while the new media-plan proposal is tried in the test markets. In that way, test outcomes can be compared with a **benchmark** from known past experiences.

Selection of test markets is always important, but this step is even more essential for media tests. The markets must be large enough to have most available media, including local television stations and, ideally, metropolitan editions of consumer magazines and business publications. At the same time, the markets should be small enough to permit management of the research study and to minimize test expenses. Finally, the markets must reflect the larger population; ideally, they are representative of the national population as a whole. Some commonly used test markets in the United States are Peoria, Illinois; Wichita, Kansas; Fort Wayne, Indiana; Baton Rouge, Louisiana; Lexington, Kentucky; Sacramento, California; and New Haven, Connecticut.

Postscheduling

After the media schedule has been drafted, other steps remain to be completed. If the media plan is prepared by an advertising agency, there are internal checks within the agency to assure quality, consistency with the overall general marketing plan, and compatibility with the agency's work standards. Larger agencies have a media board that reviews all media plans; at smaller agencies, this review may be the task of the media director.

Following approval within the media department, there is another internal agency review by a plans board, which reviews all work (media, copy, art, research) prepared by the agency before it is presented to the advertiser (client). At any of these review stages, the plan may be returned for additional work, justification, clarity, or revision.

Clearance within the agency is only the first approval, of course. The proposal must then be presented to the advertiser—perhaps first to the advertising manager or marketing director for preliminary review, and eventually to the president and other officers for final approval. Again, changes and revisions often result.

In addition, preparing an advertising media plan is only part of the task. The planning process also involves **estimation** to determine the costs of the proposed media campaign. There is also the tactical or implementation stage, during which the plan is carried out, and which involves reserving media time and space, confirming orders, sending the appropriate advertising materials, checking to ascertain that the advertising placements were correct and as ordered, authorizing payment to the media themselves, and measuring the results of the media effort.

Evaluation of the advertising media effort is also very important. This is really a research procedure that attempts to verify the adequacy of the media plan and the accuracy of its forecasts. As such, the results of this evaluation become a research tool for the continuation of the next cycle of advertising or in the formulation of a revised advertising media plan. Looking back at figure 1.4 in chapter 1 may help you to envision this cyclical outcome of the advertising media effort.

Contingencies

What if the media plan does not work? What if conditions change during the course of the campaign? What if the results are not up to expectations? A **contingency plan** covers these unexpected conditions and tries to eliminate unforeseen situations by considering all the possibilities. Many times, the contingency plan is prepared as part of the original media plan; if not, it is the next project after the actual plan is complete. Contingencies also may interact with media strategies, as is shown in figure 1.4. (Refer back to chapters 1 and 6 for an understanding of how contingencies and other uncontrollable factors may affect advertising media strategies.)

A contingency plan involves more than simply putting monies aside in a reserve fund. Usually campaign funding is so tight that setting aside any money is impossible. Furthermore, placing some of the campaign funds in a reserve demonstrates that not all the monies are required for a successful campaign, which usually is not a desired impression. A reserve for unknown events may also raise doubts about the efficacy of the media plan and about the competence of the media planner. Planning for the unexpected, rather than actually funding it, is far more logical and businesslike.

Instead of a reserve fund, there should be flexible allocations with the media budget. Plans to use radio advertising can be changed up to the last minute. Newspaper advertising may also have a short advance-ordering requirement. Some local markets may have marginal value, so their allocations can be shifted, if needed, to other uses. The media plan usually accounts for all the media funds, but some of those monies are identified as available for other uses on short notice, should they be needed.

Types of Contingencies

Four common problems can be anticipated and countered with contingency plans:

1. Sales expectations are not being met.
2. Sales expectations are being exceeded.
3. A competitor takes some action that upsets the plan.
4. Economic conditions change.

If sales expectations are not being met, more than one option is available. One course of action is to cut back on advertising, to avoid "throwing good money after bad." Another possibility is to increase advertising in an attempt to offset the disappointing sales. Still another option is to redirect the advertising, taking allocations away from areas where the item's sales are poor and investing them in areas that show more promise. Yet, the opposite is also plausible: Reduce advertising in areas where sales are adequate and use the money to supplement areas that need help.

Sales exceeding expectations can also cause problems. Sales projections should be accurate: Too low a projection is just as much an error as too high. More is involved than advertising alone. To sell more items, more must be manufactured, which requires additional raw materials, more containers and shipping cartons, possible overtime for production employees, and increased use of transportation. At the same time, shortages of an item can create consumer dissatisfaction. When Procter & Gamble introduced Sure antiperspirant, the product's popularity was greater than anyone expected, and there was insufficient manufacturing capacity. To counter the problem, Procter & Gamble took out advertisements saying that a little Sure would go a long way and encouraging consumers to conserve when using the product.

When sales exceed expectations in the midst of a new product introduction, it is not part of the plan to ask customers *not* to buy. The question is, what should be done? As long as sales are so good, it may be possible to cut back on advertising and thereby reduce expenses. An alternative might be to increase advertising to take full advantage of the newfound good luck. Larger marketing implications accompany each potential course of action, however.

Competitors can also force the use of contingency plans. A competitor may introduce a new and better product, or double its advertising, or come up with a great new campaign theme that everybody is talking about, or gain approval of a government or public review board. Any of these would require alteration of the advertising plan.

In addition to competitors, every advertiser, large and small, must continually monitor the economic situation—locally, nationally, and globally. If the economy shows a downturn, it may be necessary to decrease advertising to reflect the expected reduction in sales, or it may be desirable to increase advertising to counter the economic trend. A company could also opt to advertise other items that are recession-proof or inflation-proof, or to feature different uses or packages. During depressions and recessions, Procter & Gamble sells smaller packages, but more of them, without sacrificing total volume. At least three times in the past fifteen years,

Media Strategists: Are they for real? Position granted.

by Judy Black

Ms. Black is vice president and strategic media project manager at Bozell advertising agency.

Media is a dynamic, changing function. Influenced by many variables—political, technological, societal, economical, and others—it is evolving from a relatively isolated discipline into a fully integrated partner in marketing planning and performance.

The number and range of media options have grown dramatically over the past decade, and this trend is accelerating into the 1990s. Both the traditional media and the newcomers, as a result of advances in technology and increased competition and demand, are opening new doors every day for advertisers.

For example, a personalized news medium may be on its way—a combination computer, newspaper, and television that "knows" your interests and information needs and is able to present only what is relevant to you. Your morning newspaper may tell you about the agenda of your afternoon meeting, give you a price update on your investment portfolio, fill you in on last night's baseball game, and then discuss the implications of Gorbachev's fourth visit to New York.

With the development of interactive television, commercials will also be targeted specifically to you while your neighbor or children watch the same show on a different set and see a different ad. The Media Lab, a part of M.I.T., has assured us that these new media forms are not fantasies.

The need to comprehend and work with an altered, more complex media environment and its applications on marketing strategies has broadened the role of the media function. It also has necessitated changes in media departments' structures, operations, and professional experience requirements.

---

international events have caused oil prices to rise rapidly, with drastic implications for gasoline marketers.

If the economy swings upward, increased advertising may take advantage of it, or reduced advertising may be possible because sales are increasing anyway, in line with the prosperity. Other changes may also be needed because good economic times can bring inflation and higher media costs, along with new competitors who are buoyed by the positive outlook.

Other problems can also occur, of course. Poor manufacturing or tainted raw materials may force a product recall. Bad publicity could spoil the offering of a new service. An unfounded rumor might induce potential customers to avoid some item.

Alternate Media Plans

The key to contingency planning is to have alternate media plans prepared and ready to be used, should they become necessary. If some disaster

How do you stay on the cutting edge of such media happenings and capitalize on resulting advertising possibilities early on? There is probably no one answer to this question. Agencies have redefined the position of media-planning generalists, looked to outside consultants, or have hired specialists.

At Bozell, the addition of a "media strategist" allows for a full understanding and evaluation of the varied spectrum of changes occurring now and the trends establishing themselves for the future. The function provides for an extension of the media knowledge and information base way beyond that made possible by merely expanding the media generalist's role. It gives us the ability to prepare in-depth reports for nontraditional media and to analyze these new developments in conjunction with creative and marketing programs in tandem with more conventional media. The days when each medium was unto itself are long gone.

The strategist's view must go beyond the domestic market. Geographic boundaries will become less and less meaningful, in Europe with the advent of 1992 and elsewhere with the speed of new telecommunication technologies. This means that the number of media combinations and permutations will multiply, as will the buys available. Obviously, these types of packages will not be appropriate for all products and services.

Also under consideration is how best to achieve the proper balance between national and local media. The problem is not a new one, but with retailer power on the increase and in-store opportunities proliferating, local media efforts must be coordinated more closely than ever before with promotional tie-ins and national campaigns.

At Bozell, the focus on media strategy and exploration provides planners in all of our offices with resources to better anticipate and service clients' continually changing needs. It gives planners the background and preparation for playing a more important role in the marketing process. It makes media planning a more vital and essential part of the marketing environment.

Source: Judy Black, "Media Strategists: Are They for Real?" *Marketing & Media Decisions*, December 1989, 154.

strikes, there simply is not adequate time to begin planning all over again. Alternate media plans need to be in place. And specific individual plans may be required for *each and every* possible contingency.

Alternate media plans need to be detailed and complete. Knowing in general terms what would be done in a given situation is helpful, but it is nowhere near the specificity needed should the contingency actually occur. Basically, good contingency media plans resemble complete media plans in and of themselves because, if the unexpected events occur, these contingency plans *will become* the actual media plans.

The ideal time to prepare alternate media plans is during the regular planning process. The problem is that the planning schedule rarely allows enough time for preparation of the actual media plan, much less alternate plans. One solution is to begin working on contingency plans immediately after the regular media plan has been completed. The timing is optimal: All the necessary information is already at hand from the planning just finished, the regular

MEDIA SPOTLIGHT

13.3

Media Strategists: Are they for real? Position scorned.

by Richard Kostyra

Mr. Kostyra is executive vice president and U.S. director of media service for J. Walter Thompson advertising agency.

At J. Walter Thompson, we have rejected the idea of a single "designated strategist" for the media department. Instead, we employ a host of strategists, each assigned to a limited number of accounts. We call them associate media directors, although we could just as easily refer to them as "account strategists."

Most other advertising agencies also have account-oriented strategists, and while they may possess different titles in different shops, we believe this arrangement best serves the clients' needs. Our philosophy at JWT is that strategy is

account-driven. Appointing a "designated strategist" for the entire agency is dangerous for several reasons, not the least of which is it shifts the focus of strategic development further from the client.

The typical AMD at J. Walter Thompson—we have about twenty in our six U.S. offices—has more than fifteen years' planning experience. In most cases, he or she works on just one or two major pieces of business. As the account's chief strategist, the AMD has an intimate knowledge of the client's marketing goals, an understanding of ad strategy, and a historical perspective on the brands.

The planners draw up the actual media plans. But it is the AMDs, or the "account strategists," who are charged with establishing the media strategy and ensuring that it is both on target and exploiting opportunities to the maximum. The AMDs make all major decisions, such as (but not limited to) setting guidelines for the overall media mix, deciding whether or not to use new media vehicles, recommending whether a

---

media plan is fresh in mind, and the contingency plans can be an extension of the work on the regular plan. Doing the contingency plans then also ensures that they will be ready if and when needed, with no unnecessary delays.

Summary

Preparing a media plan is complicated, and many factors must come under consideration. The budget may not be determined by media planners, but it rigidly constrains the scope of the media effort. Media planners may be able to allocate advertising funds for various purposes even if the total sum of money has already been set.

Various media models help media planners to use established patterns of advertising efficiency and effectiveness to determine audience exposures and distribution of advertising message weights. Another type of model provides insight into the effects of advertising media and how those effects may be evaluated. Other media evaluations can be conducted using split runs, coupons, and market tests.

After the media schedule is set, postscheduling functions that must be accomplished include approval of the media plan by the media department, the adverting agency, and the advertiser; estimation of the costs of the proposed media campaign;

client should heavy-up weight during key months, suggesting flighting or pulsing patterns and so on.

But not all strategizing occurs at the account level. The media director—the department's chief strategist—gives the AMDs direction on a wide range of issues. Because he or she has a broad view of goings-on for all agency accounts, along with full responsibility for buying and research, the media director can best offer broad strategy and direction.

Our account strategists also have many resources to draw on, including the broadcast-buying groups, the media-research staff, the market-research department, and others. Often, differing opinions come from these areas. The account strategist's job is to assess each alternative, consult with the media director, and make a recommendation specific to that client.

In some cases, two different AMDs will confront the same issue, utilize the same resources, but ultimately make differing recommendations. Does this mean the system has broken down? Absolutely not. It is a recognition that each client has different priorities.

A "Guru of Strategic Development" cannot be relied on to know the intricacies of each account. He or she lacks the ongoing interaction with the client that ensures new developments will not be overlooked. With such a limited knowledge of any particular client, and what that client's competitors are up to, it is presumptuous to assume he or she can come up with truly breakthrough ideas.

Also, consider the ill will that could result from the appointment of an "official" media department strategist. If I were to establish this position at JWT, I would be sending a message to our AMDs that strategizing is no longer their responsibility—or that they are incapable of strategizing. Either way, it would be discouraging and demoralizing to them—and disingenuous.

The need for a designated department strategist suggests to me that the AMDs and the media director are not properly fulfilling their responsibilities. If this is the case, solve the personnel problem—but do not duck the issue by "changing the system."

Source: Richard Kostyra, "Media Strategists: Are They for Real?" *Marketing & Media Decisions,* December 1989, 155.

implementation of the plan; and evaluation of the advertising media effort. Also required is a set of contingency plans to ensure readiness for unexpected events that may upset the existing media plan.

Questions for Discussion

1. How is the objective-and-task method of determining advertising budgets the seeming reverse of other budget-setting approaches used in advertising?

2. How do the responsibilities differ between determining the advertising budget appropriation and allocating the budget to various uses and purposes?

3. What problems are inherent in designing and using media models?

4. What might the ideal advertising media model be like?

5. Why does advertising need a model of response functions?

6. Why do some persons want to revise the ARF model? What are the ARF model's apparent shortcomings? What changes or improvements are needed?

7. Why is advertising media testing apparently more difficult than testing, say, the creative approach?

8. Are market tests the ideal? If so, why are they not more widely used?

9. Why is a benchmark necessary in market tests?

10. Why are contingency plans needed in advertising media work? Why is not a reserve fund adequate?

11. Can any contingency plan really anticipate all the possible eventualities?

Endnotes

1. For an excellent review of media decision models, see John Leckenby and Kuen-Hee Ju, "Advances in Media Decision Models," in *Current Issues and Research in Advertising,* vol. XII, nos. 1 and 2, ed. James H. Leigh and Claude R. Martin, Jr. (Ann Arbor, Mich.: Graduate School of Business Administration, University of Michigan, 1990), 312–57.

2. Jean-Louis Jose Chandon, *"A Comparative Study of Media Exposure Models."* (Ph.D. diss., Northwestern University, 1976.

3. Pierre Hofmans, "Measuring the Cumulative New Coverage of Any Combination of Media," *Journal of Marketing Research* 3 (1966): 269–78.

4. John Leckenby and S. Kishi, "Performance of Four Exposure Distribution Models," *Journal of Advertising Research* 22 (1982): 35–46.

5. R. S. Header, J. E. Klompmaker, and J. E. Teel, "TV Audience Exposure," *Journal of Advertising Research* 16 (1976): 49–52.

6. Marshall Rice and John Leckenby, "Predicting within-Vehicle Television Duplication," *Proceedings of the American Academy of Advertising,* 1984.

7. John Leckenby and Marshall Rice, "The Decline Reach Phenomenon in Media Exposure Models," *Journal of Advertising* 15 (1986): 13–20; and John Leckenby and T. Hsu, "A Large-Scale Test of the Declining Reach Phenomenon in Exposure Distribution Models," *Proceedings of the American Academy of Advertising,* 1987.

8. Dennis Gensch, "A Computer Simulation Model for Selecting Advertising Schedules," *Journal of Marketing Research* 6 (1969): 203–14.

9. William T. Moran, "Practical Media Decisions and the Computer," *Journal of Marketing* 27 (1963): 26–30.

10. John Little and Leonard Lodish, "A Media Selection Model and Its Optimization by Dynamic Programming," *Industrial Management Review* 8 (1966): 15–23; and John Little and Leonard Lodish, "A Media Planning Calculus," *Operations Research* (1969): 3–35.

11. David Aaker, "ADMOD: An Advertising Decision Model," *Journal of Marketing Research* 12 (1975): 37–45.

12. Roland Rust, "Selecting Network Television Advertising Schedules," *Journal of Business Research* 13 (1985): 483–94.

13. For a comprehensive examination of the ARF model, see the fall 1989 *Journal of Media Planning,* devoted entirely to suggestions for updating the 1961 ARF media evaluation model.

Suggested Readings

- Banks, Seymour. "Consideration for a New ARF Media Evaluation Model." *Journal of Media Planning,* Fall 1989, 8–10.

- Green, Charles P. "A Model for Evaluating Individual's Behavior When Influenced by Advertising." *Journal of Media Planning,* Fall 1989, 16–19.

- Leckenby, John D., and Kuen-Hee Ju. "Advances in Media Decision Models." In *Current Issues and Research in Advertising,* edited by James H. Leigh and Claude R. Martin, Jr. Ann Arbor, Mich.: Graduate School of Business Administration, University of Michigan, 1990.

- Phelps, Stephen. "A Reconsideration of the ARF Media Model." *Journal of Media Planning,* Fall 1989, 2–3.

- Priemer, Gus. "A Better Media Model Starts with Understanding of How Advertising Works." *Journal of Media Planning,* Fall 1989, 29–32.

- Spaeth, Jim. "Advertising Effects and Media Planning." *Journal of Media Planning,* Fall 1989, 40–44.

PART V

TACTICAL DECISIONS

Chapter 14

General Tactical Decisions

Outline

Learning Objectives

In the study of this chapter, you will have the opportunity to:

- Observe how tactical decisions derive from the major strategy aspects of a media plan.
- Study the diverse skills that are necessary in performing the media-buying function.
- Examine how some of the major media structure the space and time units sold to advertisers.
- See some of the common rate structures and discount policies for several media types.
- Learn how buys are made for particular media.

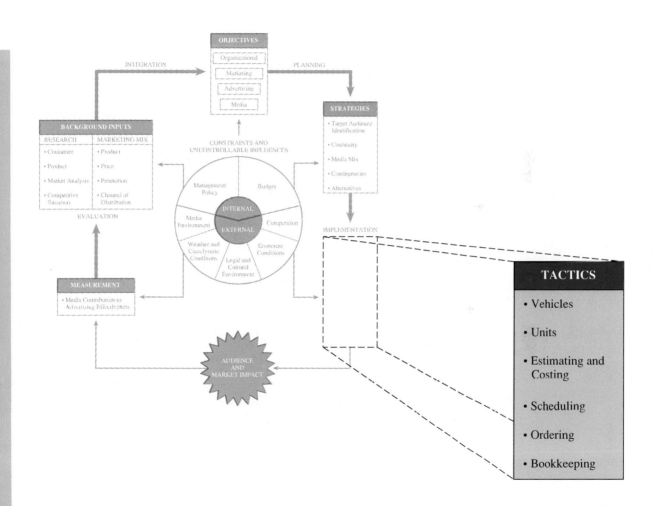

OBJECTIVES
- Organizational
- Marketing
- Advertising
- Media

INTEGRATION

PLANNING

STRATEGIES
- Target Audience Identification
- Continuity
- Media Mix
- Contingencies
- Alternatives

BACKGROUND INPUTS

RESEARCH
- Consumer
- Product
- Market Analysis
- Competitive Situation

MARKETING MIX
- Product
- Price
- Promotion
- Channel of Distribution

EVALUATION

CONSTRAINTS AND UNCONTROLLABLE INFLUENCES

INTERNAL
EXTERNAL

Management Policy
Budget
Media Environment
Competition
Weather and Cataclysmic Conditions
Economic Conditions
Legal and Cultural Environment

IMPLEMENTATION

MEASUREMENT
- Media Contribution to Advertising Effectiveness

AUDIENCE AND MARKET IMPACT

TACTICS
- Vehicles
- Units
- Estimating and Costing
- Scheduling
- Ordering
- Bookkeeping

*P*art 4 discussed the major strategic decisions that must be made in developing a media plan: setting objectives, identifying target audiences, determining scheduling strategies, deriving a media mix, and taking into account other factors. In Part 5—"Tactical Decisions"—we examine how these strategies are executed. This chapter deals with tactics in a *general* sense to explore how strategy can be effectively implemented. Subsequent chapters discuss tactics for *specific* media types: newspapers and magazines (chapter 15), television and radio (chapter 16), direct-mail and out-of-home media (chapter 17), and other media types (chapter 18).

Whereas strategic decisions commonly involve *media planning*, tactical execution is concerned with *media buying*. Although media planning is vitally important, the strategy used is only as good as the execution (how the media are purchased). Advertising and media strategy are fully dependent on how close actual schedules are to planned objectives. Although this tactical implementation phase is called media buying, it is more than just selecting media vehicles and units and placing insertion orders. The buying phase also involves audience and cost estimation, negotiation, and skillful schedule monitoring.

In many organizations, the separation of function between media planning and buying is minute. Often, the type of media used dictates the difference. In the planning of a consumer magazine schedule, for example, once the publications are chosen according to audience values, the costing of a specific schedule usually completes the media process. In spot-market broadcast schedules, however, the planning may establish broad reach and frequency goals and the needed gross rating points (GRP) to achieve them. No program or unit cost specifications are made until the buying begins; those are the buyer's duties. The rating-point goals must be translated into station availabilities, price negotiation, and the scheduling of each participation. These are duties primarily handled by media buyers when an agency has both planning and buying personnel.

Even though the responsibilities of media planners and buyers shift, the duties and skills desired in media buying are clearly recognized. In this chapter, those skills and techniques are discussed with a particular focus on how media buyers can offer the best service to the firm and the media representatives with whom they deal.

Media-Buying Skills and Techniques

Certain media-buying skills must be mastered whether the media buying is an executive or a clerical function. Certain buying duties require mechanical or procedural skills, while others demand social or human relations ability. Similarly, there are many different ways to negotiate or learn the media business, and a media buyer's personality may dictate the best approach. Media buying, when practiced expertly, encompasses a broad range of talents and skills. Beyond behaving fairly and consistently in professional relations, a buyer's technique may depend on personal perspectives.

Media Research Skills: Knowledge of Media Audiences

A primary tool of media analysis is audience research, and media buyers must become familiar with a multitude of sources. Earlier chapters, especially chapter 5, discussed the number of syndicated research reports for the major media on regular and systematic schedules. Media buyers must learn the individual format and data organization of each report since no two are exactly alike. Some circumstances also demand that buyers understand various survey methodologies to be able to evaluate discrepancies among competing reports. It takes repeated use of an audit statement or a broadcast rating book to handle the information accurately.

Beyond regularly scheduled syndicated research, numerous special audience studies are subsidized by broadcast stations or print publications. Media salespeople use these ad hoc reports to fill gaps in knowledge or to counter research studies done by competitors. Typical illustrations include when a radio station in a smaller market conducts a survey to measure program popularity, or when a magazine underwrites a readership study to determine editorial authority and influence.

The problem for media buyers is how to interpret and utilize such information. Dismissing all media-sponsored research is not the answer, but neither is blind acceptance of every research study passed across buyers' desks. Partisan research may be valid and reliable, but media buyers must know the methodology well enough to judge whether the study is objective and if it is helpful in making a decision.

Media Cost Estimation

Many advertising agencies begin media trainees in cost estimation, in part because individuals cannot contribute in media analysis until they have a good understanding of media cost policies and discount applications. Unfortunately, the learning process is complicated.

For a number of years, the advertising industry has urged the media to use standardized rate cards, discounts, and buying procedures, but such urgings have met with only modest success. Each station and publication sets rate schedules and discount policies to suit its particular needs. Situations dictate many alternatives, and media buyers must ac-

TABLE 14.1

Media Unit Cost Trends, 1987–1991 (Expressed as percent change from previous year)

Medium	1987	1988	1989	1990	1991*
Network Television (Nighttime)	3.2%	5.9%	5.00%	8.2%	5.7%
Network Television (Daytime)	−7.7	−3.4	−8.0	4.2	4.0
Spot Television	5.6	5.9	4.6	4.8	4.9
Network Radio	5.7	3.2	4.3	4.6	4.9
Spot Radio	4.4	4.0	4.5	3.6	4.3
Consumer Magazines	4.3	4.7	5.7	6.2	6.7
Sunday National Magazines	—	—	—	6.3	5.3
Cable Television	—	—	18.7	7.6	9.0
Daily Newspapers	6.5	6.0	6.1	6.1	5.7
Outdoor Posters	4.9	4.8	6.2	4.9	4.4
Business Publications	5.3	4.9	5.5	4.7	6.4
Yellow Pages	—	5.2	5.7	5.3	5.2
National Television Syndication	—	5.4	4.8	6.2	5.9

*Anticipated.
Source: Marketing & Media Decisions, 1 August 1990, 23.

custom themselves to many different ways of calculating time or space. Later in this chapter, we discuss some common formats for rate schedules and discounts.

Part of understanding how to estimate media costs means being well-versed in period-to-period media cost trends. Such expertise helps in deciding how to optimize particular media purchases. For example, if a particular medium has significant cost increases without corresponding gains in audience delivery, media buyers may be able to use such information in negotiating a buy. Table 14.1 shows the percentage change in media costs over a five-year period for several media types. That daytime network television decreased its unit costs in three of the five years could be useful to a media buyer's negotiations in this medium.

MEDIA SPOTLIGHT

Which Media Do It Best?

Most planners rely on a facility with numbers to make the case for advertising efficiency. But, when planning for R.O.I. (a measure of advertising efficiency), the planner must address not only *quantitative* evidence of dollar value, but more importantly, the *qualitative* effect of message allocation.

In simplest terms, the R.O.I. system insists not just on *more* customers (the target delivery), but on more creative advertising contact with *each* customer. The purpose, of course, is to promote a marriage of medium and message that does not countenance divorce.

The facing chart (see figure 1) illustrates the relative effectiveness of the five major media. The ratings are not intended to be definitive; they may vary with different products and campaigns.

The chart indicates, for example, that if the advertising is intended to *demonstrate the capabilities* of a product, television would probably be the best medium for the job. Television enables the advertiser to show at a glance just what the product does, and how.

In similar fashion, if the campaign involves the highly *personal* and *intimate* presentation of a product, what better medium to use than radio? It is radio's capability to stage a "theater of the mind" that allows listeners to become a part of the scene.

For products which demand an aura of *quality,* magazines readily come to mind. The comparability of meaningful, well-written, in-depth editorial that can be found in some magazines and the classic advertising placed in them for such products as fine crystal, expensive watches and luxury automobiles creates a bond of credibility

and quality that could not develop as well in any other medium.

And so it goes. Newspapers provide news of products, just as they relate news and the story behind the events. Outdoor has power to convey a message "bigger than life."

Creative media planning requires that the planner know each medium "from the inside." Radio station owners and programmers, for example, can describe their listeners' desire for jazz, country and western, and other music forms, and their need to eavesdrop on talk shows. Television programmers and managers can enhance our knowledge of the viewers' taste for sports as entertainment and the high drama of mini-series, and their insatiability for news and soap opera drama. Editors and publishers can tell us about readers' thirst for recipes, decorating ideas, financial advice and the like.

The rankings of the five major media are not invariable. They are, to a large extent, dependent upon the actual advertisement they are to carry. A beautifully executed television commercial may convey sex appeal, for example, better than even the rich color possibilities available in magazines.

A medium's ranking can also vary based on the audience's perception of that medium. Audience perceptions can change as the medium itself changes or as the "times" change. Economic conditions, lifestyle trends, and the mood of the populace can all affect a medium's ability to communicate, *with power,* a given message.

The rankings that follow are highly subjective and they invite argument. That is the true purpose of the chart—to force the planner to think about the qualities that give each medium its unique vitality. Those qualities set one medium apart from another, and give the planner freedom to exercise judgment in deciding which media do it best.

Source: DDB Needham Worldwide. Reprinted by permission.

FIGURE 1 Ratings of Effectiveness for Five Major
Media in Delivering Particular Messages
Source: DDB Needham Worldwide. Reprinted by permission.

TABLE 14.4

Open-rate structure applied to color rates for newspapers

Use b/w rate plus the following applicable costs:

	b/w 1 c	b/w 2 c	b/w 3 c
Daily, extra	$800	$1,100	$1,400
Sunday, extra	900	1,300	1,800

---

more. Other newspapers using this format may have different prices for the daily and Sunday papers, and these would be shown.

Many newspapers offer advertisers a choice of using color in their advertisements, and such rate charges also are handled and listed in *SRDS*. Color charges are called "extra" or "add-on"; that is, the cost of the advertisement in black-and-white is determined first, and then the extra charge for color is added. Color can be purchased as (1) black-and-white plus one color (b/w 1 c), (2) black-and-white plus two colors (b/w 2 c), and (3) black-and-white plus three colors (b/w 3 c). With three colors plus black, virtually *any* color desired can be achieved. For example, reproduction of a photograph that contains many different colors would require this form of color reproduction, generally called "four color" or "full color."

Table 14.4 shows the color charges for the newspaper whose black-and-white rates were given in table 14.2. Given the same example presented for table 14.2, the cost of running the 5-column by 18-inch ad, bought once a week on a weekday for 52 weeks, in *black plus two colors* can now be calculated. The extra charge for each such color ad is shown in table 14.4 to be $1,100. Since a total of 52 color ads are being purchased, the extra charge for color is $57,200 ($1,100 for b/w 2 c × 52 ads = $57,200). Thus, the total cost for this schedule of a color advertisement is $417,560 ($360,360 for b/w + $57,200 color add-on = $417,560). The cost of the ad *each* time it runs is $417,560 ÷ 52 =

$8,030. An alternate way to compute the cost of each color ad is as follows (5 columns × 18 inches × $77 per column inch) + $1,100 extra for b/w 2 c = $8,030.

Magazines

The primary reference for magazine costs is *SRDS*. One *SRDS* volume has rate information for consumer magazines and farm publications (each in a separate section), and another volume contains information for business publications.

Magazines primarily sell display space (other than classified) in page and fractional-page units, so most rates and discounts are arranged in this fashion. (Some magazines, however, also include rates in column inches or lines as well, so that a small-space advertiser can easily compute the cost.) Black-and-white rates are shown separately from color rates, and most publications show color rates *inclusive* of space charges, rather than as add-on charges. Another unique aspect of magazine rates is the charge (or absence thereof) for bleed advertisements. **Bleed** is a process whereby the illustration or graphic in the message is extended to the edge of the magazine page (no border). Some publications set a standard premium for such production, typically around 15 percent more than the space charge.

Magazine discounts for national editions are based on the frequency of insertion (issues or units used), the volume of space used (pages or page equivalents), or the volume in dollars. Table 14.5 shows the variations for one magazine. Thus, a full-page, four-color advertisement in five issues of this magazine would cost $12,000 ($2,400 per ad [the "3 ti" rate] × 5 ads = $12,000). Some magazines permit combining various sizes of units to arrive at the frequency. Thus, a schedule that calls for four full-page, four-color ads and four half-page, four-color ads would earn the "6 ti" rate; the cost of this schedule would be: (4 × $2,200) + (4 × $1,500) = $14,800.

Some publications handle the scheduling of mixed-size advertisements by allowing all space to be combined for its equivalent in pages. Often, such discounts are in addition to a frequency discount. Table 14.6 shows this. Thus, ten full-page, sixteen

TABLE 14.5

Frequency Discounts for Magazines

Black and White Rates

	1 ti*	3 ti	6 ti
1 page	$1,975	$1,785	$1,665
2/3 page	1,385	1,230	1,000
1/2 page	1,185	1,100	925
1/4 page	735	635	540

Color Rates

Black and one color:

1 page	$2,375	$1,985	$1,865
2/3 page	1,785	1,530	1,200
1/2 page	1,385	1,300	1,125
1/4 page	935	835	740

Four colors:

1 page	$2,495	$2,400	$2,200
2/3 page	2,000	1,855	1,625
1/2 page	1,800	1,725	1,500
1/4 page	1,355	1,255	1,160

*ti = times (issues)

TABLE 14.6

Frequency and Volume Discounts for Magazines

Black and White Rates

	1 ti	4 ti	6 ti	12 ti
1 page	$107,140	$104,995	$102,855	$99,640
1/2 page	57,585	56,435	55,280	53,555
1/4 page	29,465	28,875	28,285	27,400

Volume Discounts

Advertisers running at least twelve equivalent pages per contract year earn the following discount, in addition to frequency discounts:

	Discount
12 pages	3%
18 pages	4%
24 pages	5%
30 pages	6%

TABLE 14.7

Gross Expenditures Discount for Magazines

Dollar Volume	Discount Percentage
$357,000 to $713,999	3
$714,000 to $1,070,999	6
$1,071,000 to $1,427,999	9
$1,428,000 to $2,141,999	12
$2,142,000 to $2,855,999	18
$2,856,000 to $3,569,999	24
$3,570,000 to $4,283,999	30
$4,284,000 to $4,997,999	36
$4,998,000 and over	40

half-page, and sixteen one-quarter-page ads (all black-and-white) would earn the "12 ti" frequency discount as well as the "18-page" equivalent discount of 4 percent (10 + 8 + 4 = 22-page equivalent). Costs would be figured as follows: (10 ads × $99,640) + (16 ads × $53,555) + (16 ads × $27,400) = $2,291,680, less the 4 percent volume discount for the 22-page equivalent = $2,200,012.80, the total cost of the schedule.

A variation of the page-equivalent discounts may be offered on total dollars spent. A straight percentage discount may be given to advertisers once a given number of dollars is contracted for. The dollar-volume schedule in table 14.7 is from a leading consumer publication in the home service area. To arrive at the discount, the advertiser combines all size units purchased, whether in color or black-and-white, to identify the total dollars bought during the contract year. Thus, an advertiser contracting for $2,285,898 in space would earn an 18 percent discount, or $411,461.64. The total cost of the schedule would be $1,874,436.36 ($2,285,898 − $411,461.64 = $1,874,436.36).

TABLE 14.8

Black-and White Rates for Geographic Editions of Magazines

	Cost-per-Thousand Circulation		
Circulation Range	1 page	2/3 page	1/2 page
to 125,000	$14.60	$10.60	$5.60
125,000–299,999	10.20	5.80	4.00
300,000–499,999	8.80	5.00	3.50

Many magazines offer advertisers the opportunity to purchase regional or geographic space—that is, a portion of a publication's total circulation. For example, an advertiser might purchase a section of the United States (say, the southeastern states) or individual states (say, New York, California, Texas, and Illinois), or in some cases, a metropolitan market (such as New York City, Boston, Chicago, or Miami).

Presenting the costs of each geographic unit sold by some magazines could produce a bewildering listing in *SRDS*. For example, certain magazines offer over one hundred different regional areas (for example, each of fifty states, as well as fifty to one hundred major city markets). One way to handle this is to list the circulations for each geographic area that can be bought either singly or in combination, and also to provide a cost factor based on the number of thousands of circulation used. If an advertiser bought five different geographic regions that totaled 280,000 in circulation, then, from table 14.8, a full-page, black-and-white ad would cost $2,856 (280 [thousands of circulation] × $10.20 cost for each thousand = $2,856). Some publications, instead of a range of calculations, have a fixed charge for so much circulation and follow with a cost-per-thousand factor for the remaining surplus circulation. Magazines typically price the **cover po-**

sitions (there usually are three: (1) inside front cover, or second cover; (2) inside back cover, or third cover; and (3) back cover, or fourth cover) at rates that are higher than positions inside the magazine. They also usually require that cover space be full-page and in four colors. The rates are listed separately from the black-and-white and color rates.

Broadcast Media (Television and Radio)

Broadcast buying is the most lively purchase activity encountered but can also be anxious and frustrating, possibly because of the changes in programming and commodity pricing traditions that have had substantial impact on buying procedures. Also, unlike print-media planning, broadcast plans and estimates seldom include specific stations, networks, or programs. The reason generally is that someone planning months in advance cannot know which stations or networks will have the best commercial time available at the time when the campaign will be run.

The buying process begins with the media plan specifying audience targets, gross-rating-point (GRP) levels and/or cost-per-thousand (CPM) limits, and schedule periods. Media buyers inform the broadcasters of these needs, and the stations offer plans or, in the case of network television, program availabilities. Buyers then review the competitive submissions and begin to negotiate for better programs (higher ratings) and lower prices.

Negotiation involves buyers contacting competitive stations or networks and informing them of what the others have offered. It is a form of auction. Depending on supply and demand, the transaction process may reduce prices or improve availabilities, or it may be a waste of time. Once buyers are satisfied that the commercial spot or participation schedule is as close to the plan specifications as possible, insertion orders (followed by contracts) are made. The amount of time involved in the broadcast transaction process is ultimately dependent on a buyer's resourcefulness and the station or network's willingness to negotiate.

While the buying process just described fits both television and radio, and network and spot activity, there remain substantial differences among these areas in other aspects of the purchase process. The individual discussions that follow highlight some of the most distinguishing characteristics of each.

Network Television

In some ways, the network negotiation is the easiest buy, while in other ways, it is the most difficult. The process of scheduling, ordering, and shipping commercials is much simpler than it is with spot activity because, typically, there are only a few networks to deal with. On the other hand, the dollars at stake and the unstable nature of audience preference and pricing make network television buying a risk-filled activity.

The pricing for network programming today is based on the thirty-second commercial length, although other units (for example, sixty seconds and fifteen seconds) are also available. The networks assign costs on a program-by-program basis. At the same time, numerous areas of network programming operate like a commodities market, with prices fluctuating according to demand.

There is no *SRDS* for network costs because pricing is too fluid. The general ranges can be learned from trade journals, but the only accurate source is direct contact with the network.

There typically are two methods of network purchase: (1) selected-program participation or (2) scatter plan. In the **selected-program procedure,** media buyers have studied the audience histories of shows and know which audiences best match the target-prospect groups. Program candidates are located at each network, and negotiations begin. This method guarantees the desired audience characteristics and usually involves the higher-rated programs. It is a more expensive way of buying television, however, because the best prospect programs are in demand by a number of buyers, which supports higher network prices.

A considerable portion of selected-program buying in network television is handled by **up-front buying**. In this situation, buyers make arrangements to purchase programs when the programs are

first offered by the networks. For a new fall season, this usually occurs in late spring or early summer. Advertisers and their agencies work with network salespeople in determining the prices that will be paid for specific programs, the length of the schedule (say, for thirty-nine weeks), the guaranteed delivery of audiences, provisions for cancellation, and the like. Once the inventory of programs is sold during the up-front period, remaining programs are available for "scatter" buys.

The **scatter plan** works on a different theory. Here, media buyers tell the network the audience specifications and indicate the amount of money available. The network develops and offers a package of programs of various popularity and scheduling. Buyers do the same with other networks, and once the initial proposals are in, competitive negotiation begins. The network wants the advertiser's budget, and buyers want the best programs for the lowest possible price. The sacrifices on such sales are that program quality is usually uneven (one excellent show is packaged with average and even mediocre ones), and there is little schedule continuity. As a general rule, advertisers seeking more broadly defined audience prospects favor the scatter plan, while firms with narrower profiles are compelled to seek more selective programming. Figure 14.2 shows a trade advertisement for USA network.

Spot-Market Television

Spot-market television buying must balance the advantage of geographic flexibility with the logistics problems of dealing on a multistation basis with a variety of sales plans and discount arrangements. Buyers learn the necessary shortcuts to make spot buying more time efficient, but it is a demanding aspect of media buying.

Standard Rate and Data Service publishes information for many television stations in the United States, but currently, a large number of stations do not provide rates (an issue of *SRDS Spot Television Rates and Data* is likely to have the phrase, "Rates Not Submitted," in the rate section of the listing). Rate schedules that are provided give buyers a general price guide and an idea of the type

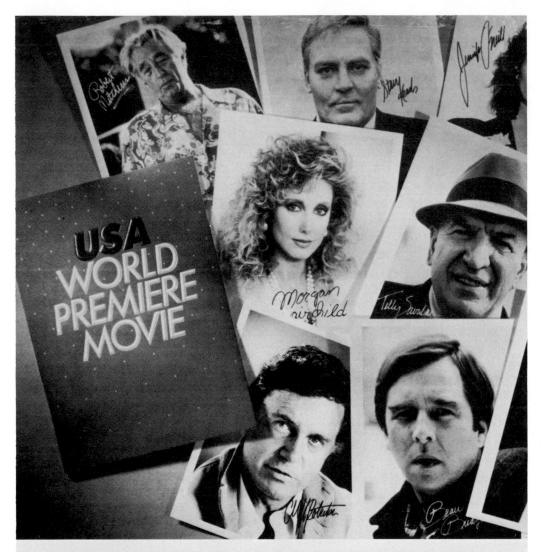

FIGURE 14.2 Trade Advertisement for USA
Network
Courtesy of USA Network.

FIGURE 14.2 Continued

of discounts used. The final word on availabilities, prices, and discounts, however, comes from each station, and spot-television buyers should never form expectations from *SRDS* alone.

Spot-television discounts are not standardized and present numerous options to broadcast buyers. The philosophy of television spot rates is twofold: The station wishes to gain as much revenue as it can from each spot placement within constraints of competitive offers, and discounts provide incentive for advertisers to spend more dollars with the station in return for lower unit costs. Stations use a number of different schemes to achieve these objectives.

Fixed Position

A unique condition in broadcast spot selling is pricing by permanence. Advertisers wanting to be guaranteed certain placements or positions can pay the so-called **fixed rate** (the highest price available for that placement) and be assured of the placement throughout the schedule.

Preemptible Positions

For many advertisers, the trade-off between the higher fixed rate and the risk of being assigned an alternative position is worthwhile. They gamble that the station will not find another advertiser willing to pay the higher fixed rate. The savings (up to 50 percent or more) are attractive. **Preemptible rates** are offered in various degrees of notice, and the conditions of notice are tied to the price. For example, one set of conditions a station might offer an advertiser is:

- The next-lowest rate under the fixed rate would require two weeks notice if a fixed advertiser is found. This means that the commercial will run for two weeks before being "bumped."

- For an even lower rate, the advertiser may receive only a one-week notice (or even less), or no notice at all (immediately preemptible).

All preemptible conditions are predicated on how high advertiser demand for time is at the time of scheduling. If the station is in heavy demand by advertisers, preemptible scheduling could be dangerous—the station cannot guarantee it will have a

TABLE 14.9

Sample Station Rate Card for Spot Television

Primetime Thirty-Second Spot Announcements

	F1	P1	P2	P3
Monday				
8:00–9:00 P.M.	$1,600	$1,500	$1,400	$1,300
9:00–11:00 P.M.	1,450	1,350	1,250	1,150
Tuesday				
8:00–9:00 P.M.	$1,600	$1,500	$1,400	$1,300
9:00–10:00 P.M.	1,700	1,600	1,500	1,400
10:00–11:00 P.M.	1,500	1,400	1,300	1,200

F1 = Fixed position
P1 = Preemptible with two-weeks notice
P2 = Preemptible with one-week notice
P3 = Preemptible without notice

supply of alternative positions. Conversely, in times of less activity, fixed prices might be unnecessary for all but very popular programs. Also to be considered in such pricing arrangements is that a price range can serve as the basis for negotiation: A skilled buyer working for a large and influential client may indeed get a schedule of commercials "guaranteed" (that is, assurances the commercials will not be bumped) for a price lower than the fixed position. Table 14.9 is an illustration of a station rate card offering several degrees of preemptibility. Listings of preemptibility can be presented in a variety of ways, as a glance through a *SRDS* reveals.

Rotation Packages

Some stations forgo advertiser selection of specific availabilities in favor of prepackaged options. These packages are a series of different shows that each participating advertiser must take on a rotation, with no substitutions. By packaging these rotations, sometimes called **orbit plans,** stations can assure more equitable scheduling for all clients. As advertisers become accustomed to these rotation

TABLE 14.10

Primetime Orbit Plan for Spot Television

$1,200 per thirty-second commercial

Position will rotate through the following programs:

Monday	"Major Dad" and "Designing Women"
Tuesday	"Rescue 911"
Thursday	"Knots Landing"
Sunday	"Murder, She Wrote"

Each commercial purchased will appear in all five positions.

TABLE 14.11

Grid Rates for Spot Television

Grid (thirty-second announcements)

	F1	P2	P1	P
1	$1,200	$1,100	$1,000	$900
2	850	800	750	700
3	650	600	550	500
4	450	400	350	300
5	250	200	150	100

F1 = Fixed position
P2 = Preemptible with two-weeks notice
P1 = Preemptible with one-week notice
P = Preemptible without notice

packages, the rotation method of selling spot television will become more accepted as a consequence of the market. Rotations among different programs and different days also might expose a greater number of different viewers. An orbit plan for a station in a particular market might appear as shown in table 14.10.

ROS (Run-of-Station)

The lowest-priced announcements are scheduled at station discretion. The advertiser, beyond requesting a certain number of commercials per week, has little or no control over the program segments or even the dayparts scheduled. In periods of low demand for station time, the **run-of-station (ROS)** advertiser may find excellent scheduling at very favorable prices. At times of high demand, ROS schedules may not even be available. This type of pricing and scheduling arrangement may be acceptable to an advertiser interested in broadly defined prospect groups and who does not have precise scheduling requirements.

Grid Rates

Grid rates are, perhaps, the ultimate in rate-card flexibility. No time periods are noted on the **grid card,** only a series of classes (grids) and prices for each class according to fixed or preemptible status. In this way, the station gives only the range of prices, committing a price only when the buyer requires availabilities. Fluctuations in audience levels and advertiser demand are accommodated without having to change the grid card. Table 14.11 shows a grid-card format.

Network Radio

Information on network radio rates is limited, and buyers tend to depend on sales representatives for costs. Presently, the approximately twenty-four radio networks in operation include: ABC (which is subdivided into the ABC Contemporary, Direction, Entertainment, FM, Information, Rock, and Talk Networks), CBS, Sheridan, and Transtar 1 and 2. Network radio programs largely consist of news and informational programming, usually of short length (five to ten minutes).

An advertiser can purchase specific programs or an ROS schedule. Some networks concentrate their programming in the 10:00 A.M. to 7:00 P.M. time period. Prices generally are given in a range (say, $2,000 to $8,000 for a thirty-second commercial), and the exact price an advertiser pays is based on negotiation.

Spot-Market Radio

Market-by-market radio pricing is similar to spot television in style of discounts and variety of rate cards. Generally, though, the rate structure offered

---

TABLE 14.12

Frequency Discounts for Spot Radio

Spot Announcements Per Week
(Sixty-second commercial)

Daypart	12 ti	18 ti	24 ti	30 ti
AMD	$375	$345	$335	$325
PMD	250	220	210	200
DT	190	180	170	160
WKND	190	180	170	160
NT	90	85	75	70

Key:
AMD = Morning drivetime (Monday–Saturday, 5:00 A.M.–10:00 A.M.)
PMD = Afternoon drivetime (Monday–Friday, 3:00 P.M.–8:00 P.M.)
DT = Daytime (Monday–Friday, 10:00 A.M.–3:00 P.M.)
WKND = Weekend (Saturday, 10:00 A.M.–8:00 P.M.; Sunday, 6:00 A.M.–8:00 P.M.)
NT = Nighttime (Monday–Sunday, 8:00 P.M.–midnight)
ti = times
Note: Thirty-second commercials usually are around 80 percent of the rate for sixty-second commercials. Thus, a thirty-second commercial bought twelve times a week in morning drivetime would cost $300 ($375 × 80% = $300).

TABLE 14.13

Package Plans for Spot Radio

Package	One-minute commercial	Thirty-second commercial
12 ti: 2 AMD, 2 PMD, 2 DT, 2 WKND, 4 NT	$2,133	$1,706
18 ti: 3 AMD, 3 PMD, 3 DT, 3 WKND, 6 NT	3,497	2,798
24 ti: 4 AMD, 4 PMD, 4 DT, 4 WKND, 8 NT	3,726	2,981
30 ti: 5 AMD, 5 PMD, 5 DT, 5 WKND, 10 NT	4,433	3,546

Key: See "Key" for table 14.12.

---

falls into two broad categories: (1) frequency discounts, based on the total commercials purchased in a period of time (usually one week) for a particular time of day (daypart), and (2) package plans. These types are illustrated in tables 14.12 and 14.13.

Some radio stations, especially those in larger markets, offer a grid-type rate plan similar to spot television, whereby any given time period has a range of rates based on the level of preemptibility and/or negotiation. Thus, in table 14.12, a grid approach might offer a morning drivetime commercial, for the twelve-times-per-week level, at $350 to $400, rather than at the single rate of $375.

In table 14.13, an advertiser wanting a schedule of twelve one-minute commercials a week could purchase a package for $2,133, and this would include two commercials in each of four dayparts and four nighttime announcements.

Out-of-Home Media

Out-of-home media consist of outdoor and transit advertising and are generally available throughout the United States. Outdoor advertising is sold by individual companies, called plan operators, that operate in a single market or by chains with many U.S. locations. Among the larger chains are such companies as the Gannett Outdoor Network and the Patrick Media Group. Transit advertising is handled in a similar way.

The basis for outdoor rental is the traffic (primarily auto and some on foot) passing the sign locations. From this count, outdoor companies project the percentage of the market covered by a given list and number of locations. Since such calculations are made on a market-by-market basis, outdoor also is sold market by market.

The cost factors for outdoor are: (1) traffic count (the higher the count, the more expensive the outdoor), (2) the size of the board, (3) whether or not illuminations (for evening use) are present, and (4) whether or not the sign accepts paper postings or painted messages. There are a number of variations, but most outdoor contracts involve the following types:

TABLE 14.14

Monthly Costs of Thirty-Sheet Posters

Market	Plant Operator	100 GRP	50 GRP	25 GRP
Los Angeles, Calif.	Gannett	$268,800	$135,600	$68,400
Chicago, Ill.	Patrick	170,906	86,172	43,526
Atlanta, Ga.	Adams	48,000	25,200	12,900
San Diego, Calif.	Gannett	43,320	21,850	11,020
Dallas, Tex.	Patrick	42,538	21,462	10,828
Orlando, Fla.	Peterson	27,000	15,480	8,280
Birmingham, Ala.	Jennings	25,201	12,601	7,169
Des Moines, Iowa	Naegele	18,480	9,240	4,620
San Angelo, Tex.	Midwest	1,860	930	465

• *Poster Panels.* The standardized **poster-panel** units are the thirty-sheet and bleed poster. The structure for these units is approximately 12 feet high by 25 feet long and accepts preprinted messages glued to the board.

• *Painted Bulletins.* **Painted bulletins** are the largest outdoor display, averaging 14 by 48 feet. These displays are usually painted onto the structure, but recent developments have permitted a variety of other applications, including fiber-optic displays, reflectorized sheets that shimmer and sparkle, and solar-powered signs.

Outdoor poster panels are sold in packages known as **showings.** Showings of various traffic intensity are offered, with the gross rating point (GRP) as the yardstick. One GRP in outdoor is equal to 1 percent of a population. A standard outdoor purchase of 100 GRPs, then, means to deliver, in one day, exposure opportunities equal to 100 percent of the market's population. Traffic studies indicate that an average 100-GRP buy reaches around 85 to 90 percent of the adults in a given market area within a month's time. Showings are also offered in 75-, 50-, and 25-GRP levels. The standard contract period for outdoor posters is twenty-eight days, with discounts offered for longer periods.

Painted bulletins, which are more costly than poster panels, typically are purchased on a location-by-location basis and usually for longer periods of time than posters, typically for one or more years. Some painted bulletins are sold on a rotary basis, whereby a particular sign is moved from site to site, typically every sixty days, to expose the message to more people.

Rates for outdoor advertising are available from the company in a particular market, as well as from the listings in *Buyer's Guide to Outdoor Advertising.* Table 14.14 shows rates for a sample of market areas. Thus, from the table, a 100-GRP buy in Atlanta would cost $48,000 for a one-month posting.

The main types of transit advertising are:

• *Inside-of-vehicle, or Car Cards.* **Car cards** are standardized units sold inside of buses and other transportation vehicles. They measure approximately 11 inches high by 28, 42, or 56 inches wide, or 22 inches high by 21 inches wide. Car cards are bought on the basis of full, half, or quarter showings (or *service*)—that is, all, half, or a quarter of the vehicles in a fleet. Rates are generally quoted for a month, with discounts granted for three-month, six-month, nine-month, and twelve-month contracts.

• *Exterior, or Outside, Displays.* The outside display is somewhat like an outdoor poster in that it is seen by pedestrians and people in automobiles. Standard size units sold for the outside of buses include such popular units as king-size, queen-size, and taillight (rear-of-bus) displays. Outside displays are sold on the basis of showings (or "runs"), usually given as 100, 75, 50, or 25, and provide a specified coverage of the population in a market. Thus, for example, a 100-showing may require eighty outside displays to reach the highest percentage possible in a market; a 50-showing might require forty units. The base time period is one month, with discounts offered for longer periods.

• *Station Posters.* **Station posters** are available in only a very few of the largest U.S. markets, where there is an extensive rapid-transit system and/or commuter trains. The posters, which are akin to small versions of outdoor poster panels, are located in the main terminal stations and at branch terminals along the route. Station posters are purchased on the basis of size (for example, one-sheet, two-sheet, and three-sheet posters, each of which is a standard size and shape) and length of time shown (typically, one month). Other forms of transit advertising include bus shelters, telephone enclosures, and taxi tops.

Summary

Decisions regarding media tactics derive from the major strategic aspects of the media plan. Tactical decisions are referred to as media buying and are vital to the success of the entire media process. Media buying involves the selection of media vehicles and units, placing insertion orders for the buys, estimating audience deliveries and costs, negotiating, and monitoring the results of scheduled buys.

Media-buying skills require the balancing of procedural capabilities with social and human relations abilities. Among the specific skills needed by media buyers are knowledge of media audiences and research methodologies. Further, buyers must be able to accurately estimate costs of alternative schedules by reading and interpreting rate sched-

ules, discount structures, and media cost trends. In addition, media buyers must have knowledge of computers and software, understand the changes that take place continually in media operations, be able to effectively negotiate media buys, and be capable of monitoring media schedules.

Newspaper space typically is sold by the column inch, either at a flat, no-discount rate, or according to an open rate, which provides discounts for the frequency and/or volume of column inches bought in a contract period. Charges for color advertising are added to the cost for black-and-white space. Magazines are priced according to the page or fractional page purchased, either in black-and-white or color. Discounts are granted for frequency of insertion and/or the volume of space bought, either in pages or gross dollar volume. Regional space bought in magazines is priced according to a cost factor based on the number of thousands of circulation delivered.

Television and radio media buys are among the most complicated types of media buying, due largely to the high level of negotiating involved and the variety of rate and discount structures offered. Spot television and radio rates often include the element of preemptibility, whereby a range of prices is given. The higher the price a buyer pays for a particular unit, the greater the assurance that the commercial will run at the scheduled time. Also, the greater the frequency of purchase of broadcast time, the less the cost per commercial. Radio and television stations also offer advertisers various package plans for purchasing spot announcements.

Among the out-of-home media, typical outdoor advertising sold by plant operators include the poster panel and the painted bulletin. Each is a standard size, and rates are determined by the amount of audience delivered and the size and nature of the ad. The gross-rating-point (GRP) method is used to designate audience size. Transit advertising mainly consists of car cards, which are inside vehicles; outside displays; and station posters, available in subway and commuter-train terminals. Each type is sold in standard units on a monthly basis, with discounts granted for longer time periods.

Questions for Discussion

1. Distinguish between media strategies and tactics, and give examples of each.

2. In what ways might social and interpersonal skills be helpful to a media buyer?

3. What are the primary skills associated with media buying?

4. Explain the difference between a newspaper offering a flat rate as opposed to one offering an open rate. Why do you think a particular paper would offer advertisers an open rate?

5. Using the newspaper rate schedule in table 14.2, determine the *total* cost for the following schedule: 4-column by 12-inch black-and-white ad run each Sunday for fifty-two weeks. What would the cost be if you bought this same schedule but added one color? (Use table 14.4.)

6. Using the magazine rate schedule in table 14.5, determine the cost of *each* ad for the following buy: one-page, four-color, bleed ad bought in five issues. (Assume a 15 percent premium charge for bleed.)

7. Using the spot-television rates in table 14.9, determine what it would cost to buy a thirty-second commercial on Tuesday evening between 9:00 and 10:00 P.M. What risks do you assume if you purchase the commercial at $1,400?

8. Why are run-of-station (ROS) rates in television and radio usually the least expensive?

9. Using the spot-radio rates in table 14.12, determine the weekly cost to run a sixty-second commercial, twenty times a week, during afternoon drivetime. What would the cost be if you switched to a thirty-second unit?

10. Using the thirty-sheet outdoor poster rates in table 14.14, determine the total cost to buy 50 GRPs in Orlando for a three-month schedule, assuming a 7 percent discount is offered for a three-month contract.

Endnotes

1. For further discussion on the use of computer software for media decisions, see "The Merge/Purge Program," *Marketing & Media Decisions,* October 1989, 48–58; "A Shopper's Guide," *Marketing & Media Decisions,* October 1989, 61–65; and Greg Clarkin, "Buying by Bytes," *Marketing and Media Decisions,* May 1990, 44–45.

2. William Wells, John Burnett, and Sandra Moriarty, *Advertising: Principles and Practice* (Englewood Cliffs, N.J.: Prentice-Hall, 1989), 305–7. For additional information on negotiation skills, see Joe Mandese, "Decoding the Deal," *Marketing & Media Decisions,* September 1989, 33–39.

Suggested Readings

- *Mediaweek's Guide to Media.* New York: A/S/M Communications, 1992. Four quarterly issues.

- Barban, Arnold M., Donald W. Jugenheimer, and Peter B. Turk. *Advertising Media Sourcebook.* 3d ed. Lincolnwood, Ill. NTC Business Books, 1989. Section 1.

- Bogart, Leo. *Strategy in Advertising.* 2d ed. Chicago: Crain Books, 1984. Chapter 11.

- McGann, Anthony F., and J. Thomas Russell. *Advertising Media.* 2d ed. Homewood, Ill. Irwin, 1988. Chapter 5.

- Sissors, Jack Z., and Lincoln Bumba. *Advertising Media Planning.* 3d ed. Lincolnwood, Ill.: NTC Business Books, 1989. Chapters 3 and 14.

- Wells, William, John Burnett, and Sandra Moriarty. *Advertising: Principles and Practice.* Englewood Cliffs, N.J.: Prentice-Hall, 1989. Chapter 12.

Chapter 15

Print Media: Newspapers and Magazines

Outline

Learning Objectives

In the study of this chapter, you will have the opportunity to:

- Learn about the classes and types of newspapers and magazines.

- Observe the newspaper and magazine characteristics used by media buyers.

- Understand how print-media rate structures affect media buying.

- See how cost comparisons are used to choose among alternative print vehicles.

- Note circulation and audience-delivery patterns of newspapers and magazines.

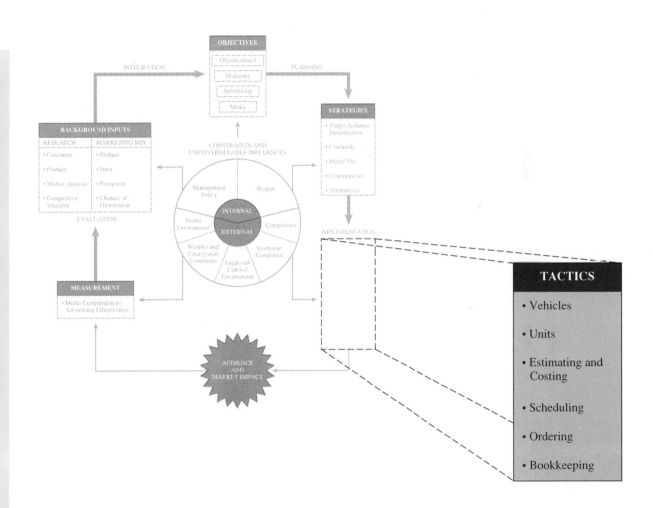

INTEGRATION

OBJECTIVES
Organizational
Marketing
Advertising
Media

PLANNING

BACKGROUND INPUTS

RESEARCH	MARKETING MIX
• Consumer	• Product
• Product	• Price
• Market Analysis	• Promotion
• Competitive Situation	• Channel of Distribution

CONSTRAINTS AND
UNCONTROLLABLE INFLUENCES

STRATEGIES
• Target Audience Identification
• Continuity
• Media Mix
• Contingencies
• Alternatives

EVALUATION

Management Policy
Budget
INTERNAL
Media Environment
Competition
EXTERNAL
Weather and Cataclysmic Conditions
Economic Conditions
Legal and Cultural Environment

IMPLEMENTATION

MEASUREMENT
• Media Contribution to Advertising Effectiveness

AUDIENCE AND MARKET IMPACT

TACTICS

• Vehicles

• Units

• Estimating and Costing

• Scheduling

• Ordering

• Bookkeeping

*C*hapter 14 was a discussion of the general aspects of making tactical media decisions. This chapter deals specifically with tactical decisions involving the print media—newspapers and magazines.

More than $42 billion annually is invested in print-media advertising. Thus, newspapers and magazines account for about one-third of all advertising expenditures, as compared with around 29 percent in the broadcast media, 18 percent in direct mail, 7 percent in the Yellow Pages, and 1 percent in out-of-home media. A large majority of that spent in newspapers—almost 90 percent—is by local advertisers, whereas the major part spent in consumer, business, and agricultural magazines is by regional and national advertisers.

Although newspapers and magazines share many common characteristics, they are sufficiently different to discuss in separate sections.

Newspapers

In terms of the total amount of money spent for advertising media, newspapers are ranked first, with over $32 billion in spending; thus, one-fourth of all media dollars are invested in newspapers. Newspapers also are one of the oldest advertising media in the United States. The *Boston News Letter* was the first regularly published newspaper in the colonies and continued publication until 1776. Other newspapers were founded during the late 1700s, but it was not until the nineteenth century that the newspaper truly became a mass medium. For example, the *New York Sun* was founded in 1833 by Benjamin Day, who looked upon publishing as a business and developed his paper as such. In the latter part of the 1800s, such publishers as Joseph Pulitzer and Horace Greeley made newspapers a dynamic force in American life.

Today, newspapers are available to just about anyone who wants to read them. More than 1,600 daily newspapers are published in approximately 1,500 cities throughout the United States. In addition, around 7,600 weekly papers are available in small communities and suburbs. About two-thirds of all adults read a daily and/or Sunday newspaper. And although newspapers primarily are published in a particular community, two of the largest circulating papers—The *Wall Street Journal* and *USA TODAY*—are national in their delivery. Table 15.1 shows the circulations of the twenty largest dailies in the United States.

Classes of Newspapers

Newspapers can be classified according to a number of different criteria, such as: (1) *frequency of publication* (daily, weekly, Sunday), (2) *page size* (broadsheet, tabloid), (3) *type of circulation* (paid, controlled), (4) *audience targeted* (businesspeople, African-Americans, Hispanics, foreign language, labor), and (5) *special sections* (comics, Sunday supplement, freestanding insert, preprint).

Based on the frequency of publication, there presently in the United States are 1,626 daily, 7,606 weeklies, and 847 Sunday newspapers. Among dailies, more than two-thirds are published as evening newspapers. Figure 15.1 shows the number of morning and evening dailies, as well as Sunday papers, for a sample of past years. The number of morning dailies and Sunday papers has increased for the periods shown, whereas evening dailies have declined (from 1,459 in 1960 to 1,125 in 1989). The net result is that the total number of daily newspapers has declined from 1,763 in 1960 to 1,626 in 1989. The number of weekly newspapers has remained fairly constant over the years.

TABLE 15.1

Twenty Daily Newspapers with Highest Circulation

Newspaper	Average Daily Circulation	Newspaper	Average Daily Circulation
1. *Wall Street Journal*	1,919,355	11. *Chicago Sun-Times*	537,780
2. *USA TODAY*	1,503,496	12. *Boston Globe*	516,981
3. *Los Angeles Times*	1,242,864	13. *Philadelphia Inquirer*	515,523
4. *New York Times*	1,209,225	14. *Newark Star-Ledger*	485,362
5. *Washington Post*	838,902	15. *Detroit News*	481,766
6. *(New York) Newsday*	825,512	16. *Miami Herald*	444,581
7. *Chicago Tribune*	741,345	17. *Houston Chronicle*	439,574
8. *New York Post*	644,738	18. *Cleveland Plain Dealer*	432,449
9. *Detroit Free Press*	622,349	19. *(Minneapolis) Star Tribune*	413,237
10. *San Francisco Chronicle*	570,364	20. *Dallas Morning News*	412,868

Source: Ratings based on circulation claims filed with the Audit Bureau of Circulations. Where newspapers report Monday through Thursday circulation and separate figures for Friday, the results are weighted averages of the two.

Newspapers also can be classified on the basis of page size. Generally, there are two sizes: **tabloid** and standard (also called **broadsheet**). Tabloids usually have an advertising page that is 10 13/16 inches wide and 14 inches deep. Each of a tabloid's five columns is 2 1/16 inches wide. The standard, or broadsheet, newspaper is 13 inches wide and 21 inches deep, with six columns of 2 1/16 inches each. The number of columns—five or six—is allocated for advertising space; the number of editorial columns may be different. Tabloids generally are concentrated in the largest U.S. cities. For example, in New York City, the *Daily News, Newsday,* and *New York Post* are tabloid size (The *New York Times* is standard). More than 95 percent of dailies are of standard size.

When classified by type of circulation, newspapers can have either **paid** or **controlled circulation.** Controlled-circulation newspapers are distributed free and generally are referred to as **shopping newspapers** or "shoppers." All of a shopper's revenue comes from advertising. Shoppers usually are distributed to certain types of homes or to a particular part of a city. Most newspapers, however, are not distributed free, and the circulation is paid for by home subscribers and newsstand purchasers.

Another way to classify newspapers is on the basis of the audience targeted. Newspapers targeted to a particular audience are often called special-interest newspapers. For example, The *Wall Street Journal*—currently the largest circulating paper in the United States—is targeted to people who have a special interest in the financial markets; *Barron's* is another example. Other newspapers—both daily and weekly—direct their attention to such groups as African-Americans, Hispanics (many of these newspapers are written in Spanish), labor members, and the like. The editorial focus is on the particular group, and advertisers may choose to reach such people within this editorial environment.

A final way of categorizing newspapers perhaps is not so much a classification *among* newspapers as it is a way to distinguish certain special sections within a newspaper. In terms of advertising space, newspaper advertisements can be viewed as being either **ROP (run-of-paper,** or run-of-press, meaning that the advertisement is printed by the newspaper

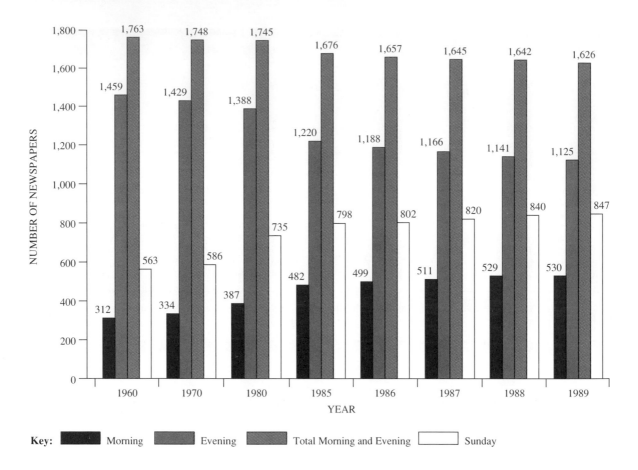

Key: ■ Morning ▨ Evening ▨ Total Morning and Evening ☐ Sunday

FIGURE 15.1 Number of U.S. Morning and Evening Dailies and Sunday Newspapers. (**Note**: The total of morning and evening papers is slightly less than the sum of morning papers plus evening papers. This is due to "all-day" papers being listed in both morning and evening columns but only once in the total. For example, there were 29 "all-day" newspapers in 1989.) Source: Newspaper Advertising Bureau. Reprinted by permission.

along with the paper's editorial/information content) or **preprint** (the advertisement is printed someplace other than at the newspaper's plant—it is *preprinted*—and then sent to the newspaper for inclusion along with the regular ROP sections).

Many newspapers distribute (typically in their weekend edition) a special section known as a **supplement** (also called a newspaper-distributed magazine). The most notable supplement examples are the national ones: *Parade, USA Weekend,* and *Sunday Magazine.* These supplements are much like magazines in that they have editorial content as well as advertising, are produced by independent media companies, and are run on glossy paper stock that permits good-quality color reproduction. They differ from magazines in that, once printed, they are shipped to newspapers throughout the country and are usually distributed by the papers along with their Sunday edition (some newspapers distribute these on other days of the week). The Sunday comics section is similarly handled, except that in recent years, it has not been used extensively by advertisers.

Another example of a special section is the **freestanding insert** (**FSI**). An FSI consists of a preprinted section that contains *only* advertisements, typically with coupons. An independent FSI company sells space to a variety of advertisers and puts all of the ads together in a section (usually tabloid size) that is then printed and shipped to newspapers throughout the country for distribution. The FSI currently is the most popular method for distributing manufacturers' cents-off coupons, accounting for almost 80 percent of all such coupon distributions.[1]

Another popular form of preprint is the **multi-page insert.** In this example of a preprint, the advertiser takes responsibility for producing four or more pages of advertising, which are printed and shipped to those newspapers on the advertiser's schedule. As with all preprints, the multi-page insert is placed into the newspaper along with the regular sections and distributed to the newspaper's circulation. This form of preprint currently is used extensively by national retailers, such as Sears, J.C. Penney, and Kmart, but is also sometimes used by local retailers.

Characteristics of Newspapers

Newspapers, like all other media types, offer advertisers both advantages and disadvantages. What may be an advantage to one particular advertiser may be a limitation to another, depending on the advertiser's goals. Thus, we discuss here a number of the characteristics of using newspapers as an advertising medium.

Market Coverage

Newspapers provide national or regional advertisers with a great deal of flexibility in levels of market coverage. For example, an advertiser could buy newspapers only in the ten largest U.S. cities, or perhaps the top twenty-five markets in the South, or only in those markets where the advertiser's distribution is strong, or in any other necessary combination of specific markets. Newspapers permit an advertiser to pinpoint the degree of market coverage desired. Even retail advertisers, operating within a limited trading area, often can purchase only a limited portion of a newspaper's circulation.

(This "zone" advertising is discussed in more detail later in the chapter.)

Aside from geographic market coverage, newspapers also provide certain coverage according to the type of audiences delivered. This is most apparent for special-interest newspapers, whose editorial approach is directed to a specific population segment. Yet, newspapers that appeal to a general audience can also, to a lesser degree, offer an advertiser some segmentation. This typically occurs through the normal "sectioning" of the newspaper—sports, business and finance, classified, food and cooking, lifestyle, and the like. (See figure 15.2.) Certain groups of people, however— for example, those under twenty years of age and those with low household income—have relatively low exposure to newspapers, which could be a limitation for certain advertisers.

Immediacy

Newspapers, especially those issued daily, generally are viewed as among the most current of media. People look to a newspaper to see what is happening *now, today,* in their community, state, and country, and throughout the world. This characteristic is useful to advertisers—national or local—who seek to convey a sense of immediacy for their product or service. A downside of this characteristic is that most newspapers have a rather short life span, typically only one day.

Community Prestige

Most newspapers have a certain amount of prestige within the communities they serve. Research shows that, when a newspaper is not available, people truly miss the newspaper's contents. This consumer attitude can be beneficial to advertisers using newspaper space.

Reader-Controlled Exposure

Many readers use newspapers to compare price, style, and variety of offerings, much as they would a catalog. Readers control when and how they go through the paper. They also can take as much time as they like in reading an ad and can refer to it later if they choose. Advertisers are likely to benefit from

OUR LARGEST CIRCULATION GAINS IN MORE THAN 20 YEARS!

1,225,189* **1,514,096***
DAILY   SUNDAY
+106,540   +80,357
(+9.5%)   (+5.6%)

The Times is now the largest metropolitan daily newspaper in the United States. Which means your Times ads now reach a larger, more responsive audience. And that's good news for both of us.

➡The faster-format **Los Angeles Times**

* 3 months ending March 31, 1990, as filed with the Audit Bureau of Circulations. 6 months ending March 31, 1990, which include the month of October when the Los Angeles Herald Examiner was still publishing: 1,210,077 daily and 1,504,540 Sunday.

FIGURE 15.2 A Trade Advertisement for the *Los Angeles Times* Encouraging Advertisers to Use Its Space
Courtesy of the *Los Angeles Times*.

the opportunity to have the advertisement exposed over an extended period of time.

National/Local Interaction

Newspapers can provide the opportunity to effectively coordinate national and local advertising. For example, a national advertiser may run an ad (perhaps one containing a coupon) on a particular day and encourage those retailers carrying the brand to also run their own ad on that day. The national advertiser may even provide the retailer with funds to assure that this happens. (This arrangement between a national advertiser and a local retailer is called **cooperative,** or "co-op," **advertising.**)

Services

Most newspapers offer advertisers a broad array of advertising and marketing services. For example, local retailers that do not have an advertising department can rely on the newspaper staff to do their entire advertisement, from planning, to artwork, to copy writing. Newspapers also typically have a "co-op" coordinator, who helps local advertisers to take advantage of the offerings of national advertisers to share space costs with the retail outlets. Many newspapers offer national advertisers merchandising services, whereby the newspaper staff calls on retail outlets and/or sends them direct-mail materials that promote the upcoming advertising. For both national and retail advertisers, newspaper research departments provide valuable information about the market they serve, readership of the paper, and consumer surveys.

Special Techniques

To stay competitive with other media, newspapers develop the necessary techniques to remain attractive to advertisers. As mentioned earlier, a **zone edition** permits an advertiser to buy only a portion of the paper's total circulation; for example, a local retail shop may have its advertisement circulate only in the northwest part of a city if that is primarily where the store's market is. This adds greatly to a newspaper advertisement's territorial flexibility.

Another technique, **total market coverage (TMC)**, permits an advertiser to reach almost all of the homes in a city. If, for example, a paper is circulated to 70 percent of homes, the newspaper may be willing to deliver extra copies of the paper—or perhaps a section of advertisements alone—to the remaining 30 percent, thus covering the market totally. It may do this by having its carriers deliver the extra copies to nonsubscribers or by mailing an advertising section to such homes.

The use of preprinted inserts, mentioned earlier, is yet another special newspaper technique. Inserts permit an advertiser to create advertising that is different from the regular advertising printed at the newspaper's printing plant. An insert can be as simple as an 8-by-10-inch sheet advertising a local pizza establishment or as elaborate as a multi-page insert with color reproductions of an automobile manufacturer's new car models.

Quality of Color Reproduction

Although the use of preprints does permit high-quality color reproduction of advertising, the advertising run in color by a paper's presses (ROP) can be of uneven quality. Some newspapers have modernized their equipment to improve such reproduction, yet others have not yet done so. If brand appearance in an advertisement is very important, an advertiser may choose to use preprints or another print medium instead of ROP newspaper advertising.

Amount of Advertising Carried

Generally, newspapers devote around 60 percent of their space to advertising and 40 percent to editorial/informational content, which means that readers are exposed to a large number of individual advertisements, with increased competition for their attention. This is especially true on Sunday and on the day when local grocery stores concentrate their

MEDIA SPOTLIGHT

15.1

A Profile of USA TODAY

Gannett Company, Inc. is one of the largest diversified news and information companies in the United States. The information presented here profiles Gannett's *USA TODAY* national newspaper.

THE NATION'S NEWSPAPER

VIA SATELLITE

Fact Sheet

First Day of Issue—15 September 1982

Readership—The Simmons Market Research Bureau survey results for 1991 report that *USA TODAY* remains the most widely-read newspaper in the nation, with a daily readership of more than 6.5 million.

Circulation—The publisher's statement to the Audit Bureau of Circulations for the six months ending March 1991, subject to audit showed an average daily paid circulation of 1,863,436, making *USA TODAY* the second largest daily newspaper in the United States.

Market Concentration—*USA TODAY* is available on the same day of publication in the top one hundred Areas of Dominant Influence (ADIs) in the United States.

Print Sites—Thirty-two in the United States, one in Hong Kong, and one in Switzerland.

Pages—Each issue has a maximum capacity of fifty-six pages, with a sixteen-page maximum of color and an eleven-page maximum for color advertising. Four-color is available in all four sections. A fifth bonus section can add twenty pages or more.

Satellite—The *USA TODAY* domestic satellite is ASC-1, located in stationary orbit 22,300 miles above the Pacific Ocean. This ASC-1 satellite plus one Intelsat satellite (Pacific Ocean region) are used for Hong Kong and Singapore transmissions. One Intelsat Atlantic-region satellite is used for Switzerland transmissions.

Transmission Time—Approximately 3 1/2 minutes for a full black-and-white page. Up to 6 minutes for each of the four-color separations for editorial color. From five to fifteen minutes for each separation for color advertising. Transmission time varies with page content.

Press Time—First-edition press start: Midnight, Monday–Thursday; 11:30 P.M., Friday

Chase-edition press start: 1:10 A.M., Monday–Thursday; 1:40 A.M., Friday

Second-edition press start: 2:10 A.M., Monday–Thursday; 2:30 A.M., Friday

Advertising—In 1990, *USA TODAY* advertising pages totaled 3,502.

Advertising Rates—Full-page black-and-white: $57,505, Monday–Thursday; $65,810, Friday; Full-page four-color: $74,757, Monday–Thursday; $85,552, Friday; (Weekend rates are higher, reflecting the weekend edition's large circulation.)

International Edition—The *USA TODAY* International Edition is in more than ninety countries in western Europe, the Middle East, North Africa, and Asia. It has a minimum of sixteen pages in two sections. *USA TODAY* International has been printed in Hong Kong since April 1988 for distribution in Asia and the Pacific. Since May 1986, the International Edition for Europe and the Middle East has been printed near Lucerne, Switzerland.

Profitability—*USA TODAY* saw its first profitable month in May 1987, six months ahead of projections. The newspaper also had a profit for the entire last quarter of 1987 and 1988. In 1990, USA TODAY was marginally unprofitable.

Staff Size—395 editorial, 2,100 total.

Headquarters—1000 Wilson Boulevard

Arlington, Virginia 22229
(703) 276–3400
Advertising Offices—535 Madison
Ave., New York, N.Y. 10022
(212) 715–5350

How USA TODAY Is Produced

1. About 425 reporters, editors, and researchers write and edit copy on 325 Atex computer terminals.

2. Main Atex computer processes copy and transmits it to phototypesetters.

3. One of three phototypesetters produces type.

4. Pages are pasted up.

5. Pages are photographed.

6. Photographs are full-page, glossy, positive prints.

7. Laser scanner converts page into electronic signal that can be transmitted to ASC-1, the satellite used for the domestic edition.

The international edition uses three satellites; otherwise, the process is the same.

8. Rooftop satellite antenna transmits signal to satellite.

9. ASC-1, stationed 22,300 miles above the equator, then transmits signal to thirty-two print sites across the United States.

10. Earth station at each print site receives the signal.

11. Signal is sent to a computer that converts the electronic signal to a laser beam that exposes film and produces a full-page negative.

Continued on p. 294

15.1 cont.

12. Film is processed, and an offset printing plate is produced.

13. Presses print copies at an average rate of eighteen thousand an hour.

14. Three hundred eighty-three trucks pick up the newspapers from *USA TODAY* print sites and transport them to 2,400 delivery trucks, which distribute them to approximately 127,000 newsracks, 500,000 homes, and 80,000 other sales points.

USA TODAY *Print Sites*

Location	Launch Date
Springfield, Va.	15 September 1982
Gainesville, Ga.	20 September 1982
St. Cloud, Minn.	27 September 1982
Tarentum, Pa.	4 October 1982
Olympia, Wash.	8 November 1982
Marin County, Calif.	15 November 1982
Pasadena, Tex.	10 January 1983 (contract site)
Fort Collins, Colo.	17 January 1983
San Bernardino, Calif.	24 January 1983 (replaced Costa Mesa, Calif. site)
Fort Myers, Fla.	9 February 1983
Port Huron, Mich.	23 February 1983
Chicago, Ill.	9 March 1983 (contract site)
Kankakee, Ill.	9 March 1983 (contract site)
Lansdale, Pa.	23 March 1983
Bridgewater, N.J.	23 March 1983
Harrison, N.Y.	11 April 1983
Mansfield, Ohio	12 September 1983 (contract site)
Farmer's Branch, Tex.	3 October 1983 (contract site)
Hattiesburg, Miss.	10 October 1983
Greensboro, N.C.	27 February 1984 (contract site)
Lawrence, Kans.	2 April 1984 (contract site)
Richmond, Ind.	10 September 1984
Phoenix, Ariz.	15 October 1984
Batavia, N.Y.	1 July 1985 (contract site)
Nashville, Tenn.	9 September 1985
Miramar, Fla.	9 September 1985

Brevard County, Fla.	16 September 1985
Norwood, Mass.	15 December 1986 (replaced Lawrence, Mass. site)
Olivette, Mo.	27 March 1988
Atlanta, Ga.	15 May 1988
Salt Lake City, Utah	29 June 1988 (contract site)
Columbia, S.C.	6 February 1989

International Sites

Switzerland (Lucerne)	5 May 1986 (contract site, replaced Rockland, N.Y. site for international edition)
Hong Kong	19 April 1988 (contract site)

USA TODAY *Spinoffs*

• USA TODAY *Baseball Weekly*—An all-baseball tabloid printed at eighteen of USA TODAY's thirty-three print sites. The newspaper includes expert analysis, team-by-team reports for Major and Minor league teams, a week of box scores, television and radio schedules and reports devoted to fans who play in fantasy leagues or collect baseball memorabilia. It publishes every Friday during baseball season and every other Friday during the off season.

• USA TODAY *Sky Radio*—A constant program wheel of live news, financial reports, sports scores and weather reports throughout the day delivered to airline passengers through the audio systems already installed on many commercial aircraft. Sky Radio will use a customized radio channel delivered to aircraft via satellite technology. Additionally, Sky Radio plans to offer live professional and college sports during evenings and weekends. Broadcasts will begin in 1992.

• USA TODAY *Update*—A news and information service consisting of eighteen executive news summaries delivered to business environments worldwide. The decisionline reports are sent electronically to the subscriber's database beginning at 4 A.M. Of the eighteen reports, thirteen are targeted to a particular profession or industry, four concentrate on general news, and one report deals in-depth with the day's top issue. Also, *USA TODAY* Update lifestyles reports, which are full-text features selected from *USA TODAY*, cover entertainment, money, and sports. *USA TODAY* Update is also available on home information networks and on Minitel, the French videotex network.

• USA TODAY *Sports Hotline*—A comprehensive two-minute report that provides late-breaking sports headlines and scoring updates from the nation's stadiums and arenas. The Hotline is updated every ten minutes to report sports news and

Continued on p. 296

15.1 cont.

scores as they happen. The Hotline is available twenty-four hours a day, seven days a week. The number: 1–900–850–1414.

• USA TODAY *Books*—A line of books developed from material that has appeared in *USA TODAY*. Among them: *Portraits of the USA; Tracking Tomorrow's Trends; The USA TODAY Crossword Puzzle Book, Volumes I & II; Desert Warriors: The Men and Women Who Won the Gulf War; The USA TODAY Cartoon Book; BusCapade: Plain Talk across the USA; And Still We Rise: Interviews with 50 Black Role Models; U.S.A. Citizens Abroad: A Handbook; The Making of McPaper: The Inside Story of USA TODAY; Window on the World: Faces, Places & Plain Talk from 32 Countries; Profiles of Power: How the Governors Run our 50 States; Truly One Nation.*

• USA TODAY *Online Library*—The Online Library allows users to research stories and infor- mation that has appeared in *USA TODAY, USA WEEKEND,* Gannett News Service, and the *Louisville Courier Journal.* The public may access this online library by calling DataTimes, Inc., in Oklahoma City, Okla., 1–800–642–2525.

• USA TODAY *Classline Today*—This four-page lesson plan aids students and teachers in the class- room as they study with *USA TODAY.* Classline Today is delivered with *USA TODAY* to schools each Tuesday and Wednesday morning.

• USA TODAY *Sports Center*—An on-line, com- prehensive sports network with everything for the sports fan. Offers statistics, boxscores, schedules, sports and news wire services, Sports Collector Exchange, injury reports and complete coverage of major sporting events. Includes fantasy base- ball, basketball, and football as well as an elec- tronic mail system, opinion polls, forums, a sports discount store, and classified ads exclusively for Sports Center users.

Source: Copyright 1991, *USA TODAY.* Reprinted by permission.

---

advertisements (generally referred to as "best food day" by the newspaper—usually, the Wednesday or Thursday edition). Since the average adult reader spends only forty to forty-five minutes with a daily paper, the opportunity for advertisement exposure is a factor to consider.

Types of Newspaper Advertising

Types of newspaper advertising can be grouped as follows:

1. Display advertising
    a. National (general) advertisers
    b. Local (retail) advertisers
2. Classified advertising
    a. Regular classified
    b. Display classified
3. Special-notice advertising (for example, legal notices, political ads)
4. Preprinted supplements

Display advertising makes up the bulk of a news- paper's main sections. Advertisements, typically with illustrative matter, appear throughout the paper, mostly for local establishments, but some for national advertisers. The size of display advertise- ments can range from very small to full page.

Classified advertising appears in the newspa- per's special classified section. Much of it comes from individuals who want to advertise something, perhaps to sell a refrigerator or stereo system. The advertising is placed according to special subhead- ings within the classified section to make it easy for readers to find the item or service sought. Much classified advertising also comes from businesses that find it useful to place their advertisement under

...OSA NEWS　　　　　　　　　　　THURSDAY, MAY 3, 1990

824. Trucks

FORD BRONCO II 1984- 4x4, V6, air, automatic, power steering, stereo, extra clean. $5650. PHILLIPS MOTOR CO. 345-8990.

FORD COURIER, 1973- New paint job; new engine. Call 553-5442.

FORD F350, 1988- Diesel, cab and chassis, 5-speed, air, power windows. $13,495. U-SAVE AUTO RENTAL 349-2510

Ford F100 1977
Camouflage hunting truck. Runs good. $950. 752-5109.

Ford F100 1977
Camouflage hunting truck. Runs good. $950. 752-5109.

FORD F-150, 1985- Short bed, V8, automatic, air, new paint. Runs and looks good. High miles. $3250. 349-1924

FORD F-250, 1986- 4x4, ¾ ton, excellent condition. Rawson toolbox. Reinforced bumpers, extras. $7800. 758-5419.

FORD F350, 1987- diesel 6.9 power and air. Excellent condition. $8500. Call after 5 P.M.

FORD F-150, 1986- Automatic with air; real clean. $5450. Dealer, 339-6450.

FORD F-100, 1978- Rebuilt 302. Automatic. Full size. $1995. Call 339-5094.

FORD F-150, 1990- 4 wheel drive, like new, 3000 mi Days 758-3015, nights 339-5367.

FORD F-250 LARIAT 1989- all available options. Big discount! Call Bill Strange at

★ **OSWALT** ★
MOTOR CO.
2115 15th St. 758-1473

FORD F-150 RANGER XLT, 1981- $3295. Ask for Steve 333-8017 or 339-7746.

Ford Ranchero
1972- Recently painted. Good motor, transmission, few minor problems. Excellent condition. $1000. 556-4554.

Ford Ranger XLT
1990, aluminum dish wheels, 2,500 miles, factory warranty, pay off. Call 333-8175

824. Trucks

FORD RANGER, 1988- 4 wheel drive. New tires. $6250. Call Dealer, 339-6450.

FORD RANGER XLT, 1988- 5 speed, air, tilt, cruise, cassette. $5450. Dealer, 339-6450.

FORD RANGER XL- 1985, automatic, power steering, air, V6, $4,300. Call 759-3113

FORD 1-TON, 1974- Dump Truck. Good condition. $2700. Call 556-6590.

FORD XL-100
1973- Without motor. $500. Call 752-8339.

GMC S15 1989
Excellent condition. 345-6492.

GMC S-15, 1989- 23,000 miles. Assume payments or $8800. Call 758-5709.

GMC S-15 SIERRA, 1987- Extended cab, air, power brakes, steering. AM-FM, 24,000 mi., $7,000. 553-4944.

GMC SIERRA CLASSIC, 1986- 4x4. Automatic, air, tilt, cruise, AM/FM cassette; short bed. Call Betty Prewitt.

DOCKINS
MOTOR CO.
308 Skyland Blvd. 345-3500

ISUZU MINI SPORT TRUCK, 1989- Take up payments. Only serious inquiries please. Call Mike 339-5207.

ISUZU PICKUP
1984, long bed, loaded, $3,250. Call 759-1146

JEEP CHEROKEE 1984- 4 door, 4x4, automatic, air, power steering, luggage rack, nice. $5650. PHILLIPS MOTOR CO. 345-8990.

JEEP PIONEER
1987, black, 2 doors, 4 wheel drive, 5 speed, 45,000 miles, $10,400. Call 758-5120.

MAZDA PICKUP, 1988- Extra Cab LX, real clean. $6250. Call Dealer, 339-6450.

NISSAN HARDBODY- Special, 1989, cloth seats, AM/FM cassette, air, sliding rear window. 556-6600 or 553-2233 ask for phillip

NISSAN KING CAB, 1984- 5 speed. New paint, new tires. Loaded. $4500. 554-0257

824. Trucks

NISSAN PICKUP, 1986- 5- speed, air, 29,000 miles. $4995. Northport Motors, 82 Bypass, 333-8151.

NISSAN TRUCK, 1986- 46,000 miles. Air conditioned. $4200. Call Ron 556-1100, 339-5108

TOYOTA- 1988, 20,000 miles, "fancy", $6995 or best offer. Call 759-1020 after 5:30 P.M.

TOYOTA- 1986, 4x4, loaded, 60,000 miles, very good condition, $6,800. Call 1-364-7939

TOYOTA EXTRA CAB 4X4, 1987- Fully loaded. Never been off road. 339-5226

TOYOTA HILUX, 1988- Air, AM-FM, bedliner, $5400. Dealer. 333-1662 or 339-6507.

TOYOTA LANDCRUISER, 1973- 4 x 4. Runs good. $2100. Call 345-2830.

TOYOTA LANDCRUISERS- 1979, $2500. 1972, $2000. Will trade. 333-0837 after 5 P.M.

TOYOTA SR5, 1981 Mags, air, super sharp! $2,995. Call 339-2879.

WILLYS PICKUP- 1950s model 4x4. Power take-off unit. No motor. Cab useable. $265. Call 349-2136.

826. Vans, Buses

Chevrolet, 1986
High Top Van. New brakes, tires, battery etc. $10,500. Call 752-6901.

CHEVROLET ASTRO VAN, 1987- Loaded, excellent condition. $10,500. 345-8539 or 759-1501, Carol.

CHEVROLET ASTRO CONVERSION VAN, 1987- low mileage, all extras. 758-0143.

826. Vans, Buses

CHEVROLET MINI VAN, 1988- Raised roof, TV, VCP, CB, blinds, table. Call 339-3279 after 5 P.M.

CHEVROLET STEP VAN, 1978- Good condition. $2500. Call 339-3057.

CHEVROLET- Vans, 1983 $1395. Ford 1984, $2250. Can be seen at, Rental Uniform Supply. Kaulooksa Ave.

DODGE CARGO VAN, 1973- runs good. $600 as is. Call 553-4766.

Dodge Van 1984
Customized, clean, 38,000 ml. $8500 firm. Call 752-9686.

DODGE
Window van, 6 cylinder, with rebuilt standard transmission. $1000. 752-3654.

FORD STEP VAN, 1970- New engine, 4-speed, good condition. $1500. Call 759-1957 or 345-6085 after 6 p.m.

PLYMOUTH VOYAGER, 1988- Black cherry, tinted windows, new mags, tires and brakes. $9500. Call 553-7051.

828. Wanted

BOOZER- Motor Co. will buy, trade or sell your car. Ask for Ray Boozer 553-6399

OLDSMOBILE CUTLASS BODY- 1976 or later model. Will pay up to $300. Call 339-8529, Clarence.

WE BUY USED CARS SHERRILL MOTOR CO. 1802 Greensboro Ave.752-6711

WE BUY JUNK CARS- from $20-$50. Call 752-8330, 556-6700 or 345-8973.

FIGURE 15.3　Classified Advertising Page Showing Both Regular and Display Classified Ads
Source: *The Tuscaloosa News*, May 3, 1990.

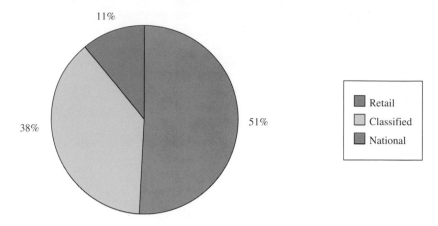

FIGURE 15.4 Newspaper Advertising Expenditures by Type

a special subhead within the section. For example, classified advertising is used extensively by realtors, automobile dealers, employment agencies, and the like. **Classified display** is advertising within the classified section that utilizes illustrative matter (including photographs) and occasional color, and in general often looks like the display advertisements found in the regular part of the paper. (See figure 15.3.)

Special-notice advertising typically is a small part of a newspaper's revenue and generally is handled differently from other types of advertising. Legal notices and government reports often are included under a special subhead of the classified section. Political advertising generally looks like most other display advertisements but usually is handled differently by a newspaper in terms of advance payment and special identification as a political advertisement.

As noted earlier, preprinted supplements differ from other types of newspaper advertising in that the newspaper has nothing to do with the production of the advertisements and serves primarily as the advertisements' distributor. This is true regardless of whether the preprint is a national Sunday supplement, such as *Parade,* an FSI of coupon advertisements, or a multi-page insert. Although most newspapers are willing to perform this distribution service, they make less money from this type of advertising and would prefer that advertisers bought ROP pages instead.

Since most newspapers earn the bulk of their advertising revenue from national, retail, and classified advertisers, figure 15.4 shows the allocation among the three. Retail accounts for the largest share—51 percent—followed by classified (38 percent) and national (11 percent).

Newspaper Rate Structure

We have already learned, from chapter 14 and earlier in this chapter, some things about a newspaper's rate structure. To summarize:

- The standard advertising unit of sale is the **column inch,** which is one column in width and 1 inch in depth. Newspapers can be of two sizes: (1) tabloid, which usually has five columns of width and 14 inches in depth, and (2) standard (broadsheet), containing six columns of width and 21 inches in depth.

- Newspapers usually price their space as either "open" or "flat." A flat rate does not permit an advertiser to earn a discount for quantity of space purchased, whereas an open rate does.

- The use of ROP color ads in newspapers is priced as an "extra" or "add-on" charge; that is, the cost of the advertising space is determined in black-and-white first, and then an extra charge for color is added. We now look at a few more items relative to rate structure.

The Standard Advertising Unit (SAU) System

Prior to the mid-1980s, national advertisers found the purchase of space in newspapers an arduous task. For one thing, tabloid and standard newspapers throughout the United States were each of varying size; for example, some standard newspapers used six columns of width for the purchase of advertising space, others used eight or nine. Buying a particular size of advertisement and having it look the same in all newspapers was difficult. Additionally, space for retailers was quoted in terms of column inches, whereas national advertising space was in agate lines (an agate line is one-fourteenth of a column inch). Thus, national advertisers buying space in their own name, as well as working with local dealers through cooperative advertising, had to be familiar with two totally different systems.

The newspaper industry adopted the **standard advertising unit** (**SAU**) system to help solve some of these problems. Thus, the number of columns is standardized (five or six), as is the width of any column (2 1/16 inch), the space between columns (1/8 inch), and the depth (21 inches for standard and 14 inches for tabloid). Column inches are used as the basis for quoting rates, and fifty-seven standard advertising sizes are available (fifty-six that fit broadsheet papers and thirty-three that apply to tabloids). Most daily U.S. newspapers, even though they may differ in page dimensions, currently use this system, and figure 15.5 shows the various size ads. Thus, the unit marked "2 × 18" is 2 columns wide (4 1/4 inches) by 18 inches deep, for a total of 36 column inches. One mechanical reproduction of the advertisement would fit every newspaper in the United States that accepts SAUs, and each newspaper would charge for exactly 36 column inches.

Premium Position Charges

Some newspapers charge extra if an advertiser wants the advertisement placed in a special position within the paper—for example, at the top, right-hand side of the back page of the sports section or, perhaps, next to reading matter (news and editorial content). To secure such special locations, the advertiser may have to pay a premium position charge of between 15 and 35 percent more than the regular space cost. Rather than pay a premium for special position, many advertisers today secure these locations by negotiating with the paper.

Retail Versus National Rates

Although both retailers and national advertisers are charged mainly on the basis of the column inches they purchase, the two typically pay dramatically different prices for the same space. In general, national advertisers are charged around 67 percent *more* than retailers for identical space. This practice, known as the **rate differential,** has been in effect for many years, and, in fact, has tended to increase gradually in recent years, despite efforts by national advertisers to get newspapers to reduce it. For example, the rate differential rose from about 55 percent in 1980 to the current level of around 67 percent.

Newspapers argue that there are logical reasons for these rate differences: (1) national advertising requires most newspapers to pay a commission to the advertiser's agency as well as to the newspaper's media representative, (2) studies have shown that lowering national rates does not result in significant increased purchases of space due to an inelastic demand situation, (3) merchandising services offered to national advertisers justify a higher rate, (4) the national advertiser benefits from the paper's entire circulation. While national advertisers and their agencies do not generally accept these as valid reasons for the size of the differential, they have not been very successful in getting newspapers to lower it. However, with demand for newspaper space lessening somewhat during the early 1990s, the national advertiser may succeed as a result of negotiating better prices.[2]

Combination Rates

In some situations, an advertiser may be given the opportunity to purchase more than one newspaper at a rate that is lower than the sum of the individual papers—that is, a **combination rate.** For example, in many cities, the same publisher owns both the morning and evening papers. A combination rate

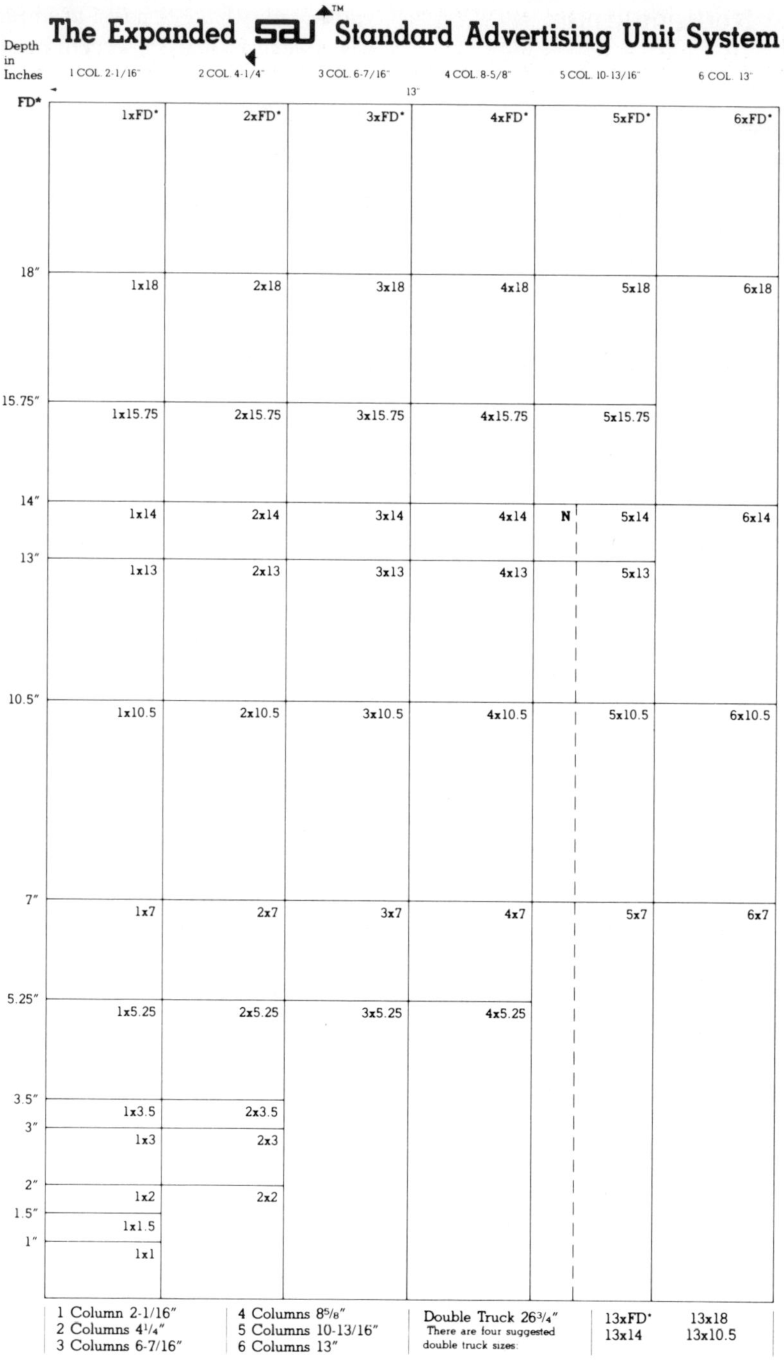

The Expanded **5ᴢ**™ Standard Advertising Unit System

Depth in Inches

	1 COL 2-1/16"	2 COL 4-1/4"	3 COL 6-7/16"	4 COL 8-5/8"	5 COL 10-13/16"	6 COL 13"
				13"		
FD*	1xFD*	2xFD*	3xFD*	4xFD*	5xFD*	6xFD*
18"	1x18	2x18	3x18	4x18	5x18	6x18
15.75"	1x15.75	2x15.75	3x15.75	4x15.75	5x15.75	
14"	1x14	2x14	3x14	4x14	5x14 N	6x14
13"	1x13	2x13	3x13	4x13	5x13	
10.5"	1x10.5	2x10.5	3x10.5	4x10.5	5x10.5	6x10.5
7"	1x7	2x7	3x7	4x7	5x7	6x7
5.25"	1x5.25	2x5.25	3x5.25	4x5.25		
3.5"	1x3.5	2x3.5				
3"	1x3	2x3				
2"	1x2	2x2				
1.5"	1x1.5					
1"	1x1					

1 Column 2-1/16"	4 Columns 8⁵⁄₈"	Double Truck 26³⁄₄"
2 Columns 4¼"	5 Columns 10-13/16"	There are four suggested double truck sizes:
3 Columns 6-7/16"	6 Columns 13"	

13xFD*	13x18
13x14	13x10.5

FIGURE 15.5 The Standard Advertising Unit (SAU) System

Source: Newspaper Advertising Bureau. Reprinted by permission.

TABLE 15.2

Column-Inch Rates, Circulations and Readers (Ages 25–49) for Example

Newspaper	Open Rate (Per Column Inch)	Earned Rate (Per Column Inch)	Circulation	Readers, Ages 25–49
A	$85	$77	320,000	420,000
B	$70	$62	220,000	360,000

generally is offered so that an advertisement can run in both newspapers at a cost noticeably below the sum of the two paper's individual rates. In fact, some newspaper companies *require* that advertising space be purchased in combination—a **forced combination rate.**

Because many newspapers today are owned by chains, this permits another opportunity for buying several papers in combination at favorable rates. An advertiser might buy two papers that are part of a particular chain, or many of them. Another situation to which combination rates may apply is where someone, perhaps a media rep firm, has put together a network of independent papers that can be sold in various combinations to an advertiser.

Comparing Alternative Newspaper Vehicles

Advertisers can compare different newspapers on the basis of their relative cost efficiency; that is, for a given amount of space cost, how many circulated copies of the paper are delivered? This type of comparison is particularly appropriate if the advertiser is considering a newspaper buy in a market with two or more competing papers. (The same newspaper also can be compared over time, from one year to the next, to see if it is becoming more or less efficient.) The typical method used to make such comparisons is the **cost-per-thousand** (**CPM**) (see chapter 7). (For those newspapers that still use the agate-line rate, the equivalent method of comparison is the **milline rate,** which is the cost per agate line per million circulation.)

Although there are alternative ways to compute a CPM, the following formula can serve as a starting point:

$$CPM = \frac{\text{Column Inch Rate} \times 1,000}{\text{Circulation}}$$

Thus, if a newspaper had a rate of $125 per column inch and a circulation of 500,000, its CPM would be:

$$CPM = \frac{\$125 \times 1,000}{500,000} = \$0.25$$

(The newspaper delivers 1,000 circulated copies for 25 cents per column inch.)

Circulation generally is used in the denominator of the CPM formula, since that information is the most readily available measure of media delivery. However, **readership** (or audience) information is available for papers in the largest fifty markets of the United States, and this usually is a more useful measure of delivery than circulation. Also, instead of the column-inch rate, it may be desirable to use the actual cost of the advertisement being purchased, taking into account any quantity discount earned. An example for a hypothetical newspaper market with two competing newspapers follows:

An advertiser is planning to buy a four-column-by-15-inch ad and will be on contract to receive an earned discount. The target market is adults, 25–49 years of age. The information in table 15.2 is available. Given the open column-inch rates and the circulations, the following CPMs can be calculated:

$$CPM_{Newspaper\ A} = \frac{\$85 \times 1,000}{320,000} = \mathbf{\$0.266}$$

$$CPM_{Newspaper\ B} = \frac{\$70 \times 1,000}{220,000} = \mathbf{\$0.318}$$

Thus, based on these CPMs, newspaper A is somewhat more efficient, delivering circulation at a lower cost-per-thousand than newspaper B.

However, CPMs based on the actual rate that would be earned with each paper and on delivery of targeted newspaper readers show somewhat different figures:

$$CPM_{Newspaper\ A} = \frac{\$77 \times 1,000}{420,000} = \mathbf{\$0.183}$$

$$CPM_{Newspaper\ B} = \frac{\$62 \times 1,000}{360,000} = \mathbf{\$0.172}$$

Here, from information that is more accurate in terms of the actual buy in this market, newspaper B is shown to be slightly more efficient than newspaper A (17.2 cents versus 18.3 cents per 1,000 target-market readers).

In this example, we could use the total cost of the ad in each newspaper, but the results would be the same. Thus, the cost of the ad at earned rates is \$4,620 in newspaper A and \$3,720 in newspaper B (60 column inches $\times$ \$77 per column inch = \$4,620; 60 column inches $\times$ \$62 per column inch = \$3,720). CPMs are \$11.00 for newspaper A and \$10.33 for newspaper B.

Circulation and Audience Delivery

As already mentioned, newspaper delivery is measured either by (1) **circulation**—the number of copies distributed in a certain way (this usually means copies that are paid for); or (2) **audience**—the number of people who can be identified as having read a certain amount of the newspaper (the terms *audience* and *readers* are synonymous).

Circulation information generally is available for virtually every newspaper published. The newspaper itself starts the process by reporting the number of distributed copies through a "Publisher's Statement." Independent auditing organizations usually verify that this information is accurate and produced according to prescribed procedures. One of the best-known auditing organizations in the print-media area is the Audit Bureau of Circulations (ABC), which was established in 1914 by advertisers, agencies, and publishers.[3] To determine a newspaper's current circulation, media people usually look in *Standard Rate & Data Service, Newspaper Rates and Data.*

Figure 15.6 shows the circulation trend of daily and Sunday newspapers in selected years. Daily newspaper circulations have not grown much over the past thirty years, and this trend is even more pronounced if population growth is taken into account. Sunday circulation has fared somewhat better, yet has remained fairly flat over the past few years. On the other hand, the circulation of weekly newspapers has grown rapidly, from 27.9 million in 1970 to the current level of around 53.0 million (a 90 percent increase!).

Audience (readership) information for specific newspapers is regularly available only for those newspapers operating in the largest fifty markets of the United States. Each year, Scarborough/Simmons publishes its *Newspaper Ratings Study,* which provides media buyers with information about the readership of specific newspapers according to a number of demographic variables (for example, gender, age, education, and income).

Information about newspaper readership in general, as opposed to the audience of specific newspapers, is available yearly through the study conducted by the Simmons Market Research Bureau (SMRB), discussed in chapter 5. In addition, various trade associations—such as the Newspaper Advertising Bureau—regularly do research that measures newspaper audiences according to many different variables.

Table 15.3 shows the percentage of adults who read a daily newspaper, according to several

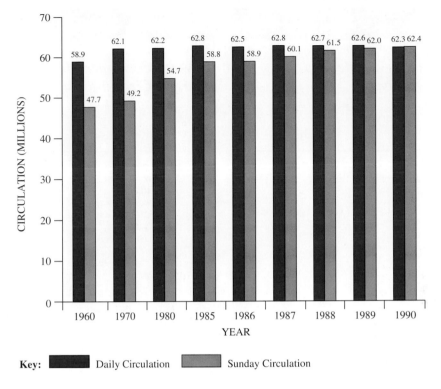

FIGURE 15.6 Circulation Trend of Daily and Sunday
Newspapers
Source: Newspaper Advertising Bureau. Reprinted by permission.

demographic categories. Thus, 62 percent of all adults read a daily paper. In demographic groupings, the highest levels of readership are among:

- Men (65 percent read, compared with 60 percent of women)
- People 55–64 years of age (69 percent)
- College graduates (77 percent)
- Persons with $50,000+ household income (74 percent)

Although the figures in table 15.3 show that a large percentage of adults read a daily newspaper, the overall level of readership generally has been declining. For example, whereas 72 percent of all adults read a daily newspaper in 1975, the figure stood at 67 percent in 1982, 65 percent in 1987, and

had dropped to 62 percent in 1990. This trend is a cause for concern among newspaper publishers.

Magazines

Magazine advertising totals around $9.9 billion annually, or 7.7 percent of total advertising expenditures. This places magazines in fourth place among the media in total dollar revenue, after newspapers, television, and direct mail.

Although magazines have been published in the United States almost since the country's founding, the medium did not become a noticeable carrier of advertising until late in the nineteenth century. Perhaps most significant in bringing this about was passage of the Postal Act of 1879, which granted second-class mailing privileges to magazines. This

TABLE 15.3

Average Weekday Readership of Daily Newspapers

Demographic Category	Percentage of Adults
By sex:	
Men	65%
Women	60
By age:	
18–24 years	53%
25–34 years	58
35–44 years	66
45–54 years	66
55–64 years	69
65 years or older	65
By education:	
College graduate	77%
1–3 years college	69
High school graduate	67
Attended high school	49
Did not attend high school	42
By household income:	
$50,000 or more	74%
$40,000 or more	73
$30,000 or more	70
$20,000–$29,999	61
$10,000–$19,999	54
Less than $10,000	42
TOTAL	**62%**

Source: Simmons *1990 Study of Media & Markets.* Reprinted by permission.

TABLE 15.4

Twenty Consumer Magazines with Largest Circulation

	Magazine	Average Circulation
1.	*Modern Maturity*	22,430,894
2.	*Reader's Digest*	16,264,547
3.	*TV Guide*	15,604,267
4.	*National Geographic*	10,189,703
5.	*Better Homes and Gardens*	8,007,222
6.	*Family Circle*	5,431,779
7.	*Good Housekeeping*	5,152,521
8.	*McCall's*	5,020,127
9.	*Ladies' Home Journal*	5,001,739
10.	*Woman's Day*	4,802,842
11.	*Time*	4,094,935
12.	*Redbook*	3,907,221
13.	*National Enquirer*	3,803,607
14.	*Playboy*	3,488,006
15.	*Star*	3,431,453
16.	*Sports Illustrated*	3,220,016
17.	*Newsweek*	3,211,958
18.	*People Weekly*	3,208,668
19.	*Prevention*	3,022,108
20.	*The American Legion Magazine*	2,956,342

Source: Paid circulation as filed with the Audit Bureau of Circulations.

Classes of Magazines

The most common ways to classify magazines are by *frequency of publication* and *type of audience* targeted. On the basis of frequency, most magazines are issued on a monthly basis, with weeklies next, and a smattering of semimonthlies, bimonthlies, and quarterlies.

On the basis of audience, *Standard Rate and Data Service* initially classifies magazines into three broad types: *consumer, farm,* and *business publications.* (*SRDS* issues two volumes providing rate information for magazines. One volume has separate sections, one each for consumer magazines and farm publications; a second volume gives information about business publications.) Consumer magazines are directed to the people who buy products and services for personal consumption. These

provided low-cost national distribution of magazines through the U.S. mail, and by the end of the 1800s, magazines had become a major advertising medium.

Today, as many as 12,000 magazines are published in the United States. According to the listings in the *Standard Rate and Data Service (SRDS)* volumes, over 2,200 magazines are directed to consumers and farmers, and around 5,000 are aimed at people in business. Table 15.4 shows the twenty largest consumer magazines in terms of circulation.

FIGURE 15.7 *Cosmopolitan* Points Out Some of Its
Uniqueness in a Trade Advertisement
Source: *Cosmopolitan*®, a publication of Hearst Magazines, a division
of The Hearst Corporation. © 1989 The Hearst Corporation.

magazines usually are paid for through a home-delivered subscription or purchased at a newsstand or other retail store.

Business magazines are aimed at people in their occupational capacity in the work force. They can be further divided into **trade papers** (available to retailers, wholesalers, and others in the channel of distribution), *industrial publications* (for product manufacturers), and *professional publications* (directed to people in the professions, such as doctors, lawyers, and engineers). (See figure 15.7.)

"Farm magazines" originally was a category used to classify a group of publications that appealed to farmers and farm families as both consumers and businesspeople. However, farm publications today primarily are aimed at the *business* of farming.

SRDS further categorizes magazines on the basis of audience targeted by placing each consumer, farm, and business magazine into a subclassification. For example, in the consumer magazine section of *SRDS* are sixty-eight subclassifications, ranging alphabetically from "airline inflight" magazines to "youth" magazines. Farm publications are subclassified into thirteen categories, including "farm organizations and cooperatives" and "poultry," whereas business magazines are placed into 174 subclasses. Table 15.5 shows a sample of consumer magazines for a selection of subclassifications.

TABLE 15.5

Subclassifications, with Selected Consumer Magazines to Exemplify

Subclass	Selected Magazines
General Editorial	*Modern Maturity*
	Reader's Digest
Entertainment	*TV Guide*
Travel/Inflight	*Delta Sky*
	TWA Ambassador
News and Business	*Time*
	Newsweek
	Money
Women's	*Family Circle*
	Ladies' Home Journal
Home Service	*Better Homes and Gardens*
	Southern Living
Romance and Movies	*True Story*
Fashion and Bride	*Glamour*
	Mademoiselle
Baby Care	*Expecting*
	American Baby
Youth	*Seventeen*
	Boy's Life
Men's	*Playboy*
	Gentlemen's Quarterly
Sports and Automotive	*Sports Illustrated*
	Field & Stream
	Car & Driver
Mechanics and Science	*Popular Science*
	Popular Mechanics

In addition to frequency of publication and audience served, magazines can be classified according to several other aspects:

- Like newspapers, magazines also can be distinguished by paid versus controlled circulation. Most consumer and farm magazines are paid for by the potential reader; however, a large number of business publications are sent free to people with a prescribed job title and function.

- Although most magazines are delivered by *traditional* means—namely, newsstands or mail—some utilize *nontraditional* delivery systems, such as hanging bagged copies on doorknobs, inserting the magazine in a newspaper, and having salespeople deliver a magazine as part of their regular sales calls.

- Most magazines are *national* in their editorial focus and delivery of audiences. However, a recent trend has been for magazines to provide a more *regionalized* offering of editorial and/or advertising circulation. Some magazines concentrate their efforts on a particular region of the country (*Southern Living*), others on a single state (*Texas Monthly*), and yet others on a given city (*Chicago*). Among those magazines that are national in their orientation, it is common to offer an advertiser only a part of the national circulation. Thus, some advertisements in *Time* magazine are seen only in certain regions, or certain states, or even specific cities.

Characteristics of Magazines

Media buyers attempt to match general attributes of magazines as a medium with the buyers' particular advertising plan objectives. We now look at some magazine characteristics.

Audience Selectivity

Perhaps the most unique attribute of magazines is their ability to reach special market segments. While some magazines are rather general in their editorial focus and appeal to large audiences—for example, *Modern Maturity,* with over 22 million circulation and 50 million readers, and *Reader's Digest,* which delivers over 16 million copies monthly and about 35 million in audience—the vast majority of consumer, business, and farm magazines are directed to very specialized target markets. For example, there are magazines that appeal to virtually every hobby, lifestyle, interest, occupational role, farming activity, and the like.

When an advertiser's target audience closely matches the audience of a particular specialized magazine, the opportunity exists to reach the target efficiently and intensively. Thus, even small-budget advertisers often can use magazines as part of their media mix (or perhaps even exclusively). Whereas a thirty-second television commercial during the

TABLE 15.6

Cost of Advertisement in Specialized Magazines

Target	Magazine	Cost of Full-Page, Four-Color Ad
Golfers	*Golf Magazine*	$42,225
Skiers	*Skiing*	$25,350
Motorcyclists	*Cycle*	$21,130
Expectant parents	*Expecting*	$34,320

evening hours can cost an average of $150,000, an advertiser would pay the rates in table 15.6 for a full-page, four-color advertisement in some specialized magazines.

Market Coverage

Magazines generally are considered national in their geographic coverage, reaching their specialized target audience, regardless of where target-audience members live and work. Yet, at the same time, a reasonable amount of territorial flexibility is available to an advertiser. This comes about in two ways. Some magazines are designed for a particular region of the United States—for example, *Southern Accents* and *Midwest Living.* Others focus on a particular state—*New Jersey Monthly* and *Kentucky Living.* And still others zero in on a single city—*San Francisco Focus, Tampa Bay Life,* and *Minneapolis Monthly.* Such magazines permit advertisers not only to reach a specific geographic target, but to do so within a publication that is editorially designed to speak to people in the area.

The other way to achieve territorial focus is through a national magazine that offers advertisers a regional split of its circulation. With this option, advertisers can choose to have their advertisements appear only in copies of the magazine going to a particular locale. Most major consumer magazines, and a number of business and farm publications, provide this opportunity. The circulation splits can be on a regional, state-by-state, or, in a few cases, individual city basis. Presently, around three hundred consumer magazines offer regional editions of some sort. *Sports Illustrated,* for example, offers seven regional editions covering broad areas of the United States (New England, the Midwest, and so on). *Time* magazine can be purchased in eleven regional areas, in each of the fifty states, as well as in fifty city markets, permitting even local retailers to use the magazine.

Some national magazines, in addition to offering regional splits, permit advertisers to buy a part of the magazine's circulation that goes only to people with certain demographic characteristics. For example, *McCall's* has a demographic edition that goes solely to women who are 50–64 years in age (it guarantees a delivery of one million to such women), and *Newsweek* will break out its circulation that delivers to 700,000 professional and managerial women. Time Warner, whose *Time* magazine has offered demographic splits for some time, offers its "Target Select" package, whereby *People Magazine, Sports Illustrated,* and *Time* provide three groups of consumers: high-income seniors (50+ years and $50,000+ income), people who have recently moved, and people who buy products or services by direct mail.[4] An advertiser's advertisement appears only in magazines received by subscribers who fit the particular demographic profile.

Prestige

Although "prestige" is a rather subjective characteristic, many analysts believe that magazines generally convey a certain prestige and credibility to the advertisements that appear within them. This probably comes about because magazines generally are attractive appearing, are valued by their readers (even passed along to neighbors and friends), and have a high-quality editorial environment. Magazines sometimes are used in an advertising schedule to impress retail dealers; for example, copies of advertisements sometimes are seen in retail stores, with a statement attached, such as "Advertised in *Reader's Digest.*" (You also might want to refer back to the section "Authority or Prestige of the Media Vehicle" in chapter 8.)

MEDIA SPOTLIGHT

15.2

Some Case Histories of How Magazine Advertising Works

Richard C. Anderson, formerly executive vice president of Needham, Harper & Steers advertising agency and now vice chairman of Lands' End mail-order firm, once defined the most important and unique value of magazines for the advertiser to be the aperture—which refers to the opening provided the advertiser by the special relationship that exists between editor and reader.

According to Anderson, "The editor/reader relationship is essentially a personal conversation between them on a group of subjects that serves the reader's interests. This is a one-on-one conversation, and in time, it creates a bond of trust, of belief, expectation, and empathy. It is through the quality of the relationship that an aperture or opening to the reader's mind and heart is created through which we (advertisers) can establish communication."

This special relationship between editor and reader, coupled with the fact that better than seven of every ten U.S. adults "prefer" that magazines carry advertising, means that advertising in magazines is functioning in an ideal environment of reader receptivity. It comes as no surprise, therefore, that magazine advertising is highly effective.

The following are just a few of the documented case histories that provide specific evidence of the power of magazines:

Vaseline Lip Therapy

Introducing a product is never easy, especially when the incumbent market leader has the high recognition and market share of a virtual generic brand. In this difficult, competitive climate, Vaseline Lip Therapy was successfully introduced with four-color spreads and pages in magazines.

According to the product manager at Chesebrough-Ponds, consumer demand exceeded even their most aggressive expectations, and they were unable to supply the product quickly enough to meet the resultant demand.

Absolut Vodka

The problem faced by Absolut Vodka was the fact that the imported vodka category was dominated by two strong, well-entrenched brands—Stolichnaya and Finlandia. Absolut had very low awareness among consumers. And Absolut was being outspent in advertising by a ratio of five to one by these leading brands. In addition, overall consumption of distilled spirits in the United States had been trending down.

To build awareness of the brand as quickly as possible and to establish a high-quality, contemporary, and sophisticated image for Absolut, a campaign ran in twenty-four magazines, focusing on the unique, distinctive shape of the bottle to generate instant and lasting visual identity.

As a result, Absolut Vodka passed Stolichnaya in 1986 to become the leading imported vodka. At current growth rates, the brand will sell over one million cases in 1987 to become the first imported vodka to ever reach that level.

National Potato Advisory Board

When potato consumption decreased because of a fattening image, the Potato Board turned to magazines to launch in 1974 an informative magazine advertising campaign to set the record straight. In a series of successive magazine advertising campaigns to provide nutritional and caloric information, the Potato Board succeeded in causing many consumers to change their minds about potatoes.

By 1985, positive attitudes about nutrition had increased by 188 percent, while negative attitudes about calories had decreased 31 percent. At the same time, per-capita consumption of potatoes had increased from 115 pounds to just over 120 pounds.

California Prune Board/California Prunes

The California Prune Board faced a thirty-year history of declining prune sales. Prunes had a serious problem—they were thought to be for older people or people with a regularity problem.

It was concluded that the usual two six-week television flights in fifteen markets would not solve the problem. To change the negative image and turn around the steady annual sales decline, for the same amount they had been spending in television, they designed a highly informative, long-copy magazine campaign to run in women's and dual-audience magazines for eight months. This campaign communicated the information about prunes having more fiber needed for general health. Most ads included a box offering serving suggestions and a recipe booklet.

The Prune Board got tens of thousands of requests for their booklet, which made them happy. What made them even happier, was the fact that, during 1986, when the advertising started running in magazines, prune sales have increased every month over the same month of the previous year by at least 10 percent.

Hallmark's Shoebox Greeting Cards

For years, Hallmark has been the market leader in greeting cards. But because of its "hearts-and-flowers" image, it had been losing some of its customers and potential customers—those interested in less conventional greeting cards.

Hallmark's solution was to develop a brand-new line of cards under the name of Shoebox Greetings, which run the gamut from witty to whimsical to risqué.

The objectives of the advertising were:

1. To broaden people's perception of the kinds of cards Hallmark makes

2. To attract new customers to Hallmark stores, particularly younger people, by creating demand for the new Shoebox line.

Actual greeting cards were put into the magazines, along with an ad. The cards were carefully chosen to appeal to each magazine's audience. Readers could actually touch the cards, open them, read and enjoy them.

Sales results have been dramatic: Hallmark has already revised its original projections upwards by more than 50 percent.

Harley Davidson Motorcycles

Harley Davidson's competition in the heavyweight category, the Japanese manufacturers, were outspending Harley in their advertising and were able to dominate the various media they used. In order to reverse a declining share of market, Harley Davidson designed a campaign utilizing multiple insertions consisting of a series of consecutive half-page color ads in the same issue of each of eleven different cycling magazines, promoting the emotional experience of owning and riding a Harley. The running of consecutive half-page ads enabled Harley Davidson to dominate the magazine issues.

The campaign has been enormously successful, generating a 4.5 point increase in market share and boosting Harley from number three to number two in the marketplace. Harley's 1986 registrations were up 17.5 percent, while the total market was down 12.6 percent.

Continued on p. 310

15.2 cont.

Fisher-Price Juvenile Furniture and Accessories

After more than fifty years in the toy business, Fisher-Price made a decision to extend its franchise beyond toys into juvenile furniture and accessories. The advertising objective was to build brand awareness on the part of new mothers and mothers-to-be, to create consumer demand, and to put pressure on the retail trade to add the Fisher-Price line. Magazines were chosen to be used almost exclusively. The

Courtesy of Magazine Publishers of America.

1986 campaign consisted of a series of full-page, four-color ads in nine magazines targeted to new mothers.

Results have greatly exceeded goals. While sales of the juvenile furniture division accounted for 5 percent of total Fisher-Price sales in 1985, they soared by 130 percent in 1986 over 1985 and now accounted for 10 percent of total Fisher-Price sales. And it is now the third largest and the fastest-growing juvenile furniture company in the nation.

Exposure Potential

In comparison to other media, magazines have a high exposure potential because they are often kept for long periods of time and used and reused for reference. Studies have shown that the reader of an average copy spends sixty-one minutes reading the magazine, is exposed an average of 1.7 times to the average page in the magazine, and spends an average of twenty-six seconds of reading time per page.[5] Another study has found that the average person picks up a monthly magazine on four different days and picks up a weekly or biweekly just under two separate days. Other studies have shown that 77 percent of adults refer to or reread something in a magazine issue that they have previously read and that around 75 percent keep the magazine on hand for future reference.

Whereas the ratio of advertising-to-editorial content in newspapers is around 60–40, magazines have for many years maintained about 48 percent advertising and 52 percent editorial. This gives magazine advertisements more exposure potential.

Quality of Color Reproduction

Magazines have long been characterized as having good-quality reproduction of editorial and advertising content, resulting from being printed on good-quality paper stock. Even those magazines distributed by newspapers, such as *Parade,* use glossy paper stock that permits good color reproduction. Advertisers can further improve quality by having advertisements preprinted on heavier, high-gloss paper stock and perhaps using special color or attention-getting inks.

In recent years, color advertising has increased while relative charges for color have decreased. In 1970, the split between color and black-and-white ads was about even (50–50), whereas currently, over 70 percent of all consumer magazine advertisements are in color.

Services

Many magazines offer extra services to advertisers (see chapters 8 and 12). These extra services may include research staffs that provide information on

MEDIA SPOTLIGHT

15.3

The "Impact" Program of Southern Living:
Innovative, Imaginative, Individualized

Southern Living magazine uses a program it calls "Impact," to delineate the types of services the magazine provides advertisers:

Southern Living *merchandising provides that extra edge, the added emphasis that helps an advertising message stand out in the minds of key southern decision makers.*

The Southern Living *merchandising staff works with you to create tailormade programs to meet your specific marketing needs. Exciting trade mailings, sweepstakes, special events, and contests enhance the initial impact of your consumer advertising message.*

Building stronger relationships between your company, your sales force or dealers, and southern consumers—that's the impact of custom merchandising from Southern Living.

Five Steps to Added IMPACT

1. The *request* is made for merchandising support in achieving a specific advertising goal, such as increased in-store displays for a new product in the southern market.

2. The *research* is done by a *Southern Living* merchandising specialist on the product and supporting ad creative, for theme development.

3. The *response* is a variety of merchandising possibilities based on a predetermined budget and time frame. Examples include a display contest, trade sweepstakes, premium mailing, and book offer.

4. The *reaction* from the advertiser in selecting a program initiates the implementation of production of printed materials, the ordering of gifts/prizes, the processing of mailing lists, and so on.

5. The *results* are carefully documented for reporting to the advertiser, and all gift/prize fulfillment is handled by the *Southern Living* Merchandising Department.

Source: *Southern Living,* Birmingham, AL.

---

readership or merchandising operations that help advertisers further promote their products or services to consumers and retail dealers.

Another service that many advertisers like is the opportunity to test their advertisements through a **split run.** In split-run testing, two or more versions of an advertisement are printed in alternate copies of the magazine. (Split-run testing also is available in many newspapers.) In each test advertisement, some offer is made to encourage replies. The assumption is that the version bringing forth the largest number of replies is superior.

Special Techniques

To attract special attention to advertisements, advertisers and magazine publishers have developed a number of special techniques, including gatefold advertisements, inserts printed on heavy stock, pop-up advertisements, musical advertisements, scent strips, and three-dimensional holograms.

FIGURE 15.8 Example of a Pop-Up Advertisement.
When the two center pages are opened, the part at the
top of the ad pops up.
Source: *In Health*, New York, NY.

Gatefolds are advertisements that fold out into a continuous number of advertising pages, usually with the idea of communicating a lot of information within a series of pages. Pop-up advertisements involve designing two facing pages so that, when the pages are opened, additional material pops out from the top of the advertisement. Figure 15.8 shows a pop-up advertisement that announces the change in title of a magazine—from *Hippocrates* to *In Health*.

Absolut vodka recently produced an advertisement that "talked" and had music to accompany. (Magazines have long had the ability to produce an advertisement that can be removed from the page and played on a phonograph.) Finlandia vodka ran a three-dimensional advertisement in the form of a hologram. Cosmetic companies have used advertisements that contain scent strips, which permit the reader to smell a particular perfume or cologne. In fact, this advertising technique has recently brought complaints from readers who are allergic to certain scents.[6] As a result of these complaints, new technology is being developed to seal in a scent so that it cannot be accidentally opened.

Magazine Rate Structure

Chapter 14 already noted several things relative to magazine rate structure. To review:

- Space normally is sold by page and fractional-page units.

TABLE 15.7

"One-Time" Rates for Shape Magazine		
Space Unit	Black-and-White Rates	Four-Color Rates
1 page	$12,950	$16,150
2/3 page	$10,000	$12,450
1/2 page	$8,100	$10,050
1/3 page	$5,500	$6,800

- Black-and-white rates and color rates are each quoted separately. That is, when looking up a particular magazine's rates in *SRDS*, one section gives black-and-white costs and another section lists costs for color units; add-on charges, noted for newspaper listings, are not used for magazines.
- Certain charges, for special types of units, may be added to the basic space cost; for example, bleed advertisements may require a premium.
- Discounts typically are given for frequency of insertion, volume of space used, and/or total dollars spent.

Table 15.7 exemplifies the use of page units and costs by showing the "one-time" (no-discount) rates for *Shape* magazine, whose editorial profile states, "*Shape* is a lifestyle magazine for the '90s woman, devoted to delivering information on the various aspects of fitness—physical, nutritional, and psychological." The table also lists the standard size units for this particular magazine. Other magazines have somewhat different fractional pages. In addition, many magazines accept advertisements that differ from the stated required sizes. In the case of *Shape* magazine:

- The cost of a four-color advertisement is around 25 percent higher than black-and-white.
- There is a built-in discount for using larger-size units; in other words, a half-page advertisement does not cost half the price of a full-page advertisement (the half-page advertisement is around 62 percent of the full-page cost).

Although other magazines are likely to have rate structures that produce different results from the ones just noted, this gives a general idea of the relationships among different size units and between color versus black-and-white advertisements.

With *Shape* magazine again as an example, the *SRDS* listing shows that: (1) the second and third covers are each priced at $18,600, and the fourth (back) cover is $20,800 (all cover advertisements must be four-color); (2) there is no extra charge for a bleed advertisement; and (3) discounts are available on a frequency basis (see table 14.5 for a sample frequency discount structure).

Premium Charges

As already mentioned, some magazines charge extra for such things as bleed advertisements and special positions. These usually are quoted as a percentage, which is added to the basic space cost. For example, *Seventeen* magazine has a bleed charge of 5 percent. A four-color, full-page ad runs $38,175.00; with a bleed, the total charge is $40,083.75. Examples of special-position charges include:

Playboy	10 percent for a guaranteed position within the magazine
Motor Trend	10 percent for a **center spread** (in the middle of the magazine)
California Bicyclist	5 percent for top or bottom of a page

Combination Rates

When a company owns several different magazines, it may offer an advertiser two or more of the magazines a **combination rate.** In effect, this amounts to a discount from the rates that would be derived by purchasing each publication separately.

For example, the Hearst Corporation, which owns a number of magazines, offers advertisers combination rates through two separate combination plans—the Hearst "Gold Buy" and "Hearst Magazines Woman Power." The latter combination involves *Cosmopolitan, Country Living, Good Housekeeping, Harper's Bazaar,* and *Redbook.* Advertisers who combine advertisements in any three or more of these publications receive a discount. Combination rates are shown in *SRDS Consumer Magazine Rates and Data* in subclass 22A— "Group Buying Opportunities."

Negotiation of Rates

Until rather recently, magazine space rates generally have not been negotiable. If a magazine, for example, had a rate of $30,000 for a particular piece of space, that is what media buyers paid for it (although, of course, any stated discounts for frequency, quantity, and so on applied). Negotiations were sometimes possible for such things as waiving certain special-position charges or providing extra merchandising support at no charge.

This situation, however, has changed dramatically within the past few years, and although the level of negotiating may not be entirely comparable to that which exists in the broadcast area, rate negotiation nevertheless does occur with noticeable frequency. The following excerpts, from an *Advertising Age* editorial, provide some insight into the issue:

A space salesman hands a prospective customer his magazine's rate card and watches as the fellow tosses it into the wastebasket. Then the customer turns to the salesman and says: "Now, let's talk. Just what will those ads cost?"

If this scene sounds extreme, it shouldn't. It exemplifies what's happening in the business of selling space these days. . . . This process, destructive as it is to the principles of selling, nevertheless is the name of today's game. . . . So today it seems the role of the rate card is just to serve as the starting point for eventually deciding what the advertiser will pay. . . .[7]

Although some analysts have suggested that rate negotiation came about due to a "soft" market— that is, a lessened demand for advertising space— and will diminish when demand improves, the more common view is that negotiation is here to stay.

Comparing Alternative Magazines

The method used to compare alternative magazine vehicles is the same as that shown for newspapers— that is, the cost-per-thousand (CPM). The formula is as follows:

$$CPM = \frac{\text{Cost of Space Unit} \times 1{,}000}{\text{Circulation (or Target Audience)}}$$

The target-audience figure is more desirable than circulation because it more accurately reflects the true efficiency of a particular magazine. Audience figures are readily available for about 150 consumer magazines from such sources as Simmons Market Research Bureau (SMRB) and Mediamark Research, Inc. (MRI).

Assume that an advertiser wants to buy one full-page, four-color advertisement in one of three women's magazines—*Good Housekeeping, Ladies' Home Journal,* or *McCall's.* The target market is "women in the 25- to 54-year-old age group." Information to compute CPMs is shown in table 15.8. The CPMs, for circulation and target market, are shown in table 15.9. Based solely on cost efficiency, *McCall's* magazine has the lowest CPM using circulation data. *Ladies' Home Journal,* however, has the lowest CPM on the basis of the designated target market.

Media buyers use these types of cost-efficiency comparisons as a starting point in deciding which of alternative vehicles they should buy. Buyers also, however, use additional criteria before making a final decision, such as:

• *The Total Size of the Target Delivered.* Advertisers who want to reach as many of the target market as possible might buy the vehicle that delivers the largest numbers, even though it is less cost efficient than other choices. In the previous example, *Good Housekeeping* might be

TABLE 15.8

Information Needed to Compute CPMs

Magazine	Full-Page, Four-Color Page Cost	Circulation	Target Readers
Good Housekeeping	$103,190	5,114,000	12,621,000
Ladies' Home Journal	78,200	5,117,000	10,000,000
McCall's	77,140	5,150,000	8,726,000

TABLE 15.9

Circulation and Target-Market CPMs

Magazine	Circulation CPM	Target-Market CPM
Good Housekeeping	$20.18	$8.18
Ladies' Home Journal	15.28	7.82
McCall's	14.98	8.84

selected by some advertisers because it delivers noticeably more targeted readers than the other two.

• *Editorial Environment.* Advertisers may decide to choose the magazine that they feel has the best type of editorial material for the brand. For example, to advertise salad dressing, an advertiser may prefer a magazine that has a large amount of its editorial content devoted to salad preparation.

• *Merchandising Support.* Certain magazines may provide better promotional offers than others, which might enhance the total effect of the advertising.

Circulation and Audience Delivery

Media buyers can find circulation information for a particular magazine in an appropriate section of an *SRDS* publication (one *SRDS* lists consumer magazines in one part and farm publications in another; a second *SRDS* provides listings of business magazines). The circulation figures are provided by the publisher, but most magazines are audited by independent auditing companies that verify the accuracy of the numbers.

Figure 15. 9 shows circulation trends during selected years for those magazines that were audited

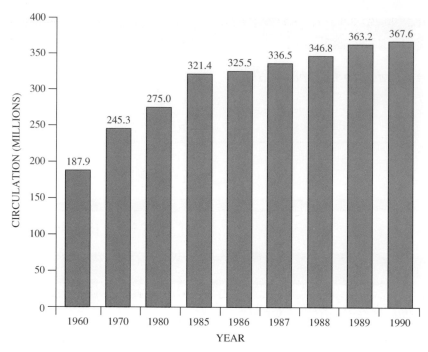

FIGURE 15.9 Circulation of Magazines Audited by
Audit Bureau of Circulations
Source: Audit Bureau of Circulation.

by the Audit Bureau of Circulations (includes consumer and farm magazines). Note in figure 15.9 that the magazine circulation trend has consistently increased for the years shown. However, circulation figures also should be considered in relationship to population growth. Thus, the circulation per one hundred adults in the population is shown in table 15.10. The table figures reflect that there was a relative downturn in circulation per adult population during the 1970s, but the trend moved back upward during the last half of the 1980s and continued at the start of the 1990s.

As already mentioned, audience information is available on a regular basis for each of around 150 consumer magazines. For such magazines, the number of readers can be classified according to three major sets of characteristics: demographics,

TABLE 15.10

Circulation Figures in Relationship to Population Growth

Year	Circulation Per 100 Adults
1960	164.9
1970	182.1
1980	178.7
1985	185.6
1986	186.6
1987	193.2
1988	196.4
1989	201.6
1990	202.2

TABLE 15.11

Demographic, Product/Brand Usage, and Psychographic Profile of Time *Magazine*

Characteristic	Audience Size
Demographic:	
Men, 18–49	9,356,000
Adults, College Graduates	7,290,000
Product/Brand Usage:	
Adult Users of Regular Cola Drinks	12,810,000
Adult Users of Coca-Cola Classic	6,943,000
Psychographic:	
Adults Who Are "Sociable"	8,984,000
Adults Who Are "Conformists"	4,982,000

Source: Simmons Market Research Bureau, 1988.

product/brand usage, and psychographics (lifestyle characteristics). Table 15.11 gives some examples of the audience for *Time* magazine.

Information about magazine audiences in general, as opposed to audiences of specific magazines, can be obtained from the same syndicated sources (for example, SMRB and MRI). In addition, the magazine industry's trade associations often do research that provides media buyers with helpful insights into overall audience and readership patterns. One such trade association is the Magazine Publishers of America (MPA). MPA studies have highlighted some of the following characteristics of consumer magazine readership:

- Ninety-four percent of adults in the United States read magazines during an average month. They read an average of 9.6 different magazine issues per month.

- Upscale, prime-prospect persons read even more magazines. Ninety-seven percent of the college-educated read over 11 issues; 97 percent of persons with $40,000+ household income and 97 percent of the professional/managerial read an average of 11 or more issues per month.

- Magazine reading is heaviest among adults, 18–44 years old, college-educated, $50,000+ household income, white-collar, and three-or-more person household—the exact opposite of television viewing.

- Sixty-two percent of all magazine reading occurs in the reader's own home.

- There is minimal variation in magazine reading by seasons.[8]

Summary

About one-fourth of all monies invested in advertising are spent in newspapers. Newspapers are classified according to publication frequency (daily, weekly, or Sunday); size (standard [broadsheet] or tabloid); type of circulation (paid or controlled); audience targeted; and special sections (ROP versus preprinted sections, supplements, freestanding inserts).

Newspapers provide advertisers with a great deal of flexibility in terms of market coverage; convey a sense of immediacy; have prestige within the community; permit a reader-controlled exposure environment; allow for national-local interaction of advertising; offer a broad array of advertising and marketing services and special techniques; have fair, but not outstanding, color reproduction quality; and contain a fairly large amount of advertising content.

Types of newspaper advertising include display advertising (national and local), classified advertising (regular and display), special-notice

MEDIA SPOTLIGHT

15.4

Ogilvy & Mather Media Executive Tom Bell Presents Some Views on Magazine Negotiation

At its very worst, magazine negotiation is agency people burning rate cards and wielding baseball bats for the pages of *Inside Print* magazine. Who in this room thinks that a buyer-seller relationship based only on implied threat and price is in the client's best interest?

But when it's good, magazine negotiation ferrets out the best *value*—that equitable combination of both price *and* quality that creates the greatest *effect* for a client's dollars.

Magazine negotiation—be it price, positioning, or added-value merchandising—was inevitable and is here to stay. For each rep in this room, the issue now is: how to make the most of negotiation.

Now why would I, a buyer, offer you, the sellers, advice on how to make negotiation work for you?

One simple reason: It's in our *mutual* clients' best interest to do so. Our job is to build *brands,* and using the *cheapest* tools isn't always the most *effective* way to build these brands.

Just study the seller-buyer relationship between manufacturers and retailers over the past decade or so. It's a very similar situation to what publishers face—and, fortunately, one from which each of you can learn.

It wasn't so long ago that ad spending commanded 60 percent of the marketing budget. Manufacturers reigned. Brand-image campaigns flourished. Magazine schedules were deeper and more continuous. The good ol' days, right?

Today, the *reverse* is true. Retailers rule. *Promotional* spending commands the budget priority ad spending once held. Brand-image campaigns have lost ground to incentive campaigns that have taught the consumer to pay for products as if they were commodities, not brands.

The resultant lower product prices have led to reduced revenues, ad budgets, and magazine schedules. All of which have undermined the *brand image,* or relationship, with consumers. In most situations, the only leverage a manufacturer

advertising, and preprinted supplements. The buying and selling of newspaper space by national advertisers has been made easier by the Standard Advertising Unit (SAU) system, yet the rate differential between national and local rates has been a problem. Alternative newspaper vehicles can be compared by computing the cost-per-thousand (CPM), which shows the relative cost to deliver one thousand circulated copies or readers. The delivery of newspapers is measured by circulation, which is the number of copies distributed in a certain way,

or by audience, which is the number of people who have read a certain amount of the newspaper.

Magazines, which consist of consumer, business, and farm publications, account for around 7.7 percent of total advertising expenditures. Characteristics of magazines include their ability to: pinpoint specialized audience segments; reach national audiences while also providing a fair amount of regional flexibility; convey a certain amount of prestige to the advertisers who use them; deliver a high exposure potential; permit high-quality color can apply to the retailer is this brand relationship with the consumer.

Our chairman, Graham Phillips, likens the brand franchise to a bank account. But instead of holding money, the brand franchise account holds consumer confidence and respect. Every time the brand is discounted, confidence and respect are withdrawn until, eventually, the account is empty. Many brands today have dropped below the required minimum balance.

How does the manufacturer escape this short-term, promotional trap? By reinvesting in its brand franchise—both its tangible and intangible assets. By convincing customers that Coke isn't just another cola, or that Levi's are not just jeans.

Each of you faces the same challenge.

It's my view that many sales reps, in their determination to adapt to the new rules of the buying game, have let their *brand-selling skills* slip. They've either deemphasized its importance in favor of the quick, easy route to the sale, or they've altogether overlooked it.

Just as the agency's job is to build and maintain strong brand franchises, so must your job be to sell the brand represented in the title of your magazine. Strong brand franchises command premium prices because people recognize and are willing to pay for quality.

Advertisers, too, will pay premiums for quality media vehicles, but only if they are convinced that the benefit to their business is commensurate with the additional cost. In other words, *value*.

But lest you think it's simply a matter of *telling* the buyer about editorial awards, heavier paper stock, average reading times, and any other tangible or intangible quality attributes of your brand, it's not. It goes beyond that to *translating* these attributes to benefits advertisers can understand in terms of *their* business, not yours. That's hard work.

What I'm suggesting is that negotiation places a greater emphasis on good ol' fashioned selling. It's knowing your magazine and the client's business inside and out, then marrying the two in a way that clients understand from *their* perspective.

If your title is worth more, then sell it. You'll be surprised how many buyers are willing to pay for quality.

Courtesy of Thomas R. Bell, Ogilvy & Mather, Chicago.

reproduction; and provide advertisers with good research and merchandising services, along with a variety of special techniques.

Magazines have a fairly straightforward rate structure, based mainly on a space unit of the page or fractional unit thereof. Advertising units in color are priced separately from those in black-and-white, and discounts typically are given for frequency of insertion, volume of space used, and/or total dollars spent. There can be extra charges for special types of units, although these can sometimes be ne-gotiated. Although magazine rates in the past have not been negotiable, the present pattern is that everything on a rate card is subject to negotiation.

Alternative magazine vehicles can be compared in terms of cost efficiency by computing the cost-per-thousand circulation or audience. The CPM comparisons usually are only a starting point in making a decision. Other factors to consider include the total size of a delivered target market, the editorial environment in which the advertising is placed, and the merchandising support a particular

Broadcast Media: Television and Radio

Learning Objectives

In the study of this chapter, you will have the opportunity to:

- Learn about the types of television and radio advertising.
- Note the television and radio characteristics used by media buyers.
- Understand how broadcast-media rate structures affect media buying.
- See how cost comparisons are computed in deciding alternative television and radio vehicles.
- Observe how broadcast audiences are measured, and note audience deliveries.

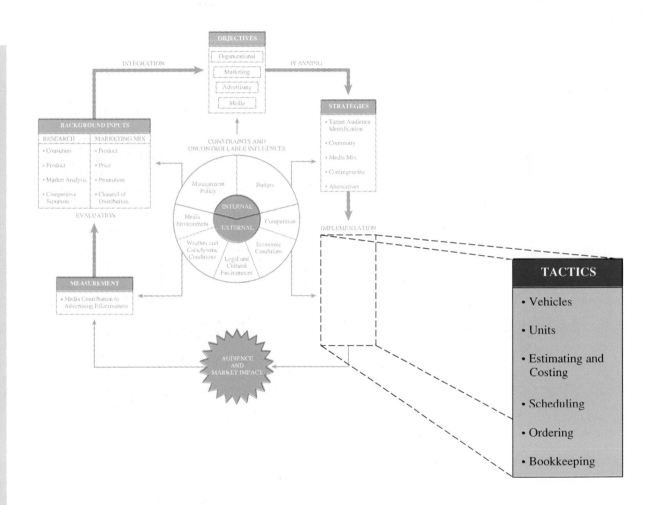

*T*his chapter discusses tactical aspects of the broadcast media. Just a few years ago, the term *broadcast* was fairly easy to define—it meant (1) the radio and television networks that distributed programs and advertising by broadcasting over-the-air signals to stations throughout the United States, as well as (2) the non-network stations that broadcast signals in a certain locale. Today, with advanced electronic technology—such as satellite transmission, cable systems, videocassette recorders, and interactive computer systems—the definition of broadcast has become more complicated. In this chapter, though, we concentrate on the more traditional components of the broadcast media—mainly radio and television, including cable television. Other aspects of broadcast advertising—for example, the commercials on prerecorded videocassettes—are discussed in chapter 18 ("Other Media"). Although like the print media discussed in chapter 15, television and radio share some features, each is discussed in a separate section.

Television

Television advertising accounts for over $28 billion of the money spent in all media, making it the number two advertising medium. Among the top one hundred national advertisers, television accounts for 69 percent of their measured media mix.

Although television technology was invented in the 1920s, the first commercial station did not begin operating until 1941. It was only after World War II ended in 1945 that consumers began to buy television sets in large numbers, although by 1950, only 9 percent of all U.S. households owned a set. This number grew to around 90 percent by the early 1960s and has been at a saturation level of around

98 percent of all households for the past several years. Currently, there are approximately ninety-three million television households in the United States. As shown in figure 16.1, 65 percent of the homes owning a television have more than one set, and 98 percent have a color set.

Among those homes that have at least one television set, around 60 percent receive their television signals by subscribing to a local cable system. Cable television's penetration will reach almost 65 percent within the next few years. Cable's growth over the past thirty years has been dramatic: Only 1 percent of all television homes received cable in 1960, but cable use grew to 7 percent in 1970, 19 percent in 1980, and 60 percent in 1991.

Types of Television Advertising

Television advertising can best be categorized as follows:

- Network
- National cable
- Syndication
- National Spot
- Local Spot
- Non-network Cable

The first four types are used predominately by national advertisers, whereas the latter two are used primarily by local firms. Figure 16.2 shows the relative allocation of total television dollars to these six categories. As noted in the figure, more than 70 percent of television dollars are placed by national advertisers, who predominately use network advertising (33.0%) or national spot advertising (27.4%). We now examine these six categories of television advertising in more detail.

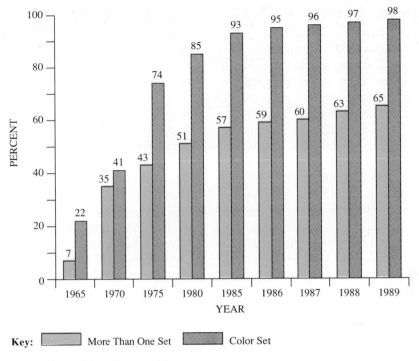

FIGURE 16.1 Percent of Television Homes with
Multi-Sets and Color Sets
Courtesy of Nielsen Media Research.

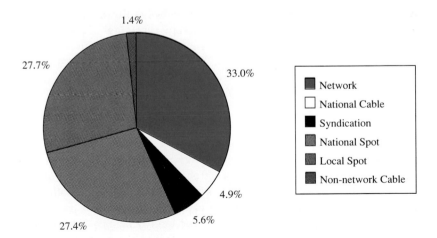

FIGURE 16.2 Allocation of Television Advertising
Dollars by Type
Source: From *Advertising Age*, May 6, 1991, p. 6. Copyright © 1991
Crain Communications Inc., Detroit, MI. Reprinted by permission.

Network

Presently, there are four major commercial television **networks**: American Broadcasting Company (ABC), Columbia Broadcasting System (CBS), National Broadcasting Company (NBC), and the Fox Broadcasting Company. In addition, there is the public television network—Public Broadcasting Service (PBS)—which in a strict sense does not air commercials but does permit program sponsorship as a means of providing company recognition (for example, on such PBS programs as "Masterpiece Theater" and "Mystery").

Network television involves tying together stations throughout the United States through some electronic means, with the primary method today being satellite transmission. A network sends its signal to an orbiting satellite, with stations in local markets picking up the signal through a receiving antenna. In turn, the local station then transmits the network signal to local viewers by broadcasting an *over-the-air* signal that individual television sets receive through their antenna system. Thus, for example, CBS broadcasts the program "60 Minutes" (including network television commercials) to around two hundred stations throughout the United States that have a contractual arrangement with CBS to carry its programming. ABC and NBC also have around two hundred stations each. Because of the range of their broadcast signal, these local stations can reach virtually every television home in the United States. Fox presently is affiliated with around 135 stations.

A network-television advertiser, often through its advertising agency, negotiates with a particular network to buy commercials on one or more of the network's programs. When a program is then broadcast to the network's affiliated stations, large numbers of viewers have an opportunity to see the commercial. Thus, network-television advertisers have the potential advantage of reaching many viewers by purchasing commercials from a *single* source (the network). As we will see later, this is quite different from buying spot market-by-market television.

National Cable

In many ways, national cable (or network cable) is quite similar to over-the-air network television. The major difference is that a cable-network program, rather than being sent to a *station* in a local market, is sent to a *cable system* in that community (currently, there are around 9,600 cable systems operating in the United States). The cable system, like a local television station, typically receives signals sent by satellite, but rather than being affiliated with only one network, it receives programs from many different cable networks (for example, ESPN, CNN, MTV, A&E, and others). The cable system then transmits its offerings, including network cable programs, to its subscribers through means of a coaxial cable wired into each subscriber's home. No over-the-air broadcast signal is sent, and to receive signals from a cable system, consumers must subscribe to the cable system's service and pay a monthly fee.

Incidentally, cable systems also typically transmit to their subscribers local over-the-air television stations, including those affiliated with ABC, CBS, NBC, and Fox, on their cable channels. Thus, cable subscribers generally not only receive cable network programs (such as those on ESPN or MTV), but also those programs appearing on the over-the-air networks. In this way, the local cable system is merely replacing the subscriber's rabbit-ears or roof-type antenna with a wired-in system.

The number of cable networks has grown dramatically in the past few years, and a recent count shows at least thirty-five such networks. Those available to 50 million or more subscribers include ESPN, CNN, USA Network, MTV, The Discovery Channel, Nickelodeon, The Nashville Network, and C-SPAN. There also are cable networks for which subscribers pay a fee over and above the cost of the basic cable offerings—so-called "pay cable," such as Home Box Office (HBO), Showtime, and Cinemax—but since these networks do not currently accept commercials, they are excluded from this discussion.

A somewhat unique type of cable network—the "superstation"—is a regular television station, operating in a local market, that sends its signal by satellite to cable systems throughout the country that choose to carry it. Currently, there are four such superstations: WTBS (operating out of Atlanta), WGN (Chicago), WWOR (New York), and WPIX (New York).

Network-cable advertising is purchased in the same way as regular network television: A commercial is purchased on a particular program at a certain time, and the program is broadcast to cable systems throughout the United States. The cable system, in turn, sends, via coaxial cable, the program to subscriber homes for possible viewing. One difference, though, is that typical cable-network programs currently have noticeably smaller audiences than those on ABC, CBS, and NBC. However, this has recently been changing, and increasingly larger audiences for many cable networks are likely in the future.

Syndication

Syndication is a type of television advertising that involves three main players: the producer-owner of a television program (syndicator), national advertisers, and local television stations (there are around thirteen hundred commercial television stations in about two hundred U.S. markets). The syndicator produces a television program, sells commercials to advertisers, and then places the program on television stations in as many local markets as possible. Typically, the syndicator attempts to sell about half the commercial time available in a program to national advertisers; the station airing the program can then sell the remaining commercial time on its own. This type of syndication is often called **barter syndication.** Under the barter syndication arrangement, syndicators must usually get their program on stations in enough markets to cover at least 70 percent of U.S. television households to be attractive to national advertisers. An alternative to barter syndication is when the syndicator *sells* the program (for what is called a cash license fee) to local stations without commercials, and the stations, in turn, sell all available time to local and/or national advertisers.

Syndicated programs include those that have not previously appeared on network television (called first-run syndication programs), such as "Wheel of Fortune," "Jeopardy," "The Oprah Winfrey Show," and "Star Trek," and those that have, such as "Dallas," "M*A*S*H," and "Three's Company." Figure 16.3 is an advertisement for a company that sells national advertising for first-run syndication programming.

National Spot

National spot advertising involves a national (or regional) advertiser buying commercials on television stations in specific markets. The term *spot* is used here in a geographical sense—advertisers "spot" those markets within the United States where they want to advertise. Advertisers might consider the use of spot advertising for a number of reasons:

- To supplement a network schedule by having *extra* commercials in certain markets (for example, although a network schedule might go to all two hundred or so television markets in the United States, advertisers may want some extra weight in, say, the top twenty largest markets).

- Network coverage may be too costly, so advertisers may decide to advertise only in the most fertile markets, perhaps adding coverage each year until they approach national delivery.

- If the product does not yet have national distribution, advertisers may advertise only in those markets where the product is available.

- Advertisers may feel it necessary to create different commercials for different parts of the country.

In purchasing national spot advertising, advertisers must first decide what markets to include in a spot-television schedule. For example, an advertiser may decide to advertise in the top-twenty largest markets (New York, Los Angeles, Chicago,

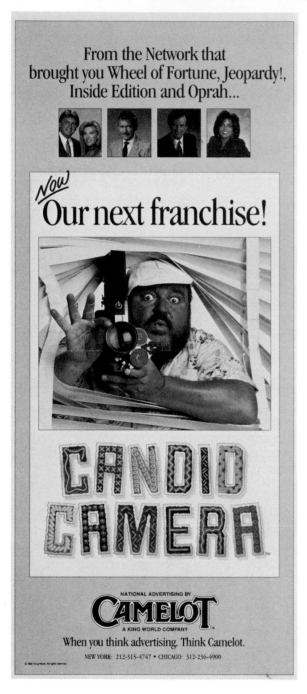

FIGURE 16.3 **An Advertisement in a Trade Magazine for a Company That Sells First-Run Syndicated Programs**
Source: Camelot Entertainment Sales, Inc., a King World company.

Houston, and so on). The advertiser must then assess what each station in each market can deliver in terms of audiences. In New York City, there is a large choice of television stations—one associated with each of the four networks and several "independent" stations (non-network). For each station used, the advertiser would have to decide in which program the commercials should be aired. These programs could be produced by the local station—for example, the "6 O'Clock News," or, if the station is affiliated with a network, the particular network show. In the latter case, the advertiser does not technically buy *within* a network-aired program because these commercial slots are reserved for network advertisers. Rather, the advertiser purchases what is called an **adjacency.** An adjacency is the time available just before or just after a network program is aired, or during a **station break,** when the network releases time to its local **affiliates.** For example, you might buy an adjacency to "Murphy Brown" on WBBM-TV in Chicago, the CBS station in that city. The commercial would be placed at either end of this thirty-minute program. When a network broadcasts a program that is longer than thirty minutes, it also releases time *during* the program to its local stations (station break), and an adjacency could also appear in this time period.

Compared with network television, national spot is considerably more complicated because, rather than buying commercials from a single source (or perhaps as many as four different networks), advertisers must deal with each station in each market. A spot-television schedule of, say, fifty different markets, could involve negotiating rates with perhaps as many as 125 to 150 different stations.

Local Spot

Local spot is akin to national spot, except that the advertiser is a *local* firm, such as a bank, department store, or supermarket. Local advertisers evaluate each television station in the local market and then make the buy. Since most television markets have only three to five stations, the decision for a local advertiser is much less complex than for a national spot advertiser.

Non-network Cable

In non-network cable television advertising, the advertiser is a local firm, and the commercial is bought through a local cable system, rather than on an over-the-air station. Cable systems typically can offer a local advertiser a wide choice of channels and programs on which to advertise, including adjacencies on cable network programs.

Characteristics of Television

In deciding whether to include television in a particular media schedule, media planners have to consider the medium's basic characteristics, including its impact, market coverage, flexibility, exposure potential, prestige, and cost efficiency.

Impact

Television has been called the medium that is most similar to personal selling. It achieves a high level of consumer impact through the combined use of moving pictures and the spoken voice. In fact, a common approach in television commercials is to have one or more people be the spokespersons for the brand, much as if they were making a personal sales call in the viewer's home. For cxample, many advertisers use a known personality—say, Candice Bergen or Michael Jackson—to "pitch" their brand. Even cartoon characters are used for this purpose—for example, Charlie Brown of "Peanuts" fame.

Market Coverage

Television has long been considered a mass-coverage medium, although this characteristic is changing somewhat with the growth of cable offerings. In terms of general availability, television is accessible to almost every person (total penetration is 98 percent; 98 percent of all homes have at least one set). On the average, each television home has a set on for around seven hours each day. During the evening hours, around 60 percent of all television homes have the set turned on to some offering. A commercial on a popular evening television program might reach as many as 18 to 20 percent of all television homes in the United States and twenty-eight to thirty million people. Some television specials (for example, mini-series, the Olympics, Super Bowl games) are seen by forty to fifty million people or more.

Broad, mass coverage of audiences has changed somewhat in recent years, primarily due to the growth of cable television. With cable, a household has many choices of program viewing—network stations, independent stations, cable networks, local cable channels, and the like. The effect of this has been to reduce audience sizes for particular programs, making television somewhat more segmented in audience delivery than it was in the past. Advertisers carefully consider this situation when they schedule their television commercials. Just a few years ago, if an advertiser wanted to reach the largest possible audience available at a particular time of day, say 8:00 to 9:00 P.M. on a Wednesday, scheduling three commercials—one each on the ABC, CBS, and NBC programs at that time—would do the trick. Today, the same advertiser with this goal would have to buy commercials on considerably more than three programs.

Flexibility

Television offers flexibility in a number of ways. For a national or regional advertiser, a choice can be made to cover the whole United States with one buy (network) or only certain areas (spot). The medium also is flexible in terms of how commercials are created and allows the use of such creative techniques as slice-of-life dramas, stand-up sales approaches, mood commercials, and the almost infinite variety of commercials that can be created with computer graphics. In addition, television provides a number of different parts of the day (**dayparts**) in which to schedule commercials, as well as a host of different program styles (for example, situation comedies, daytime soap operas, news programs, and action dramas) to choose from.

Television also, however, can be somewhat inflexible. For example, most network program commercials are sold several months in advance of a new fall television season (called **up-front buying**). If an advertiser does not make a buy at this time, relatively few alternatives may be available later. In times of high demand for television time, it also may be difficult to buy time on local stations; each station has a limited number of commercials it can sell in a day.

Exposure Potential

Television allows for the repetition of commercials, and this reiteration of the sales message helps people to become aware of a brand and knowledgeable about its attributes. On the downside, television messages are considered fleeting, since they come and go quickly, and viewers may ignore them if they are doing other things when the commercials are aired. If someone has recorded a program on a videocassette recorder (VCR)—and two-thirds of all television homes have a VCR—commercials may be ignored entirely when the program is played by using the VCR's fast-forward feature (called "zipping").

Another aspect of television's exposure potential is the number of commercials a viewer might be exposed to in a given time. Not many years ago, most commercials were one minute in length, and the number of commercials a viewer could be exposed to on a program was limited. Today, fewer than 2 percent of all commercials are sixty seconds in length; around 60 percent are thirty seconds long, and almost **35** percent are only fifteen seconds (about 3 percent are yet other lengths). Advertisers refer to this situation as commercial **clutter.** (See chapter 8.)

Prestige

In many instances, television can be considered a prestige medium because of the quality of television programming (see also chapter 8). While the "quality" of programming is an issue unto itself (some critics like programs, others do not!), many programs, especially those developed by national producers, generally use top-notch talent and spend large sums on production. Advertisers are often mindful of the effect the medium has not only on consumers, but on retailers who sell advertised brands.

Wells and his co-authors discuss the "influence" of television and state that, "It is so much a part of us that we are more likely to believe companies that advertise on television, especially sponsors of drama and educational programs like IBM, Xerox, and Hallmark Cards, than we are to believe those that don't."[1]

Cost Efficiency

Although television can be relatively cost efficient (that is, deliver an audience at a relatively low cost per viewer), the absolute cost to produce and air commercials can require large dollar sums. This may preclude low- and medium-budget advertisers from using the medium. For example, thirty seconds of network evening primetime costs an average of $150,000. Buying three thirty-second commercials a week for a six-month period would require a budget of around $12 million (and this would be in addition to the cost of producing the commercial, which might add an additional $400,000 to $500,000). Top-rated primetime shows can cost as much as $300,000 for a thirty-second commercial, and special programs, such as a Super Bowl broadcast, are even more expensive.

Table 16.1 shows how much the top-ten national advertisers spent in each of four types of television advertising. Procter & Gamble alone spent over $1 billion to advertise its brands on television.

Television Rate Structure

From the discussion in chapter 14, we know the following points about television rates:

- Virtually all television rates are negotiated between the buyer and the supplier. Generally, no published "list" shows what specific commercials cost, although some spot-television stations do provide a rate schedule in *Standard Rate and Data Service (SRDS)* that serves as a starting point for negotiation.

- Network purchases typically are for particular programs or by scatter plan.

- Spot-television rates can be fixed (guaranteed placement or position) or preemptible.

TABLE 16.1

Top-Ten National Television Advertisers

Rank	Advertiser	1990 Network-Television Advertising Expenditures (in millions of dollars)	Rank	Advertiser	1990 Spot-Television Advertising Expenditures (in millions of dollars)
1	General Motors	$598.4	1	Procter & Gamble	$303.2
2	Procter & Gamble	556.1	2	PepsiCo	284.6
3	Philip Morris	402.2	3	Philip Morris	221.2
4	Kellogg	301.3	4	General Mills	191.5
5	Sears, Roebuck	253.8	5	McDonald's	146.0
6	AT&T	244.9	6	General Motors	136.5
7	McDonald's	231.0	7	Toyota	117.6
8	Johnson & Johnson	211.4	8	Nissan	108.2
9	Ford Motor	196.9	9	Anheuser-Busch	91.6
10	PepsiCo	193.4	10	Walt Disney	86.2

Rank	Advertiser	1990 Cable-Television Advertising Expenditures (in millions of dollars)	Rank	Advertiser	1990 Syndicated-Television Advertising Expenditures (in millions of dollars)
1	Procter & Gamble	$57.7	1	Philip Morris	$113.8
2	Time Warner	50.7	2	Procter & Gamble	108.7
3	General Mills	27.4	3	Warner-Lambert	48.4
4	Anheuser-Busch	26.8	4	Grand Metropolitan	45.8
5	Philip Morris	26.6	5	Kellogg	45.3
6	General Motors	26.0	6	Unilever	42.2
7	RJR Nabisco	21.7	7	Nestle Foods	36.7
8	Sear, Roebuck	19.8	8	Coca-Cola	34.1
9	AT&T	15.3	9	Johnson & Johnson	33.4
10	PepsiCo	13.1	10	Bristol-Myers	32.6

Source: From *Advertising Age,* May 13, 1991, p. S–32. Copyright © 1991 Crain Communications Inc., Detroit, MI. Reprinted by permission.

- Rotation packages, run-of-station (ROS) commercials, and grid rates permit stations to offer advertisers pricing flexibility.

In addition, because television is a time-oriented medium, the time of day for which commercials are bought is another component of television rate structure. As mentioned earlier, the television day is divided into several time periods, called dayparts. The major broadcast dayparts (eastern standard time) typically are:

- *Early Morning*: 6:00 A.M. to 9:00 A.M.
- *Daytime*: 9:00 A.M. to 4:00 P.M.
- *Early Fringe*: 4:00 P.M. to 7:00 P.M.
- *Prime Access*: 7:00 P.M. to 8:00 P.M. (6:00 P.M. to 7:00 P.M. on Sundays)
- *Primetime*: 8:00 P.M. to 11:00 P.M.
- *Late Fringe*: 11:00 P.M. to 1:00 A.M.

Since people are exposed to television differently according to daypart, prices reflect the differing sizes of audiences delivered. The largest number of people usually watch during primetime, and accordingly, this daypart generally has the highest average prices per commercial. Of course, each program commercial is generally priced according to the specific number of people (or homes) it will likely deliver.

National advertisers using spot television may want to get an idea as to what a particular schedule might cost before negotiating with each station in each market. Most major advertising agencies provide their buyers with a rough guide to these costs, which are based on the **cost-per-rating-point** (**CPRP**). A rating point is 1 percent of the total television audience. The Leo Burnett agency shows the thirty-second spot-television costs shown in table 16.2. Thus, if an advertiser wanted to buy 75 rating points each week, during primetime in the top-fifty U.S. markets—for a ten-week schedule—the estimated total cost of such a schedule would be $7,562,250 ($10,083 per rating point × 75 rating points × 10 weeks = $7,562,250).

TABLE 16.2

Cost Per Household Rating Point for Various Dayparts

Markets	Prime-time	Daytime	Early Evening	Late Evening
Top 10	$ 4,638	$1,332	$1,536	$2,012
Top 20	6,892	1,941	2,275	3,038
Top 30	8,424	2,432	2,885	3,832
Top 40	9,304	2,726	3,239	4,346
Top 50	10,083	2,991	3,589	4,797
Top 100	12,378	3,764	4,579	6,104

Source: *Leo Burnett 1991 Media Costs and Coverage,* 11.

In buying a television schedule, the buyer also considers the length of the commercial to be bought—that is, the "unit" to be purchased. As already mentioned, most network commercials today are either fifteen or thirty seconds long. Other units, however, can be bought on network, spot, cable, or syndication—usually sixty seconds, twenty seconds, and ten seconds. On some cable channels, commercials as long as two to four minutes can be purchased. Whereas, on network television, it is common for a fifteen-second commercial to be priced at one-half of a thirty-second one, local stations generally charge an average of 70 percent of the thirty-second cost for fifteen seconds.[2] This premium charge for the shorter unit is to compensate stations for the added paperwork and technical details of handling more commercials.

As was true for the print media, television rates typically allow discounts for the amount of advertising purchased and/or the frequency and consistency of purchasing. Thus, the more commercials advertisers buy in a given period of time (say, one month), the lower the cost per unit (a "bulk" or "frequency" discount). Also, if advertisers spend more than certain dollar levels during a set period, they may be offered a "volume" discount.

Comparing Alternative Vehicles

Two methods are available for measuring the relative cost efficiency of alternative television vehicles (for example, several different programs). The first is the familiar **cost-per-thousand (CPM)** method, which is computed as follows:

$$CPM = \frac{\text{Cost of Commercial} \times 1,000}{\text{Program's Audience (or Target Audience)}}$$

Thus, if a thirty-second network commercial cost $150,000 and delivered an audience of nine million women, ages 18–49 (the target), the CPM would be:

$$CPM_{\text{Program } A} = \frac{\$150,000 \times 1,000}{9,000,000} = \$16.67$$

Similar computations for alternative programs would indicate which program is the most cost efficient. Of course, other factors, such as the total size of the audience delivered and the program context within which the commercial will be aired (for example, a situation-comedy may work better for a particular advertiser than, say, an action-drama program), are also usually taken into consideration.

The second method of comparing cost efficiency is quite similar to the CPM computation but involves using a program or station rating, rather than the actual audience size. A **rating** is merely the percent of a total audience tuned to the program or station. Thus, in the previous example, if nine million women, ages 18–49, are tuned to program A and there are sixty million women, ages 18–49, in television homes, the rating is 15 percent (9,000,000 ÷ 60,000,000 × 100, to put the answer in percent). Ratings are usually reported without showing the percent sign; thus, the rating here is simply 15. This method is called the **cost-per-rating-point (CPRP)**, sometimes also called the cost-per-point (CPP) or cost-per-rating (CPR) (see also chapter 7). The formula for computing a CPRP is:

$$CPRP = \frac{\text{Cost of Commercial}}{\text{Program's Rating (or Target-Audience Rating)}}$$

Thus, a program commercial that costs $150,000 and has a rating of 15 for women, ages 18–49, yields the following CPRP:

$$CPRP_{\text{Program } A} = \frac{\$150,000}{15} = \$10,000$$

The program with the lowest cost-per-rating-point is the most cost efficient.

To get the numbers needed for CPM and CPRP calculations for network buys, media buyers consult a **Nielsen Television Index (NTI)** report to get program audiences and ratings for a particular broadcast (say, "60 Minutes" on June 26th), or Simmons Market Research Bureau (SMRB) or Mediamark Research, Inc. (MRI) for average annual program ratings. The cost of commercials is based on the buy negotiated with the networks (or an estimate of what such costs are likely to be).

Spot-television audiences and ratings can be obtained from either a **Nielsen Station Index (NSI)** report or an Arbitron television report. Costs might be available from *SRDS* but would more likely come from discussions with particular stations. In getting cost figures for CPM and CPRP computations, media buyers must be careful to use a figure that is as close as possible to what they would *actually* pay for a specific commercial time at a particular station. For example, one station may offer better discounts.

Also, television typically is measured both in terms of *households* reached and *people* reached (and usually people with certain demographic characteristics, such as women, ages 18–49). Thus, comparisons of different stations and/or programs must be consistent in what is used for the calculations.

Measuring Television Audiences

Audience measurement began in the earliest days of commercial television, largely patterned on the type of research being done for commercial radio. Currently, two major research companies—A. C. Nielsen and the Arbitron Company—measure television audiences. Audience information is supplied for program viewing (via network and cable) by national audiences, as well as by audiences in each of the more than two hundred local markets. The A. C. Nielsen Company, through its Nielsen Media Research, measures viewing of both national programs and station viewing in local markets. Arbitron limits its service to the measurement of local market viewing.

National Program Audiences

National viewing of network and cable programs is reported by A. C. Nielsen in a series of reports, each under the Nielsen Television Index (NTI) trademark. NTI reports include extensive information about television household and personal viewing: program audience sizes and ratings, by television homes and by people in television homes, including the broad demographic characteristics of people viewing.

Figure 16.4 shows one page from an NTI *Pocketpiece* report (which reports national viewing for a one-week period). This information also can be accessed by computer. According to the figure, for Sunday evening, 24 September 1989, the CBS program "Murder, She Wrote" (broadcast between 8:00 and 9:00 P.M. eastern standard time) had an average audience of 19,060,000 households and an average audience rating of 20.7. The 20.7 rating means that 20.7 percent of all television households were tuned to this program during an average broadcast minute (20.0 percent were tuned during the first quarter hour, 20.5 percent during the second quarter hour, 21.4 percent during the third quarter hour, and 21.0 percent during the fourth quarter hour). *Pocketpiece* also shows a program "share" of 33, which means that 33 percent of all television households with their *sets on during this time period* were tuned to "Murder, She Wrote." Other parts

of the NTI *Pocketpiece* report shown provide information about some of the demographic characteristics of the *people* who tuned in to "Murder, She Wrote." Part of the NTI service includes a report on the home-video market—cable viewing and the use of videocassette recorders.

Nielsen's NTI reports are produced from data collected from a sample of around four thousand television households in the United States. The households are selected according to a sampling procedure that ensures that they are representative of all television homes in the country (of which there currently are about ninety-three million). Individuals in these sample households indicate to what program they are tuned at a particular time by pressing a button on an electronic recording device called the Nielsen **people meter.** The people meter is installed on each television set in NTI sample households. Each household member is assigned a button by which he or she records viewing (there also are buttons for visitors). Users are instructed to press the button "on" or "off" each time they are viewing a program (for example, they press "off" when they leave the room to get a snack). The people meter provides minute-by-minute records of television viewing by household members and visitors. The device can be used at the television set or via a remote unit. Figure 16.5 shows the Nielsen people meter and people using it.

Presently, Nielsen Media Research is testing the use of "passive" people meters, which would eliminate the requirement that a person press a button to record viewing. Instead, the device uses a form of artificial intelligence hardware/software, whereby a person's presence in a room can be detected and recorded. If perfected, the passive people meter could record viewing on a second-by-second basis, and especially at the time a particular commercial is aired.

A-16
Nielsen **NATIONAL TV AUDIENCE ESTIMATES** **EVE. SUN. SEP. 24, 1989**

TIME	7:00	7:15	7:30	7:45	8:00	8:15	8:30	8:45	9:00	9:15	9:30	9:45	10:00	10:15	10:30	10:45	11:00	11:15
HUT	53.3	55.2	56.8	58.2	60.1	61.9	63.3	64.6	66.7	67.7	67.4	66.6	63.8	62.5	60.5	57.7	51.1	44.3

ABC TV — ←LIFE GOES ON→ → FREE SPIRIT · HOMEROOM ← — ABC SUNDAY NIGHT MOVIE THE PREPPIE MURDER (PAE) — →

	7:00	7:15	7:30	7:45	8:00	8:15	8:30	8:45	9:00	9:15	9:30	9:45	10:00	10:15	10:30	10:45	11:00	11:15
AVERAGE AUDIENCE	9,210				9,580		8,010		14,000									
(Hhlds (000) & %)	10.0	9.3*		10.8*	10.4		8.7		15.2	13.7*		15.8*		15.7*		15.5*		
SHARE AUDIENCE %	18	17*		19*	17		14		24	20*		24*		25*		26*		
AVG. AUD. BY 1/4 HR %	8.7	9.8	10.6	11.1	10.2	10.6	8.5	8.9	13.6	13.8	15.7	15.8	15.9	15.6	15.6	15.5		

CBS TV — ← 60 MINUTES → ←MURDER, SHE WROTE→ ← [ISLAND SON SPEC (PAE)] → ← [WOLF SPEC] →

	7:00	7:15	7:30	7:45	8:00	8:15	8:30	8:45	9:00	9:15	9:30	9:45	10:00	10:15	10:30	10:45	11:00	11:15
AVERAGE AUDIENCE	17,040				19,060				14,640				11,700					
(Hhlds (000) & %)	18.5	16.9*		20.0*	20.7	20.2*		21.2*	15.9	15.5*		16.2*	12.7	13.1*		12.3*		
SHARE AUDIENCE %	33	31*		35*	33	33*		33*	24	23*		24*	21	21*		21*		
AVG. AUD. BY 1/4 HR %	15.7	18.0	20.1	20.0	20.0	20.5	21.4	21.0	15.4	15.7	16.5	16.0	13.2	12.9	12.5	12.1		

NBC TV — (1) [ALF TAKES NETWORK (7:25-8:00) (PAE)] · SISTER KATE · MY TWO DADS ← — [SNL 15TH ANN. SPC] — →

	7:00	7:15	7:30	7:45	8:00	8:15	8:30	8:45	9:00	9:15	9:30	9:45	10:00	10:15	10:30	10:45	11:00	11:15
AVERAGE AUDIENCE		5,990			8,200		10,870		18,700									
(Hhlds (000) & %)		6.5		6.4*	8.9		11.8		20.8	19.3*		21.1*		22.1*		21.1*		17.7*
SHARE AUDIENCE %		11		11*	15		18		33	29*		31*		35*		36*		37*
AVG. AUD. BY 1/4 HR %	13.6	6.9	6.1	6.7	8.6	9.3	10.9	12.8	18.5	20.0	20.6	21.6	22.4	21.8	21.4	20.9	19.8	15.6

	7:00	7:30	8:00	8:30	9:00	9:30	10:00	10:30	11:00
INDEPENDENTS (INCL. SUPERSTATIONS)									
AVERAGE AUDIENCE	11.5	12.6	14.2	14.8	15.7	11.4	9.6	7.7	6.0
SHARE AUDIENCE %	21	22	23	23	23	17	15	13	13
SUPERSTATIONS									
AVERAGE AUDIENCE	2.3	2.3	1.9	2.2	2.5	2.8	2.4	1.9	1.7
SHARE AUDIENCE %	4	4	3	3	4	4	4	3	3
PBS									
AVERAGE AUDIENCE	1.5	1.6	2.4	3.0	1.7	1.8	1.2	1.2	1.0
SHARE AUDIENCE %	3	3	4	5	3	3	2	2	2
CABLE ORIG.									
AVERAGE AUDIENCE	6.8	8.6	7.2	6.5	5.6	5.4	4.9	4.4	3.8
SHARE AUDIENCE %	12	15	12	10	8	8	8	8	8
PAY SERVICES									
AVERAGE AUDIENCE	2.7	2.5	3.7	4.1	4.1	3.5	3.5	3.1	2.5
SHARE AUDIENCE %	5	4	6	6	6	5	5	5	5

U.S. TV HOUSEHOLDS: 92,100,000   For explanation of symbols, see page B.
(1) NFL GAME 2, VARIOUS TEAMS AND TIMES, (PAE), NBC, (MULTI SEGMENT)

FIGURE 16.4 A Page from the Nielsen Television Index *Pocketpiece* Report, Showing National Television Audiences, Ratings, and Shares for the Evening of 24 September 1989
Courtesy of Nielsen Media Research.

FIGURE 16.5 The Nielsen People Meter Measures Which Specific Individuals Are in a Room Where a Television is On
Courtesy of Nielsen Media Research.

Local Audiences

Nielsen measures local television audiences in around 220 markets and reports findings in the **Nielsen Station Index (NSI)** reports. One section of an NSI report is shown in figure 16.6. The information provided for a particular market is extensive.

The audience information in an NSI report comes from a randomly selected sample of both listed and unlisted telephone households in each local market. Most selected households fill out television viewing **diaries,** showing their viewing activity during one week of a four-week measurement period. In the nation's largest markets, meters are used to record viewing patterns. Measurement of local television viewing is done at least four times a year in all markets—November, February, May, and July (four weeks are measured in each month), with very large markets also measured at other times of the year.

Arbitron provides a similar local-market-audience service through the use of diaries in most markets, with meters in the largest fourteen. Figure 16.7 shows a sample Arbitron diary, with explanations as to how viewers are to record their viewing.

In defining the two hundred or so markets in which measurements are made, Nielsen and Arbitron each assign a county to only one television market. A **television market** is an unduplicated geographical area to which a county is assigned on the basis of the highest share of the viewing of television stations."[3] Nielsen refers to such television markets as **designated market areas (DMAs)**, whereas Arbitron calls television markets **areas of dominant influence (ADIs)**.

Although Nielsen Media Research is perhaps the major supplier of national television audience data, providing program information on a *daily* basis, national audience figures can also be obtained from SMRB and MRI. These two services, though, rather than showing program audiences on a particular day, report the general program audience sizes for a given year. Also, SMRB and MRI give not only the total audience size of a nationally broadcast program, but show audience sizes according to viewers' demographic and psychographic characteristics, and according to whether viewers are product users (and, in many cases, *brand* users).

MEDIA SPOTLIGHT

16.1

A Description of Nielsen Media Research's Nielsen Homevideo Index (NHI)

Nielsen Homevideo Index (NHI) is the Nielsen service that conducts research into all aspects of the home-video market. This includes reports on the major satellite networks, local cable systems, and videocassette usage.

Cable Reports

For example, the quarterly *Nielsen Cable Activity Report (NCAR)* provides national meter ratings for pay-cable networks, superstations and supported cable networks, other cable originators, and over-the-air television within the cable universe and total United States. On the local cable scene, NHI conducts customized telephone coin-

Courtesy of Nielsen Media Research.

cidentals for cable systems, resulting in ratings data for use in advertising sales. Another syndicated product, the *Pay Cable Report,* measures viewing in pay-cable households and is released four times a year, with each Nielsen Station Index (NSI) sweep period.

Videocassette Data

NHI is the only source for the *Video Cassette Recorder Usage Study,* a report that profiles the behavioral and attitudinal aspects of the VCR households based on an in-depth, three-month diary survey. The *VCR Usage Study* addresses the subjects of commercial deletion, recording, playback, videocassette rental, purchase, and more.

Local Market Services

In addition to all these syndicated reports, NHI has been providing custom-designed studies to clients across the country to supplement current NSI data. These studies, such as demographic profiles of the cable community within a designated market area (DMA), have helped in establishing a clearer picture of broadcast station presence on cable systems in all markets. C.O.D.E., NHI's *Cable Online Data Exchange,* holds detailed subscriber counts and carriage information on every cable system in the United States, over ten thousand to date.

NHI is the source for expert research and the most current information in the areas of cable, pay-cable, and VCRs. For more information on how you can use NHI services, contact your Nielsen representative.

Daypart Section

EASTVILLE

The table shows a Nielsen Station Index (NSI) report with columns for METRO HH, DAYPART TIME (ETZ) STATION, DMA HH (SHARE TREND), DMA RATINGS (PERSONS, WOMEN, MEN, CHILD), DMA CUME RATINGS, PERCENT DISTRIBUTION, and TV HH RATINGS IN ADJACENT DMA'S.

MON.-FRI. 4.00P-6.00P

METRO HH	DAYPART TIME STATION	RTG	SHR	SHARE TREND MAY '85	FEB '85	NOV '84	JUL '84	PERSONS 18+	WOMEN 18-34	18-49	18-49	25-54	18+	WKG	12-24	FEM 12-24	PER 18+	MEN 18-34	18-49	25-54	TRS 12-17	CHILD 6-11	PER 2+	WOMEN 18+	18-49	WKG	MEN 18+	18-49	CHD 2-11	PERCENT DIST MET	HOME DMA	#1	#2	#3	#1	#2	#3
2 6	WAAA 61 I	2	6	5	6	5	6	1	1	1	1	1	1				1		1		1	3	4	5	4	5	3	3	4 16	60	100						
9 27	WBBB 5 A	9	28	30	29	26	33	2	2	3	7	3	3	4	3	2	1	4	1	1	2	2	1	16	23	16	14	15	8	3	53	94	4	1		2		
8 24	WCCC 8 C	7	21	19	19	19	15	4	3	3	5	4	4	4	3	5	4	3	3	3	3	5	2	3	19	22	22	18	15	15	15	64	96	2		1	1	
4 13	WDDD 3 N	4	13	13	14	17	17	2	2	2	3	2	2	2	2	2	2	2	2	3	1	1	13	14	11	10	11	8	9	57	98	1			1	
3 10	WEEE 19 I	2	8	3	NR	NR	NR	2	1	1	2	2	2	2	1	1	1	1	1	3	2	1	8	7	10	6	5	7	12	74	98	2				
3 9	WFFF 43 I	3	8	11	13	16	13	1	1	1	1	1	1	1	1	1	1	2		1	1	3	7	7	12	7	9	8	5 38	46	74	8	10		2	1	
1 4	WGGG 25 P	1	3	3	4	3	2														2	2	2	1	1	1	12	79	99	1				
	HBO	1	2	3	4	2	2	1	1		1						1	1		1			2	1	2	1	2										
<< 33	HUT/PUT/TOT.*	32		31	43	35	29	13	13	14	20	16	16	17	17	12	19	17	13	11	10	11	11	23	21	21	56	58	56	49	45	40	70						

6.00P-7.30P

METRO HH	DAYPART TIME STATION	RTG	SHR	MAY '85	FEB '85	NOV '84	JUL '84	PERSONS 18+	18-34	18-49	18+	25-54	18+	WKG	12-24	FEM	PER	18-34	18-49	25-54	12-17	6-11	2+	18+	18-49	WKG	18+	18-49	2-11	MET	HOME	#1	#2	#3	#1	#2	#3
2 4	WAAA 61 I	2	4	4	3	3	2	2	1	2	2	1		1		1		2	1	1		1	1		4	4	5	4	5	7	2	58	99	1			1		1
17 37	WBBB 5 A	16	36	36	34	32	36	5	6	7	12	6	7	7	8	4	3	10	4	5	6	7	3	2	31	40	30	31	33	24	13	58	97	1	1		1		1
13 27	WCCC 8 C	12	26	27	26	26	22	5	6	7	9	5	6	7	7	7	4	7	5	5	6	6	3	1	23	28	24	25	25	22	8	58	96	2			1	2	1
6 13	WDDD 3 N	5	11	11	14	13	15	1	2	2	3	1	2	2	2	1		3	1	2	2	2	1		12	14	10	12	14	10	4	62	97	2			1	
2 5	WEEE 19 I	1	2	4	1	NR	NR	1	1	2	3	1	1	2	1	1	1	2	1	1	1	1	1	1	7	6	8	7	5	7	11	59	99	1				
5 10	WFFF 43 I	4	9	11	15	17	15	2	2	2	2	2	2	3	3	2	4	3	1	2	2	2	5	5	6	13	11	13	10	9	10 24	46	71	7	13		2	2
1 1	WGGG 25 P	<<		1	1																											72	98	2				
	HBO	1	2	3	3	2	2	1	1	1	1	1		1	1	1	1	1	1	1	1	1			4	4	3	4	4	4								
<< 47	HUT/PUT/TOT.*	45		48	64	56	44	19	22	24	32	20	23	26	26	18	17	28	18	20	21	23	18	12	66	71	64	66	67	61	52							

#1 = NORTHVILLE   237,060
#2 = WESTVILLE   599,400
#3 = SOUTHVILLE   180,430

1 WBBB's average quarter-hour DMA audience for Mon.-Fri. 4:00-6:00PM was a 9 rating and a 28 share. This means 9% of the DMA TV households were viewing WBBB, which represents 28 percent of all TV households viewing.

2 32% of all DMA TV households were viewing in an average quarter-hour in this daypart.

3 WCCC's share of audience grew from 15% a year ago to 19% in the previous Nov., Feb. and May reports to its current 21%.

4 7% of the women 18+ in the DMA watched WBBB in the average quarter-hour Mon.-Fri. 4:00-6:00PM.

5 The PUT (Persons Using Television) level includes all reported demographic viewing. Note here, 20% of all women 18+ in the DMA were in the average quarter-hour of this daypart.

6 38% of the children 2-11 watched WFFF at least one time during the Mon.-Fri. 4:00-6:00PM daypart.

7 53% of WBBB's Station households (explained in Point 12) were located in the Metro Area, while 94% were in the home DMA area. 4% were located in the adjacent DMA #1, Northville.

8 WBBB achieved a 2 rating in adjacent DMA #1, Northville, in this daypart.

9 31% of Metro TV households viewed WBBB at least one time during this daypart.

10 29% of the DMA TV households viewed WBBB at least one time during this daypart.

11 438,000 unduplicated (weekly cumes) TV households viewed WBBB at least once per week during the daypart.

12 Station WBBB delivered a total of 133,000 households in an average quarter-hour Mon.-Fri. 4:00-6:00PM. This represents all viewing to the station, not limited to any pre-designated geography.

FIGURE 16.6 Example of a Nielsen Station Index (NSI) Report Showing the Viewing of Television Stations in "Eastville"
Courtesy of Nielsen Media Research.

NSI AVERAGE WEEK ESTIMATES — EASTVILLE — DAYPART SUMMARY

WEEKLY CUME CUR MET HH %	CUR DMA HH %	JUL '85 STAT TOTAL HH	DAYPART TIME STATION	HH	PERSONS 2+	18+	WOMEN 18+	18-34	18-49	25-49	25-54	50+	WKG	FEM 12-24	PER 12-24	MEN 18+	18-34	18-49	25-49	25-54	TEENS 12-17	GIRLS	CHILD 2-11	6-11
51	52	53		54	55	56	57	58	59	60	61	63	64	65	66	67	68	69	70	71	73	74	75	76
			MON.-FRI. 4.00P-6.00P																					
8	8	115	WAAA	26	37	16	10	6	8	7	7	2	3	2	5	6	3	4	4	4	4	1	17	11
31	29	438	WBBB	133	165	159	105	15	31	25	31	74	17	9	12	54	7	13	11	15	4	3	1	1
31	26	398	WCCC	98	146	115	70	21	38	30	32	32	15	19	31	45	19	27	21	23	18	12	13	9
21	19	296	WDDD	61	90	73	45	12	18	13	16	27	10	13	20	28	7	14	11	13	11	8	6	3
16	11	161	WEEE	36	52	31	20	10	17	14	15	3	7	10	18	11	7	8	7	8	12	7	9	7
17	17	330	WFFF	51	90	27	17	10	13	11	12	4	6	8	18	10	6	8	6	7	14	6	48	31
5	4	59	WGGG	14	18	5	3	2	3	3	3		1		2	2	1	1			1		13	1
	3		HBO																					
74	73		HUT/PUT/TOT.*	419	597	426	271	76	129	103	116	142	59	63	107	156	50	76	60	69	65	37	106	63
			6.00P-7.30P																					
7	7	95	WAAA	27	40	33	18	9	13	13	14	5	5	2	10	14	10	13	8	8	4	1	3	1
50	47	692	WBBB	237	339	320	189	31	62	52	64	127	47	16	27	131	20	46	39	50	10	6	9	5
37	35	517	WCCC	176	253	234	133	26	61	53	60	72	41	15	29	101	27	48	40	48	12	7	8	5
23	20	291	WDDD	76	103	97	52	4	17	16	19	35	11	3	9	45	6	10	13	17	4	2	2	2
12	9	135	WEEE	28	45	32	20	14	17	10	11	4	10	11	16	12	8	10	7	7	5	4	8	5
19	17	349	WFFF	79	130	72	46	20	34	27	31	12	19	22	34	26	10	19	16	18	24	15	34	27
		32	WGGG	6	8	8	3				3		1		1	5		1		1				
	5		HBO																					
85	84		HUT/PUT/TOT.*	629	919	796	461	104	204	170	199	258	132	69	124	335	82	153	122	149	59	36	64	45

Reference markers: **9** **10** **11** **12**

The Daypart Section enables users to:

- Analyze the viewing audience of each station by time of day.
- Generally evaluate the performance of rotation schedules sold on a broad daypart basis.
- Evaluate the overall "reach" (cumulative audience) of each station for the various time periods.
- Analyze a station's ability to cover the market area and adjacent markets (Spill-Out data).
- Generate specific target audience shares by station and time period.
- Tabulate TV usage in the market by target audience.
- Compare station's present share of audience performance to its past performance (Share Trend Guide).

FIGURE 16.6 Continued

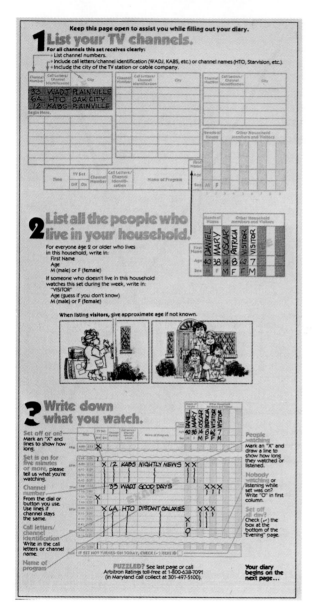

FIGURE 16.7 Page from an Arbitron Television Diary Explaining How Viewers Are to Record Their Television Usage
Source: THE ARBITRON COMPANY. Used with permission.

Audience Delivery

The following are some selected items of television audience delivery from Nielsen Media Research:[4]

- The television audience increases throughout the day, reaching a peak between 8:00 and 10:00 P.M., when around 60 percent of all households have their set on.

- Late-afternoon and early-evening audiences are lower in summer than in winter. Early-morning and late-night audience levels do not show much change from season to season.

- The average U.S. television household can receive almost thirty-one channels, including those available via cable services. Only 7 percent of households are limited to a choice of between one and six channels; 51 percent can receive thirty or more channels.

- The average number of hours of household viewing per day (seven hours) has not changed appreciably in the past six years.

- The total number of persons in television households has increased, from 200.17 million in 1975–1976, to 224.44 million in 1985–1986, to 235.23 million in 1989–1990. The proportion of adults (18 years and older) versus nonadults (ages 2–17) is 77 percent to 23 percent.

- Households that viewed television the most had the following characteristics:
  - Three or more people in the household (59 hours, 45 minutes of television usage per week)
  - Under $30,000 household income (52 hours, 59 minutes)
  - Cable subscribers (59 hours, 38 minutes)
  - Nonadults in household (58 hours, 43 minutes)

- Generally, younger children view television more than do older children, women more than men, and older adults more than younger men and women. For example, women who are 55 years or older view an average of 41 hours, 19 minutes per week versus 29 hours, 16 minutes

TABLE 16.3

Rank Order of Television Programs, by Demographic Group

Women 18+	Men 18+	Teens 12–17	Children 2–11
1. "Roseanne"	1. "NFL Monday Night Football"	1. "A Different World"	1. "Bill Cosby Show"
2. "Bill Cosby Show"	2. "60 Minutes"	2. "Bill Cosby Show"	2. "A Different World"
3. "Golden Girls"	3. "Cheers"	3. "Wonder Years"	3. "Full House"
4. "Empty Nest"	4. "CBS NFL Football Game 1"	4. "Roseanne"	4. "Roseanne"
5. "Murder, She Wrote"	5. "Roseanne"	5. "Who's The Boss?"	5. "Wonder Years"
6. "Cheers"	6. "Bill Cosby Show"	6. "Doogie Howser, M.D."	6. "Hogan Family"
7. "A Different World"	7. "L.A. Law"	7. "Cheers"	7. "Family Matters"
8. "60 Minutes"	8. "Murder, She Wrote"	8. "Coach"	8. "Alf"
9. "Dear John"	9. "Unsolved Mysteries"	9. "Head of the Class"	9. "Who's the Boss?"
10. "L.A. Law"	10. "CBS NFL Football Game 2"	10. "Hogan Family"	10. "Perfect Strangers"

Courtesy Nielsen Media Research.

for those 18–34 years of age; for men, the comparable figures are 38 hours, 22 minutes versus 24 hours, 51 minutes.

- The most popular evening for television is Sunday night, followed by Monday, Tuesday, Thursday, Wednesday, Saturday, and Friday.

- Situation-comedies are the most-watched program type in primetime. Feature films are second, suspense/mystery drama third, and general drama fourth.

- Individual television programs vary in their appeal to demographic groups. For example, table 16.3 shows the top-ten programs for their respective categories in November 1989.

Radio

Radio accounts for almost $9 billion in advertising expenditures, with more than 75 percent of this by local advertisers. When commercial television took root at the close of World War II in 1945, some analysts thought that radio would no longer be a viable medium. However, radio has remained vibrant, largely as a result of switching its focus from na-

tional advertisers to local firms. In addition, radio has prospered through the development of new broadcast technology, such as FM and FM-stereo broadcasting.

After radio became established as an advertising medium in the early 1920s, advertising expenditures rose through the 1920s, 1930s, and 1940s to $624 million by 1952. Then expenditures started to drop off and did not rise again until 1956; by 1958, spending had passed the previous high.

Of all the media types available today, radio is the most pervasive in terms of total potential audience. Presently, 99 percent of all households in the country have at least one working radio (television is available to 98 percent). More than 541 million radios are in use, for an average of more than two radios per person and almost six radios per household. Because of the large number of radios available in automobiles, trucks, and other vehicles, as well as the wide use of battery-operated radios, the medium is attended to by people just about *everywhere* (even at work, where almost twenty-one million radios are located!).

Over 12,000 radio stations are licensed by the Federal Communications Commission (FCC) to

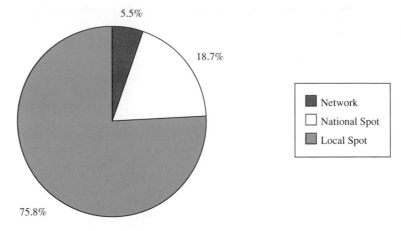

FIGURE 16.8 Allocation of Radio Advertising
Dollars by Type
Source: From *Advertising Age,* May 6, 1991, p. 16. Copyright © 1991
Crain Communications Inc., Detroit, MI. Reprinted by permission.

operate in the United States. Of these, 5,226 are commercial AM stations and 5,175 are commercial FM stations. In addition, there are 1,712 noncommercial stations, many of which announce regularly those companies that contribute to their operation.

Types of Radio Advertising

Radio advertising is considerably easier than television to classify. The major types are network, spot, and local. When compared to television in terms of usage by national versus local advertisers, radio is primarily a local medium. Figure 16.8 shows that local advertisers account for 75.8 percent of all radio dollars, with national advertisers spending 18.7 percent on spot radio and only 5.5 percent on network.

Network-radio advertising is akin to television except that there are no cable-radio networks. There presently are, however, twenty-six networks that involve interconnecting stations, through telephone lines or by satellite transmission, in local markets. These networks, with their number of affiliated stations, are shown in table 16.4. Stations in local markets often are affiliated with more than one network to provide programming diversity. As shown in table

16.4, the three major television networks each own radio networks as well. ABC, for example, operates six different radio networks. Until recently, ABC sold advertising separately on each network; it now offers advertisers various "packages" of stations: Prime, Platinum, and Galaxy, reaching adults ages 25–54; and Genesis and Excel, reaching young adults, ages 18–34.[5]

The over ten thousand commercial radio stations in local markets, whether affiliated with a network or not, primarily focus their advertising sales on local advertisers. They attempt to secure national spot advertising primarily through media representatives (see the discussion of media "reps" in chapter 2). Since it would be cumbersome for national advertisers to buy commercials on several stations in each of many markets, **nonwired networks** were formed. Nonwired networks are not comparable to radio networks because they do not provide *programming*. Rather, they are assembled by radio rep firms, who can then offer national advertisers a package of stations, which greatly simplifies the buying process.

In addition to network, spot, and local classifications of radio advertising, stations can be classified according to their programming "format," such as adult contemporary, news/talk, classical, rock,

TABLE 16.4

Networks and Number of Affiliated Stations

Network	Number of Affiliates
ABC Excel	105
ABC Galaxy	990
ABC Genesis	330
ABC Platinum	1,580
ABC Prime	1,640
ABC Special Programming	2,000
Business Radio Network (BRN)	80
CBN Radio Network	312
CBS Radio Network	440
CBS Spectrum Radio Network	600
CMN "Concert Music"	41
Dow Jones Report	40
Financial News Network (FNN)	65
NBC Talknet	300
Sheridan Broadcasting Network (SBN)	150
SBN Sports Network	185
STRZ Entertainment Network (SBN)	250
Unistar Power	205
Unistar Programming	2,000
Unistar Super	1,004
Unistar Ultimate	1,029
Wall Street Journal Radio Network	105
Westwood MBS (Mutual)	1,000
Westwood NBC	500
Westwood Source	110
Westwood One	4,450*

Source: *Mediaweek's Guide to Media*, third quarter, 1991.
*Cumulative total of network *programs*.

TABLE 16.5

How AM and FM Stations Program By Format

Format	AM	FM
Adult Contemporary	15.6%	28.5%
Country	23.6	22.7
Religion/Gospel	11.9	3.8
Contemporary Hit Radio/Top 40	2.7	15.8
Oldies	8.4	4.5
Middle of the Road	7.7	2.2
Talk	6.8	0.2
Album-Oriented Rock (AOR)	1.0	6.2
Easy Listening	1.5	5.4
News	5.4	0.2
Spanish	3.2	1.0
Big Band/Nostalgia	3.4	0.7
Urban Contemporary	1.4	2.2
Diversified	2.3	0.8
Classic Rock	0.6	2.5
Black	1.9	0.7
Agricultural	1.6	0.8
Jazz	0.5	0.9
Classical	0.4	0.8

Source: *Radio Facts for Advertisers, 1990*, Radio Advertising Bureau, 38. Reprinted by permission.

Characteristics of Radio

Among radio's basic characteristics are the following:

Audience Selectivity

Perhaps radio's most important characteristic is its ability to deliver a selective audience as a result of programming format. For example, big band/nostalgia and news formats will reach an older audience than will a classic rock format. Spanish-speaking stations will largely reach Hispanics. In addition, people can be reached at specific times of the day—say, on their way to and from work. The downside here is that, with so many stations in each market programmed to reach a selective audience, the total audience size can be quite small. For an advertiser to reach the size of audience desired may involve buying commercials on many stations.

and country. Table 16.5 shows the percent of AM and FM stations according to their programming format. Thus, adult contemporary and country music formats dominate both AM and FM stations.

Further, stations broadcast either on the AM (amplitude modulation) band or FM (frequency modulation) band. The frequency a station is assigned on the AM or FM band, along with the power of the station (such as 250 watts or 50,000 watts) and the height of its transmitter, affect the distance the station can cover in reaching listeners.

MEDIA SPOTLIGHT

16.2

"Radio . . . What Would Life Be Without It"

The Radio Advertising Bureau sponsored a campaign called "Radio . . . What Would Life Be Without It" to promote radio as a medium to listeners and advertisers. The information that follows about the campaign was sent to stations. Figure 1 shows a script from a sample radio commercial for the campaign, while figure 2 shows a campaign print ad.

Everybody Has a Story About Radio

A recent widow survives her loneliness by listening to the radio throughout the day.

A teenage girl dances her moods away to the beat of rock on the radio.

A soldier survives Vietnam by listening to Armed Forces Radio.

Everybody has a story about radio that reveals the strong emotional pull it has on all our lives.

Stories like these are the heart and soul of a new advertising campaign created to enhance the image and raise the perception of radio's value in the minds of radio listeners and advertisers.

There are stories from well-known personalities like Willard Scott, recording artists Debbie Gibson and Richie Havens, and stories from real people like a widow and a Vietnam veteran.

There are funny stories, sad stories, dramatic stories, passionate stories all in response to the statement: Radio. What would life be without it.

Perception Improves Reception

Psychological research has proven that the more people talk about radio, the more they realize the deep emotional attachments they have to the medium.

They start to see that radio is more like a trusted friend than any other medium.

It cuts through their boredom.

It relieves their loneliness.

It fills their empty moments with song or talk.

It lets them escape from day to day pressures.

It's a vital link to other people, to their communities, to the world.

They realize that life wouldn't be nearly as rich or as rewarding without the radio.

The purpose of this new campaign is to improve the image of radio by bringing these deep-seated feelings to the forefront of every listener's mind.

Not by telling them what they feel, but by helping them discover the feelings within themselves. The stories are the catalyst for this discovery. And with this discovery, they'll have a deeper, more intimate appreciation of the vital role radio plays in their lives.

And Now a Word to Our Sponsors

How will all this help your station? How will it get advertisers to commit more of their advertising dollars to radio?

First, remember, an advertising manager, a media buyer, an ad director, anyone who controls the purse strings is also a radio listener. This ad

WILLARD SCOTT

(:53 with :07 Live Copy Tag)
RFC-02-53/07
As Recorded Script

SINGER: *RADIO . . .*
RADIO . . .

WILLARD: Hi, hey this is Willard Scott. Hey I love the radio—being a radioman was one of my earliest dreams and to this day there's nothing I like more than sitting on a porch, sipping an ice tea and listening to some nice relaxing music on the radio. It's like passing time with an old friend. And if you think about it, the radio is a vital part of all of our lives. It's a companion for an eighty-year-old recuperating from surgery, it's the way a thirteen-year-old gets up for a party, and it lets a father and son spend a few pleasant hours together listening to a ballgame. It touches all of our lives, and if you're like me, you'd probably feel a giant hole in your life without it.

SINGER: *RADIO . . .*
RADIO . . .
WHAT WOULD LIFE BE . . .
WHAT WOULD LIFE BE WITHOUT IT.

LIVE COPY TAG: (:07—See attached suggested copy)

FIGURE 1 Script from a Sample Radio Commercial for the Campaign
Courtesy of Radio Futures Committee.

campaign will put radio in the forefront of their minds. They'll understand the power of radio in their lives and the lives of everyone around them.

And they'll realize that by putting more of their advertising on the radio, they'll reach people on this deeper level.

To help marketers translate this campaign to their professional demands, we'll run ads in trade magazines and in major national newspapers featuring opinion leaders in the marketing community. These ads will make the connection between the personal stories and the needs of

Continued on page 346

16.2 cont.

marketers. They'll allow the opinion leaders to tell their own success stories about marketing through radio.

They'll show that radio is as vital to the life of a business as it is to the life of a consumer.

With this two-pronged approach, agencies and businesses will see the connection between consumers' attachment to the radio and what radio can do for their business. They will become more open to our sales presentations and, in the end, shift more advertising dollars into radio.

Realize the Rewards

By participating in this breakthrough program, you will help raise the awareness of the value of radio that much quicker, and you will start to realize the benefits that much faster.

You will help radio gain top-of-mind awareness and improve its image in the minds of consumers and advertisers.

You will help build a strong sense of pride in an industry that deserves it.

And you will help everyone realize just how good a friend radio really is.

Radio. What would life be without it.

Courtesy of Radio Advertising Bureau.

FIGURE 2 Campaign Print Ad Used in Trade Publications to Promote Radio as an Advertising Medium
Source: Radio Advertising Bureau.

Immediacy

Radio has the ability to deliver information with a sense of immediacy. For example, more people tune to radio in the morning for news information than to other media types—42 percent for radio versus 31 percent for television and 18 percent for newspapers.[6] Radio also has a short lead time for commercial placement.

Flexibility

Radio offers advertisers good flexibility since a national advertiser can use network or spot radio to achieve whatever geographical coverage is required. In addition, the creative format used in commercials can be flexible and varied, from straight, spoken announcements to using music, sound effects, and/or humor to create a particular mood or to emphasize a point. Another aspect of radio's flexibility is its "mobility." There are few places radio cannot go—it follows the listener from room to room, can be heard in the car on the way to work or shopping, goes to the beach, is listened to at work, and can often be heard within a retail store.

Among radio's negatives, though, is the lack of visuals, which may affect the creative opportunity. Product demonstration is virtually impossible, and clear brand identification is often difficult.

Exposure Potential

Radio generally is considered a high-frequency medium—that is, an audience can be reached with a great deal of message repetition. If a particular station delivers a high percentage of the audience desired by an advertiser, it usually is cost efficient for the advertiser to deliver a high frequency to get across the content of the commercial. For example, if advertisers bought eighteen commercials a week on each of three stations in the top two hundred markets of the country, they would reach 47.9 percent of the total audience an average of 3.4 times a week, or 79.9 percent of the audience an average of 8.2 times in four weeks.[7]

However, radio's exposure potential can be lessened by the fact that messages are fleeting and may be missed entirely or heard only partially. Part of this circumstance is a result of the fleeting nature of the medium itself, and part of it is due to the clutter caused by the number of commercials aired.

Cost Efficiency

Individual commercials on many radio stations and networks are quite low-priced in comparison to other media types. For example, the CBS station in New York City—WCBS—has drivetime one-minute commercials available for around $600. In a much smaller market—say, Emporia, Kansas—a similar spot goes for as little as $20. Thirty-second network commercials range from about $9,000 on the ABC Prime Network to $1,000 on the ABC Galaxy network. In addition, radio commercials usually are

| TABLE 16.6 |

Top-Ten Product Categories, As a Percent of Total Spot-/and Network-Radio Expenditures

Rank	Product Category	Percent of Total Spot and Network Combined
1	Food Products	17.0%
2	Automotive	13.4
3	Consumer Services	11.3
4	Travel and Shipping	8.1
5	Beer, Ale, Wine	6.2
6	Retail Stores (National)	5.8
7	Drugs and Health Care	5.3
8	Publishing and Media	4.2
9	Gasoline and Oil	2.8
10	Apparel	2.7

Source: Radio Advertising Bureau, *Radio Facts for Advertisers, 1990,* 42. Reprinted by permission.

quite inexpensive to produce. Radio cost-per-thousands (CPMs) likewise are generally low. For example, CPMs among adults for network radio average around $4.50; spot-radio adult CPMs, in the top-fifty markets, is about $5.00.

Table 16.6 shows the ten most advertised product categories by national advertisers using spot and network radio. Food products head the list, followed by automotive brands and consumer services. Table 16.7 shows how much the top-ten national advertisers spend on network and spot radio. Sears spent more than $107 million in spot and network, and was number one in the network-radio category. Philip Morris led spot advertisers with almost $43 million in spending.

TABLE 16.7

Top-Ten National Radio Advertisers

Rank	Advertiser	1989 Network-Radio Advertising Expenditures (in millions of dollars)
1	Sears, Roebuck	$71.0
2	General Motors	35.3
3	Procter & Gamble	24.2
4	AT&T	19.8
5	U.S. Government	17.8
6	City Investing	17.4
7	Cotter & Company	16.0
8	Warner-Lambert	14.3
9	Campbell Soup	14.0
10	Kmart	13.6

Rank	Advertiser	1989 Spot-Radio Advertising Expenditures (in millions of dollars)
1	Philip Morris	$42.7
2	Anheuser-Busch	42.1
3	Chrysler	40.3
4	General Motors	39.5
5	Sears, Roebuck	36.1
6	PepsiCo	33.4
7	Southland	33.2
8	Grand Metropolitan	26.6
9	News Corporation	24.8
10	Delta Air Lines	18.3

Source: From *Advertising Age,* September 26, 1990, pp. 61, 64. Copyright © 1990 Crain Communications Inc. Detroit, MI. Reprinted by permission.

Radio Rate Structure

From the discussion of broadcast rates and discounts in chapter 14, we know that:

- Both network and local station buys typically are negotiated between the buyer and seller. Although rates sometimes are published in *SRDS* for radio stations, they usually serve only

---

WMOP
1953
OCALA
COUNTY: Marion

Country Music

NAB BROADCASTERS   **RAB**

Location ID: 4 RLST FL   Mid 009325-000

WMOP Radio, Inc.
Box: 3930, 343 N.E. First Ave., Ocala, FL 32678. Phone 904-732-2010. FAX: 904-732-6261.

FORMAT DESCRIPTION
WMOP: MUSIC: Country, current & goldies, for adults 25+. FEATURES: Farm, horse race results. NEWS: at :60 & :30 AP. Contact Representative for further details. Rec'd 3/28/89.

1. PERSONNEL
National Sales Manager—Carol Carpenter.
General Manager—Carol Carpenter.
Operations Director—Capps Sutherland.

2. REPRESENTATIVES
Southern Spot Sales, Inc.

2A. NETWORK/GROUP AFFILIATION
Affiliated with KBS.

3. FACILITIES
5,000 w.; 900 khz. Stereo. Non-directional.
Operating schedule: 5:45 am-10 pm. EST.
Primary signal coverage: Ocala, Belleview, Dunnellon, Gainesville.

4. AGENCY COMMISSION
15/0.

5. GENERAL ADVERTISING REGULATIONS
General: 1, 2, 3, 4, 5, 8.
Rate Protection: 10b, 11b, 12b, 13b, 14b.
Cancellation: 20a, 21a, 23.

TIME RATES
No. 21 Effective December 1, 1990.
Received November 30, 1990.

6. SPOT ANNOUNCEMENTS

PER YR:	1x	121x	301x	721+
1 min	17.65	16.50	15.75	15.00
30 sec	12.75	12.00	11.25	10.50

7. PACKAGE PLANS
TAP—ROS 6 AM-7 PM

PER WK:	14 ti	21 ti	35 ti	70 ti
1 min	14.00	13.50	13.00	12.75
30 sec	9.75	9.25	9.00	8.75

For Agri information, see Agri section.

FIGURE 16.9 Page from *Standard Rate and Data Service,* Showing Spot Radio Listing for a Station in a Particular Market
Source: Standard Rate and Data Service.

as a starting point for discussion. A sample page from *SRDS Spot Radio Rates and Data* is shown in figure 16.9.

- Spot-market radio rate structures typically involve either (1) frequency discounts, whereby the cost per commercial goes down as the number of commercials purchased (per week) goes up; or (2) package plans, where an advertiser purchases a specified number of commercials throughout a broadcast day for a stated price. Some stations offer the grid-level form of pricing, similar to television.

Further, stations divide their broadcast day into various dayparts and price their commercials according to the level of audience delivered during these time periods. Although each station sets its own dayparts, the following gives a general idea:

- *Morning Drivetime (AMD)*: 6:00 A.M. to 10:00 A.M.
- *Daytime (DT)*: 10:00 A.M. to 3:00 P.M.
- *Afternoon Drivetime (PMD)*: 3:00 P.M. to 7:00 P.M.
- *Evening or Nighttime (NT)*: 7:00 P.M. to midnight
- *Overnight*: Midnight to 6:00 A.M.

Sometimes, all of Saturday and Sunday are grouped together as a "weekend" time period. Since most radio stations deliver their largest audiences during **drivetime,** this time period usually commands the highest costs per commercial.

To get a rough idea of what a particular spot-radio schedule would cost an advertiser, media buyers can use a cost-estimating guide. As was the case for television, these guides are based on the cost-per-rating-point (CPRP). One such guide is shown in table 16.8. Thus, the CPRP to reach teens in the top-fifty markets would be $1,618. A schedule aimed at teens that called for fifty rating points a week for twelve weeks would cost $970,800 ($1,618 × 50 × 12).

Most radio units are thirty seconds or sixty seconds. For network radio, a thirty-second commercial typically is one-half the cost of a minute unit. Local stations, however, usually charge relatively more for the thirty-second spot, typically around 80 percent of the minute cost. Thus, a $100 charge for one minute probably would cost approximately $80 if a thirty-second commercial was chosen instead.

TABLE 16.8

Cost-Estimating Guide, Based on Cost-Per-Rating-Point

| Markets | Cost Per Metro Area Rating Point | | |
	Men, 18+	Women, 18+	Teens, 12–17
Top 10	$1,687	$1,598	$678
Top 20	2,392	2,252	968
Top 30	3,022	2,839	1,266
Top 40	3,448	3,241	1,442
Top 50	3,834	3,602	1,618
Top 100	4,914	4,592	2,123

Source: *Leo Burnett 1991 Media Costs and Coverage, 13.*

Comparing Radio Vehicles

To make cost comparisons among alternative radio vehicles, media buyers use the CPM and/or CPRP methods discussed earlier for television. For example, given the information in table 16.9 for a particular daypart, three different radio stations in a market can be compared in terms of cost efficiency. The same formulas given earlier in the chapter for television allow computation of CPMs and CPRPs shown in table 16.10. Thus, KXXX is the most cost-efficient station for a target of adults, 25–49 years old. However, station KYYY delivers the largest *number* of targeted persons, which could cause media buyers to choose it over the more efficient station.

Audience Measurement and Delivery

Radio audiences are measured both nationally and in local markets. National audiences are determined by RADAR (Radio's All-Dimension Audience Research). A RADAR survey involves a sample of more than twelve thousand people, who

TABLE 16.9

Cost Comparisons of Three Radio Stations

Station	Cost of One-Minute Commercial	Audience Size (Adults, 25–49)	Rating (Adults, 25–49)
KXXX	$150	4,700	1.5
KYYY	300	7,400	2.4
KXYZ	110	3,000	1.0

TABLE 16.10

CPMs and CPRPs for the Three Radio Stations in Table 16.9

Station	CPM	CPRP
KXXX	$31.91	$100.00
KYYY	40.54	125.00
KXYZ	36.67	110.00

are telephoned and asked to recall their radio listening for the past twenty-four hours. RADAR issues a number of reports each year that describe national listeners of radio. Some of the audience deliveries from these reports are discussed later in this section.

Listening in local markets is provided by two measurement services—Arbitron, Inc. and Birch Radio. Arbitron samples listeners in individual markets by asking respondents to complete a one-week diary of listening habits. Surveys are conducted four times a year—winter, spring, summer, and fall—each for a twelve-week period. Figure 16.10 shows a sample page from an Arbitron radio diary.

Each market surveyed does not necessarily include all four time periods—for example, some smaller markets may be measured only once during the year. Arbitron issues local market reports that provide information on each station's audience sizes and ratings for various dayparts. Buyers of spot radio use these reports to determine which station or stations to buy in a market.

Birch Radio provides information for over 250 radio markets. Birch uses a recall telephone-interview technique to obtain information from sample respondents, who report their "yesterday" listening of radio. Respondents are asked to recall the stations heard yesterday within each daypart, beginning with the morning, 5:00 A.M. to 10:00 A.M. For each station, respondents report the exact start and stop times of listening, as well as the location of listening—in home, in car, or in another away-from-home location. To get cumulative listening over an entire week, Birch also asks respondents who listened to a particular station yesterday if they likewise listened to that station the "day before yesterday."

Birch issues a number of different reports that provide information on various aspects of station listening. Figure 16.11 is a page from the Birch Radio *Quarterly Summary Report* for persons ages 12 and over in the Albany/Schenectady/Troy (New York) metropolitan area (MSA). In other Birch reports, information is given for (1) AQH Persons (PRS), (2) AQH Persons (PRS) Rating (RTG), (3) AQH Persons (PRS) Share (SHR), and (4) Cume Persons (PRS). These four terms are defined as follows:

• *AQH Persons*—The number of persons in the audience during an average quarter hour (AQH) of a given radio station.

• *AQH Persons Rating*—The number of AQH persons expressed as a percentage of all such persons in the area's population.

• *AQH Persons Share*—The number of AQH persons expressed as a percentage of all radio listeners at a particular time.

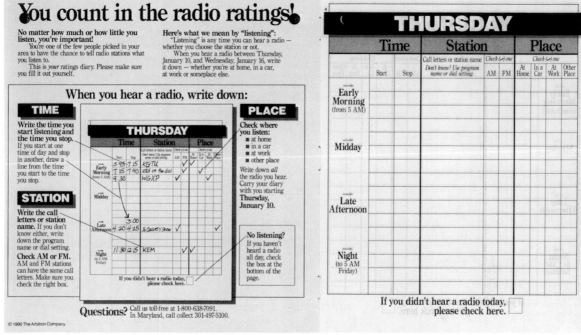

FIGURE 16.10 **A Page from an Arbitron Radio Diary**
Source: THE ARBITRON COMPANY. Used with permission.

• *Cume Persons*—The number of different persons who have reported hearing a given station for five or more minutes during a given daypart.

As mentioned earlier, the RADAR® survey reports on national audiences. Some general information on radio audience delivery, as provided by the Radio Advertising Bureau from RADAR studies, follows:[8]

• During an average week, 96.3 percent of all Americans twelve years or older listen to radio. The percent for teens, ages 12–17, is even higher—99.0 percent. Each day, almost four out of five adults (77.3 percent) listen to radio. See figure 16.12.

• The percent of people reached by radio according to various dayparts, Monday through Sunday, is as shown in table 16.11.

• Eighty-six percent of all car commuters are reached weekly by radio; 68 percent of adults listened to the radio *every time* they used their car during their last ten car trips.

TABLE 16.11

Percent of People Reached by Radio

Daypart (Monday–Sunday)	Men, 18+	Women, 18+	Teens, 12–17
6:00 A.M. to 10:00 A.M.	88.7%	85.7%	91.2%
10:00 A.M. to 3:00 P.M.	83.8	85.6	86.3
3:00 P.M. to 7:00 P.M.	83.6	80.9	92.0
7:00 P.M. to midnight	65.3	62.0	86.0
Midnight to 6:00 A.M.	44.4	38.4	51.3
24 hours	**96.9%**	**95.3%**	**99.0%**

Source: Calculated by the Radio Advertising Bureau from Radar® 40, Fall 1989, Volume 1, Copyright © Statistical Research, Inc. 1989.

ALBANY/SCHENECTADY/TROY NY MSA
JUNE 1991 - AUGUST 1991

Trends
PERSONS 12+

AVERAGE QUARTER HOUR SHARE TRENDS - READ ACROSS

	MON - SUN 6:00AM-MIDNIGHT					MON - FRI 6:00AM-10:00AM					MON - FRI 10:00AM-3:00PM					MON - FRI 3:00PM-7:00PM					MON - FRI 7:00PM-MIDNIGHT				
	SUM 90	FAL 90	WIN 91	SPR 91	SUM 91	SUM 90	FAL 90	WIN 91	SPR 91	SUM 91	SUM 90	FAL 90	WIN 91	SPR 91	SUM 91	SUM 90	FAL 90	WIN 91	SPR 91	SUM 91	SUM 90	FAL 90	WIN 91	SPR 91	SUM 91
WABY	2.6	1.9	2.6	1.1	2.1	2.3	2.9	1.9	.7	2.9	3.3	2.2	3.4	.4	2.1	3.0	2.1	3.5	1.2	1.9	1.0	1.0	1.3		.7
WAMC-FM	2.1	2.7	2.0	2.9	2.1	2.7	3.6	2.0	2.4	2.7	1.1	1.8	2.4	3.0	1.9	2.3	4.0	3.6	4.4	3.5	1.0	1.7	1.0	2.7	.5
WCAN-FM				.1	.1									.1									.1		
WCDB-FM	.6	.5	.2	.3	.2	.5	.3	.1	.6	.1	.3	.2		.3		1.2	.5	.1	.1	.5	1.4	1.3	.3		1.0
WCKL*	.6	.5		.3	.4	.7	.4	.2	.7	.7	.7				.5	.5			.3	.1	.3				
WCSS*	.3	2.0	.7	1.4	.2	.6	2.2	1.1	2.1	.5	.5	1.8	.2	1.5		.1	2.0	.3	1.1						
WEQX-FM	.9	1.5	.7	1.3	1.5	.8	1.5	.7	1.5	1.5	1.1	1.7	1.1	1.3	1.6	1.1	1.7	.8	1.6	1.6	.6	1.2		1.2	.7
WFLY-FM	11.4	11.8	12.4	13.0	15.1	9.5	12.1	9.9	10.4	9.7	9.6	10.6	11.6	11.3	15.3	11.3	13.2	13.0	14.3	17.8	15.8	11.5	14.7	12.7	15.0
WGNA	.8	.4	.7	.3	.2	.6	.3	.5	.3	.1	.2		1.2	.5	.1	.9	.2	.1	.6	.1	1.7			1.1	
WGNA-FM	12.7	10.2	10.8	8.6	8.5	13.2	10.1	11.4	7.4	8.8	15.0	11.5	11.3	9.3	8.2	12.2	10.8	9.2	8.3	9.5	10.7	8.2	7.5	6.7	5.7
WGY	5.9	8.7	9.1	7.2	7.8	8.9	9.3	13.8	9.5	9.9	2.8	8.1	5.9	4.7	9.0	4.3	8.2	7.7	5.1	5.2	8.2	11.2	11.6	11.5	8.6
WGY -FM	6.9	6.8	5.3	4.1	5.7	5.4	4.6	3.7	4.1	7.7	6.7	7.3	6.6	4.5	7.5	7.3	7.1	5.8	5.0	4.6	11.3	8.8	4.0	2.7	2.6
WHAZ	.6		.5	.2	.2	.6		.4	.2	.7	1.3		.9	.1	.2	.8		.6		.4					.1
WHRL-FM	.7	.8	.6	.3	1.0	.5	.3	.5	.4	.6	.9		.2		1.4	1.2	1.0	.4	.2	1.3	.1	2.6	1.4	.2	.3
WKLI-FM	6.5	6.4	6.8	5.7	5.4	7.0	6.6	5.6	6.7	6.5	6.9	8.5	7.3	6.1	5.1	5.6	6.1	8.5	5.7	4.9	5.6	5.2	8.3	6.2	6.8
WKOL-FM	.2	.2	.4	.6	.3	.2	.6	.3	.6		.2	.3	.5	.8	.5	.4	.1	.1	.6	.2				.9	.5
WMHT-FM	2.2	1.8	2.2	2.0	1.6	2.5	1.1	2.0	2.7	1.3	1.8	1.9	1.8	1.6	1.3	2.2	2.5	1.6	1.7	2.5	3.5	2.6	2.7	1.5	1.6
WPTR	1.5	2.2	2.0	1.3	1.4	2.8	3.5	3.0	1.8	2.1	1.5	3.1	2.3	.9	1.2	.9	2.0	1.6	1.1	1.3	2.0	1.3	1.1	3.3	2.1
WPYX-FM	11.4	8.3	7.1	7.3	7.4	8.8	9.0	6.9	6.9	5.5	11.2	7.9	6.2	7.9	8.0	14.1	8.4	8.4	8.5	7.0	11.0	7.3	8.3	7.4	8.0
WQBK	2.5	1.8	2.9	3.0	3.0	2.5	2.9	3.6	4.5	4.7	3.0	.6	3.2	3.9	2.9	3.0	2.2	2.5	1.5	1.7	2.3	1.7	2.8	2.7	2.7
WQBK-FM	4.9	7.5	5.3	9.9	6.8	4.2	6.3	4.4	10.8	7.7	5.9	9.5	6.0	10.5	6.1	5.4	7.1	6.8	8.3	6.2	2.5	7.1	4.9	7.1	7.3
WQKZ-FM				1.2	.3									1.6	.5				1.2	.3				2.6	.3
WQQY-FM	.5	.5	.2	.3	.4	.4	.6	.7	.2	.5	1.1	.9	.1	.2	.7		.9	.1	.6	.5	.8	.4			.7
WROW	.9	1.1	.5	1.2	.7	1.2	1.6	1.0	1.6	1.3	.7	.8	.3	1.7	.2	.5	.5	.6	1.2	.5		.7	.8		.5
WROW-FM	6.3	5.0	7.1	7.1	5.9	7.1	3.9	6.6	5.8	5.0	6.2	4.5	8.7	9.2	5.1	7.7	4.1	6.6	7.9	7.4	3.0	6.8	5.5	2.3	4.8
WRPI-FM	.3	.2	.2	.3	.1	.1				.2	.4	.2	.1			.6	.2	.1	.5	.1	.7			1.5	
WSHQ-FM	.6	.8	.1	.5	.4	.1	.4	.1	.2	.4	.6	.9		.1	.3	.1	.4		.9	.2	.3	1.2		1.7	.4
WSHZ-FM	.5	1.0	.9	1.2	.7	.6	.6	.5	1.5	.6	.1	1.1	1.8	1.6	.4	.5	.6	.9	.9	1.1	1.4	.1		.2	.4
WSSV-FM	1.1	1.4	.7	.4	.7	1.2	1.5	.8	.4	.6	1.4	2.4	.8	.5	1.1	.7	1.1	1.0	.6	.4	.4	1.3	.3	.3	1.3
WTRY	3.5	1.5	3.3	2.5	1.7	4.9	2.9	5.0	3.3	2.7	4.4	.1	4.0	3.9	1.2	2.9	1.0	2.5	2.7	1.2	2.0	.7	1.3	1.5	1.8
WVCR-FM	2.8	2.2	3.5	3.3	3.4	3.2	1.8	3.5	2.5	2.8	1.6	1.3	2.0	3.0	2.0	2.3	2.2	3.1	3.0	3.5	5.9	3.2	7.2	6.8	7.8
WVKZ-FM	2.0	4.5	4.3	5.1	6.0	1.4	4.1	2.2	3.4	3.7	1.7	5.0	4.2	4.0	6.3	1.8	4.8	5.1	6.4	6.6	.7	5.0	8.8	7.6	7.7
WFAN				.6	.1				2.0	.3				.3					.3	.1				.3	
WJIV-FM	.2	.6	1.2	.2	.1	.1	1.0	1.2	.3	.3	.1	.5	1.3	.4	.2	.5	.3	.8				.4	3.1	.3	
WPDH-FM				.3	.3				.1	.6					.1				.6	.6				.8	.1
PUR	16.0	15.6	16.7	16.3	16.7	21.3	21.6	23.1	22.7	20.7	20.4	17.9	20.5	20.7	20.4	17.9	17.6	19.8	19.2	18.9	9.8	9.6	9.8	9.1	10.6

+ DENOTES HISPANIC FORMAT. SEE ADVISORY ON PAGE IV.
* ESTIMATES ADJUSTED FOR ACTUAL BROADCAST SCHEDULE

BIRCH RADIO
COPYRIGHT 1991 BIRCH/SCARBOROUGH RESEARCH CORP.

PAGE 4

FIGURE 16.11 Sample Page from Birch Radio *Quarterly Summary Report*
Source: Birch Scarborough Research, Copyright 1988, 1991. Reprinted by permission.

- Radio's share of audience among ages 12 or more by location of listening, for an average twenty-four-hour period, Monday through Sunday, is: 46.8 percent at home, 24.8 percent in cars, and 28.4 percent at other places.

- The average weekday time spent listening to radio is:

Men, 18+	3 hours, 30 minutes
Women, 18+	3 hours, 20 minutes
Teens, 12–17	2 hours, 26 minutes

- Radio listening is greater than television viewing from 5:00 A.M. until 5:00 P.M.

Summary

Television is the number two medium in terms of total advertising investment and is in first place among major national advertisers. Television advertising is categorized as network, national cable,

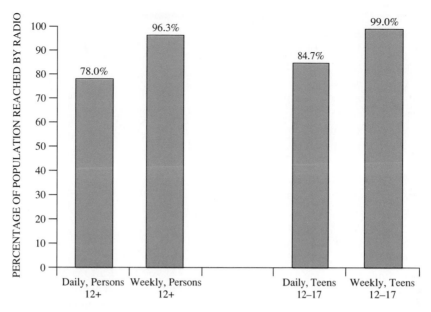

FIGURE 16.12 Percentage of U.S. Population
Reached by Radio
Source: Statistical Research, Inc., Westfield, NJ.

syndication, national spot, local spot, and non-network cable. The first four types are primarily used by national advertisers, whereas the latter two are used mostly by local companies.

Television's basic characteristics include its ability to: (1) combine sight and sound, allowing the medium to have a high level of impact on viewers; (2) provide users with a high level of market coverage; (3) offer flexibility in terms of regional coverage and creative technique, although it is often less manageable in terms of scheduling and availability; (4) deliver commercials repetitively so that a sales idea can be effectively communicated; (5) provide prestige for advertisers; and (6) offer good cost efficiency, although requiring large absolute dollar outlays.

Television is a fairly complicated medium to use, primarily because most aspects of buying are negotiated between buyers and sellers. The prices charged for television time are based on the size of audience delivered—with audience size varying according to the daypart used—and length of the commercial. Thirty-second and fifteen-second commercials are the major units used. Alternative television vehicles can be compared in terms of cost efficiency with either the cost-per-thousand (CPM) or cost-per-rating-point (CPRP) method. Each method requires knowing the cost of a commercial and its audience delivery, either in total audience size or by a relative measure of size—namely, the rating.

National television audiences are measured daily by the A. C. Nielsen Company through its use of people meters, which electronically record when a set is on, to what channel it is tuned, and who was in the room with the television set. Average audiences over an entire year are reported by Simmons Market Research Bureau and Mediamark, Inc. Local television delivery is provided by Nielsen and Arbitron, primarily by having sample respondents record their viewing in a diary.

Radio advertising consists of three types: network, spot, and local, with the latter category predominating; more than three-fourths of all radio advertising is purchased by local firms. More than 99 percent of all households are equipped to receive radio.

The basic characteristics associated with radio are its ability to: (1) provide a highly selective audience as a result of specialized programming formats; (2) deliver information with a sense of immediacy; (3) offer flexibility of geographical coverage, creative content, and mobility in terms of where it can be listened to; (4) deliver repetitive messages, thus giving an advertiser high frequency; and (5) provide cost efficiency, in terms of both absolute and relative costs.

Like television, radio rates are, for the most part, negotiated, and the pricing of time units is based on audience delivery. For most stations, the drive-time dayparts—morning and evening drive—are the most expensive. Alternative radio vehicles can be compared with the same methods used for television—CPM and CPRP.

The measurement of national radio audiences is provided by the RADAR® survey, which issues a number of reports each year that show listenership patterns. Data are gathered from telephone interviews. Local radio markets are measured by two competing services—Arbitron and Birch. Arbitron uses a diary method to collect listenership; Birch uses a recall telephone-interview technique, asking respondents to report their "yesterday" listening of radio stations. Both services issue reports that show audience sizes, ratings, shares, and cumulative listening to radio stations in a number of markets.

Questions for Discussion

1. Why might a national advertiser decide to use spot television in the media schedule?

2. How does syndicated television differ from network television? From spot television?

3. Why do you think cable television has grown so dramatically over the past twenty years? Will this growth trend likely continue? Why or why not?

4. On what basis are the rates for radio and television set?

5. Do you feel that people meters are better than diaries for measuring television viewing? Explain your reasoning.

6. Why is buying spot television and spot radio considered more complicated than buying network television and network radio?

7. How can a medium such as television be considered cost efficient when a single thirty-second evening commercial can cost $150,000?

8. What is the difference between the Nielsen Station Index and the Nielsen Television Index?

9. What characteristic do you think is the most important for radio? Why?

10. Compare the cost efficiency of the following two radio stations:

Station	Audience Size	Rating	Cost of Sixty-second Commercial
WAAA	6,345	2.1	$210
WBBB	4,050	1.4	150

Endnotes

1. William Wells, John Burnett, and Sandra Moriarty, *Advertising: Principles and Practice* (Englewood Cliffs, N.J.: Prentice-Hall, 1989), 259.

2. See Wayne Walley, "Local TV Cuts Rates for :15s," *Advertising Age,* 5 June 1989, 37.

3. Wells, Burnett, and Moriarty, *Advertising,* 258.

4. Nielsen Media Research, *Nielsen Report on Television, 1990.*

5. Wayne Walley, "ABC Radio Revise Targets Cable," *Advertising Age,* 4 June 1990, 39.

6. *Radio Facts for Advertisers, 1990,* Radio Advertising Bureau, 28.

7. *Radio Facts for Advertisers, 1990,* 20.

8. *Radio Facts for Advertisers, 1990,* 4–7, 9, 15.

Suggested Readings

• Abernethy, Avery Mark. "The Accuracy of Diary Measures of Car Radio Audiences: An Initial Assessment." *Journal of Advertising Research* 18, no. 3 (1989): 33–39.

• Dunn, S. Watson, Arnold M. Barban, Dean M. Krugman, and Leonard N. Reid. *Advertising: Its Role in Modern Marketing.* 7th ed. Chicago: Dryden Press, 1990. Chapter 17.

• Kaatz, Ronald B. *Cable: An Advertiser's Guide to the New Electronic Media.* Chicago: Crain Books, 1982.

• McGann, Anthony F., and J. Thomas Russell. *Advertising Media.* 2d ed. Homewood, Ill.: Irwin, 1988. Chapters 6, 7.

• Russell, J. Thomas, and W. Ronald Lane. *Kleppner's Advertising Procedure.* 11th ed. Englewood Cliffs, N.J.: Prentice-Hall, 1990. Chapters 8, 9.

• Shimp, Terence A. *Promotion Management and Marketing Communications.* 2d ed. Chicago: Dryden Press, 1990. Chapter 13.

• Sissors, Jack Z., and Lincoln Bumba. *Advertising Media Planning.* 3d ed. Lincolnwood, Ill.: NTC Business Books, 1989. Chapters 10, 11.

• Wells, William, John Burnett, and Sandra Moriarty. *Advertising: Principles and Practice.* Englewood Cliffs, N.J.: Prentice-Hall, 1989. Chapter 10.

Chapter 17

Direct-Mail and Out-of-Home Media

Outline

Learning Objectives

In the study of this chapter, you will have the opportunity to:

- Understand the types of direct-mail and out-of-home media.

- Observe the direct-mail and out-of-home characteristics used by media buyers.

- Examine the factors that are considered in buying direct-mail, outdoor, and transit advertising.

- Learn something about the preparation of direct-mail and out-of-home media.

- Observe how audiences of direct mail and out-of-home media are measured.

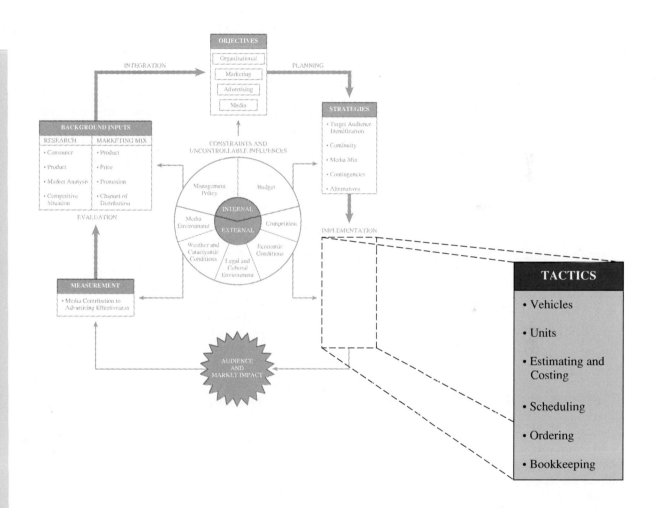

*T*he two previous chapters discussed four "traditional" media types—newspapers, magazines, television, and radio—which collectively account for over 60 percent of all measured media expenditures.

Print and broadcast media involve a combination of editorial, informational, and entertainment content, along with advertising that is, in effect, adjacent to the content the medium is intended to carry.

The types of media discussed in this chapter—direct mail, outdoor, and transit (the latter two of which often are referred to as out-of-home media)—consist only of the advertising itself, with no news or entertainment material to help attract an audience.

Direct Mail

For the past fifty years, **direct mail** has generally ranked second or third among the measured media in total advertising dollars spent. For many years, it was ranked second only to newspapers, but television's rapid growth in the early 1960s resulted in direct mail becoming the third largest medium in 1964. It has retained this position since that time.

In 1775, Benjamin Franklin headed the first U.S. post office. Major growth of the U.S. Postal Service and of direct-mail advertising came in the nineteenth century. Penny postage after 1850 encouraged use of the mails to distribute advertising materials, and after the Civil War, notices, circulars, and almanacs became popular. Catalogs started to appear toward the end of the century, as improvements in printing enabled advertisers to illustrate clearly the products being offered. Early catalogs—for example, the first Montgomery Ward catalog, which consisted of one hundred pages when distributed in 1872—brought to rural and small-town communities information about products that people wanted but could not buy at the few general stores available to them. Today, catalogs are sent to people in virtually every type of community—rural, small-town, suburban, and urban markets—and offer the ease of shopping by mail or by calling an 800 number and placing a credit-card order. Currently, the U.S. Postal Service delivers almost fourteen billion catalogs annually.

Before discussions of some of the tactical aspects of direct-mail advertising, a few terms often mentioned in conjunction with direct mail need to be clarified. **Mail-order advertising** involves any method of selling in which the product is promoted through advertising (such as magazines or newspapers) and ordered by customers through the mail (or by telephone). The normal retail channel of distribution is bypassed, and no personal selling is involved. Thus, mail order is a way of doing business and can involve any number of different media types, including direct mail. About 10 percent of all retail sales are by mail order.

Direct marketing is an interactive system of marketing that uses one or more advertising media—including direct mail—to effect a measurable response and/or transaction at any location.[1] It is one-on-one communication between a marketer and a consumer by phone, mail, personal visit, and so on, with responses to the offer directly measurable.

Direct response is a specific advertising technique whereby the advertising, regardless of the medium used, seeks an immediate action or response. The response could be an order, an inquiry about the product or service, or a visit to a retail store. Among direct-response advertisers, direct mail presently is the major medium used. As shown

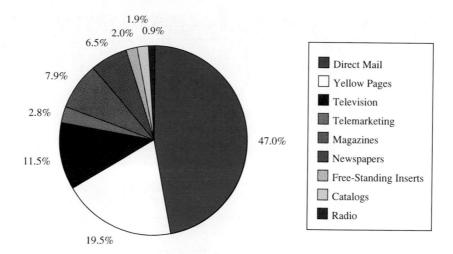

FIGURE 17.1 Use of Various Media by Direct-Response Advertisers
Source: Data from *Advertising Age,* March 30, 1988, p. 45, Crain Communications Inc., Detroit, MI.

in figure 17.1, 47 percent of the total media dollars spent by direct-response advertisers is for direct-mail advertising, followed by Yellow Pages directory advertising (19.5 percent).

Although the concepts just discussed may involve direct mail as an advertising medium, they are not in and of themselves media types and, thus, are not discussed further. Direct mail, on the other hand, is an advertising medium that involves distributing the advertising message through the U.S. Postal Service or some other direct-delivery service (for example, United Parcel Service or Federal Express). The message can have any number of objectives—from direct action (such as a sale [direct response]), to intermediate goals (such as providing information or changing attitudes).

Types of Direct-Mail Advertising

Direct mail can involve a virtually endless number of message formats. Creativity and the dollars available usually are the only limiting factors. Even if a direct-mail idea does not meet U.S. Postal Service regulations—say, because of its size—a private

delivery service usually can be used. Nevertheless, most direct-mail advertising takes certain common forms.

Sales Letter

The sales letter is one of the most frequently used forms of direct mail. Through the use of computers, the respondent's name can be inserted into the letter's text to provide the ultimate in personalization. Figure 17.2 shows a personalized sales letter (memorandum) used by Allstate to solicit customers for its group accidental death and dismemberment insurance plan. The letter—along with a leaflet explaining the plan's benefits, a brief message from the Chairman of the Board of Allstate, and a reply envelope—was sent to holders of Sears charge accounts.

Leaflet

A leaflet is usually a single printed sheet that explains a product or service more fully than a sales letter and often is included in a mailing along with a sales letter. Leaflet costs can vary dramatically, depending on the quality of paper used and whether or not color is used for illustration.

RE: Group Accidental Death and Dismemberment Insurance Plan for
SearsCharge Accountholders

FROM: Charles F. Thalheimer
Assistant Vice President

TO: 0004
Xxxxx Xxxxxxxx
XXX Xxxxxxxxx Xxxx
Xxxxxxxxxx, XX XXXXX

MEMORANDUM

This memo is to notify you that, as a SearsCharge Accountholder, you are guaranteed eligible to enroll in an Accidental Death and Dismemberment Insurance Plan being offered to members of the SearsCharge Accountholder Group.

Under this Insurance Plan, you're covered for up to $500,000 in Accidental Death and Dismemberment benefits - depending on the type of accident, loss and plan chosen - 24-hours-a-day, anywhere in the world. And, the cost is affordable!

The Insurance Plan protects you as a driver or a passenger in a car; as a pedestrian struck by a vehicle; as a passenger on any public transportation such as a plane, train, ship, or bus; even at home, at work, or while engaging in sports.

PROTECTION FOR THE XXXXXXXX FAMILY

That's important. It means you can enroll for additional coverage providing separate benefits for your spouse and all eligible children, for an affordable amount more. With this Family Coverage, they'll be protected against all the same risks you would. And when you look at the most recent accident statistics on the back of this memo, you'll agree that this kind of protection is important!

More good news. The Insurance Plan is so affordably priced, you may well want to choose our Better Plan coverage which offers over DOUBLE THE GOOD PLAN BENEFITS!

If you want the most insurance for your money, pick the Better Plan with Family Coverage included. That's the Plan we recommend, and it's one with which we know you'll be very well protected.

Please read over the Important Provisions and the enclosed Brochure for full details of coverage and costs; including exclusions, limitations and termination of the Insurance Plan. Then, take advantage of your Guaranteed Eligibility to enroll as a SearsCharge Accountholder in the Insurance Plan of your choice now ... today. You'll be giving your family protection that could make a world of difference to them if something happened to you.

As a SearsCharge Accountholder, we hope you don't let this opportunity slip by.

Charles F. Thalheimer
Assistant Vice President
Allstate Life Insurance Company

DHK331AB Copyright© 1989, Allstate Life Insurance Company

Allstate® ENROLLMENT FORM

Allstate Life Insurance Company
Group Accidental Death and Dismemberment Insurance

Here's How to Enroll:

1. Darken the appropriate oval for the coverage you desire. (Choose "Family Plan" if you wish to include your spouse and all eligible children.)
2. Sign, date and return this form in the post-paid envelope today.
3. Send no money now. You may return the Certificate of Insurance within 30 days of receipt and owe nothing. Or, if you decide to keep the insurance in force, you'll be billed monthly on your SearsCharge Account.

YES, enroll me for the plan I've selected and bill the monthly charge to my SearsCharge Account. I understand coverage takes effect on my first regular Sears billing due date following the date Allstate processes this enrollment; that Sears will first deduct the insurance charge from my monthly Sears payment and then apply the remainder to the balance due on my Sears Account; and that Sears helps maintain and service this insurance program and is entitled to compensation from Allstate Life Insurance Company, its subsidiary, for doing so.

Note: Under the terms of the Master Policy, beneficiaries are designated as stated on the back of this enrollment.

X _____
Signature of SearsCharge Accountholder (listed above)   Date Signed
DHA874AB   Copyright© 1989, Allstate Life Insurance Company

XXXXXXXX XXXXXXXXXXXXX XXXXXXX
XXXXX XXXXXXXX
XXX XXXXXXXXX XXXX
XXXXXXXXXX, XX XXXXX

170A

COVERAGE DESIRED
Fill in Only One Oval

Family Plan		Individual Only	
Better Plan ($500,000 max.)	$9.90 a month	Better Plan ($500,000 max.)	$6.50 a month
Good Plan ($200,000 max.)	$4.45 a month	Good Plan ($200,000 max.)	$2.95 a month

FIGURE 17.2 A Personalized Sales Letter for Allstate's Group Accidental Death and Dismemberment Insurance Plan
Courtesy of Allstate Life Insurance Company.

Booklet

While similar to a leaflet, a booklet contains several pages and is appropriate when a considerable amount of complicated information must be communicated. For example, a gasoline company that wants to convey information about car care might mail a booklet to prospects, or an automobile manufacturer might send to recent car purchasers a booklet about the servicing of the car at a local dealership. A booklet that contains many pages that are bound together (for example, with center staples) and is elaborately produced can be called a **brochure.**

Folder

A folder is larger than a leaflet and is often printed on heavier paper stock. It is typically on a single sheet of paper, although usually oversized, and is folded to reduce the mailing's total size. If the name and address of the prospect can be placed in an open area of the folder, the folder can be a **self-mailer.** Folders can be fairly economical to produce and provide a large amount of information.

Broadside

A broadside is even larger than a folder, and when entirely unfolded, takes on the appearance of a poster and can dramatically illustrate the advertised product. Broadsides can be sent to dealers to use as store point-of-purchase displays or, perhaps, to be posted on the store's outside windows. Although used extensively for advertising to retail dealers, they also can be sent to ultimate consumers, who might post them on a wall in the home or office.

Circular or Flyer

A circular/flyer is a widely used form of direct-mail advertising, primarily because of its low cost to produce. Circular/flyers are similar to leaflets in that they are printed on a single sheet of paper. They look less elaborate than leaflets, however, because they generally are printed on lighter paper stock and are less likely to have extensive color reproduction and illustrations.

Postcard

Postcards are, perhaps, the simplest form of direct mail and are often used to convey announcement-type information. A local department store, for example, might send a postcard to its charge-card holders, announcing an upcoming sale. Some postcards are folded over along a perforation and contain a second, reply card that can be returned to place an order or to secure additional information. Postcards provide advertisers with a time advantage—they can be produced and mailed quickly and are relatively inexpensive.

Catalog

A catalog is like a booklet or brochure in that it usually contains many pages. But its main function is to serve as a reference book, to be kept until the consumer decides to place an order by mail or by calling an 800 number. The catalog serves as a buying guide to be used over a certain period of time. Many companies that use catalogs derive all or most of their sales from this source, and some do not have any retail outlets. L. L. Bean, Lillian Vernon, and Lands' End are examples of companies that primarily are "catalog retailers." For example, L. L. Bean has about 90 percent of its total company sales from mail order. Yet, a number of advertisers who use catalogs extensively also have many retail stores as well. Examples include such retailers as Sears, Roebuck, The Sharper Image, Victoria's Secret, Bloomingdale's, and Brooks Brothers (whose mail-order volume is about 15 percent, with 85 percent from retail stores). Catalogs also are used by business-to-business advertisers because catalogs can provide a wealth of technical details. Figure 17.3 shows the cover and inside pages from a Lillian Vernon catalog.

FIGURE 17.3 Cover and Inside Pages from a Lillian Vernon Catalog
Courtesy of Lillian Vernon®.

Characteristics of Direct Mail

Most direct-mail users believe that this medium has a number of positive attributes, including:

Selectivity

The most unique characteristic of direct mail is its ability to deliver a highly selective audience. Whereas the coverage of most mass media seldom corresponds exactly with the audience an advertiser is trying to reach, in the case of direct mail, the advertiser can build, at least theoretically, the precise circulation desired. In fact, direct-mail specialists often use the term *precision targeting* to describe the medium because the *advertiser* determines to whom the mailing is to be sent, not a publisher or broadcast company, as is the case with print and broadcast media. For example, Porsche Cars North America, in wanting to target upscale prospects for its car, mailed 200,000 test-drive invitations to a list of high-income people. The mailing included a poster showing a Porsche 944 bearing a license plate

with the recipient's name.[2] Securing a precise-target mailing list is usually possible, although sometimes it may be difficult.

Personalization

Computers allow direct-mail advertising pieces to be personalized to include a recipient's name within the letter, as well as additional individualized information. (See figure 17.2 for an example of a personal sales letter.) For example, an advertiser might include different content based on, say, in what city or state a person lived. Or a direct mailing to a particular farmer could identify the types of farm activities in which the farmer is engaged. For example, an advertiser of a herbicide that can be used on several different crops would probably send material to a corn farmer that is different than that mailed to a soybean farmer. The ability to provide such individualization can mean that individual readership is increased, as is the advertising's impact.

Coverage Intensity

The coverage of direct mail can be at whatever degree an advertiser desires. For example, if necessary, a mailing could be planned for delivery every day for a certain period of time. If more than one delivery a day is desired, the U.S. Postal Service could be bypassed and a private carrier used.

Related to this characteristic is *timeliness*. Direct mail can be scheduled to be delivered on a particular time schedule. For example, an advertiser may want materials to be received by dealers or consumers just before certain holidays or seasons of the year. With direct mail, delivery schedules can be determined with a fair amount of precision.

Flexibility

As shown earlier in the chapter, direct mail can involve a number of different formats, from a simple postcard to a large catalog. This gives an advertiser a great deal of flexibility in terms of how much is spent, the extent of information provided, and the type of impact achieved. In addition, geographic distribution of direct mail is highly flexible. A mailing can be sent to people throughout the United States, or only in certain states or cities. Advertisers can even send direct mail only to certain postal zip codes, and since they can find out the general characteristics of people living in a zip code—for example, average income—targeting flexibility is enhanced.

Measurable Response

Since much direct-mail advertising requires a direct response from a recipient—a mail-order or telephone sale, or a request for more information—the effect of the mailing can be determined fairly easy. This characteristic also allows advertisers to test different creative techniques. One creative treatment, for example, can be mailed to half of a test sample, with the other half receiving an alternative approach. The one producing the largest number of responses would then be used in the full mail-out. This is analogous to split-run advertising in newspapers or magazines. Also, if multiple mailings are sent to people over a period of time, names of prospects who do not eventually respond or place an order can be removed from the mailing list.

Cost Efficiency

Direct mail can be either a high or low-cost medium, in absolute dollars, depending on the format used and the extent of the distribution. The key is whether a particular mailing is cost efficient on a relative basis—that is, the cost per reader. Obviously, the quality of the advertiser's mailing list can be a large factor in this determination: The more precisely the list matches prospects, the greater the efficiency in reaching the target. Since response to a mailing can often be measured quickly, the list can be "fine-tuned" to eliminate those who do not respond, thereby increasing efficiency.

Buying Direct Mail

Given its unique nature, direct mail is bought in a somewhat different manner than previously discussed media. A buyer of print or broadcast media deals with a specific media vehicle, such as the *New York Times, Mademoiselle,* "Roseanne" on the ABC television network, or radio station WHBF-FM. In return for the price paid for the advertisement or commercial unit, the media vehicle delivers an audience that the buyer hopes will efficiently reach a targeted group of consumers. The costs involved for a direct-mail advertisement, on the other hand, involve: (1) production, (2) delivery, and (3) mailing list.

Production

Production costs include everything involved in preparing a direct-mail piece for mailing at a particular time, including concept development and design, artwork, photography, printing materials and labor, computer programming and processing, labeling, sorting, bundling, and envelope sealing.

The advertiser can be directly involved in this phase of the process or may choose to pay an outside specialist, such as a direct-mail advertising agency. Whoever is responsible—whether advertiser or agency—is likely to work with a number of different suppliers—artists, photographers, talent agencies, computer processing companies, printers, and the like.

Production costs, of course, vary according to the type of format used. A personalized computer-generated letter can range from about $40 per thousand to over $200 per thousand, based on the size of the letter, the paper stock used, whether printed on one or two sides, and the quantity printed. A double postcard (self-mailer, with return card) can cost between $17 and $70 per thousand; a folder, between $23 and $70 per thousand; a brochure, from $15 to over $100 per thousand; and a broadside, between $60 and $250 per thousand.

Delivery

Although direct-mail advertising can be distributed through private carriers, the U.S. Postal Service presently handles around 97 percent of the total, with 3 percent by alternative means. However, as postal rates continue to rise, experimentation with private carriers is likely to continue, and their share of the total volume may grow. The U.S. Postal Service presently delivers around sixty-six billion pieces of direct mail annually, including almost fourteen billion catalogs.

An advertiser distributing direct mail through the U.S. Postal Service has a choice of sending the materials either first-class or third-class mail. Third-class rates are significantly lower than those for first class and are the predominant means of delivery. Thirty-nine percent of all mail is sent third-class. Third-class rates are broken down into several subcategories, based on the number of pieces mailed, their total weight, whether bundled according to zip code, and the like. Generally, rates are sufficiently complicated that a mailer is advised to confer with the local postmaster before undertaking a mailing. To mail a 4-ounce catalog via current third-class rates would cost 24.1 cents per catalog, but this will likely increase in the near future (prior to the rate change in 1988, the 4-ounce catalog cost 18.6 cents to mail).[3] If the next rate increase is the same as the last—about 30 percent—the 4-ounce catalog will cost more than 31 cents per piece.

Mailing List

Many direct-mail experts consider the quality of the mailing list to be critical to the success or failure of a particular mailing. Thus, advertisers must take special care in deciding to whom the piece should be mailed. Advertisers can develop their own mailing list or secure one from someone else.

Advertisers who decide to develop their own list can use a number of possible sources:

- Automobile registrations
- Building permits
- Business directories
- Charge-account holders
- City directories
- Government directories
- Newspaper announcements (for example, a department store might develop a list of people who announce their engagement in the newspaper to encourage them to register in their china, silverware, and crystal glass departments)
- Property-tax lists
- Reply or warranty cards (manufacturers of appliances, electronic equipment, cameras, and similar goods often ask buyers to send back a card recording their purchase)
- Yellow Pages directories

Although many advertisers, especially local firms, develop their own mailing list, a problem associated with this approach is keeping the list current. People move, marry, change jobs, get divorced, remarry, have babies, or die. Businesses change their name, move, or go out of business; new businesses are started. Also, a list source may contain "duplicates," whereby the same person or household is listed more than once. To avoid waste deliveries, advertisers need a system of purging these duplicates. All of these problems require that an advertiser continually monitor the list and update it regularly.

The more common method of securing a mailing list is to buy or rent one. Companies that compile and maintain various mailing lists, using a host of sources, are called **list houses** or **list brokers.** They typically publish a catalog that describes their lists, including the number of names available and the cost for using a list. Rates can be quoted as a flat cost—that is, a set price for the entire list of names

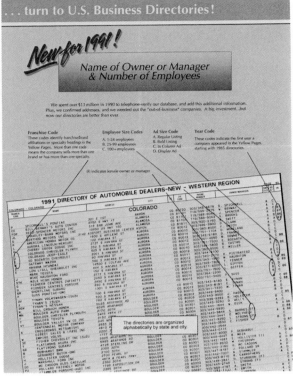

FIGURE 17.4 Cover and Inside Page from the American Business Directories Catalog of Direct-Mail Lists

Source: American Business Directories, Division of American Business Information. 5711 S. 86th Circle, Omaha, NE 68127. Reprinted by permission.

and addresses—or as a cost-per-thousand-names on the list (often shown as /**M**—per thousand—in the catalog). Usually, the more specialized the list, the higher the cost per thousand names. Some highly specialized lists, for example, can cost more than $1,000 per thousand, but the average rental list is usually around $40 to $50 per thousand names. Figure 17.4 shows the cover and an inside page from the American Business Directories catalog. This list house offers over twelve hundred mailing lists that are compiled from nationwide Yellow Pages directories.

Standard Rate & Data Service (SRDS) publishes bimonthly *Direct-Mail List Rates and Data,* which catalogs more than thirteen thousand business, consumer, and farm mailing lists available for rental. The "Master Index" classifies lists by sub-

ject/topic. For example, assume the target prospects are black Americans. The subject index shows "Black Citizens" to be in Class 538 ("Ethnic"). Class 538 in the book notes a large number of list houses that provide various lists of people with ethnic affiliations. Several companies specifically provide lists of black Americans. Each such listing should be evaluated to determine which list house provides the type of individuals that best meet the targeting criteria. Figure 17.5 shows a *SRDS* page from "Class 538, Ethnic."

Cost Allocations

Having discussed the three cost areas of a direct-mail piece, we can now look at how an average catalog's costs are broken down. Table 17.1 shows how

536 Epicurean & Specialty Foods
538 Ethnic

WINDSOR VINEYARDS—cont

6. METHOD OF ADDRESSING
4-up Cheshire labels. Pressure sensitive labels, 6.00/M extra. Magnetic tape, (9T 800/1600), 20.00 flat fee.
4-up Cheshire labels. Pressure sensitive labels, 6.00/M extra. Magnetic tape (9T 800/1600 BPI), 20.00 nonreturnable fee.

8. RESTRICTIONS
Sample mailing piece required for approval. Rental is for one-time use only.

11. MAINTENANCE
Updated monthly.

WINE BUYERS

Location ID: 10 DCLS 536   Mid 054127-000
Business Data Service, Inc.

1. PERSONNEL
List Manager
Best List Management Corp., 5030 Champion Blvd., Suite 6240, Boca Raton, FL 33496. Phone 407-496-1086. FAX 407-496-1432.

2. DESCRIPTION
Buyers of better wines who participated in rebate promotions by mail; 50% female, 48% male, 2% unknown.

3. LIST SOURCE
Respondents.

4. QUANTITY AND RENTAL RATES
Rec'd June 4, 1991.

	Total Number	Price per/M
Total list	1,246,712	*65.00

(*) Publishers/fundraisers, 40.00/M.
Selections: age, dwelling type, state, SCF, ZIP Code, 3.00/M extra; key coding, 1.50/M extra.
Minimum order 5,000.

6. METHOD OF ADDRESSING
Magnetic tape, 20.00 flat fee.

8. RESTRICTIONS
Sample mailing piece required for approval.

WINE DIGEST

Location ID: 10 DCLS 536   Mid 050579-000
Wine Digest.

1. PERSONNEL
List Manager
Saavoy List Management, 277 Forest Ave., Suite 100B, Box 1765, Paramus, NJ 07652. Phone 201-967-5777.

2. DESCRIPTION
Subscribers to a publication of reviews on wines of the world; mostly male; ages 25-55.
Average unit of sale 30.00 yearly.
ZIP Coded in numerical sequence 100%.

3. LIST SOURCE
Direct mail.

4. QUANTITY AND RENTAL RATES
Rec'd May 16, 1991.

	Total Number	Price per/M
Total list	32,000	70.00
Hotline (monthly)	10,000	+5.00

Selections: state, SCF, 3.00/M extra; ZIP Code, 6.00/M extra; keying, 2.00/M extra.
Minimum order 5,000.

5. COMMISSION, CREDIT POLICY
20% commission to recognized brokers.

6. METHOD OF ADDRESSING
4-up Cheshire labels. Pressure sensitive labels, 7.00/M extra. Magnetic tape, 25.00 nonreturnable fee.

8. RESTRICTIONS
Sample mailing piece required for approval.

THE WINE ENTHUSIAST

Location ID: 10 DCLS 536   Mid 035588-000
The Wine Enthusiast.

1. PERSONNEL
List Manager
D-J Associates, 77 Danbury Rd., P.O. Box 2048, Ridgefield, CT 06877. Phone 203-431-8777 FAX 203-431-3302.

2. DESCRIPTION
Mail order catalog buyers of and inquirers about wine racks, temperature-controlled vaults, wine games, corkscrews, crystal, wine-related art, etc.; 70% men; average age 45.
Average unit of sale 246.00.

3. LIST SOURCE
95% direct mail.

4. QUANTITY AND RENTAL RATES
Rec'd July 3, 1991.

	Total Number	Price per/M
Buyers (last 24 months)	185,000	*95.00
Last 6 months	115,000	+10.00
Last 12 months	125,000	+5.00
Paid catalog requests (6 months)	394,000	55.00

(*) Fundraisers/publishers, 65.00/M.
Selections: state, SCF, ZIP Code, sex, 5.00/M extra; keying, 2.50/M extra; buyers 50.00+, 20.00/M extra; 75.00+, 25.00/M extra; 100.00+, 35.00/M extra.
Minimum order 5,000.

5. COMMISSION, CREDIT POLICY
20% commission.

6. METHOD OF ADDRESSING
4-up Cheshire labels. Pressure sensitive labels, 7.00/M extra. Magnetic tape (9T 1600 BPI), 25.00 fee.

8. RESTRICTIONS
Sample mailing piece required for approval. Signed list rental agreement.

11. MAINTENANCE
Updated monthly.

(D-C)

WINE TIMES

Location ID: 10 DCLS 536   Mid 050662-000
The Wine Enthusiast.

1. PERSONNEL
List Manager
D-J Associates, 77 Danbury Rd., P.O. Box 2048, Ridgefield, CT 06877. Phone 203-431-8777. FAX 203-431-3302.

2. DESCRIPTION
Subscribers to a magazine on wine enjoyment and wine education; 80% men.
Average unit of sale 36.00.

3. LIST SOURCE
50% direct mail; 50% bind-ins.

4. QUANTITY AND RENTAL RATES
Rec'd July 2, 1991.

	Total Number	Price per/M
Total list	58,000	75.00

Selections: state, ZIP Code, SCF, sex, 5.00/M extra; keying, 2.50/M extra.
Minimum order 5,000.

6. METHOD OF ADDRESSING
4-up Cheshire labels. Pressure sensitive labels, 7.00/M extra. Magnetic tape (9T 1600 BPI), 25.00 fee.

8. RESTRICTIONS
Sample mailing piece required for approval.

(D-C)

WOLFERMAN'S

Location ID: 10 DCLS 536   Mid 024912-000
Wolferman's.

1. PERSONNEL
List Manager
JAMI Marketing Services, Inc., 2 Blue Hill Plaza, Pearl River, NY 10965. Phone 914-620-0700. FAX 914-620-1885.
All recognized brokers.

2. DESCRIPTION
Mail order buyers of English muffins, preserves, teas, gift baskets; 75% women.
Average unit of sale 42.00.
ZIP Coded in numerical sequence 100%.

3. LIST SOURCE
85% direct mail; 15% space ads.

4. QUANTITY AND RENTAL RATES
Rec'd July 24, 1991.

	Total Number	Price per/M
Total list	479,504	*85.00
Last 12 months	270,670	
Last 6 months	96,811	90.00
Hotline (quarterly)	29,948	95.00
Hotline (monthly)	10,000	
Gift buyers (last 12 months)	135,335	85.00
Gift recipients (last 12 months)	194,617	60.00

(*) Fundraisers and publishers, 20% discount.
Selections: keying, 2.00/M extra; state, SCF, 3.50/M extra; sex, 5.00/M extra; ZIP Code, 6.00/M extra; business buyers, multi-buyers, credit card, 10.00/M extra; dollar: 25.00+, 10.00/M extra; 50.00+, 20.00/M extra; dollar cumulative: 50.00+, 10.00/M extra; 100.00+, 15.00/M extra; 250.00+, 20.00/M extra.
Minimum order 5,000.

5. COMMISSION, CREDIT POLICY
20% commission to all recognized brokers. Orders cancelled after mail date require payment in full.

6. METHOD OF ADDRESSING
4-up Cheshire labels. Pressure sensitive labels, 7.00/M extra. Magnetic tape (9T 1600), 25.00 nonreturnable fee.

THE WOODEN SPOON

Location ID: 10 DCLS 536   Mid 034094-000
The Wooden Spoon, Inc.

1. PERSONNEL
List Manager
D-J Associates, 77 Danbury Rd., P.O. Box 2048, Ridgefield, CT 06877. Phone 203-431-8777. QWIP 203-431-3302.

2. DESCRIPTION
Mail order buyers of specialty cookware and gourmet gadgets; mostly women.
Average unit of sale 45.00.
ZIP Coded in numerical sequence 100%.
List is computerized.

3. LIST SOURCE
Direct mail.

4. QUANTITY AND RENTAL RATES
Rec'd July 22, 1991.

	Total Number	Price per/M
(13-24 months)	32,516	*85.00
12 months	51,186	+5.00
6 months	40,417	+10.00
3 month	19,298	+15.00

(*) Publishers/fundraisers, 65.00/M.
Selections: state, ZIP Code, SCF, 5.00/M extra; key coding, 1.50/M extra; dollar amount: 20.00+, 5.00/M extra; 30.00+, 10.00/M extra; 40.00+, 15.00/M extra; 50.00+, 20.00/M extra.
Minimum order 5,000.

5. COMMISSION, CREDIT POLICY
20% commission to recognized brokers.

6. METHOD OF ADDRESSING
Pressure sensitive labels, 7.50/M extra. Magnetic tape, 25.00 fee.

8. DELIVERY SCHEDULE
Five Days.

8. RESTRICTIONS
Sample mailing piece required for approval.

11. MAINTENANCE
Updated quarterly.

(D-C2)

538 Ethnic

IRA
Ethnic Groups
Since 1971
CALL 800-548-9959
FAX 214-771-3244

Affiliated Active Jews

Location ID: 10 DCLS 538   Mid 031905-001
Member: D.M.A.
A.B. Data Ltd.
8050 N. Port Washington Rd., Milwaukee, WI 53217.Phone 414-352-4404, Toll free, 800-558-6908. FAX 414-352-3994.
NOTE: For basic information on the following numbered listing segments 1, 5, 6, 7, 8, **see A.B. Data, Ltd. listing under classification No. 552.**

2. DESCRIPTION
Members of and donors to Jewish conservative, orthodox and reform congregations and women's organizations.
ZIP Coded in numerical sequence 100%.
List is computerized.

3. LIST SOURCE
Local organizational rosters.

4. QUANTITY AND RENTAL RATES
Rec'd July 20, 1991.

	Total Number	Price per/M
Total list	393,367	40.00
Women	193,944	45.00
Community	127,517	+7.50
Women's groups	19,074	
Reform	40,008	
Orthodox	70,413	
Conservative	134,640	

Selections: state, ZIP Code, SCF, city, keying, 5.00/M extra; affiliation, 7.50/M extra; age, income, 10.00/M extra. Phones 15.00 extra.

11. MAINTENANCE
Updated quarterly.

AMERICAN HISPANICS/PERFORMANCEDATA SYSTEM
TRW

Location ID: 10 DCLS 538   Mid 037963-000
TRW Marketing Services.
P.O. Box 851918, Richardson, TX 75085.Phone 214-699-1271, Toll free, 800-527-3933. Fax: 214-437-1611.

1. PERSONNEL
Nat'l List Sales—Raelyn Wade.
Broker and/or Authorized Agent
All recognized brokers.

2. DESCRIPTION
Hispanic Americans by name at home address.
Selections available: Hispanic surname, gender, dwelling type, head-of-household.

3. LIST SOURCE
Public records.

4. QUANTITY AND RENTAL RATES
Rec'd July 31, 1991.

	Total Number	Price per/M
Total list	11,026,029	*20.00
Head of household	5,853,061	
Women head of household	1,268,085	+2.50
Total women	4,595,156	
Total men	5,379,118	
Income, 75,000.00+	1,128,675	+3.50
50,000.00+	4,729,218	
35,000.00+	8,004,785	
15,000.00+	10,922,320	

(*) Quantity discounts per/M.
Selections: exact age, 13/M; phone number, 50.00/M extra; families w/children by age range and/or gender, 7.50/M extra; presence of children, 6.50/M extra; radius select, 5.00/M extra; marned, length of residence, inferred age ranges, sex, household status, 2.50/M extra; SMACS data (census), carrier route sort, prioritizing, state, ZIP code, SCF, county, census/BG/ED, SMMA, SMSA, Arbitron, Nielsen, 2.00/M extra; PRIZM, 10.00/M extra; Acorn, 22.00/M extra; height, weight, corrective lenses, 20.00/M extra; resequence/breaks, keying month/year of birth, key coding, 1.00/M extra; splits, .50/M extra. ZIP tapes, 25.00 flat fee.
Minimum order 250.00 (includes all select charges).

5. COMMISSION, CREDIT POLICY
20% commission available to all qualified brokers on base price only. Orders cancelled within ten days of mailing date charged full price orders; already processed and cancelled before ten days of mailing date subject to 5.00/M running charge and stock.

6. METHOD OF ADDRESSING
4-up Cheshire labels. Pressure sensitive labels (under 50,000), 6.00/M extra; (over 50,000) 5.00/M extra, 3 x 5 cards 15.00/M extra. Magnetic tape (9T 1600/6250 BPI), IBM compatible, 15.00 nonrefundable fee, running charge 5.00/M extra.

7. DELIVERY SCHEDULE
Five working days.

Direct Mail - Consumer Lists

FIGURE 17.5 Page from *Standard Rate and Data Service's Direct-Mail List Rates and Data*
Source: Standard Rate and Data Services.

Percentage Allocation of Costs for an Average Catalog Direct-Mail Piece

Cost Category	Percent of Total Cost
Creative	
Includes preliminary roughs, copywriting, and comprehensive layouts	3.7%
Art and Preparation	
Mechanical art, typography, repros, photography, model fees, color separations, proofs, and stripped-in print films	9.0
Printing and Binding	
1,750,000 catalogs, black plate changes, orderform key changes	39.6
Computer Processing	
Reformatting, data conversion, merge/ purge, code and run labels, miscellaneous reports and analyses	2.7
Lettershop Production	
1,750,000 catalogs	2.8
Allocated Fees	
Consultants' development time; oversight and review; fulfillment and systems time; travel, phone, etc. expenses	6.6
Postage	
First-class rate for 30,000; third-class bulk rate for 1,720,000	21.3
Mailing Lists	14.3
Grand Total	**100.0%**

Source: *Marketing & Media Decisions,* August 1989, 105.

one particular direct-marketing firm estimates relative cost allocations. Note that production costs here are subdivided into creative, art and preparation, printing and binding, computer processing, lettershop production, and allocated fees, and these costs are 64.4 percent of the total. Thus:

Production	64.4%
Delivery (Postage)	21.3
Mailing List	14.3
	100.0%

Preparing Direct Mail

Several major stages are involved in preparing a direct-mail package:[4]

1. Decide on the type of direct mail, and develop the basic format.

2. Write copy and select artwork.

3. Decide on printing methods, select paper, and set up schedules with the printer.

4. Develop or secure mailing lists.

5. Work out mailing costs and schedules.

6. Address and mail.

Many of the stages involve technical knowledge of paper finishes and weights, printing processes, postal rates and requirements, computer processing, and the like, and the advertiser must have this knowledge or secure it from a specialist. Given these complexities, many advertisers today use outside direct-mail specialists to handle all or most of their direct-mail program. Several advertising agencies concentrate solely on direct mail and direct marketing. Some of the larger, full-service advertising agencies recently have established departments, or separate companies, to handle this type of advertising.

MEDIA SPOTLIGHT

17.1

Case History of Creative Test for Allstate Motor Club's Direct-Mail Packages

The Allstate Motor Club Spring Creative Test, soliciting the standard membership package, consisted of three cells: two new creative packages and the control package.

The objective for the test was threefold:

1. Explore various new creative approaches through copy and design.
2. Outperform the control package by cost per sale and/or overall response rate.
3. Create awareness that the Allstate Motor Club's Emergency Road Service is superior in comparison to other motor clubs.

The following research was taken into consideration:

- The current membership profile consisted of mostly males and married. Almost half were employed, while a significant number were retired. Average age was fifty-five.

- Renewal decisions were based on satisfaction with service, security, and towing.

- The five product features considered most important were: 800 number for emergency road service, towing costs, changing of flat tires, dead battery assistance, and cost of dues including spouse.

- A competitive analysis revealed several key benefits that provided definite product differentiation for Allstate Motor Club, including: one countrywide 800 number, choice of dispatch or reimbursement, ability for member to be towed anywhere without mileage restrictions, towing

of recreational vehicles/motor homes/camping trailers/pickups at no additional cost. Both member and spouse are protected no matter what car they are driving. Allstate Motor Club is a national club, so it does not have state or regional restrictions.

- A review conducted of past Allstate Motor Club tests showed that certain key elements were apparent in all packages, those being: red, white, and blue colors; guarantee; competitive chart "laundry list" of benefits; testimonials; and a plastic temporary membership card.

Based on this research, two copy platforms were developed. In both cases, the copy approach heavily emphasized the emergency road service benefit, but each package had a copy platform that was totally distinct.

The first creative package, titled "Customer Service," placed a greater emphasis on recognizing the customer. Testimonials, reflecting good service, were used throughout the package. It also contained a push toward "satisfaction guaranteed." This package was very simple in design and utilized the red, white, and blue colors traditional to Allstate Motor Club. The outer envelope contained a reader involvement device. A special flap was designed to look like a car door. The prospect was asked to open the flap—or door—to get into the package.

The second creative package titled "Facts," combined statistics and customer service. The reasoning behind testing a facts approach came from the knowledge that Allstate Motor Club and Allstate Accidental Death & Dismemberment (AD&D) insurance buyers were similar in demographic profiles. Therefore, the Motor Club creative package utilized a copy approach similar to the long-standing control package for AD&D, which was also called the "Facts" kit. This package was very busy, with lots of information about Allstate Motor Club. The eye-catching brown kraft envelope demanded attention in the mailbox because of the check and plastic card showing through the window. Each of seven checks inside the package were made out to be used for one of the Motor Club benefits, and the dollar amounts reflected the Motor Club membership limit for the benefit. The reverse side of the checks is where the facts came into play. A small factual paragraph was written on the reverse side, along with a corresponding testimonial adding credence to the fact. This package also utilized the red, white, and blue color scheme and played up the guarantee.

All of the packages (the red, white, and blue "Control," "Customer Service" and "Facts" kits) were soliciting new memberships in the standard benefit plan. One additional new creative package was developed to solicit new memberships in the deluxe/higher-limit benefit plan and was called, quite appropriately, the "Deluxe" kit. The deluxe plan on its own had previously only been successfully marketed as an upgrade to existing standard coverage; it had never been successful in solo efforts. This "Deluxe" package was designed to reverse this trend.

A variety of Sears and Allstate policyholder lists were also part of the test, and the final test grid is shown in figure 1. The results of each cell (indexed) are shown in table 1.

Continued on page 370

PACKAGE	SEARS LIST	ALLSTATE POLICYHOLDER LIST
Facts	X	X (Nth Name Select)
		X (55+ Age Group Select)
Customer Service	X	X
Deluxe		X (Nth Name Select)
		X (Female Group Select)
Control	X	X

FIGURE 1 Final test grid
Courtesy of Allstate Life Insurance Company.

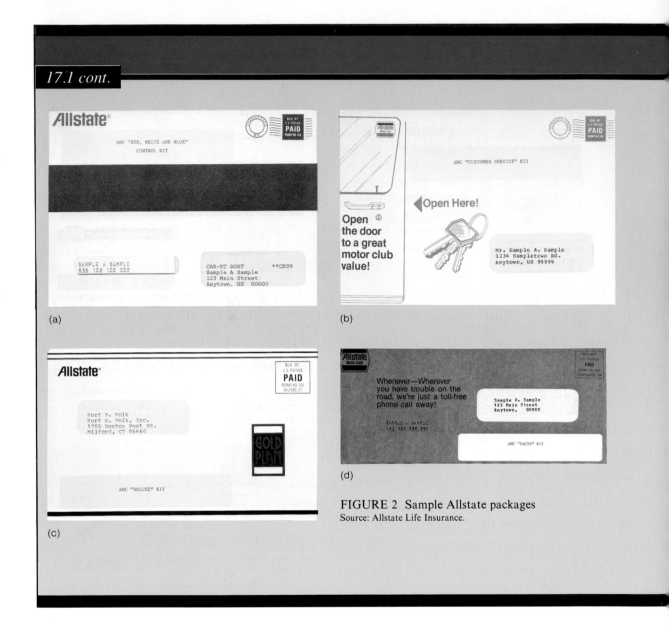

FIGURE 2 Sample Allstate packages
Source: Allstate Life Insurance.

(e)

After segmentation, the rollout (distribution) was comprised of a combination of the "Facts" and "Control" packages to both Sears and Allstate lists. The overall projected rollout response rate was 79.4 percent higher than the overall untargeted test response, with some rollout segments as high as 114.1 percent over the test response. Also, it should be noted that this was the first time in nearly five years that something other than the red, white, and blue "Control" was rolled out.

All in all, this was a very successful test that produced one of the largest Allstate Motor Club rollouts of all time. Figure 2 shows some of the packages discussed.

Courtesy of Allstate Insurance Company.

TABLE 1

Results of Each Cell

Package/List	Indexed Response Rate
Overall Test Response	100.0
Facts (Nth Name–Sears)	83.5
Facts (Nth Name—Allstate)	147.8
Facts (55+ Group—Allstate)	192.7
Customer Service (Sears)	62.1
Customer Service (Allstate)	89.9
Deluxe (Nth Name—Allstate)	42.8
Deluxe (Female Group—Allstate)	38.5
Control (Sears)	98.5
Control (Allstate)	143.5

Outdoor

Some historians consider **outdoor advertising** the oldest form of advertising, dating back over four thousand years to engravings on Egyptian temples. Egyptian merchants used stone tablets, called "stelae," in which they cut sales messages and placed them along public roads hundreds of years before Moses. Centuries later, in Rome and Pompeii, decorated walls known as "albums" had painted advertising on them. With the invention of the printing press in the fifteenth century, and lithography three hundred years later, came the earliest outdoor posters, much like those used today. By the mid-1800s, outdoor posters were being produced by famous artists, such as Manet and Toulouse-Lautrec, who were commissioned by advertisers in the United States.[5]

Today, outdoor-advertising expenditures total over $1 billion, with 59 percent of that placed by national advertisers and 41 percent by local firms. In some foreign countries, where the number of media is limited or where the rate of literacy is low, outdoor advertising is among the most important of all media types.

In recent years, the growth of outdoor has been somewhat limited as a result of legislation and societal attitudes. The Highway Beautification Act of 1965 limited the placement of outdoor advertising to within 660 feet of interstate and major federal highways. The effect of this act has only recently begun to have an impact, primarily because Congress did not adequately provide funds for the removal of signs. Perhaps even more restrictive for growth have been local laws and ordinances that place a variety of limits on the use of outdoor. More than five hundred cities have enacted billboard-control regulations. Some cities, for example, specify the number of postings permitted within a city; other localities restrict the distance required between structures; and yet other locales prohibit construction of any new billboards. Most sessions of Congress, especially recently, have seen new legislation introduced to control what is typically called "visual pollution." A current bill under consideration—the Surface Transportation Assistance Act of 1991—would ban new outdoor advertising along the 150,000-mile National Highway System and nearly 300,000 miles of rural secondary highways.[6]

Various environmental groups have attacked outdoor advertising because of visual pollution, while some pressure groups have focused on eliminating advertising for certain products, such as tobacco and alcohol, since the outdoor advertisements for these products are readily seen by minors. Tobacco and alcohol products alone recently accounted for 35 percent of overall outdoor spending, making them likely targets. In an attempt to prevent further detrimental legislation, the Outdoor Advertising Association of America (OAAA), an industry trade association, recently issued new guidelines on tobacco and liquor bill-board placement. OAAA recommends that its members voluntarily limit "the number of billboards in a market that may carry messages about products that cannot be sold to minors."[7] In addition to restricting the number of billboards, the guidelines also recommend a ban on such signs within 500 feet of schools, hospitals, and places of worship.

Types of Outdoor Advertising

In a general sense, anything that can be seen by people who are out-of-home could be considered outdoor advertising. As such, outdoor advertising could include a sign designating a retailer's store, an herbicide advertisement painted on the side of a barn, or a blimp flying over a used-car lot. Here, however, we discuss only the three standard types of outdoor advertising: (1) posters, (2) painted bulletins, and (3) electric spectaculars.

Posters

Posters are the oldest type of standard outdoor advertising and consist of an advertising message printed on sheets that are then pasted onto a structure. For posters (also referred to as **billboards** or **poster panels**) to be used by a wide variety of advertisers, national as well as local, their size must be standardized.

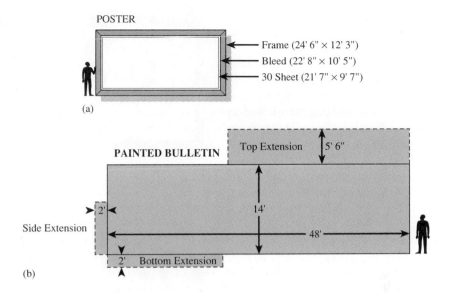

FIGURE 17.6 Standard Sizes of (a) Thirty-Sheet and Bleed Posters and (b) a Painted Bulletin.

The standard poster panel *structure* is 12 feet, 3 inches by 24 feet, 6 inches, which includes the frame or molding (300 square feet total). The paper panels that are pasted onto the structure are of two standard sizes: thirty-sheet and bleed (where the printed matter goes right up to the structure's molding). The dimensions of these sizes are shown in figure 17.6a. The term thirty-sheet does not mean that the poster is made up of thirty sheets of paper (although an earlier type, called a twenty-four-sheet poster, was, in fact, printed on twenty-four different sheets of paper). Rather, because of the larger size of today's printing presses, a thirty-sheet or bleed poster usually is printed in eight to twelve sections. Posters are lithographed or silk-screened by a printer and shipped to the outdoor company in a particular market. They are then prepasted and applied in sections to the structure at the location.

In addition to thirty-sheet and bleed posters are eight-sheet posters, or "junior panels." These have a structure that is 6 feet high by 12 feet wide (72 square feet, including the molding). The pasted panels, usually two or three sheets of paper, are 5 feet by 11 feet. Junior poster panels typically are located on secondary arteries, urban locations, and areas of high visibility.

Painted Bulletins

Painted bulletins are more custom-made than posters. They are either painted by hand in an outdoor company's studio and then put up in sections on location, or painted directly at the location. The standard size of painted bulletins is 14 feet by 48 feet (672 square feet), and they are thus noticeably larger than a thirty-sheet or bleed poster. Although the basic structure on which a bulletin is mounted is 14 feet by 48 feet, many bulletins extend over the top, bottom, and sides of the structure, adding even more visual impact. Figure 17.6b shows these dimensions, with typical extensions.

Painted bulletins typically are much more expensive per unit than posters. Since producing enough bulletins to cover a market entirely could be cost prohibitive, outdoor companies often offer an advertiser a rotary bulletin, which means that the bulletin is moved every sixty or ninety days to a different location to assure market coverage. However, an advertiser also can buy a permanent bulletin, which remains stationary.

Currently, producers of painted bulletins are experimenting with different techniques. For example, one company has developed a computer that paints the bulletin, thus eliminating the need of an artist to hand paint each unit. Fiber optics are being used to create outdoor displays with dramatic impact at night; this technique can create virtually any color, change colors in sequence, and provide an illusion of motion. Some advertisers have experimented with mounting reflectorized disks or sheets on painted bulletins to make the copy sparkle or shimmer, so as to create an illusion of motion and texture.

Figure 17.7 shows poster panels and painted bulletins.

(a)

Spectaculars

Although highly dramatic, **spectaculars** are only a small part of total expenditures in outdoor advertising. An electric spectacular is an outdoor display, of bulletin size or larger, in which the advertising copy is presented in a spectacular fashion through the use of specialized electrical and mechanical devices. These large, illuminated, often-animated signs usually are located in and around big cities. In New York City, for example, spectaculars dot Broadway's "Great White Way." Spectaculars are custom-made to fit high-traffic locations, usually are extremely expensive to produce and maintain, and are bought on a long-term contract, usually for at least several years.

(b)

Characteristics of Outdoor

In deciding whether to use outdoor advertising in a media mix, media planners and buyers consider some of the following basic attributes of the medium:

FIGURE 17.7 (a) Posters and (b) Painted Bulletins. Notice how the illustrative matter on the painted bulletin extends over the structure of the frame.
Source: (a) State Farm Insurance Companies. (b) Client: The Des Moines Register, Des Moines, IA. Agency: Muller & Company, Kansas City, MO. Reprinted by permission.

Mass Coverage

Outdoor advertising is a mass-oriented medium in that it can provide mass coverage of the population in a market. On average, a 100-gross-rating-point (GRP) showing reaches around 88 percent of an area's adults in a thirty-day period. Outdoor advertising not only delivers a large percentage of the population in general, but likewise does so for most demographic segments. For example, low-income people are reached as readily as upper-income ones, a variety of educational levels are delivered, as are people with diverse occupations. Outdoor can deliver these audiences because of the highly mobile nature of the U.S. population and the fact that posters are available in about seven thousand cities and towns.

Although primarily used for mass coverage, outdoor advertising can provide certain types of audience selectivity. For example, many advertisers use the medium to target certain groups, such as Hispanics or African-Americans. If such individuals are located predominantly in a certain area of a city, outdoor postings can be limited to these areas. Retail establishments, such as restaurants, motels, and food stores, likewise can focus their outdoor advertising on areas where their prospects travel.

Table 17.2 shows outdoor advertising expenditures by product categories. Tobacco products alone account for $293 million of outdoor spending.

Impact

As discussed earlier, outdoor advertisements can be large and dramatic: An oversized painted bulletin may occupy as much as 1,000 square feet of space. With colors, lights, and special materials, an outdoor advertisement can do an excellent job of capturing a passerby's attention and conveying a quick image of brand identification. Since most people pass the same locations often over a period of time, outdoor also can provide an advertiser with high repetition of message content. The average frequency for 100 GRPs is over twenty-eight times in a thirty-day period; thus, the average person in a

TABLE 17.2

Top-Ten Categories of Outdoor Advertising Expenditures

Category	1990 Ad Dollars (in millions)
Tobacco	$292.7
Retail Stores and Products	195.1
Business Services	162.6
Entertainment	130.1
Automotive	97.6
Beer, Wine, & Liquor	86.7
Travel	75.9
Miscellaneous	43.4

Source: Computed from *Mediaweek*, 8 July 1991, 27.

market is potentially exposed to the message 28.5 times each month.

On the other hand, outdoor messages can be quite fleeting. Typically, a person has only a few seconds to note and comprehend the intended communication. Thus, outdoor postings are not very successful at communicating a *lot* of information. Consumers have no chance to browse leisurely, as they do with newspapers, magazines, or direct-mail pieces, or to see the product demonstrated, as they do on television. Designers of outdoor advertisements usually understand this characteristic and handle it by keeping the message short and using large, dramatic illustrations. If a more in-depth sales message is needed for a product, an alternative medium should be considered.

Flexibility

Outdoor advertising can be purchased in almost every community, providing media planners with extensive geographic flexibility. Also, as indicated earlier, certain groups can be targeted in a certain part of a city or a local firm can limit its locations to that part of the city where it can reach its prime prospects, thereby resulting in flexibility in the type of audience delivered. Where the cost of using painted bulletins is especially high, a rotary plan serves to reduce overall costs and still provide wide reach.

By using one or more types of outdoor advertising, an advertiser has considerable flexibility in terms of cost, creative technique, and impact achieved. Posters provide an opportunity to deliver a standard message a large number of times, while painted bulletins and spectaculars permit a more dramatic form of communication.

Cost Efficiency

In terms of absolute costs, outdoor advertising is a high-cost medium, especially for a national advertiser who wants to reach a wide market. For example, to buy poster panels, at the 100-GRP level, in the top one hundred markets costs around $4 million *per month*; 50 GRPs, which deliver a reach of around 84 percent and a frequency of fifteen per month, would still cost over $2 million per month for these one hundred markets. A 50-GRP buy of thirty-sheet posters in Los Angeles costs around $155,000 per month. Of course, the smaller the market, the less the cost: Knoxville, Tennessee, ranked as the eighty-first U.S. market, would cost about $9,000 per month, and Columbia, South Carolina (ranked one-hundredth), costs around $5,500 per month. To these space costs, the advertiser must add the cost to produce the posters; this usually is around 15 to 20 percent of the space costs. A painted bulletin delivering 5 GRPs daily costs around $39,000 in Los Angeles, $1,685 in Knoxville, and $1,400 in Columbia.

Although high in absolute costs, outdoor nevertheless can be fairly low in relative cost—that is, the cost-per-thousand. A typical CPM for a poster-panel buy is between 60 and 90 cents; average CPMs for bulletins are between $1 and $2. Of course, any measure of relative cost efficiency must be weighed against the type of impact that a medium provides. When outdoor advertising fits a particular communication need, and the desire is to deliver mass coverage of the targeted market, the medium can indeed be efficient.

Buying Outdoor

As mentioned in chapter 14, the basic insertion unit for outdoor posters is the gross rating point (GRP). GRPs are the daily effective circulation generated by poster panels divided by the market population (and multiplied by 100 to put it in percent); the term is used interchangeably with **showing,** which was used in earlier years by the outdoor industry. **Daily effective circulation** is the audience that has an opportunity to see an advertising structure in a twenty-four-hour period. Thus, the formula to compute a GRP showing is:

$$\text{GRPs (Showing)} = \frac{\text{Daily Effective Circulation}}{\text{Market Population}} \times 100$$

Posters generally are bought in multiples of 25 GRPs—100, 75, 50, and 25. Thus, a 100-GRP buy delivers as many daily exposures in a market as the population in that market. In a city of a million population, a 100-GRP buy delivers one million exposures each day. A 50-GRP showing delivers exposure opportunities equal to 50 percent of a city's population.

This does *not* mean that 100 GRPs reaches *every person* in a city. Exposures involve *duplication*—that is, the same people who are exposed more than once in a day. If a person passes a poster panel twice in a day, that is considered **two** exposure opportunities. As mentioned earlier, 100 GRPs will reach, on average, about 88 percent of all adults in a market, and this level of delivery requires a posting of thirty days.

To determine the daily effective circulation, traffic studies must be made to measure delivery at any given location. Further, studies are made to determine how many different locations throughout a city are needed to provide a given level of delivery, such as 100 GRPs. The number of poster locations required for a certain delivery varies, depending on the city's population, its physical size, the extent of its roads, and the traffic patterns throughout the city.

MEDIA SPOTLIGHT

17.2

When United Dairy Industry Association® Wanted Real Visibility . . . They Went Outdoor

Outdoor Advertising: It's a natural environment for success. Here's how Outdoor Network, USA proved it for the Dairy Industry:

Source: Dairy Industry/Gannett Outdoor Group.

BACKGROUND/OBJECTIVE

- The United Dairy Industry Association (UDIA) has taken an active role in promoting the nutritional benefits of dairy products.
- The "Real Seal" logo is the symbol used to instantly identify calcium-rich dairy products for consumers.
- Outdoor advertising seemed like an ideal medium for the "Real Seal" message—"Real dairy products carry this seal."
- Outdoor was tested to see how a poster might enhance UDIA media plans.

STRATEGY

- Test markets were established in Rochester, New York, and Scranton, Pennsylvania, between 15 May and 15 September 1988.
- "Real Seal" outdoor advertising ran at a weight level of 25 GRPs; during the same period, fluid milk advertising was running on television and radio at similar levels in both markets.

TEST METHODOLOGY

- The research study consisted of two waves (pre- and post-outdoor campaign) of personal, mall-intercept interviews in both test markets.
- Respondents were adults, 18–54, who were residents of each test market metropolitan area, involved with at least half of household's grocery shopping.
- At least two hundred respondents per wave, per market, were interviewed.

RESULTS

- By the end of second-wave testing, the "Real Seal" outdoor poster campaign had helped increase awareness and recognition of dairy products by up to 10 percent.
- The action standard set by UDIA—a statistically significant increase at the 90 percent confidence level—was surpassed in several instances:

In Rochester:

Aided recall of advertising for dairy products .... +10%

Unaided recall of "Real Seal" .... +6%

In Scranton:

Unaided recall of advertising for dairy products .... +5%

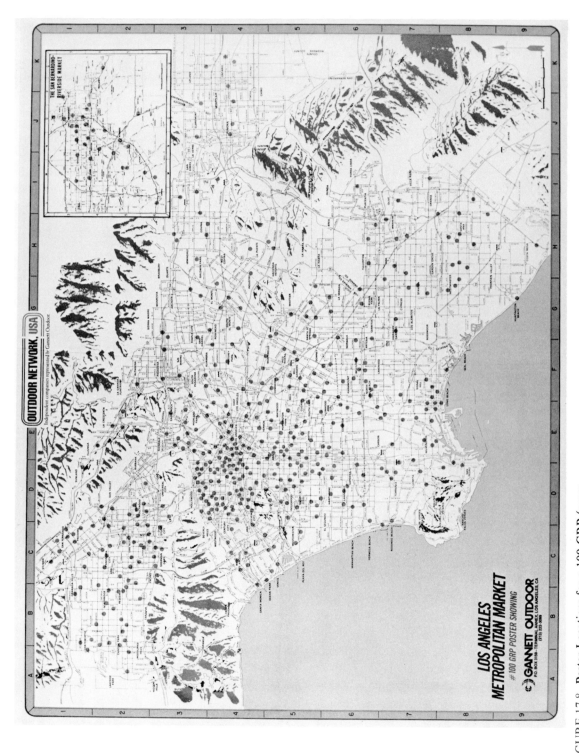

FIGURE 17.8 Poster Locations for a 100-GRP (gross-rating-point) Showing in Los Angeles

Source: Gannett Outdoor Group.

TABLE 17.3

Number of Regular and Illuminated Panels Needed for 100 GRPs for Several Markets

Rank (by Pop.)	Market	Regular Panels	Illuminated Panels
1	Los Angeles, Calif.	60	420
19	Phoenix, Ariz.	44	44
26	Denver, Colo.	16	62
37	San Antonio, Tex.	16	52
49	Memphis, Tenn.	27	53
55	Birmingham, Ala.	16	52
65	Tulsa, Okla.	21	24
77	Omaha, Nebr.	4	42
87	Baton Rouge, La.	20	20
97	Mobile, Ala.	21	21
115	Des Moines, Iowa	16	32
145	Macon, Ga.	20	10
170	Huntsville, Ala.	20	28
189	Gainesville, Fla.	5	5
212	Cedar Rapids, Iowa	9	14
257	Wichita Falls, Tex.	7	7
296	Bloomington, Ind.	8	8
315	Lawrence, Kans.	4	5

(Figure 17.8 shows a map of Los Angeles, with dots representing poster locations of a 100-GRP poster showing from the Gannett Outdoor Company.) Further, because of nighttime driving patterns, some poster panels require illumination, and some do not (called "regular" or "nonilluminated"). Table 17.3 lists the number of regular and illuminated panels needed for 100 GRPs for several markets. Note that a market's rank in terms of total population does not relate directly to the number of panels needed for a 100-GRP delivery.

The standard time period for the purchase of outdoor posters is thirty days. Typically, discounts are given based on the total volume purchased, as well as for advertising on a continuous basis. Thus, the monthly cost for a three-month showing is less

per month than if only a one-month showing is purchased. Painted bulletins usually are bought for at least a twelve-month period, and two- and three-year contracts are fairly common. Likewise, because of the expense of their production and erection, spectaculars are bought for long periods of time.

Information about outdoor costs for markets throughout the United States is available in the *Buyers Guide to Outdoor Advertising.* A sample page from this source is shown in figure 17.9. Note that the number of illuminated and regular (nonilluminated) posters required for each GRP showing is given, as well as the monthly costs.

If the poster buyers for a national advertiser want to get an estimate of total costs before looking up each market's rate in *Buyers Guide,* they can use a cost estimator like the one shown in table 17.4. The table shows that 100 GRPs in the top-fifty markets of the United States costs $3,263,042 per month.

Outdoor advertising is bought on a market-by-market basis from an outdoor company (called a "plant operator") within a city; some locales have more than one company operating in the area. A number of companies, however, operate in several markets, thus permitting multiple-city buys from the same source. The Gannett Outdoor Group and the Patrick Media Group are examples. Gannett also operates the "Gannett Outdoor Network, USA," which is a network affiliation of around forty-four different companies, providing an advertiser the opportunity to buy more than 370 markets across the United States with a single contract. This type of network greatly simplifies the buying of outdoor.

Audience Measurement

Due to the nature of the medium, audience measurement in the outdoor industry is somewhat unique. The basic method involves a **traffic count**— counting the number of pedestrians and vehicles, mostly automobiles, that pass outdoor locations during a certain time period. A **load factor** of 1.75 persons per vehicle is usually applied to a vehicle to estimate the number of persons in the audience.

Chapter 17

PLANT NO.	MARKET NO.	MARKET NAME	COUNTY NAME	POP.	EFF. DATE	GRP/ SHOW	POSTERS NON ILL.	POSTERS ILL.	COST PER MONTH	DIS.
3080.0 DOWDY	12520	TALLADEGA CO MARKET BIR	TALLADEGA	72.8	04/01/88	100	22		6050.00	23
						75	18		4950.00	23
						50	12		3300.00	23
		-Sub Markets (Sold Separately) CHILDERSBURG, AL LINCOLN, AL MUNFORD, AL SYLACAUGA-MIGNON MARKET, AL TALLADEGA, AL								
4435.0 LAMCOR	12550	TALLASSEE MOT	ELMORE-TALLAPOOSA	4.8	09/01/88	100	2		525.00	68
						50	1		275.00	68
7160.0 TALTON	12800	THOMASVILLE MOB SEE MARKET NO. 01-02980**	CLARKE	5.8	09/01/88	100	3		750.00	32
						50	2		500.00	32
						25	1		250.00	32
3110.0 DURDEN	12990	TROY MOT	PIKE	14.8	09/01/87	100	2	2	970.00	
						50	2	1	745.00	
						25		1	260.00	
6015.0 ATRIC	13099	TUSCALOOSA, AL TUS SEE MARKET NO. 01-13100**	TUSCALOOSA	75.6	03/01/89	100	3	7	3024.00	57
						75	3	5	2384.00	57
						50	2	4	1818.00	57
						25	1	2	919.00	57
6015.0 PATRIC	13100	TUSCALOOSA METRO MARKET TUS	TUSCALOOSA-BIBB-FAYETTE GREENE-HALE-LAMAR-MARION PICKINS	260.3	01/01/88	100	24	8	8696.00	57
						75	18	6	6599.00	57
						50	12	4	4385.00	57
						25	6	2	2214.00	57
		-Sub Markets (Sold Separately) ALICEVILLE, AL CENTREVILLE, AL EUTAW, AL FAYETTE, AL MOUNDVILLE, AL REFORM, AL SULLIGENT, AL TUSCALOOSA, AL WINFIELD, AL								
4435.0 LAMCOR	13190	TUSKEGEE MOT	MACON	12.2	09/01/88	100	3		775.00	68
						50	2		530.00	68
						25	1		275.00	68
3110.0 DURDEN	13250	UNION SPRINGS MOT	BULLOCK	5.0	09/01/87	100	3		660.00	
						50	2		455.00	
						25	1		240.00	
7160.0 TALTON	13300	UNIONTOWN MOT	PERRY	2.0	09/01/88	100	2		500.00	32
						50	1		250.00	32
7160.0 TALTON	13570	WAGARVILLE MOB	WASHINGTON	.3	09/01/88	100	1		250.00	32
4435.0 LAMCOR	13650	WEDOWEE ATL	RANDOLPH	1.7	09/01/88	100	1		255.00	68
3080.0 DOWDY	13690	WESTOVER BIR SEE MARKET NO. 01-01527** SEE MARKET NO. 01-12120**	SHELBY	3.0	09/01/88	100	1		275.00	23
4435.0 LAMCOR	13700	WEST POINT, GA.-LANETT, ALA. MKT. COG	TROUP, GA-CHAMBERS-HARRIS GA	25.2	09/01/88	100	4		1030.00	68
						75	3		780.00	68
						50	2		530.00	68
						25	1		275.00	68
4435.0 LAMCOR	13900	WETUMPKA MOT SEE MARKET 01-09450**	ELMORE	2.9	09/01/88	100	1		265.00	68
3110.0 DURDEN	13940	WICKSBURG DOT	HOUSTON	.6	09/01/87	100	2		455.00	
						50	1		240.00	
3080.0 DOWDY	13950	WILSONVILLE BIR SEE MARKET NO. 01-01527**	SHELBY	.7	09/01/88	100	1		275.00	23
6015.0 PATRIC	13965	WINFIELD, AL TUS SEE MARKET NO. 01-13100**	MARION	4.0	03/01/89	100	1		259.00	57

ADI CODE SEE NOTE TO BUYER
**FIRST TWO DIGITS INDICATE STATES

GRP GROSS RATING
POINTS EXCEPT *** = SHOWING

FIGURE 17.9 Sample Page from *Buyers Guide to Outdoor Advertising*
Source: Leading National Advertisers/Arbitron.

TABLE 17.4

Outdoor Poster Cost Estimates

Markets	100 GRPs			50 GRPs		
	Number of Regular Panels	Number of Illuminated Panels	Monthly Cost	Number of Regular Panels	Number of Illuminated Panels	Monthly Cost
Top 10	525	2,171	$1,431,585	273	1,133	$768,620
Top 20	772	2,943	1,921,633	395	1,523	1,012,749
Top 30	975	3,977	2,554,730	494	2,054	1,338,109
Top 40	1,182	4,542	2,905,736	596	2,341	1,517,447
Top 50	1,446	5,129	3,263,042	732	2,638	1,704,376
Top 100	2,292	6,527	4,147,191	1,185	3,384	2,172,390

Source: Institute of Outdoor Advertising.

Several organizations measure outdoor audiences. The Traffic Audit Bureau (TAB) is a tripartite organization, with representation from advertisers, agencies, and outdoor companies. As an auditing organization, TAB validates outdoor companies' claims of capacity (number of boards), quality (space position value), and quantity (authenticated number of potential viewers passing each board daily). TAB audits a market at least once every three years and has established the standards by which audience measurement is conducted.

Audience Measurement by Market (AMMO) provides reach and frequency information on a market-by-market basis, including demographic breaks by age, sex, and income, for over 550 markets and uses circulation data obtained from TAB to develop audience figures. AMMO is affiliated with the Institute of Outdoor Advertising (IOA), the marketing, research, and promotion arm of the standardized outdoor industry. Until recently, outdoor measurement was primarily limited to the 210,000 posters in the United States, but the nation's 50,000 painted bulletins now are also included.

National audiences of outdoor advertising are provided on a yearly basis by Simmons Market Research Bureau (SMRB). Not only are reach and frequency figures given by standard showing sizes, but the information is categorized according to a particular product category. For example, advertisers can note the outdoor audience delivery for users of "diet soft drinks" (and, indeed, for several hundreds of other product categories as well).

The Out-of-Home Measurement Bureau (OMB) provides audience measurement of eight-sheet posters and other unique units, such as transit shelters and airport terminal ads. OMB was established in the late 1970s to provide information on out-of-home units that were not being measured by TAB and AMMO. At the time of OMB's formation, TAB was not interested in measuring other than thirty-sheet and bleed poster audiences.

A number of changes have occurred recently in the measurement part of the outdoor industry. For example, TAB and OMB merged in 1990 as the Traffic Audit Bureau for Media Measurement.[8] The new organization measures a broad array of outdoor types and is not limited to regular posters and painted bulletins. Further, the industry currently is working on a new measurement system that will provide more accurate audience information through the development of a more precisely derived load factor.[9]

(a)

(b)

FIGURE 17.10 Interior Transit Advertising
Courtesy of Transportation Displays Incorporated.

Transit

Of all media types discussed so far, **transit** is the smallest in terms of dollars spent—presently, about $225 million annually. Yet, the transit medium is quite pervasive, appearing in and on more than seventy-five thousand vehicles—buses, subways, and commuter trains—in around three hundred urban markets.

Transit advertising began in 1831 when an enterprising conductor in New York attached an advertisement to his streetcar. These first transit advertisements were handbills suspended from streetcar ceilings and fastened to interior walls.[10] Local advertisers were among the first users of transit advertising. As early as 1850, the dry-goods firm of Lord & Taylor used car cards as part of its advertising program.[11] By 1895, transit advertising was available in fifty-four cities and nine thousand vehicles, with annual expenditures estimated at $2 million. By then, national advertisers were noted users of transit. In 1899, the famous "Campbell's Kids" promoted Campbell's Soup through advertisements inside transit vehicles, and Wrigley's introduced its new "spearmint" flavor of chewing gum in a test of transit advertising in Buffalo, New York.[12]

In recent years, transit advertisements have made somewhat of a resurgence, with packaged goods becoming a major category. For example, Colgate-Palmolive used bus advertisements for its Ajax household-cleaner line:

simply because we wanted a high-frequency campaign to get the Ajax name out there . . . [and] . . . because most of our audience works during the day . . . [thus,] . . . running more fifteen-second TV commercials . . . wasn't the answer.[13]

Types of Transit Advertising

As was the case for outdoor, there are a number of types of transit advertising, but we discuss here the three standard types: (1) inside-of-vehicle advertisements, or car cards, (2) outside transit displays, and (3) station posters. (Some of the less standard types of transit are discussed in chapter 18.)

Car Cards

Inside buses and subway cars are racks above the windows that hold a standard advertising **car card,** measuring 11 inches high and either 28, 42, or 56 inches wide. In addition, some interior advertisements measure 22 inches high and 21 inches wide, and these are usually placed on the partition behind the driver's seat and the partitions adjacent to the exit door. Figure 17.10 shows examples of interior ads.

Outside Transit Displays

The ads on the outside of public transportation vehicles, sometimes called traveling displays or posters, are somewhat like an outdoor billboard in that they are seen by pedestrians and people in private vehicles. Like interior transit, **outside transit displays** are available in standard sizes—super king-size, king-size, queen-size, headlight, taillight, hightail, and rear displays. These are shown in figure 17.11.

The *super king-size* display, appearing on the street-side of the bus, is the largest type available and measures 30 inches high by 240 inches (20 feet) wide. The *king-size* poster appears on both the curb- and street-sides of the bus and is 30 inches high by 144 inches wide. *Queen-size* displays usually appear on the curb-side of the bus and are 30 inches high by 108 inches wide. Appearing on the front and rear of buses are *headlight* displays (21 inches by 44 inches), *taillight displays* (21 inches by 72 inches), *hightail* displays (15 1/2 inches by 63 inches), and *rear* displays (14 inches by 60 inches, with a bottom poster of 17 1/2 inches by 50 inches).

Station Posters

Station posters are primarily available in the eleven U.S. markets that have commuter trains and/or rapid-transit systems, such as subways. The posters are located on subway and train platforms, as well as in the track areas of major rail terminals. They also can now be seen in many airport terminals. The standard station posters are *one-sheet,* measuring 30 inches wide by 46 inches high, *two-sheet* (46 inches by 60 inches), and *three-sheet* (42 inches by 84 inches) (see figure 17.12).

Characteristics of Transit

The basic characteristics of transit as an advertising medium include the following:

Mass Coverage

Transit advertising generally delivers broad coverage of a market area. The largely mobile nature of the population provides opportunity of exposure to outside displays by people on foot, on bicycles, and in their automobiles. People who use mass transportation are potentially exposed to interior transit and/or station posters virtually every workday.

Transit reach and frequency levels in many markets approximate those delivered by outdoor advertising. Thus, between 85 and 90 percent of the total adults in a city may be reached in a month's time. Those riding on a transit system will be reached an average of twenty times each month. The typical rider spends more than sixty minutes each day in a vehicle.

Although generally considered a mass medium, transit also can be used to reach people with specific characteristics. For example, a certain transit route may have a high percentage of high school or college students; another may serve blue-collar workers who go to and from factories; and yet another may transport white-collar employees into the central business district. Station posters and interior advertisements bought on commuter trains may effectively reach professionals. In this way, transit can pinpoint targets for both national and local advertisers.

Message Impact

Outside displays and station posters can effectively use dramatic illustrations and color to provide much the same type of impact as that achieved by outdoor advertising, although the size of the ads is smaller. If brand identification is important, a dramatic picture of the package can communicate effectively. Interior car cards provide the opportunity to communicate an in-depth message because of the time a person spends in the vehicle.

Flexibility

Transit advertising is considered a flexible medium in that it offers a fairly wide choice of types and sizes, which permits versatility in the creative treatment used. National advertisers can achieve geographic flexibility by using only certain markets—for example, by limiting their transit advertising to large markets in the northeastern part of the United States. Local advertisers might choose to limit their buy to certain routes within the city.

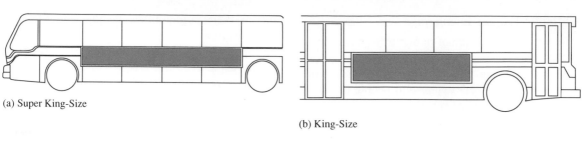

(a) Super King-Size

(b) King-Size

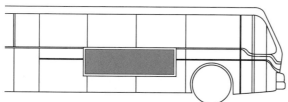

(c) Queen-Size

(d) Headlight

(e) Rear

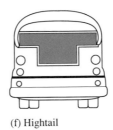

(f) Hightail

(g) Taillight

(h)

FIGURE 17.11 Types of Outside Transit Displays.
(a) Super King-Size. (b) King-Size. (c) Queen-Size.
(d) Headlight. (e) Rear. (f) Hightail. (g) Taillight.
(h) Photographs of samples.

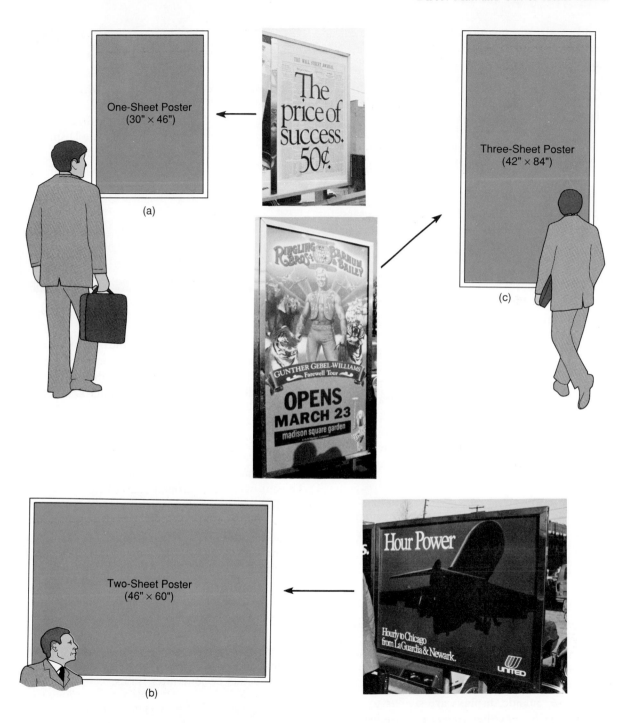

FIGURE 17.12 Transit-Station Posters. (a) One-sheet poster. (b) Two-sheet poster. (c) Three-sheet poster.
Courtesy of Transportation Displays Incorporated.

And as already mentioned, national and local advertisers can pinpoint certain targeted groups who use a particular route.

Cost Efficiency

Transit advertising costs generally are fairly low in terms of absolute costs. For example, a king-size display in a medium-sized market costs around $2,000 to $3,000 per month. Given the large number of people reached, most transit buys deliver extremely high cost efficiency; thus, CPMs are quite low, generally less than 25 cents per thousand for car cards and 75 cents per thousand for outside displays.

Buying Transit

Inside-of-vehicle car cards are bought on the basis of full, half, or quarter *showings* or *service*. Full service means that every vehicle in a transit system will carry one car-card advertisement; half service means one card in half of the vehicles in a fleet; and so on. It is also possible to buy *double* service—two cards in every vehicle. Rates are generally quoted for one month of service, with discounts granted for three-month, six-month, or twelve-month contracts. For example, an 11-inch-by-28-inch car card bought full service in a medium-sized market might have the following rate structure:

One Month	Three Months	Six Months	Twelve Months
$3,000	$2,850	$2,650	$2,330

Thus, a six-month schedule would cost $15,900 (6 × $2,650). The six-month rate of $2,650 per month is 88.3 percent of the one-month rate.

Outside displays are bought on the basis of showings (or *runs*), and these are usually given as 100, 75, 50, or 25. The gross rating points (reach multiplied by average frequency) for a 100 showing are twice that of a 50 showing. Each level of showing is related to the number of display units bought. In this sense, outside displays are similar to outdoor advertising in that they indicate the delivery of a particular buy. Discounts are granted for purchasing beyond the one-month base rate in the same way as that shown for car cards.

TABLE 17.5

Transit Advertising Cost Estimates

Markets	11″ × 28″ Car Cards, Full-Service, Monthly Cost	King-Size Outside Displays, 100 Showing, Monthly Cost
Top 10	$111,330	$588,845
Top 20	151,925	795,799
Top 30	201,295	910,751
Top 40	212,482	1,007,199
Top 50	220,812	1,086,641
Top 100	279,769	1,376,774

Rates for interior and exterior transit are available in *Transit Advertising Association Rates & Data,* a publication published by the industry's trade association. Rates also are available from companies that specialize in selling transit advertising (and often outdoor as well) in particular markets. These companies usually lease the advertising space from the municipal authority that operates the transit system. An advertiser wanting to get a rough estimate of transit costs for a national buy can consult rate estimates, such as those shown in table 17.5. Thus, it would cost around $220,812 per month to buy full service of an 11-inch-by-28-inch car card in the top-fifty markets of the United States, and a 100 showing of king-size outside displays in the top-fifty markets would cost approximately $1,086,641 per month.

In the few markets in which station posters are available, they are sold either on an individual basis or by showing. Cost schedules are not standardized to the same extent that they are for interior and exterior transit. Rates for station posters are usually supplied by the company representing the rapid-transit system or commuter trains.

Audience Measurement

The measurement of exterior transit audiences is done by TEAM (Transit Estimated Audience Measurement). The service provides estimates of the audience delivery of exterior transit advertising in local markets by computing reach and frequency figures. The calculations of reach and frequency are based on a seven-day diary of exposure opportunities kept by consumer panels. The delivery of interior audiences is based on the number of transit riders of a particular system.

Summary

Direct mail, outdoor, and transit differ from the print and broadcast media in that no editorial, informational, or entertainment content accompanies the advertising.

Direct mail has accounted for a large share of total advertising expenditures for the past fifty years. Direct mail takes many forms, but the most common include sales letters, leaflets, booklets, folders, broadsides, circulars, postcards, and catalogs. The most unique characteristic of direct mail is its ability to deliver a selective audience. It also can be personal and flexible, can provide whatever level of coverage is needed, allows for careful measurement of response, and can be cost efficient, depending on how used. The cost of a direct mailing is derived from three sources: production, delivery, and mailing-list charges.

Outdoor advertising has a long history, dating back four thousand years to the Egyptian civilization. It is a relatively minor medium today, although outdoor advertising expenditures total over $1 billion annually. Outdoor's growth has been somewhat limited as a result of federal statutes and local laws and ordinances.

Three standard types of outdoor advertising are: posters, painted bulletins, and spectaculars. Poster panels, such as the eight-sheet, thirty-sheet, and bleed type, involve preprinted sheets of paper that are pasted onto a standard-sized structure, whereas painted bulletins are hand-painted and then affixed to the structure. Bulletins today are being produced with a variety of techniques and on varying surfaces. Spectaculars are highly customized through the use of electrical and mechanical devices. Outdoor advertising is noted for providing mass coverage of the population in a market, imparting dramatic impact, delivering geographic flexibility, and although being high in absolute costs, yielding very good cost efficiency.

The gross rating point (GRP) is the basic insertion unit for outdoor showings and represents the percent exposure of the population in a city. The standard showing for outdoor posters is one month, with discounts for longer periods of time, whereas bulletins and spectaculars typically are purchased for at least one year, often longer. Outdoor is bought on a market-by-market basis from local plant operators. Audiences are measured by a variety of organizations, including TAB, AMMO, OMB, and SMRB.

Transit advertising began in 1831 and today accounts for around $225 million in ad sales. The three standard types of transit advertising are interior car cards, outside transit displays, and station posters. Each type consists of several standard-sized advertising units. Transit delivers broad coverage of a market area, although it can be purchased in a way to reach special market segments. It can provide dramatic message impact, permits flexibility of coverage, and is low in both absolute costs and cost efficiency.

Interior car cards are bought on the basis of the number of vehicles in a transit system—double, full, half, and quarter service. Outside displays are purchased in a manner similar to outdoor and are based on the delivery of a market's population, such as 100, 75, 50, or 25 showings. Station posters are available in only the largest markets, where rapid-transit and commuter rails exist, and are bought by showings or on an individual basis. Transit ads typically are bought for a one-month period, with discounts available for longer contracts. Audience delivery, in the form of reach and frequency estimates, is provided by TEAM.

Questions for Discussion

1. Describe how direct mail differs from other advertising media, especially print media.

2. How is direct marketing different from direct-mail advertising?

3. Assume you are the direct-mail advertising expert for an automobile company and have decided to use a *sales letter* to reach prospective buyers of a new model (choose any car model you would like to advertise). Write the sales letter and a brief justification of your strategy.

4. Examine a current issue of *SRDS Direct-Mail List Rates and Data*. What mailing-list sources are available to reach "advertising agency executives"? How many such names does each source provide, and what are the costs of renting the lists?

5. If you were an outdoor company in a city, and the city council was considering a law that would ban all outdoor postings within the city limits, what arguments would you make against such a law?

6. Under what conditions might advertisers use outdoor and/or transit as a *primary* medium in their advertising campaign?

7. Describe the ways in which transit advertising is similar to outdoor advertising. How are they different?

8. In what ways are car cards different from outside displays? From station posters?

Endnotes

1. Definition of direct marketing is provided by the Direct Marketing Association. See Bob Stone, *Successful Direct-Marketing Methods,* 4th ed. (Lincolnwood, Ill.: NTC Business Books, 1988), 3.

2. Janice Steinberg, "Direct Mail Becoming Hottest Incentive Conduit," *Advertising Age,* 24 July 1989, S-4, S-6.

3. See Nancy Youman, "To Major Mailers, Rising Rates Spell 'Alternative Delivery,' " *Adweeks' Marketing Week,* 19 March 1990, 2.

4. See S. Watson Dunn, Arnold M. Barban, Dean M. Krugman, and Leonard N. Reid, *Advertising: Its Role in Modern Marketing,* 7th ed. (Chicago: Dryden Press, 1990), 461; for a detailed discussion of preparing direct mail, see Stone, *Successful Direct-Marketing Methods,* Chapter 14, "Techniques of Creating Direct-Mail Packages," 310–48.

5. For a further discussion of outdoor advertising's history, see Budd Buszek, *Planning for Out-of-Home Media,* rev. ed. (New York: Traffic Audit Bureau, 1987), Chapters 1, 7.

6. Eric Weissenstein, "Bush Widens Outdoor Ad Ban Bill," *Advertising Age,* 25 February 1991, 53.

7. See Alison Fahey, "Outdoor Sets Limits," *Advertising Age,* 25 June 1990, 57.

8. See Alan Radding, "Outdoor Faces Its Flaws: Measuring Bureaus Mend Fences to Push Medium Forward," *Advertising Age,* 9 October 1989, S-1.

9. Alison Fahey, "Outdoor Eyes Better Measurement," *Advertising Age,* 5 June 1989, 28.

10. Buszek, *Planning for Out-of-Home Media,* 115.

11. George T. Clarke, *Transit Advertising* (New York: Transit Advertising Association, 1970), 12.

12. Clarke, *Transit Advertising,* 14.

13. Laurie Freeman and Allison Fahey, "Packaged Goods Ride with Transit," *Advertising Age,* 23 April 1990, 28.

Suggested Readings

• Clarke, George T. *Transit Advertising.* New York: Transit Advertising Association, 1970.

- Dunn, S. Watson, Arnold M. Barban, Dean M. Krugman, and Leonard N. Reid. *Advertising: Its Role in Modern Marketing.* 7th ed. Chicago: Dryden Press, 1990. Chapter 18.

- McGann, Anthony F., and J. Thomas Russell. *Advertising Media.* 2d ed. Homewood, Ill.: Irwin, 1988. Chapters 10, 11.

- Russell, J. Thomas, and Ronald Lane. *Kleppner's Advertising Procedure.* 11th ed. Englewood Cliffs, N.J.: Prentice-Hall, 1990. Chapters 12, 13.

- Sissors, Jack Z., and Lincoln Bumba. *Advertising Media Planning.* 3d ed. Lincolnwood, Ill.: NTC Business Books, 1989. Chapters 10, 14.

- Stone, Bob. *Successful Direct-Marketing Methods.* 4th ed. Lincolnwood, Ill.: NTC Business Books, 1988.

- Strauss, Steve. *Moving Images: The Transportation Poster in America.* New York: Fullcourt Press, 1984.

- Wells, William, John Burnett, and Sandra Moriarty. *Advertising: Principles and Practice.* Englewood Cliffs, N.J.: Prentice-Hall, 1989. Chapters 16, 17.

Chapter 18

Other Media

Outline

Learning Objectives

In the study of this chapter, you will have the opportunity to:

- Learn about the types, characteristics, and buying of directory advertising.

- Discuss specialty advertising—what it is, its characteristics, and how specialties are bought.

- Examine the types and attributes of "nonstandard" out-of-home media.

- Observe the various types of in-store media and learn how they are used.

- Note how a number of other miscellaneous media can fit into a media mix.

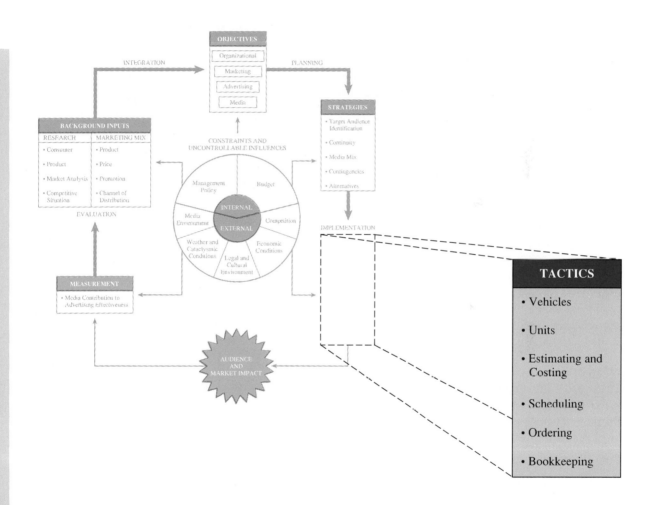

*P*revious chapters have examined those media types that typically are considered for use in most media schedules. Yet, these media do not exhaust all possible choices. This chapter focuses on a number of these "other" media types, such as directories, advertising specialties, other out-of-home media, in-store media, and miscellaneous media types, including motion picture advertising and trade shows. Some of these media have been available to advertisers for many years, while others have been developed only recently.

Directories

Although most people associate **directory advertising** with the Yellow Pages in the telephone book, over 6,500 classified directories of various sorts are published annually in the United States. These directories are used by businesspeople, as well as consumers seeking information about products and services.

The first telephone directory was published in 1878, after the opening of the world's first commercial telephone exchange in New Haven, Connecticut. The complete directory was a single sheet of paper listing fifty customers under seven classified headings: residences; physicians; dentists; stores, factories, etc.; meat and fish markets; hack and boarding stables; and miscellaneous. In the 1890s, publishers began to use yellow paper to distinguish classified directory sections from the alphabetical sections, which gave rise to the name **"Yellow Pages."**

Estimating how much is spent on directory advertising is difficult, but Yellow Pages advertising (by far the biggest category) itself accounts for over $8.9 billion in advertising sales. Of this amount,

TABLE 18.1

Percent Increase in Annual Advertising Expenditures Over the Period 1980–1990, by Media Type

Medium	Percent Increase 1980–1990
Yellow Pages	207.8%
Direct Mail	207.7
Television	149.9
Radio	135.7
Consumer Magazines	116.0
Newspapers	107.7
Outdoor	87.5
Business Publications	71.7
Farm Publications	65.4
All Media Combined	**141.6%**

Source: Computed from data collected by Robert J. Coen of McCann-Erickson, Inc. and reported in various issues of *Advertising Age.*

about 87 percent is spent by local advertisers, and 13 percent comes from national advertisers. Over the past ten years, Yellow Pages advertising has grown by a greater percent than any other medium. Table 18.1 shows these growth rates.

Types of Directory Advertising

Directory advertising can be of varying shapes and forms. Some common forms of Yellow Pages advertising are:

• *Display Advertisements*. These are usually from one-eighth page to a full page and usually are distinguished by an illustration. The advertisement can be black printing on yellow paper, or some or all of the print can be in color, typically red. A new patented process called "Markolor" gives the appearance of full-color printing but uses only black and red ink on yellow paper.

• *Trademark Headings*. Included in such advertisements is a trademark or logotype of the retail store, or of the brand or brands the store carries. National advertisers often buy such advertisements in a directory to include the brand logotype and a listing of local dealers carrying and/or servicing the brand. For example, national gasoline dealers often provide a listing of their local dealers (typically with the national trademark at the top of the advertisement) under "service stations" in the Yellow Pages.

• *Space Listings*. These appear in a listing column and allow for varying amounts of information to supplement the business listing of firm name, address, and phone number. They are bought in varying column lengths, such as 1 inch or 1 1/2 inches.

• *Regular Listings*. These form the bulk of most advertisements found in a directory and provide the name, address, and phone number of the advertiser. This type can be modified to include a *semi-bold* or *bold* listing of the company name.

Figure 18.1 shows some of the typical types of directory advertising.

A number of innovative types of directory advertising are also currently being used and tested. One type is referred to as "talking Yellow Pages," in which information is transmitted electronically via telephone lines (a form of data transmission called **audiotex**). One of the largest U.S. directory companies—Donnelley Directory—has had an audiotex-enhanced directory since 1987 and now operates it in thirteen states. Donnelley estimated that thirty million consumers had called its talking Yellow Pages service by the end of 1989.[1] In all, talking Yellow Pages services are available in more than 160 cities, with advertising revenues around $160 million. Similar to this type of directory are *fax directories,* which take advantage of the growing use of facsimile machines, and *cellular Yellow Pages,* targeted to the cellular telephone industry (see figure 18.2).

Another new type is the *minidirectory,* which is designed to fit in briefcases or glove compartments. Minidirectories can provide specialized services or be miniaturized versions of the original, larger Yellow Pages.[2] A new directory innovation, aimed at increasing national advertising, is the use of "brand-sell" or "billboard" advertisements, which are targeted to sell specific brands to consumers, rather than promote specific businesses that carry the brands. This type is being tested by Pacific Bell Directory in California.[3]

Characteristics of Directories

Perhaps the most unique attribute of directory advertising is that it is "directional;" that is, it points the customer to the store where the product or service is available. It can be the final link in the buying cycle: After seeing advertisements in other media urging them to buy a particular brand, consumers turn to directories to decide where to buy.

Similarly, directories reach prospects when they usually are ready to buy. Most users do not look in a directory until they need a particular product or service. The directory helps them to determine which outlets are available, and by using the telephone, they can easily get additional information that helps in making a purchase decision.

Directories are widely used and reach large numbers of people. One study showed that almost 90 percent of all adults use the Yellow Pages at least once in the course of a year when they are considering a purchase. Over 77 percent of adults refer to the Yellow Pages in a typical month, with 59 percent using it in a typical week, and 18 percent on an average day. The typical adult user refers to the Yellow Pages over three times each week. Figure 18.3 is an advertisement for the Yellow Pages by the industry's trade association.

(a)

(b)

(c)

(d)

FIGURE 18.1 Common Types of Yellow Pages Advertising. (a) Display ad. (b) Trademark heading. (c) Space listing. (d) Regular listings (including semi-bold and bold).
Courtesy of Yellow Pages Publishers Association.

Directory advertising is relatively flexible in terms of creative treatment, although this is not one of its strong points. The number of units that can be used, though, is large enough to permit variety, and the medium also provides a national advertiser with geographic flexibility. The advertiser can choose from around six thousand Yellow Pages directories that cover most U.S. cities. The national advertiser can use directories to supplement a basic appeal advertised in another medium; some magazine advertisements and television commercials encourage prospects to check their local Yellow Pages to find the nearest dealer who carries the brand.

Directory advertising has some limitations. Most advertisements serve primarily to remind consumers of the existence of a store or product, although it is possible to include more varied sales appeals in a large display advertisement. Currently, most directory advertisements are printed in black, with perhaps red as an additional color. To make an advertisement stand out on the page, the advertiser

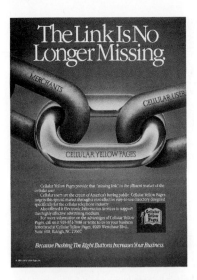

FIGURE 18.2 An Advertisement in a Trade
Magazine for Cellular Yellow Pages
Source: Cellular Yellow Pages.

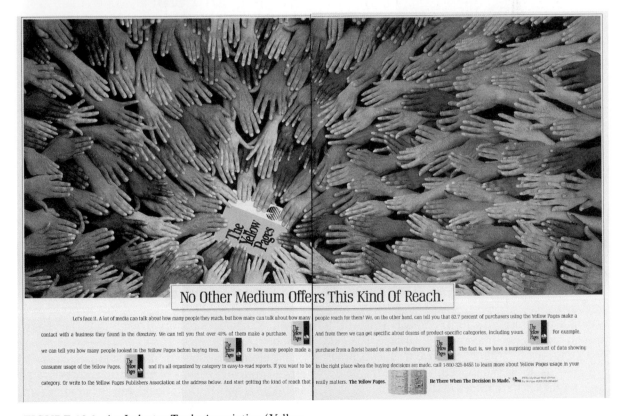

FIGURE 18.3 An Industry Trade Association (Yellow
Pages Publishers Association) Advertisement for the
Advantages of the Yellow Pages
Source: Created by Martin/Williams, Inc. for Yellow Pages Publishers
Association. Reprinted by permission.

FIGURE 18.4 Advertisement for Company That Specializes in Preparing Yellow Pages Advertising
Courtesy of Ketchum Advertising/San Francisco. David Wolfe, Copywriter, Jay Talwar, Account Executive.

TABLE 18.2		
An Estimate of the Cost of Trademark Ads and Bold Listings in Directories		
Markets	Trademark Ad	Bold Listing
Top 50*	$345,000	$73,000
Top 100†	510,000	113,000

*About six hundred directories.
†About nine hundred directories.

Buying Directory Advertising

As with other print media, directory advertising is bought according to the space unit desired and the length of time the advertisement is to be run. As mentioned earlier, standard units are available for the Yellow Pages, including display advertisements of specified page or fractional page size, trademark headings, space listings, and bold, semi-bold, and regular listings. Advertisements are contracted for the issue length of the directory, typically one year.

Most of the companies that publish directories—primarily the large, regional telephone companies, such as BellSouth, Nynex, Southwestern Bell, and Ameritech—have their own sales staffs that sell advertisements primarily to local, but also national advertisers. Each directory issues a rate card, listing the price for various units and information about producing the advertisement. An estimate of national directory advertising costs is given in table 18.2.

In addition, several firms are authorized sales representatives (ASRs) of the various directories, and ASRs work with national and regional advertisers and their advertising agencies. These sales

must design the message carefully. (See figure 18.4 for an advertisement by a company that specializes in preparing Yellow Pages advertising.) If "Markolor" proves to be efficient, this could add much impact to directory advertisements in the future.

Directory advertising is noted for having a long message life, usually one year, which provides for repeated exposure. On the other hand, each message must be created with the idea that it will be around for a long time, and the advertiser should be careful not to "date" an advertisement. Prices are unlikely to be mentioned, although the advertiser might encourage people to call for the latest prices.

The blast of fresh air your Yellow Pages need.

There's a change in the wind.

L.M. Berry NYPS has developed into a company even better positioned to respond to the fundamental changes occurring in the national yellow pages industry. And, to reflect this shift in direction, we have a new name. Now you can call us Berry Network, Inc.

What's the new name mean? It means we're much more than a yellow pages company. We're a marketing partner committed to integrating Yellow Pages planning into your strategic marketing process.

As your partner, we bring you the benefits of our vast resources which connect us to every aspect of the industry. Berry Network, Inc. is a Yellow Pages Agency as well as an Authorized Selling Representative, working both directly with advertisers and through advertising agencies to serve a broader range of customer needs.

So if you're ready for a company that combines bold new enthusiasm with proven expertise, call Dave Tremain at 1 800 543-3330 (1 800 762-4844 OH). Ride the wind to Berry. We're the blast of fresh air your Yellow Pages need.

Berry
NETWORK, INC.

FIGURE 18.5 Trade Advertisement for a Yellow Pages Authorized Sales Representative
Source: Berry Network.

representatives assemble rates and data information, as well as research information on the effectiveness of directory advertising. (See figure 18.5 for an advertisement of an ASR firm.) An ASR firm sends orders through a network of directory publishers, thus consolidating the billing for an advertiser or its agency. The advertiser can buy just a few or literally thousands of directories from one source and gets a single contract for the total buy.

The Yellow Pages Publishers Association (YPPA) is the industry's trade association, with more than three hundred telephone-directory publishers and ASR firms. YPPA provides advertisers and agencies with a central source of market information, promotional materials, rates and data publications, and assistance useful in the analysis of national Yellow Pages advertising. YPPA recently developed a rate card for "brand-sell" advertisements and hopes that the "brand-sell" innovation will lead to more packaged-goods ads in Yellow Pages directories.[4]

One of the current problems with directory advertising is the lack of syndicated research that measures delivery and effectiveness in ways comparable to some of the other media. The YPPA established a task force to investigate the situation but concluded that "although book-to-book comparison offers certain industry members potential advantages, the association does not recommend the adoption of syndicated intramedia research on an industry basis."[5] Improved measurement of the medium is likely in the near future, however.

Specialty Advertising

Specialty advertising dates to 1886, when an Ohio printer sought ways to supplement his company's income. He came up with the idea of imprinting school book bags with the name of a business. He reasoned that children would carry the bags all over town as moving billboards and, hence, would increase the visibility of the advertiser. He succeeded in selling his idea to a local shoe store, and the specialty advertising industry was born.[6]

The terms *specialty advertising* and *advertising specialties* are catchall classifications that include a variety of items carrying the advertiser's name and address and, frequently, a short sales message. The specialty items are usually inexpensive and are often given to a preselected audience. The donating company hopes that, if the key ring or letter opener is useful, the recipient will be reminded of the donor many times a year and will feel kindly toward the

MEDIA SPOTLIGHT

18.1

The "Walking Fingers" Logo Used to Promote the Yellow Pages

The most instantly recognizable mark in the Yellow Pages is the "walking fingers" logo first used by AT&T in the 1960s. Yet, for some reason, the company did not trademark the unique logo, leading many to speculate as to why. Some have said that the communications giant simply forgot to trademark the logo, an answer that seems unlikely. Others say that the failure to trademark the logo was a conscious, planned decision on the part of AT&T.

"I became the president of the National Yellow Pages Service Association in 1975," said Fred E. Smykla, now executive director emeritus for the Yellow Pages Publishers Association (YPPA). "We went to AT&T to purchase all of the contract material we needed to use for the national Yellow Pages plan. We specifically asked (AT&T) if we could get license to use the walking fingers. They told us that there was no need to get a license because it was in the public domain. In fact, they encouraged any publishing company to use it," he explained. "I think they knew what they were doing. They were trying to make people aware of this advertising medium," said Smykla. "It has become the mark of the medium and, in that respect, I think they did a good job."

Was their decision not to trademark the logo a curse or a blessing for the industry? On one hand, the ubiquitousness of the mark has helped to create an overall identifying image for the industry. On the other hand, with the large number of directories and publishers in a given market—each legally able to use the walking fingers logo—it is hard for consumers to differentiate between directories.

BellSouth Advertising and Publishing Company (BAPCO) is trying to change all that. It filed for registration of the walking fingers logo in 1985, and the case is proceeding.

"We've taken the position that the walking fingers in our specific area refers to the telephone company," said Vincent Sgrosso, vice president and general counsel of BAPCO. "We're not attempting to create a trademark. We already have one. All we're doing is registering our trademark."

As Sgrosso explained, BellSouth hopes to register what he called the company's "common-law trademark" of the walking fingers in the nine-state area in which it offers telephone services. Other companies would be free to use the mark outside of BellSouth's telephone service area but, within

that area, BellSouth would be the sole legal owner of the walking fingers.

While at least twenty-two parties are contesting BAPCO's filing—from RBOCS to independents—the outcome of the case may have the biggest impact on independents. If its filing is approved, what will BAPCO say, for example, to a large, independent publisher that has operated in its area—and has used the walking fingers logo—for the past fifteen years?

"We'll say we have the mark, and they have been using the mark inappropriately," Sgrosso replied.

Source: *Link,* March/April 1990, 19. Reprinted with permission of the Yellow Pages Publishers Association.

firm and its product or service. According to the industry's trade association—Specialty Advertising Association International:

Specialty advertising is an advertising, sales promotion, and motivational communications medium which employs useful articles of merchandise imprinted with an advertiser's name, message, or logo. Unlike premiums, with which they are sometimes confused, these articles (called advertising specialties) are always distributed free—recipients don't have to earn the specialty by making a purchase or contribution.[7]

Specialty advertising accounts for over $5.0 billion in annual sales, about half as much as that spent on Yellow Pages.

Types of Advertising Specialties

The over fifteen thousand different advertising specialties are somewhat difficult to organize into a few categories. Generally, though, the medium consists of five types: (1) calendars, (2) writing instruments and desk accessories, (3) wearable items, (4) business gifts, and (5) other imprinted specialties.

Calendars have been a major type of specialty advertising for many years, although their popularity today is perhaps not what it once was. They are primarily used by local businesses, such as beauty salons, banks, dry cleaners, auto repair shops, and the like. If used by a recipient, calendars communicate the advertiser's name, and perhaps a brief sales message, all year.

Writing instruments and desk accessories are a popular form of advertising specialty because of their value to the recipient. Pens, pencils, rulers, notepad holders, marker pens, paperweights, and desk organizers all represent this category.

Wearable specialty items include hats, visors, sweatbands, jackets, scarves, aprons, watches, sunglasses, fragrances, name tags, and gloves. T-shirts currently are very popular with advertisers as a wearable specialty item.

Business gifts are not, in a strict sense, advertising specialties because they are seldom imprinted with an advertising message; rather, they are often personalized with the *recipient's* name. However, specialty-advertising counselors assist their clients with executive gift programs to such an extent that the category is among the leading in the industry. About two-thirds of all business gifts are purchased through specialty-advertising distributors.

The term *business gift,* can be confusing in a discussion of specialties unless it is more precisely defined. After all, a set of all-leather luggage, a Rolex watch, or a case of French wine might also be considered a business gift. However, the usual definition of a business gift is as follows:

Business (or executive) gifts represent that category of the advertising-specialty industry which includes nonimprinted products (sponsor identification typically accompanies the gift) in the $5 to $25 range of value.[8]

Business gifts typically are used by companies to show appreciation for past business and to influence a group of select buyers in the hope of future business.[9] The gift serves as a reminder of the giver and can include a wide variety of products, many of which are simply more expensive versions of other imprinted items. For example, a company may distribute ballpoint pens with the company imprint, costing perhaps less than one dollar each, to a large group of its customers, yet provide a Hallmark wood-grain pen, costing $20 to $25, to its special customers.

Specialty items not fitting into one of the previous categories can simply be grouped as "other imprinted specialties." This catchall category includes thousands of different miscellaneous items, such as:

- Bookmarks
- Money clips
- Golf ball markers
- Golf tees
- Calculator cases
- Clocks
- Flashlights
- Cork removers
- Paper hand fans
- Mug insulators
- Bumper stickers
- Eyewear retainers
- Auto sun protectors
- Candle holders
- Knives (for example, steak, pocket)
- Luggage tags
- Golf divot fixers
- Calculators
- Trivets
- Phone cords
- Thermometers
- Drinking glasses
- Tape measures
- Balloons
- Stadium seats
- Tote bags
- Key rings
- Beverage coasters
- Card cases
- Shoehorns
- Bookends
- Pocket planners
- Maps/travel guides
- Nail files
- Coffee mugs
- Tire gauges
- Shoelaces
- Vinyl cushions
- Trash bags

Excluding business gifts, the relative amount spent on specialty advertising types is:

Percent of Total

- Calendars 8%
- Writing Instruments/
  Desk Accessories 25
- Wearables 20
- Other Imprinted Specialties 47

Characteristics of Specialties

One of the important characteristics of specialty advertising is its ability to preselect the targeted audience. Like direct mail, the advertiser controls the delivery of the message; and as such, the message can be directed to either a large, fairly heterogeneous audience or to a small, select one. There is thus little waste circulation, which is especially important if a costly specialty item is being used.

Another important attribute of the advertising specialty is its long life. Calendars present the opportunity for exposure over a full year. Studies have shown that a high percentage of people receiving advertising specialties were still using them six months later.[10] The medium also provides high exposure opportunity. Every time an individual looks at a firm's calendar or wears an imprinted T-shirt, he or she is reminded of the company's name and perhaps some slogan attached to it. A study by Schrieber & Associates showed that nearly 40 percent of all persons receiving advertising specialties could recall the name of the advertiser as long as six months after receiving the specialty. Perhaps even more important are the findings of an A. C. Nielsen study showing that all other things being equal, people are more likely to patronize a business that has given them an advertising specialty than one that has not.[11]

Specialties can also provide an advertiser with a great deal of flexibility. They can be issued just about anytime and can be tied to special promotions, such as a store's anniversary. The advertiser can choose from specialties that are fairly expensive to items costing only a few cents, which allows for flexibility in terms of the advertising budget. In addition, specialty houses have thousands of items to choose from and can even provide specific items on request. The number of items delivered, as well as to whom they are given, provides flexibility in terms of audience coverage.

The brevity of the specialty's message might be considered a limiting factor. Many specialties allow for only the name, address, and telephone number of the advertiser, although some, such as certain wearable items, can contain more extensive messages. Another limiting characteristic is that the cost per prospect reached may be high: A specialty item costing 50 cents yields a cost-per-thousand of $500, and a $25 business gift results in a CPM of $25,000!

MEDIA SPOTLIGHT

18.2

Two Case Histories of the Use of Specialty Advertising

Dodge, Warren & Peters Insurance Services, Inc., Torrance, California

Objective: To increase new business by motivating employees and securing referrals from existing clients.

Strategy and execution: To recover income lost by premium reductions, the Torrance, California, agency embarked upon a new business campaign directed to its sales force and their families, employees, and present clients. The promotion stressed that the targeted individuals were "One of a Kind." An incentive contest for the sales force was announced at a kickoff meeting. Each salesperson was given an engraved walnut desk pen set, a personalized leather correspondence holder, a catalog of prize merchandise, and rules for the contest. The pen sets were also given to clients who had referred business to the agency. Other clients were issued a gold pocket telephone index with a message encouraging them to refer new customers. Those who did received an imprinted executive pocket knife and, later, a desk diary. To encourage spouses to spur their mates to greater efforts, the prize catalogs were mailed to the salespersons' homes. Each month, a miniature pocket tool was also mailed to spouses as a reminder. The tools were also mailed to office employees, who were encouraged to assist their bosses to reach their goal and thus qualify for a $100 cash prize. At the awards banquet, salespeople who achieved their "One of a Kind" goals were presented a gold record plaque. All staff members received personalized coffee mugs.

Results: Commission sales of $330,000 during the three-month promotion exceeded goal by 147 percent, reported the agency president. Eight of the agency's twelve salespeople surpassed their assigned goals, four by 125 percent.

The Dallas Morning News, Dallas, Texas

Objective: To increase newspaper circulation and to improve public relations.

Strategy and execution: The circulation department targeted newlyweds and parents of newborn babies for the subscription drive and compiled a list of thirty thousand names from courthouse records. To each newlywed couple in the circulation area, the paper mailed a congratulatory card with an apothecary jar. *The Morning News* graphics appeared on the jar, and a headline announced, "Texas has a new bride and groom." A few weeks later, the telemarketing department followed up with a sales call. A baby T-shirt was the specialty chosen for parents of newborns. Illustrated with the paper's front page, the T-shirt proclaimed, "Texas has a new star." A letter and subscription card accompanied the specialty, and the telemarketing department called later to verify receipt of the gift and to secure a subscription order.

Results: The paper was said to have achieved a 17.6 percent increase in subscriptions from newlyweds and a 22.7 percent increase from new parents.

Photos and text courtesy of Specialty Advertising Association International.

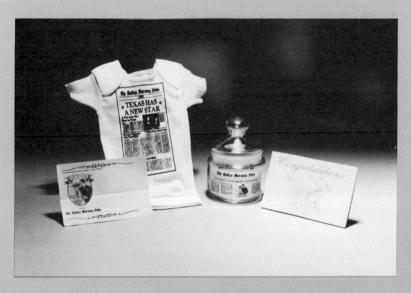

Buying Specialty Advertising

Buying specialty advertising is similar to buying direct mail in that the advertiser, or a specialist hired by the advertiser, has primary responsibility for making the purchase; no independent publisher or broadcast company is involved.

Three main business categories make up the specialty-advertising industry through which the buying activity takes place: (1) suppliers, (2) specialty-advertising counselors or "distributors," and (3) direct-selling houses.

Suppliers make up the production end of the business. They manufacture, import, imprint, or otherwise produce the myriad of specialty-advertising items. Some limit their activity to one or only a few items, but most produce a variety of advertising specialties. Many suppliers, though, limit their manufacturing to a single material, such as plastic, wood, metal, ceramics, paper, or leather. A vinyl supplier, for example, may have a complete line of vinyl products, ranging from inexpensive key tags to costlier underarm portfolios.[12] Approximately two thousand firms are the industry's primary suppliers. A few are well-known manufacturers of brand-name products, but most are small, privately owned companies.

Distributors are the sales companies that represent the many industry suppliers. They are independent agents who call on prospective advertisers to sell them specialties, but they also provide counseling on how the medium can fit into an overall advertising program. They present an advertiser with ideas for using specialty advertising to achieve certain marketing and advertising objectives. Once an advertiser is sold, distributors help to coordinate the copy, art, and distribution plans; secure the specialties from the appropriate supplier; and have the specialties shipped to the advertiser. Thus, they provide a full counseling service for the client (advertiser). Approximately eleven thousand such firms are in operation.

Direct-selling houses are a combination of supplier and distributor. They produce many of their own products and sell them to advertisers through their own sales forces. They supplement the products they produce themselves by buying from other suppliers and thus can offer their clients a large array of items. The dozen or so direct-selling houses are usually among the largest in the industry.

The industry trade association is the Specialty Advertising Association International (SAAI). Its approximately four thousand firms consist of around one-third suppliers and two-thirds distributors, along with direct-selling houses and general marketing firms that have an interest in specialty advertising. SAAI's main functions are to enhance the marketing environment for its members and to facilitate the operation of their businesses. SAAI sponsors trade shows, provides industry-wide public relations, maintains legislative liaison with Congress and federal regulatory agencies, and distributes research findings and educational materials.

Other Out-of-Home Media

In chapter 17, we discussed the standard types of outdoor and transit advertising—posters, painted bulletins, electric spectaculars, interior car cards, outside displays, and station posters. Here, we look at some other types of out-of-home media.

Types

In addition to the standard type of station posters, a number of other units, such as *dioramas* and *kiosks,* can be purchased in subway, bus, train, and airport terminals. Dioramas come in a variety of sizes and shapes and usually have backlighting to provide added impact. One popular size is 43 inches high by 62 inches wide, with the advertisement placed behind sheets of clear or diffused plexiglass (see figure 18.6).

Kiosks also come in different sizes, such as a vertical island kiosk (33 inches wide by 45 inches high), a horizontal island kiosk (57 1/2 inches wide by 43 3/4 inches high), and a cylindrical island kiosk (45 inches high by 36 inches wide). Kiosks may have backlighting, and some have headers above the kiosk to call attention to the advertising units in them. Kiosks are used extensively in airport terminals.

FIGURE 18.6 Dioramas and Clocks Are Used in
Public Transportation Terminals
Courtesy of Transportation Displays Incorporated.

Also available in terminals are *station clocks.*
These typically are lighted and range in size from
46 1/2 inches wide by 21 1/2 inches high to
30 1/2 inches wide by 14 inches high. In addition
to an analog or digital clock, there is an adjacent
advertising message (see figure 18.6).

A newer form of advertising in terminals is called
"Metrovision." "Metrovision" involves mounting 25-
inch high-resolution television color monitors in
high-traffic passenger areas of bus, train, or transit
depots. Each monitor displays forty still frames at
fifteen seconds per frame, repeated every ten minutes for twenty-four hours a day. The content shown
includes travel information; news, weather, sports,
and business programming; and advertisements.
Advertisements are bought from "Metrovision" for
a minimum of three months and are available in
about a dozen markets.[13]

Another type of out-of-home advertising is
shopping-mall displays. These are two-, three-, or
four-sided freestanding kiosks, some of which are
backlit. They measure 46 inches by 60 inches or 40
inches by 50 inches. Located in high-traffic areas
in shopping malls, they afford coverage at the timely
decision-making stage.

Bus-shelter displays are a popular form of out-
of-home media because of their exposure to both
pedestrians and people in vehicles. They include the
advertisements placed on the outsides of a shelter
as well as within the shelter. Typically, they are en-
cased in plexiglass for protection from weather and
measure 42 inches wide by 68 inches high (see figure
18.7). Shelter advertisements are sold by the
number of units purchased, with a base showing of
one month. The more units purchased, the lower the
cost per unit; also, discounts are given when units
are purchased for more than one month. Since shelters are not available in many cities, an alternative
is to purchase advertising on a *bus bench.* For example, a local insurance agency can have a bus
bench painted to include the name of the company,
its address and phone number, and perhaps a brief
sales message.

Taxicabs provide another opportunity for out-of-
home advertising. Typical units are those mounted
on the tops of taxis (14 inches high by 48 inches
wide) or on the trunk of the cab (13 inches by 49
inches). Taxi tops consist of a triangular frame with
advertisements on each side and often have backlighting so they can be seen at night (see figure
18.7). Similarly, *trucks and vans* can be outfitted
to display advertisements—on each side of the
truck/van, on the back, and on top. These are referred to as "moving billboards," and as such, share
many characteristics with outdoor posters. This type
of out-of-home advertising usually is limited to
about a half-dozen large cities, where there is high
pedestrian and vehicular traffic. Truck advertisements can be quite large, up to the equivalent of a
thirty-sheet outdoor poster.

FIGURE 18.7 Bus Shelters and Taxicabs Provide
Opportunity of Exposure to Pedestrians and People in
Vehicles
Courtesy of Transportation Displays Incorporated.

FIGURE 18.8 Advertisement on a Public Telephone
Enclosure Panel
Courtesy of Transportation Displays Incorporated.

Public telephone advertisements are placed on
the faceplates or enclosure panels of pay telephones. The telephone can be located inside a
building, such as a transportation terminal, on the
outside of a building, or along a roadway. An advertisement on the faceplate provides exposure opportunity to the telephone user, whereas enclosure-
panel advertising can potentially be seen by anyone
passing the unit. Enclosure advertisements vary in
size, but a typical form is 26 inches wide by 50
inches high. The advertisements usually have backlighting. (See figure 18.8.)

A variation on pay-phone advertising is a
"BellBoard" kiosk, developed by a new media company, Electric Avenue. "BellBoard" is a kiosk unit
that houses a pay phone and a 13-inch high-
resolution video screen that can display up to twenty
still-frame color advertisements. An advertiser buys
a six-second advertisement that plays on the screen
thirty times each hour, twenty-four hours a day; the
present cost is around $100 per month at each
"BellBoard." In addition, the kiosk has regular en-
closure-type panels on which advertising can be
placed.[14]

Other out-of-home media include a number of
related items called "specialty forms." For example, *skywriting* was used over fifty years ago to
spell out the words "PEPSI COLA" with special
cloudlike exhaust from an airplane. Airplanes also
can be used to pull a *banner,* with an advertiser's
name and message, and are often seen over college
football stadiums on fall Saturday afternoons.
Blimps can be used to pull an advertising banner,
or messages can be printed on the side of the blimp.
For example, Anheuser-Busch Companies has a
blimp painted to resemble its Sea World of Florida's star attraction, Shamu the killer whale.[15] The
blimp is used in Florida and in the Northeast.
Goodyear Tire Company is world famous through
its use of blimps.

Yet another out-of-home specialty form is the *freestanding inflatable*. These usually are quite large, are filled with gas to make them remain aloft, and thus can be seen over quite long distances. They can be produced in virtually any form and shape—say, a giant soft-drink can, an automobile, or a cartoon character—and are then tethered to a retailer's store or at some high-traffic point in a city. *Hot-air balloons* also are often painted with an advertiser's logotype. Each of these specialty forms is sufficiently unique that media buyers must seek out the various specialized companies in the field to determine format, costs, how to produce the advertisements, and the like.

Characteristics

Other out-of-home media share many of the same characteristics as those noted for the standard media of the industry. Thus, they typically provide for the mass coverage of a market. The population's high mobility and availability in many different places means that these media reach a high percentage of a city's population and usually with a high degree of message frequency.

Through the use of color, high-quality photography and printing techniques, as well as lighting, these other out-of-home media types can have a dramatic impact on viewers. Further, many—such as inflatables, moving billboards, blimps, "Metrovision," and "BellBoards"—are unique, which attracts attention.

Given the large number of different types available, other out-of-home media provide advertisers with much format flexibility: the variety of sizes, shapes, and styles—each with varying costs—allows for much individual choice in the media mix used. Because most of these types are bought on an individual basis, advertisers are free to choose where the advertisements will be placed.

In general, other out-of-home media are quite cost efficient, yielding low CPMs. When advertisers are targeting a broad-based, diversified group of prospects, the opportunity for large exposures results in favorable cost efficiencies. Even for low-budget advertisers, absolute costs can usually be kept within a reasonable range.

In-Store Media

In-store media can be grouped into three categories: (1) point-of-purchase displays, (2) shopping carts and bags, and (3) in-store television and radio.

Point-of-Purchase Displays

In one sense, all types of in-store media could be classified as "point-of-purchase," but the term is used here to describe the more traditional kinds of advertising found within a store.[16] Other in-store advertising efforts—such as the use of shopping carts and television monitors—are newer forms (many are still in an experimental stage) and merit special discussion.

Point-of-purchase (P-O-P) advertising displays are those developed by brand goods manufacturers and distributed to retailers with the hope that they will be used to deliver an advertising message to consumers at the time of purchase. Total expenditures for P-O-P advertising are difficult to estimate precisely, but around $14 to $15 billion probably is spent annually for this medium.

The continuing trend toward self-service in retail outlets means that advertisers must depend heavily on effective in-store displays to communicate the merits of their brands. Point-of-purchase displays often are designed to reinforce a basic advertising theme carried out in other media, yet in many instances, such units tell the whole brand story. Studies have shown that anywhere between two-thirds and four-fifths of all supermarket purchases are in-store decisions, adding to the importance of point-of-purchase advertising. Because the retailer is the final link in the chain of communication with the consumer, in-store displays can be extremely effective if the material is well planned.

For the manufacturer, the problem is twofold: first, to design a display that meets the needs of retailers while also having an impact on consumers; and second, to induce retailers to take advantage of it. Retailers' biggest problem is to decide how much to use of the mass of material they receive—they cannot possibly use it all without cluttering their store. Fortunately, many studies have shown that

TABLE 18.3

Results of POPAI Research

Store Managers of:	Percent Stating That "P-O-P Attracts Attention and Increases Sales"	Percent Stating That "Most or Almost All Manufacturer-Supplied P-O-P Is Used"
Mass Merchandisers	89.5%	53.0%
Convenience Stores	95.0	78.0
Chain Drugstores	93.4	60.0
Automotive Stores	91.6	75.0

retailers believe that the use of point-of-purchase advertising increases sales and attracts consumer attention in their stores. These studies have largely been conducted by the industry's trade association, the Point-of-Purchase Advertising Institute (POPAI). For example, POPAI research has revealed the information in table 18.3.[17] As shown in the table, a very high percentage of the store managers surveyed—90 percent or more—felt that point-of-purchase advertising was useful in attracting attention and increasing store sales. Over half said that they use most or almost all of the P-O-P materials supplied, with three-fourths or more of the automotive- and convenience-store managers so stating.

Types of P-O-P

Any kind of display that can be used in a retail store (or on outside windows and doors) can properly be called point-of-purchase advertising. The variety of such material is almost endless. Among the more popular types of P-O-P are:

- Banners
- Cash-register units
- Clocks
- Counter units
- Floor stands
- Aisle displays
- Overheads and mobiles
- Pole displays
- Electronic displays
- Racks
- Wall units
- Testers/Sampling units
- Window/door units
- On-product units
- Signs
- Shelf units and shelf extenders
- Interactive units

Some displays, such as a clock, are permanent. Displays can be constructed from a variety of materials—for example, paperboard, wood, metal, and plastic. Light and motion are often added for attention-getting value. Figure 18.9 shows a variety of displays, and figure 18.10 is a trade advertisement for a company that produces a particular type of P-O-P display for advertisers.

Use of P-O-P Advertising

Basically, advertisers spend money on P-O-P advertising to take advantage of its inherent communication ability. Whether or not used in conjunction with other media, point-of-purchase advertising can convey the entire sales story—and does so at the point closest to purchase. It also can be used to remind prospects of a campaign theme or product benefit, or to emphasize uses of a brand or certain details that differentiate the brand from competition. Point-of-purchase advertising displays also can be used to build brand and corporate images. They can help provide technical details of a product, or may make the brand appear luxurious or unique or modern, or may associate the brand with fun or fashion or an exotic location.

P-O-P displays may help a brand to secure a better location in a store by raising the product closer to eye level, by increasing the amount of shelf space devoted to it, or by moving it nearer a choice spot like the checkout counter. Some displays actually dispense the brand, such as from a

(b)

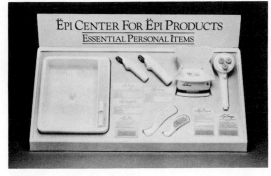

(c)

(a)

FIGURE 18.9 Several Different Point-of-Purchase
Advertising Displays
Courtesy of Point-of-Purchase Advertising Institute.

(d)

self-standing bin or a countertop display, in addition to providing an advertising message. P-O-P displays also can dispense in-store coupons or instructional literature.

The wide choice of P-O-P displays allows for much flexibility in cost, and given the high delivery that can be obtained from certain locations in a store, the medium can be quite cost efficient. However, in addition to the actual cost of producing displays, the advertiser must consider what might have to be paid to retailers to secure space within the store. Such charges, or "allowances," can be either direct payments for display space or may take the form of price discounts. When asked, "What percentage of the time do you receive an allowance for using manufacturer-supplied point-of-purchase

FIGURE 18.10 MediaOne Is a Company Supplying a
Particular Type of P-O-P Advertising
Courtesy of Media One, Inc. 150 E. 58th Street. N.Y. N.Y. 10022.
(P.O.P. Advertising in Supermarkets, U.S.A.)

FIGURE 18.11 Advertisement for a Company Selling
Shopping-Cart Ads in Kmart Stores
Courtesy of STRATMAR.

signs and displays?" Only 20 percent of mass-
merchandiser and convenience-store executives answered "never." Among chain drugstore people, the
figure was 28 percent, whereas a majority of
automotive-store executives—53 percent—said
"never."[18]

Shopping Carts and Bags

In-store advertising media also include the advertisements placed on shopping carts and shopping
bags. Shopping carts have been available to advertisers for a number of years. A frame is attached to
the part of the cart facing the user or to the front
of the cart; advertisements are inserted into the
frame. One company—ActMedia—specializes in
this type of advertising in around twenty thousand

stores, and advertisers can buy on a national or regional basis, generally for a cost-per-thousand of
between 70 and 85 cents (space costs only). The
frames permit an advertisement of 10 inches by 7
3/4 inches. Customers potentially are exposed to
the advertising throughout their use of the cart. The
advertisement for Stratmedia in figure 18.11 explains the use of such advertising in Kmart stores.

Another company, ADDvantage Media Group,
recently introduced on a national basis its "Shoppers Calculator." This system involves hooking a
solar-powered calculator onto a shopping cart so
that shoppers can tally their purchases; the print
advertisement placed alongside the calculator already has been used by such advertisers as Coca-
Cola and Pepsi-Cola.[19]

A new innovation in shopping-cart advertising is
the use of *video monitors* mounted on a cart. For
example, one system that has been market tested is
"VideOcart," developed by Information Resources,
Inc. A 6-inch-by-8-inch screen is mounted on a cart
and provides viewers with commercials as they move
through the store. Messages can even be triggered
according to the aisle in which the cart is located
at a particular time. Tests have shown that
"VideOcart" advertisers can achieve average sales
gains of 33 percent.[20] By early 1991, "VideOcart"
was in fifty stores, and company executives estimated it would be in five thousand stores in the top
twenty-five markets by the end of 1994.[21]

Shopping bags also can be used as an advertising medium. Of course, retailers for many years have placed their company names and logotypes on their bags. Today, though, shopping bags sometimes carry the imprint of a brand sold by the store. For example, the Eastman Kodak Company has used shopping bags to imprint a picture of its film and camera products. Usually, the shopping bag has the retailer's name on one side and the brand advertised on the other.

In-Store Television and Radio

One of the newest, and still somewhat experimental, types of in-store media involves television monitors that carry brand advertising in the store. Several companies are testing this method of advertising. For example, Turner Broadcasting System and ActMedia recently introduced "Checkout Channel," which has television monitors placed at supermarket checkout counters. As consumers stand in line, they have the opportunity to see news, weather, sports, business, and consumer programming provided from Cable News Network (CNN) and Headline News, along with advertising. Apple Computer, Inc. and Advanced Promotion Technologies, Inc. use Macintosh II computers, laser disc players, color video monitors, and thermal printers to provide store shoppers with ten-second promotional messages run at checkout counters while customers' items are being scanned.[22]

Another video form is to show an animated, computer-generated commercial on television monitors that are placed strategically throughout supermarket aisles. Shoppers' Video and Nynex Computer Services Company have developed this type of system, which is available in around four thousand supermarkets nationally. Test results show that more than 65 percent of consumers said that the video advertisements reminded them of forgotten grocery items, and 27 percent said that the advertisements caused them to switch from their current brand to the advertised one.[23] The fifteen-second commercials shown on Shoppers' Video can be changed to promote price specials and also can be tied to other in-store events. Messages are bought

FIGURE 18.12 Trade Ad for Shoppers' Video, an In-Store Television Medium
Courtesy of Advertising Graphics Network.

on a four-week cycle and can be purchased for an entire network of stores in one market or on a store-by-store basis. Advertisers who have used the system include Procter & Gamble, General Mills, and Kraft General Foods. A trade advertisement for Shoppers' Video is shown in figure 18.12.

Studies have shown that in-store video can be a highly effective medium, especially for certain groups of people. One expert made the following observation:

Not surprisingly, children and teenagers are the easiest groups to capture [with in-store video]. They are the video generation. MTV, Nickelodeon, and Saturday morning cartoons have prepared them to pick up quick hits of information.

Men from 25–50 years old are a good target. They tend to be more likely to look than women in that same age group. In any shopping environment, the strategic positioning of video units can increase the exposure rates to a specific demographic audience.[24]

In-store radio has been available for a number of years. One of the largest companies providing this type of service is POP Radio Corporation, which pipes prerecorded taped music and advertising messages into retail stores. The programming has the effect of a live FM broadcast, including the disc jockey. An advertiser can place a thirty-second commercial during each broadcast hour, with packages bought on a monthly basis. Programming is for twelve hours a day, thus providing a total of 360 messages in a month. The cost to run commercials is around $12 per store for one month. Thus, using the entire network of approximately six thousand stores would result in a monthly cost of approximately $72,000. Estimates of the number of shopper impressions received from POP Radio show a cost-per-thousand of around 40 cents (without production charges).

Miscellaneous Media

Included in this section is yet another set of "other" media types that do not readily fit into previous classifications.

Motion Picture Advertising

Advertising in motion picture theaters, often called "cinema advertising," has been available in the United States since 1897.[25] Its popularity comes and goes, and there has been a resurgence since the late 1980s. Of the approximately 24,000 theater screens in the United States, of which 17,500 show first-run movies, most accept advertising. Cinema advertising has been used extensively for many years in Europe, where television commercials are less common than in the United States.

One of the largest companies selling motion picture advertisements in the United States is Screenvision Cinema Network, a company founded in 1976 by Mediavision of France, the largest cinema advertising firm in the world. Screenvision sells over $25 million of advertising annually through its network of more than 6,100 screens in over two hundred markets. The company limits the number of commercials shown to three, which are presented before the movie begins. Cineplex Odeon, which operates almost 1,200 movie screens, is another company that sells commercials in its theaters. The cost for advertising on Cineplex's screens is around $140,000 for a four-week period. National Cinema Network offers an alternative to cinema advertising in that it sells advertisers "cinema billboards," which are ten-second slides rather than live-action commercials. The company places advertisements on about 3,100 screens. Many cinema advertisers are local businesses, but a number of national advertisers also use the medium, including American Express, the California Raisin Advisory Board (with its "talking raisins" commercials), the U.S. Marine Corps, Toyota, Puma athletic shoes, Volkswagen, and General Motors' Oldsmobile Division.

Motion picture advertising provides advertisers with a number of advantages. For one thing, there is a captive audience, and the advertising is difficult to avoid. For these reasons, cinema-advertising experts recommend that the advertisements be as entertaining as possible and that hard-sell techniques be avoided. When American Express used a commercial similar to its television advertising, viewers expressed their dislike.

With typically only three commercials shown, each usually sixty to ninety seconds in length, cinema advertising is noticeably less cluttered than television advertising. The large visual of the advertisement, coupled with a powerful sound system, allow the advertising to have dramatic impact. Studies have shown that about four out of five viewers remember the advertisement twenty-four hours after seeing it.

Also to be considered, however, is that cinema advertising usually does not permit extensive message repetition and reaches only a certain percentage of the population. For example, studies show that the average moviegoer attends about eight

TABLE 18.4

Movie Attendance by Age Group

	Percentage Who Have Attended a Movie in Last Ninety Days
18–24 years old	44%
25–34 years old	38
35–44 years old	37
45–54 years old	27
55–64 years old	21
65 years or older	14
Total Adults	**31%**

Source: *Mediaweek's Guide to Media*, third quarter, 1991, 76.

movies a year, thus yielding a low average frequency of exposure. About 30 percent of all adults attended a movie in the last ninety days, although, as shown in table 18.4, the percentages vary noticeably according to age.

Perhaps the most pertinent disadvantage of motion picture advertising is the possibility of alienating the audience who have paid to see the movie. Recent research on this issue is somewhat inconclusive. For example, the Walt Disney Company, which along with Warner Brothers presently prohibits movie theaters from showing on-screen commercials before its films, found from its research that 90 percent of people surveyed did not want commercials shown in movie theaters.

On the other hand, a Gallup study found that only 44 percent favor a ban on movie commercials, with 35 percent opposing such a ban, and 21 percent undecided.[26] The Gallup study further asked those favoring a ban on advertisements whether they would continue to favor a ban if it meant an increase in admission price. Under this scenario, half of the group said they would still oppose advertisements if the price increase was 50 cents; only 26 percent said they would continue to favor a ban if

the price increase was $1; and for a $2 price increase, opposition shrank to 15 percent. Research by Screenvision showed that two-thirds of moviegoers said they would not like to see movie advertising when they were interviewed *before* going into the theater; but when interviewed upon *exiting* the theater, two-thirds of the audience said they liked the commercials shown before the movie.[27]

Videocassette Commercials

The use of prerecorded videocassettes as an advertising medium can be dated to 1987, when a sixty-second commercial showing fighter pilots drinking Diet Pepsi in midflight appeared on the home-video version of the movie *Top Gun*. Since then, videocassettes have been used by a number of advertisers, including Diet Coke at the beginning of the *Batman* video, a ninety-second commercial for Procter & Gamble's Downy brand on *The Wizard of Oz*, Nestle's on *Dirty Dancing*, Jeep on *Platoon*, a Snickers commercial on *Moonstruck*, and Pizza Hut on *The Land before Time*.

With around two-thirds of all homes owning a VCR, and increasing percentages of people buying and renting videocassettes, the medium seems logical for increased future use. Yet, some problems are associated with such advertising. The major issues deal with how people feel about such commercials and whether they view them. For example, a Gallup study found that two-thirds of people interviewed said commercials at the beginning of a video were either "very annoying" (36.3 percent) or "somewhat annoying" (31.2 percent); 32.5 percent found such advertisements "not at all annoying."[28] When asked whether they watched the commercial on a video, 57 percent said they did, whereas 42 percent said they used fast-forward to "zip" through the advertisement (1 percent were not sure how they handled the situation).[29] Many advertising media experts believe results such as these will limit future growth.

Another way in which videocassettes are being used as an advertising medium is when advertisers buy a program from a producer, add commercials,

FIGURE 18.13 Advertisement for "Channel One"
Courtesy of Whittle Communications L.P.

and distribute the tape either free or as a premium offer. For example, Hallmark Cards offered a thirty-minute "Creepy Classics" videocassette as a Halloween promotion, charging $4.95 for the video with any $5.00 purchase of Hallmark products. A variation on this theme was even used by a political candidate running for Congress in a California district. The candidate distributed free to voting households 110,000 videos containing an eight-minute political advertisement.[30] No programming material appeared on the tape.

"Channel One"

"Channel One," a medium launched in 1990 by Whittle Communications, is a twelve-minute daily television news program seen exclusively in junior high and high schools throughout the United States.

Included in the programming are two minutes of commercials—four thirty-second units. The system began operations in early 1990 in about one thousand schools, is currently in over eight thousand schools, and expects to reach over fifteen thousand schools in the next few years.[31] To date, advertisers have included Burger King fast-food restaurants, Snickers candy bars, Head & Shoulders shampoo, Levi Strauss leisure wear, and Wrigley chewing gum. Figure 18.13 is an advertisement for "Channel One."

"Channel One" has met opposition from a number of groups, especially state education bodies who feel that commercials should not be shown in classrooms. It may also face competition from cable systems, such as Turner Broadcasting System's Cable News Network (CNN), which likewise is planning a similar form of news programming, but without commercials.

Whittle Communications also provides a similar medium, "Special Reports Television" ("SRTV"), in twenty thousand physicians' offices. Begun in fall 1990, "SRTV" features family-oriented information and entertainment programming. Hour-long programs are divided into eight segments, such as travel and health, that are changed twice a month. Each "SRTV" hour has about fifteen minutes of commercials. "Channel One" and "SRTV" could be considered a special type of "in-store" television advertising.

Sports and Theatrical Events

At least three categories are included in the sports and theatrical events media type: (1) *programs* sold or distributed free at sporting events and the live performances of theater plays, concerts, and the like, (2) stadium *scoreboards,* and (3) *poster-type* advertisements in sports stadiums and theater lobbies. While these types could be classified elsewhere in this book—as regular print advertising and as a special type of out-of-home—they are sufficiently distinct as to warrant special discussion.

Most college and professional sports events have a program that contains information about the game and the players, as well as both local and national advertising. The group sponsoring the sporting event usually has a sales staff to sell space to local advertisers; advertising sales representatives typically sell national advertisers. Space is sold in page and fractional-page units. As is the case for magazine advertising, discounts are given for frequency and quantity of advertising purchased during a contract period. By the same token, print advertisements are available in programs for live plays, musicals, concerts, ballets, and other events—from local community theater productions to Broadway plays.

Stadium scoreboards, especially in college and professional sports arenas, are today quite intricate, usually with elaborate lighting effects that are computer-driven and capable of producing dramatic commercials. Also, scoreboards usually have fixed advertising display units on their frames. The athletic departments of colleges and companies owning professional teams sell advertising to local and national advertisers.

Stadiums have a host of other locations where poster-type advertising can be placed, and similar posters also are often available in theater lobbies. These advertisements are similar in appearance to transit-station posters. Other opportunities for advertising in sports arenas include the fences of a baseball stadium (especially in the minor leagues), which often host painted bulletins, and the walls around an ice-skating arena, which can be painted with an advertising message. Madison Square Garden in New York, in addition to some of the types already mentioned, sells large dioramas (approximately 6 feet wide by almost 4 feet high) in the promenade and tower.

Trade Shows

In one sense, trade shows and exhibits can be considered a form of sales promotion rather than strictly an advertising medium. Yet, the display booths and exhibits used at trade shows often contain advertisements, and accordingly, they are included here as a type of advertising medium.

Trade shows bring together in a single location a group of suppliers who set up exhibits of their products and services from a particular industry or discipline in an effort to reach both businesspeople and ultimate consumers. The event usually is held in an exhibit hall, often specially designed for such events, or a convention center or hotel. Trade shows can range in size from only fifteen to twenty exhibitors to over one thousand exhibits and more than 100,000 attendees. The trade show provides excellent opportunities for marketers to promote and sell their products and services through display and demonstration, as well as by providing exposure to advertising themes. Customers are able to examine the product in its natural setting and to make comparisons with competing products. Exhibitors can enlarge their dealer contacts and distribute samples and advertising literature.

Trade shows are particularly useful in promoting new products or innovations in existing products or services. They are especially important in fields in which technical innovations are appearing at a rapid rate. For example, trade shows dealing with computer hardware and software are very popular with both businesses and consumers.

A great deal of professional skill is required to design exhibits effectively, and many companies hire trade-show specialists to design and build their displays (see figure 18.14). Usually, however, *company* personnel work at the trade-show booth, showing the product, answering questions, handing out sales and advertising literature, and sometimes taking orders.

Audiotex and Videotex

Two newer forms of alternative media are audiotex and videotex. **Audiotex,** mentioned earlier in the chapter with regard to "talking Yellow Pages," involves an advertiser leasing telephone lines from such companies as AT&T, MCI, and Sprint and delivering messages to people who call an 800 or 900 number. Messages can be heard by the caller with no other action required, or they can be "interactive." In the case of an interactive system, the callers can request certain information by pressing buttons on their touch-tone phone. For example, a multiproduct company might deliver a general message at first and then permit the caller to request specific

Imagine this...

EUROPEAN SOCIETY OF CARDIOLOGY CONGRESS, STOCKHOLM

as a turnkey rental exhibit... anywhere in the world.

Feeling the pinch of budget and travel constraints, yet still have the need to put your best foot forward in the international healthcare marketplace? Impact Exhibits, with more than a decade of global marketing experience, can rent you a custom-designed tradeshow exhibit to showcase your company anywhere in the world.

And there's more! Impact's award-winning design team is backed by a quality-oriented, nonstop service and support staff that can help you surround

your one-of-a-kind exhibit with a wide range of value-added marketing services... from pre-show planning and training to lead management and fulfillment.

Discover why SmithKline Beecham and others entrust their corporate images to us. For more information on Impact Exhibits and our worldwide rental program, call **1-800-321-1148** today or write Impact Exhibits, Inc., P.O. Box 558, Dayton, New Jersey 08810.

IMPACT
EXHIBITS, INC.

FIGURE 18.14 Trade Advertisement for a Firm That Designs Exhibits
Courtesy of Impact Exhibits, Inc., Dayton, NJ 08810.

brand information. In cases where the company sells its products directly to consumers, such as a catalog house, the caller can even place an order.

Calls placed via a 900 number are typically paid for by the caller, although some companies using these lines cover some or all of the cost. Advertisers using audiotex include Lever Brothers, RJR Nabisco, Kraft General Foods, Kimberly Clark, and Anheuser-Busch. Although audiotex is often used for consumer promotions, such as contests, sweepstakes, and games, it is increasingly being used to deliver regular advertising messages.

Videotex is an interactive electronic system in which data and graphics are transmitted from a computer network over telephone lines and displayed on a subscriber's computer terminal or television screen. To access videotex, a person must subscribe to a videotex service and have the necessary hardware, usually a computer equipped with a modem. Subscribers can receive a wide range of services, including news, weather, and sports information; at-home banking and financial services; travel schedules and reservations; real estate listings; and buying and ordering information. Because videotex is an interactive system, subscribers can ask for additional information, including advertising messages, and actually place orders for products and services.

One of the largest videotex systems operating today is Prodigy Services Company, a joint venture of IBM and Sears, Roebuck. Started in 1988, Prodigy has 460,000 subscribers in forty markets who pay a flat monthly fee, and over two hundred advertisers are using the system.[32] Prodigy subscribers see teaser advertisements at the bottoms and sides of their screens, and they can then access the full advertisement for more complete information. Each advertisement consists of a specified number of screens. Current advertising charges are $11,500 per month for a five-screen unit and $16,000 per month for fifteen screens.

One of the limiting features of videotex systems is that there presently are only about six million homes equipped with a personal computer and modem. This number, however, will likely increase notably in the future, especially as new information appliances become available, such as a "voice-data telephone."

MEDIA SPOTLIGHT

18.3

How Advertising Agencies Participate Profitably in Trade Shows

by Jenny Tesar

The trade-show medium has changed dramatically during the past ten years, evolving into the most cost effective and dynamic of all direct-marketing media. Corporations of all sizes and in all industries have recognized that trade shows are major selling opportunities. It is not uncommon, for instance, for a company to write 50 percent or more of its annual sales at one or two shows.

Maximizing selling and other marketing opportunities available at trade shows requires the application of many of the same creative marketing techniques used in advertising and other similar endeavors. In recognition of this, many companies are turning to their advertising agencies, who are marketing experts, for assistance in their trade-show programs.

Concurrently, many agencies have recognized the potential value to them of involvement in the trade-show industry. Indeed, a recent study found that "84 percent of ad agencies felt that trade shows [are] a valuable and important sales/marketing tool." It has become evident that agencies *must* be knowledgeable about trade shows and how to effectively use them if they are to provide complete marketing services for their clients. These findings are supported and illustrated by ten case studies conducted for the Trade Show Bureau. The studies, of advertising agencies actively involved in their clients' trade-show programs, contain numerous examples of specific ways in which the agencies have been instrumental in helping their clients utilize the trade-show medium for maximum productivity. The clients cover a broad range of industries, from heavy trucking to pharmaceuticals. If they have a common denominator, it

is in the appreciation by their corporate executives of the tangible benefits to be derived from well-thought-out and well-executed marketing programs.

Many Types of Involvement

An advertising agency can help clients utilize trade shows in numerous ways:

• **Unified image.** A company that involves its agency in its trade-show program ensures that all marketing media present one unified image of the company. "Because the show is usually just one communications vehicle in a larger mainstream, you want to present the same message to your marketplace at the show as you do in advertising and public relations materials. This means that the show has got to have the same style and say the same things—it shouldn't be doing its own thing," says William O'Neal, president of O'Neal & Prelle. In the case study of his agency, O'Neal illustrates this point by describing how the agency created a theme and visual motif for one of its clients. Even the systems engineers who demonstrated the client's products at a show followed a script that had the same structure and the same story told by ads and literature.

• **Setting objectives.** Agencies can provide objective input as they assist clients in developing trade-show schedules, defining objectives for each show, and selecting the exhibit designer and producer. Often, involvement goes much further. For instance, when Fleishmann & O'Connor Marketing, as part of developing a comprehensive marketing program, planned a client's trade-show program, the agency's responsibilities included evaluation of sixty-four shows the client might enter, recommendations on booth size and location, development of configurations for five different booth sizes, and the creation of lead-tracking forms.

Continued on page 418

18.3 cont.

• **Preshow promotion.** Preshow promotion campaigns are an essential yet often-overlooked ingredient of a successful trade-show program. Among the examples of effective preshow programs detailed in the case studies is one developed by Anderson & Lembke, which took an unconventional route to achieve 100 percent turnout of its client's prospects at a key trade show. "Ironically, the resounding success of the campaign cost us business in the short run," says Hans Ullmark, the agency's executive vice president. "Our campaign was so effective that the factory stretched to its limits to meet production demands. The follow-up advertising campaign is, for the time being, on hold."

• **Increased visibility.** "Since we are also responsible for our client's advertising and collateral material, it is easy for us to see that these are well coordinated, both in timing and in appearance," says Quinten Barclay, president of Cummings Advertising. "Still another aspect we contribute is the organization of press conferences in conjunction with trade-show participation. Here we have been involved from facilities arrangements to the writing of presentations. Most of the time, we handle all the arrangements, including speech writing and food-and-beverage service. We have even made arrangements to transport editors from their hotels to the press conference."

• **Added value.** Agencies can help increase exhibitors' visibility through the creative use of show dailies, seminars, and other activities. "We're talking about added value—of making an exhibitor's $10,000 worth $20,000 or $100,000 worth $200,000," says Katrine Barth, president of The Barth Group. "Many [corporate] exhibit managers have more than enough to worry about. Their time is taken up with shipping and setup and assembling a sales staff and dozens of other responsibilities. The fine details that could increase the value of their trade-show participation are what an agency can best handle for them."

• **Training, motivation.** Many agencies have the resources to develop effective training and motivational programs. In one program developed by Shapiro & Conner, the objective was to get independent reps to bring their five top customers to the client's exhibit. Successful reps were rewarded with all-expenses-paid vacations. "If you spend $50,000 or more for a trade-show exhibit, why not spend an extra few thousand dollars to ensure that the $50,000 was well spent," says the agency's president, Alan Shapiro.

• **Special events.** An agency's creative talents can be especially helpful in planning and organizing hospitality functions. In any business, many long-term relationships can be nurtured or solidified in a social environment. Even in hospitality

Summary

Directory advertising includes the familiar Yellow Pages, started in the 1890s, as well as other consumer and business directories. Yellow Pages advertisements are of varying shapes and forms. Common forms are: display advertisements, trademark headings, space listings, and regular listings that may contain semi-bold or bold type. New innovations include "talking Yellow Pages," where a person can access directory advertising by telephone, minidirectories that fit in briefcases or glove compartments, and "billboard" advertisements for national brand goods advertisers. Directory

functions, however, it is important to reinforce the exhibitor's name in the mind of current and potential customers. Simms & Mclvor did this by subtly and amusingly incorporating the names of its client's products in scoreboard messages displayed during a Super Bowl party for orthopaedic surgeons. The party, held at the New Orleans Super Dome, attracted 4,132 of the 7,500 surgeons at the convention and was the highlight of their trip. Yet "costs were deceptively low," says agency president Patrick Mclvor.

• **Market research.** Trade shows offer a superb opportunity to learn the thinking of clients, prospects, and show attendees in general. Many agencies spend a significant amount of time at trade shows in which their clients participate. One of their objectives is to assess the impact of their clients' exhibits. "It's only through personal observation that I can determine whether a client's exhibit is working, is doing what we wanted it to do," says Keith Sanderson, vice president/general manager of Andrews/Mautner. Sanderson also visits his clients' competitors to learn what they are doing, then turns around and offers constructive recommendations to his own clients.

Type of Involvement Varies

All the agencies in the case studies develop advertisements and other promotional materials in conjunction with their clients' trade-show programs. But while some also provide such services as exhibit design and setup, others work in partnership with the client's exhibit design firms. "There should always be a close association between the agency and the exhibit house," says Alan Hutchings, a partner of Barbeau-Hutchings. "If just the client works with the exhibit house without the input of the agency, they're not going to have the same feel for what should be at the booth in order to draw people in."

Although the types of trade-show services provided to clients vary significantly from agency to agency, all those interviewed for the case studies agree that there are significant contributions to be made in this area. "Involvement at some level is necessary, I think, if an agency wants to do a decent job for its clients," says Steve Swanbeck, president of Forum Communications. "Trade shows are a marketing vehicle whose time has come in this country. They offer many advantages to a company eager to market its products or services . . . and many opportunities to advertising agencies eager to expand the services they provide their clients."

Source: Courtesy of the Trade Show Bureau.

advertising is characterized as being "directional" in that it directs a person to the store where a product is available. It reaches customers when they are ready to buy, is widely used by large numbers of people, can deliver repeated exposures over a year, is flexible in terms of geographic coverage, but primarily serves to provide only reminder-type messages. Advertising is bought from the directory publisher's sales staff or through an authorized sales representative (ASR).

Advertising specialties are useful articles of merchandise imprinted with an advertiser's message and given away to customers or potential customers. Over fifteen thousand different specialty items are available, including calendars, writing instruments and desk accessories, wearable items, business gifts, and "other" imprinted specialties, such as key rings, flashlights, and coffee mugs. Specialty advertising is noted for its ability to preselect a targeted audience, thus resulting in little waste circulation. The medium provides high exposure opportunity through its continued use over long periods of time and allows much flexibility in when and how it is used. The brief nature of the advertising communication, however, can be a limiting factor. Advertisers typically buy specialty advertising from distributors, who represent a number of manufacturer suppliers. Distributors provide a full counseling service in the effective use of the medium. A few companies are direct–selling houses, and they produce their own items as well as sell them to advertisers.

In addition to the standard types of out-of-home media, transportation terminals may contain dioramas, kiosks, clocks, and television monitors showing advertising. Kiosks can also be located in shopping malls. Other forms of nonstandard out-of-home advertising include displays on bus shelters, taxicabs, trucks, vans, and pay-telephone faceplates and enclosure panels. Skywriting, airplane banners, blimp advertising, inflatables, and hot-air balloons are also specialty forms of out-of-home media. These out-of-home media, like the standardized part of the industry, provide mass coverage, yield dramatic impact, allow for flexibility in a media mix, and typically are cost efficient.

In-store media consist of point-of-purchase displays (such as aisle displays, shelf units, and floor stands), shopping carts and bags, and in-store television and radio. Studies have shown that a high percentage of retailers believe that point-of-purchase displays increase sales and attract the attention of store shoppers. A new form of shopping-cart advertising is the use of a video monitor that shows commercials as a shopper pushes the cart through the store. Similarly, television monitors mounted near shopping aisles and at the checkout counter broadcast programs and commercials. In-store radio is used to present music, news, and advertising to shoppers.

Among other, miscellaneous media are motion picture advertising and videocassette commercials.

Likewise, "Channel One" and "Special Reports Television" permit advertisers to buy commercials that are shown in schools and doctors' offices. Advertising also can be purchased in a number of ways at sporting events and theatrical productions: in printed programs, on stadium scoreboards, and on poster-type advertisements in sports arenas and theater lobbies. Trade shows allow prospects to see a product demonstrated, to learn of new product introductions, and to secure sales materials, including advertising. Among the newer types of miscellaneous media are audiotex and videotex. Audiotex delivers advertising messages to people via their telephone, whereas videotex provides verbal and visual communication via a personal computer or television monitor. Both can be interactive in that they permit a user to selectively access specific information.

Questions for Discussion

1. Look in a Yellow Pages directory at some sample advertisements. What characteristics of the advertisements do you feel are most effective? For which type of advertisers is this medium best suited? What types of advertisers use trademark headings?

2. Why is specialty advertising so popular with certain advertisers?

3. Look around your apartment, house, or dorm room to see if you have some advertising specialties, and if so, bring them to class. What type of specialty items do you feel are particularly useful as an advertising medium? Why?

4. What are the most important reasons an advertiser might use nonstandard, out-of-home media in a bus, rail, or airport terminal? In a shopping mall?

5. Visit several local supermarkets, drugstores, and discount merchandise stores. Make a list of all of the different types of in-store advertising you see. Which type or types do you feel are most effective? Why?

6. Are shopping-cart video monitors and in-store television advertising likely to be successful? Give your reasoning.

7. Assume you are a representative of Screenvision Cinema Network, the company selling motion picture advertising in the United States. A local group has been picketing theaters that show commercials, and you are asked to address this group at their next meeting. Prepare a five- to ten-minute speech that will convince them to change their minds about cinema advertising.

8. Will advertising on videocassettes increase or decrease in the future? Why? By the same token, do you feel "Channel One" will be successful or unsuccessful? Why?

9. How effective is stadium scoreboard advertising? Why would an advertiser use this medium?

10. What is your prediction about the future use of advertising on audiotex and videotex? What underlying factors would you consider in making a prediction?

Endnotes

1. "What Is Electronic Publishing?" *Link,* January/February 1990, 28.

2. Diane M. Shister, "The Yellow Pages in 1990," *Link,* November/December 1989, 40.

3. Shister, "The Yellow Pages in 1990," 45.

4. Patricia Strnad, "Yellow Pages Group Offers Brand Buys," *Advertising Age,* 2 April 1990, 1.

5. Wally Wood, "Seeing Red Over Yellow Pages Research," *Marketing & Media Decisions,* April 1989, 120–21. Also, see Carol Hall, "Numbers, Please: As Publishers Reach Out for National Ad Dollars, Their Lack of Objective Research Takes on Greater Importance," *Marketing & Media Decisions,* August 1989, 97–102.

6. *Specialty Advertising, the Medium That Remains to Be Seen* (Irving, Tex.: Specialty Advertising Association International, not dated).

7. "Specialty Advertising Fact Sheet" (Irving, Tex.: Specialty Advertising Association International, not dated).

8. Richard F. Beltramini, "Measuring the Effectiveness of Business Gifts" (Unpublished paper, 1989), 1–2.

9. Beltramini, "Measuring the Effectiveness," 2.

10. William Wells, John Burnett, and Sandra Moriarty, *Advertising Principles and Practice* (Englewood Cliffs, N.J.: Prentice-Hall, 1989), 290.

11. *Specialty Advertising,* 3.

12. *Preference Building, the World of Specialty Advertising* (Supplied by the Specialty Advertising Association International, not dated).

13. See pamphlet by DDB Needham, "A Reference Guide to Alternative Media Forms," 3 February 1988, 3.

14. Bob Geiger, "New Medium Rings a Bell," *Advertising Age,* 20 March 1989, 50-E.

15. *Advertising Age,* 16 July 1990, 29.

16. Parts of the material in this section come from S. Watson Dunn, Arnold M. Barban, Dean M. Krugman, and Leonard N. Reid, *Advertising: Its Role in Modern Marketing,* 7th ed. (Chicago: Dryden Press, 1990), 470–72.

17. See the series of reports: "Retailer Attitudes on P.O.P." (Englewood, N.J.: Point-of-Purchase Advertising Institute, for Mass Merchandisers, Convenience Stores, and Chain Drugstores, not dated).

18. "Retailer Attitudes on P.O.P."

19. Alison Fahey, "Advertising Media Crowd into Aisles," *Advertising Age,* 18 June 1990, 18.

20. Ira Teinowitz, "VideOcart Starts to Roll for IRI," *Advertising Age,* 8 January 1990, 30.

21. Scott Hume, "Improved VideOcart Starts Test," *Advertising Age,* 12 November 1990, 66. Also see "High-tech Advances in Food Aisles," *USA Today,* 25 April 1991, 1D.

22. Robert McMath, "In-Store Devices Are Popping Out All Over," *Adweek's Marketing Week,* 9 July 1990, 57. Also see Michael Burgi, "Turner, Actmedia Roll In-Store TV," *Advertising Age,* 20 May 1991, 40.

23. Laurie Petersen, "On a Roll, Shoppers' Video Links with Nynex," *Adweek's Marketing Week,* 2 July 1990, 8.

24. Paco Underhill, "In-Store Video Ads Can Reinforce Media Campaigns," *Marketing News,* 22 May 1989, 7.

25. *Mediaweek's Guide to Media,* third quarter, 1991, 75.

26. Scott Hume and Marcy Magiera, "What Do Moviegoers Think of Ads?" *Advertising Age,* 23 April 1990, 4.

27. Marcy Magiera, "Advertisers Crowd onto Big Screen," *Advertising Age,* 18 September 1989, 10.

28. Scott Hume, "Consumers Pan Ads on Video Movies," *Advertising Age,* 28 May 1990, 8.

29. Hume, "Consumers Pan Ads."

30. Steven W. Colford, "Video Ads: Sign of the Future for Politicians," *Advertising Age,* 23 October 1989, 28.

31. Scott Donaton, "Whittle Nets May Get Boost," *Advertising Age,* 19 August 1991, 4.

32. Alison Fahey, "Videotex Hard-Sell," *Advertising Age,* 30 April 1990, 54; and Alison Fahey, "Prodigy Loads Up," *Advertising Age,* 10 September 1990, 24.

Suggested Readings

- Dunn, S. Watson, Arnold M. Barban, Dean M. Krugman, and Leonard N. Reid. *Advertising: Its Role in Modern Marketing.* 7th ed. Chicago: Dryden Press, 1990. Chapter 18.
- Fletcher, Alan D. *Yellow Pages Advertising.* Rev. ed. Chesterfield, Mo.: American Association of Yellow Pages Publishers, 1987.
- Gaw, Walter A. *Specialty Advertising.* Chicago: Specialty Advertising Association International, 1972.
- McGann, Anthony F., and J. Thomas Russell. *Advertising Media.* 2d ed. Homewood, Ill.: Irwin, 1988. Chapter 11.
- Russell, J. Thomas, and Ronald Lane. *Kleppner's Advertising Procedure.* 11th ed. Englewood Cliffs, N.J.: Prentice-Hall, 1990. Chapter 14.
- Shimp, Terence A. *Promotion Management and Marketing Communications.* 2d ed. Chicago: Dryden Press, 1990. Chapter 16.
- *Specialty Advertising, the Medium That Remains to Be Seen.* Irving, Tex.: Specialty Advertising Association International, not dated.
- Wells, William, John Burnett, and Sandra Moriarty. *Advertising: Principles and Practice.* Englewood Cliffs, N.J.: Prentice-Hall, 1989. Chapters 11, 17, 18.

PART VI

THE FUTURE

Chapter 19

Trends and Projections

Outline

Learning Objectives

In the study of this chapter, you will have the opportunity to:

- See how future developments may affect current advertising planning.
- Learn what changes are currently occurring in the structure of the advertising business.
- Understand the new media technologies and how they may simultaneously simplify and complicate media planning.
- See how the advertising media industry is growing, and examine its prospects for future growth.
- Explore advertising media employment possibilities.
- Learn about the growing importance of international advertising.

As with any kind of planning, media strategies deal with the future. When media planners select the media and vehicles to be used for an advertising campaign, they are really trying to predict which channels will best carry the advertising message. For example, television ratings are not available until *after* the programs are run, so scheduling television commercial time involves trying to predict actual audience levels. Similarly, all advertising media planning, estimating, and buying involve predictions.

Because of this need to deal with the future, advertising media planners and buyers must know and understand current business trends as well as future projections. Future concerns may focus on the advertising business itself, changing media technology, the use of computers in media planning and buying, changes in the media measurement, the growth of the media business, and international involvement, all of which can affect how well plans and strategies will mirror actual development. We now examine each of these future concerns in greater detail.

Advertising Business Trends

Like any dynamic operation, the advertising business is constantly changing and shifting, so advertising strategies must change, too. Advertising agencies gain accounts and lose other accounts. Advertisers decide to change the direction, scope, and purpose of their advertising efforts. Media alter their advertising rates. Commercial time is already taken by another advertiser, so plans must shift to take advantage of what is still available. In this section, we look at some of the changes faced by agencies and also by advertisers.

Agencies

In recent years, many of the significant changes have occurred within the advertising agencies themselves. Some agencies that already were comparatively large have become even larger, through a variety of means. Even a very large advertising agency experiences significant growth when it acquires a very large new account: When the largest U.S. advertising agency—Young & Rubicam, Inc.—was awarded the advertising account for the U.S. Army recruitment efforts, the Army account was the largest in the agency's New York headquarters office; the Leo Burnett USA agency gained its largest account when it took on the advertising for McDonald's.

One long-standing concern of agencies has been the use of **in-house** or simply **house agencies**—that is, advertiser-owned and -controlled advertising agencies. House agencies have been used especially by packaged-goods marketers, who have frequent product improveness and who wish to maintain strict advertising confidentiality. The trend toward house agencies comes and goes, and nobody can be certain whether their popularity will grow.

Similarly, separate media buying services outside of advertising agencies have grown and waned in cycles of popularity. Originally, these services were formed by independent media planners and buyers, whose experience and singularity of function could provide greater media economies. Eventually, advertising agencies countered by making their media departments stronger and media work more of a long-term career opportunity. Some advertisers prefer to use full-service advertising agencies, particularly when the agencies offer full marketing services as well. Other advertisers may be better served buying their advertising services

MEDIA SPOTLIGHT

19.1

Growth of Performance-Based Agency Compensation

Performance-based compensation for advertising agencies is rapidly replacing the 15 percent fixed-commission system that has historically supported advertising agencies. In the past, agencies generally opposed performance-based compensation, contending that too many factors other than advertising influence sales. Now a survey of agencies and advertisers has found that a majority of them support performance-based compensation. According to the study's author, researcher Nancy Salz, it is "not just a money issue; it's a way-of-working-together issue."

Other findings from the survey:

- Only 15 percent of the advertisers reported paying their agencies on product performance, but 65 percent said they favored such systems.

- Of the agencies, 62 percent also endorsed the concept.

- Of those companies using performance-based compensation for their agencies, 82 percent said that the quality of their advertising had improved. The remainder indicated no change in advertising quality.

- The same fraction—82 percent—said that performance-based compensation had improved motivation among their agencies and account managers.

- Among the agencies who are paid according to performance, only 40 percent said that their advertising had improved, 55 percent said that their work had not changed, and 5 percent admitted that their work had grown worse.

- Among the advertisers, 45 percent said that performance-based compensation had increased their sales. An identical percentage said that it had no effect on sales.

Source: From Randall Rothenberg, "Basing Pay on Results Gets Support," *New York Times*, 7 June 1990.

piecemeal from media buying services and other similar functionaries.

Some advertising agencies started as specialized shops, dealing only with particular kinds of businesses, but eventually grew into larger, more general agencies. Other agencies began as small, personal shops that concentrated on, for example, outstanding advertising copywriting, but their success attracted more advertiser clients and caused them to expand. One approach to this expansion involves hiring more people to work at the agency. Another approach might be to open additional offices, often in more than one city. Sometimes, growth involves expanding existing departments, while at other times, it involves adding new departments to service new client needs.

In recent years, one trend in agency growth has involved the merger of two agencies to form a larger shop. The belief tends to be that the two merging agencies can benefit from some sort of synergy, by complementing one another's strengths and experience. Merged agencies may also recognize greater economies of scale because management of two agencies under the same organizational structure may be more cost effective.

Some of these mergers have worked out quite well, and the new firm has thrived right from the beginning. In other cases, however, the usual problems of mergers—involving duplication of some types of functions and personnel, along with smaller-than-anticipated savings from economies of scale—have developed. In addition, determining who is senior within the joined organizations is often difficult, as is creating new organizational charts and reporting channels. Salaries and ranks carried over from the formerly separate firms also must be equalized.

One very significant advertising agency change has come with the declining use of the commission system, which was discussed in chapter 2. At one time, most agency work was financed by a standard 15 percent commission on the costs of media placement. For many years now, experts have predicted the decline of the commission system. Now that decline has begun, it has not only brought the long-anticipated shift to fee payments and cost-plus payments for agencies. Several large advertisers have begun using performance-based compensation for their agencies. In some cases, agency income is based on clients' sales; in other cases, various measurements of advertising success, such as readership, recognition, and recall of advertisements, are used to determine how much an agency is paid.

Some supporters of performance-based agency compensation recommend judging performance by subjective criteria, such as client satisfaction, rather than by sales or store traffic. Yet, these kinds of factors are very difficult to measure. What scale should be used? What measurement tool should be developed or adopted, and does it really measure the characteristic that is of concern in establishing goals and accomplishments? What is a fair starting point? Is some benchmark needed? What might constitute an adequate increase in these rather nebulous factors?

No matter what measures are utilized, with performance-based compensation, advertising agencies producing superior advertising receive higher compensation than those that produce mediocre advertising. (A background perspective on the commission system and advertising agency compensation is provided in chapter 2.)

Advertisers

Advertisers, the agencies' clients, have also changed in recent years. Advertisers have grown larger: Through its acquisitions of other large advertisers, such as Kraft Foods, Miller Brewing Company, and General Foods Corporation, Philip Morris moved ahead of other large advertisers, such as Procter & Gamble, to become the largest advertiser in the world.

Advertisers have also become more involved in multinational operations, trying to streamline and coordinate advertising efforts. IBM once used several agencies throughout the world but, for example, is now moving toward using a single agency in most of Latin America. Other advertisers may merge their advertising to a single agency to achieve closer control over the advertising campaigns, to promote greater creative continuity from one place to another, and, perhaps, to save money spent for advertising. (International advertising is discussed in more detail later in the chapter.)

Just the opposite, however, can also occur. At the same time it was merging advertising operations in other parts of the world, IBM was also splitting its U.S. advertising account to be served by two separate and individual advertising agencies. The company's former agency had lost its principals (that is, its founders and major officers), who left to form their own new agency. IBM decided not to stay with the former agency and not to go to the newly formed agency, but instead went to two totally different agencies than it had used before. One of the new agencies took over the corporate portion of the account, and the other new agency took on the product-oriented advertising. Because IBM's advertising account was split between two agencies, the entire IBM advertising operation will not be at risk in the future as it was when IBM's former agency was experiencing personnel changes.

A very recent development is for an advertiser to place its own executives at the advertising agency to work on the advertiser's account. The first such instance of this new kind of arrangement was when Lotus Development Corporation, the computer software company, selected Hill, Holliday, Connors, Cosmopulos of Boston as its advertising agency. At the same time, two creative directors at Lotus were assigned to work 40 percent of their time as part of the agency's creative team, helping to develop the creative portion of the Lotus advertising campaign.

Media Buy Lines: The Agencies' Position

In my work as executive director for L.I.A.N. (Leading Independent Agency Network), I've noted a definite trend for medium to large agencies to establish their media operations as separate profit centers handling media for nonclients. The L.I.A.N. agencies are typical of agencies in the $50- to $500-million range since our group includes leading independent agencies in major markets, such as New York, Los Angeles, Atlanta, and Dallas.

There are two basic reasons for this trend. First, agency commission income is being reduced; and second, some media-buying services are making a handsome profit.

There's no question that many major clients are reducing their commissions downward from the former "standard" of 15 percent. The Association of National Advertisers found that many companies are operating at 10.5 percent or less, and my recent consulting work with five of the nation's top-ten advertisers confirms the survey data.

Agencies need to make up the loss. But if they trim media departmental costs too low, their work will suffer and their clients will fall prey to media-buying services. The better alternative is to set up their department as a profit center by handling media work for other nonagency clients and even for noncompetitive agencies.

In the L.I.A.N. group of agencies, well over half are already in the process of doing just that. They are also going a step further by combining their media resources into a separate network-television subsidiary headed up by Steve Auerbach of Ally & Gargano and by making regional buys for the other L.I.A.N. agencies in their home regions. Here's what several L.I.A.N. agencies feel about the concept:

Errol Dengler of Wyse Advertising in Cleveland launched a division known as Pinnacle Media in July 1988 and increased the agency's media volume with media-only clients. "One of the benefits of Pinnacle Media's success is that it enables us to reinvest the incremental dollars back into our media operation," he says.

Dawn Sibley, executive vice president of Ally & Gargano, New York, says that, in addition to their network-television subsidiary, they began buying spot television for political advertisers and for nonagency clients of the MCA Consulting Group. She acknowledges the advantages of the extra income but also says, "This kind of work broadens the horizons of our media professionals and encourages an entrepreneurial spirit."

Jack Shubert, who has recently joined Earle Palmer Brown, claims, "There's no reason major agencies shouldn't be better at buying media than media-buying services—if they make up their mind to invest their income in building a stronger media department."

He should know, since for twenty years before coming to Earle Palmer Brown, Shubert was vice president and general manager of Advanswers, which was the first major agency-backed buying service. In fact, when Gardner Advertising, the parent company, folded last year, Advanswers announced several new clients and topped $300 million in capitalized fees.

And so it goes. The agencies I've been in contact with are enthusiastic about taking on media work for nonagency clients. Agency full-service clients should also welcome it, providing it doesn't detract from their work. And it shouldn't.

When I was at Ralston Purina, we worked with Advanswers, Ally & Gargano, and several other agencies that performed media work for nonagency clients. We found these agencies did such a highly professional media job for us that we were pleased to see them build up their media departments to place even more media.

Source: William M. Claggett, "Buy Lines: Agencies or Services?" *Marketing & Media Decisions,* May 1990, 114.

Media Buy Lines: The Services' Position

Ad agencies have been critical of buying services since they first appeared on the scene some twenty years ago. Now that buying services are prospering and many agency media departments are in flux, some agencies' departments are trying to reshape themselves into structures that look suspiciously like buying services. One of their primary targets is other agencies.

I predict this effort will fail because of some very fundamental problems involving conflicts, confidentiality, and logistics. Let's look at it from the client side.

You're a midwestern company with a local ad agency, and you want to make a spot buy in the New York market. So your agency hands the project over to their affiliated agency in New York to do the buying. At that point, your costs, your buying criteria, your whole business becomes an open book to an outside agency.

Furthermore, if the New York agency has a conflicting piece of business, they can't do the buy. If they don't have conflicting business, it's a sign that they may not know your business or they're not big enough to do the buy effectively. So in that respect, the idea of L.I.A.N.'s "confederation" is somewhat self-defeating.

Now let's look at it from the agency's point of view.

You're a midwestern advertising agency, and your client wants to make a spot buy in the New York market. Are you really going to feel comfortable turning over your hard-won account to a third party? Are they really going to work as hard on the buy as they would on their own business? And when even the once-gentlemanly agencies have taken the gloves off and gone after one another's clients, are you really going to allow another agency to get cozy with your clients?

Even allowing that these obstacles aren't insurmountable, there's the added problem of billing and payment. With more than one agency now in the picture, things can get very complicated. And that means more room for mistakes. No wonder the issue has yet to be resolved on any kind of standardized basis.

What bears serious scrutiny are the reasons why agencies, in particular, are forced to take this action in the first place. By turning to other agencies for their buys, these shops are, in effect, confessing that they can't buy out-of-town markets as effectively as they'd like. Otherwise, they wouldn't be looking for other people to do their buying for them.

Finally, there's the issue of getting the best person for the job. Agencies, particularly the larger ones, have become more volatile and less secure. Many veteran media people have merged, consolidated, and squeezed dry to extract every last nickel for the all-important bottom line. Salaries have been crunched in the process. Under these circumstances, why in the world would an excellent planner, buyer, or media director want to bet his or her future on such an agency?

Buying services, on the other hand, are booming. Most are being run by former advertising agency media people with the foresight to have seen the way the business was heading. And they've been able to attract talented media people away from the agencies.

Source: Ethel Rosner, "Buy Lines: Agencies or Services?" *Marketing & Media Decisions*, May 1990, 115.

MEDIA SPOTLIGHT

19.4

Major Advertisers Try Computer Network Service As a New Advertising Medium

[The PRODIGY *service is an online service from a partnership of IBM and Sears, Roebuck that presents information and advertising from some 200 advertisers and merchants.]*

A long list of well-known firms are participating in the PRODIGY computer service. Prodigy senior vice president Ross Glatzer said, "The increasing audience for the PRODIGY service has created a market that interests a wide variety of companies. Major ad and sales promotion agencies are also seeing the value of this powerful new medium."

Advertisers and marketers are attracted by the demographic profile of PRODIGY service members. Members have a median age of 42, a median household income of $72,000 and a large proportion of women and children—a group advertisers want to reach.

Audi, BMW, Chrysler, Ford, Ford Trucks, Mazda, Mercury, Subaru, and Volkswagen are advertising new model brochures and dealer information.

On the editorial side, *Road & Track* magazine and WGBH's [a Boston public television station] well-known "Last-Chance Garage" provide aid to car owners, and members can trade information about cars on the "HOMELIFE" bulletin board.

Spiegel, J.C. Penney, Sears and many other merchants and direct marketers are selling tens of thousands of products.

United Airlines, NCL, British Tourist Authority, and other travel providers offer information about their products on the service. Travel editorial features on PRODIGY include the EAASY SABRE^{sm} airline, hotel and car reservations system, a travel bulletin board, travel columnists, and an online version of the Mobil Travel Guide.^{sm}

New home-banking services have been added by leading institutions. Electronic banking allows busy PRODIGY service members to pay bills, check statements, and transfer funds twenty-one hours a day, 365 days a year. Home banking is being offered in local markets, but a new product, BillPay USA, provides online bill payment nationwide.

"We are very excited that a wide variety of advertisers, merchants, and other marketers have found new ways to use the power of interactivity to meet the needs of their customers, and to attract new customers as well," Glatzer said.

Source: "200 Advertisers, Banks, Insurance Firms and Merchants Share Rollout Excitement," In Prodigy "Action News & Insights for Creative Marketers," September 1990 (Vol. 1, no. 2), 1–2.

Changing Media Technology

The world is changing more rapidly than ever before, and much of the change is occurring in the mass media. While media planners and buyers must deal with these media changes, they can also take advantage of new technology to help them do their jobs faster and easier. These newer technologies also interact with the tactical decisions that were discussed in Part V of this text.

Sometimes, the media themselves are part of the changing technology, which makes new media opportunities available to advertisers. For example, cable television has experienced tremendous growth

(a)

(b)

FIGURE 19.1 Advertisements Demonstrating the
Growth of Independent Television
Source: Assoc. of Independent Television Stations 1990 Creative by
Fallon-McElligott. Reprinted by permission.

in the past decade, and major advertisers now use
cable as a standard advertising medium. Concomitantly, broadcast ratings services have begun to include cable in their audience surveys. Cable
television also adds to the broadcast times available
to media buyers. Because cable television generally
offers smaller and more selective audiences than do
the major broadcast networks, advertisers can reach
a more homogeneous audience with a more specific
message and with less waste circulation. At the same
time, television network audience levels have declined because of cable competition, home videotape viewing, other competitive media, and the
growth of other recreational and leisure activities.
(Figure 19.1 displays advertisements that demonstrate the growth of independent television.)

With this shift in television-use patterns may
come changes in television's ability to reach large
general audiences. For decades, television has been
a primary marketing tool in the packaged-goods industry, but with the decline of network audiences
and the changes in television viewing habits, this use
of television will certainly be reexamined.

(c)

One exciting new media opportunity is advertising on computer networks. Prodigy, a joint venture of Sears, Roebuck and IBM, offers information
about travel, clothing, automobiles, and many other
items that can be researched and sometimes even
purchased through the Prodigy network. More than
two hundred advertisers are providing information

Why settle for an ad your customers read when you can have one they talk to.

Discover the interactive phone line for local businesses. Only from New York Telephone.

Picture this. Suddenly, people are passing by "the other guy's" ads and going straight to yours! Better yet, more customers than ever are calling to place orders, find out prices, get the information they want, 24 hours a day. Thanks to 394-service from New York Telephone.

While your competitors are closed, you can get more leads...make more sales...bring in bigger profits. Want to make it in New York? Just pay attention to the numbers.

A 394-number can help you get ahead. And stay there. You can change your recorded messages anytime you want. As often as you want. Or use a live salesperson. It's *that* flexible!

394-numbers are local, too. No area code needed for calls from New York City, Long Island, Westchester. So millions of potential customers know they're calling a business in New York. Not a "service center" halfway

across the country. An 800- or 900-number can't give you that!

They can't keep you as lean, either. 394-numbers cost your business less than any 800- or 900-number. Put a 394-number in your ad. Put your business ahead of the competition.

Get the inside story on 394-service. And find out what smart telemarketing can do for your bottom line. It's all connected for you in our free brochure. There's no obligation, of course. Just call

1 800 526-3982 Dept. 70

We're all connected.

New York Telephone
A NYNEX Company

READER SERVICE NO. 10

©1990 New York Telephone

FIGURE 19.2 An Advertisement Promoting a New Telemarketing Service for Advertisers
Source: New York Television.

and advertising through Prodigy, creating an entirely new advertising media opportunity.[1]

The development and growth of other new media types is providing additional avenues for advertising. Advertising is now included on some motion picture rental videotapes, where the advertising helps to promote the sale of the video and may partially underwrite the cost of the movie. New ideas for places and items that may be able to carry advertising are developed every day. (See figure 19.2.)

How these newly developed media may cause some changes in media channel priorities for advertisers is unknown. Certainly, however, marketers will consider any new developments that offer better targeting, less clutter and competition, greater economies, and more control.

Use of Computers in Media Planning and Buying

Computers have attracted special attention in the advertising media business because they offer so many ways to save time, money, and effort while simultaneously combining media facts and information. With the huge memory capacity of newer personal computers, a media planner can have the entire media library, all the media records, and every clients' history and media plan available—right on the office desk. Some aspects of applying computers to media problems were outlined in chapter 14.

Much of the media information that once was available only from thick books and periodical publications can now be accessed through computer networks. On-line information about products, purchasers, media habits, available media, prices, and demographic characteristics can be "called up." This information may come directly from the source, such as a syndicated research firm, or via computerized data banks that store all kinds of information that subscribers can access. Using data banks or on-line computer systems, a media planner can try various combinations of media and vehicles, calculate anticipated costs, match special messages with certain audiences through selective media channels, manipulate various reach and frequency levels, check the availability of desired broadcast times, and even keep a running total of monies committed and accumulated audience figures. (Again, you may wish to refer to earlier discussion about computer applications in chapter 14.)

Changing Media Measurements

How media audience sizes are measured is growing somewhat more complicated. Television viewing once itemized the percentage of households using television (known as **HUT**). Now the percentages of people using television (**PUT**) and women using television (**WUT**) also are measured. Because television viewing levels appear to be declining, advertisers have become concerned about how to reach large audiences. In one two-month period, the Nielsen ratings service indicated that two million fewer Americans were viewing television than previously. These people are not just viewing something else—such as cable or home videos or a new network—they simply are not watching television at all. The networks naturally have taken corrective measures, deemphasizing the importance of television ratings while also stating that the ratings services had been grossly undercounting the viewing levels.

Some major television networks have proposed that, instead of charging according to the rating for a program, the television rates should be based on how well a program does relative to overall general viewing trends, over anywhere from a three-year to an eight-year period. Thus, if a program's audience declined, but did so at the same rate as the decline in general viewing, the advertiser would pay just as much as if the program maintained its original ratings counts. As might be expected, advertisers and their agencies have not been uniformly enthusiastic about this proposal, and some have vigorously resisted the change.

While media audience measurement is becoming more refined and more accurate, more improvements are likely in the future. Some changes may involve more cross-referencing between media habits and purchasing patterns. Greater study of the possible correlations among advertising media and advertising creative approaches may also be proposed. Finding some way to predict audience media usage, rather than tracking it after it occurs, would also prove valuable.

Media Growth

Expenditures for advertising in the United States have been increasing at a faster rate than general consumer price inflation. One estimate is that advertisers may now spend more than $140 billion dollars a year in the United States.[2] Although the local retail advertising market has been rather static of late, regional and national advertising investments have continued to climb. As media costs es-

---

> ## MEDIA SPOTLIGHT
> ### 19.5
> ### Cost of Color Ads
>
> In its first study of print production costs, the American Association of Advertising Agencies found that color ads are about two-and-a-half times as expensive as black-and-white ones. In 1989, the average four-color, one-page magazine ad cost $15,660 to produce; the average black-and-white ad cost $6,224.
>
> Source: Randall Rothenberg, "Media Business," *New York Times*, 30 May 1990.

---

calate, advertisers and agencies search for ways to save money, increase efficiency, and control total advertising costs. Much of this task falls to the media operation.

Expenditures

To put the cost of advertising in perspective, each year more than $570 is spent on advertising per person in the United States. That is more than $1.50 each day for each and every U.S. resident. To a small extent, the increased advertising expenditures are the result of having more media and vehicles available, which result in more opportunities for spending. But the media have also increased the prices charged for advertising (see table 19.1).

To keep costs down, advertisers have begun to buy smaller advertisements, especially in the form of shorter broadcast commercials. While thirty-second commercials were standard a few years ago, more advertisers are now trying fifteen-second and even briefer broadcast announcements. Advertisers have also found that using less than a full page of newspaper space can still dominate the reader's attention while saving some of the money that would be required to purchase the entire page. In addition, advertisers may choose to concentrate advertising in a few media, which adds frequency (often

TABLE 19.1

Index of Advertising Media Cost Trends (1985 = 100)

Cost	Index	Five-Year Change
Network Television		
Daytime	75	Down 25%
Nighttime	131	Up 31%
Spot Television		
Primetime	130	Up 30%
Daytime	100	Unchanged
Network Radio	157	Up 57%
Spot Radio	114	Up 14%
Consumer Magazines	131	Up 31%
National Sunday Supplements	132	Up 32%
Business Publications	128	Up 28%
Newspapers	138	Up 38%
Outdoor	141	Up 41%

Source: *Marketing & Media Decisions*, June 1990.
Note: Comparisons are to a base of 1985 costs, as of the first quarter of 1990. No assessment of value is implied, only actual prices for advertising time and space.

preferable to additional reach) and earns larger discounts from the advertising price (thereby saving the budget).

Media buyers also negotiate lower prices, sometimes by buying a combination of advertisements for more than one client advertiser. Close examination of cost-per-thousand or cost-per-rating-point comparisons helps media buyers to find the most efficient vehicles. Calculating the number of actual prospects or product users for a particular service or product who can be reached through a certain media vehicle, rather than the total audience size, can also help locate a more efficient media vehicle.

The overwhelming number of announcements and messages in the mass media has resulted in media **clutter.** One "solution" has been to buy more messages, sometimes using shorter and smaller messages to compensate for the cost of buying more, but the result is even greater clutter, possibly along with increased prices because of the increased demand for advertising time and space. More sophisticated advertisers look for alternate media availabilities or narrower targets. Some advertisers are even using alternatives to advertising: The amount of money spent on nonadvertising promotions has been increasing far faster than advertising expenditures.

Employment

One way to control costs is to employ fewer persons. Where advertising agencies once hired an average of ten employees for each million dollars of clients' advertising billings, now there may be only one or two persons working on that advertising effort. Of course, part of the apparent reduction is not a reduction at all: While inflation may have increased the cost of advertising, the amount of advertising may not have increased; thus, the number of agency employees may not have declined as much as the cost of advertising went up. Still, cutting employment costs is one way to combat general rising advertising costs.

But with more types of media, more vehicles, more nonadvertising promotions, and more complications in the way that business is conducted, there are still many opportunities for advertising media people. The total number of persons employed in advertising, and especially in advertising media positions, may have declined, and the use of computers and other more efficient approaches may require fewer personnel, but capable individuals can always find interesting positions.

Advertising is still very much a young person's business. Even though the total number of opportunities in advertising agencies may be declining, new opportunities continue to arise. Capable persons can find challenging positions in the advertising media business, and young persons can make an impact at an earlier stage of their professional development.

MEDIA SPOTLIGHT

19.6

Taxes on Advertising

One continuing future threat to advertising is a tax on advertising itself, which local and state governments searching for new sources of revenue often explore. Opponents, including the advertising industry, point out that such a tax may violate the constitutional right to free speech and a free press.

One state that tried such a tax suffered quick and dramatic declines in advertising revenues, as expected. But one unanticipated change was that large advertisers stopped holding business meetings in that state, costing its tourism industry huge sums of revenue. As a result, the advertising tax was dropped.

Still, other states continue to consider taxes on advertising. To avoid problems, several states have considered taxes only on certain aspects of advertising. One popular proposal has been taxing Yellow Pages advertising, with the hope that the free-speech and free-press issues will not come into play if directory advertising is the only target.

Source: Based on Steve W. Colford, "Yellow Pages Tax Fear Spreads," *Advertising Age*, 10 September 1990, 35.

International Advertising

Most large firms and many smaller ones are now engaged in multinational or international sales and marketing. As a result, their advertising must also consider multiple nations, cultures, languages, and markets. The most obvious problem in international advertising involves whether to use the same basic messages and appeals in several countries or whether to develop individual campaigns for each locale. A related concern is how well the advertising messages translate from one language to another.

There are also media concerns in dealing with international advertising transfers. Not all media are available commercially in all countries: A television advertising campaign for Coca-Cola may not be usable in countries that do not have commercial television. Similarly, some countries emphasize certain media, such as cinema advertising (advertising in movie theaters, projected onto the screen before or between films), that are not widely used in the parent country.

Another advertising media difficulty arises in trying to locate reliable information about some countries' media. Good demographic information about audiences and target groups may not be available. In some cases, reliable advertising rate guides are not published, and there is no guarantee that the sizes of audiences claimed by the media vehicles are truthful and actual.

Then there is the matter of taste and permissibility. Some countries think little of nudity in the mass media, while other cultures consider nudity in advertising a personal affront and morally incorrect. As a result of these kinds of problems, an advertising campaign may not be carried in some locations, or it may be edited or censored, yet media buyers are still responsible for ordering the advertising media time or space, possibly from a remote location.

Another potential problem of international advertising involves the different ways of working and communicating in different cultures. A media manager might insult a Japanese businessperson by offering to shake hands. A gift of flowers to a foreign media buyer might be received wrongly because the colors of the flowers may be related to death and illness in the media buyer's culture. Even using another person's first name, or ordering the wrong food at dinner, or eating with the wrong hand may have negative consequences. Once a potential customer feels insulted, it is difficult, if not impossible, to regain confidence and carry on a business relationship.

MEDIA SPOTLIGHT
19.7

Unusual Places for Advertising

Shave the modern way
Fine for the skin
Druggists have it
Burma-Shave

In the fall of 1925, Allan Odell put up a series of four 36-inch-wide signs bearing that jingle along a road leading out of Minneapolis to promote his brushless shaving cream.

His son later recalled advertising professionals said Odell's idea wouldn't work. But it did.

It helped sell Burma-Shave first in Minneapolis and then nationwide, as the distinctive ad signs sprouted along highways nearly everywhere.

It also helped change advertising.

The assumption behind the Burma-Shave ads was that people puttering along in their Model-T Fords would pay as much attention—maybe more—to the road signs as they did to ads in newspapers, magazines, and on the radio.

Despite the tremendous growth of those media in the past sixty-five years—and television—the assumption behind the Burma-Shave signs still is held by advertisers: Consumers will look at and remember messages conveyed in unexpected environments.

In the past decade, as traditional media have become increasingly cluttered and expensive, the number of alternative or nontraditional ad media has exploded.

In 1989, the one hundred largest advertisers spent $19.2 billion on traditional, measured, media advertising. Another $14.9 billion was spent on unmeasured advertising.

The unmeasured category includes such "mainstream" vehicles as sales promotion, direct marketing, and point-of-purchase. But it also includes a growing number of unexpected ad environments. Among them:

• A California company offers ad space on Arm Guard, a sleeve drivers can wear to protect their left arm from sunburn.

• Boudreau/Darque will put your ad in the bottom of golf cups with its Ad-in-the hole.

• Another company, J'atoo, will reproduce corporate logos or add themes as removable, waterproof tattoos.

• Perhaps the ultimate in unexpected ad environments, public restrooms offer unused space on walls or stall doors.

Not all the new ad opportunities are unexpected. The nontraditional sector also includes the growing range of in-store media—such as overhead signage and the VideOcart screen on shopping carts—as well as advertising in movie theaters or high school gymnasiums.

But that explosion of opportunities also has created new problems for those companies selling nontraditional media and for agencies and advertisers evaluating the increasing options.

As with traditional media, the key words driving nontraditional media are environment, audience, cost, and research.

"You do have to look for alternative ways to communicate a client's message. It's no secret that it's become more difficult to reach consumers," says Chris Vlahos, who has researched nontraditional media as media director at Lord, Sullivan & Yoder, Columbus, Ohio. "There certainly are a lot of new options. But you have to put yourself in the position of the consumer in evaluating them," he says.

"I think we've heard pitches for ads just about anywhere you can name," he says. "I think restroom ads are the ultimate in irritating. There should be *some* escape from advertising."

The alternative-media companies say they are aware of the potential for backlash against advertising perceived as intrusive. Many of the most successful new ad media have been developed in conjunction with new services.

Checagau Communications has created a vehicle it calls the GuidePoster. Targeted to upscale travelers and tourists, it is a detailed city map and a guide to high-end restaurants. The company has produced a GuidePoster for Chicago, sponsored by Sears, Roebuck and Company's Discover Card, is preparing a second, for San Francisco, and is contemplating creating similar city-specific products.

Because GuidePoster provides a service as well as ad space, "we've encountered very little hesitation by potential advertisers," says Checagau partner Robert Gifford.

Many top advertisers who have tested the waters in nontraditional media are impressed with formats available both here and overseas. Colgate-Palmolive Company uses mobile cinema—trucks that go into villages and run short movies and commercial messages—with success internationally.

"That medium is very powerful," says Clay Timon, vice president/worldwide advertising. "We're able to run four-minute, very educational commercials." Samples of Colgate products also are distributed through the trucks.

Many nontraditional media companies agree they must offer more than just additional ad space to avoid the "irritation factor" and to succeed.

"A key element is that our programs are perceived as beneficial," says David Rieff, director of marketing and operations at MarketSource, which offers ad-supported programs at colleges.

One is the Campus Source, a communications center that includes a monthly calendar of on-campus events, an LED message screen, and a color, backlit ad.

"Campus Source is a communications medium that also is an ad medium," Rieff says.

The promise of communicating with an audience not easily reached through traditional media is the lure that has spurred the growth of nontraditional media. MarketSource estimates college students represent $33 billion in discretionary spending, yet have lower-than-average exposure to many traditional media. As a result, several companies offer ways to put ad messages in front of that audience.

To interest major advertisers, however, a nontraditional media company needs to have the right numbers. "You've got to have a sufficient number of locations to make it worthwhile," Rieff says, adding his program is on 1,600 campuses.

Liz Conn, associate media director at D'Arcy Masius Benton & Bowles, Chicago, contends it still takes audience numbers to attract her clients to a nontraditional medium.

"If there's no research at all to support an ad opportunity, it's at an immediate disadvantage," she says.

"But clients are open-minded about the opportunities. And for every bad idea out there, there's a good one."

Source: From Scott Hume, "Bounty in Most Unusual Places," in *Advertising Age,* August 27, 1990, S–1 and S–14. Copyright © 1990 Crain Communications Inc., Detroit, MI. Reprinted by permission.

MEDIA SPOTLIGHT
19.8

Coupons Come of Age

Couponing, the promotional technique that dominated the last two decades, is entering a new phase. Its boom years are probably over, due in part to the fact that few major product categories have yet to enter the field. As a result, coupon services and publishers/mailers, like other media, are turning to added-value ideas to give their option a fresh spin. Meanwhile, retailers look for ways to make the most of all those coupons while paying the least.

The best sources differ on current coupon growth trends but agree that it is slowing. Although all the figures are not tabulated for 1989, two of the services that keep a close track on coupons have made some early predictions. Summary Scan (a recent acquisition of the Advertising Checking Bureau) has predicted a mild 2 percent growth in the number of coupons distributed for 1989, but Carolina Manufacturers Service (CMS) sees a healthier 9 percent increase, with a somewhat more modest 5 percent increase predicted for 1990 (see figure 1).

The industry has taken action to thwart misredemption in several highly publicized moves. Last year, local authorities, manufacturers' security managers, CMS, Mc3 (a coupon fulfillment operation), and postal inspectors teamed up

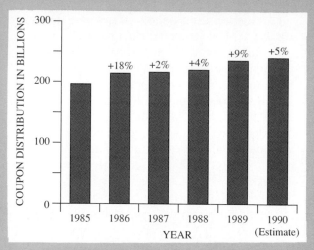

FIGURE 1 Report on Coupon Growth
Marketing and Media Decisions.

to catch foreign felons in Florida, counterfeiters in Texas, and Larry Krasnick, the all-time king of the misredeemers, who attempted to rip off $44 million in coupons.

In a related effort to clean up "unintentional" improper redemptions, the Food Marketing Institute (FMI), Washington, D.C., published a twenty-four-page booklet, titled *Guidelines on Hard-to-Handle Coupons*. It is a very specific set of do's and don'ts on coupons, including a recommended size—6 inches long, with tolerance to

Investment in international advertising is growing at a faster pace than domestic advertising. U.S. advertisers already spend more on international advertising than they do on advertising in their own country, and the annual spending increase is higher as well.[3]

In Conclusion

To stay on top of all the trends and projections examined in this chapter, media planners and buyers must keep current in the business and must react to changing business conditions. While the advertising trade press can be helpful, individual planners and buyers must keep an eye on what is

3 inches, by 2 1/2 inches in width, with tolerance to 2 1/16 inches—endorsed by the Grocery Manufacturers of America.

In-ad coupons seem to be making a comeback, but to mixed reaction. To some, they are a good device for the retailer to offer brand-name savings at little or no direct cost to the chain involved. But compared to those controlled, printed, and placed by manufacturers, in-ad coupons run the risk of serious errors.

CMS, one of the leading coupon redemption service companies, has developed a set of guidelines to avoid accounting and trade relation problems, resulting in a white paper that has been presented to Kelloggs, Hunts-Wesson, Kraft, and several other CMS clients.

There appears to be a trend to shorter coupon expiration dates and a concurrent trend to fewer coupons with "no expiration date." Summary Scan reported in 1989 that only 5 percent of the coupons it monitored had no expiration date. CMS analysis of coupons nationally shows over half have expiration dates of six months or less.

The coupon media lineup is not expected to change drastically for the next year or two. Certainly, freestanding inserts (FSIs) will continue to account for over three-quarters of all coupons distributed. According to Ken Bortner, president of Product Movers/Quad Inserts, FSI pages for the combined insert publishers at Bortner's division of the Rupert Murdoch empire were up 10 percent. Newspaper run-of-paper (ROP) (both black-and-white and color) will probably remain the second most frequent place to find coupons, followed by direct mail.

Both selective/targeted direct mail and various techniques of coupon distribution at retail could make real breakthroughs in the 1990s. The Savings Spot, an interactive in-store computerized display that dispenses coupons and was introduced in Atlanta in 1989, continues expansion to North Carolina and Florida early this year and other markets in the fall. U.S. Suburban Press, Inc., a network of one thousand smaller suburban newspapers, adds markets not covered by the three national FSIs. And Citicorp P.O.S. Information Services has a long-term plan to build a data base of names and addresses that includes both demographics and purchase histories. The project is tied to the service's in-store frequent-shopper program.

Source: Russ Bowman, "Coupons Come of Age," *Marketing & Media Decisions*, February 1990, 74.

occurring in their businesses and everyday personal and business interrelationships.

The advertising business is growing smaller in some ways—through mergers, through increased operating efficiencies, through the use of new media and new technologies, and in the number of persons who work in agencies and for advertisers. But at the same time, the business is growing more complex, and more money is being spent. While local retail advertising rates may be static, regional and national advertising levels are still increasing. And while domestic advertising may not be growing as rapidly as it once did, international advertising is increasing more than ever. The basic point is that the advertising industry needs good people now as much as ever. No matter what the changes, new

MEDIA SPOTLIGHT
19.9

Looking for a Few Good Planners

Like other agency departments, media generally has experienced significant downsizing in recent years. However, many media managers expect to increase their staff within the next year, according to an informal, anonymous survey of fifteen media-department heads conducted recently by *Marketing & Media Decisions*. A third of the respondents said they had added to their staff last year, a third said they were flat, and a third said

they were down. But nine said they planned to hire additional people this year, while four said they would be flat, and only two said they would make further cuts.

Asked what their current department staffing-to-billings ratios were, responses ranged from one media staffer for every $2 million to one per $6 million. The average was one person per $4.3 million in billings. By discipline, there was an average of one planner per $17 million and one buyer per $15 million.

Source: Joe Mandese, "Looking for a Few Good Planners," *Marketing & Media Decisions*, April 1990, 21.

challenges mean that talented, hard-working, capable individuals continue to play an essential role in the advertising business, and especially in the media portion of the advertising world.

Summary

This chapter explores the present and future of the advertising media business. Both the media and advertising itself will be impacted by changes that already are occurring.

First, the advertising business is changing in the way that advertising agencies are hired, staffed, and organized. Although the agency commission system has been slowly declining in importance for many years, the shift to alternate forms of agency remuneration is now much more rapid and far-reaching. Some advertisers even want their own staff people represented among agency personnel.

Changing media technology brings opposing forces into play. The use of computers and new access to media information can somewhat simplify media planners' tasks, but the huge increase in the amount of working data also makes the job much more complicated. New media are developing, offering greater segmentation and thus increased efficiencies, yet this increased ability to target comes at the expense of a more simplified general approach.

Not only are the media and their audiences changing—the way in which audiences are measured is also in flux. Both the measurement techniques and the numerical formats are undergoing an evolutionary transition. The need for increased specificity in audience counts and definitions is fueled by the increasing costs for advertising and the concomitant increases in required advertising investments by advertisers.

Rising advertising costs create pressure to purchase less expensive advertising units, resulting in more advertisements crowded into the same time segment; the clutter that results is countered by scheduling more commercial time, adding to the clutter problem, rather than alleviating it. To fight cost increases, agencies are reducing the number of employees required to prepare advertising campaigns, yet there remain outstanding opportunities for energetic and capable individuals.

One method of growth is to expand overseas. International advertising is growing rapidly. Yet, other cultures have different standards: Not all advertising can simply be transported whole to another country. Even the media availabilities and opportunities differ from one country to another.

With all the change that is occurring, in the advertising business and elsewhere, the ambitious advertising media manager must stay abreast of transitions, both to keep the advertising current and efficient and to maintain his or her place in the changing advertising business.

Questions for Discussion

1. What are the advantages and disadvantages of merging advertising agencies?

2. Why is it difficult to gain an accurate estimate of the amount of advertising done in the mass media each year?

3. Why has the agency commission system declined? What advantages are provided by the newer alternative—agency compensation systems?

4. What is gained by an advertiser having its own executives work on its account at an advertising agency? Are there any drawbacks?

5. Why haven't computers been able to take over the entire task of media planning?

6. Because of language and culture problems, international advertising obviously complicates creative-message development in advertising. Does international advertising also bring problems for media-planning development in advertising?

Endnotes

1. *Interaction: News & Insights for Creative Marketers,* September 1990, 1–4 (a newsletter from PRODIGY).

2. Randall Rothenberg, "Slow Growth Projected for Spending," *New York Times,* 15 June 1990, D15.

3. Rothenberg, "Slow Growth."

Suggested Readings

- Hume, Scott. "Bounty in Most Unusual Places: Unexpected Media Hard to Measure, Often Startlingly Effective." *Advertising Age,* 27 August 1990, S-1 and S-14.

- Jugenheimer, Donald W. "Forecast for Future Advertising Strategies." In *Strategic Advertising Decisions,* edited by Ronald D. Michman and Donald W. Jugenheimer. Columbus, Ohio: Grid Publishing, 1986.

- Leigh, James H., and Claude R. Martin, Jr., eds. *Current Issues & Research in Advertising.* Ann Arbor, Mich.: Division of Research, Graduate School of Business Administration, University of Michigan, annual issues.

- Levin, Gary. "It's Tough Not to Work by the Numbers: Agencies Grow Frustrated by Hard-to-Quantify Ad Systems." *Advertising Age,* 27 August 1990, S-2 and S-4.

- Rotzoll, Kim B., and James E. Haefner. *Advertising in Contemporary Society.* 2d ed. Cincinnati, Ohio: South-Western Publishing, 1990.

- Steenhuysen, Julie, ed. "Special Report: Non-Traditional Media." *Advertising Age,* 27 August 1990.

Advertising Media Terms

Included in the "Glossary" are the terms in bold-face type in the text and other terms in general use in the field of advertising media.

A

Account executive: Advertising agency manager who oversees and/or coordinates work on an account; also, term for a media representative.

Account supervisor: Advertising agency executive who oversees work on several accounts.

Accumulation: See "cumulative audience."

Accumulative audience: See "cumulative audience."

Across the board: A program that is broadcast at the same time period every day. See also "strip programming."

Adjacency: A program or a commercial announcement that is adjacent to another on the same station, either preceding or following the other.

Advertising impression: A possible exposure of the ad message to one audience member of a media vehicle.

Affiliate: A broadcast station that grants to a network an option of specific times for broadcasting network programming, in return for compensation.

Agate line: Newspaper advertising space one column wide by one- fourteenth of an inch deep; often referred to simply as "line"; somewhat obsolete because most newspapers now use column-inch measurements of advertising space, especially for national advertising.

Agency commission system: Usually 15 percent, allowed to advertising agencies by media on the agencies' purchase of media space or time.

Agency recognition: Acknowledgement by media owners that certain advertising agencies are good credit risks and/or fulfill certain requirements, thus qualifying for a commission.

Agency of record: Advertising agency that coordinates an advertiser's promotion of several products handled by more than a single agency. See also "blanket contract."

Air check: Recording a broadcast to serve as an archival or file copy.

Allotment: The number and type of outdoor posters in a showing. See also "showing."

Alternate sponsorship: Two advertisers who sponsor a single program; one advertiser sponsors one week and the other sponsors the alternate weeks. See also "crossplugs."

American Research Bureau (ARB): One of several national firms engaged in radio and television research; the founder of Arbitron ratings.

Announcement: An advertising message that is broadcast between programs or an advertisement within a syndicated program or feature film; any broadcast commercial, regardless of time length, within or between programs, that presents an advertiser's message or a public service message. See also "station break," "participation," "ID," and "billboard."

Annual rebate: See "rebate."

Area of dominant influence (ADI): Arbitron measurement area that comprises those counties in which stations of a single originating market account for a greater share of the viewing households than those from any other market; similar to Nielsen's designated market area.

Audience: Persons who receive an advertisement; individuals who read a newspaper or magazine, listen to a radio broadcast, view a television broadcast, and so on.

Audience accumulation: The total number of different persons or households who are exposed to a single media vehicle over a period of time. See also "cumulative audience."

Audience composition: Audience analysis expressed in demographic terms or other characteristics.

Audience duplication: Those persons or households who see an advertisement more than once in a single media vehicle or in a combination of vehicles.

Audience flow: The movement of a broadcast audience's attention from one station to another when the program changes, measured against the audience that stays tuned to the same station or network to view the new program. *See also* "holdover audience."

Audience profile: The minute-by-minute viewing pattern for a program; a description of the characteristics of the people who are exposed to a medium or vehicle. *See also* "profile."

Audience turnover: That part of a broadcast audience that changes over time. *See also* "audience flow."

Audimeter: A. C. Nielsen Company's automatic device attached to radio or television receiving sets that records usage and station information. *See also* "people meter."

Audiotex: Advertising messages delivered to people calling an 800 or 900 telephone number.

Availability: A broadcast time period open for reservation by an advertiser, in response to an advertiser or agency's initial inquiry; slang term is "avail."

Average audience: The number of broadcast homes tuned in for an average minute of a broadcast.

Average exposure: The average (mean) number of times that each audience member has been exposed to an advertisement.

Average frequency: *See* "average exposure."

Average net paid circulation: Average (mean) number of copies that a publication distributes per issue.

B

Back to back: Two broadcast programs or commercials in succession.

Barter: An advertising medium that sells time or space in return for merchandise or other nonmonetary returns; also, a television programming offer where a station is offered a syndicated program in exchange for commercial positions within the program.

Basic rate: *See* "open rate."

Benchmark: Baseline measurement against which future measures are compared.

Billboard: An outdoor poster; cast and production information that follows a broadcast program; a six-second radio commercial; a short commercial announcement, usually eight or ten seconds in length, at the start and close of a program, announcing the name of the sponsor.

Billing: The value of advertising that is handled by an advertising agency on behalf of its clients (often called "billings"); the process of issuing invoices for media space and time that have been purchased.

Blanket contract: A special rate or discount granted by an advertising medium to an advertiser who advertises several products or services through more than one agency.

Bleed: Printing to the edge of the page, with no margin or border.

Block: Consecutive broadcast time periods.

Booking: Scheduling a broadcast program or commercial.

Brand Development Index (BDI): An individual market's contribution to brand sales; a comparative measure of a brand's sales in one market, compared with other markets; used to decide the relative sales value of one market versus another. *See also* "Category Development Index."

Brand management/Product management: Marketing function or organizational structure that places an individual or small team in charge of all marketing for a single product or brand.

Break: Time available for purchase between two broadcast programs or between segments of a single program. *See also* "station break" and "chain break."

Broadcast Advertisers Report (BAR): A commercial broadcast monitoring service available on a network and market-by-market basis.

Broadsheet: Full-sized newspaper page, rather than tabloid.

Brochure: Type of direct-mail advertising that contains many pages bound together and elaborately produced.

Budget allocation: Dividing advertising media dollars into categories, such as groups, media types, regions, and so on.

Bulk discount: A discount offered by media for quantity buys. *See also* "quantity discount."

Bulk rate: *See* "bulk discount."

Business card: A small print advertisement, announcing a business, that does not change over time. *See also* "rate holder."

Business paper: A publication intended for business or professional interests.

Buy: The process of negotiating, ordering, and confirming the selection of a media vehicle and unit; as a noun, the advertising purchased from a vehicle.

Buyer: *See* "media buyer" and "media planner."

Buy sheet: The form used by a media buyer to keep track of the data on a media selection buy.

C

Call letters: The letters that identify a station—for example, WBZ-TV.

Campaign: A specific, coordinated advertising effort on behalf of a particular product or service that extends for a specified period of time.

Car card: Transit advertisement in or on a bus, subway, or commuter train car.

Card rate: The cost of time or space on a rate card.

Carryover effect: The residual level of awareness or recall after a flight or campaign period; used to plan the timing of schedules.

Cash discount: A discount, usually 2 percent, by media to advertisers who pay promptly.

Category Development Index (CDI): An individual market's contribution to total category sales by all marketers; a comparative market-by-market measure of a market's total sales of all brands of a single product category; used to evaluate the sales potential of a market for a product category or a brand. *See also* "Brand Development Index."

CC: The conclusion of a broadcast—for example, this program runs 11:30 P.M.–CC.

Center spread: An advertisement appearing on two facing pages printed on a single sheet in the center of a publication. *See also* "double truck."

Chain: A broadcast network; also, a newspaper or magazine group of single ownership or control.

Chain break (CB): The time during which a network allows a station to identify itself; usually a twenty-second spot (slang "twenty"); now often a thirty-second spot plus a ten-second spot, with twenty seconds remaining for identification.

Checking: The process of confirming whether an advertisement actually appeared.

Checking copy: A copy of a publication that is supplied by the medium to show that an advertisement appeared as specified.

Circulation: In print, the number of copies distributed; in broadcast, the number of households within a signal area that have receiving sets; in outdoor, the number of people who have a reasonable opportunity to see a billboard.

City zone: A central city and the contiguous areas that cannot be distinguished from it.

City zone circulation: The number of newspapers distributed within a city, rather than in outlying areas.

Classified advertising: Advertising that is set in small type and arranged according to categories or interests.

Classified display advertising: Classified advertising of a larger size than most other classified advertising, possibly with headlines, illustrations, and so on; classified advertising with some of the characteristics of display advertising. *See also* "display advertising."

Class magazines: Special-interest magazines with desirable up-scale audiences.

Clearance: Coverage of national television households by the number of stations (or markets) accepting a network program for airing; also, gaining available time on stations to carry a program or commercial.

Clear time: The process of reserving time or time periods with a station or network; checking on available advertising time.

Clipping bureau: An organization that aids in checking print advertising by clipping the advertisements from print media.

Closing date: The final deadline set by print media for advertising material to appear in a certain issue; in broadcast, the term *closing hour* may be used.

Closure: A sale resulting from following up on an inquiry from direct-mail advertising.

Clutter: Overabundance of advertising media.

Column inch: Publication space that is one column wide by 1 inch high, used as a measure of advertising space.

Combination rate: A special discounted advertising rate for buying space in two or more publications owned by the same interests.

Commercial impressions: The total audience, including duplication, for all commercial announcements in an advertiser's schedule. *See also* "gross impressions."

Confirmation: A broadcast media statement that a specific time is still open for purchase by an advertiser who is preparing a broadcast advertising schedule.

Consumer profile: A demographic description of the people or households that are prospects for a product or service. *See also* "target group."

Contiguity rate: A reduced broadcast advertising rate for sponsoring two or more programs in succession—for example, an advertiser participating in two programs running from 7:00–7:30 and then 7:30–8:00 may qualify for a contiguity rate.

Contingency plan: Fallback plan for unexpected situations.

Contract: Written agreement, between agency and advertiser, advertisers and media, and so on.

Control: A research test group left untreated, against which the change in the treated (experimental) group is measured.

Controlled circulation: Circulation that is limited to persons who qualify to receive a publication; often distributed free to qualified persons.

Cooperative advertising: Retail advertising that is paid partly or fully by a manufacturer; two or more manufacturers cooperating in a single advertisement; slang term is "co-op."

Cooperative announcement: Commercial time that is made available in network programs to stations for sale to local or national advertisers.

Cooperative program: A network broadcast that is also sold on a local basis and sponsored by both national and local advertisers—for example, "The Tonight Show." *See also* "network cooperative program."

Corporate discounting: Incentives offered to advertisers with numerous brands of products; all of a corporation's advertising schedules are combined for a larger discount level.

Cost-per-point: *See* "cost-per-rating-point."

Cost-per-rating: *See* "cost-per-rating-point."

Cost-per-rating-point (CPRP): The figure that indicates the dollar cost of advertising exposure to 1 percentage point of the target group, audience, or population. *See also* "rating point." Also known as cost-per-point (CPP) and cost-per-rating (CPR).

Cost-per-thousand (CPM): A dollar comparison that shows the relative cost of various media or vehicles; the figure indicates the dollar cost of advertising exposure to a thousand households or individuals.

Coverage: The number or percentage of individuals or households that are exposed to a medium or to an advertising campaign.

Cover position: An advertisement on the cover of a publication, often at a premium cost; first cover—outside front cover; second cover—inside front cover; third cover—inside back cover; fourth cover—outside back cover.

Cowcatcher: A brief commercial announcement at the beginning of a broadcast program.

CPM/PCM (cost-per-thousand per commercial minute): The cost-per-thousand of a minute of broadcast advertising time.

Crossplugs: In alternating sponsorships, permitting each advertiser to insert one announcement into the program during the weeks when the other advertiser is the sponsor, maintaining weekly exposure for both. *See also* "alternate sponsorship."

Cumulative audience (slang "cume"): Cumulative broadcast rating; the net unduplicated audience of a station or network during two or more time periods; also used to describe how many different households or people are reached by an advertising schedule; also called accumulative audience, net audience, and unduplicated audience; technically, a cumulative audience includes those persons who were exposed to any insertion of an advertisement in multiple editions of a single vehicle, whereas an unduplicated audience includes those persons who were exposed to any insertion of an advertisement in a combination of vehicles or media, counting each person only once.

Cumulative reach: The number of different households exposed to a medium or campaign during a specific time.

Cut-in: The insertion of a local commercial announcement into a network or recorded program.

D

Daily effective circulation: The audience that has an opportunity to see an outdoor advertising structure in a twenty-four-hour period.

Dayparts: Specific segments of the broadcast day—for example, daytime, early fringe, primetime, late fringe, late night.

Deadline: The final date for accepting advertising material to meet a publication or broadcast schedule. *See also* "closing date."

Dealer imprint: Inserting a local dealer's identification into nationally prepared advertising.

Dealer tie-in: A manufacturer's announcement that lists local dealers; not the same as co-op.

Delayed broadcast (DB): A local station broadcasting a network program at a time other than its regularly scheduled network time.

Delivery: The ability to reach or communicate with a certain audience or number of people by using a particular advertising schedule; the physical delivery of a publication.

Demographic characteristics: The population characteristics of a group or audience.

Designated market area (DMA): A term used by the A. C. Nielsen Company to describe an area based on those counties in which stations of the originating market account for a greater share of the viewing households than those from any other area—for example, Lake County, Illinois, belongs to the Chicago DMA because most household viewing in Lake County is or can be ascribed to Chicago stations, rather than to stations from Milwaukee or any other market. *See also* "area of dominant influence (ADI)."

Diaries: Records maintained by consumers to track purchase patterns and media usage.

Digest unit: *See* "junior unit."

Direct advertising: Advertising that is under the advertiser's complete control, rather than through some established medium—for example, direct mail, free sampling, and so on.

Direct-mail advertising: Advertising sent by mail; also used to describe advertising in other media that solicits orders directly through the mail.

Direct marketing: Sales made directly to the customer, rather than through intervening channels; includes direct mail, direct advertising, telemarketing, and so on.

Direct matching: Identifying media-vehicle selection directly from consumer information, rather than attempting to match the demographics of a target group with those of an audience.

Direct response: Advertising technique whereby the advertising, regardless of medium used, seeks an immediate action or response.

Directory advertising: Advertising that appears in a buying guide or directory; advertisements in a store directory—for example, Yellow Pages advertising.

Display advertising: Print advertising that is intended to attract attention and communicate easily through the use of space, illustrations, layout, headlines, and so on, as opposed to classified advertising.

Display classified advertising: *See* "classified display advertising."

Double spotting: *See* "piggyback."

Double spread: *See* "two-page spread."

Double truck: Slang term for a print advertisement that uses two full pages side by side, but not necessarily the two center pages, usually for a magazine advertisement. *See also* "center spread" and "two-page spread."

Drivetime: Radio broadcast time during morning and evening commuter rush hours.

Duplicated audience: Those persons exposed to an advertising campaign in more than one media vehicle.

E

Earned rate: The advertising rate actually paid by the advertiser after discounts and other calculations.

Effective frequency: Level or range of audience exposure that provides what an advertiser considers the minimal effective level, and no more than this optimal level or range; also called effective reach.

Effective reach: Those reached with at least minimum frequency. *See also* "effective frequency."

Estimation: Process of calculating approximate cost of possible media schedule or of media affordable by media budget.

F

Facing: A billboard location with the panels facing the same direction and visible to the same lines of traffic.

Fair share: Allocating advertising dollars to markets based on their indexed weights.

Fixed rate: An advertising rate for advertising time that cannot be taken away or "preempted" by another advertiser; usually the highest advertising rate; commonly used in broadcast advertising.

Flat rate: A print advertising rate that is not subject to a discount.

Flight scheduling: Concentrating advertising within a short time period; an advertising campaign that runs for a specified number of weeks, followed by a period of inactivity (see also hiatus), after which the campaign may resume with another flight; also known as flight saturation.

Floating time: *See* "run of station."

Forced combination rate: A policy that requires newspaper advertisers to buy advertising space in both morning and evening newspapers owned by the same interests within a market.

Forcing distribution: Using advertising to increase consumer demand, thereby inducing dealers to stock a product; now seldom used.

Fractional page: Print advertising space of less than a full page.

Fractional showing: An outdoor advertising showing of less than number 25. *See also* "showing."

Free circulation: A publication sent without charge, often with controlled circulation.

Freestanding insert: Print insert comprising a separate element or unit, rather than as regular part of publication.

Frequency: The number of times that an average audience member sees or hears an advertisement; the number of times that an individual or household is exposed to an advertisement or campaign (frequency of exposure); the number of times that an advertisement is run (frequency of insertion).

Frequency discount: A reduced advertising rate offered by media to advertisers who run a certain number of advertisements within a given time.

Fringe time: Broadcast time periods preceding or following primetime; television time between daytime and primetime is called "early fringe," and television time immediately following primetime is called "late fringe."

Full run: When one transit-advertising car card is in every transit bus or car.

Full-service agency: Advertising agency that provides complete range of advertising functions.

Full showing: The number of outdoor posters needed to reach all of the mobile population in a market at least once within a thirty-day period. *See also* "gross rating points." Also called a number 100 showing. *See also* "showing."

G

General magazine: A consumer magazine not aimed at a special-interest audience.

Geodemographics: Research that blends social/ economic data into U.S. markets.

Giveaway: A free offer; a broadcast program that offers free gifts as prizes.

Grid card: Spot-broadcast advertising rates in matrix format to allow a station to set rates based on current audience ratings and advertiser buying demand—for example:

	60 seconds	30/20 seconds	10 seconds
A	$250	$175	$125
B	245	172	123
C	240	170	121
D	230	165	120
etc.	. . .	. . .	. . .

Gross audience: The total number of households or people who are "delivered" or reached by an advertising schedule, without regard to any possible duplication that may occur; also called total audience.

Gross billing: The cost of advertising at the highest advertising rate; the total value of an advertising agency's space and time dealings. *See also* "billing."

Gross impressions: The total number of persons or the total number of audience impressions delivered by an advertising schedule. *See also* "gross audience."

Gross rate: The highest possible rate for advertising time or space.

Gross rating points (GRP): The total number of broadcast rating points delivered by an advertiser's television schedule, including overlap, usually in a one-week period; an indicator of the combined audience percentage reach and exposure frequency achieved by an advertising schedule; in outdoor, a standard audience level upon which some markets' advertising rates are based.

Gutter: The inside page margins where a publication is bound.

H

Half run: Transit-advertising car cards in half the buses or transit cars of a system.

Half showing: A number 50 outdoor showing. *See also* "showing."

Head of household: The person within a family or household who is responsible for the major purchase decisions; sometimes, male and female heads of household are considered separately.

Hiatus: A period during a campaign when an advertiser's schedule is suspended for a time, after which it resumes.

Hitchhiker: A broadcast advertising announcement at the end of a program that promotes another product from the same advertiser.

Holdover audience: Those persons tuned to a program who stay tuned to that station or network for the following program.

Horizontal cume: The total number of different people who were tuned to a broadcast station or network at the same time on different days of the week.

Horizontal publication: A business or trade publication that is of interest at one level or to one job function in a variety of businesses or fields.

House agency: An advertising agency that is owned or controlled by an advertiser.

House organ: A company's own publication.

HUR: Households using radio. *See also* "sets in use."

HUT: Households using television. *See also* "sets in use" and "PUT."

I

ID (Identification): A spot-television commercial eight to ten seconds in length during a station break; the last two seconds of the visual time may be reserved for showing the station call letters ("station identification"); a ten-second broadcast commercial announcement, sometimes referred to as a "ten."

Impact/Impact value: Special media quality that attracts notice and comment; the degree to which an advertisement or campaign affects its audience; the amount of space (full-page, half-page, and so on) or of time (sixty-seconds, thirty-seconds, and so on) that is purchased, as opposed to reach and frequency measures; also, the use of color, large type, powerful messages, or other devices that may induce audience reaction. *See also* "unit."

Impressions: *See* "gross impressions."

Independent station: A broadcast station not affiliated with a network.

Index: A numerical value that is assigned to quantitative data for ease of comparison.

Individual location: An outdoor location that has room only for one billboard.

In-house agency: *See* "house agency."

Insert: An advertisement that is enclosed with bills or letters; a print advertisement, one-page or multi-page, that is distributed with the publication and may or may not be bound into it.

Insertion: Agreement to place an advertisement in an advertising vehicle.

Insertion order: A statement from an advertising agency to a media vehicle that accompanies the advertisement copy and indicates specifications for the advertisement.

Integrated commercial: A broadcast advertising message that is delivered as part of the entertainment portion of a program.

Irritation factor: Broadcast commercial viewed so frequently as to alienate audience. *See also* "message wear-out."

Island position: A print advertisement surrounded by editorial material; a print advertisement not adjacent to any other advertising; a broadcast commercial scheduled away from any other commercial, with program content before and after; often offered at premium advertising rates.

Isolated 30: A thirty-second broadcast commercial that runs by itself and not in combination with any other announcement; usually found only on network television.

J

Junior unit: A smaller page size print advertisement run in a publication with a larger page size, with editorial matter around it in the extra space; similarly, a *Reader's Digest*-size advertising page in a larger magazine—usually called a "Digest unit."

K

Key: A code in an advertisement to facilitate tracing which advertisement produced an inquiry or order.

L

Life: The length of time an advertisement is used; the length of time an advertisement is judged effective; the length of time a publication is retained by its audience.

Lifestyle profiles: Classifying media audiences on the basis of career, recreation, and/or leisure patterns or motives.

Limited-service agency: Advertising agency specializing in only one or a few functions.

Linage: In print, the number of agate lines to be used for an advertisement or for a series of advertisements; now made somewhat obsolete by the declining use of agate-line measurements. *See also* "agate line."

Line rate: The print advertising rate established by the number of agate lines of space used; somewhat obsolete because of the declining use of agate-line measurements.

List broker/List house: An agent who prepares and rents the use of mailing lists.

Load factor: Number used in outdoor advertising to estimate the average number of people in an automobile passing outdoor structures.

Local rate: An advertising rate offered by media to local advertisers that is lower than the rate offered to national advertisers.

Log: A broadcast station's record of its programming.

LOH (ladies of the house): A term used by A. C. Nielsen Company in some of its reports, referring to female heads of households.

M

M: One thousand.

Magazine concept: Buying a certain number of broadcast announcements from a station with a certain guaranteed audience level, without selecting the specific times or programs.

Mail-order advertising: Advertisements intended to induce direct ordering of merchandise through the mail; the advertisements themselves are not necessarily distributed through the mail and may appear in other advertising media.

Make-good: A repeat of an advertisement to compensate for an error, omission, or technical difficulty with the publication, broadcast, or transmission of the original.

Market: *See* "target market" and "target group."

Marketing concept: The assumption that the ultimate consumer or user plays an important role on *both* ends of the marketing channel.

Marketing mix: The essential factors that can be manipulated in formulating a marketing effort.

Market potential: The reasonable maximum market share or sales level that a product or service can be expected to achieve.

Market profile: A geographic description of the location of prospects for a product or service; sometimes used instead of target profile. *See also* "target market" and "target profile."

Market share: A company or brand's portion of the sales of a product or service category.

Mat service: A service to newspapers that supplies pictures and drawings for use in advertisements; entire prepared advertisements may be offered; "mat" is slang for "matrix."

Maximil rate: An agate line of advertising space at the highest milline rate; somewhat obsolete as the usage of agate lines has declined.

Media (singular, "medium"): Go-between or intermediary, joining an advertisement to an audience.

Media buyer: The person responsible for purchasing advertising space or time; often skilled in negotiation with the media.

Media-buying service: Business that orders media time and/or space for advertisers, in lieu of using an advertising agency.

Media commission system: *See* "agency commission system."

Media mix: Use of a combination of advertising media.

Media planner: The person responsible for determining the proper use of advertising media to fulfill the marketing and promotional objectives for a specific product or advertiser.

Media representatives: *See* "reps."

Media type: Broad, general categories of communications channels—for example, newspapers, radio, television.

Media vehicle: *See* "vehicle."

Merchandising: The promotion of an advertiser's products, services, and the like to the sales force, wholesalers, and dealers; promotion other than advertising to consumers through the use of in-store displays, guarantees, services, point-of-purchase materials, and so on; display and promotion of retail goods; display of a mass media advertisement close to the point of sale.

Message distribution: Measurement of media audience by the successive frequency of exposure—for example, saw once, saw twice, and so on.

Message wear-out: Overexposure to an advertising message.

Metropolitan area: A geographic area consisting of a central city of 50,000 population or more, plus the economically and socially integrated surrounding area, as established by the federal government; usually limited by county boundaries; slang term is "metro area."

Metro rating: The broadcast rating figure from within a metropolitan area.

Milline rate: A comparison of the advertising line rates of newspapers with uneven circulations by calculating the line-rate-per-million circulation; determined by multiplying the line rate by one million and then dividing by the circulation; now somewhat obsolete because of the declining use of agate-line measurements and advertising line rates.

Minimil rate: The cost of an agate line of advertising at the lowest possible milline rate; somewhat obsolete as the usage of agate lines has declined.

Mood programming: Maintaining a single approach or characteristic in broadcast programming.

Multi-page insert: A type of newspaper advertising where the advertiser prints four or more pages and ships the insert to newspapers for distribution along with the regular pages of the paper.

N

NCR (or NCIR) (no change in rate): Used when some other format or specification change has occurred.

Net: Money paid to a media vehicle by an advertising agency after deducting the agency's commission; slang term for "network."

Net unduplicated audience: The number of different people who are reached by a single issue of two or more publications. *See also* "cumulative audience."

Network: In broadcast, a grouping of stations; an organization that supplies programming to a group or chain of stations.

Network cooperative program: A network program with provisions for inserting local commercials. *See also* "cooperative program."

Network option time: Broadcast time on a station for which the network has the option of selling advertising.

Newspaper syndicate: A firm that sells special material, such as features, photographs, comic strips, cartoons, and so on, for publication in newspapers.

Next to reading matter: A print advertising position adjacent to news or editorial material; may be at premium rates.

Nielsen: The A. C. Nielsen Company; a firm engaged in local and national television ratings and other marketing research.

Nielsen Station Index (NSI): A rating service for individual television stations.

Nielsen Television Index (NTI): A national television rating service, primarily for network programming.

Nonwired networks: Broadcast stations grouped by sales representative firms for combined advertising sales.

O

O & O (owned and operated) station: A broadcast station that is owned and operated by a network.

Objective: Goal intended to be attained.

One-time rate: *See* "open rate."

Open-end transcription: A transcribed broadcast with time for the insertion of local commercial announcements.

Open rate: The highest advertising rate before discounts can be earned; also called basic rate and one-time rate.

Orbit: Broadcast commercials gathered around a certain time, theme, or type of programming.

Orbit plan: A plan offered by a television station to an advertiser that involves a group of programs in which commercials will be shown.

OTO (one time only): A commercial announcement that runs only once.

Outdoor advertising: Advertising that is placed primarily on standardized structures in the form of posters and painted bulletins; also includes electric spectaculars.

Outside transit displays: Standard-size advertisements that are placed on the outside of mass-transit vehicles.

Overrun: Additional copies of an advertisement beyond the number actually ordered or needed; extra copies to replace damaged outdoor posters or transit car cards.

P

Package: A series of broadcast programs that an advertiser may sponsor.

Package plan discount: A spot-television discount plan for buying a certain number of spots, usually within a one-week period.

Packager: An individual or company that produces packaged program series; also called syndicator.

Paid circulation: The number of print copies purchased by audience members.

Painted bulletin: Outdoor advertising where the advertisement is painted onto a standard frame.

Panel: A single outdoor billboard.

Partial showing: An outdoor showing of less than number 25.

Participation: A commercial announcement within a broadcast program, as compared with one scheduled between programs; also called participating announcement.

Participation program: A broadcast program with each segment sponsored by a different advertiser.

Pass-along readers: Readers of a publication who acquire a copy other than by purchase or subscription. *See also* "secondary audience."

Pay cable: Cable-television programming for which the audience must pay or subscribe.

Penetration: The percentage of households that have a broadcast receiving set; a measure of the degree of advertising effectiveness; the percentage of households that have been exposed to an advertising campaign.

People meter: Slang for a broadcast ratings measurement device that records individual audience members who are present during a program.

Per-issue rate: A special magazine advertising rate determined by the number of issues used during the contract period; similar to a frequency discount, except not based on the number of advertisements but, rather, on the number of issues in which an advertising campaign appears.

Piggyback: Slang for two of a sponsor's commercial announcements that are presented back to back within a single commercial time segment—for example, two thirty-second commercials in a sixty-second time slot; also called double spotting.

Pilot: A sample production of a proposed broadcast program series.

Plans board: An advertising agency committee that reviews campaign plans for clients.

Plug: A free mention of a product or service.

Pod: A group of commercials during a broadcast break.

Point-of-purchase advertising (P-O-P): Promotions in retail stores, usually displays.

Position: The location of an advertisement on a page; the time when a program or commercial announcement will run in a broadcast; special positions may cost premium prices.

Positioning: Where the product, service, or idea will ideally be categorized in consumers' minds.

Poster panel: Outdoor advertising where the advertisement is printed on pieces of paper and pasted on a standard frame.

Potential audience: The maximum possible audience.

Preemptible rate: An advertising rate subject to cancellation by another advertiser paying a higher rate, usually in broadcast; the protection period varies by station and ranges from no notice to two-weeks notice or more. *See also* "fixed rate."

Preemption: Cancellation of a broadcast program for special material or news; the right of a station or network to cancel a regular program in order to run a special program; a commercial announcement that may be replaced if another advertiser pays a higher or "fixed" rate.

Premium: An item offered to help promote a product or service; a higher-cost advertising rate. *See also* "premium price."

Premium price: A special advertising rate, usually higher, for special positions or other considerations.

Preprint: Advertising material that is printed in advance of the regular press run, perhaps on another printing press with greater capability for color.

Primary audience: Individuals in the print-media audience who purchase or subscribe to the publication. *See also* "secondary audience."

Primary household: A household that has subscribed to or purchased a publication.

Primary listening area: The geographic area in which a broadcast transmission is static-free and easily received.

Primary readers: Those persons who purchase or subscribe to a publication; readers in primary households.

Primary research: Research that has not been done before or is not available in suitable form from some other source.

Primetime: The hours when television viewing is at its peak; usually, the evening hours.

Product allocation: The various products assigned to specific times or locations in an advertiser's schedule, where more than one brand is advertised; the amount of the advertising budget allocated to individual products.

Product management: *See* "brand management."

Product protection: A time separation between the airing of broadcast commercial announcements for competitive goods or services.

Profile: A term used interchangeably with audience composition to describe the demographic characteristics of audiences.

Program compatibility: Broadcast programming or editorial content suitable for the product or service being promoted; suitability of the advertisement or campaign theme with program content.

Progressive proofs: A test press run of each color in the printing process.

Projected audience: The number of audience members calculated from a sample survey of audience size; the number of broadcast viewers, either in total or per receiving set, based on the sample for the rating percentages.

Promotion: Any form of publicity, advertising, and so on.

Prospect targets: Target audience and target group combined, using a less restrictive term. *See also* "target group."

Publisher's statement: The certified circulation of a publication, attested to by the publisher and subject to audit.

Pulp magazine: A publication, usually printed on low-quality paper, with sensational editorial material—for example, a mystery, detective, or television/movie magazine.

Pulse scheduling: *See* "wave."

Purchase cycle: Length of time between purchase and re-purchase of an item.

PUT: Persons using television.

Q

Qualified circulation: The distribution of a publication that is restricted to individuals who meet certain requirements—for example, member physicians are qualified to receive *The Journal of the American Medical Association.*

Qualified reader: A person who can prove readership of a publication.

Quantity discount: A lower advertising rate for buying a certain amount of space or time.

Quarter-run: One-fourth of the car cards required for a full run in transit; a card in every fourth transit-system vehicle.

Quintile: One-fifth of a group; usage in advertising often refers to audience members who have been divided into five equal groups (quintiles), ranging from the heaviest to the lightest media-usage levels.

Q-Sort: A research method using statements categorized by respondents to determine opinion or attitude.

R

Rate: A charge for advertising media space or time.

Rate book: A printed book that provides advertising rates for several media vehicles—for example, *Standard Rate and Data Service.*

Rate card: A printed listing of advertising rates for a single media vehicle.

Rate differential: The difference between local and national advertising rates in a vehicle.

Rate guarantee: Media commitment that an advertising rate will not be increased during a certain calendar period.

Rate holder: A small-print advertisement used by an advertiser to meet contract requirements for earning a discounted advertising rate.

Rate protection: The length of time that an advertiser is guaranteed a certain advertising rate without an increase.

Rating: The percentage of the potential broadcast audience that is tuned to a particular station, network, or program; the audience of a vehicle expressed as a percentage of the total population of an area.

Rating point: A rating of 1 percent; 1 percent of the potential audience; the sum of the ratings of multiple advertising insertions—for example, two advertisements with a rating of 10 percent each will total 20 rating points.

Reach: The total audience that a medium actually reaches; the size of the audience with which a vehicle communicates; the total number of people in an advertising media audience; the total percentage of the target group that is actually covered by an advertising campaign.

Reader interest: An expression of interest through inquiries, coupons, and so on; the level of interest in various products.

Readership: The percent or number of persons who read a publication or advertisement.

Readers-per-copy (RPC): The number of persons exposed to each copy of an issue of a publication.

Reading notice: A print advertisement intended to resemble editorial matter.

Rebate: A payment that is returned by the media vehicle back to an advertiser who has overpaid, usually because of earning a lower rate than that originally contracted.

Reminder advertising: An advertisement, usually brief, that is intended to keep the name of a product or service before the public; often, a supplement to other advertising.

Rep: A media representative; slang term for a national sales representative.

Replacement: A substitute for a broadcast commercial announcement that did not clear the original order—that is, was not broadcast as specified on the advertiser's order.

Retail trading zone (RTZ): The geographic area in which most of a market's population makes the majority of their retail purchases.

Roadblock or roadblocking: Slang term for placing television announcements at the same time on two or more networks or on several stations in a single market; used to remedy channel switching during a commercial break.

ROP color: Color printing that is done during the regular press run.

Rotation: Using different advertisements in a certain time period or publication to enhance audience interest; running a broadcast commercial in various time slots.

Run-of-paper (ROP): Advertising that is positioned anywhere in a publication, with no choice as to where, specifically, the advertisement will appear. Also known as run-of-press.

Run of station (ROS): Broadcast commercial announcements that can be scheduled at the station's discretion; in some cases, the advertiser can specify or request certain time periods—for example, ROS 10:00 A.M.–4 P.M., Monday–Friday.

S

Satellite station: A broadcast station in a fringe reception area, to boost the effective range of the main station's signal.

Saturation: An advertising media schedule of wide reach and high frequency, concentrated during a time period to achieve maximum coverage and impact. See also "flight scheduling."

Scatter plan: Commercial announcements that are scheduled during a variety of times in broadcast media; usually, the advertiser is permitted to specify general time periods during which the commercials will be scheduled; also called scatter package.

Schedule: A list of advertisements or media to be used in a campaign; a chart of the advertisements that have been planned.

Schedule and estimate: A data form submitted by an advertising agency to the advertiser prior to a firm media purchase; contains price and audience goals and a proposed schedule.

Secondary audience: The members of a print-media audience who do not subscribe to or purchase the publication. *See also* "pass-along readers."

Secondary listening area: The outlying area in which broadcast transmissions are subject to fading or static; in television, the Grade 3 signal contour.

Secondary research: Information that has already been collected.

Selected-program procedure: The purchase of network television advertising whereby specific programs (for example, "60 Minutes") are selected by the buyer.

Self-liquidating point-of-purchase: A display for which the retailer pays part or all of the costs.

Self-liquidating premium: An item for which the cost is paid by the customer; the price that the consumer pays covers the premium's manufacturing cost.

Self-mailer: A direct-mail item that is mailed without an envelope.

Semantic differential: A research method using bipolarized adjectives to determine opinion or attitude.

Sets in use: The percentage of households that have broadcast receiving sets that are operating at one time within a market area; because many households have more than one receiving set, "households using television" (HUT) and "households using radio" (HUR) are the current common terms.

Share of audience ("share"): The percentage of sets in use (and, thus, of HUT or HUR) that are tuned to a particular station, network, or program.

Share-of-voice (SOV): Percentage of all competing product messages controlled by one brand; share of category advertising within a market.

Shopping newspaper ("shopper"): A newspaper-like publication that is devoted mainly to advertising and is often distributed free to shoppers or to households.

Short rate: Money owed to a media vehicle by an advertiser to offset the rate differential between the earned rate and the lower contracted rate.

Showing: The number of outdoor posters necessary to reach a certain percentage of the mobile population in a market within a specified time; many outdoor markets are now purchased by gross rating points. *See also* "full showing" and "gross rating points."

Sixty: Slang for a one-minute broadcast commercial announcement.

SNR (subject to nonrenewal): Commercial time available for purchase if the current advertiser does not renew.

Soap opera: Slang for a continuing broadcast dramatic serial, usually a daytime program.

Space buyer: The person who is responsible for purchasing advertising in newspapers, magazines, and business publications, and sometimes outdoor and transit. *See also* "media buyer."

Space position value: A measure of the effectiveness of an outdoor poster location.

Specialty advertising: An advertising medium that involves the use of articles (such as ballpoint pens) with the company name and message on them.

Spectacular: A large outdoor lighted sign.

Split run: Testing two or more print advertisements by running each only to a portion of the audience, usually in a single issue.

Sponsor: An advertiser who buys the exclusive right to the time available for commercial announcements in a given broadcast program or segment.

Spot: The purchase of broadcast slots by geographic or station breakdowns; the purchase of slots at certain times, usually during station breaks; the term *spot* can refer to the time used for the commercial announcement, or it can refer to the announcement itself.

Standard Advertising Unit (SAU): Prescribed space units for newspaper advertising.

Standard Metropolitan Statistical Area (SMSA): *See* "metropolitan area."

Station break: The time between broadcast programs to permit station identification and spot announcements; slang for a twenty-second broadcast announcement.

Station clearance: *See* "clear time."

Station identification: The announcement of station call letters, usually with broadcast frequency or channel, and station location.

Station option time: A broadcast time for which the station has the option of selling advertising.

Station posters: Advertisements consisting of posters in transit stations.

Strategy: Plan or approach to achieving goals and objectives.

Strip programming: A broadcast program or commercial that is scheduled at the same time of day on successive days of the week, either Monday through Friday or Monday through Sunday. *See also* "across the board."

Supplement: A newspaper section in magazine format; also called magazine supplement or magazine section or newspaper-distributed magazines.

Sustaining period: A period of time during an advertising campaign when advertisements are used to remind the audience of the product or service or of the campaign; often, a time of reduced advertising expenditures following the introductory flight.

Sweep: The period of the year when a ratings service measures the broadcast audience in the majority of the markets throughout the country—for example, surveys that are scheduled for November 2–24 are referred to as the "November sweeps."

Syndicated program: Broadcast program that is sold to individual stations, rather than appearing on a network.

Syndication: Selling the same service, such as research, to a variety of clients, who thereby share the costs.

Syndicator: Television program distributor who works with reruns or new programs on a market-to-market basis. *See also* "packager."

T

Tabloid: A newspaper of the approximate size of a standard newspaper folded in half; slang term is "tab."

Tactics: Implementation or execution of a strategy.

Tag: Dealer identification, usually added to the end of a broadcast commercial announcement, to indicate where the product or service being advertised can be purchased in the local market.

Target audience: *See* "target group."

Target group: Those persons to whom a campaign is directed; those individuals with similar characteristics who are prospects for a product or service; also called consumer profile.

Target market: The geographic area or areas to which a campaign is directed; the areas where a product is being sold or introduced; also called market profile.

Target profile: A demographic description of the target groups, often including the geographic target markets.

TBA (to be announced): Used as a notification in broadcast program schedules.

Tearsheet: A publication page with an advertiser's message, sent to the advertiser for approval or for checking.

Teaser: An advertisement that precedes the major portion of an advertising campaign and is intended to build curiosity.

Telemarketing: Selling by use of telephones, either initiating the calls or receiving orders.

Television market: *See* "Designated market area" and "area of dominant influence."

Ten: Slang for a ten-second broadcast commercial announcement.

Test marketing: Conducting an experiment to determine the optimal marketing approach.

TF: A newspaper insertion order abbreviation for "till forbidden"; in other words, run the advertisement until told to stop.

Thirty: Slang for a thirty-second broadcast commercial announcement.

Throwaways: Free shopping newspapers.

Tie-in: *See* "cooperative advertising" and "dealer tie-in."

Time buyer: The person responsible for purchasing advertising on radio and television. *See also* "media buyer."

Time period rating (TPR):   The rating for a particular broadcast time period, regardless of the program that was broadcast during that slot.

Time sheet: A form used by a time buyer to keep track of the data on a media buy; also called a buy sheet; also, the form used to keep track of how advertising agency personnel use their time, for application in billing purposes.

Total audience: The number of all the different homes or individuals who are tuned to a broadcast program for six minutes or longer.

Total market coverage (TMC):   Using advertising to reach all households in a market, or as near to all households as possible.

Tracking studies: Research that records the marketing track or record for a brand or category.

Trade paper: A specialized publication for a specific profession, trade, or industry; another term for some business publications.

Traffic count: The number of persons who pass an outdoor panel location.

Transit: Advertising that is placed within and on the outside of mass transit vehicles (for example, buses, subway cars), as well as posters placed in subway and commuter rail stations.

Trim size: The final magazine page size, after it is trimmed.

Turnover: The frequency with which the audience for a broadcast program changes over a period of time. *See also* "audience turnover."

Twenty: Slang for a twenty-second broadcast commercial announcement; also called a chain break or station break.

Two-page spread: A single print advertisement that crosses two facing pages; also called double spread or double truck. *See also* "center spread" and "double truck."

U

Unduplicated audience: The total number of different people who are exposed to an advertisement or campaign through multiple insertions in more than one media vehicle. *See also* "cumulative audience."

Unit (advertising unit):   The form and context in which an advertisement appears in a media vehicle—for example, full-page, half-page vertical, center spread, black-and-white, back cover, two-color, thirty-second commercial, ten-second ID, and so on.

Up-front buying: Initial purchasing of network television advertising by firms wishing to have optimal selection of available programs; reserving advertising time on network television programs when the seasonal schedule is first announced; this tactic often requires longer schedules and higher prices.

Usage level: Classifying media audiences by the amount of the product or service they use.

V

Vehicle (media vehicle):   An individual outlet of an advertising medium, such as a certain magazine or a specific broadcast station or program.

Vertical cume: The total number of different people who were tuned to successive broadcast programs.

Vertical publication: A business or trade publication that is of interest to all levels or job functions within a single business or profession.

Vertical saturation: Many broadcast commercial announcements scheduled throughout the course of a single day; generally designed to reach a high percentage of the broadcast audience.

Videotex: Interactive electronic system in which data and graphics are transmitted from a computer network over telephone or cable lines and displayed on a television or computer terminal screen.

Volume discount: Lower broadcast advertising rate based on dollar amount, rather than amount of time purchased. *See also* "quantity discount."

W

Wait order: An instruction or request to delay publication of a print advertisement; also but seldom used in broadcast.

Waste circulation: The readers of a publication who are not prospects for the product or service being advertised; advertising in an area in which the product or service is not distributed.

Wave: Pattern of high and then low levels of advertising.

WUT: Women using television.

Y

Yellow Pages: Special type of directory advertising that is available in a special section of telephone directories throughout the United States.

Z

Zoned edition: When newspapers offer an advertiser the opportunity to deliver an advertisement to only a portion of the newspaper's total circulation—for example, to only part of the city.

Index